SOE
in the
Low Countries

ALSO BY M. R. D. FOOT

Gladstone and Liberalism (with J. L. Hammond, 1952)

British Foreign Policy since 1898 (1956)

Men in Uniform (1961)

SOE in France (1968)

(ed.) *The Gladstone Diaries 1825–39* (2 vols, 1968)

(ed.) *War and Society* (1973)

(ed. with H. C. G. Matthew) *The Gladstone Diaries 1840–54*

(2 vols, 1974)

Resistance (1977)

Six Faces of Courage (1978)

MI9 (with J. M. Langley, 1980)

Holland at War against Hitler (1990)

(ed. with I. C. B. Dear) *The Oxford Companion to the*

Second World War (1995)

SOE: An Outline History 1940–46 (1999)

SOE
in the
Low Countries

M. R. D. FOOT

humanum est errare

ST ERMIN'S
PRESS

A *St Ermin's Press* Book

First published in this form in Great Britain in 2001
by *St Ermin's Press*
in association with Little, Brown and Company

Copyright © 2001 by St Ermin's Press and M. R. D. Foot

The moral right of the author has been asserted.

A CIP catalogue record for this book
is available from the British Library.

ISBN: 1-903608-04-X

Typeset in Garamond by M Rules
Printed and bound in Great Britain
by Clays Ltd, St Ives plc

St Ermin's Press
in association with
Little, Brown and Company (UK)
Brettenham House
Lancaster Place
London WC2E 7EN

Contents

Illustrations

The three CDs: Nelson, Hambro, Gubbins.
Some London staff: Keswick, Knight, Bingham, Dobson.
Opposition: Rauter, May, Poos, Giskes.
Some victims: Ras, van Os, Beukema toe Water.
Taconis, Lauwers, Terwindt, Ubbink, Dourlein.
'King Kong', Celosse, Tazelaar, Faber.
'Bull', Floor, Livio, Todd, Brinkgreve, Austin.
Del Marmol and Pire in conference; containers in polderland.

Author and publisher alike are grateful for leave to reproduce these photographs: for Sir Frank Nelson, to Gervase Cowell; for Rauter, May, and Poos to the Rijksinstituut voor Oorlogsdocumentatie, Amsterdam; for del Marmol and Pire, to Editions Duculot; for Ras, van Os, Beukema toe Water and the containers in polderland, to the resistance museum in Amsterdam; and for the rest, which are from SOE files, to the Controller, Her Majesty's Stationery Office.

Maps

The fourth map is reproduced from *European Resistance Movements 1939–1945* (Oxford: Pergamon Press, 1960).

Author's Note

'Greater experience, as anyone knows who has tried to make the simplest thing in any medium, introduces more difficult problems'; René Hague was quite right.[1] Work nearly forty years ago on *SOE in France*, work over twenty years ago on a general study of resistance to nazism, and a great many talks with former participants in secret work have combined to complicate as well as to illuminate the present study.

The passage of time has eliminated most of the witnesses. Though my access to former members of SOE was sharply restricted when I wrote the earlier book, I was able while I prepared it to see several key figures, both on the staff and from the sharp end in the field. I then saw a larger proportion of former members of SOE than the Gallup organisation finds it necessary to see of the voting population when it conducts a national opinion poll. This time round, hardly any are left in a state to say much of historic importance. Instead of meeting representatives of each main class of secret agent – organiser, W/T operator, sabotage instructor – and talking to them in detail, I have only had chance meetings with a few agent-survivors and stalwarts on the staff. This would matter less, had the shattered archives been more complete. For this book, I have tried to rely to some extent on an understanding of how the secret war was run at the time, rather than on the firmer professional base of documents; this cannot be helped.

---

1 René Hague, 'David Jones: a Reconnaissance', in *The Twentieth Century* clxviii (July 1960), 37.

The earlier book was written when the mere wartime existence of secret services, other than the Special Operations Executive, was still unavowable. In the slightly more relaxed air of the 1990s, I have sometimes needed to discuss several of them; but must emphasise that anything I say about them is based on the published sources that I quote, or on SOE's archives, or on my own inferences, not on official access to their papers.

The whole history of SOE, hitherto a specialised and secret subject, will shortly fall in line with the rest of the twentieth century's military history; for SOE's surviving archives – about one-eighth of what was committed to paper at the time – are now in process of being released, after laundry, to the Public Record Office, where they can be found under the symbol HS.

It is unusual in military histories to go into quite so much detail; but SOE was not a usual military formation, and detail was often decisive for the success or failure of any attempt to cope with the unusual conditions SOE's agents had to face.

No apology is made for the episodic roughness of much of the narrative that follows, for a series of more or less harrowing anecdotes was often all that secret staffs in London had got to work on, at the time, about what was happening in nazi-occupied Europe.

Proust wrote of one of his minor characters: 'He lived in the world of approximations, where people salute in a void and criticise in error, a world where assurance, far from being tempered in ignorance and inaccuracy, is increased thereby.'[2] This mirrors exactly the regular view of secret services; this book is meant to redress the balance, if only a little.

There were a couple of incidents in the Belgian story of just the sort that any government might be shy at having to admit.[3] The Dutch débâcle, public for over fifty years, far too big to hide, is not one of which either English or Dutch governments can be proud; though the discussion below may help to show it to have been a simpler and stupider tale than some commentators have tried to make out.

---

2 Marcel Proust, tr. C. K. Scott-Moncrieff and Terence Kilmartin, *Remembrance of Things Past* (Penguin, 1983), i. 827.
3 Pages 247–8, 310–12.

It needs emphasis that this book is not a history of resistance in the Low Countries; it is an account of the work of a British secret service – one of several – which tried to encourage active resistance there, in the forms of sabotage and subversion. While attempts are made to describe the difficulties 'in the field', as London called nazi-occupied Europe, the author's normal angle of sight is from SOE's headquarters in Baker Street; not a usual, but I believe a significant, perspective.

I have paid some attention to the sensibilities of survivors and of relatives – suppressing at one point the name of an agent who was murdered and of his two W/T operators, one of whom shot him in the presence of the other – but have normally left the raw facts to stand for themselves, where they can be established.

Naturally I have tried to quote documents correctly; a duty rather than a virtue. Readers deserve notice of one small point: for uniformity's sake, I have omitted full stops between the initials of acronyms, when they were present in the original; reading for instance CIGS instead of C.I.G.S. There are too many acronyms in this book (see the list on pages xvi–xviii); histories of modern secret services have to be riddled with them.

A few points about names also need to be cleared up early.

Typically enough for a body that was often organised in haphazard ways, SOE had two N sections, one for work into the Netherlands, the other to run naval affairs in the Far East;[4] but there will be no further need to refer either to the naval one, or to another and quite different body, N section of A Force, which ran escape lines in the Mediterranean for MI9.

The second point may affect feelings nearer home. Following then normal practice, I shall use 'Holland' and 'The Netherlands' interchangeably to refer to the whole of the same kingdom; when I need to refer to the specific provinces of North or South Holland within it, I will make it plain. In wartime, outside the foreign office, the English used 'Holland' almost universally.

---

4 See Charles Cruickshank, *SOE in the Far East* (1983), 100–2. There is a list of useful books on pages 514–24. All are published in London unless otherwise noted. Publication details of books found in Appendix 7 are not repeated in the footnotes.

Thirdly, as this book is written in English about events that took place half a century ago, I stick to place names familiar to readers of my own generation, instead of using the current Dutch equivalents. Should this book go into a Dutch translation, Antwerp, Bastogne, Bruges, Liège, Louvain, Malines, Mons, Namur can become Antwerpen, Bastenaken, Brugge, Luik, Leuven, Mechelen, Bergen, Namen. No Englishman is ever likely to talk about the legend of the Angels of Bergen or the Bergen retreat, nor any American parachutist to recall the siege of Bastenaken.

On the whole, I have omitted ranks, which in any case were of slight importance in a body in which a rear-admiral and a full general served under a squadron leader. Survivors still alive will hardly mind being treated as historical figures, without courtesy prefix. In the carefully structured armed forces of 1940–5, forenames were seldom used, except between close friends. It would mislead readers to adopt the modern habit, overload this book with forenames, or call Churchill 'Winston' or Gubbins 'Colin'.

Some aspects of my own background may affect my handling of this history. In 1941–2 I happened to be billeted at a country house near Reading, where I met at dinner several notables from the Belgian and Luxembourg governments in exile including MM Spaak, Gutt and Bech. Only many years later did I discover that my host, Basil Marsden-Smedley, was a member of the Special Operations Executive, of which I had not then heard. Later in the war, I handled secret and top secret – but not ultra secret – intelligence at Combined Operations Headquarters; learned to parachute, as intelligence officer of the Special Air Service Brigade; and managed to conceal any connection with intelligence during an uncomfortable hundred days as a prisoner of war. In 1972 I married a wife who is Dutch by birth; her father, already then a retired cabinet minister, had been in prison, and her brothers on the run, during the war. I have an adequate reading knowledge of Dutch, French and German. In 1989 I was chairman of a three-day conference in London on Anglo-Dutch relations from 1940 to 1945, an event that brought me into contact with numerous Dutch citizens, some of them of great eminence.[5]

---

5 I edited the proceedings: *Holland at War against Hitler*.

Military historians share a weakness with sergeant-majors: they like things to be orderly. Wars are not orderly. As Wavell once put it, 'war is always a far worse muddle than anything that can be produced in peace'.[6] So readers need to remember the proverbial fog of war as they peruse what follows; rational men may have made rather too many rough places plain. Yet the running will not all be smooth. Resistance, viewed through the haze of news media myth, and through such books as Steinbeck's *The Moon is Down* or Vercors's *Silence de la Mer*, now seems to have been splendid. It is easy to forget that at the time it was dangerous, difficult and dull all at once; frequently it was also downright nasty. These pages have to include several examples of its nastiness.

There is not much glory to be found in them; glory, in any case, fades fast enough. Yet scientific history ought not to be so dry as to leave no sense in its readers of what an extraordinary business a world war is; some of this may be conveyed below.

Heroism is no more enough than patriotism. Several heroes and many patriots will appear below; few of them got adequate support. Staff officers' incompetence and plain treachery threw away too many good lives. Friendship and admiration for Louis de Jong, David Stafford and the late Henri Bernard have not I hope blinded me to their occasional slips. To them, as to all the other authors cited as such, I am – as is usual among historians – most grateful.

I am grateful too to Gervase Cowell and Duncan Stuart, successive SOE advisers to the Foreign and Commonwealth Office, for much patience and forbearance; and particularly to their secretary Valerie Collins, who has borne without complaint many extra office burdens I have laid on her. I am also particularly grateful to Varinda Walters of the Cabinet Office historical section, for devoted attention to strange names in a bad handwriting.

I acknowledge the leave of the controller, HMSO, to publish all the extracts below from official correspondence and telegrams; most of them have by now reached the Public Record Office.

The staff at the British Library, the London Library, the Rijksinstituut voor Oorlogsdocumentatie in Amsterdam and the

---

6 Earl Wavell, *The Good Soldier* (1948), 120.

Centre de Recherches et d'Etudes Historiques de la Seconde Guerre Mondiale in Brussels (since renamed) have all been most helpful; and Maartje Romme, my niece-in-law, gave me an invaluable long loan of one of the family's copies of de Jong's great work, repeatedly cited below. Michael Sissons, my agent, has been most helpful and most patient.

Unattributed translations are my own.

I must also record how grateful I am to the secret archive clerks, whose identity – even whose location – I have never been tactless enough to inquire, who have responded promptly over nine years to numerous and sometimes fractious requests.

My greatest debt is to my wife, for years of unstinted encouragement.

Though the events described in this book took place over fifty years ago, all passion about them is by no means spent. Although old men now, some survivors still tremble with long-cherished rage when they recall what their enemies did to their friends, or how some they had taken for friends turned out enemies and betrayed them. Authors attempting this subject still walk on egg-shells.

M.R.D.F.
Nuthampstead
4 August 1998

POSTCRIPT

This book was finished two and a half years ago; needed time to be cleared by various authorities; and has had to wait its turn to be published. This gives me the chance to record further obligations of gratitude, and to add a few books to the book list.

One of these books, the virtual in-house history of SOE by W. J. M. Mackenzie, completed in 1948 but graded secret until fifty years later, is a masterwork, crammed with insights into the body's worldwide activities, and is henceforward the starting-point for every book or article devoted to it.

I am much indebted to Linda Osband of St Ermin's Press for

pulling the book into final shape; to Peter Winfield of *The Economist* for the maps; to Adrienne Fell for typing the index; and to my son Richard for saving me from a foolish mistake.

M.R.D.F.
Nuthampstead
20 February 2001

Abbreviations

AA	anti-aircraft
A/CD	one of CD's chief assistants
AD/E	head of SOE in NW Europe
AD/P	one of CD's chief assistants
AGRA	Amis du Grand Reich Allemand
AI	air intelligence
AL	Armée de la Libération
AMP	Armée de Milice Patriotique
AS	Armée Secrète
BBO	Bureau voor Bijzondere Opdrachten
BdS	Befehlshaber der Sicherheitspolizei
BEF	British Expeditionary Force
BI	Bureau Inlichtingen
BS	Binnenlandse Strijdkrachten
BSS	Bayswater security section
BVT	Bureau Voorbereiding Terugkeer
C	head of MI6
CD	executive director of SOE
CID	Centrale Inlichtingsdienst
COSSAC	chief of staff to the supreme allied commander
CS.6	Corellistraat 6
D/CE	SOE's director of counter-espionage
D/F	direction-finding
DNB	*Dictionary of National Biography*
D/R	SOE symbol
D/R.LC	SOE symbol

duplic	duplicated
DZ	dropping zone
ed., edn	editor(s), edition
EU/P	section for Poles abroad
F	independent French section
FIL	Front de l'Indépendence et de la Libération
Gestapo	geheime Staatspolizei
GFP	geheime Feldpolizei
ID	Inlichtingen Dienst
JIC	Joint Intelligence Committee
KdN	*Het Koninkrijk der Nederlanden in de Tweede Wereldoorlog*
KP	Knokploegen
LB	Légion Belge
LC	Low Countries
LCS	London Controlling Section
LO	Landelijke Organisatie
MEW	Ministry of Economic Warfare
MI5	security service
MI6	secret or special intelligence service
MI9	escape service
MI10	intelligence on enemy equipment
MI14	intelligence on German army
MIR	war office operations branch
MNB	Mouvement National Belge
MVT	Bureau Militaire Voorbereiding Terugkeer
N	Netherlands section
NRA	nothing recorded against
NSB	Nationaal Socialistische Beweging
OD	Orde Dienst
OMBR	Organisation Militaire Belge de la Résistance
Orpo	Ordnungspolizei
OSS	Office of Strategic Services
OTP	one-time pad
PF	personal file
PP	parliamentary papers
PRO	Public Record Office
PWE	Political Warfare Executive

RAF	Royal Air Force
RIOD	Rijksinstituut voor Oorlogsdocumentatie
RN	Royal Navy
R/T	radio telephony
RUSIJ	*Royal United Services Institute Journal*
RVPS	Royal Victoria Patriotic School
RVV	Raad van Verzet
SAS	Special Air Service
SD	special duties
SD	Sicherheitsdienst
SFDets	Special Force Detachments
SFHQ	Special Force Headquarters
SHAEF	Supreme Headquarters, Allied Expeditionary Force
Sipo	Sicherheitspolizei
SIS	MI6
SOE	Special Operations Executive
SS	Schutzstaffel
STS	Special Training School
T	Belgian section
tpt	teleprint
tr	translated, translator
TS	typescript
TSC	typescript copy
V/CD	one of CD's chief assistants
Verdinaso	Verbond van Dietse Nationaal-Solidaristen
VNV	Vlaams National Verbond
W/T, WT	wireless telegraphy

I

Introduction

'Its reputation lags behind its performance'[1]

This book describes the work of the Special Operations Executive (henceforward SOE), the worldwide British secret service in charge of sabotage and subversion, into German-occupied Holland, Belgium and Luxembourg in the years 1940–5.

The story lies, on the whole, on the margin of allied and German strategy; Germany's wartime allies, Italy and Japan, hardly figure in it. It includes some intricate passages of betrayal and disaster, and one substantial clandestine triumph.

In German strategy, the prospective value of the Low Countries lay in the routes they provided for turning the Maginot Line; and in the chance their invasion gave for drawing allied troops forward towards Antwerp – for this would weaken the allied left centre before Guderian's decisive strike for the mouth of the Somme. Once they had been conquered, as they rapidly were, Holland was a useful source of food, and both Holland and Belgium of skilled forced labour, for Germany. They provided some of the airfields from which the Luftwaffe flew during the battle of Britain and the subsequent 'Blitz' on British cities. Moreover, the main railway line Cologne-Namur-Paris ran on to the new U-boat bases on the Biscay coast of France, from which Dönitz waged with almost fatal effect the battle of the Atlantic.

In the much longer term, nazi theorists envisaged incorporating the Dutch, the Luxembourgers and the Flemings – all of whom they

---

1. Report on SOE's organisation, 1942: see page 37.

Europe (part) in 1942

thought Nordic – into their Thousand-Year Reich, of which the frontier would shift westward to the Meuse, or to the Scheldt, or even to the coast west of Ostend; the Walloons, the French-speaking Belgians, could be thrown in with the French in a client state. Meanwhile, so long as the war went on, the Low Countries made a convenient glacis – an open space across which attackers on the German homeland could be bombarded.

When in 1944 the ground attack of operation 'Overlord' followed repeated and continuing allied air attacks, many German suppliers for the Normandy front used Belgian and some used Dutch railways, canals and roads. Eisenhower's strategy, and an uncharacteristically rapid retreat by the German army, secured the overrunning of most of Belgium in a few days, but the momentum of that astonishing advance was not maintained. A brief pause led to a further leap, operation 'Market Garden', checked at Arnhem; after which Holland's strategic role was slight, though its people's sufferings were intense.

Unlike the battle for France, which was crucial both in 1940 and in 1944, the battle for the Low Countries was usually marginal. Only twice in SOE's lifetime did the principal combatant powers concentrate on a major objective in them: the allies, in the attack that foundered at Arnhem in September 1944 – which was only meant to be a series of stepping-stones for an attack on the Ruhr; and the Germans, in their abortive advance through the Ardennes on Antwerp three months later ('the battle of the Bulge') which never got half way. Yet at the margin, as readers will see, the secret war had excitements of its own.

For a few ghastly days in May 1940 Holland received such heavy and sudden blows from the Wehrmacht that it succumbed; Belgium did not do much better. For a few spectacular days in September 1944 Belgium was overrun by Eisenhower's advancing armies, which soon got stuck in southern Holland. Round some small towns in Belgian Luxembourg the fate of the war in the west seemed to hinge about Christmas 1944; though Hitler's Ardennes offensive was not in reality the danger into which it was inflated by a staff scare at the time, later perpetuated in newspaper myth.

Otherwise, it needs to be said early, the strategic importance of the Low Countries seemed slight. Yet it had been for centuries a principle of English foreign policy that no other great power should dominate the mouths of the Scheldt, the Meuse and the Rhine. Edward III, Elizabeth I, William III and Anne had all fought wars – the two kings had fought in person – to uphold this principle; under George III, England had fought a protracted world war against revolutionary and Napoleonic France to reassert it. Dutch neutrality had been precious to the English during the next world war – now commonly, wrong-headedly called 'the first' – against Wilhelm II's Germany, because this neutrality helped to protect the principle. This war was vividly within the memory of anybody over thirty-five years old in 1940; to many of whom in this island, the loss of Belgium and Holland in a few weeks to the Wehrmacht seemed an almost personal affront.

France rivalled Yugoslavia as a centre of SOE's attention; indeed only into Yugoslavia were more stores sent under SOE's auspices than were sent into France.[2] The Low Countries, by comparison, lay in a backwater. Holland's cardinal economic importance to Germany before and during the world war of 1914–18 was not repeated next time round; Holland, Belgium and Luxembourg became conquered provinces, ripe for exploitation by the wartime economy of the Reich.

Every military historian must consider terrain, early. Terrain is perhaps not quite the *mot juste* for the Netherlands. The Dutch all know from childhood how much of their country lies below sea level, and how fragile it is, because its safety from the sea depends on a long-elaborated, highly complicated dyke and drainage system. All through the years of exile, this fragility was ever-present to the Dutch government in London; in the closing months of the war, the dykes again came to the forefront of anxiety.

The Netherlands are – were already then – remarkably easy to move across, if one sticks to the many admirable roads, or goes by train; but it is hardly possible to travel secretly across country there, even on horseback, even by motor-bicycle, because of all the water obstacles. Most of these are too deep to wade, many are too wide for

2. *Franco-British Studies* 2 (Paris, autumn 1986), 25–6; *Proceedings of the RAF Historical Society* 5 (Bristol, February 1989), 14.

a horse to jump; swimming, seldom silent, leaves the swimmer drenched and cold. Both by road and by rail, there are endless openings for control; control was a nazi speciality, as it is in all tyrannies. In fact, in Holland the Germans did not bother much about road controls, except on the great Moerdijk bridge, although no one at SOE's headquarters in Baker Street knew this. However, all the Frisian Islands and the big islands between Flushing and The Hook soon became prohibited areas, into which no one could go – or was supposed to go – without a German permit. In the early 1940s the Netherlands presented terrain unsuitable for rural guerilla, which became an SOE speciality; and neither the Dutch nor SOE were ready for urban guerilla.

The terrain of Belgium, north of the Sambre and the Meuse, consists also of countryside much cut up by watercourses, particularly west of the Scheldt, and of even more heavily populated townscape. In the south-east lie the forested, rolling hills of the Ardennes – less built up, fuller of hiding places, less easy to control – extending into most of Luxembourg. Though better territory for rural guerilla, the Ardennes are short of easily findable dropping zones (DZs) for parachute supply. This forced some of the Belgians back on urban guerilla, with interesting results.

The Low Countries at war were unlike their neighbouring France. Large areas of central and southern France, such as the heath and marshland of the Sologne, the great *causses* of Poitou and the Limousin, the rugged country of the Massif Central, were ill equipped with fast roads and difficult to police. In them maquisards could live, wander, even mount attacks in comparative ease.[3] The Ardennes apart, nowhere in the Low Countries, not even the Dutch Veluwe, provided such splendid terrain for SOE.

Belgium, even with the Ardennes, was the most densely populated country in Europe; Holland came a close second. Holland had nearly nine million inhabitants in 1940, Belgium had nearly 8,300,000. Over 100,000 people lived in the following four Belgian cities:

---

3. H. R. Kedward, *In Search of the Maquis* (Oxford University Press, 1993), is a seminal study.

Brussels, with over 900,000 inhabitants, Antwerp with over a quarter of a million, and Ghent and Liège with just over 160,000 each. Three Dutch cities, Amsterdam (at nearly 800,000), Rotterdam and The Hague each had over half a million. Utrecht, Haarlem, Groningen and Eindhoven all had over 100,000; Nijmegen, Tilburg, Enschede and Arnhem well over 80,000. Luxembourg had fewer than 300,000 inhabitants, one in five of whom lived in the capital. To lay out their sizes in tabular form,

Luxembourg had 998 square miles / 1,628 km^2
Belgium had 11,775 " " / 18,820 km^2
Holland had 12,865 " " / 19,515 km^2 (land area);

while Great Britain had 89,041 square miles /143.914 km^2, an area three and a half times as large as all the Low Countries put together, holding a population of over 45,000,000, well over twice as numerous.

Caesar's Gallic war advanced the frontier of the Roman empire as far as the left bank of the Rhine, which cuts across the Low Countries. Six times since they have all been united under a single ruler; never for long. Augustus's advance into the new province of Germania, which reached the Elbe, ended in AD 9. Charlemagne's empire covered all the Low Countries; so did Charles V's; neither lasted.

The names of Campin, van Eyck, Memling, Vermeer, Rubens and Rembrandt testify to the grandeur of Flemish and Dutch painting, a vital element in north European culture; Magritte and Mondrian upheld the tradition in the twentieth century. The buildings of Brussels, Amsterdam and a dozen other cities testify also to the Low Countries' cultural standing. Moreover, they have been much fought over: Flanders used to be called the cockpit of Europe. The name of one village, Fleurus near Charleroi, has been given to as many as four battles.[4]

The Dutch still recall their Eighty Years' War, begun in 1568, fought to throw off Habsburg supremacy. Their United Provinces

---

4. Cf Richard Holmes, *Fatal Avenue* (Cape, 1992), 250.

next made the world shake: Amsterdam was for a while its commercial capital, and Dutch ships ruled the seven seas. Once they towed the pride of the Royal Navy out of the Medway, and have galleries to prove it in the Rijksmuseum at Amsterdam.

The Habsburgs long controlled the Austrian Netherlands, sharing much of the land of modern Belgium with the prince-bishopric of Liège – then independent. Revolutionary and Napoleonic France overran all the Low Countries, to which Napoleon allotted nineteen *départements* in an imperial France of which he thrust the frontier through to the Baltic. Dutch and Belgian soldiers played a part in his final overthrow at the battle of Waterloo in 1815, at which the Prince of Orange was wounded. The Congress of Vienna, building barriers against French expansion, placed all the Low Countries in a single Kingdom of the Netherlands under the Prince of Orange's father, King Willem I.

This kingdom in turn split apart in 1830, when street fighting in Brussels brought on a civil war between the Dutch and the Belgians; who seceded to form a separate kingdom under George IV of England's son-in-law, Leopold of Saxe-Coburg, a secession recognised in a treaty negotiated by Lord Palmerston in 1839.[5] This treaty declared Belgium a perpetually neutral state, under a joint and several guarantee given by Austria, France, Prussia, Russia and the United Kingdom. Under it, the eastern half of the grand duchy of Luxembourg remained part of both the Kingdom of the Netherlands and the Germanic Confederation, which broke up in the German civil war of 1866. Next year the grand duchy was declared neutral also; and in 1890 it again became independent.[6]

Napoleon III's ambitions to secure territory in the Low Countries were held in check, partly by British diplomacy and partly by Prussian arms; in the Franco-Prussian war of 1870–1 the Low Countries' only role was to intern soldiers who strayed across the border. Thereafter they held aloof from what A. J. P. Taylor has called

---

5. C. Parry (ed.), *Consolidated Treaty Series* lxxxviii (New York: Oceana, 1969), 411–26.
6. See page 353.

the struggle for mastery between great powers that culminated in war in 1914.

The French had several years' warning of the German plan to attack France across Belgium; and ignored it, believing it to be a plant. British efforts to alarm the Belgians by drawing their attention to the vast German railway sidings near Belgium's eastern border were also fruitless. In August 1914, as another Great War began, the Germans conquered all of Luxembourg and most of Belgium, while leaving Holland neutral; it took four years and a quarter, and a worldwide coalition, to drive them out. At the start of this war, 100,000 Belgians took refuge in Holland;[7] presage of a larger future exodus that went the opposite way.

At the end of this Great War the German Kaiser, Wilhelm II, lost the confidence of his officer corps and bolted by train to neutral Holland. The western allies wanted him for trial as a war criminal. The Dutch would not compromise their neutrality by handing him over; he thus evaded justice. This made the Dutch unpopular with the allies, but preserved their sense of integrity. Holland was admitted, after a moment's hesitation, as a founder member of the League of Nations, but the Dutch did not sign the treaty of Versailles; the Belgians did.

From SOE's later angle of sight, it mattered that Belgium in the early 1940s was full of men and women who had tasted occupation before, and of men who had tasted battle – neither taste is agreeable, nor quickly forgotten – while the Dutch had tasted neither since Boney's day. No Dutchman had fired a shot in anger in Europe, unless in a private quarrel on a duelling-ground, between 1832 and 1936; the mere thought of doing so was unthinkable to many Dutch politicians and officials. There were a few survivors who had fought against the British in South Africa in 1899–1902; none of them young enough to exert any military, or important enough to wield any political, influence. Seven hundred Dutchmen went to fight in the International Brigades in Spain, where 430 of them are buried.[8]

---

7. *Grote Winkler Prins* xiii (Amsterdam, 1983), 133c.
8. Dr L. de Jong, *Het Koninkrijk der Nederlanden in de Tweede Wereldoorlog* (henceforward de Jong, *KdN*), i. 482.

In the scales of diplomacy none of the Low Countries carried much weight, not least because their armed forces were so feeble. By 1939 those of land-locked Luxembourg amounted to 400 gendarmes, nearly half of them reservists. The Dutch, with colonies in the East and West Indies, had a small navy to protect their sea-borne trade. It included one elderly sizeable coast defence ship with 11″ guns, out east, and four light cruisers. They also had a small air force, with few up-to-date aircraft; and an army of eight weak home defence divisions, with no experience and not a single tank. The Belgians had just abolished their navy. They had a similar small air force; and their army ran in 1939 to seven infantry and two horsed cavalry divisions – larger than the army of the United States. It included as many as ten tanks. The German army then had over 2,500.

All three small states had vast goodwill towards mankind, and sound Christian feelings towards their neighbours, but they exerted little actual power in the maelstrom into which Stalin, Mussolini and Hitler whirled Europe in the late 1930s. Indeed, their passion for neutrality worked against the taking of precautions that in hindsight look sensible against impending German attack: precautions urged on them by, among others, MIR, a small branch of the War Office's general staff – one of the seeds from which SOE grew[9] – but urged in vain.

Luxembourg remained frankly indefensible, relying on its neighbours' goodwill and respect for treaties: 'sanguine!', Mr Gladstone would have said, on Hitler's visible record. Both Holland and Belgium made a positive fetish of neutrality. The more nazi Germany rearmed and behaved aggressively, the farther the Dutch and the Belgians went out of their way to avoid giving their great eastern neighbour any offence.

Nearly sixty thousand refugees fled from nazi Germany in 1933, the year the nazis came to power; over half of them Jewish – 5,000, of whom 3,000 were Jewish, into Holland, and about half that number into Belgium. The Dutch government reckoned that by

---

9. See page 25.

April 1938, 32,000 refugees had reached their soil from Germany, 25,000 of them Jewish; of whom 8,000 (undifferentiated) had moved on.[10] Their arrival embarrassed Dutch officials, who did not want to offend the German government by open offers of asylum from it; there were awkward incidents in country villages, when refugees who thought they had walked through safely, avoiding the nazis' strict controls on exit by main road or rail, encountered their first Dutch policeman or customs guard. There was plenty of sympathy for them in Dutch private families; and one political row. On 20 February 1934 eight young German citizens were arrested at a meeting at Laren, near Hilversum; four of them were packed off back to Germany and the other four deported to Belgium. One of these last, later famous, was Willy Brandt, who described the event as 'cringing servility before the powerful Third Reich'.[11]

In October 1936, when the civil war in Spain that provided a dress rehearsal for the impending world conflict was already three months old, King Leopold III of the Belgians issued a formal public affirmation of his country's strict adherence to neutrality. This effectively revoked the Franco-Belgian alliance of 1920 that had resulted from the Great War. Repeated messages from the British and the French, conveyed formally and informally by diplomats, service attachés and businessmen both to the Belgians and the Dutch, urging them to prepare against an impending German attack, were rebuffed: the two neutral countries did not even yet concert together what line they would follow. Belgium stuck to the concept of armed neutrality as an adequate defence, while lacking the arms to sustain it; Holland stuck to being neutral.

Neither Belgium nor Holland took any part in the Anschluss, the union of nazi Germany and catholic Austria in March 1938. From the Munich conference of September 1938 they were also excluded, as indeed were the Czechs and Slovaks who were the immediate sufferers, as well as the Hungarians and the Poles who were short-term gainers from it, and the Soviet Union which was treated as if it, too, was a minor power that could be neglected. In

---

10. Bob Moore, *Refugees from Nazi Germany in the Netherlands 1933–1940* (Dordrecht: Nijhoff, 1986), 21, 81.
11. *Ibid.*, 149.

the subsequent disruption of Czechoslovakia they had no say; nor were they covered by Prime Minister Chamberlain's guarantees, all of which applied to eastern Europe. In the run-up to world war, through the nazi-soviet pact of 23/24 August 1939 and the consequent German attack on Poland on 1 September, none of the Low Countries had any part to play beyond that of appalled spectator.

Leopold III had hoped to do better. He had prepared, with Dutch, Luxembourger and Scandinavian support, an appeal for world peace; but when he made it, in a broadcast on the evening of 23 August, Ribbentrop's arrival in Moscow to sign the pact overnight stole the world's headlines.

The Dutch armed forces mobilised in two stages, on 24 and 28 August; the Belgian on the 25th. Early on 1 September Hitler unleashed the German attack on Poland, which brought on British and French declarations of war on Germany on the 3rd. In western Europe, eight months of stand-by followed for armies and air forces alike, enlivened by occasional alarms.

Mobilisation in the Low Countries was little troubled by dissidence. Holland included some small groups that were actively pro-nazi; so did Belgium. Anton Mussert's Nationaal-Socialistische Beweging (NSB) had secured 4.21 per cent of the Dutch vote in the general election of May 1937, and thus had four seats in each of the two Dutch houses of parliament. In a free country, Mussert was allowed his say; his prospects of power, without support from abroad, were nil. The same was true of Léon Degrelle, who led the rexist movement among the Walloons. The rexists had secured twenty-one seats in the lower chamber of 177 members in the 1936 elections, but – after an upset with the Roman Catholic authorities – only four in a chamber enlarged to 200 in the elections of April 1939. They also had four seats in the 1939 senate. The Vlaams Nationaal Verbond (VNV) under Staf de Clercq advocated fascist views in northern, Flemish-speaking Belgium with slight success – they won seventeen seats in the chamber and twelve in the senate in 1939 – but were also remote from power. A Dutch and Flemish splinter party, the Verbond van Dietse Nationaal-Solidaristen (Verdinaso), had still less appeal and still fewer adherents; the Dutch Zwaarte Front was even more obscure.

In each country there was also a small communist party, affiliated to the Comintern. The Belgian communists had nine deputies in the chamber, and three senators, after the 1939 general election. The Dutch communists, like the Dutch nazis, also commanded about 4 per cent of the popular vote. In the 1937 elections, following the directives of the seventh world congress of the Comintern in 1935, they made common cause with the Dutch socialists and ran no separate candidates. By 1939 they had over 9,000 party members, nearly half of them in Amsterdam, and some standing in the trade union movement.

Notionally, these communists had given some thought to what an underground struggle against an oppressor might be like. Moreover, their hard core had had recent practical combat experience in the International Brigades in Spain. They all performed a prompt political somersault, on Moscow's orders, to conform with the nazi-soviet pact. Their discipline held, though their popularity suffered.

Religion was more important in Europe, as a social cement and as a guide to conduct, half a century ago than it is today. Communists, though anti-Christian in their beliefs, often held to their Marxist tenets with exemplary piety; and practically every Belgian communist had been baptised a Roman Catholic. The Dutch had a Roman Catholic minority over two million strong, a Protestant majority which included the royal family and almost all civil servants, and over a million citizens who had declared themselves of no religion in the census of 1930.

The gift for looking officials straight in the eye, and lying to them, which comes easily to the criminal classes – especially to con-men – does not sit well on a puritan conscience; many Dutch citizens could not manage it. It was one of the gifts SOE tried to teach,[12] but is not easily taught; it comes as second nature to those born devious. This needs to be counted among the obstacles to SOE's success in the Low Countries.

Once Poland had been overrun by Germany and Russia, and the western front dozed in *Sitzkrieg*, the king of the Belgians took

---

12. See page 46.

another diplomatic initiative. Having cleared the scheme with the Pope, the kings of Denmark and of Sweden and the president of Finland, he visited The Hague on 6 November, and next day he and Queen Wilhelmina of the Netherlands issued a joint appeal to England, France and Germany, proposing their own good offices to establish an equitable peace.[13]

This was a reasonable but not a well-timed appeal. The English and the French no longer trusted anything Hitler had to say because he had deceived them so often already. Hitler was one of the rare men who had enjoyed the Great War; having gone to war again in September, he found he still enjoyed it, and kept pressing his generals to get on with it. Besides, 7 November was the eve of his failed *putsch* in Munich in 1923, and he was busy preparing his usual memorial speech. This speech was greeted by a bomb, which burst in the meeting-hall a few minutes after he had left it. Of this bomb he may have had forewarning; as he may have had forewarning of a smaller but more successful *putsch* at Venlo, on the Dutch-German border, on the 9th.

The Venlo affair, though an embarrassment both to the government and to SIS, the secret or special intelligence service, is now too well known to be swept under the carpet.

In the mid 1930s the Gestapo managed to penetrate SIS's office at The Hague; from which C – Admiral Sinclair, the head of the service – found it convenient to run most of his agents in place in north-west Europe. C suspected Gestapo successes, not only there; and arranged for Claude Dansey, his man in Rome, to appear to be drummed out of the service for malversation of funds. This enabled Dansey to set up a parallel organisation, called Z. On the outbreak of war in September 1939 Z's men joined or rejoined C's.

Z's man in Holland, Sigismund Payne Best,[14] was already under close Gestapo watch. Dansey had known him when both of them

---

13. Text in *Keesing's Contemporary Archives*, 3799, from *The Times* for 8 November, 8d; and see Lord Keyes, *Outrageous Fortune* (2 edn, Tom Donovan, 1990), i. 97.
14. *The Times* obituaries, 27 September, 16g; 2 October 14g; and 26 October 21h, 1978.

worked under the original C during the Great War. In August 1939 Best and C's head of station in Holland – R. H. Stevens, late of the Indian army – found themselves in touch with a group of anti-nazi Germans, headed (they understood) by a general, whom they had not yet identified. SIS did not hug this secret to itself. The prime minister, the foreign secretary and his permanent under-secretary were kept fully informed, and in October Chamberlain reported progress to the War Cabinet.

Best and Stevens confided what they were doing to the head of Dutch intelligence, Major-General J. W. van Oorschot, who provided them with an escort, Dirk Klop, an army subaltern whose English was fluent. Klop was present at some interviews with junior Germans and saw the texts of several British-coded messages, which van Oorschot's expert read easily. On 9 November Klop went with Best, Stevens, and Best's chauffeur[15] to a meeting with a more senior German. On the way to it, Stevens jotted down and put in his pocket a list of the agents he must get out of Holland quickly if there was trouble.

The rendezvous was at a café slap on the Dutch-German frontier, beyond the Dutch customs control point, at Venlo. There all four men – Klop mortally wounded – were abruptly bundled over the border into Germany by a carload of thugs. The principal with whom they had been dealing turned out in fact to be Walter Schellenberg, a twenty-nine-year-old major in the Sicherheitsdienst (SD), the nazi party security service.

One at least of the captives, threatened with torture, talked all too freely. From him the Germans got all that he knew about the structure, functions and staff of MI6, the secret or special intelligence service (SIS).[16] The incident is rumoured nearly to have cost Stewart

---

15. Identified in *The Times*, 19 February 1948, as Jan Lemmers of The Hague.
16. See Christopher Andrew, *Secret Service* (1985), 432–9, as well as de Jong, *KdN*, ii. 80–116, and *The Times*, 10 November 1939, 8b, and 22 November 1939, 8d. This last article cited a communiqué Himmler had signed on the previous day, which identified the Venlo captives as Best and Stevens, officers of the British Secret Service, and held them responsible for the Munich bomb. Cullum A. MacDonald, 'The Venlo affair', in *European Studies Review* viii (October 1978), 445–64, spells out the War Cabinet's involvement.

Menzies the succession to Sinclair's post as C;[17] Sinclair, for some months unwell, had died on 4 November.[18] Certainly it left on Menzies's mind a strong distaste for dealings with anybody German who claimed to be a dissident from nazism; with unhappy later results. It also provided the Germans with the ghost of an excuse for their aggression six months later.

Poland had already vanished from Hitler's map of Europe, carved up in the fourth partition, of September 1939, between Germany and the USSR. The Scandinavian campaign of the spring of 1940 left the neutral Low Countries still more apprehensive; for where they lay on the map laid them open to invasion when next the Germans decided to turn on the French.

Every army staff officer in western Europe had pored over the history of the Franco-Prussian war of 1870–1 and of the Great War of 1914–18. Every staff officer, like every serious newspaper reader, knew that the French had fortified the Maginot Line between themselves and the Germans, but this seemingly unbreakable barrier of steel and concrete ran only from the Swiss border to the southernmost edge of Belgium: it stopped at Longuyon. Efforts to extend a fortified line along the French side of the frontier, from Longuyon past Sedan, Maubeuge and Lille to Dunkirk, were visibly in progress during the winter of 1939–40, and as visibly incomplete.[19] Clearly some variant on Schlieffen's plan of 1905 – an attack across Flanders on the French left – was a more feasible way to turn the Maginot Line than a cast through Switzerland.

Whether or not to invade Holland as well as Belgium was much debated among the Germans. Wilhelm II's Germany was more cautious than Hitler's; the Third Reich was ready to go the whole hog.

---

17. Private information.
18. *Dictionary of National Biography* (henceforward *DNB*), *Missing Persons* (Oxford University Press, 1993), 604–5. Menzies also figures in *DNB 1961–1970* (1981), 749–50.
19. In March 1940 the *Daily Mail* published a thirty-two-page *War Atlas*, which had in its back pocket an 'Air-view Map of the Western Front', about 30″ × 36″, showing the line as complete: an interesting fragment of propaganda.

Before the new world war was a fortnight old, Churchill as First Lord of the Admiralty went on record on 12 September 1939 at a War Cabinet meeting that he 'considered the attitude of the Belgian Government indefensible' as it continued to ban staff talks or reconnaissance missions aimed at impeding a German attack.[20] Leopold III, wiser than his ministers, managed to take a few steps behind their backs; acting not as monarch, bound to follow their advice, but in his other constitutional role as commander-in-chief. He had for some months past been in touch privately with Gamelin, the French commander-in-chief, whom he provided personally with every detail the French requested about Belgian topography and troop dispositions. Gamelin did not mention this to the British.[21]

Leopold also sent a private emissary to London, to sound out the War Cabinet through his old friend Admiral of the Fleet Sir Roger Keyes. As C was ill, the War Cabinet consulted Sir Vernon Kell, the original head of the security service, still in post; having risen from captain to knighted major-general since 1909.[22] Kell sent Guy Liddell – a connexion, appropriately enough, of Alice in Wonderland[23] – over to Brussels to probe the emissary's *bona fides,* which were intact. The end result was one three-day secret reconnaissance in March 1940 by a British general of the line the British Expeditionary Force (BEF) proposed to take up on the River Dyle. The rest of the Belgian king's initiatives drained into the sands of indecision.

Not until early in 1940 did Dutch and Belgian ministers creep far enough out of their separate hutches of neutrality to start discussing, even with each other, what steps it might be sensible to take jointly to ward off a German attack; and the discussions resulted in nothing

---

20. PRO CAB 65/1, quoted by Martin Gilbert (ed.), *The Churchill War Papers* (Heinemann, 1993), i. 79.
21. Keyes, *op. cit.*, i. 115–16, 121, 125–6.
22. Gilbert, *op. cit.*, i. 207–8. For Sir Vernon Kell, see *DNB Missing Persons*, 370–1. Keyes, *op. cit.*, i. 128–9.
23. For Liddell, see *The Times*, 6 December 1958, 8e, and 21 January 1989, 3c.

beyond mutual reproaches. Tentative soundings were also made with the British and French commanders; so tentative, on the land and air sides, that none of the essential staff work was even begun, and even the Admiralty only managed a few provisional plans.[24] The German general staff handled things differently.

Repeatedly, through late autumn, winter and spring, Hitler ordered his generals to activate *Fall Gelb* – Case Yellow – the main westward attack; and was then persuaded to cancel the order, usually on account of bad weather. Each order and counter-order was promptly passed on by Hans Oster, a senior personage at the Berlin headquarters of the Abwehr, the German armed forces' secret service, to his friend Colonel Sas, the Dutch military attaché. Their reports became so frequent that no one took them seriously any more at The Hague. However, Oster's message of 9 May was genuine. By the end of that month the Low Countries had once more come under a single ruler: Hitler.

Early on 10 May 1940, with no shred of official previous warning, Germany invaded all three of the neutral Low Countries; as well as attacking belligerent France. German parachutists landed near the royal palace on the outskirts of The Hague, aiming to kidnap Queen Wilhelmina; her bodyguard, aided by her son-in-law, managed to repel this attack. Indeed, almost all the Germans' airborne efforts into Holland failed. The rest of the Dutch armed forces had hardly any successes to report; with their peaceable mentality and inferior weaponry, they were rapidly overwhelmed.[25]

The Dutch parliament was in recess. The cabinet held an emergency meeting in The Hague on the morning of 10 May, at which Dr de Geer, the prime minister, was in such a state of anxiety that he could not work a dial telephone. The queen's nerve was steadier, and she gave what leadership she could; but achieved no control over the invaders. On 13 May, during an air raid on the Hook of Holland, she embarked in a British destroyer, HMS *Hereward*, hoping to travel to still uninvaded Zeeland and pursue the battle from there. Naval

---

24. De Jong, *KdN*, ii. 252–69.
25. For a full account of this brief campaign, in Dutch, see H. Amersfoort and P. H. Kamphuis (eds), *Mei 1940*.

necessity, against which even queens have no power, took her to Harwich instead, and she had to throw herself on the hospitality of her remote cousin King George VI.

She had not so much as a spare blouse with her; but she did bring her great seal, and was accompanied by a senior Dutch official whose consent was needed for any Dutch act of state to be legal.[26] Any German regulations imposed on the Netherlands thus could have no validity in Dutch law.

One of the earliest decisions of Churchill's newly formed War Cabinet was to offer asylum to Wilhelm II, who was living in exile at Doorn, east of Utrecht. He was closely related to the English royal family, for his mother had been Edward VII's elder sister; even if he had gone to the bad. After two days' reflection, he turned the offer down,[27] and congratulated Hitler instead. He remained under virtual house arrest, now with SS sentries, till he died of old age on his ancestor George III's birthday, 4 June 1941.

German intelligence about the Low Countries was full, indeed complete: except that the nazis had no concept of how unwelcome they were going to be. For example, Fort Eben Emael, on the Albert Canal just south of Maastricht, a key point in the eastern defences of Belgium, had been erected in 1932–4 in consultation with two German engineering firms; every last detail of its construction was therefore available to Belgium's newest enemy. Not till long afterwards did it become known that Hitler himself had decided the minutest details of the airborne attack on it. Though the subaltern in charge of that attack arrived several hours late, his chief sergeant had rapidly bottled up the defenders, who soon gave in.[28]

The Belgian army had little more success than the Dutch at repelling the expanding torrent of the Wehrmacht's armour; but the fighting went on for a fortnight longer, and ravaged more of the country. There was no Belgian equivalent to the raid on Rotterdam that brought the Dutch to surrender in short order, and no repeat in

---

26. A point in constitutional law for which I am indebted to Herman Friedhoff: see his *Requiem for the Resistance*, 27–8.
27. Gilbert, *op. cit.*, i. 1276, 1277n.
28. Holmes, *op. cit.*, 298.

1940 of such an atrocity as the burning of Louvain university library in 1914; though the new library was set on fire by German shells, most of it survived. But this time there was no protracted formal stand on Belgian soil.

Instead, there was a colossal – if only temporary – shift of population. Frightened by what they feared from the Germans, nearly a quarter of Belgium's inhabitants bolted, before, or in case, or as the battle passed their homes. Some only went a few miles; two million entered France, where some cast up near the Pyrenees. On 28 May, in circumstances long fiercely disputed, Leopold III surrendered.[29]

Section D of the Secret Intelligence Service (SIS), from which SOE in part derived,[30] was a vigorous but short-sighted body. No one in it had looked far enough ahead to envisage the German overrunning of the Low Countries: nothing had been prepared there in the way of stay-behind parties or dumps of sabotage stores.[31]

MIR did a little, though only a little, better than Section D. At least its head, J. C. F. Holland,[32] realised that there was a problem worth study, and consulted the Admiralty about what might need to be demolished, in the way of heavy cranes and other harbour facilities, if the Germans were about to overrun the ports on the east side of the North Sea. After these talks, on 15 October 1939 he sent to the British military attachés in Brussels and The Hague lists of vulnerable points.[33] The attachés had trouble getting anyone in either country to pay attention, for Dutch and Belgians alike were passionately attached to their neutrality.

MIR, planning gloomily for the worst case, envisaged three field companies of the Royal Engineers as necessary for the work that would need to be done. In the end the task was reduced to disposing of stocks of stored oil, for which a single unit sufficed: Kent Fortress Company, RE.

---

29. Keyes, *op. cit.*, i. 308–94, a sturdy defence of the king, now holds the field.
30. See page 25.
31. SOE whole world war diary, i. 3.
32. See *DNB Missing Persons*, 322.
33. MIR war diary for that day, in SOE HQ 71.

That company sailed to Holland, reaching The Hook at 16:30 on 10 May 1940, with a detachment two hours later at IJmuiden. No one met the party at The Hook, but they picked their way through the general confusion to Rotterdam, where they started a colossal oil fire. The Boyes anti-tank rifle, only of use against the lighter tanks, pierced oil storage containers easily; the flames were several hundred feet high. The IJmuiden party blew up oil tanks in Amsterdam, under heavy small-arms fire, on Tuesday the 14th, and helped destroy dock installations on their way out. There were no engineer casualties, though Commander Hill, RN, who helped them rescue thirty-six tons of gold, was killed by a mine.[34]

Another engineer detachment, probably from the same company, went to Antwerp in mid-May and 'successfully discharged its duties',[35] presumably by setting another oil fire; now that the frail bark of neutral status had been shattered for Belgium as well as Holland.

Here is a typical instance of the tale half told, out of which so much of the popular history of SOE is built. On the same last boat from Holland that carried the Kent Fortress Company, there travelled also one of SOE's principal founding figures, who has had little publicity: F. T. Davies, then a Grenadier major in MIR. In David Stafford's memorable words, 'In peacetime, Davies was a wealthy director of Courtauld's, a flamboyant, volatile character of great energy and ruthlessness.'[36] Tommy Davies shared with George Taylor the distinction of supplying SOE with most of the brightest of its original ideas. Like Taylor, he had plenty of friends in the City, from one of whom he got the indispensable introduction. He had crossed to Amsterdam on the 12th, and got hold – even during the Whitsun bank holiday weekend – of some directors of the Bank of the Netherlands. After making safe record of the owners, they spent the next day and a half destroying several million pounds' worth of American bearer bonds.[37]

---

34. PRO WO 166/3549, the company's war diary, 15 May 1940. See also de Jong, *KdN*, iii. 162–4; photographs of oil fires, *ibid.*, at 321, 448–9.

35. MIR war diary, May, appx 2.

36. *Journal of Contemporary History* xxii(ii) (April 1987), 310.

37. MIR war diary, May 1940, appx 2; private information.

Tommy Davies thus did much better in removing resources from under the nazis' noses than did the better-known emissary from Section D, M. R. Chidson. Chidson's task was to secure as many industrial diamonds as he could from the Amsterdam diamond merchant quarter, which was the world centre for the trade; the bank holiday prevented him from extracting more than £1,250,000 worth, because 'a very large part of the stock' was shut away behind time locks until Tuesday.[38]

Chidson, Lawrence Grand's only assistant when Section D was first founded, had a Dutch wife, knew Holland well, and had had plenty of experience in the intelligence world; his previous post had been that of passport control officer at The Hague. He had learned to fly, aged twenty, in 1913, had been shot down over the western front two years later, and had had some three years as a prisoner of war. A. F. Rickman, whose early sabotage effort in Sweden miscarried,[39] was his brother-in-law. His coup with the diamonds was recorded in a book, and reappeared in his obituary;[40] Davies's larger coup with the bearer bonds has remained untold. Chidson received an immediate DSO; Davies's surviving friends treasure his memory.

Rumour and war go together. The suddenness of the German attack on 10 May multiplied rumour's chances of spreading; no one on the losing side was ready to admit how utterly they had been outwitted and outgunned. Rumour put the blame on a fifth column of secret nazi supporters. Stories of lights in windows, arrows in fields, parachutists dressed as priests or nuns, ran all over the Low Countries, and much farther afield; so in particular did the story of poisoned chocolates, handed out to children by strangers.[41]

Practically all of this was myth. Bohle, head of the nazi Auslandsorganisation who was supposed to have been running it all,

---

38. Report signed by Chidson, 10 March 1947, 3; in his PF.
39. See Charles Cruickshank, *SOE in Scandinavia* (Oxford University Press, 1986), *passim*.
40. David Walker, *Adventure in Diamonds* (Evans, 1955); *The Times*, 4 October 1957, 13c. None of SOE's files on diamond dealing appear to have survived.
41. Louis de Jong, *The German Fifth Column in the Second World War*, 66–94.

testified on oath at Nuremberg that he had had no special arrangements at all.[42] De Jong, in an early investigation, found 'no
indication that *reichsdeutsche* guests living in Holland or Dutch
national socialists rendered active support in that campaign in any
organized relation to the military or to any considerable extent'.[43]

However, Sir Neville Bland, the British minister at The Hague,
who had himself been present while bombs and parachutists were
falling round him, took quite a different view in May 1940. He
broadcast on the BBC about the many Germans who had been lurking in Holland, waiting to do Hitler's will, and had done it by
spreading confusion and dismay. The confusion and dismay, hindsight now makes clear, were Bland's own; but his was an influential
view. He had been at Eton and King's College, Cambridge; he was a
knight and a senior diplomat; in the inner circle he was known to
have been a close friend of Admiral Sinclair, the late C;[44] his word
thus carried extra weight. It is now clear that he was talking nonsense;
at the time, he and many others thought the contrary.

The fifth column, in short, was a myth; but SOE was founded, in
a tearing hurry, in July 1940 to turn this myth into reality if it could.
While nobody in SOE ever did hand out poisoned chocolates to
children, or descend by parachute dressed as a nun, the misdirection
of German columns, the marking of targets for allied forces and
repeated acts of sabotage were precisely tasks that its agents undertook. It was founded on a double misconception: that subversive
activity had played a vital role in the *Blitzkrieg* victories of 1939–40,
and that the nazis' dirty tricks could promptly be played back against
them.[45] It was founded moreover at a moment when general opinion
on the continent was sure that the war was virtually over; an opinion
not shared on this side of the Channel.

The second chapter of the present writer's *SOE in France*, entitled
'What SOE was', has stood the test of time. Some more details were
given in his more recent and less official *SOE: An Outline History*,

---

42. *Ibid.*, 140, quoting *The Trial of German Major War Criminals*, x. 20, 24–5.
43. De Jong, *German Fifth Column*, 186.
44. Private information.
45. See the perceptive comments by C. M. Andrew in Foot, *Holland at War*, 98–9.

repeating oneself is tiresome. Some points about SOE previously unpublished, or peculiar to the Low Countries, are still worth attention. It was a secret service, then inadmissible in public like the others, at work in parallel with the older security, intelligence and decipher services. It was founded in July 1940, on Churchill's instructions, to act offensively in enemy-occupied territory:[46] to 'set Europe ablaze', in the now hackneyed phrase, by sabotage and subversion. Forty years ago, preparing *SOE in France*, the present writer proposed to append to it Neville Chamberlain's Cabinet memorandum of 19 July 1940: a proposal at once vetoed, for the document dealt largely with another body, the Home Security Executive, not then officially held to be a suitable subject for public discussion. Hinsley and Simkins referred to it freely in 1990 in their official history of wartime security, and Chamberlain's paper – 'treasured by SOE as its founding charter'[47] – is now in published print.[48]

Dr Hugh (later Lord) Dalton was minister in charge until February 1942, under the cover of being Minister of Economic Warfare; thus giving a Labour minister control of a secret service, to balance in the wartime coalition the strongly conservative controllers of the security and intelligence services, Lords Swinton and Halifax; later replaced by Duff Cooper (who died Viscount Norwich), under the distant wing of Sir John Anderson (who died Lord Waverley), and by (Sir) Anthony Eden (who died Earl of Avon); all conservatives also.[49] Dalton pushed his Low Countries sections, like the rest, hard for the results by which he set such store, which always seemed to elude him – not only in the Low Countries. A rumour, not borne out by surviving archives, has it that he was kicked upstairs to the Board of Trade in 1942 because MI5 had caught him using SOE's telephone-tapping facilities to spy on his colleagues in the Labour

46. PRO PREM 3/409/1 has some interesting new details on SOE's origins, including Churchill's suggestions of Lords Cork, Trenchard or Vansittart as its executive heads, from which Attlee deflected him.

47. Foot, *SOE in France*, 8.

48. W. J. M. Mackenzie, *The Secret History of SOE* (St Ermin's Press, 2000), 753–5.

49. (Sir) F. H. Hinsley and C. A. G. Simkins, *British Intelligence in the Second World War: iv, Security and Counter-Intelligence* (1990), 74, 173.

Party.[50] Were this true it would account for his replacement by another strong conservative, Lord Selborne, who as Lord Wolmer had been one of the handful of MPs who had voted with Churchill on the India question in 1932–5; it would also account for Churchill's notorious, and otherwise inexplicable, comparison of the Labour Party to the Gestapo during the general election of 1945.

Selborne was a less stern taskmaster than Dalton; though he sometimes required details of operations, he never tried to control them closely. He took more notice than Dalton had done of the governments in exile, co-operating as far as he could with the Dutch, and wrestling against the apparent inertia of the Belgians.

SOE was formed by conflating, hastily, Section D of the secret intelligence service, MI6;[51] MIR; and a semi-secret propaganda branch of the Foreign Office, called EH or CS, which in 1941 became a separate service, the Political Warfare Executive (PWE). L. D. Grand, the head of Section D, and Sir Campbell Stuart, the head of EH, were soon moved away from SOE by its incoming masters; and Holland, the head of MIR, also moved on, because his regiment – the Royal Engineers – offered him an overdue promotion which, as a regular soldier, he thought he must accept.

SOE took over from MIR the concept of sections – MIR had called them bureaux – to work into separate countries. Groups of adjoining country sections were placed under supervising directors, members of SOE's governing Council. These directors were a good way above the battle, but could offer leadership and advice.

At first the Low Countries sections – N for the Netherlands, T for Belgium and Luxembourg – came under the lively eye of Charles Hambro, banker and businessman. He had shown extraordinary promise early: he took seven Winchester wickets for six runs when captain of Eton XI in 1915, won a Military Cross in the Coldstream Guards before he came of age, and had been general manager of the Great Western Railway.[52] At first his main concerns in SOE were

---

50. Private information; Ben Pimlott's notable *Dalton* is not at its strongest on SOE.
51. SIS's continued official existence, which dates back to 1909, was admitted in Parliament by the prime minister on 6 May 1992 (Parl. Deb. 6s. ccvii. 65).
52. See *DNB 1961–1970*, 476–7.

with Scandinavia, where he earned his knighthood in 1941. In November of that year he was promoted to be deputy director of all SOE, under Sir Frank Nelson[53] and (Sir) Gladwyn Jebb,[54] and passed control of the Low Countries – as well as several other sections – to Harry Sporborg, the lawyer, another of SOE's formidable senior figures.[55]

Sporborg saw at once that his own fief was too large; he could no more give every part of it the attention it deserved than Hambro had been able to do, and like Hambro he then wanted to concentrate on Scandinavia. So he set up one more rung on the staff ladder, to be called D/R, between himself as regional director and the country sections concerned, to oversee operations into France and the Low Countries.

Six months later Sporborg too changed jobs. Jebb and Nelson, like Dalton, left SOE in the first half of 1942. Hambro succeeded Nelson as CD, executive director, and took Sporborg as his political deputy. The control of western Europe passed to (Sir) Colin Gubbins, a regular soldier, already director of operations and training; described by Jebb as the lynch-pin of the whole organisation.[56] Gubbins joined SOE in November 1940. Within six months he had inspired Jebb, above him on the staff ladder, to put up a strongly aggressive paper on what SOE could achieve to the chiefs of staff, and was exercising a continual impulse towards aggression all through SOE's training structure and on as many country sections as he could reach. He, too, energetic and capable far beyond the common run, had a great deal else on his plate; and was glad to pass his western European sections over to his fellow-gunner E. E. Mockler-Ferryman (known as AD/E in SOE) when 'the Moke' returned in apparent disgrace from Algiers in March 1943.[57] AD/E, as the director in charge of north-west

---

53. *Ibid.*, 788–9.
54. Later Lord Gladwyn. *Times* obituary, 25 October 1996, 23a.
55. See *DNB 1981–1985* (1990), 380–1.
56. Final report by Jebb to Sir Alexander Cadogan, 6 May 1942, 19; signed typescript in HQ 59. For Gubbins, see *DNB 1971–1980* (1986), 367–8, and Sir Peter Wilkinson and Joan Bright Astley, *Gubbins and SOE*.
57. The disgrace was apparent rather than real: see Hinsley *et al.*, *British Intelligence in the Second World War*, ii. 757–63. Mockler-Ferryman is also noticed in *DNB 1971–1980*, 573–4.

Europe, was responsible for France, the Low Countries and Scandinavia.

The first D/R, whose name was withheld from *SOE in France* at his own request lest its appearance should harm his career in the City, was David Keswick. His brother (Sir) John played a prominent role in SOE in the Far East, where the family had for some time been established in the great firm of Jardine, Matheson. Like Gubbins, he had been born in Yokohama; but as he was five years younger – born in 1901 – he just missed the Great War, all through which Gubbins fought. Much Hambro's junior at Eton, Keswick was also a banker, a partner in Samuel Montagu from 1930. As SOE's man in Nigeria, he had played a part in 'Postmaster', a successful old-fashioned cutting-out operation.[58] He had a Franco-Jewish grandmother who came from Provence; spoke fluent French; and took a keen and informed interest in French politics. It was always on the French rather than on the Low Countries' wing of his cares that his main attention was fixed.

After operation 'Torch' established in November 1942 an allied headquarters in Algiers, Keswick moved to it, as political adviser to SOE's 'Massingham' base.[59] He was succeeded as D/R by (Sir) Robin Brook. Brook had been a star pupil of J. M. Keynes at King's College, Cambridge, and Dalton – also a King's man – had brought him early into SOE, in the minister's immediate entourage. When Dalton left, Brook remained, working close to Hambro. He combined high intelligence with tact as well as originality. He too became much interested in French politics, and after a year as D/R started to look out for a deputy to take detailed charge of the Low Countries, while he gave most of his own mind to the several sections working into France.

C was persuaded to release Paymaster Lieutenant Commander P. L. Johns, RN, who had in the early war years been his anchor-man in Lisbon, to take over supervision of both N and T sections, with the symbol of LC; though Johns did not become available until late in 1943.

---

58. See J. E. A[ppleyard], *Geoffrey* (Blandford Press, 1946), 71–109.
59. His *Times* obituary – on 14 April 1976, page 21f – confined what it said of his war career to the remarks that he 'was employed on staff duties' and reached the rank of lieutenant-colonel in the King's Own Scottish Borderers.

There are two types of secret staff officer, the balls of fire and the quiet men. SOE was full, perhaps over-full, of balls of fire: enthusiasts who enjoyed cutting corners, riding rough-shod over bureaucrats' rules, producing sudden and startling results. Philip Johns was emphatically a quiet man, one who might secure equally startling results, but less suddenly, and leaving fewer ruffled tempers behind him as he pursued his carefully planned way.[60]

Shortly before the allied re-invasion of north-west Europe, operation 'Overlord', began on 5/6 June 1944, Brook moved out of SOE's main headquarters to the elbow of General Eisenhower, the supreme allied commander, and spent the rest of the European war in charge of a Special Force Headquarters (SFHQ) at Supreme Headquarters, Allied Expeditionary Force (SHAEF). As 'Overlord' developed, the system of control of resistance in north-west Europe needed frequent readjusting (described in chapter viii below).

Several leading intellectuals served in or near SOE; Ayer, Casson, Dunbabin, Joll, Namier, Hugh and R. W. Seton-Watson, Talbot Rice, Woodhouse and Zaehner among them. None of these had anything to do with the Low Countries, where most of the staff officers who decided the details that counted had been business managers or junior diplomats before the war. The great multinationals, already playing their roles in the world economic order, several of them with Anglo-Dutch or Anglo-Belgian connexions, were notably absent: Shell, Unilever, Philips, Cockerill, Sofina hardly any of them appeared, except on target lists.[61] None of SOE's Low Countries opponents were noted intellectuals, either; but some of them had been professional policemen, whose methodical training turned out useful.

One of SOE's leading principles was to be flexible, to avoid set patterns and fixed rules; this applied to staff as well as to agents. Neither T section nor N section ever had the same head for as long as two years together. These, and the rest of the section staff, will be discussed below; as will the Belgian and Dutch staffs in exile with whom they needed to work.[62]

---

60. See his war autobiography, *Within Two Cloaks*.
61. But see pages 140, 394.
62. See pages 78–90, 231–8.

It is worth remark that a strict security ruling within SOE, with which the security service MI5 concurred, forbade heads of country sections – or their seniors – from visiting enemy-occupied territory; on the ground that they knew far too much, and so could not be exposed to capture, which might endanger far too many agents. The rule was hardly ever broken; never, in the Low Countries. André Dewavrin, who headed de Gaulle's secret services in exile, thought it immoral not to be ready to take the same risks as his agents,[63] and twice parachuted into occupied France – returning safely each time; N and T sections' heads prudently put safety and obedience before morality.

In the autumn of 1940 SOE's headquarters settled at 64 Baker Street, Marylebone; the building was taken over from the prison commissioners, and is today a motor-car showroom on the ground floor with offices above. At Norgeby House, almost opposite, N and T sections shared the building with F section, and – when the post was created – with D/R and his staffs. It is a mark of the density of the cloud of unknowing in which SOE staff lived that there seems to have been no interchange of gossip, even in the women's cloakrooms, between these various staffs; this did not make the shocks of various disasters any more easy to bear, but did security good rather than harm.[64] S, M and AD/E, who were successively in charge of the Low Countries sections, all worked in 64 Baker Street, only a few paces away; the signals and cipher staffs were in Michaelhouse, a furlong south of Norgeby House. All of them thus started close to each other, but some way removed from the seat of government in Whitehall.

Most of the few civil servants in Whitehall's civil departments who were aware of SOE's existence looked at it askance. Jebb and Nelson spent much of their working time in SOE explaining to other officials what, and how secret, SOE was, and how promptly and how secretly any requests that came from it for help were to be handled.

With the Treasury, then as so often Whitehall's leading depart-ment, there were no upsets. In an age of accountancy, it is worth

---

63. *Souvenirs du Colonel Passy* (Monte Carlo: Solar, 1947), i. 138.
64. Cp Themistocles Marinos, *Harling Mission – 1942* (Athens: Papazisis Publications, 1993), 20, for a similar degree of secrecy even in gossiping Cairo.

recording that SOE was not much bothered by money. Its officers received the pay of their rank, but paid no income tax.[65] Prospective expense never seems to have been a barrier to any of SOE's enterprises. Agents going into occupied territory – 'into the field' was the usual phrase – took with them adequate sums in local currency. Much of this had been looted by undisciplined elements of the BEF, retreating towards Dunkirk through Flemish towns and villages in which the banks had just been bombed open, and rescued from them in turn by the Pay Corps.[66]

For instance, money for a sudden journey by taxi should always have been available for an organiser in the field; but were taxis to be had, in remote areas or even, at times, in cities? Moreover, few agents in the Low Countries came from the social strata in which taxi-taking was then common form. There were security doubts about taxi-taking, too, in a police state, which only a nimble and far-seeing agent in a large circuit would have taken measures to overcome.

SOE had in J. J. Venner, its director of finance, a professional accountant – ranked as a Group Captain, RAF – with a genius for handling money. He put in to the Treasury, as early as 22 April 1941, requests for up-to-date French, Belgian and Dutch currency notes in small denominations.[67] The following table, compiled from a thick folder of jottings, gives some idea of the comparative effort SOE put into these three countries:[68]

spent	by 27 August 1942	by 28 September 1944
in French francs	£156,554.16.1	£758,937.9.3
in Belgian francs	£41,907.4.4	£69,766.6.11
in Dutch gulden	£25,530.6.4	£56,239.5.0

The £126,005.11.11 SOE had so far spent in Dutch and Belgian money was no vast drain on the secret service account; from which, in seventy-nine slices, Venner drew from time to time all through the

---

65. George Millar, *Maquis* (2 edn, Pan, 1956), 14.
66. Private information.
67. HQ 161, grants.
68. *Ibid.*

war. He never met any but the mildest inquiry from his paymaster about whether these expenses were really necessary.[69]

Neither the navy nor the air force ever thought of charging SOE for the costs of moving agents or stores. The War Office supplied the bulk of the stores, again without charge; civilian contractors, paid direct by SOE – often in cash – supplied most of the rest.

Up to mid-August 1942, the British government paid – through SOE – the salaries and expenses of SOE agents sent to the Netherlands; thereafter the Dutch government in exile bore half the cost, and for this Selborne sent an appreciative letter of thanks to Prince Bernhard.[70] The Belgian government in exile, with the resources of the Belgian Congo at its disposal, covered operational expenses in Belgium, and paid the salaries of Belgian – though not of British – agents operating there. By 1943, ten million Belgian francs' worth of US dollars were being dispatched to Belgian resistance monthly, through SOE channels, and then reconverted into local currency on the black market.[71]

From SOE's angle, the Foreign Office – unlike the Treasury – was a prominent obstacle to effective subversive action. After all, it was staffed by diplomats, whose whole existence revolved around settling differences by discussion, not by force of arms; while SOE was essentially a fighting service. SOE's first and best historian once remarked that 'From the Foreign Office point of view SOE was an intrusive nuisance with an infinite capacity for diplomatic mischief',[72] a view still not quite extinct. This attitude towards it was not confined to the Foreign Office; it was common in the service ministries that handled the more conventional armed services.

Early in the Great War, Asquith's Cabinet and Sir John French's GHQ had leaked like sieves. Lloyd George's War Cabinet was smaller, and Haig's GHQ duller, but round both there were still many gossips. Next time round, Society was less powerful and less talkative, and great service headquarters had become aware of discretion. However, there was still a large coterie, mainly uniformed, aware of impending events, for in both the War Office and the Air

---

69. HQ 159–63.
70. 17 August 1942, typed copy in Holland 1.
71. History xxxiv. 41.
72. Mackenzie, *op. cit.*, 339.

Ministry about forty busybodies in each had arranged, by the end of 1940, to see, in clear, a copy of every message that entered the building. Most of them belonged to the same service clubs, where over a late whisky they liked to exchange news of the day. Luckily for SOE, messages for the cover addresses of MO1(SP) and AI 10 fell outside this large net, as did messages for other secret services; luckily for the country, signals to the Admiralty – where SOE was called NID(Q) – were more securely handled. Part of SOE's shaky reputation with posterity can be traced back to under-informed speculations in clubs.

For all Jebb's and Nelson's efforts to get it established, SOE had many enemies in Whitehall. Enmity several times went beyond mere grumbling, or reluctance to help, and reached the stage of a proposal to abolish SOE altogether; the earliest of these came in May 1942. Churchill's support sustained SOE; it did not survive six months beyond his fall from power in July 1945.

In London at least SOE was spared various embarrassments that affected its outstation in Cairo, ranging from a too sprightly junior officer, through a too talkative senior one, to dark tales of penetration by a Comintern agent.[73] The London governments in exile gradually built up social standing. Most of them, to keep abreast of each other, got their legations' accreditation to St James's up-graded to embassies; Queen Wilhelmina, like King Haakon of Norway, kept up some degree of state on national holidays. The Belgians, having no monarch with them in London, were less well equipped for state occasions, but the Belgian colony in exile sustained an active social life. Their cabinet's neighbour in Eaton Square, Mrs L. S. Amery, went out of her way to arrange luncheon and evening parties, so far as bombardment allowed, for the benefit of exiles from Europe as much as for exiles from India.[74] Of the governments in exile there will be only too much to say later.

SOE – its SO2, operational, branch in particular – had early troubles, digging itself into a position in the secret world from which it

73. Foot, SOE, 187; Artemis Cooper, Cairo in Wartime (Hamish Hamilton, 1989), 71; David Martin, Patriot or Traitor (Stanford, California: Hoover Institution Press, 1978), 118–24.
74. Private information.

could work at all. It took time and trouble for MI5 and MI6 to get used to the presence of another, co-equal secret service at their elbows; and besides security and intelligence, there were several other secret services in being. They covered escape, signals, censorship, decipher and deception. Political warfare, at first part of SOE and called SO1, also became a separate service, on being hived off from SOE in August 1941. Of it there will be a little more to say later;[75] some of the others are worth a moment now.

SOE had little to do with the decipher service, that worked – mainly at Bletchley Park – under the cover name of the Government Code and Cypher School (GC & CS).[76] Till the closing weeks of the war, there was hardly any Enigma or *Geheimschreiber* traffic that affected SOE in the Low Countries; because the Germans there did their work with each other, and with Berlin, by telephone or teleprinter, or in the Gestapo Enigma key that even GC & CS could not read.[77] In those closing stages, C – who took responsibility for GC & CS – saw no need to alter the existing system, by which Ismay, Churchill's military assistant, showed once a week any ultra secret messages that bore on SOE to one of the few men at SOE's headquarters who were on the prime minister's list to read them. The list seems already to have vanished down the gulf of time; but may be supposed to have included by 1944 Gubbins; Sporborg, his deputy; Barry, his chief of staff; Boyle, his head of intelligence; and Mockler-Ferryman.[78]

SOE's dealings with the Radio Security Service were also slight, although adequate to establish whence sets were operating.[79] Neither the Belgians nor the Dutch took much notice of the advice the

---

75. E.g. pages 291–21, 271, 303, 317, 336.
76. The strategic aspects of its work are described in Hinsley *et al.*, *op. cit.*, summarised in a single volume by Hinsley (HMSO, 1993); see also Ronald Lewin, *Ultra Goes to War* (Hutchinson, 1978), and F. H. Hinsley and Alan Stripp, *Code Breakers* (Oxford University Press, 1993).
77. Hinsley *et al.*, *op. cit.*, ii. 658.
78. Private information. Intelligence officers in SOE's L section also received ultra secret material in 1940–2, but from the War Office, not direct from Bletchley; they knew it was highly reliable, but did not know its source (a point I owe to Dr Mark Wheeler).
79. No papers on this subject have been available to me.

English constantly offered them: to keep quite separate the tasks of intelligence-gathering, escape, sabotage, and propaganda. No citizen of either (or indeed of any) occupied country, once determined to resist, was going to miss any chance of doing so that offered; unless previously exposed to some training in what the secret experts thought indispensable.

Among the several secret services at work in London there were frequent staff arguments about which of them should handle what. On the occupied spot, no one drew fine distinctions. The splendid Berthe Fraser at Arras, who hid escapers, stored explosives, and gathered intelligence – all at once[80] – had dozens of unconscious imitators, all over occupied Europe. Only those of them in the Low Countries who had links with SOE, and whose names or details happen to have survived in its archives or in the reliable published studies, can be mentioned below; and many figures of national reputation will have to be left out. Such characters as Louis d'Aulnis and Walthère Dewé are omitted, not because they are believed unimportant, but because their vital work had nothing to do with SOE. George Behar, later Blake, the SIS officer who defected to the KGB, is also omitted because there is no reliable evidence to show that he was in touch with any form of resistance until he was brought out of Holland along an escape line that was not part of SOE.

SOE's links with MI5 were close and cordial. SOE's security branch, of which almost all the survivors remain properly silent about the past, was partly staffed with officers seconded from MI5; so that 5's experts could easily be called in when a security problem appeared.[81] The little branch of MI5 called B1a, which ran back the agents the Abwehr imagined it had lodged in Great Britain, was sometimes consulted by SOE's country sections about doubtful incoming messages.[82]

SOE's security staff included some sections of the field security police, who kept – had to keep – a close eye on agents under training, watching their drinking habits and inspecting their mail. They

---

80. See Foot, *SOE in France*, 147, 267, 368n.
81. E.g. page 181.
82. Conversations with Sir J. C. Masterman, 1977; but see pages 168–90.

may have had some advice from the censorship staff, although no papers remain to say so.

MI9, the escape service, was of course involved with the Low Countries, into which allied aircraft often crashed; so was DF section of SOE, which ran the service's own escape lines for agents. Both in Belgium and in Holland there were extensive local arrangements for hiding those whom the nazis hunted; Anne Frank's diary provides a world-famous example of how well – and how badly – such plans could develop. Out of Belgium several escape lines ran; notably 'Comet', run by brave and cautious young women between Brussels and San Sebastian. With 'Comet' MI9 did maintain touch, though not control. Most of the other lines out of Belgium seemed suspect, both to MI9 and to MI5. The German security services did indeed make several attempts to feed double agents onto them; two of them highly successful. MI9 made one attempt before 1944 to start up a line running out of Holland; SOE acted as travel agent for this, and it failed.[83]

MI9 worked under the wing of MI6, which will have to figure repeatedly below. There has been a lot of misunderstanding and confusion, on both sides of the North Sea, about the supposed and the actual roles of SOE and of SIS; moreover rumours continue to abound about how badly they got on with each other. In some countries – Italy, for example – they got on splendidly together; in the Low Countries, for some years they did not.

There is nothing odd about this: bad relations between rival secret services are no less usual than bad relations between rival ships' crews, or army regiments, or football supporters. SIS could give one sound professional reason for distrusting SOE: if SOE did its work properly and provoked active unrest, it would certainly attract enemy police attention; this might hamper SIS agents as they attempted their own quite different work, of observing and reporting the enemy's doings, for which they needed calm and quiet.

Part of MI6, its Section D – the D is supposed to have stood for destruction – was split off from it to help form SOE, in the earliest stages of the new body's creation; in such circumstances of haste and

---

83. See pages 156–8. On MI9 in general, see M. R. D. Foot and J. M. Langley, *MI9*.

confusion as to create a fair amount of ill feeling. Personal clashes sometimes made things worse. 6's history has in any case been handled, in discreet detail, with that of the decipher service – the tail that wagged the dog – by abler authors than the present writer, using a firmer archival base.[84] It is symbolic of the relation between the two services that whenever SOE's whole world war diarist referred to C – sometimes meaning the individual, usually meaning his organisation – he habitually followed the initial with a full stop.

No history of SOE can be complete that omits the role of Colonel Dansey, the wartime assistant chief of SIS – C's *éminence grise,* by all accounts a far more powerful personality than C himself – who after one catastrophic admission in his own teens became a by-word for silence and security.[85] Dansey's hand rocked the cradle of the infant SOE. Sir Frank Nelson, the first CD, had belonged to his Z organisation; so, by the bye, had the first T. Dansey had no official position in SOE, but he had a desk in Baker Street – as C's liaison officer – as well as one in Broadway, and had the whole of SOE's W/T traffic before him daily; certainly up to the summer of 1942, probably thereafter as well. Moreover, an agreement made as early as 15 September 1940, only relaxed – reluctantly – in October 1943, laid down that any intelligence SOE collected 'must be passed to C', even before being circulated inside SOE.[86]

Dansey left little personal trace in SOE's archive – he was too wily; and too angry, once the genie had escaped from the bottle of signals constraint and soared out of his direct control. However, his presence can sometimes be sensed in the background. To confuse the plot further, there was another C. M. Dansey in SOE – Cyril Maurice, not Claude Edward Marjoribanks – an Essex-born bank clerk thirty years Sir Claude's junior (the knighthood was conferred in 1943), who went from school to fourteen years' work as a coding clerk in Samuel Montagu's bank, whence he joined SOE in 1940. He

---

84. Hinsley *et al., op. cit.*
85. On the admission, see Richard Ellman, *Oscar Wilde* (Penguin, 1988), 382–3, 426, where he is misnamed 'Philip Danney'. The biography of him by Anthony Read and David Fisher, *Colonel Z* (1984), is not based on official sources. There is a summary of his career in *DNB Missing Persons*, 171–2.
86. Mackenzie, *op. cit.*, 95; Hinsley *et al., op. cit.*, iii(i). 463.

rose to be a major on the General List and the head of SOE's main line ciphers; he won golden opinions for steadiness and competence from Nicholls and from Gubbins.[87]

Claude Dansey's extraordinary hold on the secret machine of state was so firm that it ensured, all through the war, C's priority over SOE whenever there was any possibility of a clash: for example, MI6's coded messages – however wordy – always took priority over SOE's – however brief – when there was a shortage of available BBC broadcasting time,[88] and it was always MI6 that took priority over SOE when there was a shortage of available aircraft sorties. C moreover laid down that his agents were never to share an aircraft with those of any other secret service; a rule rigidly observed till 1944, and not often relaxed then.

Dansey also, like the senior men in SOE, was much involved with the course of the secret war in France; and with grand strategy; and with Anglo-American relations. He, like them, normally had no time to concentrate on the problems of the Low Countries.

Early in 1941 Cowgill of MI6's Section V – under whose wing Philby later dug himself in to pilfer MI6's archive – tried to keep SO2 from hearing about arrivals in this country from abroad, and had to be called to order by C himself: from mid-March SO2 was more fairly treated.[89] Yet not until 14 May 1942 did SOE's Council receive an assurance that SOE would be treated on an equal basis with SIS at the MI5 reception centre, the Royal Victoria Patriotic School (RVPS) at Wandsworth, through which almost all arrivals in Great Britain from the continent were channelled: therefore, an important secret service recruiting patch.[90]

A few weeks later, J. C. Hanbury-Williams of SOE and E. W. Playfair, brought in from the Treasury to help him, put in a thirty-six page report to Selborne on how SOE was organised. They found themselves 'much disturbed by the tone of petty bickering and sniping which one finds' in SIS's letters to SOE, which they had sampled

---

87. His PF.
88. E.g. France 223, Communications, 9 July 1944.
89. Security 20. On Cowgill, see *Intelligence and National Security*, ix (April 1994), 345–53, and Hayden B. Peake and Samuel Halpern (eds), *In the Name of Intelligence* (Washington, DC: NIBC Press, 1994), 387–90.
90. HQ 6, Council minutes 1941–2.

for a random fortnight.[91] The present writer felt much the same when trying in 1961 to probe the history of secret sea operations into France in 1940–2.[92] Decent veil best drawn.

SOE had little to do with the deception service, called the London Controlling Section (LCS), which grew out of another of J. C. F. Holland's bright ideas,; indeed, nothing in the Netherlands and hardly anything in Belgium. Several versions of the Dutch catastrophe present it as a piece of calculated deception: all are mistaken.

The sober truth – too sober to suit anyone in search of a hot story – is that SOE was rigorously excluded from almost all the major deception schemes. It was of some help to LCS in Greece in operation 'Animals', part of the cover for the invasion of Sicily in July 1943; but its role shortly thereafter in operation 'Starkey' in France, ill conceived and too hastily mounted, was a failure. The small, intensely secure group who composed the LCS rightly mistrusted SOE, as nothing like as secure as themselves. After 'Starkey', the head of LCS – Colonel Bevan, uncle of the Lord Lucan who vanished – resolved not to use so unsure an instrument as SOE again, if he could help it;[93] and only did so once, with critical tactical effect, in Belgium in June 1944.[94]

Those who think the 1942 Plan for Holland was a deception scheme do not understand the Plan for Holland; those who think the *Englandspiel* was a British deception do not understand deception. This will need treatment in detail later, but deserves to be set down early.[95]

At least the local police system in the Low Countries was comparatively simple. The Dutch had only two services, the town Politie and the country gendarmerie, the Maréchaussée; the Belgians four – police, police judiciaire, gendarmerie (*rijkswacht*), and sûreté nationale: contrast the fifteen different police forces of Vichy France.[96]

91. Hanbury-Williams and Playfair to Selborne, Most Secret, duplic, 18 June 1942, 11, in HQ 60.
92. These have now gone public: see Sir F. Brooks Richards, *Secret Flotillas*.
93. Conversation with him shortly before his death in 1978.
94. See pages 360–1.
95. See pages 131–4 and chapters II and III.
96. All listed in Security 16A, interrogators' *aide-mémoire*, 21.

The German police set-up was imposed on top of the local ones. The occupying armed forces brought with them the geheime Feldpolizei (GFP), military police who wore large brass breastplates over their field-grey uniforms: as conspicuous, and as formally fierce, as the red or white or blue-hatted military police of the British or United States or Soviet armies. Backing them, usually in plain clothes, was the Abwehr, the armed forces' security branch, answerable to Hitler through Admiral Canaris in Berlin. Often in rivalry with the Abwehr, reporting to Hitler through Himmler, was the Sicherheitsdienst (SD) of the SS, intricately interpenetrated with the geheime Staatspolizei or Gestapo. In 1942, responsive to Himmler's growing power in the Reich, the GFP were brought under the SD; two years later, so was the Abwehr.

There will be more to say of German counter-espionage later.

SOE's relations with the Soviet secret service, then called the NKVD, were never easy. In the Low Countries, an unhappy incident made them even stickier than usual, and may be disposed of here.

A few agents, codenamed 'Pickaxes', were sent from the USSR to Great Britain for transit into western Europe. It fell to SOE to act as their travel agent. Their Soviet controllers had already given them parachute and W/T training, to minimise contact with members of any British secret service: several of them deserted, vanishing from the secret world altogether.[97] Gubbins retained bitter memories of Bolshevik excesses from the Archangel campaign of 1919, and looked on them with disdain; but appreciated how much the western allies owed to the Red Army, which from mid-1941 held the bulk of the Wehrmacht in play. He therefore insisted on full SOE support for every 'Pickaxe'; even while the NKVD pursued secrecy so far that nothing was to be said about 'Pickaxes' to other British or Soviet authorities, in Moscow or in London; let alone to the governments in exile; and even while the Foreign Office questioned the wisdom of forwarding 'Pickaxes' at all.[98]

Two reached Glasgow on 11 May 1942, after an adventurous voyage on HMS *Bulldog*. One was a professor of languages, a former

---

97. Whole world war diary, viii. 2978, 21–23 November 1941.
98. *Ibid.*, xii. 3260–1, March 1942.

preacher, in his middle sixties, carrying Swiss papers. He spoke fluent Dutch, French, English, German, Danish, Norwegian and Swedish, and a little Russian, all with a strong Dutch accent. He claimed to have been a personal friend of Lenin's and of Nehru's, and had not the least notion of security. With him was his son, Dutch-born of a German mother who had recently died; he was a good-looking, blue-eyed, teetotal, non-smoking twenty-two year old, who had left two younger brothers in Moscow. SOE called them 'Burgundy' and 'Barsac'. Their surname was probably Kruyt.[99]

They missed the May moon because of bad weather. 'Barsac' was dropped successfully on 21 June, in a clearing in the woods north-west of Apeldoorn. His father followed three nights later, on to a large field about twenty miles south of Liège. Each went, by some fool's or knave's error, with the other's personal luggage.[100] 'Barsac' came on the air a month later to report that this had caused him grave inconvenience: no wonder.

Peter Kuznetsov, alias 'Sauternes', alias 'Kuhn', an earlier 'Pickaxe', had been wounded on the night of 27/28 December 1941, when the aircraft that had tried to drop him and a friend into Belgium crashed on its return to England, killing his companion. When he recovered, he was dropped on 29/30 November 1942 on to 'Barsac's' landing ground, with some clothes for that agent as well as a W/T set and a mission of his own. As he was German-born, in his middle thirties, and spoke no Dutch at all, SOE understood that he intended to proceed into Germany;[101] though early in March 1943 the NKVD mission in London told SOE that he wanted some stores dropped where he had landed. By the time these stores had been packed, the RAF had banned flights to the area.

SOE does not seem to have heard of 'Burgundy' again; though de Jong established that he broke a leg on landing, was soon thereafter arrested by the Germans, and shot dead by his captors.[102] 'Sauternes'

---

99. That at least is the name given them by van der Stroom, *Nederlandse agenten*, 28, following de Jong, *KdN*, v. 782n and ix(ii). 808–9. SOE's whole world war diary called 'Barsac' Kravets and his father 'von Krumin' (xiv(ii). 3950).

100. Russia 13.

101. Russia 30.

102. De Jong, *KdN*, ix(ii). 808.

fell into German hands in Holland in July 1943, and managed to commit suicide.[103] 'Barsac' survived unarrested – indeed he survived the war – but seems to have had little if any clandestine success. In May 1944 he handed a cipher message for the Soviet embassy in London to an SIS agent in Holland; provoking SOE to telegraph to its man in Moscow: 'IN UNLIKELY EVENT OF OUR BEING APPROACHED BY DUTCH GOVERNMENT WE SHALL DENY THAT WE HAVE DROPPED PICKAXES . . . ESSENTIAL YOU TAKE SAME LINE WITH N.K.V.D.'[104] – a suitably confused note on which to end this muddled story.

Wheels within wheels: even inside a secret service, though there is a common pool of knowledge about what it is for and how it works, everyone does not know everything. It was common knowledge in SOE that a wallet full of papers, usually forged for secret incomers, was something without which no one could pass the street controls that were thought to abound in nazi-occupied Europe. It was also common knowledge in SOE that forgery was among the special skills which the London Poles had brought with them into exile. SOE's country sections working into north-western Europe sent all their requests for false papers to EU/P section – the one that dealt with Polish minorities outside Poland – as a matter of course.

Outside EU/P section it was not at all widely known that for Holland this was only a cover: Dutch papers were beyond even EU/P's capacities. The section passed all Dutch requests on, promptly, to Station IV W of SIS;[105] if IV W already had urgent work for SIS on hand, it was not SOE that got priority. Nor was the work of SOE always deftly handled; some of the products were downright bad.[106]

Belgian and Luxembourg papers were less difficult, and EU/P could turn them out quite readily. Agents in Belgium often carried

103. *Ibid.*
104. Tpt in Russia 30.
105. History xxv, false documents section; Holland 4. Photographs of typical Dutch identity cards in de Jong, *KdN*, v(i). 448–9.
106. See pages 108–9. Two specimen Dutch identity cards, one genuine and one forged, are in History xlix. 310(ii).

their own identity cards, bearing their real names. These would be likely to see them through any police check, unless their previous absence from the country had been officially noticed; but might bring ghastly troubles for their families if they were caught *in flagrante delicto*. So an agent out on a job preferred to carry forged papers.

Agents working into Belgium were supplied, as a stop-gap, with London-forged papers to see them through their first few days; they were then expected to use local resources to provide proper cover.[107] The novelist Frederick Forsyth assures us that 'Brussels has a long tradition as the centre of the forged identity-card industry and many foreigners appreciate the lack of formalities with which assistance in this field can be obtained'.[108] Such forgeries could seldom be backed by a genuine birth certificate, on which a policeman making a full check would insist; but they were not meant to stand up to a full check. As a retrospect put it, 'so long as papers looked sufficiently good so that in themselves they did not excite suspicion, that was all that really mattered.'[109] Belgian identity cards, unlike French or Dutch, did not include a fingerprint; this made them the more easy to forge.

Preferably, a forged card covered someone else's genuine identity – in spite of the extra risks. Those agents who had friends in the business world were sometimes able to find senior managers in big firms that worked for the Germans, who would take them on as nominal – or even actual – travellers, and provide supporting papers: this made excellent cover.[110]

This was one of the points at which card-carrying communists had a large advantage over SOE, for the Comintern's forgery branch was exceptionally skilled: agents equipped by its outstations could travel without a tremor through almost any control the enemy cared to mount.

As the historian of the false document section once remarked, 'The only way to learn this subject is to grow up with it.'[111] This was

---

107. History xxxiv B, Belgium (supplement), 9, TS.
108. *The Day of the Jackal* (Hutchinson, 1971), 70.
109. History xxxiv, Technique of the agent, 15, TS.
110. History xxxiv B. 18.
111. TS in History xxv. 5.

true not only of forging false papers, but of every other facet of the clandestine world; yet the time to grow up with it was unavailable for SOE's wartime agents, who had to follow their own understanding of how the world worked. Not all of them were mature enough to understand it well: hence some palpable errors. Few of the staff were much better placed than the agents: hence several more.

There are many references in SOE's whole world war diary to the presumed insecurity and indiscretion of other nationalities; an attitude that can be taken as universal. Just as the British did not quite trust the Dutch or the Belgians, the Belgians and the Dutch did not quite trust the British; this did not make for smooth running of secret affairs. Once real successes had been scored, trust could become solid; this took time.

Recruiting policy was the same in T and N sections as it was in the rest of SOE. That is, the original staff were drawn in by their pre-war friends or acquaintances – there was no other safe way to recruit – and then either brought in more friends, or put out trawls through MI1 for anyone who might speak the right languages. Each section, if it was lucky, might pick up agent recruits at the RVPS. As MI5 ran the RVPS, security checks at it were sound; but SOE had competition there from MI6 and MI9, who were both recruiting also. Even within SOE, F was not above trying to poach French-speaking Belgians from T.

The foreign business and journalistic communities in London were soon stripped of likely helpers. Armed forces in exile might well provide recruits, but would have of course to be approached through the ministers in charge of them – a source of repeated troubles.

Many young adults were also anxious to volunteer for special service, in spite of being warned of the fate that might await them if they did. Few of these would-be heroes and heroines found their way into T or N section; the great majority of the agents SOE sent in to the Low Countries were Belgian or Dutch citizens, who had made their escape – or were abroad at the moment of catastrophe in May 1940 – and were eager to return.

It was to the credit of this rather haphazard recruiting system that it could secure agents as resourceful as Blondeel or as brave as

Brinkgreve; on the other hand, it must indeed have been faulty to have taken on anybody half as wicked as 'Goat' or half as obtuse as some of the heads of N section.[112]

In the 1980s and 1990s there was some research, and much discussion, in continental Europe about the class composition of resistance movements. SOE's agents covered, in the Low Countries as in France, the whole range of class distinction, from peasants and proletarians to noblemen, priests and courtiers. No amount of metamarxist wrangling can obscure the plain fact: what turned men and women into resisters was a matter of chance rather than of class. Class standing or class aspirations had nothing to do with it; what counted was having the opportunity – and the courage – to act.[113] As one of F section's saboteurs, from an old English recusant family, put it at the time, 'real courage was beyond nationality and class'.[114]

The training system was devised by Tommy Davies in SOE's earliest days, and needed little revision.[115] It might be likened to a series of sieves of which the meshes got finer and finer. Davies originally planned to train raiding parties and longer-term agents separately; as Combined Operations Headquarters developed to run the Commandos, this part of Davies's plan could quietly be dropped. The rest worked, up to a point, well.

Potential agents were first looked over at a preliminary training school, at a requisitioned country house – one for each country section – in southern England. Nearby villagers gathered they were would-be commandos, not yet entitled to the coveted green beret. The teaching staff and conducting officers from the country section consulted together about whether the students would be suitable for secret work; anyone obviously unfitted for it could at this stage be posted off somewhere else.

---

112. Pages 311–12, 326, 409–12 below.
113. See V. Janssens, one of Walthère Dewé's regional organisers, in G. Drigeard and C. Kesteloot (eds), *La Résistance et les Européens du Nord* (Brussels, 1996), ii. 130.
114. Hugh Dormer, *War Diary* (Fisher Press, 1995 edn), 108.
115. Note by G. Cowell at back of *UK Establishments* (June 1992).

Those who passed this stage went next to a fiercer paramilitary school in Arisaig, in the western highlands of Scotland, near to Gubbins's childhood home.[116] The main building is now a luxury hotel, but wartime conditions were tough; one Dutch agent at least found it 'a most depressing place'.[117] There, beyond stiff physical training, they learned silent killing, living off the country, rock climbing, the use of small boats, and how to use plastic explosive and small arms. At both stages, students were treated more as country-house guests than as soldiers. They slept between sheets and were called by batmen in the mornings, instead of being rousted out of their blankets by buglers or NCOs. There were no parades; there was plenty to eat and drink, at a common table and bar; the lecturers' tone was friendly, gentlemen chatting to gentlemen. Informal classes, half-a-dozen strong, gave students every chance to absorb and to discuss what was taught.

Students were expected to be able to use all kinds of British, German, Dutch and Belgian small arms, to clean them and to clear stoppages on them; they became extra familiar with the sten submachine gun, produced from June 1941 by the million to suit a recommendation from Gubbins for an ideal ambush weapon. The sten was not a good gun; but it was cheap – it only cost thirty shillings (£1.50, then $7.20). With its short barrel, it was inaccurate at ranges of more than a few feet; and it was likely to let off a round if jolted, a deadly vice in the secret world.

There is now a full description of the sten in print, with line drawings by a French architect; nothing could be clearer.[118] Many other aspects of SOE's work, once intensely secret, are laid out in the same excellent book; and though its author had France primarily in mind, everything in it except the account of Hudson pick-ups applies with equal force to the Low Countries. Pistols, tommy guns, carbines, rifles, silencers, hand-held anti-tank weapons, and various types of knife, grenade and incendiary are described and admirably illustrated there as well.

For security's sake, agents at these schools were usually given cover names so that, if one later fell into enemy hands, there would be no

---

116. See Foot, *SOE in France*, 54–6.
117. P. Dourlein, *Inside North Pole*, 81.
118. See Pierre Lorain, ed. David Kahn, *Secret Warfare*, 118–21.

repercussions on his fellow agents' families. According to one of them, the Dutch among them dutifully used the cover names when within earshot of the staff, but when they were by themselves reverted to their real names which, coming from comparatively small communities, they all knew perfectly well.[119]

Though Dorothy Sayers had derided the practice as feeble well before the war,[120] SOE in its early years followed MI6's habit of giving people cover names with initials that matched their real ones. This dated back to the ample days of the gentry before 1914, when one carried one's initials in one's hat, on one's handkerchiefs, on one's card case, on one's underclothing, on one's binocular case, on one's suitcase; it had saved gentlemen inconvenience, but hardly applied to non-commissioned officers in the Dutch and Belgian armies.

Again, at the Scottish stage the less promising could be quietly returned to their previous units. The rest went to a merchant's house in Altrincham, near Manchester, for parachute training; dropping into Tatton Park from Whitley aircraft based at Ringway.

Survivors from these Group A courses next went to Beaulieu, on the edge of the New Forest, to begin Group B training. It was then made clear to them that they were to become secret agents, and they picked up as many tricks of the Great Game as they had time and wits to absorb. They learnt for instance a few simple password phrases, exchangeable with a pause during the phrase (a trick given away at the turn of the century in Kipling's *Kim*). 'You come on behalf – of whom?' 'I was sent here by – Léon.' 'Ah you can hardly mean – Degrelle' was the sort of way that two Belgians could establish they were both working for T. They also had more routine training on German organisation, equipment and counter-espionage methods; and were sent off on a two- or three-day exercise in some English provincial town, in which they had to make a notional attack on a real target, or perform such a task as borrowing a chief constable's motor car; and might if indiscreet be picked up by real policemen for cross-questioning.[121]

---

119. Sworn interrogation of Ras of N section, 19 January 1944, as reported in a photocopied KGB file.
120. In *Hangman's Holiday* (Gollancz, 1933), 194–5.
121. See Cyril Cunningham, *Beaulieu*.

Some of them then went to Thame Park for ten weeks for intensive training as wireless operators; others to Brickendonbury in Hertfordshire, where G. T. Rheam expounded the mysteries and techniques of industrial sabotage. Rheam taught in small classes; teaching at Thame Park began in small classes, but ended up more intensively, with one-to-one tutorials and practices.

M. R. Jefferis, one of the stalwarts of MIR, had produced even before the war began a brief, clear pamphlet on 'How to use High Explosive', widely read in SOE and still more widely distributed by its agents.[122] A few tips from Jefferis on how to tackle railway lines were included in Gubbins's forty-page *Partisan Leaders' Handbook*, a tactical guide he wrote in the spring of 1939 and never had occasion to revise.[123] That pamphlet and the more wide-ranging one he wrote beside it, *The Art of Guerilla Warfare*,[124] were basic texts in SOE's schools, translated into many languages,[125] and widely distributed by parachute; when he wrote them, he must have realised that copies were likely to fall quite soon into enemy hands, as they did. They provided thoroughly down-to-earth training in how pupils at SOE's schools were to behave as active agents; and they were infused, as all SOE's teaching was, with the need to be aggressive. Aggression and secrecy, shackled tight together, became the core of successful agents' characters.

No pretence was made at Beaulieu that everything agents would be called on to do in the field would be legal; they all knew that much of it would be illegal under local nazi-inspired regulations, and that in international law their own status, performing acts of war in plain clothes, would be illegal also. They were equally certain that, as sound patriots, they were right to act illegally. Problems lurk here for the moralist, over which the historian need not linger.

Hitler gave his Wehrmacht an assurance, even before the war began, that he would extract it from any difficulties it got into over

---

122. French translation in Marc Leproux, *Nous, les terroristes* (Monte Carlo: Solar, 2v, 1947), i. 278–88. I am grateful to Sir Peter Wilkinson for correcting my misattribution of this pamphlet to Gubbins in *SOE in France*, 4. For the rest of Jefferis's war career, see Stuart Macrae, *Winston Churchill's Toyshop*.
123. Text in appx 2 below.
124. Text in HQ 64.
125. Sixteen are listed in Foot, *SOE*, 14.

operations that appeared illegal – doubts had been raised about dress-
ing soldiers in Polish uniforms[126] – but did not live to keep his
promise. There was no need for Churchill to offer a similar assurance
to SOE. Rheam, teaching sabotage, and the Beaulieu staff, teaching
subversion, took a pragmatic English view of military necessity; they
may have recalled the tag *inter arma silent leges*.

Hitler changed his mind in the middle of the war. Annoyed by incidents at Dieppe and by Appleyard's raid on Sark,[127] he put out his
notorious commando order, promising short shrift for anyone caught
working against him behind the battle fronts, whether in uniform or
not.[128] SOE agents could thereafter expect nothing but the severest
treatment if they fell into enemy hands. SAS troops, equally, were
aware that they would be lucky indeed to return alive after capture: as
six, out of a hundred-odd taken prisoner in 1944–5, did.

Beaulieu's most difficult and most important task lay in character
training: turning civilians and ordinary soldiers alike, inspired by
the aggression they had learned at Arisaig, into devoted calculating
saboteurs and killers. This cannot have been easy; and it is now clear
that, with many of the Dutch and some of the Belgians who passed
through it, Beaulieu, in this aspect at least of its training, failed.

Much of Beaulieu's advice, here as in other matters, was plain
commonsense. 'Do not be clever or abusive.' 'Avoid replies that lead
to further questions.' 'Deny everything you cannot explain.' 'Do not
express personal affection or interest in anybody.' 'Have a simple
straightforward story and stick to it.'[129]

Much of SOE's training was sternly practical. Parachuting was
unforgettably actual; plastic went off with a real bang, and at Arisaig
it could be applied to a real locomotive on a real railway line. At the
end of their Beaulieu course, students went on an excursion in which
they were liable to actual arrest, and real interrogation in real police
stations. And yet – and yet: no amount of training could simulate
properly what life was going to be like in nazi-occupied Europe. To

126. Lahousen diary, 17? August 1939, photocopy TS in Brussels archive (see page
     514) 4 WE 1.
127. See Foot, *SOE in France*, 186–7.
128. *The Trial of German Major War Criminals*, iv. 2, dated 18 October 1942.
129. History xxx(i), A6. 4–5, duplic.

this major defect in the system no remedy was ever found; it seems to have weighed extra heavily on agents in the Low Countries.

New though SOE believed itself to be, and original as many of its most inspiring officers were, the principles of irregular war remain just as they were in Machiavelli's day – or indeed in Boudicca's – however much technical changes affect the ways they are applied.

Some of the methods that SOE used were by no means as new as itself. Many routine devices of secret and semi-secret tactics, taught at Arisaig and Beaulieu, had been set out by Aeneas Tacticus, a Greek commentator on warfare writing before 350 BC.[130] Wellington had co-operated usefully with Spanish-speaking guerillas during the Peninsular War; Cochrane had fought alongside others during the liberation of South America from Spanish rule; Holland's researches in MIR had thrown up several twentieth-century irregular campaigns, fought by Irish, Arabs, Chinese and Spaniards. Moreover, T. E. Lawrence's *Seven Pillars of Wisdom*[131] provided an idiosyncratic textbook; even though later scholarship and later reflexion cast doubt on its complete authenticity.[132]

Beaulieu tried to teach how to behave, if captured, under enemy interrogation. Hardly anyone who taught this subject had himself been through this disagreeable experience[133] at the hands of a Gestapo questioner;[134] but care and imagination could help. Students were plucked from bed at Beaulieu in the small hours, and hustled by a soldier in German army uniform (who rather enjoyed the task) into a bleak room with bright lights; where they were grilled. Some students at once recognised their tormentors as friends on the staff, and took the affair lightly; others were more properly impressed.

---

130. The 1928 Loeb *Aeneas Tacticus: Works* was available to SOE; there is a more modern translation by David Whitehead (1990).
131. Cape, 1935.
132. See references in M. R. Elliott-Bateman (ed.), *The Fourth Dimension of Warfare* and *Revolt to Revolution*, and private information.
133. Personal knowledge: I was one of the lucky SAS six.
134. Bernard Hanauer, active in SOE's efforts into the Dutch East Indies – which this book does not treat – had been released after a spell in Dachau, and must have had some practical advice to offer; of which there is no trace in the PF for him.

A captured secret agent was in a far weaker stance at interrogation than was the normal prisoner of war. As he was caught in plain clothes, he was ill placed to claim his rights under the 1929 Geneva Convention,[135] which covered the treatment of men in uniform.

Prosper Mérimée, friend of the great librarian Panizzi, when he commented on sixteenth-century manners 300 years later, remarked that a week's dissimulation could be wholly undone by a moment's folly.[136] For a secret agent working against the Gestapo or the NKVD, the rules of prudence were still stricter: however long one had behaved impeccably, a moment's folly was likely to be fatal. Himmler tried not to allow allied agents any leeway at all. Motorists today are, or ought to be, aware of the same point; in days when motor cars were less nearly universal than they now are in prosperous countries, the point was less well known. It was certainly less well taken, by too many of the Gestapo's prisoners.[137]

On first being arrested, an agent gave his current cover name, as found on the identity card he carried. One of the Germans' first aims was always to establish his real name. This the agent often did his best to conceal, knowing that reprisals were likely to fall on his family; this would give his enemies their first excuse for turning nasty. The hard man and the soft would take turn and turn about, while the prisoner got no rest, no sleep; after two or three days, one or the other of his interrogators had usually succeeded in finding out who he really was, and a good deal else as well.

A first-class agent, even during these travails, would keep an eye open for any chance to escape; such chances, in a Belgian, Dutch or German police building, were not many. But almost every agent had had one lecture at least, at Beaulieu, from one of MI9's experts; several of whom had practised what they preached about escape techniques during the previous world war. Their leit-motif was always, escape quickly: for with every hour, every day, every week that passes in enemy hands, the tighter the net is drawn round the prisoner, and the less fit he is mentally for life outside it.

---

135. PP 1930/31. xxxvi. 471 ff, Cmd 3941.
136. Prosper Mérimée and Louis Lacour (eds), *Oeuvres complètes . . . de Brantôme* (Paris, 1858), i. 41.
137. Cp de Jong, *KdN*, ix(ii). 848.

Again, so far as can now be perceived, this was not one of the subjects where Beaulieu did best, so far as the Low Countries were concerned. On a few agents the shock of arrest had so disorienting an effect that they talked, only too fast and only too freely: thus providing a mass of material that could be used to unnerve their companions and successors.

The training staffs did what they could. They scarcely ever let anyone through to the field who was quite unfit by character for so exacting a task. Yet they knew far too little about life and manners in occupied Europe. This was certainly one of the points where bad relations between SIS and SOE – often made worse by clashes of jarring personalities – harmed SOE's efforts; even SIS was not as perfectly informed as legend supposed. Occasionally, weak or distant relations between SOE and the Low Countries authorities in exile made things worse.

The gulf between the directing staff and the combatants actually doing the work, familiar already in Shakespeare's day,[138] was extra wide in the secret world; even when things went as they should. When things went wrong, as they too often did, the gulf became absolute. Day-to-day life in prison at Haaren or day-to-day torture in Mauthausen were as inconceivable in Roehampton or Eaton Square as in Baker Street or Beaulieu.

N's and T's agents, like most of SOE's agents in Europe, had to work among populations thoroughly infiltrated by the enemy secret police; many of them did not even have that officer status which was sometimes found to generate a minimum degree of respect, if they fell into enemy hands.

Though most of N's agents, when recruited, were sergeants or corporals in the Dutch army, most of them were given what SOE's administrators, tidying up at the end of the war, called courtesy commissions – never gazetted – as second lieutenants on the General List. Few of them had ever lived in an officers' mess or thought of themselves as other than subordinate. Why some were chosen for this small distinction, and others were not, cannot now be established. Larger sections in SOE made a rule, that they would commission all

---

138. *I Henry IV*, Act I, sc. iii, ll. 28 ff.

their agents in the belief that officer status would be a help to those
who were taken prisoner. This belief rested on blissful ignorance of
how savage SS policemen could be. For daily life in the hands of the
SS, there is now a startlingly accurate account in English by a
Dutchman who spent three years behind bars for the offence of
having had a clerk who – unknown to him – was trying to start up a
resistance group.[139]

Another security problem arose when training was done, but no
chance of actual work was yet open. SOE, nicknamed by its enemies
Stately 'Omes of England, had some fine country houses, such as
Audley End by Saffron Walden where the future Mrs Gladstone had
been brought up; named STS 43, Audley End was an agreeable point
at which to mark time while waiting to go on operations, its role in
1941–2. So, though less grand, was STS 61, Gaynes Hall by St
Neot's near Huntingdon, seat for a century and a half of the Duberly
family. It was requisitioned from its owner, Mrs Duberly, elderly,
energetic and inquisitive, who tried to settle in a cottage on the
estate so that she could see what this great house had been taken over
for; the cottage had to be requisitioned too.[140]

Yet many of N's and T's agents were bored by country-house life,
and begged for leave in London; which, with a little pocket money,
they got. In a free society, they could not be kept on too short a leash;
and tended to congregate in some of the many pubs, clubs and dance
halls that welcomed allied troops. The Dutch, the Flemish and the
Walloon communities in exile were all small; most of them knew
most of the others by sight at least. Not many of the efforts of SOE's
training staffs to instil into their students from the Low Countries
that they had joined a *secret* service had much effect.

The next technical problem was to find the right means of travel: sea,
land or air.

The tireless Lieutenant-Commander Gonin, RN, had noted early
that the Great War had not been decisive; and foresaw that an enemy
might have one day to be engaged on any of the coasts opposite

---

139. Floris B. Bakels, tr. Herman Friedhoff, *Nacht und Nebel.*
140. HQ 151, *passim.*

England. In the years 1922–38 he took his family on a bathing holiday on beaches practicable for a major sea-borne landing, everywhere between Den Helder and Brest; he then estimated the gradient of every beach; and reported his findings to NID.[141] All the Dutch and Belgian beaches were gentle, some of them almost flat; therefore unsuitable for easy clandestine landings from the sea. Only at Flushing, opposite Flushing, and at Den Helder was there deep water close inshore. Both ports were heavily fortified by the Germans, and the coast opposite Flushing was a dead end. No one in Coastal Forces at Harwich, Dover or Yarmouth, or in SOE's little naval base west of Southend at Leigh-on-Sea, had quite the nerve that led Andrew Croft to land agents on the inner side of a quay in Genoa.[142]

Moreover, the coastline of the Low Countries came under strict guard early; the northern Dutch islands apart, and they had difficulties of their own, well known to readers of Erskine Childers's matchless *The Riddle of the Sands*.[143] In practice, sea landings turned out to be impossible in Belgium,[144] and all but impossible in Holland.[145]

It was impractical even to think of sending many agents into the Low Countries overland: it took too long, and there were too many obstacles on the way. L. A. L. Humphreys who ran DF, SOE's private escape line section, worked at a more leisurely tempo and on a longer-term view than F or T or N: he did sometimes send men in across the Pyrenees. He made one attempt to help N by sending an agent by felucca to the south coast of France, but this too miscarried.[146]

MI9 had various land lines which ran out of Belgium, at least, southward towards Spain and eventual freedom; as the Germans

---

141. Personal knowledge; every Admiralty coastal docket on this area requested by COHQ in 1942–3 began 'Lt-Cdr Gonin bathed here in [date] and estimated the beach gradient at', etc. His wife is said to have hated it.

142. See his *A Talent for Adventure* (Hanley Swan, 1991), 190–2.

143. (1903).

144. See pages 229–30, 264.

145. See pages 82, 85, 103, 124, 139.

146. See pages 148–9.

became well aware. Several more amateur groupings were awash with double agents. Once the best line, 'Comet', moved the whole crew of a shot-down heavy bomber from the Dutch-Belgian border to Gibraltar in a week;[147] these were seven lucky young men, not in SOE, in the hands of experts. 'Comet' and 'Pat' specialised in aircrew, and so were hardly available for SOE. SOE's own lines were, as we shall see, of limited use.[148]

For, however he moved, the land traveller had several frontiers to cross; even if he escaped being managed by the enemy secret police, he had to pass through the normal police and customs controls, or secure the services of smugglers. Belgium, France, Holland, Portugal and Spain all then came under police-controlled regimes in which movement was restricted and supervised; difficult countries for anybody to cross, extra difficult for able-bodied men, ostensibly liable for forced labour in Germany, travelling under false identities. SOE was at least able, sometimes, to supply agents with well-forged *Rückkehrscheine*, chits that declared them to have worked in Germany already and to have been released on grounds of ill health.[149] *Ausweise* – passes to cross the internal frontiers in France (one round the north and west coasts; one separating the *départements* of Nord and Pas-de-Calais from the rest; and the demarcation line separating off Vichy's zone)[150] – were best obtained locally.

As neither land nor sea entry could be relied on, SOE had to take to the air: its agents normally went in by parachute from RAF bombers. Parachuting carried with it the task of training agents in how to do it – no complicated business: it can be fixed in three or four days,[151] and at a pinch agents could make their first drop directly on operations.[152] No one elderly or delicate could be expected to undertake it, though one elderly soviet agent attempted

---

147. Foot and Langley, *op. cit.*, 71.
148. See pages 170–1.
149. History xxxiv. 14–15. Cf also Ellic Howe, *The Black Game*, 14–20, 198–205.
150. See maps at end of Foot, *SOE in France*.
151. Personal knowledge.
152. Cp page 395.

it,[153] and so did many women, four of whom dropped into the Low Countries for SOE.[154] Such people could be sent into France by light aircraft, which could land and take off unobtrusively;[155] this method was seldom available to SOE in the Low Countries.

In retrospect, it looks as if SOE might have made more use than it did of 161 squadron's light aircraft to move agents in and out of fields not too far from the Belgian border. This could sometimes be managed,[156] but seems to have been too complicated for frequent use.

A further consequence followed from the unavailability of sea or air pick-up: agents who wanted to come back and report, or agents who deserved relief, had to travel over land, aiming for Lisbon or Gibraltar. This was at best a risky, tedious and time-consuming business; worst for the Dutch, who had all Belgium to cross as well as France and Spain.

Flights into the Low Countries were less straightforward than the nearness of the targets might have suggested. At least they were comparatively short: there were none of those ten- or even twelve-hour flights in unheated, uncomfortable aircraft that were normal for operations into Czechoslovakia or Poland. Yet the land over-flown was unusually heavily defended, for it lay athwart the shortest air route from England into Germany, and therefore bristled with heavy and light anti-aircraft guns, radar stations, and night-fighter bases.[157] It was therefore a danger area for aircraft on special duties, which had to fly low to drop parachutes. So strong and so dense in fact were the German AA defences that only a single SOE pick-up operation was attempted from the Low Countries, in November 1941. That was a failure;[158] no more were mounted, in spite of efforts by N and T section staffs to secure them.

Clandestine sorties were begun gingerly by 419 Flight RAF from

---

153. See page 40.
154. See pages 370, 376–7, 404, 421.
155. See Hugh Verity, *We Landed by Moonlight*.
156. E.g. page 330.
157. The RAF talked of the Kammhuber line, after the Luftwaffe general who commanded it: see R. V. Jones, *Most Secret War* (Hamish Hamilton, 1978), 264–79.
158. See pages 268–9.

various airfields in East Anglia. In February 1941, renumbered 1419, the flight settled on Newmarket racecourse, where in August it became 138 squadron. In February 1942 it was joined by 161 squadron, and next month the two of them moved to Tempsford, where they stayed till the late spring of 1945.

Tempsford, between Bedford and Cambridge, has been called Bomber Command's foggiest and soggiest airfield.[159] The main railway line from London to Edinburgh and the Great North Road both overlook the site, but it was well camouflaged, and the Luftwaffe left it alone. It has now reverted to farm land, but the farmer has left standing the bleak brick shed in which agents received their final briefings.

The aircraft these squadrons flew are set out elsewhere:[160] Whitleys at first, replaced gradually by Halifaxes, which in turn were replaced by Stirlings in May 1944; there were never many. Shortage of dropping aircraft was indeed, the world over, one of the main brakes on SOE activity. Early in 1944 the shortage was lessened in north-west Europe because some other sources became available, as 'Overlord' came nearer and even the air chiefs appreciated the role that SOE might play in it. Two special duty squadrons of the US air force worked often into France, and occasionally into Belgium, though never into Holland.[161] The aircraft of 38 Group, RAF Transport Command, of which the main task was moving airborne troops – it was almost always 38 Group that carried SAS parties to work – also had the necessary skills in pin-point navigation, and could sometimes help SOE out; as could, occasionally, Stirling squadrons of Bomber Command.

Shortage of aircraft plagued SOE; but had there been many more aircraft, SOE would have come up against a shortage still harder to remedy: not many men, and hardly any women, were capable of living in protracted clandestinity.

---

159. See *Proceedings of the Royal Air Force Historical Society* 5 (Bristol, 1989), 12, 16.

160. Table in Foot, *SOE in France*, 76.

161. W. R. Craven and J. L. Cate, *The Army Air Force in World War II*, iii. ch. xiv (Chicago: University of Chicago Press, 1951); History v A, *Special Duty Operations in Europe*, appx H4.

Bomber Command disliked detaching aircraft for special duties, as operations for the secret services were called; not only out of normal inter-service jealousy, strong though that was, but also because such work could only be done by bright moonlight: for over half each month, therefore, every aircraft so detached was held to be an idle asset.

The Air Ministry insisted that no dropping zone was used for a parachute operation until a reasonable recent air photograph of it had been passed by AI 2c, the branch there that handled SOE, and seen by the pilot. By 1942 there was plentiful air cover of western Europe, so there were no security troubles about photographing particular points.

There was a catch, unknown in England at the time. Just as the British Y service was able to give Fighter Command a few minutes' extra advance notice of bomber attacks on south-east England in the late summer of 1940, because Luftwaffe pilots could be heard chatting to each other as they taxied out for take-off, the German listening services often heard 138 squadron aircraft – of which they recognised the R/T call signs – talking to Tempsford flying control on afternoon flying tests, and were able to forewarn the Abwehr of probable clandestine activity that night.[162]

By 1943 Tempsford had settled into a drill, for briefing agents and for kitting them out for despatch; most of the drill had been in use from the beginning, and is worth setting down.

Agents were usually dropped in parties of two, three, or four; sometimes, alone. Larger drops were generally thought insecure. They were driven to Tempsford, from Audley End – only some twenty-five miles away – or Gaynes Hall, still closer; or from London; in a large staff car with a FANY driver, sometimes after a farewell dinner with N or T. N or T might himself go as far as Tempsford with the agents to brief them; failing him, a conducting officer – usually a friend from training school days – would go instead. Agents had already been briefed on their false identities, and their supporting cover stories, with which they had become

---

162. Henry Probert and Sebastian Cox (eds), *The Battle [of Britain] Re-Thought* (Shrewsbury: Airlift Publishing, 1991), 66; extra interrogation of Giskes, 27 June 1945, 2, duplic in Holland 22.

thoroughly familiar. At this last moment, they were handed their operation orders, to read, memorise and hand back. Any doubts or questions were settled on the spot; and they were given a last chance to back out, if they wanted. By this stage backing out had become almost impossibly awkward.

Next they were armed, with knives or handguns or both, as they wished; and equipped with three sets of pill – 'knock-out drops', stupefying pills which might be usable against an opponent into whose drink they could be slipped; benzedrine, handy for keeping awake for unusual hours or on arduous journeys; and a single cyanide capsule, one bite on which brought death within five seconds, for use in drastic emergency. Then, usually with an overall over their clothes and a parachute harness over that, there was nothing more to do beyond meeting the aircrew and climbing up into the plane.

Parachuting and container-landing techniques used to be secret. SOE played a sizeable part in developing them; they have now become common form. Details of them can be studied in a recently released War Office manual, issued in 1951 and made public in 1982.[163] The army was long suspicious of air supply and of air-mobile forces;[164] SOE was not alone in being looked at askance by senior soldiers. SOE's dropping methods did not vary widely from the army's; though as SOE's requirements for stores were odder, it made more use of packages than the army did. Results here were not always perfect; the Low Countries, yet again, suffered from seldom being at the focus of strategic attention. For instance, the first N section wireless operator to be sent into Holland was fobbed off with a set that had been faultily wired up.[165]

Parachute accidents, only too common in the early days of the craft,[166] were mercifully rare where T and N were concerned: none

---

163. See T. B. H. Otway, *Airborne Forces* (1990 reprint by Imperial War Museum), 403–4, 407–12. Otway had fought in Normandy. Original in the PRO WO 277/21.
164. Cf Major-General John Frost, *2 Para Falklands* (Buchan and Enright, 1983), 15–16.
165. See page 110.
166. Cf *Souvenirs du Colonel Passy*, i. 139

fatal in training, and only four in action. Of these two had unhappy consequences; they happened to early wireless operators, one in each section.[167] Accidents to parachutes carrying stores were not uncommon, a frequent cause of grief; and several agents broke an ankle on landing.

Though SOE detested routine on principle, RAF aircraft on special duty flights into the Low Countries were bound to some routines by the density of the opposition. Flights into Belgium normally approached from the west, crossing the enemy coast through a gap in the flak defences at Le Crotoy, at the mouth of the Somme; while flights into Holland approached from the north over the Afsluitdijk and the Zuyder Zee (now shrunk to the IJsselmeer). Navigators reckoned on being able to pinpoint their position at the coast, at any rate, and to run by dead reckoning to the neighbourhood of the dropping zone if cloud or ground haze prevented map reading – as they often did.

Often, again, aircraft could not find the reception committees they sought; sometimes they did find them, but got the wrong signal from the ground, and therefore made no drop. Occasionally the reception committee turned up, but the aircraft did not; either because fog had prevented it from taking off in England, or – less likely – because it had been shot down on the way. Rarely, engine or instrument trouble forced aircraft to turn back before they reached their dropping zones; Tempsford's maintenance was unusually sound, but the aircraft of the early 1940s were all fairly fragile.

Those who think, as many writers seem to do, that a parachute drop is like a shower of rain, something that simply falls out of the sky, should consider Mackenzie's remark: 'The full procedure for a single [air-to-ground] operation in its final form involved twenty-three stages and seven different authorities' in north-west Europe.[168] In the light of Murphy's proverbial Law – 'if it can go wrong, it will' – it is surprising that any operation survived all twenty-three stages intact; and these were only the staff stages, which took no account of stress of weather or pressure from enemy

167. See pages 122–3, 248.
168. Mackenzie, *op. cit.*, 366.

police. There were also countless difficulties at the receiving end – troubles about curfew-breaking, transport, storage[169] – quite apart from the possibility that the whole operation was a put-up job, put up by the enemy police: as was too often the case.

It was a nice question, constantly debated, whether agents were best parachuted blind, or to a reception committee.

If dropped blind, the parachutist had an immediate problem: location. Where was he? Till he knew, he could do nothing useful; and he was lucky if it only took him the rest of the night to find out. At best, he dropped into country that he knew already, and could recognise by moonlight from the air more or less exactly where he was. Much more usually, he could not be sure of his whereabouts within twenty miles or so.

Moreover, he might have trouble finding his kit, which was dropped from the same aircraft as himself, but not always on the same parachute. It might have fallen in another field; it might have been damaged by the drop. It had to be found instantly, and its parachute – as well as his own – hidden; or else the police would know there was an enemy stranger about. From the spring of 1944 onwards, agents could use a leg-bag – that is, could carry their kit in a rucksack or small case – dangling below them on a stout cord attached to their knee; a useful aid to parachuting in the dark because the cord slackens just before one touches the ground.[170]

If dropped to a reception committee, the trouble about location vanished; worse might easily follow. Curfew, hated by the common people of England for many centuries, applied all over the occupied Low Countries, and was strictly policed in towns. Members of a reception committee would have to break it, to get to the dropping zone, and would have to move any new arrivals through it, or have somewhere safe and warm enough to spend the rest of the night, not too far away. Worse still, reception committees might appear friendly, but in fact be run by the other side: a nightmare that sometimes came true.

---

169. Cf M. R. D. Foot, *Resistance*, 56.
170. Personal knowledge. Why was this device passed on so late to the Americans? See Stephen E. Ambrose, *Band of Brothers* (New York: Simon and Schuster, 1992), 64–5.

C. R. Tice, already a major in the Royal Welch Fusiliers in his early twenties, deserves mention here. He became SOE's chief airfield liaison officer with the RAF, based at Tempsford but helping out at several 38 Group airfields as well. He only flew once to the Low Countries, to Belgium in July 1944, but took part in several other operational flights, one of them as early as October 1941. He was brisk, decisive, energetic, a quick solver of minor practical problems; and he knew a lot about parachuting, because he had been an instructor at SOE's school at Altrincham before he went to Tempsford.[171] He provides an instance of the useful kind of staff officer, who sorts difficulties out instead of creating them. SOE needed men and women of this type because so much of its work lay out at the margins of normal service activity.

In 1942, 138 squadron aircraft were fitted with 'Rebecca', a direction-finding device that worked to 'Eureka' on the ground.[172] After a shaky start, some use was made of 'Eureka' in Belgium: three sets were established in the Ardennes, from each of which pilots could make short runs on dead reckoning to nearby dropping zones, and were found 'very helpful' in 1944.[173] 'Eureka's' history in Holland was less happy: 'the organisers in the field, through lack of training, had little faith in it, and after a bad blind drop on Eureka, when the load fell into the sea, they lost faith in it altogether.'[174] In the last spring of the war, a few better-trained and better-informed organisers were found to make good use of it for last-minute supply drops; but meanwhile at least two sets had been delivered straight to the Abwehr, as agreeable a present to enemy signals intelligence as the S-phone.[175]

An inaccurate wavemeter was used when the earliest 'Rebeccas' and 'Eurekas' were set up; several 'Eurekas' were distributed to the field, and could not be recalled, before the mistake was noticed. Both SOE and the RAF managed to live with the results.[176]

*

---

171. His PF.
172. History ix, appx 10, 1; useful diagrams in Lorain, *op. cit.*, 100–1.
173. History ix, appx 10, 4.
174. *Ibid.*
175. See pages 64, 129.
176. History ix, appx 10, 8.

Once an agent had safely reached occupied Europe, and had solved the problem of where he (or she[177]) was going to live, a vital problem remained: how to communicate with headquarters in England.

Direct post did not work. Neither side's postal authorities would accept letters, telegrams or packages, or admit telephone calls, addressed to the other.[178] Indirect contact by post, through someone in a neutral country who could pass on messages, was not unthinkable, but was bound to be slow, taking weeks at least, perhaps months, to produce any result.

Both in N and T section agents were given an address to memorise, in Sweden or in Switzerland, to which they could send an innocent-seeming postcard, signed with a prearranged codename, which could at least announce their safe arrival, and perhaps a working address or a point of contact; they were warned that nothing would happen through this channel quickly.

N and T section had one advantage over most of SOE's other country sections, which arose from the Low Countries' closeness to England: some use could be made of pigeon post. Nowadays this raises a smile; but it was extensively used by the German intelligence services, all over Europe, and was not quite useless to SOE[179] or indeed to SIS.

Pigeon politics, which were intricate, can be omitted. The army and the RAF ran rival pigeon services; SOE made use of the army's, and an army pigeon expert – Captain Kleyn – used to go to Stradishall or Tempsford to deliver pigeons just before agents left. Though this was only a one-way service, and was by no means totally

---

177. So few of the agents SOE sent to the Low Countries were women – three went to Holland and two to Belgium – that the author hopes today's feminists will forgive him for writing, as a rule, in the male gender only.

178. By a freak, a German operator forgot – it is said – to cut off the teleprinter connexion from the Ministry of Propaganda in Berlin to the London office of the *Völkischer Beobachter*, to the great advantage of SO1 and PWE in turn, who twice a day received Goebbels's routine broadcasts to the whole of the German press.

179. SOE file Security 21, draft retrospect prepared by MI5 in June 1945. George Starr, alias Colonel Hilaire, one of F section's leading agents in France, went to that task from being quietly *embusqué* as a pigeon post sergeant in St James's Park.

reliable, it was better than nothing. It provided at least a means of knowing that an agent had landed safely; and he might get a chance to send valuable information as well, if he acted fast – the longest he could hope to keep a pigeon by him was ten days, and it was usually wise to dispatch it homeward within two.

English pigeons, of course, had to be used; just as well, for some Belgian ones are supposed to be at the origin of that term of contempt, 'twerp'.[180]

Few actual messages sent by pigeon from the Low Countries seem to have survived in SOE's archive; but there are several mentions of the method, and one case of a party shot down on their way into the field with as many as fifteen brace of winged companions.[181] This was as late as July 1944; pigeons were still being dropped into Belgium on 15 September.[182]

Radio – often then, and usually in these pages, called wireless – remained an indispensable but dangerous resource. Four sorts were then available: radio telephony (R/T), wireless telegraphy (W/T), navigational aids (i.e. 'Eureka'), and radio direction-finding, renamed radar during the war and not employed by SOE – though German radar stations might be targets for sabotage.

R/T had only just emerged as readily usable in war by 1940. German air and armoured units used it with lethal success in the *Blitzkrieg* in Poland and France. During the battle of Britain that followed, R/T touch between fighter pilots in combat, and with their controllers, proved a battle-winning factor on the side of the RAF.[183] The United States Army had developed a walkie-talkie – a light portable R/T set usable by men walking about – by the autumn of 1939, but none was available east of the Atlantic till 1945.[184] Moreover, from a secret service point of view, there was one vital objection to R/T: it was readily intercepted and therefore not normally secret at all.

---

180. *Spectator*, 2 April 1994, 31c.
181. Eddy de Roever, *Zij sprongen bij maanlicht*, 59.
182. PRO AIR 27/956, 161 squadron ORB, f. 203.
183. Personal knowledge, from a month's experience in Hornchurch operations room in 1940.
184. HQ 147, *ad fin.*

SOE developed an R/T set, called the S-phone, which was bulky but efficient, and reasonably secure: it was so narrowly directional that conversations over it were not at all likely to be intercepted. It was a portable ground-to-air or land-to-sea telephone; talking on it was as clear as talking to someone in the same room, if the range was right. Tommy Davies conceived it, in the summer of 1940; it took SOE's Radio Communications division about eighteen months to perfect,[185] with the refinement added that someone standing next to the user could not hear what was being said. Like so many former secrets, it is illustrated by Lorain.[186]

Absurd though at first it might seem, there was also available – one way only, outwards from London – the great engine of the BBC. It was T section that proposed, in February 1941, the use of coded messages in BBC broadcasts to the continent; even before SO2 had persuaded SO1 of the need for a Belgian freedom station to broadcast at all.[187] By June 1944 it was possible for the BBC to send out scores of messages in a single night, gibberish to those who did not know the codes. It was not difficult – as both sides discovered – to convey a simple message by the insertion of a single phrase into a particular programme. This was all best prearranged with agents before they left for the field, but could be set up later by signal.

Like so many weapons, this one was double-edged: as both SOE and SIS found to their cost, when N section was gulled into guaranteeing the bona fides of a double agent who thereupon penetrated an intelligence circuit.[188]

The bulk of SOE's wireless traffic with the continent was by W/T. For most of its first two years of existence, it had to live with a rule laid down by SIS which maintained that the business of clandestine W/T communication was so esoteric that such newcomers as SOE could not handle it. To start with, all SOE's W/T equipment and ciphers were handed out by SIS, of which the home station handled all the traffic – with no increase in the cipher staff. This naturally caused delays, which in turn caused friction. Nelson complained to

---

185. Page 1 of that division's history, TSC in History xxv.
186. Lorain, *op. cit.*, 96–7.
187. Whole world war diary, ii. 232–3, 20 February, and iii. 314, 6 March 1941.
188. Page 127.

Jebb in March 1941 of four-day delays incurred on telegrams from the eastern Mediterranean; and of C's habit of holding some messages up for anything up to a week, while their contents were considered in his office before being passed across to their addressees.[189]

The staff of SOE were not alone in finding the signals branch of SIS cantankerous and at times incompetent. De Gaulle's original head of secret services remarked just after the war that 'SOE's technical services proved themselves much more comprehensive and more competent than those of the Intelligence Service'.[190] This was one of the major points of friction between SOE and SIS. On 1 June 1942 SOE cut free. From that date it took charge of its own wireless affairs, made its own sets, used War Office ciphers and then devised its own, and trained its own operators – at Thame Park, east of Oxford. Its main home stations were nearby, at Grendon and Poundon on the Oxfordshire-Buckinghamshire border. At the time they were deadly secret. A wiring diagram of one of them is now in print, compiled by the tireless Lorain.[191]

Lorain also devotes nearly half his book to discussions and illustrations of clandestine wireless sets, and of various cipher methods used by SOE. The cumbrous early sets provided by SIS were replaced by the autumn of 1942 by SOE's A Mark II, and from 1943 by the B Mark II, each of which fitted neatly into an attaché case, then as now a normal sight in the office district of any large town, and not eye-catchingly out of the ordinary in the country. These were transceivers – that is, they could both send and receive. They worked on a short wavelength, between 3 and 15.5 megacycles a second, precisely determined by a crystal – an object about the size and shape of a two-pin electric light plug – inserted by the operator when he started up the set.

Miniaturisation had hardly begun. The tiny transmitters now mounted in spacecraft were not yet known; an A Mark II had a power output of about five watts, a B Mark II developed thirty at least. Their signals were often so weak that only operators with

---

189. Whole world war diary, iii. 334, 9/10 March 1941.
190. *Souvenirs du Colonel Passy,* ii. 185 n, tr., cf *ibid.*, 181–91.
191. Lorain, *op. cit.*, 174. See also Foot, *SOE in France*, 103–5.

exceptionally keen hearing could pick them up at home station at all. They worked only on AC; operators sometimes had to have recourse to pedal generators.[192] Moreover, all these sets were liable to goniometry – direction-finding; a German speciality. Much emphasis was therefore placed, in training, on the need to keep messages short. A few experts had already devised how to send very short messages, that only involved being on the air for inside a minute; they were neither in SOE nor in SIS.[193] High-speed transmission was already known to journalists in sophisticated countries, who used it for teleprinting; it was not till 1944 that a journalist in Denmark thought of applying it to SOE's wireless traffic, and such transmissions – now, apparently, a commonplace of clandestine life – were unavailable in the Low Countries for the war against Hitler. SOE's operators there tried to keep their transmission times down to five or ten minutes; and knew that if they stayed on the air for as long as twenty, they would be liable to prompt arrest. Yet if one had managed, several times over, to transmit for twenty minutes without mishap, one might easily get careless, do it again, and so get caught.

At first operators were tied to fixed schedules, which the English ones called skeds among themselves. Leblicq for instance was to have come on the air, using the call sign NYT to home station's RCA, at these Greenwich mean times:

Mondays at	1400
Wednesdays at	1930
Fridays at	2100
Sundays at	2030[194]

Fixed schedules provided points round which an operator's life rotated; they also made life simpler, once they had been understood, for the enemy's efficient direction-finding service.[195] Some years passed before the system became flexible enough for operators to be able to call up at less regular intervals, or better still at any time.

---

192. History xxxi(i). A16, 2, duplic.
193. Private information.
194. E to T, 1 July 1941, initialled TS in Belgium 128.
195. Cp Foot, *SOE in France*, 103–4, 324, 368.

As for ciphers, agents were taught the Playfair code as a mental exercise, but were forbidden to use it on the air. It is a simple substitution-code on a 25-letter word square; easily learned,[196] but almost as easily broken: as readers of Dorothy Sayers's *Have His Carcase*[197] will remember. It might still be usable, even useful, in the field for traffic that was urgent and not deadly secret.[198]

That book codes were used early can be inferred from a list of the items to be dispatched with the ill-fated Leblicq on operation 'Moonshine' in July 1941. It begins:

'W/T Set
Parachute
Novel
Automatic Pistol .32'.[199]

Operator and home station held identical copies of the same book, which could lie inoffensively on the operator's bedside table; the opening figures of a message indicated where in the text coding for it was to begin. Notoriously, the Abwehr was supposed still to be using a book code in the summer of 1942;[200] SIS abandoned it, and so did SOE.

Operators moved on to a single or double transposition cipher, based on some unforgettably simple poem, assisted by one or two strips of figures.[201] They were urged to memorise the strips of figures, as well as the poem; but too many of them did not trust their memories to retain the figures in the correct order, and jotted them down somewhere handy. This was a useful habit for interrogators, if they were captured; when they were likely to have their poems browbeaten or tortured out of them as well.

---

196. See David Kahn, *The Codebreakers*, 198–202.
197. Gollancz, 1932
198. Example, from Paris 1944, in Foot, *SOE in France*, 332.
199. TSC at back of Belgium 128. For 'Moonshine', see pages 247–9.
200. Many legends have built up round a pair of Abwehr spies, then in Cairo, who spoke no English but had a copy of Daphne du Maurier's *Rebecca*, of which the purchase was traced back to the German military attaché in Lisbon. See J. Eppler, *Geheim Agent im Zweiten Weltkrieg* (Preussisch Oldendorf: Schütz, 1974), 324–6.
201. See Lorain, *op. cit.*, 68–74, for a lucid exposition, with examples.

A safeguard existed, so that home station would know if an operator had been captured and had had his code squeezed out of him: the security check. This was of much more use in theory than in practice. Many SOE country sections, including F and N, regarded it as a tiresomeness introduced into the smooth working of SOE by MI6's mistrusted experts; and often ignored it. Leo Marks, SOE's young cipher expert, described it at the end of the war as 'merely a gesture to give the agents confidence'.[202]

The checks were purely routine ones. If pressed hard, a captured agent was to confess to one of them, called the bluff check: he was to make a transmission error on every umpteenth letter. However hard he was pressed, he was not supposed to reveal his true check, which was simply a mistake of the same kind made at a different interval. A security expert, commenting on the 'Bishop' case – a protracted German attempt to play back the set of an F section wireless operator captured in south-western France – went so far as to say, in July 1943, that 'The omission of the security check seems to be a common feature of nearly all the country sections' wireless traffic (on my recent experience I should regard it as much more suspicious if the security check were invariably included).'[203] Moreover reception was often so bad that messages arrived littered with mis-hearings or mis-transcriptions: this helped to make the system appear unreliable to its users.

By 1944 refinements had been added: each W/T operator had a separate arrangement with home station, about where he would insert anodyne words or phrases in his messages, or about words to indicate that a deliberate error was impending. The simpler system had meanwhile helped to cause damage.

Another kind of security check may be useful: a prearranged trick question and answer. Base asks, for example, 'Would you like some whisky?' Any reply but 'Send Aunt Agatha my love' means trouble. This cannot safely be used more than once; and is not proof against an agent who has changed sides, as a few did. Ideally, each operator knows a different trick question and answer and none are written down; real operators, like real staff, are not ideal.

---

202. History xxxiv, 20.
203. France 132.

T section did arrange a trick question and answer, but with far too many operators at once. To the inquiry '*Avez-vous besoin du savon?*' the only right response was '*Il y a suffisament de poires ici.*'[204] Someone must have been captured with this in writing, or betrayed it; for when in September 1942 T heard of an operator's arrest through MI6, and sent the trick question, he got the correct reply.[205] This put T, and indeed SOE, off this sort of check.

From 1943 onwards – warned by several disasters, in several countries – SOE's signals staff took to recording every operator's individual sending touch, so that dubious transmissions could be compared with ones known to be authentic. This system, known as fingerprinting, was far less accurate than the anti-criminal device of which it took the name. Many of the girl operators at home station knew SOE's operators in the field extremely well, because the two of them had practised together for weeks on end; but it turned out only too easy for enemy signals clerks to imitate prisoners' sending styles.[206]

A much sounder safeguard was also introduced in 1943, on Marks's initiative: the one-time pad (OTP). This consisted in principle of a silk sheet of random letters or numbers – or both – which the agent took with him, of which home station held the only other copy. After he had used a strip of letters or numbers on his sheet, the agent could cut it off and burn it, thus leaving nothing useful for the enemy to capture. OTP at last provided a safe and foolproof cipher system; and much increased the reliability of the groups that used it. For the purpose of SOE in the Low Countries, it arrived rather late.

Secret resistance in the 1940s, once a familiar subject, is now fading like so much else in the past into obscurity. A few notes on its nature are needed to close this introduction.

In every country the nazis occupied, even Austria, they managed to make themselves unwelcome in the end, however warmly they had been received at first. Myth now has it that they were resisted everywhere, even that there was a European resistance movement; myth is

---

204. 'Do you need soap?' 'There are enough pears here.'
205. War diary xxii. 34, 68.
206. Cp pages 145, 154, 280.

not history. Resistance to them, which indeed became widespread, varied greatly, in time and place and method; different countries, with different histories, took the shock of occupation in different ways, and the differences are as marked as the similarities.

Historical comparisons, always tricky, are sometimes dangerous; let an historian, writing of men and women who faced grave dangers, nevertheless attempt a comparison or two.

Among the governments in exile in London, the Dutch was certainly stronger than the Belgian, and less cantankerous – less a perpetual source of trouble to its hosts – than the Polish; none of the three could compare with the Norwegian for stability or for readiness to help the allied cause or to de Gaulle's Free French – not officially recognised until October 1944 – for capacity to exasperate the prime minister and the foreign secretary.

Dutch resistance was unlike Danish or French or Belgian. The Dutch introduction to being occupied was much more violent than the Danish, and ran contrary to what the Dutch people had been hoping for. The Danes put up virtually no initial fight at all; most of them took several years to decide that, after all, they would resist. In Belgium, as in northern France, the bulk of the car-owning population – much smaller than today, and comprising the governing, managerial and administrative classes – fled: blocking the roads for troop movements, and aggravating the sense of national disaster. In the Netherlands in May 1940 there was no chance for such people to bolt, even if they wanted to do so, for the initial German onslaught on 10 May reached right through to the coast, leaving no route for escape by land.

It is too easy to confuse the pattern, now familiar, of resistance in, say, France or Yugoslavia with what happened in the Low Countries: each of which reacted differently. The racial antagonisms that beset occupied Yugoslavia hardly affected Belgium.[207] The Belgians did to some extent work in parallel with the French: that is, at first most people took the practical, realistic view, and accepted defeat as a *fait accompli*. A few Belgians, out of political enthusiasm or mere greed, flung themselves at once into full co-operation with their new

---

207. See page 233.

masters; while a few more detested them from the start, worked for their eventual downfall, and in the end brought the bulk of their compatriots over to their side.

The Dutch handled things another way. They too had their instant collaborators, and their share of double agents. Yet about a million citizens – one in eight of the population – knew from the start that they were already resisters in spirit and in truth, who only waited for the moment to become resisters in action as well. This provided SOE with a splendid chance; which, first time round, it muffed.

English readers who keep abreast of the secret history – so far as it is known – of the mid- and late-twentieth century will recall the names of Maclean, Burgess, Philby, Blunt, Blake, Prime; they will not need to be reminded that the prevalence of double agents is not confined to the Low Countries. Nor will Americans who recall the Snowman and the Falcon, or the more recent Ames case. In an age of volatile electorates, the readiness of men of strong but unstable character to change sides should surprise nobody. Had the nazis succeeded in conquering England, dubious characters this side of the North Sea would have been ready to help them. In spite of Churchill's proud and valid boast that the nation was as sound as the sea is salt, half-a-dozen bad apples would have been enough to rot the barrel – as they were in Holland and in Belgium. We can be glad we were spared the temptation.

Of this book's central characters, agents who parachuted by night into enemy-occupied territory to help subvert nazi rule over the Low Countries, hardly any had the sort of startling success that sometimes fell to their opposite numbers in such other countries as France or Greece or Norway; but they were all of them brave, beyond the common run. All were volunteers; this sort of work is no task for a conscript. They deserve credit from posterity for having dared to try to outface the Gestapo, even if some of them, once in Gestapo hands, did not live up to their own or their comrades' hopes. None of us can be sure that we would have done any better in their often impossible fixes.

An official SHAEF assessment of SOE's role in the liberation of France confirmed that it had been of essential importance.[208] No

---

208. Foot, *SOE in France*, 402 and n.

such claim can be made for it in the Low Countries; but in Belgium it provided at least plenty of arms and of hope, as well as presenting the allies with the prize of a great port, almost intact; while in Holland, after a horribly sticky start, it arrived at a workmanlike conclusion.

Such questions as whether the Belgians were better or worse than the Dutch at the business of resisting, or whether SOE gave better or worse service to one country or the other, are not worth asking: it is always a mistake to try to compare the incomparable. One or two sets of figures are worth setting out side by side all the same.

Prospective agents were told, at an early stage, that their chances of survival were thought to be about evens – in north-west Europe: the risks and the rate of loss were much lower in the Balkans. F section, working to the south-west of the Low Countries, sent 470-odd agents into France, of whom 104 – fewer than one in four – did not return.[209] (Of the 39 women it sent in, 13 – one in three, included among those 104 – were killed.) T section sent 182 agents to Belgium, of whom 61 – one in three – were killed, in action or in enemy hands. Three more were wounded before they could start work; and 23 survived arrest. N section is notorious for its severe rate of loss, and indeed 46 of the first 53 agents it dispatched did not survive; the final balance was less dreadful than the myth. Of a total of 137 agents sent to Holland, 66 failed to return: just as had been predicted at the start.[210]

A current fashion among military historians discusses what experience in battle was like. For SOE's agents, battle was continuous: they could never safely let down their guard, even when half asleep.[211] They were more alarmed than ordinary soldiers, and for longer, and for better reason: they were less exposed, as a rule, to shot and shell, but much more exposed to anguish, doubt, and the risk of torture. Nasty as prisoner-of-war camps could be, concentration

---

209. The 104 names on the F section memorial at Valençay, Indre, unveiled in May 1991 on the fiftieth anniversary of F section's first successful drop which took place nearby, were quarried out by the industry of Lieutenant-Colonel J. D. Sainsbury, OBE, TD.
210. An attempt at a nominal roll of agents sent is in appendices 3–4, page 473 ff.
211. Cf page 218.

camps were infinitely worse. That was where most of SOE's Low Countries captives were sent: the worst part of the bad regime against which they fought. There, the need to stay alive at all absorbed the full attention of almost everybody.

Otherwise, the bulk of agents' day-to-day attention had to concentrate on maintaining the pretence that they were dutiful subjects of the occupying power that they were planning to help overthrow. One of the most accomplished of their tutors in this task at Beaulieu, in the autumn of 1941, was Kim Philby,[212] marking time till there was an opening for him in SIS; he spoke from the heart.

As early as 18 June 1942, two learned commentators on SOE – Hanbury-Williams and Playfair, reporting to the new minister about how the body was organised – remarked that 'its reputation lags behind its performance'; this remains true. They rightly added in their next sentence that SOE 'has in the past, and to some extent still has, something of a bad name'.[213] SOE's bad name will not be much refurbished by the pages below, but there were entries to be made on the credit as well as the debit side of its ledger.

Secrecy was unavoidable, even indispensable in SOE, which was a secret service; much of it, certainly, was both necessary and desirable. Sometimes, in retrospect, it looks as if there was too much of it: a certain paradox attaches to the attempt to raise whole peoples to throw out their occupiers without something being done in public. No secrecy, no surprise, it is true, and the springing of surprises was one of SOE's strongest cards. Yet, as the original incorporation of EH which became the PWE into SOE made clear, in the closing stages at least of any campaign of liberation there would be a role for posters, leaflets, broadcasts, other forms of propaganda.

Agents received some training in this at Beaulieu, hardly with useful results in the Low Countries. There, the staff officers involved, both in Baker Street and in the governments in exile, were weighed down – perhaps too heavily – under a cloak of secrecy.

---

212. Conversation with Yvon Morandat, 1969.
213. *Op. cit.*, 3, duplic in HQ 60.

Staff officers in SOE stuck rigorously to a drill of addressing each other on paper only by their symbols – 'AD/P to V/CD through D/R' and so on. Any security value this might have had was much diminished by the habit most of them retained of putting their own initials at the foot of everything they wrote.

SIS was in full sympathy with SOE on one point at least: the despatch of agents to the field was held to be so highly secret a matter that staff officers of governments in exile were kept well clear of it. They were allowed a say – sometimes a large say – in settling what agents' tasks were to be, and their advice was useful when it came to preparing cover stories; but it was not they who drew up the operation orders, and not they who accompanied the outgoing agents to their airfield. Quite a palaver was made of the secrecy of the dispatching system; though many foreign staff officers had been through Ringway, to help earn their agents' confidence, they were supposed not to know Tempsford's name or location, not revealed till 1944.

SOE and SIS were by no means isolated in secretiveness. In the very week of Germany's surrender, the secretary to the Cabinet was still refusing to release even to members of the War Cabinet either details of SOE's raid on Vemork, which had scuppered Hitler's advance towards an atomic bomb, or a mere mention of 'C', the title by which the inner circle had for years referred to the head of MI6.[214] And the ten thousand-odd men and women who hugged to themselves for twenty-nine years what the decipher staff had been up to at Bletchley Park knew that they had a secret worth keeping.

Resistance in the Low Countries, indeed throughout Europe, was intricate as well as dangerous. Some sixty years ago, Nowell Myres concluded his study of the history of England in the century and a half after the Romans left with a passage which he dropped from later editions because scholarship had cleared up so many points. Resistance history is still obscure enough for the transfer of this passage to bear on it today:

---

214. Bridges to Selborne, with a copy to Sporborg, top secret, 3 May 1945, in Selborne papers, 21.

The conflicts are too complex, the issues too obscure, the cross-currents too numerous, and the decisions too local, to make possible the application of any single formula to their solution; and it is at least reassuring sometimes to remember that, if we found such a formula, we should unquestionably be wrong. *Uno itinere non potest parveniri ad tam grande secretum.*[215]

---

215. 'So large a secret cannot be reached down a single road.' R. G. Collingwood and J. N. L. Myres, *Roman Britain and the English Settlements* (Oxford University Press, 2 edn, 1937), 456. Myres's Latin is from Symmachus, *Patrologia Latina* database (Cambridge: Chadwyck-Healey, 1994), 016.831.10.

II

Dutch Catastrophes
1940–2

'If stories are suppressed, lessons cannot be learned from them'[1]

'A historian must often be content to suspend judgement and to leave obstinate problems unanswered'[2]

For the Dutch an old-fashioned view of monarchy prevailed: at the moment of catastrophe, the queen provided leadership. On her instructions, her cabinet followed her to London, where they got off to a shaky start as a government in exile. They were formally accepted as such on 21 May.[3] These were the same men who had taken such care to preserve Dutch neutrality in the summer before the war began, and through the *Sitzkrieg* that had followed in the west. Belligerence was now forced on them: too sharp a change of attitude for some. They were none of them young; only one, van Kleffens, the foreign minister, had brought his wife with him. None of them had the battlefield experience that had left so strong a mark on Churchill, Attlee, Dalton, Eden, Cooper, Gubbins, Hambro, Lyttelton, Macmillan, Menzies, Sinclair and so many other figures in the ruling class in London; because the Netherlands had clung to neutrality during the Great War. An early lampoon by a more bellicose Dutch exile called the cabinet 'the shivering sisters'.[4]

---

1. Bernard Fergusson (Lord Ballantrae), *The Watery Maze* (Collins, 1961), 29.
2. H. R. Trevor-Roper (Lord Dacre), *Hermit of Peking* (Penguin, 1993 edn), 25.
3. De Jong, *KdN*, ix(i). 8–9.
4. Foot, *Holland at War*, 21.

De Geer, the prime minister, regarded the struggle as hopeless from the start, and gave it up after three months; in August he took his leave of the queen, took ship for Portugal, and found his own way home. Dijxhoorn, the minister of defence, not much more combative, held on until the following summer. Normally Dutch cabinets take weeks, months even, to form; this was an emergency. On 23 August 1940 the queen instructed Professor P. S. Gerbrandy, a tiny but resolute Frieslander, her minister of justice, to take over as prime minister;[5] he obeyed. His new colleagues were sworn in on 3 September.

The various Dutch republics had not quite been of one mind during the Eighty Years' War in their desire to get rid of the Spaniards, and their citizens cherish diversity of belief as one of their strongest principles. Even during the war against Louis XIV, the United Provinces had seldom been united in much; and their fusion at the end of the great war against Napoleon into part of a single kingdom had not lasted twenty years before the kingdom split. The tendency to fission seems to be as strong in Dutch politics as in Irish or in Indian. The Dutch politicians and civil servants who went into exile with their queen, or escaped later to join her, brought these fissiparous leanings with them; plenty remained in the Netherlands to bedevil the tasks of resistance.

Inter-secret-service rivalries now and then upset the British secret effort; not only the British were affected by them. Just as relations between the OSS and the FBI, or the NKVD and the GRU, were not always smooth, SIS and SOE had tiffs – quarrels – downright antagonisms; and the same syndrome applied, on a smaller scale, to the Dutch in exile. Their intelligence and subversive services were first placed in separate hands, then combined under a regular marine officer who did not seem to understand either properly, and then separated again; which did not make for efficient working.

In principle, the intelligence service was to work with MI6, and the subversive service gradually learned to work with SOE.

The first Dutch intelligence service in exile, the Centrale Inlichtingendienst (CID), was contemporary with SOE. It was founded, under Francois van 't Sant who had Queen Wilhelmina's

---

5. Unnumbered note in RIOD.

ear, on 19 July 1940, the day SOE's charter was signed. Van 't Sant handed over to R. P. J. Derksema, noted for incompetence,[6] on 14 August 1941. In parallel with CID, the Dutch created an office for special affairs, the Bureau voor Bijzondere Aangelegenheden, which ran from 8 February to mid-June 1941 under Dijxhoorn, but seems to have been entirely ineffective.[7]

Derksema was replaced as head of CID on 5 February 1942 by Colonel M. R. de Bruyne,[8] who was already in charge of a new Dutch subversive service. This was the Bureau Voorbereiding Terugkeer (BVT), the office for preparing the return to the Netherlands, set up on 20 December 1941 by the navy minister in exile Vice-Admiral Furstner[9] – hence his choice of a marine, just back from the Far East, to command it. De Bruyne also had a marine captain at his elbow, Henricus Lieftinck, who had come out of Holland in May 1940 in charge of 800 captured German parachutists.[10] De Bruyne had no direct experience himself of the German occupation of his country at all.

Outside both these services there was for a time an informal group that amounted to a third, run by a young Dutch naval officer in exile, Erik Hazelhoff Roelfzema. Nominally he came under CID but in practice he did what he chose, protected by van 't Sant and by Gerbrandy in turn. He and the CID each despatched eight agents; six of his, five of theirs, did not return. He had the panache, the enterprise, the push-and-go of a seventeenth-century buccaneer; not much protection against a twentieth-century police state. One of his surviving agents, Pieter Tazelaar, did a second mission, this time for SOE, and survived again,[11] dying in July 1993. Hazelhoff Roelfzema went over to a further distinguished career as a Mosquito pilot in the Dutch air force.

---

6. De Jong, *KdN*, ix(ii). 853–4.

7. F. A. C. Kluiters, *De Nederlandse inlichtingen – en veiligheidsdiensten*, 102–3.

8. Duplication of names is incessant in the secret world, as in the open. He is in no way to be confused with H. B. A. de Bruyne, 'Bo-Peep' in MI9. He signed his wartime letters as de Bruyne; modern purists spell him as de Bruijne.

9. Snapshot in de Jong, *KdN*, iii. 432.

10. Kluiters, *op. cit.*, 372.

11. Pages 412–14.

So used did the British become to the presence of Dutch service airmen that the one German who ever escaped from them in England once passed himself off at a Derbyshire airfield – he was in flying kit, an international uniform – as a Dutch pilot who had crash-landed near by, and got as far as strapping himself into a Hurricane cockpit before he was detected.[12]

On 1 July 1942 BVT was redesigned. Still under de Bruyne, it became the Bureau Militaire Voorbereiding Terugkeer (MVT), the military office for preparing return. BVT had come under the navy; MVT came under the army. On 1 June Van 't Sant had taken charge of CID again, to lighten de Bruyne's workload; on 12 August he handed it over nominally to the prime minister, Gerbrandy, who set A. J. H. Lovink the diplomat to run it for him.

On 28 November 1942 the CID was dissolved, and replaced by the Bureau Inlichtingen (BI), news bureau, under H. G. Broekman, a captain in the Dutch army reserve who had already been an important figure in resistance in Amsterdam before he escaped across the North Sea in September 1941. A heart attack forced him to resign in July 1943; his successor, Dr J. M. Somer, a major in the Dutch East Indian army, had also had clandestine experience, running an intelligence circuit in Brabant,[13] and retained his post to the end of the war.

De Bruyne did not. Often distracted from secret work by marine-corps business, he resumed his career as a full-time marine in mid-March 1944, when it was MVT's turn to be dissolved. The Bureau voor Bijzondere Opdrachten (BBO), the bureau of special operations, under Major-General J. W. van Oorschot replaced it. Van Oorschot was less of an amateur at this sort of work than de Bruyne, for in 1939 he had headed GSIII, the intelligence section of the Dutch general staff, and had thus been present at the margin of the Venlo incident; after which he had been dismissed by a still passionately neutral government. He had reached London – with difficulty – on 11 May 1940 as head of a liaison mission, leaving too many papers behind him, which a friend managed to burn before the Germans searched his house.[14] He left the day-to-day

---

12. K. Burt and J. Leasor, *The One that Got Away* (1956), 135 ff.
13. De Jong, *KdN*, ix(ii). 807.
14. *Ibid.*, iii. 409.

work of BBO in the hands of Kas de Graaf, a recent evader from Holland, who unlike himself had practical experience of resistance life in occupied Europe.[15] De Graaf in turn was succeeded by J. Klijzing, a police inspector from The Hague, in the autumn of 1944.[16]

By that time Prince Bernhard had taken command, *in absentia,* of the Binnenlandse Strijdkrachten (BS), the fighting forces of the interior: as will be laid out in chapter viii.[17]

All these Dutch arrangements were complicated enough; the secrecy in which the British arrangements were shrouded at the time has made it less easy to understand what went on, on both sides of the North Sea. In 1948 Dr Somer, the former head of BI, testified at length to the Dutch parliamentary commission of inquiry into the policy of the wartime government in exile. Unhappily, he described SOE as the English intelligence service; and did not do so to shield SIS, to which he referred a few minutes later.[18] He also described Rabagliatti of SIS as the superior of Bingham in SOE:[19] another manifest error. Rabagliatti certainly carried more weight in the secret world than Bingham did, but in no sense commanded him. It seems likely that, out of the cloud of unknowing in which officers of SIS then liked to live, Rabagliatti said something that confused Somer and never tried to clear up the confusion, which has become widespread in the Netherlands.

The first effort SOE made to put an agent into the Netherlands foundered, perhaps because it was too indirect. He was briefed in London, but then despatched westwards to the Dutch colonies in the Antilles, where he was to add some extra polish to his cover story before he found his way back through Iberia; he faded out quietly in Central America.[20]

15. See pages 211–20.
16. All these arrangements are summarised in van der Stroom, *Nederlandse Agenten,* 6–13, and described in detail in Kluiters, *op. cit.*
17. See pages 385–6.
18. *Enquêtecommissie Regieringsbeleid 1940–1945* (henceforward *Enq.*), iv C-1, 12–13.
19. *Ibid.,* 15b.
20. Whole world war diary, iv. 623, 17 April 1941.

Another attempt, also made well before N section was founded to take charge of SOE's Dutch affairs, did manage to put an agent into Holland, by sea, but nothing came of it. J. van Driel was a merchant seaman, who knew the morse code and learned to work one of C's bulky W/T transmitters. With it, he was set early on 28 August 1940 to row ashore in a dinghy from a light craft off Oostvorne, south-west of the Hook; but it was already daylight when he neared the beach. A German patrol-boat approached him. He slipped his W/T set overboard, and spun a cover story that he had deserted his ship and wanted to go home; the Germans accepted it, and let him go.

His mission was to make touch with resistance-minded elements among the Dutch trade unions; he had memorised several addresses. All the men he approached took him to be a German agent, out to provoke trouble; indeed, one of them handed him over to the SD. His luck then changed back; he was again able to present himself as an injured innocent, and to talk his way out of German hands. He then lived out his cover story, went home and faded out of history.[21]

N section – usually called in Holland SOE-Dutch – was inaugurated on 20 December 1940, when the diplomat R. V. Laming took charge of it.[22] He came from a family of English shipbrokers who had lived in Holland for centuries; he was Dutch-born himself, at Rotterdam in 1887, and at school there. He read medicine at Amsterdam, where he was a prominent oarsman, but took no degree. Bad eyesight kept him from combat during the Great War, which he spent in Holland, helping administer blockade. Thereafter he cultivated a wide circle of friends, in the triangle Bergen-Zürich-Lisbon, and rose to commercial counsellor at The Hague in the late 1930s. He was thus well known to Sir Neville Bland, who had been a year senior to Dalton both at Eton and at King's; moving no doubt in different sets. More important for his posting to SOE, Laming was known both to Hambro and to Keswick; and his

---

21. See de Jong, *KdN*, iv. 706n, ix(ii). 856–7, xiii(ii). 100. No trace of this mission survives in SOE's archives at all.
22. Whole world war diary, i. 33.

extensive knowledge of the Dutch business world made him an obvious choice for the job.[23]

Diplomatic immunity brought him and his Dutch wife, whom he had married in 1934,[24] safely out of conquered Holland; he had spent a few months as director of the empire division of the department of overseas trade.[25] He brought into the section wide and detailed knowledge of Dutch commerce, history, customs and language – his Dutch was perfect – and a full acquaintance with old-fashioned diplomatic drill: he habitually referred, for example, to code words familiar to those with whom he worked, however clear it was from his context what he meant. He was over six feet tall and weighed seventeen stone (108 kg); something of an imposing presence.

Unluckily, he brought into the section, besides his knowledge, a quarrel dating back twenty-four years with a crucial figure among the Dutch who accompanied Queen Wilhelmina into exile: her treasurer and head of secret intelligence, van 't Sant. Laming and van 't Sant had taken opposite sides over a treason trial in Rotterdam in 1916, and had never been able to forgive each other.[26] Hence the stiff first fence Laming, as N, had to cross: the Dutch authorities in exile did not want to know he existed. Hence too, no doubt, the tone of SOE's war diarist, who first mentioned van 't Sant – in December 1940 – as an 'unsavoury individual', 'a man of extensive but malign influence' 'who made it impossible to obtain the services of Dutchmen of military age'.[27] De Jong has explained at length the private reasons the queen had for trusting van 't Sant's discretion and skill.[28] A policeman by profession, van 't Sant had in the mid-1930s exposed himself to much calumny to cover up a scandal in the royal family. In May 1940, by a further sacrifice, he had left his wife and daughter behind in Holland. He did not release to SOE much of

23. I am grateful to his nephew James Laming for information about the family.
24. *Who Was Who 1951–1960* (1961), 633a.
25. His thin PF.
26. R. J. Laming, R. V.'s nephew, to C. M. Woods, 17 November 1985; in R. J. Laming's PF.
27. Whole world war diary, i. 33.
28. De Jong, *KdN*, ix(ii). 811–36, especially 820–6.

what he knew about conditions in Holland, and shared to the full several cabinet ministers' dread that any sort of subversive activity would lead to unacceptable reprisal.

During their first winter of exile, the Dutch cabinet changed their minds. Encouraged by their monarch, they came to approve the need for anti-nazi activity by the summer of 1941. Yet when Laming saw Prince Bernhard in May 1941, and the prince made it clear that he was convinced of van 't Sant's integrity, Laming had to reply that this was not a man to whom he would entrust the lives of his friends, even at the request of the queen herself.[29] A few days later he was able to minute CD that van 't Sant 'has been successfully sidetracked' and would have no chance to interfere directly in SO2's affairs;[30] the indirect damage remained. For excellent private reasons, the Dutch royal family trusted van 't Sant; nothing SOE or SIS could say or do had any prospect of dislodging him from the queen's confidence. SOE learned, rather slowly, that this was part of the cross it had to bear.

The high-born Dutch who went into resistance – many did – were all devoted monarchists, and made their approaches to the queen; who referred them to van 't Sant; who detested Laming, and hence SOE. Hardly any of the leading men in Dutch society who escaped to England came anywhere near N section, which had to make do with whomever it could find. Brave and devoted though almost all N's agents turned out to be, it needs to be stressed that hardly any of the first and unluckiest fifty had any military or social standing, and that their quality was not always of the highest.

Laming observed early that Queen Wilhelmina, Prince Bernhard and Professor Gerbrandy had all come round to favour active and drastic opposition to the Germans, and puzzled over how this offensive spirit could be transmitted to lower and more sluggish levels of the Dutch in exile.[31]

His diplomatic and commercial training led him to favour reconnaissance by a businessman, or by the captain of a coastal steamer.

29. N to AD/A, secret, 14 May 1941, TS in Holland 1; repeated in whole world war diary, vii. 1734–5.
30. N to CD, 26 May 1941, in Holland 1.
31. Whole world war diary, ii. 46, 14 January 1941.

No such scheme worked. Much of the spring of 1941 was taken up with a project called 'Serbonian' – aptly enough, as it turned out, for it sank into a bog of ineptitude. A timber-boat's captain, plying intermittently between Delfzijl and Stockholm, was to have been SOE's emissary, but nothing came of it.[32] The suspicious-minded can infer that some other secret service nobbled him.

In the early summer, Laming's nephew Dick was drawn by the formidable Gus March-Phillips into a plan for using the sailing sloop *Maid Honor* as a sort of Q-ship. She was to hover off a Dutch port, entice a small German warship alongside, and overpower it with a Blacker bombard: a project the Admiralty banned.[33]

N also had hopes of small-boat operations, on or off the Frisian Islands; these too came to nothing, in spite of devoted efforts by his nephew, and the purchase of two fishing boats, one unremarkable in northern and the other in southern Dutch waters. Late on 30 June the first of these boats, east bound across the North Sea with two agents on board for an operation called 'Rhodium I', had the bad luck to be overflown at close range by three German fighters, while her captain was in process of painting one name out and another name in; and after a further close inspection from the Luftwaffe next morning sailed prudently back to Yarmouth.[34]

Laming had a head-on clash with Hambro over policy. He was sure that Holland, which he knew intimately, was too crowded with people who knew each other too well for secret work there to be feasible; Hambro overruled him and sent him back to the Foreign Office. He was commercial counsellor in Beirut for eighteen months, and in the same post with the Dutch in exile from November 1943; returning to The Hague in mid-June 1945, and retiring in 1948. He died in 1959.[35] Charles Cecil Blizard succeeded him as N.

Blizard, who sometimes used the alias Blunt at work, was born in 1897 in north London and at Mill Hill School until 1915; he fought through the rest of the Great War as a subaltern in the Middlesex Regiment and then in the RAF. He went into business and became

---

32. Holland 41.
33. Richards, *Secret Flotillas*, 95.
34. TSC of report in Naval 12A.
35. FO List, 1948, 270a; talk with his nephew James, 1997.

export manager of the Morgan Crucible Company. He was a good linguist, with fluent Dutch, French, Italian and Spanish, as well as some German, Portuguese, Romanian and Swedish. He re-entered the army in 1939, and was assistant military attaché at The Hague from January 1940 until the German invasion. He came out safely with the rest of the legation's staff. He then held intelligence posts in the War Office until 6 December 1941, when he entered SOE at Laming's elbow. On 19 December he became N; Laming stayed on for three months more, called NA.

His seniors in SOE thought highly of Blizard. Brook minuted on 3 December 1942 that he was 'An outstandingly capable and successful section head who is exactly suited to his post';[36] Gubbins concurred, calling him 'an able and excellent officer'.[37] Marshall-Cornwall and Gubbins both regretted it when Blizard signed out of SOE on 24 February 1943;[38] the War Office insisted on posting him to civil affairs. De Jong, like Homer, can nod: he did not move to the Italian section of SOE, but to lecture to future members of AMGOT in Italy.[39]

Near the end of his six months' absence, he telephoned Brook to inquire on what sort of terms he could return; indicating that he did not want to displace his successor Bingham. Brook envisaged him as head of 'a sub-Directorate, combining the Netherlands and Belgian Sections' – the post, in fact, that went next year to Philip Johns; although 'these countries were radically different and even opposed in their politics and clandestine organisation', they did form a bloc on the flank of the impending invasion, 'astride important communications into northern France'.[40] However, civil affairs promoted Blizard full colonel, and he dropped the idea of returning to SOE.

He did, though, retain one connexion with N section: he married into it. He had parted from his first wife, and married on 1 May 1943 Sibyl Irene Bond, who was many years younger than himself. She became a second subaltern in the ATS on joining N section in

---

36. MS in Blizard's PF, 3 December 1942.
37. Signed TS in *ibid.*, 20 January 1943.
38. *Ibid.* For Marshall-Cornwall, see *DNB 1981–1985*, 267–9.
39. Contrast de Jong, *KdN*, ix(ii). 805.
40. War diary, xlviii(i). 121, 2 July 1943.

March 1942, and remained in it till the end of the war; earning golden opinions for her conscientious work from her last section head.[41] Her original duties were hardly more than clerical, but she came to take over the business of allotting prospective agents to training courses and preparing them to go to the field; and it was largely to her that the gloomy task fell of taking dead agents' belongings back to their families after the war. After marriage, she continued to use her maiden name at work.

As soon as he entered SOE, Blizard persuaded MI5 to release the man who had been running the RVPS, an Anglo-Dutchman called Seymour Bingham, born at Rotterdam in 1898 and as bilingual as Laming. Bingham had read engineering at Delft, and had gone straight into business without pausing to take a degree; he had managed a furniture factory near Amsterdam for some years before the war. In the autumn of 1939 he joined the British consulate at Amsterdam, in the junior post of pro-consul; it was he who guided Commander Hill through that stricken city in May 1940.[42] He emerged safely, with the rest of the diplomatic staff; and his languages – he spoke fluent French and German as well as perfect Dutch – made him a useful recruit to the expanding security service.

Bingham, with the symbol NO, turned out an energetic but somewhat eccentric second-in-command to Blizard. His abrupt and emphatic manner seemed, to some of his colleagues, too abrasive; there was something dislikeable about him, and a surviving subordinate said simply, long afterwards, 'I thought he was a fool.'[43] Aptly enough, it was on All Fools' Day 1943 that Bingham officially took charge of N section,[44] which he had already been running *de facto* for five weeks. He was meant to be in charge *pro tem.*, till Blizard came back; but Blizard stayed away. So dislikeable was he that N section under him cannot have been what the navy would have called a happy ship; and his manners did no good to its relations either with the Dutch government, or with MI6.

41. MS report by R. I. Dobson in her PF, 12 March 1945.
42. See page 21.
43. Conversation in 1992.
44. Note in his PF.

His replacement by R. I. Dobson in the spring of 1944, when disaster had become manifest, is explained below.[45] Dobson saw the war out.

N had several subordinates worth mention. Captain L. L. Loewe, a regular army officer seconded to the Foreign Office for duty as a passport control officer in Holland in 1938–40, had been a colleague of Laming's before the war, and was four years his junior. He spent a year in N section, from February 1941, and seems to have made himself agreeable to some of the section's Dutch acquaintances, but moved on (when Laming left) elsewhere.

J. W. G. Kay, a twenty-four-year-old Intelligence Corps subaltern when he joined N section from the Joint Intelligence Committee (JIC) in June 1941, at least knew something of the enemy, for he had spent the academic year 1936–7, on leaving Winchester, studying at Heidelberg and Munich.[46] He had fluent French and Dutch as well as German, and spent eighteen months with N as interpreter and conducting officer. For most of 1943 he was elsewhere, but he rejoined the section as operations officer that October, moving over to 2 Special Force Detachment in the spring of 1944.

Laming brought into the section in the autumn of 1941 another consular acquaintance, John Dennis Kuipers, born in Cheshire in 1918 and largely brought up in Holland, who was bilingual in English and Dutch as well as speaking fluent French and German; he was a qualified pilot as well. He soon adopted the name Killick in the office, and moved on from the care of sabotage training to the task of section signals officer. From mid-February 1943 he had 'Mr Oliver' to help him – B. H. Olink, who was Dutch by birth at Almelo in 1910, had lived in Great Britain with a British wife since 1936, and had been naturalised in 1940. He was a businessman in peacetime – managing director of a busy merchanting firm – and bilingual in English and Dutch; in the summer of 1944 he took over control of W/T traffic – so far as the country section had any say in it – from Killick, and ended the war a captain.

In mid-1942 Blizard brought in from the Wimbledon Home

45. Page 206.
46. M. S. Leigh (ed.), *Winchester College 1884–1934: A Register* (Winchester: P. & G. Wells, 1940), 540.

Guard W. E. Mills, who had been a clerk in his pre-war firm, and was a more than competent linguist with fluent French, Spanish, Italian and German as well as some Danish, Portuguese and Dutch. Mills, as NA, handled such PWE business as affected N section, and was a general office manager and factotum; it was he who completed the first draft of the section history.

There were four Dutch-speaking conducting officers in the section. One, J. A. C. Rupert, had been born Dutch, in 1910, and naturalised British when he came of age. He was tall, good-looking, well mannered; at Arisaig he was described as the 'ideal type of accompanying officer'. Unluckily, his temperament turned out too open for secret-service work. Late in July 1942 he left SOE, at his own request, for airborne forces, and survived the war.

Roy Snewing succeeded him – they overlapped by ten weeks. Snewing had picked up fluent Dutch in two and a half years as a fashion buyer for C & A in Holland during the 1930s; he had joined SOE as a twenty-six-year-old Intelligence Corps subaltern, and quickly learned to make himself useful.

Frank Dawson, another likeable man, had picked up fluent French and Dutch, and a close knowledge of most towns in the Low Countries, while he ran the pre-war Workers' Travel Association. He was conducting officer for N from late 1941 to late 1943, when he left for SOE's L section and the post of trade union adviser.

Alfred Charles Parr, a year younger than Rupert, joined N as a civilian in mid-1942 when the BBC released him from monitoring Dutch broadcasts. 'Pleasant, quiet chap, obviously reliable,' Selwyn Jepson noted at his initial interview. He dressed as a second lieutenant, General List, on joining the section, was commissioned early next year, and ended the war as a captain. His tubby, bespectacled figure looked vaguely Dutch; the years as a journalist before the war had developed plenty of commonsense.

Marks's strictures on the lack of knowledge of Dutch by N's staff – 'only one member of the Directorate spoke it'[47] – are thus not borne out by the facts.

By the spring of 1944 Mockler-Ferryman had an OSS colonel, Joe

---

47. Foot, *Holland at War*, 131.

Haskell, at his elbow, and there was full OSS-SOE co-operation in the training of the three-man 'Jedburgh' teams which were to para-chute in and stiffen resistance in western Europe when its invasion began; a dozen of these teams were to be devoted to the Low Countries. Conformably, one OSS officer joined N section in December 1943. He was Derek G. Mortlock, born of British parents in Jamaica in 1914, who had been an infantry captain in the United States Army, and an east coast steelbroker before America entered the war. Gubbins testified in September 1945 to the meticulous hard work he had done, first as assistant to N's operations officer and in that task himself from January 1945; there is hardly anything else in his personal file.

There was just one secretary in the section, Elsie French, who spoke Dutch. She at least spoke it perfectly, for she had been born in The Hague of British parents and was brought up bilingual. She had been one of Marks and Spencer's clerks in Michaelhouse before SOE requisitioned it; joined the service, aged eighteen, in October 1941; worked devotedly hard, and pleased everybody. She joined Prince Bernhard's staff at the end of the war.

Close friends can run secret operations in extra safety; for they can recognise each others' voices if they can talk, each others' turn of phrase if they have to write; they can refer back to old friends and old enemies by nicknames their present enemy is sure not to know; and it is all but impossible to run one of them back to another, without the friend at the receiving end spotting at once that some-thing has gone wrong. Unhappily, social and national barriers were too steep for the first three Ns – or the Dutch interested in N's affairs – to be on such terms with many N section agents. Although several of the conducting officers got on with the students, there was not much warmth of feeling between the students and any of the first three section heads; to whom their agents remained strangers.

It is worth setting out who SOE's opponents in Holland were.

Posterity does not often care for detail. Of the myriad of nazi and para-nazi wartime leaders, not many are now remembered. Hitler, Himmler, Goering, Goebbels, Hess, Speer, Rommel are unforgotten names; the rest are fading out of public memory. This book can try to rescue a few from obscurity; starting at the top, yet recalling that – as is usual in modern wars – critical steps are often taken by junior figures.

Hitler himself made it clear from the start that he would give short shrift to any local interference with his plans. The day before the invasion, in a directive on how to treat occupied countries, he ordered: 'Hostile activities by the population (freebooting, sabotage, passive resistance, politically motivated withdrawal of labour) are to be suppressed with full severity.'[48]

He proposed to humiliate France, and to demote her from Great Power status to the second rank; the re-annexation of Alsace and Lorraine was as automatic in 1940 as in 1945. Of the fate of the Low Countries, he and his followers had thought less. The Dutch, so the nazis supposed, would quite soon come to appreciate the role laid down for them in nazi racial myth: that of associate Aryans, not quite full-blooded, but close cousins of the Germans, with whom they would gradually assimilate as the thousand-year Reich developed.

The local nazi chieftain, the *Reichskommissar*, was Artur von Seyss-Inquart, an Austrian who had co-starred with Hitler in the drama of the Anschluss in March 1938. Hitler picked him for this governor-general's task, to which he came from the post of deputy governor in occupied Poland. Like the republic of Poland and the kingdoms of Norway and Yugoslavia, the kingdom of the Netherlands vanished from the nazi world map.

Beside Seyss-Inquart, who was in charge of civil affairs, stood the armed services' commander, the Luftwaffe General F. C. Christiansen. Neither was much involved with SOE, though each was naturally opposed to any body that sought to interrupt the smooth running of what was – though the phrase was never used – a German colony.

Under Seyss-Inquart, the leading figure from SOE's angle of sight was Hanns Albin Rauter, also an Austrian by origin, who had been picked by Hitler himself to be the colony's SS chief, with the rank of *Obergruppenführer* – lieutenant-general, Heydrich's rank – and wide

---

48. L. Nestler *et al.*, *Europa unterm Hakenkreuz* (Berlin: Deutscher Verlag der Wissenschaften, 5v, c. 1991), iv. 93, tr.

responsibilities. Born in Klagenfurt in 1895, Rauter had been severely wounded as an infantry soldier in the Habsburg army on the southern front; not so severely as to keep him from *Freikorps* combat against both south Slavs and Hungarians in the aftermath of the Great War. By 1929 he was chief of staff of the Heimatschutz on the Austrian far right, and was a natural for the SS. He overtopped most other men in stature – he was nearly two metres tall – and in energy: three years elapsed between the two spells of leave he allowed himself during the next world war, and he worked a seven-day week, with neither rest not churchgoing on Sundays.[49]

Though he made himself work, he was spared the climatic rigours of the eastern front, or the stresses of supervising killing-grounds in person, which were at one point too much even for a killer as notorious as Bach-Zelewski.[50] Instead, he helped to supply the victims. He had no god but Greater Germany, and looked to Hitler and Himmler as its prophets. He had first met Hitler, in Munich, as far back as 1921,[51] and had become an instant convert. As a devout nazi, he busied himself with the persecution of the Dutch Jews. He did not love SOE either, and his name crops up here and there in its records. On 30 November 1944, for example, he was reported as 'holding a special court martial at which the prisoners are to be interrogated about the dropping of arms'.[52] No file on him seems to survive in British hands, though the Dutch hold his files in thousands. A vast archive was captured intact at the war's end; for no one would destroy it without his authority, and he was not at that moment in a state to give many orders.[53] It is now held by the Rijksinstituut voor Oorlogsdocumentatie (RvO or RIOD), the state institute for war documents in Amsterdam, and throws floods of light on nazi colonising methods. Its security content is on the thin side, for most of the files on captured agents were held at a lower level, and burnt.[54]

---

49. De Jong, *KdN*, iv(i). 80.
50. See Christopher R. Browning, *Ordinary Men*, 25.
51. De Jong, *KdN*, iv (i). 78.
52. History cx for that date.
53. See pages 416–17.
54. See page 378.

Under Rauter, there were four successive Befehlshaber der Sicherheitspolizei (BdS), police commanders of security. The first, Hans Nockemann, who came from Aachen, had spent the years 1935–40 in the SD's head office in Berlin. He had a total staff of some 700.[55] He did not last long. Spontaneous Dutch demonstrations, all over Holland, on 29 June 1940 – Prince Bernhard's birthday – showed such enthusiasm for the exiled royal family that Nockemann was dismissed (he died of wounds on the eastern front eighteen months later[56]).

His successor, Dr Wilhelm Harster,[57] was an ardent Bavarian nazi, who had distinguished himself already as BdS of Innsbruck and of Cracow, and had been about to take up the same post in Brussels when Himmler sent him to The Hague instead. Rauter testified to his energies at his desk, and to his quickness of mind. De Jong thought him not to have been a sadist; a captured allied agent (not of SOE's) whose fierce interrogation he supervised formed the contrary impression.[58] He got on well with Seyss-Inquart, and ran his parallel police force with strict precision for three years. As he spoke a little Italian, he was transferred to Italy in the autumn of 1943.

His successor, Erich Naumann, a Saxon, was a thug rather than an intellectual. He had left school at fifteen; moved from the SA to the SS after Röhm's murder in 1934; headed the SD in occupied Austria, and for a few weeks in occupied Poland; and was posted to The Hague as a rest cure, after a hectic winter killing partisans by tens of thousands in an *Einsatzgruppe* on the eastern front.[59] Rauter found him a far less satisfactory subordinate than Harster, and sacked him on 1 June 1944, replacing him with Dr Eberhard Schöngarth.[60]

Schöngarth just missed the Great War – he was born in 1903 – but had been old enough to fight in a *Freikorps* just after it; had graduated early into the nazi party; gave it up for a while to read law; rejoined in February 1933, and moved promptly into the SS. He had

---

55. De Jong, *KdN*, iv(i). 86–7.
56. *Ibid.*, 290.
57. Snapshot in Jelte Rep, *Englandspiel*, at 28.
58. De Jong, *KdN*, iv(i). 291–3; private information.
59. *Ibid.*, iv(i). 539–41.
60. *Ibid.* vii(ii). 1274–5.

already served as BdS in 1940–2 in the rump of occupied Poland, persecuting Poles and Jews; had been present at Heydrich's notorious conference held in Interpol's headquarters at Wannsee, which decided on the 'final solution'; and had just been persecuting partisans in the Balkans. Harster, a non-smoker like Hitler, hardly drank; Schöngarth by this stage in the war drank (and no wonder) a great deal, often being noticed the worse for drink while at work by his underlings. Even for a Gestapo man, he was unusually merciless; and a decision of Hitler's in July 1944 gave him extra powers of life and death over captured resisters.[61]

It was Harster who recruited his fellow-Bavarian, *Sturmbannführer* (Major) Joseph Schreieder, to head his section IVE, which was in detailed charge of counter-espionage and counter-sabotage: therefore SOE's direct opponent. Schreieder, short and tubby, born in 1904, was a thoroughly unmilitary figure – he said in 1945 that he had never attended a parade in his life[62] – but he was a professional policeman. He had been a guard on the Swiss frontier at Bregenz after the Anschluss, and his post-war ambition was to rejoin his wife and two boys at Lindau, and re-start criminal investigation in Bavaria.

Hermann Giskes, his opposite number in the Abwehr, gives an account worth recall of their first meeting, in the autumn of 1941: 'A small, almost bald man with a heavy round head who extended a flabby, well-manicured little hand. . . . Slightly protruding, rat-like eyes gave lift to the pasty face, and the nose betrayed the delights of the bottle. The whole well-fed man exuded joviality, his slightly provincial accents emphasising the note of southern warmth.'[63]

One of Schreieder's assistants, Otto Haubrock, was personable and quick-witted enough – he once claimed himself – to have picked up a Dutchman who was a British agent by falling into talk with him in a bar, recognising the cigarette he was offered as one of a sort the British parachuted in, making the man tipsy, putting him up for the night at an SD flat, and arresting him over breakfast.[64] This may only

---

61. *Ibid.*, x(i). 67–9.
62. 29 July 1945, interrogation by 21 Army Group, 17; in his PF.
63. H. J. Giskes, *London Calling North* Pole, 31–2.
64. History xlix. 309.

have been a story spun to impress a captive; but the same man claimed that agents carried fountain pens, knives, scissors, watches, even pencils, of uniform make, which the SD had learned to spot at a glance;[65] just as 'Xavier' in the Ain used to say that he could recognise London's agents by their shoes.[66] Bright schoolchildren would recognise the syndrome; it is not a point to SOE's credit.

Nazi theory seemed to indicate that the Sicherheitspolizei's (Sipo's) task was to check signs of internal discontent, while the Abwehr's was to deal with subversion stimulated from abroad; that at least was Giskes's reading of his own role.[67] Giskes was head of the Abwehr's section III F for counter-espionage in the Low Countries.

He was Gubbins's contemporary, born in 1896; he too had fought all through the Great War. He spent the 1920s and most of the 1930s in a family tobacco business, which fell on hard times in the Great Depression; he had been in the Abwehr since 1938, and had had a year in Paris before being posted to The Hague in midsummer 1941. Though a nominal nazi, he had the manners and the instincts of a gentleman: this made him an exception in the wartime company he had to keep.

A few of his subordinates also deserve mention.

Willy Kup, born in Germany about 1905, had a genial manner, suitable for his pre-war profession; like his father, he had been an innkeeper. For some years before the war began he had kept a pub in Holland, and picked up fluent Dutch. He was a burly man with close-cropped dark hair, who usually worked in plain clothes. 'His dress and careful appearance', said Giskes, 'were those of a well-placed official or businessman, and his healthy, open face gave an impression of satisfaction with himself and the world. Not even the most suspicious minded could mistrust his approachable and winning personality.'[68] He was a sergeant in the Abwehr – like the more famous Bleicher in Paris – and acted as cut-out with several double agents, whom Giskes did his best not to meet in person.

One of Giskes's and Schreieder's handiest subordinates was Ernst

65. *Ibid.*
66. Interview of 13 January 1945 with J. P. Archambault, 6; TSC in France 175.
67. Giskes, *op. cit.*, 14. Cp *Enq.*, iv A. 565–7, iv B. 36.
68. Giskes, *op. cit.*, 46.

May, a calm, cheerful, grey-eyed, burly Swabian born in 1905, who was a *Kriminalobersekretär* – that is, a detective sergeant – in the Ordnungspolizei (Orpo), seconded to the Abwehr and to the SD. Schreieder had known him at Bregenz before the war, and testified that he had been well known as a life-saver on the Bodensee.[69] Though the Orpo was separate from the Gestapo or the SD, it often co-operated closely with these more notorious bodies;[70] such a secondment was normal enough. May seldom wore uniform; he was an expert in secret wireless techniques, and had a flair for decipher. He turned out an extremely thorough, affable, knowledgeable interrogator, wholly unexcited and inexhaustibly patient.

Another man on Giskes's staff with whom N section had only too much contact was Richard Christmann, alias Arnaud or Arno. Many refugees from Alsace or Lorraine in 1870 were father or grandfather to ardent figures in French resistance; Christmann's family and loyalties went the other way. Born near Metz late in 1905, he moved as a child with his parents and sisters into Weimar Germany, and was brought up a German; but he posed in Holland as a refugee from France, who made a living on the borders of legality as a dealer in diamonds. He seems to have worked in turn for the French and the German secret services, settling down from 1940 to 1945 with the latter. Plausibility was his long suit; and he did his best to endear himself to the allies – while remaining loyal to Germany – by helping shot-down American aircrew to evade from the Low Countries to Paris, which he knew well.

Not many British citizens speak Dutch. N Section's staff included several, but hardly any of the cipher staff had even a smattering of it. Laming, Blizard and de Bruyne agreed to the use of English, rather than Dutch, for agents' operation orders and for the bulk of the W/T traffic. This, it is now clear, handed a trump to the enemy; for awkward phrasing, if any occurred in the playing-back of captured sets, could be put down to the agents' lack of fluent English. It was not in fact a card the Abwehr needed to play. Giskes had picked up good English in the tobacco trade; and he had at his

---

69. *Enq.*, iv B. 43.
70. See Browning, *op. cit.*, for an account of the Orpo's share in massacres in Poland in 1942.

elbow a businessman in his forties, called Huntemann, who spoke English as well as Laming spoke Dutch.

Lauwers, the first of N's captured operators to play his own set back – to save his own and his friends' skins – came to find Huntemann excellent company, and fancied he had learned his English in Kenya; Huntemann told his interrogators at the end of the war it had been Nigeria; either way, it was perfect.[71] Between them, they settled the English texts of the messages sent over Lauwers's set to N. The operator did his best to make them sound as stilted and Germanic as he could, a tone N was not sensitive enough to pick up.

For all their displays of force, and all their undoubted successes, the German police forces were not all that well informed about their secret opponents. Their success at Venlo made them over-confident: they thought thereafter that they must have the secret service taped. Neither of the captives at Venlo knew enough about decipher to endanger the war-winning triumphs at Bletchley Park, of which Rauter never heard. Both the SS and the Abwehr were slow to appreciate SOE as an entirely separate service from SIS, which acted independently. The Germans got as far as taking in that sabotage was separately organised from intelligence-gathering; but believed – this they probably picked up from SOE's prisoners in Haaren and Fresnes – that it was organised by the War Office. Even here, they were so under-informed that they believed SAS – which was indeed, remotely, under War Office control – to be a uniformed wing of SOE.[72]

Some of the Dutch could see for themselves what they ought to do, and did it, unprompted. In particular, the close-knit Calvinist seagoing community, in the islands of Zeeland and round the mouths of the great rivers, had watched with foreboding what they regarded as the triumph of evil in Germany; had been shaken, but not disrupted, by the terror attack on Rotterdam; and had the nerve as well as the chance to act. At Wilton-Feyenoord, a big shipyard at Vlaardingen

---

71. Conversation with Lauwers, 25 April 1995; Holland 22.
72. It is so shown in an organigram circulated in typescript by Frontaufklaerungs-kommando 306 on 11 February 1945; a reference I owe to Mark Seaman of the Imperial War Museum, who provided a photocopy.

between Rotterdam and The Hook, some of the more far-sighted hands had begun caching stocks of small arms and explosives from 1938, in case things went too far wrong.

When things did go thoroughly wrong, the survivors went back to work; with a difference. Two sizeable warships had been on the stocks for some years, and were nearing completion. Originally, they had been designed as heavy cruisers, but a pre-war government, passionately devoted to neutrality, had scaled down their armament; they were to be light cruisers. The Kriegsmarine requisitioned both, and ordered Wilton-Feyenoord to hurry. Propeller-makers put an extra sharp edge on the screws; as the armour-plating was fitted, an imperceptible extra half-millimetre was filed off the edge of each sheet; and so on. When in January 1941 the first of them put out for sea trials, and was worked up to a speed above twenty knots, she vibrated so much that the captain slowed down and returned to harbour, lest she foundered at once.

No one in the yard could find anything wrong with her. The Gestapo knew better. They at once diagnosed sabotage, and made numerous arrests. Most of the first batch of martyrs of Dutch resistance, executed after the great spontaneous strike that started in Amsterdam in February 1941, came from Wilton-Feyenoord.[73]

The last execution in the Netherlands had taken place in 1861; the death penalty had been abolished there in 1870. Executions were therefore extra shocking to the Dutch, because so unfamiliar.

Normal Dutch political life had come to an abrupt standstill with the occupation. Neither house of parliament met again until after the defeat of Germany; nor did provincial or city councils. All parties, except the detested NSB, were banned in July 1940.

Late in that month, a body called Nederlandse Unie, Dutch Union, was set up by three well-meaning men who called for national co-operation to face the changed world. By the end of the year, as German propaganda reported, some 800,000 people had joined it; hardly any of them renewed their subscriptions, as it achieved nothing.

*

---

73. Information from Dr Hans Hers, who had worked in the yard, 1991.

N section made only one contribution of any originality to 'Claribel', SOE's scheme to devise means of hindering '*Seelöwe*' (Sealion), the Germans' plan to invade England. Of course the Netherlands would be involved here, with their large ports, if only to mount the follow-up convoys after a beach-head had been established. Yet Laming's only positive suggestion, after he had listed port, road, rail and telephone targets he judged too big to tackle, was that as many agents as possible should keep ringing up as many official German and Dutch numbers as they could discover, so as to hamper the tasks of embarkation by keeping the telephone permanently engaged.[74]

No wonder that Laming was invited to resume his career in diplomacy; though he carried to the grave the belief that he had been uprooted from N section through an intrigue of van 't Sant's.[75] 'Claribel' was stood down on 25 March 1942.[76]

Two early troubles beset Laming: the reluctance of the official Dutch in exile to help him, and hence the difficulty of finding any agents to put into training at all. Even when he did find some men who seemed trainable, they did not always stay – or want to stay – the course. 'Three of the best students', as he described them, defected early.[77]

Bernard ter Haar, who had taken a law degree at Leyden and worked for Heineken's breweries, was one of the energetic young Dutchmen whom Laming met and persuaded to begin training as an agent. Unhappily, the more ter Haar saw of N section and of the training staff, the less confidence he felt in either; the section staff lost confidence in him as well. Minor troubles blazed up in September 1941 into a day-long row with the section head; after which ter Haar and two friends, J. B. Hazewinkel and F. de Boer, were released back into the Dutch army in exile.[78] They swore oaths of secrecy; ter Haar survived to pass on to the post-war inquiry and to de Jong some

---

74. Paper of March 1941 in Holland 37.
75. De Jong, *KdN*, ix(ii). 858.
76. Note that day by AD/L – that is, D. R. Guinness – in Holland 37.
77. N to M, 26 November 1941, at the start of a summary of the section's failures; initialled TS in HQ 45.
78. Ter Haar PF.

profoundly pessimistic views about how little N section knew of the facts of life in occupied Holland.[79]

Laming hoped to make some use of a Dutchman called Spruytenberg, who lived at Bellaria in Switzerland and seemed to be able to travel easily to and from Holland; nothing came of this.[80]

His section had to make do with whom it could find. As will appear below, it found two mechanics for its earliest agents; followed by privates and sergeants from the Dutch army in exile, a small but steady flow of volunteers from the mounted police, naval petty officers, a recent Cambridge graduate, several students, a baker, a tailor, some carpenters and a few men of distinction.

For all their diversity of origin – several came from South Africa, a few from South America, one from Manila – all these potential agents needed training in the same schools. N section's preliminary school, STS 4, was at a country house deep in the Surrey countryside at Winterfold, by Cranleigh; midway between Guildford and Horsham. (After July 1943 it housed STS 7, a student assessment board.) West Court at Finchampstead, Berkshire, STS 6, and Gumley Hall near Market Harborough in Leicestershire, STS 44 (afterwards 41), were later alternatives. Those who passed this course went on to Arisaig, to Ringway, to Beaulieu, and if time and need allowed to Brickendonbury or Thame Park.

A typed forty-page pamphlet of advice on how to behave in the clandestine world, circulated among intelligence and escape agents in the Netherlands, began with the obvious, necessary warnings: never carry an address book; never carry a map; if arrested, talk readily, but give no names or addresses away; if caught with compromising papers on you, play the idiot; remember that all the enemy knows about you, he knows from your own lips.[81] SOE's agents should have acquired all these rules at Beaulieu.

Codenames in SOE's early days were random, as codenames should be. By the autumn of 1941, each country section drew a block of less random ones from the inter-services security board. N

---

79. De Jong, *KdN*, ix(ii). 857–8; *Enq.*, iv A. 465–7.
80. Notes in Germany 153.
81. I am grateful to Colonel Walter L. Pforzheimer, who made this document from his unrivalled collection available to me.

section here had bad luck: it was to name its agents after vegetables. Marrow, Turnip, Sprout, Broadbean were the sorts of name that staff officers applied to the glum heroes they speeded forward into danger. The next group of names N drew was of games. Quoits and Ping-pong were not much more dignified. Thirdly, they had loud noises: Bang, Belch and Squeak were no better.

On one front SOE was able to make some distinct impact on Holland: black broadcasting. This was handled by the Dutch branch of SO1, SOE's propaganda outfit, originally part of the Foreign Office; not by N section, which was the Dutch branch of SO2, which dealt with actual operations. SO1 split away, in August 1941, to form the PWE; in the previous month, its Dutch branch had started up a successful short-wave black broadcast, called De Flitspuit (the Flyspray: elderly readers will recall the insecticide Flit).

It was named by Meyer Sluyser, a vigorous Dutch journalist in exile who wrote most of the copy for it,[82] and was in constant touch with Laming, to whom he was introduced by Dalton's friend, the international secretary of the Labour Party.[83] It rapidly overtook the more formal and official broadcasts of Radio Oranje in the interest it aroused among the occupied Dutch; many of whom believed it to be sending from somewhere on Dutch territory.

This was a start, at least, towards shifting opinion; yet not much could be done in the way of active subversion without arms. The Dutch army's stocks, already obsolescent in 1940, were all confiscated. There were hardly any of the mining or quarrying industries from which, in many other occupied countries, dynamite could be stolen. Arms and explosive supply therefore involved contact with Great Britain: far from easy, as the Dutch coast was soon well fortified. Though a few agents were slipped in by sea for SIS, quite early on,[84] SOE in spite of two years' hard work failed to open up sea channels for arms.

Land channels for arms were out of the question. Air supply was bedevilled by technical and by staff difficulties, even before the Germans took a hand. The technical troubles were four: the shortage

82. De Jong, *KdN*, v(i). 150–2.
83. *Enq.*, iv A. 471.
84. See E. Hazelhoff Roelfzema, *Soldaat van Oranje '40–'45*, 106 ff.

of aircraft; the shortage of remote areas where drops could be made unnoticed; the far too many points for enemy controls, at Holland's numberless bridges; and the sheer danger for dropping aircraft of having to fly low near one of the world's heaviest concentrations of flak. The staff troubles were three: poor co-ordination between N section and the shifting Dutch authorities in charge of irregular warfare; lack of understanding, by both the British and the Dutch in London, of what life in occupied Holland was actually like – this hampered choice of targets and of tools for attack; above all, pressure of time.

Most of SOE's senior staff were too far above the mêlée of despatch and operations to have much direct responsibility for what followed; but some, even if not much, of the blame for the catastrophe does rest on the first minister in charge, Hugh Dalton. Dalton had a bullying manner, charming though – like so many bullies – he could try to be in private; and kept urging on his juniors the need for results, to keep SOE's record up with SIS's and with the other fighting services. In a competitive society, he was only too keen a competitor, and the haste he urged on N section may have helped to bring on premature activity, with fatal results.

It is widely believed that the many Dutch agents who fell into German hands were sent to Holland on purpose, to suit some deep-laid English deception: an intriguing notion, but false. No possible English interest could be served, in any way, by their loss; it was no subtle trick. It was a ghastly run of mistakes.

If a simple explanation offers, there is no need to hunt for a complicated one. The simple truth is that, for a while, N was entirely deceived.

For fifteen months, the Germans controlled almost all of SOE's work into the Netherlands, and much though not all of SIS's; and, to that extent, deceived the British completely: just as, all through the war, MI5 controlled all of the Abwehr's work into Great Britain, and deceived the Germans completely. It deserves remark that the British secured a much larger benefit from their prolonged success than the Germans did from their less lasting one. For, in part through turned-round Abwehr agents, the British were able to mount several successful deceptions, culminating in 'Fortitude', which saved thousands of lives in 1944 by assuring the success of the Normandy landings; while all that the Germans got out of their captives was evidence – only too much of it – that enabled them to go on playing their particular local trick.

The local trick did bring them one strategic advantage that mattered: it severely delayed the organisation and arming of Dutch active resistance, which was thus unable to exert as much impact as, say, French resistance once the allied invasion of western Europe began in June 1944.

Repeated efforts to insert agents by small boat, either direct on to the coast between the Hook of Holland and Den Helder, or through the intricacies of the Frisian Islands, all failed in the summer of 1941. At last, on 7 September, Laming was able with the RAF's help to send in a pair of agents by parachute, on a reconnaissance called 'Glasshouse'. They were called 'Ab' and 'Cor' – good short names for wireless traffic; but neither was a wireless operator. Their surnames were Homburg and Sporre. They jumped, blind, near Utrecht; missed each other on their dropping zone; but soon met, in that city, and at once found themselves in difficulty about where to live.

They had of course received the universal warning against making any sort of contact with their own families, but felt, having found several expected friends' doors closed, that they must break orders. They spent a few days with an uncle of Sporre's, Jan Martens, at his cigar shop in Haarlem.[85] They then went their separate ways.

Less than three weeks after they landed, Seyss-Inquart mentioned to Hitler in an interview a recent increase in sabotage, and was ordered to counter-attack sharply, taking plenty of hostages and if need be shooting a few;[86] it would be agreeable to SOE's supporters to suppose that the increase was due to Homburg and Sporre, but the timing is rather tight. Much more probably, it was due to Dutch communists, who since the start of Hitler's attack on the USSR on 22 June had been released from the bonds of the nazi-soviet pact, and had by early September begun to get an act together.

(Huib) Albert Homburg – 'Ab' – was a garage mechanic from IJmuiden, who had reached England with two friends in March,

---

85. Rep, *op. cit.*, 51; snapshot of shop, *ibid.*, at 142.
86. Nestler, *op. cit.*, iv. 163: report on 1 October of interview on 26 September 1941.

having managed to slip out of his home harbour in a rowing boat with an outboard motor; he was then aged twenty-three. He was bright and energetic, but knew no more of the secret world than he had picked up in a week at Beaulieu and a sabotage course.

In conformity with what became a normal drill, the British – not the Dutch – provided him with a list of addresses at which he might usefully call.[87] All, in his case, were friends of Laming's. Not one of them was prepared to stir a finger. Homburg got involved instead with friends of the heroic Lodo van Hamel,[88] a regular Dutch naval officer who had fought his way out in May 1940, fought again at Dunkirk, and gone back to Holland that August to start up the Inlichtingsdienst, the Dutch intelligence organisation that was to work hand in glove with MI6. Van Hamel was soon arrested – the Germans tried and later executed him – but his friends carried on. They deluged Homburg with leaflets and requests to carry back to London.

Luckily for him, he had none of their papers on him when he was suddenly arrested in Amsterdam on 8 October 1941: for a banal reason. He had had toothache and had just paid a second visit to a dentist, whom he wrongly thought secure, when two Dutch detectives arrested him as he walked away.

He was at once handed over to the Gestapo, stripped to his underclothes, and interrogated briskly, first in Amsterdam and then – with his clothes back on – at the Binnenhof in The Hague, where Rauter had his Dutch headquarters. (What would occupied Londoners have made of the Sicherheitsdienst working out of the Palace of Westminster?) Even when beaten up, Homburg made no damaging admissions. He was locked away in Scheveningen prison, just north of The Hague: the building Dutch resisters came to nickname the Orange Hotel.[89] He was not put on trial, but was told he had been sentenced to death. Early on Friday, 24 October, he made a prompt, classic escape. Having sharpened his spoon into a chisel with a fragment of stolen razor blade, he whittled away the plaster above his window frame, and managed to squeeze out into the yard; and so away over a couple of walls.

---

87. Lieftinck's account, *Enq.*, iv A. 488.
88. Photograph in de Jong, *KdN*, at iv(ii). 689.
89. Photographs in *ibid.*, at viii(i). 252–3.

Two days later, early in the morning again, he called at a friend's house in The Hague: the de Haas family took him in. Johannes de Haas had met him earlier on a reserve officers' training course before the war, and had recently offered him help. Thence he regained touch with Sporre, whom he judged to have been much too indiscreet in his approaches to other potential resisters. The two of them waited one night on a prearranged beach near his hiding-place; they and the boat failed to meet.

Cornelis Sporre ('Cor'), a thirty year old of great mechanical aptitude, had had one useful contact: with Jan Bottema ('Brandy'), one of Laming's pre-war acquaintances, a fortyish master mariner and eel fisherman who worked from his home at Zoutkamp along the Frisian coast. Bottema had worked for five months for MI6's Section D, before it got absorbed into SOE, and left the impression that he was a first-class man on several SOE officers.[90] Sporre was able to meet him and to hand over some money to him.[91] Laming strongly approved his scheme for moving agents in and out through the Engelsmanplaat, an uninhabited Frisian sandbank, but nothing came of it. Nothing came either of projects to use some empty corner of the Lauwerszee, the bay west of Zoutkamp,[92] since reclaimed as land.

Sporre then set off – to England, he hoped – with W. B. Schrage, an MI6 agent whose wireless operator had been caught at his set at the end of August.[93] They secured a sailing boat, and without a word to Homburg sailed on 19 November from Petten (now a seaside camping village), fourteen miles south of Den Helder. They vanished. Presumably the North Sea swallowed them up, as it swallowed up so many adventurers; though SIS and SOE had to assume that they might have been picked up by a German sea patrol.

Homburg was developing clandestine antennae fast. Through his sister's husband, who lived in IJmuiden, he made touch with Taconis

---

90. Notes of mid-September 1940 in his PF
91. Note by Homburg, 20 April 1942, TSC in Holland 36. Van der Stroom, *op. cit.*, omits Bottema.
92. Notes of mid-September 1940 in his PF.
93. Van der Stroom, *op. cit.*, 16.

(of whom more shortly): one of the two agents SOE had sent in to find out what had become of him and of Sporre. To Taconis he mentioned, as a possible future meeting-place for agents, the cigar shop in Haarlem where Martens would respond to the password 'bow and arrow'. And he persevered with his inquiries in the port, which led him to better success than Sporre.

He persuaded de Haas and another friend, Johannes Buizer, to hide with him on an IJmuiden trawler, the *Beatrice*. While she was at sea, they persuaded the captain to sail west, and chance the minefields; they reached Yarmouth safely on 17 February 1942, with a mass of intelligence of interest to MI6, MI9 and SOE.

As Homburg had been so thoroughly looked over by the Gestapo, there was no question of sending him back on another secret mission. He was allowed to transfer to the free Dutch air force, in which he was commissioned; and in which he met his death in action, a few weeks before the war in Europe ended.

N continued to hanker after a sea link; several more agents were shortly sent to look for one, but none that lasted was ever found. The air remained. Another pair of agents left by air on an operation with the ill-omened codename of 'Catarrh', on 7/8 November 1941. From 'Catarrh' bad trouble for SOE derived, from a mixture of incompetence in London and treachery in Holland.

Exactly a month before these two agents departed, Wavell used a good phrase to the National Defence Council of India: 'what are now called Fifth Column methods but used to go by the simpler name of treachery'.[94] Treachery was their undoing.

The 'North Pole' or *Englandspiel* catastrophe, long known and long taught in spy schools as an example of what should not be done, first came to public knowledge in Holland in 1948 during the parliamentary committee of enquiry's investigation into the conduct of the government in exile in London. Next year an account of it by the Abwehr officer who had helped control it appeared in Dutch. The English version of this was published in London by Kimber in 1953: H. J. Giskes, *London Calling North Pole*. A more recent English public received a treatment of it, as a disaster beyond mitigation, in

---

94. Sir Archibald Wavell, *Speaking Generally* (Macmillan, 1946), 91.

a programme devoted to it by a BBC television series on SOE broadcast in the winter of 1984–5.

No attempt can be made to excuse the inexcusable, but there is
more to be urged in SOE's defence than viewers of that programme
might have gathered from it.

Terrain was extra difficult, as we saw at the start: part heavily built
up; much intersected with waterways, in town and country alike,
which hindered rapid secret movement. The quality of the agents
could not always be of the highest; and one or two of them were
more helpful to their captors than they need have been, with disastrous results for the rest. Moreover, the hardest stage in getting a
subversive organisation set up is usually the first; and it was at that
first, hardest stage that N section came unstuck.

At the time the enemy was taken – correctly – to be powerful; and
also – wrongly – to be well organised. Germans since Bismarck's day
have been proverbial for order and efficiency; any unit that encountered the ordinary German soldier acquired prompt and painful
respect for his competence as a fighting man. Yet it later became clear
that the nazi state was badly structured for fighting a long war; and
that Hitler's *penchant* for setting up rival authorities which overlapped extended to his secret and police services. Indeed, rivalry
between the Sicherheitsdienst and the Abwehr became so fierce that
in the end the SD not only swallowed the Abwehr up but executed
Canaris, its head: far worse than any of the inter-secret-service squab-
bles that sometimes plagued the allies.

Unhappily for SOE, in 1942–3 these two German services got on
amicably together at the working level in the Netherlands. Giskes
and Schreieder each had the sense to see that if they co-operated, they
would do much better than if they wrangled; although they fell out
with each other in the end. Of the two, an agent who saw only too
much of them both survived to record the opinion that Giskes was
much the brighter.[95]

They ran the affair jointly. From November 1942 they each had a
villa at Driebergen, a small town in the woodland between Utrecht
and Doorn, conveniently close to the Luftwaffe's fighter headquarters.

---

95. Lauwers: see *Enq.*, iv A. 583.

They took some trouble to play back the many W/T sets they captured from the parts of Holland where the agents they simulated were
supposed to be at work, lest the English direction-finding system,
notoriously efficient, noticed anything amiss.

They did not carry this practice quite as far as a perfectibilitarian
would have done: they worked the sets from the comparative comfort of a wartime office, instead of venturing out into private houses
or open country. The British secret services were not then sophisticated enough to notice that all N's agents seemed to be transmitting
from towns, and that every one of the towns from which the transmissions came included an Abwehr headquarters. Giskes listed the
sites after the war: The Hague, Scheveningen its northern suburb,
Noordwijk, Amsterdam, Driebergen, Utrecht, 's-Hertogenbosch and
Rotterdam.[96] All except 's-Hertogenbosch, which is close south of the
Maas, lay north of the great rivers; and all were grouped in the most
populous quarter of the kingdom. Agents supposed to be operating
in the south or north-east notionally left their operators behind,
communicating with them by courier.

Commandos briefed for the 'Hardtack' raids on the coast of
north-west Europe in the winter of 1943–4 were told, if a choice of
prisoners offered, that 'NCOs are preferable to officers (who will not
talk) or privates (who know too little)':[97] exactly the policy pursued
by their enemies during the *Englandspiel.*

'Catarrh' consisted of two agents, Taconis and his wireless operator
Lauwers. At Newmarket racecourse, just before they left England,
they were handed false papers to cover their false identities; and
were appalled to spot an elementary mistake on both their identity
cards. N knew of the mistake already: a pregnant phrase in the war
diary for 4–6 November says this operation 'will be carried out
provided the agents are prepared to accept such identity cards as
are now available'.[98] The pair of royal lions in the watermark,
instead of facing each other, faced the same way. Lauwers said
afterwards that his lions were so ill-drawn that they looked more

---

96. RIOD, Doc. I-542, secret interrogation of Giskes, 1 November 1946, 35.
97. PRO, DEFE 2/352, 25 September 1943 (duplic).
98. Whole world war diary, viii. 1914. Cp *Enq.*, iv A. 460, 473.

like hobby-horses.[99] Their conducting officer brushed aside their protests at this scandalous error, remarking – truly, as it turned out – that those papers would not be their undoing.

SOE's tailors had hardly done better for them than SIS's forgers. Their clothes looked Dutch all right, but were identically the same. A tall, slender man and a short, stocky one were each wearing suit, shirt, tie, socks, shoes, hat of precisely the same shade, pattern and cut; even their briefcases matched.[100] So turned out, they thought it prudent to live well apart; Taconis settled in Arnhem, Lauwers in The Hague.

Thijs Taconis, born in Rotterdam in 1914, had been working on mathematics and physics at Leyden university, and escaped to England in a fishing smack in May 1940. He spent the next winter in Canada, as a private with the Dutch military mission; volunteered for more active work; and was trained by SOE as a saboteur.

A glance at his complexion revealed that he had some East Indian blood. Many of the Germans who met him later, fascinated as they were with racial myth, remarked on his being *ein Halbblut*, a half-breed. Nobody could then have heard Dr Jones's 1991 Reith Lectures, in which he expounded how very few – five, six or seven – of the hundred-thousand-odd genes that influence human form and character affect skin colour.[101]

The wireless operator, H. M. G. Lauwers ('Ebenezer'), a year Taconis's junior, born in Amsterdam, had been working in the rubber industry in Singapore before the war. After the invasion of Holland he too sought an active role, and found his way from Manila to England. Derksema refused to take him on for Dutch intelligence, in the belief that five years' absence from Holland would make him too conspicuous. He did well at wireless training, and got on well with his organiser, who was an acting sergeant. He was a private with a courtesy second lieutenant's commission.

Flying Officer Murphy dropped them at seven minutes past midnight on 7/8 November 1941[102] near Ommen, east of Zwolle. They

---

99. *Ibid.*, 580.
100. *Ibid.*, 468, and de Jong at Oxford resistance conference, 1962, 6.
101. Steve Jones, *The Language of Genes* (Harper/Collins, 1993), 18.
102. PRO AIR 27/956, 138 squadron operational record book, 9v.

had a dual mission: to find out what had happened to Homburg and Sporre, and then simply 'to start the organisation of the Dutch underground movement'.[103] Lauwers's set survived the drop, but would not work. There turned out to be a wiring fault in it, eventually traced and repaired for him by a helpful Leyden student whom Taconis had known in a pre-war youth movement.[104] The syndrome was not unknown in other secret services: the sets the Soviet Union parachuted in to its celebrated 'Red Orchestra' in Germany also failed to work.[105] It was not until 3 or 4 January 1942 that Lauwers was able to send his first message.[106] Some people in SOE later thought this initial delay suspicious; it was only accidental. He was on the air, on and off, for two months and a day as a free man; by mid-February he was on the air almost every day.

He had to begin by reporting an unhappy mistake by SOE, one extra hard to believe in today's world of global banking transactions, but an example of how deep the gulf was in 1941 between England and occupied Europe. To ease their first steps in Holland, over trivial purchases, these agents were given plenty of silver coin. When they tried to use it, they discovered that a nazi rule had withdrawn it from circulation: they thus became conspicuous, the last thing they wanted. Luckily, no Dutchman reported it to authority; but it gave them a jolt.

Taconis and Lauwers were both aware, as Lauwers said at the end of the war, that early Dutch resistance organisations were full of stool-pigeons: that is, creatures trying to work their passage to comfort under the occupiers by betraying acquaintances who thought of opposing them. The two agents therefore took extra trouble about whom they confided in; until Taconis, in a hurry, made a slip. Long afterwards, Lauwers put their small group's disaster down to Taconis's

---

103. Signed TS in Lauwers PF, 30 May 1945.
104. De Jong, *KdN*, ix(ii). 936; Rep, *op. cit.*, 70.
105. Christopher Andrew and Oleg Gordievsky, *KGB* (Hodder and Stoughton, 1990), 205–6.
106. Whole world war diary, x(i). 2605, 9–10 January 1942. Lauwers's own final report, 30 May 1945, TSC in his PF, puts the date as late as 3 February. The RAF special duties operations history, VA. 241, puts his first message in December 1941; this must be a mistake.

disciplined obedience to the orders he got from London; and described his organiser as a splendid man who had got pushed by N into premature activity, for which they were not yet ready.[107]

Taconis knew Captain van den Berg, a retired infantry officer who belonged to the nascent Ordedienst, a widespread movement loyal to the queen in exile. It was van den Berg who put Taconis, and through him Lauwers, in touch with another reserve officer, Teller, from whose flat in The Hague Lauwers sometimes transmitted.

Taconis mentioned to van den Berg that he urgently needed a lorry to move some stores away from an impending drop. Van den Berg produced a friend who ran a small transport firm; this friend, with a con-man's affability, took Taconis in. His name was Ridderhof; he was an established, salaried double agent who took his orders and his pay from Kup of the Abwehr. Shakespeare, who knew about con-men, went on record centuries ago: 'One may smile, and smile, and be a villain.'[108]

In strict security theory, Taconis should have reported van den Berg's, Teller's and Ridderhof's full names, addresses and dates and places of birth to SOE, so that MI5 and MI6 could run checks on them before he went any further – certainly before he let Lauwers transmit from Teller's flat, or lend his pistol to van den Berg, or borrow a lorry from Ridderhof. It is unlikely that, at so early a stage, a check would have thrown up anything more than the usual 'NRA' – nothing recorded against. In any case, Taconis reckoned he had not time to make one. Van den Berg turned out in the end an innocent dupe; Ridderhof was a traitor.

The double agent has an ancient, if dishonourable, place in the history of secret activities; some devout Catholics, for example, suppose that one was used to betray or even provoke Guy Fawkes's plot.[109] As recently as 1915, one had penetrated without much trouble Edith Cavell's escape line, which ran from Brussels north to the Dutch border; and thus brought on her arrest and death.[110] Details

---

107. Conversation with him, 25 April 1995.
108. *Hamlet*, Act I, Sc. V, l.108.
109. See Antonia Fraser, *The Gunpowder Plot* (Weidenfeld and Nicolson, 1996), 156–8, for what did happen.
110. Cp. S. Theodore Felstead, *Edith Cavell* (Newnes, 1940), 56–67.

of this case were well known to the Abwehr and the SD, as they were to MI5 and MI6; they cannot possibly have been overlooked at Beaulieu. Yet training a man at Beaulieu was not an automatically successful process, from which he would emerge waterproofed against any devices the Gestapo might shower on him. Here was another instance of N section's troubles over getting hold of the best types of Dutchman: not all N's agents had the mental stature for coping with men as shrewd as Giskes, Schreieder and May.

Rauter wrote to Daluege, the head of the Orpo, to wish him a merry Christmas (an odd gesture between devout pagans), and boasted that – thanks to sixty death sentences, forty-five of which had so far been carried out – Holland was now a model, orderly, occupied country.[111]

Early in 1942, Ridderhof told Kup that men he knew expected an aircraft shortly, from England, to drop them some sabotage stores near Assen. Kup reported this to Giskes, who said he could tell that one to the Marines, in the phrase – since famous – '*Gehen sie zum Nordpol mit solchem Geschichten!*'[112] The Abwehr codenamed the consequent operations '*Nordpol*', North Pole, in memory of this remark. The parallel SS codename was '*Englandspiel*' – the game against England – still in common use in Holland, where the idea seems prevalent that the German and the English secret services were playing a game, in which they used live Dutchmen as counters without much caring what happened to them.

From the English point of view it was not a game; it was a howler.

The aircraft from England did turn up, on 27/28 February 1942, and (so Lauwers reported at once) dropped two containers to a reception by Taconis.[113] A week later, at 18.30 on Friday, 6 March, Lauwers had a schedule – a prearranged time for sending a message. He proposed to use the best transmitting site he had found, the flat of the Tellers – who had become his friends – in the Fahrenheitstraat in The Hague. He had enciphered three brief messages. One of them

---

111. Nestler, *op. cit.*, iv. 172, 20 December 1941.
112. 'Take stories like that to the North Pole!': Holland 15, 'Report on the investigation into the "Nordpol" affair', duplic, 2. De Jong, *KdN*, v(i). 96, has almost the same phrase in writing.
113. Whole world war diary, xi(ii). 3150.

contained a nugget – false, as it happened – of naval intelligence: the cruiser *Prinz Eugen*, damaged (by HMS *Trident*) a fortnight earlier off Norway, was said to be in dock at Schiedam.

It was so cold that Lauwers sat down to his set in his overcoat, with a blanket over his knees. A minute or two before half-past six Teller, his only look-out man, came in to report that there were three police cars at the street corner. Lauwers took for granted that this was a D/F team, which would pick him up the moment he started to transmit; so he and Teller left, leaving it to Mrs Teller (who was pregnant) to drop the transmitter out of the window into the rose bed below.

They strolled up the street, but had hardly gone a furlong when one of the police cars drew up beside them; they were at once arrested and separated. A search of Teller's pockets revealed, of course, the flat's address. A search of Lauwers's pockets revealed his three cipher texts, which he had not found time to destroy. Some of the police took him back to the block of flats; there was his transmitter, visible in the gloom, caught on the laundry-lines of the flat below the Tellers'.[114]

Lauwers gave only his current false name and actual address. One of the police party, an Orpo subaltern called Heinrichs, carefully briefed by May, took his three messages off to a side table, while Lauwers continued not to answer questions.

Twenty minutes later Heinrichs looked up, smiling, and remarked, 'Ah, I see the *Prinz Eugen* is now in Schiedam.' At the Dutch inquiry, both May – who should have known – and Schreieder, as well as Heinrichs, testified that a break-in, even with so simple a code, could not possibly have been made in twenty minutes.[115] Heinrichs was bluffing; but the bluff shattered Lauwers. He never dreamed that the message about the cruiser had been planted on him, through Ridderhof; and had to suppose that the code in which he had trusted was transparent.

He now admitted to being a parachuted wireless operator and indeed – according to Kup[116] – promptly declared himself ready to

---

114. J. Schreieder, *Das war das Englandspiel* (hereafter Schreieder), 102, has it protruding from a snowdrift on the ground.
115. *Enq.*, iv A. 576–7.
116. *Ibid.*

work with the Germans. He surrendered his code at once;[117] but gave nothing away about his organiser, on whose trail the enemy police were already busy. Three days later, the Sipo quietly picked up Taconis near Arnhem.[118]

May suggested that, as Lauwers had missed his schedule on the 6th, he might send his three messages whenever he was next due to transmit. This Lauwers, wavering, at first refused to do. For several days he was off the air, wrestling with conscience and shock; further unnerved by a few old telegrams May found in his rooms, and by interviews with the imperturbable Giskes. Giskes put it to him that his life was forfeit, as a spy caught in the act; but that his life, and his friend Taconis's life as well, would be spared if he conformed with his captors' wishes. This was the first he had heard of Taconis's arrest; the point brought him round, and he sent his three messages. His sending style was normal.

Lauwers, writing in 1947, said he began his transmission on 12 March; Schreieder said the same to the enquiry commission; de Jong concurs.[119] SOE's war diary is specific: 15 March.[120] The war diarist may this time have made a slip.

His long silence had raised an alarm in N section: what could have happened to him? When he came through after all, there was immediate, joyous relief; the section was back in touch with its only operator, and its work into Holland could now unfold.

One of Blizard's juniors in N section pointed out that Lauwers's next message, about a new DZ, contained no security checks at all; and was told not to bother about trivia, at the start of great events.[121]

Giskes and May cross-questioned Lauwers about these checks at length; and here the operator thought he had a stroke of good luck, when so much of the rest of his luck was bad. In two of the first three broken messages, the first bluff check happened to fall on the third

---

117. *Ibid.*, 582.
118. More colourful account, buttressed by passages in direct speech, in Rep, *op. cit.*, 118–23, places this arrest earlier, in Arnhem.
119. Lauwers in Giskes, *op. cit.*, 185; *Enq.*, iv B. 30; de Jong, *KdN*, ix(ii). 940.
120. xii. 3385.
121. Conversation with Smewin, 31 August 1994.

letter of the word STOP; and Lauwers believed he had persuaded May that his only check was to send, once a message, STEP or STIP or STUP instead of STOP. N section, like F section, did not bother about security checks at all, regarding them as an irritating quirk of C's, with which nobody in SOE needed to trouble. They might all the same have noticed that up to the long break in his transmission Lauwers had kept strictly to the rules, and thereafter had used no checks whatever, mis-spelt STOP apart. In any case the checks were so mechanical that May, or any other reliable decoder, could unravel them by plodding through back traffic, all recorded by the Orpo as a matter of routine.

One extra point needs notice here: Blizard's whole mind may not, in March 1942, have been on his job. His first marriage had by now ended, and he was in process of introducing his future second wife to the section: she joined it on 31 March.

The Germans thought Lauwers worked for the British intelligence service;[122] not a point on which he felt it necessary to correct them, and a cause of confusion both to them at the time and to many later students of 'North Pole'. It was indeed true that he had been ordered to set up a small, secure news-gathering body, once he had settled in;[123] this was no sort of rivalry with SIS. Laming wanted a readily available source of up-to-date news for De Flitspuit, the black broadcasting station,[124] which he was helping SO1 to run. Experience had made clear that nothing was coming quickly through normal secret intelligence channels.

On 19 March London indicated that it could send a sizeable sum, 5,000 guilders, with the next agent, if it would be useful; Lauwers's reply that 'he did not need the money'[125] reassured London further that he was behaving normally. (By the end of April he declared himself ready to accept it after all.)[126]

Just as Goetz in Paris was, for six weeks, cleverer than Buckmaster

---

122. *Oorlogsdocumentatie '40–'45, vijfde jaarboek* (Zutphen: Walburg Pers, 1994), 194.
123. *Enq.*, iv A. 467.
124. *Ibid.*, 477–8.
125. Whole world war diary, xii. 3384, dated 22 March 1942.
126. *Ibid.*, xiii(ii). 3674.

in London, and received eighteen F agents dropped slap into the arms of the Gestapo,[127] Giskes and Schreieder in Holland were cleverer than Blizard and Bingham in England, and secured almost everybody those two sent across: not just for six weeks, but for fifteen months. Moreover, Buckmaster's dead losses were well counterbalanced by over two-score active agents, hard at work;[128] while, for that year and a quarter, Giskes and Schreieder all but scooped the N section pool. N section's effort unravelled slowly, but surely. Its reply to Lauwers's group of three supervised messages asked him for a ground on which Taconis could receive another agent. Giskes and Schreieder agreed a ground; Huntemann drew up the message; Lauwers, not seeing what else he could do, sent it.

It is worth recalling some factors, beyond mischance and stupidity, that put N into trouble. One is that Blizard and his team were in a hurry. SOE's Polish, French and Belgian sections, at least, seemed to have plenty to report; this made N section inclined to cut corners, in its anxiety to catch up with the others – a human, if unprofessional failing. Such phrases as 'most urgent that this party should get going'[129] were common in the traffic with the field.

The initial lack of enthusiasm by the Dutch authorities in exile seemed to Blizard to have acted as a brake on the section's development. Laming, still obsessed by his long-standing feud with van 't Sant, had felt this even more strongly.

Certainly the original Dutch reluctance helps to account for the comparatively low personal quality – accompanied by junior rank and low social standing – of some of the agents N did have available. There was a knock-on effect here, too: these were not men of the stature of a Yeo-Thomas or a 'Trotsky' Davies, who on being barked at by a nazi boss would bark back. Several of them turned out docile under enemy questioning; which made it harder for their stouter-minded colleagues.

The goose/swan syndrome was important too. N section, like many others, had faith in its agents; the profound scepticism of such

---

127. Foot, *SOE in France*, 335.
128. *Ibid.*, appx H.
129. Whole world war diary, xiv(ii). 3974, 26 May 1942.

professional secret service men as Kell or Dansey was not shared by Laming, Blizard and Bingham, still less by their juniors. The flywheel effect became perceptible, as well; once a process had been set in motion – in this case, the process of parachuting agents in to pre-arranged receptions – and everybody had got used to it, it was extra hard to stop abruptly.

'North Pole' is often recalled as a disaster of SOE's, from which SIS took care to withdraw its skirts. The point therefore needs emphasis that a serious mistake by each of two SIS agents had much to do with landing SOE in the soup.

For on 31 August 1941, at Bilthoven near Utrecht, a German direction-finding team captured the twenty-year-old J. J. Zomer at his set; and, with him, the text of about a hundred messages he had exchanged with London since his arrival in mid-June by parachute, both in cipher and in clear.[130] Zomer himself was an uncommunicative prisoner, and played his set back in such a way that van 't Sant at once concluded that he was in enemy hands, but all those messages were a godsend to Sergeant May, who worked over them thoroughly.[131]

Moreover, three weeks before Lauwers's arrest the Germans had captured W. J. van der Reyden, whom Hazelhoff had put ashore near The Hague on the previous 9 December.[132] Van der Reyden said nothing about his security checks, and May's effort to play his set back therefore at once failed; but otherwise he did not behave as a perfect prisoner should. On the contrary, in the course of several long talks with the sergeant he expounded the whole of SIS's systems for coding messages[133] – the systems to which SOE was at the time bound.

De Jong, in a celebrated passage, picked on SOE's neglect of Lauwers's neglect of security checks as the 'capital blunder',[134] the

---

130. Van der Stroom, *op. cit.* 16; shot in Oranienburg, 11 May 1942. Cp. *Enq.*, iv A. 570. Not to be confused with Dr J. M. Somer, later head of BI.

131. De Jong, *KdN*, v(ii). 891–2, 1118.

132. Van der Stroom, *op. cit.*, 21; Hazelhof Roelfzema, *op. cit.*, 117–21.

133. RIOD Doc. I-1103, typed report signed by May, 23 September 1946; *Enq.*, iv A. 565, 569–70, iv B. 47.

134. De Jong, *KdN*, v(ii). 920, tr.

fons et origo malorum from which the whole catastrophe derived. While most of the blame rests with SOE, some rubs off on to SIS as well.

The combined use of what Zomer did, and what van der Reyden said; of what Lauwers did, and what Baatsen their next captive said; gave the Germans a promising start. By luck and judgement together, they soon increased their grip on N's work.

Ridderhof, meanwhile, was paid a bonus of 2,000 florins for having got the whole business going.[135]

How completely N was taken in – Giskes constantly had his doubts – emerged in mid-April. N then warned Lauwers that he was about to send in some special apparatus – in fact, an S-phone – for another agent; 'this apparatus must not fall into wrong hands'. Moreover, he sent in a container full of explosive coal, one of the proudest products of SOE's camouflage department; and a list of immediate objectives for discreet sabotage – 'shipping and ship-building, factories engaged on work vital to the enemy, rubber, leather, textiles, timber, paper, oil and petrol stocks, military stores, food for Germany and enemy motor transport' as well as mainline railways:[136] an invaluable set of hints for German security staffs.

N section might fairly claim to have been unlucky, as well as unobservant, in having Lauwers's set turned round against it. It now proceeded to compound its error by making and repeating two professional mistakes.

Too many of its agents received the same advice about where they might turn if they found themselves in a fix. Once one agent had been frightened or indiscreet enough to give this address away, he put his comrades into peril. This was how the severe mishap of the 'Catarrh' arrests turned into the disaster of the *Englandspiel.*

Moreover, many agents made a mistake from which a more careful staff would have saved them; another mistake that did not only endanger themselves: they carried with them into occupied Holland the names and addresses of probable helpers – as was only to be

---

135. RIOD, Doc. I-542, Giskes *procès-verbal* of April 1947, 5.
136. Whole world war diary, xiii(ii). 3673, 16 April 1942.

expected – but instead of memorising them, they wrote them down. Schreieder in old age had still got, and showed to his acquaintance Hers, several of the little notebooks in which the agents had carried these fatal jottings.[137]

Not far away, SOE's and indeed other secret services' agents in France were expected to carry a great deal in their heads: beyond their bogus personal life stories, organisers would need to know where and when they were to meet their wireless operators, and eventually to recall not only the exact sites of several – perhaps scores – of dropping zones, but also the map reference and the BBC messages of each. N section judged this sort of feat to be quite beyond its agents' grasp; but did not take in how dangerous it was to commit a lot to paper instead.

Agents were indeed warned against writing addresses, names or telephone numbers down, but not sharply enough; so that too many of them scrabbled with success inside their parachute harness, after emplaning, and jotted down – lest they forget – what they would have been wiser to memorise.

N section was undone not only by incompetence in London, but also by friendliness and decent behaviour in the field: an intelligible, normally a laudable, but in this context a disastrous line of conduct. As Rabagliatti, his MI6 adviser, said once to Hazelhoff, 'In this business there's no such thing as straightforward. Honesty and all that, splendid! But in this game all it does is kill people.'[138]

Nine more N agents, most of them in their early twenties, went into Holland in the early spring of 1942. By midsummer one was dead, one was on the run, and all the rest were locked up in the same German prison: mostly because they thought that a double agent who said he was a friend's friend was telling the truth. One went by the late February moon, seven by the March/April one, and one by boat in the mid-April dark spell.

On the night of the Bruneval raid, 27/28 February – that is, before Lauwers's arrest – George Dessing ('Carrot') parachuted blind into

---

137. Conversation with Hers, 6 August 1993. Schreieder died on Christmas Eve 1990. He mentions this error in his book: Schreieder, 205.
138. Hazelhoff Roelfzema, *op. cit.*, 131. Photograph of Rabagliatti, *ibid.*, before page 97.

Holland, by himself. He was a stocky thirty-two-year-old bachelor accountant, who had worked in Vienna as a youth, moved on to South Africa and travelled to England, when he heard of the invasion of his homeland, to join the Dutch army in exile. He joined SOE in April 1941. He did not get on well under training with his fellow students, and indeed had a spell in the cooler at remote Inverlair after a drinking bout; but emerged penitent, and was thought suitable for a lone mission: although his spells speaking German and Afrikaans meant that he no longer spoke perfect Dutch.[139]

He had two tasks: to reconnoitre a sea landing point near the mouth of the Maas, and to make touch with trade unionists. He found the coastline unapproachable, but did meet some trade unionists. He helped one of them, the left-winger Levinus van Looi, to distribute the underground newspaper *Verzet* (Resistance). Oddly enough, it was his bad accent that made van Looi trust him.[140] Moreover, he met a leading socialist, Koos Vorrink,[141] who provided him with some microphotographed papers that he eventually brought back to London for the queen: for Dessing, unlike most of his colleagues, escaped arrest.

We must return to the catalogue of casualties.

On 27/28 March A-A. Baatsen ('Watercress') was dropped to a reception north-east of Steenwijk that London thought Taconis organised. Baatsen was a photographer, born in Amsterdam in 1918, who had joined SOE as a Dutch army corporal; he was a courtesy second lieutenant. Under training he got on badly with his fellow students, and raised some security alarms; but then seemed to turn over a new leaf, and buckled down to detailed work on telephone and teleprinter sabotage, which he was to carry out near The Hague.[142]

He was received by Ridderhof – who had fortified himself for the occasion so heartily that Giskes forbade him to attend any more drops – and by two of his friends, Dutch policemen called Poos and Slagter. A Wehrmacht infantry platoon, armed to the teeth, was

---

139. *Enq.*, iv A. 479.
140. *Ibid.*, iv C. 1008.
141. Photograph in de Jong, *KdN*, at iv. 591.
142. N to D/R, 31 January 1942, typed copy in Baatsen PF.

posted round the dropping zone, just in case; so was a troop of light AA guns, with orders not to fire unless the aircraft dropped bombs. It dropped a container as well as a man. While Ridderhof, Poos and Slagter welcomed the man, Giskes walked over to the container; fearing it might be booby-trapped, he opened it himself. It was full of sabotage stores. The aircraft that dropped Baatsen never returned to base.

Baatsen took his arrest particularly badly, as any highly strung and energetic man might well have done. With the advantage of half a century's hindsight, it is worth emphasising that SOE's security staff might have laid even more stress than they did on the importance of picking for agent duty only unruffled types of steady character.

Schreieder recalled that Baatsen had been furious at his prompt arrest; and had fallen immediately for an interrogator's trick. On being told – quite untruly – that he had been betrayed by a German agent in London, he behaved as if everyone in that city was his enemy, and poured out to his captors a torrent of detail about where he had been trained, and how, and by whom.[143] This laid a solid foundation of knowledge on which Schreieder and Giskes could base later interrogations of any more agents they might catch; many of whom they unnerved by the extent of the detail of their understanding of their captives' recent past.

Giskes and Schreieder reported their successes to Rauter, who passed joyful word upwards; and was impressed by what he heard of Baatsen's task. If, he wrote to Himmler, Baatsen was sent orders to carry out specific fragments of teleprinter sabotage near The Hague on a particular date, it would be a certain indication of an imminent allied invasion:[144] a curious piece of wishful thinking, a vice not confined to N section.

On the same night that Baatsen dropped, the RAF made a separate delivery of three containers to Holland; collected without loss or effort by the Abwehr, and duly receipted by Lauwers in his schedule on the 28th.[145]

---

143. Schreieder, 124–8.
144. De Jong, *KdN*, v(ii). 921–2.
145. Whole world war diary, xii. 3384.

Dubito, ergo sum – I doubt, therefore I survive – was an indispensable motto for agents; SOE's country section staff might have made much more use of it also. Neglect of it by N now compounded his error in dispatching Baatsen; he thought he had taken care enough to separate the parties he was sending in, but turned out mistaken.

On the following night, the RAF dropped two more pairs of agents for N, blind, into Holland. One of these pairs, called 'Turnip', had twice tried to drop already. The 'Turnip' leader was Leonard Andringa, a fresh-faced blond saboteur aged twenty-eight; who – according to Rep – had been in England since 1937, training to be a priest.[146] Jan Molenaar, a policeman four years younger, was his wireless operator.

They were not lucky. On 26 January they had taken off from Newmarket; found their dropping zone covered in snow; and refused to drop. Exactly the same thing happened on 3 March.[147]

The normal airborne forces drill is brusque: any parachutist who refuses to jump has his wings ripped off, and is sent straight back to the unit from which he came. Agents did not wear wings in plain clothes; and N accepted 'Turnip's' judgement as sound. The two could not have helped leaving traces of their landing in the snow, and might thus have imperilled their mission from the start. Indeed, this was how a gamekeeper had recently stumbled on the two men SOE sent to Czechoslovakia to dispose of Heydrich:[148] a point unknown, of course, to N section.

Late on 28 March they took off again, from Tempsford to which 138 squadron had just moved. The snow had melted; this time they dropped, blind. A third agent who was with them, 'Leek', on a separate mission, thought the neighbourhood too populous and refused to join them.

The DZ was near Hellendoorn, west of Almelo in Overijssel province. Bad luck continued to dog them: Molenaar had a bad parachute accident. He landed, extra heavily, against a stone trough, damaging his spine and breaking both his legs. He was

---

146. Rep, *op. cit.*, 135, 137.
147. PRO AIR 27/956, 138 squadron ORB.
148. See Callum Macdonald, *The Killing of SS Obergruppenführer Reinhard Heydrich* (Macmillan, 1989), 128–9, 142–3.

fully conscious, but in excruciating plain. Quite sure that Andringa had no hope of finding him secret medical help in a hurry, he reached for his lethal tablet, and it worked.

Andringa left him where he lay, but buried his own parachute and the W/T set, keeping the crystals and the code. He missed the signal plan, which the Germans later found in one of Molenaar's pockets.[149] He found digs in Utrecht; and before long fell victim to a piece of neat detective work by Schreieder.

On the same night as this unlucky pair, but from another aircraft, two more agents dropped a dozen miles east of Deventer – supposedly also blind: 'Lettuce' and his wireless operator 'Trumpet', both tall men – six feet three each. 'Lettuce', G. H. G. Ras, had a recent degree in economics from Caius, Cambridge, and had been working as an agent for Heineken's beer[150] before he volunteered for the Dutch army in exile. He made an exceptional mark on the training staff – J. W. Munn remarked on his 'very likeable personality'[151] – and intended to start up sabotage groups in Utrecht province, arranging also DZs for their stores. 'Trumpet', H. J. Jordaan, had also had some higher education in England, at Manchester, where he had been studying the textile trade. The Dutch navy in exile had given him his wireless training.

He managed to send a little traffic, such as his report on 19 April that he and Ras 'WERE DROPPED ENTIRELY WRONG PLACE BUT BOTH SAFE'.[152] He added, cryptically, 'IDENTITY CARDS HAVE NO WATERMARK ARE CHECKED BY GESTAPO': a point SOE can be presumed to have passed over to SIS.[153]

A week later, two more agents parachuted in: 'Leek', who had refused to jump with 'Turnip', and his assistant 'Leek II'. Barend Kloos was a twenty-eight-year-old Rotterdammer, who had given up a good job as a shipping agent in Saigon to join the free Dutch

---

149. History cx, agents sent 1942, 2.
150. The Heineken company is rumoured to have kept careful notes, which it smuggled over to London, of the delivery addresses for all the many orders it received from Wehrmacht units as they arrived in Holland.
151. Typed scrap in Ras PF.
152. Tpt in his PF; identity check not given.
153. Cp page 41.

army, and had thence reached SOE in May 1941; where Munn found him 'Very intelligent and thorough' as a pupil.[154] 'Leek II' was Hendrik Sebes, a tailor from Dordrecht, born in 1919, who had recently married. They too dropped blind, on 28/29 March; they were to work in Overijssel,[155] and in particular to sabotage engineering firms at Hengelo.[156]

In the dark period that followed the early April moon, N managed for once to send in an agent by sea: J. H. M. de Haas, Homburg's friend and fellow escaper, whose task it was to organise a sea ferry for SOE – if he could. It is well known that agents might, several times over, emplane for a parachute drop and then be brought back to base without dropping, either because there was no reception committee, or none that the pilot could find, when one was expected; or because the weather closed in on the way to the DZ; or, more rarely, because the aircraft developed a fault that made pressing on too risky. Similar hitches were known at sea; de Haas encountered them. Worsening weather scuppered his voyage, on the night of 11/12 April;[157] the MTB carrying him encountered an enemy convoy, and lost too much time evading it, on the 16/17th; and finally put him ashore, as 'Potato', on the 18/19th.[158] His was the only instance of an N section agent put in by sea; but the section continued to hanker after opening up a sea route, in the belief that many more stores could be passed through one than there was hope of dispatching by air. All these agents going into Holland on reconnaissance, to sound out adherents and to form sabotage groups, were intended by N as the advance guard of something more formidable.

On 24 April London sent a message to 'Trumpet' that 'the present general contacting was bad for security and must stop';[159] quite true, but sent too late.

---

154. Typed scrap in his PF.
155. All these statements of intention come from History cx.
156. N to D/R, 12 February 1942. TSC in 'Leek' folder in Holland 35.
157. Whole world war diary, xiii(i). 3675, sends him ashore on this date. De Jong, *KdN*, ix(ii). 949, and van der Stroom, *op. cit.*, 30, have him parachuted on 9 April, when there was no moon.
158. Holland 38. 'Potato' folder, reports of 17 and 19 April 1942. Giskes, *op. cit.*, 95–6, also gets both date and method right.
159. Whole world war diary, xiii(ii). 3678.

On 27 April London told Taconis, through Lauwers's set, to go to the cigar shop in Haarlem, and drop into conversation the catch phrase 'bow and arrow'. Giskes could make nothing of this. Schreieder tried a chat with Taconis in his cell. 'Bow and arrow', he was astute enough to say, meant nothing to him; but he let slip the name of a cigar merchant in Haarlem called Martens. A few moments with a telephone directory gave Schreieder an address.[160]

Poos went there and mentioned 'bow and arrow'. Martens – who, remember, had never been to Beaulieu or received any other kind of training for secret work – replied that Bow, de Haas, was not there; but would his visitor care to speak to Bow's friend Akki, who was sitting right there at the back of the shop? Akki was Andringa, from whom Poos at once extracted de Haas's address; and Andringa and de Haas were both arrested next day.

They too were told that they had been betrayed from London; they too believed it. They too added to the Germans' pile of data on the workings of SOE. Worse, Andringa mentioned that he was to meet four agents on 1 May in the bar of the Terminus hotel in Utrecht.

He was taken there by Poos, who posed as secret agent 'Dick', and – according to Rep – kept prodding him in the back with a pistol.[161] The agents were sitting, two and two, at separate tables; Ras and Kloos were pulled in, Jordaan and Sebes slipped away. In one of Ras's pockets the Germans found Jordaan's telephone number, through which they reached him; and arrested him after he had revealed to a supposed friend where he was next to meet Sebes. Sebes joined the others on 9 May.[162]

Andringa also mentioned another bar rendezvous, when later in the month N told him to make touch with 'George'. They were to meet at noon on the following Wednesday at 'De Leidse Poort', a café-restaurant in Amsterdam. Andringa went there; so did George Dessing. Dessing recognised Andringa, with whom he had trained; but noticed that he had with him a stranger to Dessing, who stuck

---

160. Schreieder, 133.
161. Rep, *op. cit.*, 146–7.
162. De Jong, KdN, ix(ii). 948–50.

to him like a leech, and was in fact Giskes's man Poos. The two N agents went through the charade, rehearsed at Beaulieu, of falling into conversation without seeming to know each other. Dessing slipped off to the men's room; so did Andringa – followed at once by his leech. Dessing gave it up, and walked out; so did Andringa, onto a pavement so crowded that he managed to separate himself by a pace or two from his shadow and hiss the single word 'Gestapo'.

Dessing took the hint and walked off smartly, taking the usual steps to make sure he was not being followed. He hung about all summer in Amsterdam, but failed to make contact with anybody; in September he decided to make for Switzerland. It took him another seven months. On 13 April 1943 SIS wrote to inform SOE that Dessing – under his cover name of Dirksen – had reached there on the 10th.[163] On 21 April, at 5.35 in the morning, SOE received an overnight telegram about him from its man in Berne, which included this passage: 'SAW A[NDRINGA] AT BAR RENDEZVOUS BUT A WARNED HIM TO KEEP AWAY AS HE WAS ACCOMPANIED BY GESTAPO OFFICER.'[164]

Nobody seems to have picked this up.

While Dessing was on his way back from Switzerland, by slow stages and with several delays, not all his fault, a message he had sent earlier reached London through a Belgian intelligence channel; again, with a significant phrase in it: 'THINGS HAVE GONE WRONG WITH MOST OF THE OTHER PARACHUTISTS.'[165] Once more, no alarm was taken.

When on 3 September 1943 he at last returned to this island, passing smoothly through the controls, and delivering Vorrink's documents, SOE's special security section cross-questioned him at length. 'I could not help regarding this man with some little suspicion,' his interrogator reported; supposing that 'he did practically nothing in Holland, and is rather ashamed of it'.[166] A similar opinion was expressed by the first serious London inquirer into the

---

163. War diary, xlviii(i). 90, Berne to London, 10 April 1943.
164. Local 173 cipher telegram, tpt in Dessing PF.
165. Note 27 August 1943, *ibid.*
166. D/CEGA to N, 22 September 1943, *ibid.*

troubles: 'CARROT was not in my view a resourceful agent.'[167] Dessing was happy to spend the rest of the war working in the Dutch ministry of finance in exile.

He deserves credit from history for having rung an early alarm bell, even if N was too deaf to hear it.

N section had meanwhile made a crass, though not a unique error: a similar floater was committed two years later, several times over, by a staff officer in F section.[168] Jordaan assured the Germans that he had no security checks; and refused to work his set for them, or to demonstrate his sending style. They rose to the challenge. One of May's clerks sent a message in Jordaan's code explaining that he had hurt his wrist too badly to send himself, but had managed to find an assistant. N's reply told him to instruct the new operator in the use of security checks. This made Jordaan so angry that he complied.[169]

The Germans now had two lines open to London. Soon they had more. On one of these two earliest lines, van der Waals, a radio ham who competed with Ridderhof for the title of most useful Dutch double agent in German pay, was able to arrange for Radio Oranje in London to broadcast a phrase that authenticated himself to an intelligence group started up by van Hamel, which he was trying to penetrate: with fatal success. De Jong, who later set all these disasters down in his great book, was working for Radio Oranje at the time; none of that team had any inkling that they were helping the Gestapo's work.[170]

This was not the only occasion when they were tricked into doing so.[171]

Himmler visited Holland in May 1942, and swore 800 Dutchmen into the Waffen-SS at a ceremony held in the zoo at The Hague. He made encouraging remarks to Rauter and to Harster, and had an

167. 'Survey of Dutch operations during 1942/1943', 1; initialled TS of 15 December 1943 in Holland 19.
168. Cp Foot, *SOE in France*, 329–30; and, for the same error elsewhere, Richards, *Secret Flotillas*, 591.
169. Whole world war diary, xv. 4310, June 1942; de Jong, *KdN*, ix(ii). 950.
170. *Ibid.*, 952 and n.
171. See pages 163, 165.

interview with Baatsen;[172] 'North Pole' of course was still then in its early stages, not the success it gradually became. He also had a friendly talk with the Dutch police colonel in charge of Amsterdam, Tulp, who was happy to work hand in glove with Rauter. Himmler, Rauter and Tulp were once photographed together at a parade just outside the Rijksmuseum.[173]

Heydrich accompanied Himmler, and is said to have had a long talk with Jordaan; he also took one of the captured sten guns for a range test.[174]

When a pair of Czechoslovak agents, trained by SOE, managed to mortally wound Heydrich on 27 May 1942, it was not only in Prague that the SS went on the rampage. The SOE agents already in German hands in the Netherlands were closely interrogated about whom they had seen during their training; not all of them were silent. Several reported that they had seen Czechoslovak parachutists at Ringway, and Czechoslovak saboteurs at Brickendonbury; one of them, Taconis, explained how he thought the detonator of the bomb that killed Heydrich had worked.[175]

On 29 May one of Lauwers's telegrams reported 'that they had two helpers now working in Germany at the Schiess Machine Factory in Dusseldorf'.[176] This was a response to several suggestions from N that 'Catarrh' might be able to make touch with Dutchmen sent on forced labour into Germany, and so be able in the end to hamper production by the German armaments industry. This was one of SOE's main preoccupations, all through the war, deriving from its Ministry of Economic Warfare (MEW) cover; however, it was not through 'Catarrh' that any advances were going to be made on this hidden front. Indeed presumably it was useful to the German security authorities to get this forewarning of a chink in Germany's armour.

---

172. Giskes, *op. cit.*, 87.
173. *Oorlogsdocumentatie '40–'45 Derde jaarboek* (Amsterdam?: Walburg Pers, 1992), 29.
174. Schreieder, 254.
175. SD report made at The Hague, 24 June 1942, in Czechoslovakia 37. I am particularly grateful, for this reference as well as for much other official kindness, to C. M. Woods.
176. Whole world war diary, xiv (ii). 3974–5.

The Germans meanwhile went back to 'Turnip's' DZ, dug around, and found the hidden W/T set, which May soon had working, as if by a friend of Andringa's; codenamed 'Gilgal' till September 1942, when SOE's security section changed his name to 'Swede'.[177] With 'Gilgal's' help, Giskes and Schreieder composed, Huntemann translated and Blizard believed a modest run of telegrams signed Turnip, for Andringa, which indicated that he was getting on quietly with forming sabotage groups; and that more help would be useful.

Accordingly, two more saboteurs, 'Beetroot I and II', parachuted in on 29/30 May 1942, Herman Parlevliet – only half an inch shorter than Ras – and Antonius van Steen. Parlevliet, born in 1916 at Baarle-Nassau, the Belgian enclave south-east of Breda, was a quiet, efficient NCO in the Dutch mounted police; van Steen, four years older and still quieter, was another. They were to set up sabotage groups in Limburg. They were not dropped blind; they went, London supposed, to a reception by Andringa, but were in fact received by Poos and Slagter on the Steenwijk DZ.

They brought a lot of wireless equipment with them: two 'Eurekas', and a transmitter and codes for de Haas. As an obliging signaller had written down the security checks with de Haas's codes, the Germans acquired their next set. (May testified to the enquiry commission that he usually found agents' codes in writing.)[178] The newcomers had the sense to say that they had no idea what the 'Eurekas' were for. One was sent off straightaway to Berlin, where it made an intriguing present for the experts;[179] and within a few weeks May had gained enough of the confidence of one of his prisoners to discover how to work the other. London obligingly explained when and where to use it.[180]

N's next pair for Holland, van Rietschoten and Homburg's fellow escaper Buizer ('Parsnip' and 'Spinach'), were dropped east of Deventer on 22/23 June 1942. Van Rietschoten, whom Hoets remembered as a promising young oarsman,[181] had made a simple,

---

177. War diary, xlviii(i). 30, 18 September 1942.
178. *Enq.*, iv B. 17.
179. Cp Giskes, *op. cit.*, 102.
180. War diary, xlviii(i). 7, misnaming it 'Rebecca'.
181. Pieter Hans Hoets, *Englandspiel ontmaskerd*, 11.

adventurous escape from Holland nine months earlier. Aged twenty, he and another student from Delft had bought a canoe with a sail, taken it to Katwijk for the weekend, and simply walked down to the shore after dark, carrying it, just after a patrol had passed by. They sailed due west, and landed at Aldeburgh. He was recognised at the RVPS by Laming, who knew his parents slightly;[182] was trained in anti-shipping sabotage by Rheam, so that he could tackle the plentiful targets in the province of South Holland; and took the Beaulieu course from the House in the Wood. Buizer meanwhile had been at Thame Park, improving his W/T skills; he had already worked as a radio-telegraphist in Holland.

As he had not been to Beaulieu, Buizer was easy prey for Schreieder and Giskes. He and van Rietschoten were both arrested by their reception committee; Buizer made no difficulties about either his code or his security checks; the Germans thus acquired a fresh channel. (Van Rietschoten's fellow escaper in 1941 joined Hazelhoff Roelfzema and was soon killed in action.) Buizer will be familiar to readers of Marks's book under his signals codename, 'Boni'.[183] From now on, the coding department of SOE began to be suspicious of the Dutch traffic; these suspicions gradually deepened, till by midwinter 1942–3 they were hardening into certainty.

Poos, still posing as a resister, had meanwhile kept up his acquaintance with Martens at the Haarlem cigar shop; Martens remained unaware of Andringa's fate, as Poos had taken the trouble to arrest him elsewhere. Through Martens, Poos managed to hear of a projected escape by sea from Ijmuiden of Homburg's brother Piet; who was arrested, with several friends, shortly before they had meant to depart.

Worse followed 'Parsnip's drop. On 26/27 June 138 squadron dropped near Steenwijk G. L. Jambroes ('Marrow'), and J. Bukkens, his wireless operator, who were to be the liaison between the Dutch government in exile and the Orde Dienst (OD). High hopes were placed in the OD, both by its organisers in Holland and by the queen and her advisers in London. Its object was to secure an orderly transfer back of power to

---

182. Undated MS note in his PF in Laming's hand.
183. See Leo Marks, *Between Silk and Cyanide*, 99–101, 124, 146, 204–9, 230–6, &c.

the proper Dutch authorities, when the Germans left. Most of these hopes were ruined by the *Englandspiel*, some had crumbled already, in early arrests. Some of these early arrests had already become known in London, through various sources, both to the Dutch in exile and to the British; including a mass execution of seventy-two people, widely reported.[184] They might have induced more caution than they did into any approach to the OD.

'Marrow's' task was first of all to explain to the OD the Plan for Holland, which had been drawn up in London, and which was to put military teeth into any political schemes the OD might have prepared.

This is the point at which the *Englandspiel* ceased simply to be a disaster for SOE, and got entangled both with Dutch politics and with world strategy. For 'Marrow' dropped, at de Bruyne's insistence, not blind, but to a reception committee; and not to a waiting N agent as expected, but to Poos and Slagter. The Germans were thereafter in charge of the Plan for Holland, and could make sure it did not turn out as London had intended.

Some still believe that the Plan for Holland was foisted on the Dutch in exile by SOE, to suit some British deception so devious that it has never come to light.[185] This was not so. It was concocted jointly by the British and the Dutch; when it came to detailed planning, by Blizard and de Bruyne. The initiative, it is true, may have been British. As early as 19 July 1941 the war diary envisaged 1,000 saboteurs, and a secret army of 5,000 men, in the Netherlands. Six weeks later, on 22 August, Hambro minuted to Nelson that a secret army would eventually have to be raised there, with the full co-operation of the exiled government in London; though that need not deter SOE from running sabotage parties meanwhile with the pick of the best men to be had.[186]

Gubbins moreover, in charge of SOE's training and all its current operations, had made a point of befriending de Bruyne. They lunched or dined together about once a month, apart from their

---

184. C. M. Schulten, *Verzet in Nederland 1940–1945*, 129.
185. E.g. de Jong, *KdN*, xiv(ii). 606; or Hoets, *op. cit., passim*.
186. Whole world war diary, vi(i). 1199, and vii. 1739. CAB 121/305 includes Dalton's letter to Churchill of 16 July 1941 (duplic) with a mass of supporting figures.

official meetings;[187] Gubbins enjoyed good food and drink,[188] and certainly tried to use these occasions to instil into de Bruyne his own ideas about how subversion and sabotage could be organised. There is reason to believe de Bruyne was not his readiest pupil.

The main concern of the Dutch in exile in 1942 was the fate of their empire in the East Indies, overrun by the Japanese with atrocious ease. Many staff officers and civil servants, who formed part of the government machine in exile, had relatives and close comrades in those captured islands, and could hardly get news of their fates. This did not improve their judgement. All the same, it is surprising that no one thought of passing on to de Bruyne Brooke the CIGS's circular letter of 2 June 1942, advising the exiled governments how to plan sabotage, which put SOE 'squarely on the map'.[189] He first heard of it when Gubbins showed him a copy in mid-November, nearly six months after it had been issued.[190]

Moreover, he was the object of constant, jealous sniping from other staff officers among the Dutch in exile. Menzies, who did not share Gubbins's personal friendship with him, remarked in October that 'it was well known that [his] statements were apt to be tainted as also were the statements by various Dutch officers about [him]'.[191] De Bruyne was also, as became clear after the war, in a considerable muddle himself about what his BVT was supposed to be for. He told the commission of inquiry that his orders from government were to make touch with, and to strengthen, the resistance movements in the Netherlands, but to take no part at all in sabotage;[192] this cannot have been a doctrine Gubbins preached to him.

The plan was a common effort, directed to a common end: the expulsion of nazi forces from the Netherlands. Blizard certainly consulted D/R from time to time, and was continually kept up to the

---

187. According to Gubbins's appointments diary, now in the Imperial War Museum. I am most grateful to Lady Gubbins for a preview.
188. Wilkinson and Astley, *op. cit.*, 48–9.
189. *Ibid.*, 112.
190. *Enq.*, iv A. 503.
191. War diary, xlviii(i). 33.
192. *Enq.*, iv A. 484.

collar by Gubbins; who in turn followed the orders of the Chiefs of Staff. De Bruyne, equally certainly, now and then consulted Furstner, and was continually inspired by his queen. She of course was too discreet to say anything specific in her memoirs; de Bruyne, like Furstner, Gubbins, Blizard and Bingham, left none. In the English as in the Dutch case, only the most general guidance was given from above. N section and the BVT tackled all the donkey work.

The section history is specific: 'In April a plan was worked out known as the "Plan for HOLLAND" . . . It was elaborated in collaboration with the Dutch and Col. de BRUYNE spent much time in discussing it with us, so that co-operation between SOE Dutch Section and his office was very close.'[193]

The plan was a good one. It married Gubbins's general principles of irregular warfare to the specific needs of Holland. In its first version, SOE's, it was sent over to de Bruyne's office 'for consideration and discussion' in April 1942;[194] this took over two months.

The object was to create and arm a secret army of Dutchmen, with tasks the section history set out:

PHASE A.
(a)   The disruption of enemy communications on or soon after D-Day [for the main invasion of the continent], according to the strategic plan and the tactical situation.
(b)   The prevention, by this disruption, of the removal to Germany of Dutch locomotives and rolling-stock.
PHASE B.
(a)   After D-day, the provision of direct support, behind the enemy's lines, to forces in the field.
(b)   The prevention of demolition by the enemy;
      (i)   of objectives (bridges, power-stations, dock facilities etc.) which the advancing Allied armies will wish to use.
      (ii)   of other objectives constituting scorched-earth policy.[195]

---

193. History cx, 1942, [2].
194. *Ibid.* [3].
195. *Ibid.* Revised version, in Dutch, dated 12 June 1942, in Hoets, *op. cit.*, 194–6.

Jambroes, who was to diffuse the plan, was a thirty-seven-year-old petrol engineer who had been teaching physics in a girls' school at Zaandam in the autumn of 1940, and had already had some experience of undercover work; including several months on the run.[196] As he had served as an officer in the Dutch army, he was spared the paramilitary schools.[197] He went to parachute school and for a fortnight to Beaulieu, and then after a week in London and a night at Gaynes Hall straight into the field. He had reckoned that his life in Holland, on the run, had not been worth much, and was ready to risk it again;[198] he had hardly reckoned on being received by an enemy.

The capture of Jambroes and Bukkens marked a turning-point in the *Englandspiel*. Bukkens made no kind of secret about his codes, any more than Jambroes did about his orders. Neatly, Giskes and Schreieder solved the problem of pretending contact with the OD. For some weeks they sent, in Jambroes's codename, via Bukkens's transmitter, temporising messages about how Jambroes was finding his feet and sounding out potential helpers. Then, in mid-August, they had him report that unnamed 'experienced men in the Secret Army Organisation had advised him not to attempt to make contact in the higher spheres of the Secret Army Organisation, which had been partly broken up through recent arrests, and the remainder partly discovered and shadowed. The organisation was riddled with informers and it would be sometime before it found its feet again.'[199] Would London agree to his organising and supplying sabotage groups, later expandable into a secret army, himself? London concurred, and poured agents steadily into the trap.

This was bad enough; Jambroes went on to let out his final instruction, which was to get into touch with the senior working intelligence agent in Holland; who happened – here is the small-country syndrome at work – to be well known to Bukkens. The consequences were not likely to endear SOE any more closely to SIS.

---

196. RVPS report, 28 March 1942, TS in his PF.
197. History cxii.3.
198. *Enq.*, iv A. 503.
199. 18 August 1942, reported in war diary, xlviii(i). 19; cp de Jong, *KdN*, ix(ii). 955.

One more agent went in that summer to join the rest in captivity, in response to simulated reports from Kloos about how he was opening up chances for secret work in Overijssel: the Brooklyn-born G. J. van Hemert ('Leek A'), son of a Dutch leather merchant, who had spent most of his short life – he was born in 1920 – in Holland, including six years at the Montessori school at 1 Corelli Straat, Amsterdam. He had been working in Amsterdam as an insurance clerk until May 1941, when he secured a passport to return to the USA; when he was persuaded to volunteer for special service in Europe, joining SOE at Christmas, and being trained as a wireless operator as well as a saboteur. His instructors noticed how quiet and secure he was.[200]

He was dropped, supposedly to Taconis, on 23/24 July 1942, with an urgent message: 'Catarrh' was to prepare an attack on the German navy's transmitter masts at Kootwijk, west of Apeldoorn, from which German U-boats waging the battle of the Atlantic received some of their orders. This operation, to which the Admiralty attached importance, was codenamed 'Feather'; Blizard sent an order on 6 August – his eighty-sixth message to 'Ebenezer' – for it to be carried out 'at the earliest possible moment'.[201]

This put Giskes and Schreieder in a fix; out of which they clambered nimbly. 'Ebenezer' came up on 12 August, in his sixty-seventh message, to report that 'FEATHER had been started on the night of the 9th and had ended in complete failure. When approaching the main objective, two men ran into a land mine, thus alarming the guard, who shot and wounded one of our men. A total of five men were missing.'[202] Newspaper reports – carefully fudged, of course, by the Germans – later added credence to this story.[203]

This triggered off London's thanks 'for this striking proof of their great courage and high morale', great regrets, and inquiries after all possible details.[204] For weeks thereafter London could be kept busy with putative arrangements for bringing away by sea, with 'Potato's'

200. Typed chits in his PF.
201. War diary, xlviii(i). 15.
202. *Ibid.*
203. Giskes, *op. cit.*, 104; de Jong, *KdN*, ix(ii). 969–72; *Enq.*, iv B.51.
204. War diary, xlviii(i). 15–16.

or 'Brandy's' help, the fictional 'Fred', a friend notionally attributed to Taconis who had been in charge of the equally notional raid. This canard was still flapping its wings in December, and was not finally put down till February 1943.[205]

As N remarked in a paper of 6 August, laying out a difference of opinion with MI6, 'In a small and densely populated country like HOLLAND, in which so many people know each other, it is quite impossible to prevent the crossing of lines however carefully they may be grouped at the London end.'[206] During this summer relations between MI6 and SOE, at least where Holland was concerned, seem to have been more strained than usual – each service feeling it was under-informed by the other. On the enemy side, life was more calm.

The summer of 1942 was high summer indeed for the Third Reich. Though the United States had entered the war, they had not yet made any impression east of the Atlantic; the Wehrmacht's advances into the almost limitless expanse of Russia seemed almost limitless also, probing towards the Volga and even the Caucasus. The west, by comparison, was quiescent; the reconnaissance in force at Dieppe on 19 August was repelled with almost contemptuous ease. The sense of being comfortably installed, for an indefinite future, settled on German security staffs. They examined their captives thoroughly, and at leisure. Schreider, gifted – as so many in the intelligence world were – with an exceptional memory, reconstructed when it came to his turn to be interrogated a systematic list of as many as a hundred questions, to be put in a set order to every prisoner of his *Englandspiel.*[207]

Giskes had friends enough in the Luftwaffe to be able to hunt for likely dropping zones at leisure from a Fieseler Storch light aircraft,[208] a facility allied airborne staff would have envied.

---

205. *Ibid.*, 56, 76.
206. TSC, 7, in 'Kale's' PF.
207. Those interested in interrogation techniques may care to read this questionnaire, which is printed in full in appx 5, page 503. It is already familiar to the Dutch, for he repeated it to their post-war commission of inquiry: *Enq.*, iv B. 40–2.
208. Schreider, 222.

As for securing the prisoners, Poos and Slagter arranged an informal drill; it worked only too well. One of them walked up to the newly arrived agent, as he struggled out of his parachute harness, and exchanged a password with him – prearranged over the captured W/T sets. The other double agent meanwhile collected the torches that had guided the aircraft in. All three of them – or all four, if two agents had arrived – walked over to the edge of the dropping zone; where they paused to chat. Friends, also in plain clothes, were on hand to bury the parachutes and to collect any containers or packages. The pause lasted, on one excuse or another, for an hour or so; during which the new arrivals, unguarded in the elation that follows a successful night drop and delighted to be back in their own country, were gently pumped to find out their real names and their real tasks.

Suddenly, each agent found himself pinioned from behind, and handcuffed. An SD party, headed by a Hamburg boxing champion, had stolen up silently the other side of the hedge; and then moved fast, to make sure that the agent neither drew a weapon nor bit on his lethal tablet.

A car drive to The Hague or to Driebergen followed, during which Giskes or Schreieder would explain to the agent that this style of reception was normal. Routine interrogation then began at once, and ran on if need be for three or four unbroken days and nights of questioning. When one agent (not of SOE's) told the post-war commission of inquiry that he had been grilled continuously for 110 hours – over four days – Schreieder commented that the BdS's personal leave had to be sought to go on for more than three days.[209] Agents, once drained of data, were then dispatched to prison in Haaren seminary, north-east of Tilburg;[210] where May would sometimes turn up, to pursue points of detail with the wireless operators; and where the prisoners could indeed see for themselves that men they had trained with had fallen into the same trap.

Early in these interrogations they were all promised that their lives would be spared – a useful lubricant, to open up discussion with men trained to be silent. The promise, as originally given by Giskes to

---

209. *Enq.*, iv A, 342.
210. Photograph in de Jong, *KdN*, at viii(i). 186.

Lauwers as 'North Pole' began, was formally confirmed by the Reich's security headquarters in June 1942.[211] It went the way of many other nazi promises, later; but it served its purpose – it encouraged agents to talk. Schreieder indeed maintained that it was a useful as well as a legitimate interrogator's choice, to treat captives in a friendly way instead of using the ferocity that the name of the Gestapo had already made only too well known.[212] His matter-of-fact, avuncular tone unnerved only too many of his captives, who had been trained to expect the quite different treatment that, in the bitter end, they received.

Among the stores dropped, in blind faith, straight into the Germans' hands were several S-phones.[213] Though SOE's craftsmen had invented these devices, it had no monopoly in them; SIS used them quite often, in conjunction with the Havoc flight of 161 squadron, relying on the narrowness of their directional beam to assure security. Neither service had properly appreciated that, though S-phones were safe at a distance, they were interceptible within a mile of the point of use; as the Germans had discovered by the end of 1943. In October 1944 they arrested a senior BI agent in Leyden because he had been using an S-phone, and killed him later.[214] SAS had by then discovered that, at any rate on a set they borrowed from SOE in France, a low-flying aircraft's end of an S-phone conversation could be heard over a moving circle of ground a quarter of a mile (400m) across.[215]

The captured sets cannot have failed to be interesting to German signals intelligence officers; yet SOE never in fact used them to verify the security of their agents in Holland. Historians are bound to ask, why not?

F Section unravelled within nine minutes a game the Gestapo had run against them with success for nine months, by flying Gerry Morel over Lorraine with an S-phone: he heard an unmistakably German instead of an unmistakably Canadian accent, and the

---

211. Giskes, *op. cit.*, 98.
212. Schreieder, 154.
213. See page 139.
214. De Jong, *KdN*, ix(ii). 847.
215. Paul McCue, *SAS Operation Bulbasket* (Leo Cooper, 1996), 109.

doomed 'Archdeacon' circuit – in enemy hands from its inception – was therefore wound up.[216] Why was some similar step not taken in the Netherlands?

Presumably because the RAF – sensibly enough – disliked the idea of time spent flying to and fro, quite low down, over some of the world's heaviest anti-aircraft defences; the Havoc flight, which operated over sea, was reserved for SIS. SIS, too, might well blame SOE for the loss of the BI agent in Leyden.

N in fact sent the S-phones in for use from shore to ship, rather than from land to air; pursuing the mirage of a secure sea supply line, which was still dancing before his eyes all through the autumn of 1942.[217] DF section used shore-to-ship S-phones efficiently in its 'Var' line on the north coast of Brittany in 1943–4;[218] technically, this was a discreet success. But N never got his opening. All his efforts to establish sea lines, or sea pick-up and set-down operations – 'Potato' in April apart, before 'North Pole' was fully organised – came to nothing. Giskes and Schreieder went along with him in preparing the arrangements, down to minute details of place, time and signal; and then pulled back at the last moment, usually pleading (truly or not) unexpected new guard posts close to the point involved. They found it much simpler to work by air than by sea; it saved them a whole swathe of extra complications with the German navy; and N could do nothing but, unknowing, conform with his enemy's desire.

The case of Isak de Groot was an odd one and deserves a pair of paragraphs. He was a Dutch timber merchant, born in 1898, who had been working in the Baltic when the war began, and had had some disagreeable experiences in German hands in Finland in the autumn of 1941. N section took him on, on May Day 1942, and trained him as a saboteur and propagandist. Under the cover name of Buurman, or the codename 'Asparagus', he figures often in N section's war diary for the summer and autumn of 1942. He was to have been put ashore from a small boat on the Engelsmanplaat, and moved forward by Bottema. His work, designed jointly with X (the

216. Foot, *SOE in France*, 331–3.
217. War diary, xlviii(i). p*assim*.: e.g. pages 24–5, 37–8.
218. Richards, *op. cit.*, 218–23.

German) section, was to have been to forward propaganda material, and instructions in elementary sabotage, to Dutch forced labourers who had to work in German factories: in principle, a useful form of pinprick attack on the nazi war economy. He was to have taken it up through whatever fragments he could find still in existence of the pre-war Dutch trade unions: a corner of Dalton's legacy to SOE, unless it was simply an idea of Frank Dawson's.

All the messages about de Groot's intended journey into Holland went straight to the Germans. Luckily for him, it did not suit the Germans (as we have just seen) to open up a sea line at all, and for months they put N and the navy off with minor excuses. He was judged too fat to be parachuted. In mid-December 1942, N inquired of S and of D/R what the chances would be of stowing him away on a boat to Delfzijl, or of sending him by Lysander to northern France, and then forward with an MI9 guide. Nothing came of any of these proposals. De Groot was left kicking his heels in London, or on refresher courses, all through 1943; got married; fell ill; and was prostrated by having his house in West Kensington bombed, on 20 February 1944, the day after he was posted out of SOE.[219] De Jong adds that he was dropped at last, on an MI9 mission, in December 1944.[220]

As early as 30 April 1942 Gubbins expressed to Hambro the uncertainty felt by the Dutch authorities in London about which groups in the Netherlands were reliable; he hoped soon, with de Bruyne's help, to send someone across to make sure.[221] This was probably the origin of the fated 'Kale' mission.

'Kale' and 'Bill' were the codenames of K. W. A. Beukema toe Water, one of N's most distinguished agents. He was a chemical engineer working for Shell, born in Java in 1909; a reserve lieutenant in the Dutch army; and a mountaineer. His powers of leadership and outgoing personality were attractive to SOE's training staff; he was thought outstandingly good at Arisaig.[222] He was

---

219. His PF.
220. De Jong, *KdN*, ix(ii). 971.
221. M to CD, 30 April 1942. TSC in Holland 1.
222. Typed note in his PF.

dropped on 24/25 September 1942, with a companion, the twenty-year-old Cornelis Drooglever Fortuyn ('Mangold'), 'a typical carefree Dutch student' as he seemed to the RVPS when he reached there early in 1942.[223] Drooglever Fortuyn was a nephew of van Lidth de Jeude, one of Gerbrandy's ministers, and the son of a banker; he had escaped from the Netherlands with Baron d'Aulnis, finding their own way across the Pyrenees.

These were men of weight: Beukema toe Water (whom it will be simpler hereafter to call 'Kale') was by a long way the most formidable agent N had yet dispatched. Yet he too, like his operator, was in enemy hands before he left his dropping zone: Poos and Slagter were waiting for them both.

The arrangements for pinioning them did not go perfectly smoothly. Drooglever Fortuyn got a moment's notice of trouble impending; and used it to hurl away into the darkness the book – an Anglo-Dutch pocket dictionary – on which his personal code depended. Schreieder took a party of policemen back to the DZ at first light; they searched every blade of grass for a stone's throw round the point of arrest, and found the book.

Even so, the agent refused to explain how to use it. 'Kale' notionally sent his traffic through operators provided, equally notionally, by 'Turnip'. He was supposed to take over from Jambroes, whom Drooglever Fortuyn was supposed to exfiltrate from Holland as best he could; neither of these plans could come to anything.

The arrangements to drop 'Kale' were made – London supposed – with Jordaan. On the same night, two other agents were dropped, supposedly to Jambroes: Roelof Jongelie ('Parsley') and Adriaan Mooy ('Cauliflower'). Jongelie, already grey-haired at thirty-nine, was a Dutch naval officer who had earlier been in charge of degaussing at Soerabaya. He had a semi-political mission: Gerbrandy charged him with reinforcing Jambroes's earlier message to the OD, that this was not a time for party quarrels and that all the Dutch should pull together.[224]

He had a separate mission to the sub-section of the OD that dealt

223. RVPS report 5226, 19 January 1942, TSC in his PF.
224. His PF.

with intelligence. SOE provided him with four-and-a-half closely typed pages of instructions about this, including the comment that 'your position is not that of a "spy" but more or less that of a reflector and sieve' between this branch of the OD and the Dutch government. To avoid any chance of misunderstandings, all his traffic was to be in Dutch.[225] One cannot help wondering why SOE was undertaking part of SIS's work.

The undertaking did not get far; Jongelie too was arrested on arrival. He was unco-operative with his interrogators, beyond letting slip the remark that Bukkens was to tell home station that 'Erica arrived safely' (according to Schreieder) or (Giskes's version) that 'the express left on time'. Giskes noticed a gleam in Jongelie's eye when he agreed to send this message, so suppressed it. Instead, the Germans sent word through Bukkens's set that Jongelie had hurt his neck in a heavy landing; and killed him off, notionally, a week later.[226]

Mooy, much younger – born in 1919 – had been a gunnery cadet officer for the Dutch East Indian army when the war began, and had had to make two tries at getting out of Holland: the first landed him in a labour camp in south-west France, from which he ran away; the second took him via Switzerland to Brazil. He had been less than five months in England. His training had included a week's Lysander course, in which 161 squadron judged him one of their star pupils. No one seems to have noticed the oddity of training a man in these techniques from a section to the area of which it remained RAF policy not to mount pick-ups at all.

He too was arrested on their DZ. Giskes sidestepped his mission neatly, by reporting through 'Trumpet' – as if from 'Kale' – in mid-November that Jambroes and Bukkens had both been killed in action by German police who raided Bukkens's set.[227] This closed down one of the W/T lines available to Giskes; he had several more.

Later that moon, on 1/2 October, N arranged one more drop, this time for a single agent, Arie van der Giessen ('Cabbage'). He came from a family of shipbuilders at Krimpen, at the mouth of the IJssel;

225. TSC of 15 August 1942, 2, 5, in 'Parsley' sub-file of Holland 38.
226. De Jong, *KdN*, ix(ii). 976–8; Giskes, *op. cit.*, 108; Schreieder, 258–62.
227. War diary, xlviii(i). 43–4.

stood over six feet tall; and weighed in at fourteen stone (eighty-six kilograms). He knew Rotterdam well, as he had spent part of his schooldays there, before he went to work in English shipyards; and was to have helped van Rietschoten organise sabotage in South Holland province.

Nothing, of course, came of this; Poos and Slagter were waiting for him too. He brought with him a large torch; London provided elaborate instructions about where it was to be delivered in Amsterdam.

So far as N could make out, nothing much came of this either: Lauwers sent word through on 11 October that 'The man who received it was very cautious and thought he might be in danger. All contact with him had therefore been broken off' – to N's approval two days later.[228] N was thus convinced of a proper degree of caution exercised by his agents in the field; things did not look quite the same to the Germans.

For May had opened the torch, gingerly, and found wrapped round the batteries a hundred 100-florin notes, and a well-forged identity card for a twenty-eight-year-old Dutchman.

Van der Waals again made himself useful. He presented himself, with the torch as guarantee, as a newly parachuted agent; took in his new acquaintance, whom he recognised from the photograph on the identity card; and thus secured the arrest on 6 October of W. J. Niermeyer, who had been working for six months for CID and MI6,[229] and was indeed at the moment – according to de Jong[230] – 6's only active agent in the Netherlands.

The Germans appreciated the need to time his arrest carefully, lest London should suspect its cause – that N section had become an unreliable travel agent. Their knowledge of security checks was now advanced enough for them to work out what his must have been; they then played his set back several weeks more.[231] SOE had no reason to hear of his arrest; and if SIS noticed that it had followed on their use of SOE as messenger-boy, they made no comment to SOE (or none that has survived on paper).

228. War diary, xlviii(i). 22, 37.
229. Van der Stroom, *op. cit.*, 25–6.
230. De Jong, *KdN*, ix(ii). 891.
231. *Ibid.*; Schreieder, 268–71; *Enq.*, iv B. 51.

SOE's doubts had yet to develop. On 11/12 October the RAF brought off a stores drop to 'Eureka' (still misnamed 'Rebecca' in the war diary) without a moon. N believed Andringa to have received it, and SOE's D/Air, Group Captain Grierson, described the fact as 'most gratifying' in a letter to the Air Ministry.[232]

Lauwers's plight commands sympathy: he had suddenly found himself having to co-operate, to save his friend Taconis's life, with an enemy he still detested. For over seven months he transmitted for the Germans, in his usual sending style. At each transmission one or two Orpo signallers hovered over him, to make sure he only sent the text in front of him. All the same, he tried to send some warning.

As a guard against chance interception, SOE's operators imitated the commercial traffic of the time, using five-letter morse groups for the main text, and a then familiar set of three-letter operating signals called the Q-code. Most exchanges concluded with QRU, which meant 'I have nothing further for you'. Lauwers took to sending CAU instead; and to sending GHT instead of QSY when he wanted to change frequency, as he often did.

Neither C's operators nor SOE's – the change-over was made on 1 June 1942 – appeared to notice.

Lauwers persevered. He tried to insert into the jumble of random letters that began and ended each message the phrase 'WORKED BY JERRY SINCE MARCH SIX'; as the Germans allowed him no vowels among his random letters, this was not a success either.[233]

Once, in October 1942, he found that the text he was to transmit included the group CARGS. Reception that day was bad; so, as drill laid down, he sent each five-letter group twice; and home station then sent him R – meaning 'received' – before he went on. Instead of sending CARGS CARGS he sent CAUGH CAUGH; got his R; and sent T, followed by GR3 – meaning 'I have made a mistake', and then CARGS CARGS. Home station responded not with R but with RRRRRRRRRRRR; which he took to mean 'I quite understand'.[234]

He was an amateur; his face lit up. One of his Orpo companions

---

232. War diary, xlviii(i). 28–9.
233. See Giskes, *op. cit.*, 175–200, an epilogue by Lauwers.
234. Spelled out in detail in *Enq.*, iv A. 840.

noticed, and reported to Giskes; who at once took Lauwers off keying himself. An Orpo operator who had often listened to his touch imitated him perfectly thereafter; home station perceived no change.

No wonder this incident left Lauwers with the assurance that London knew he was in enemy hands. Marks opined, over fifty years later, that all the operator who had sent the string of Rs meant was 'Get on, get on, get off the air'.[235]

The only trace N section's war diary shows of this is a mention (in EBENEZER 99 of Trafalgar Day) that Lauwers was now so busy that he 'would like to engage a spare operator whom he could fully guarantee'. When this operator, called 'Tom', came up a week later, London complained that 'the morse was bad' – to Lauwers's astonishment, as 'Tom' had had twenty years' practice;[236] he was accepted later.[237]

Once a message reached SOE's home station it was deciphered, and then transmitted by a signal clerk – usually by girls in their late teens – straight onto a teleprinter to Baker Street. The clerks' first care was to leave the random letters out altogether, before beginning to break the message's five-letter groups down into separate words. So the only people in England who saw Lauwers's warnings were decipher clerks and transmission clerks, all quite junior, all busy, and all preoccupied with doing their job exactly right: theirs not to *read* what passed under their eyes.

Brook (D/R) recalled, over forty years later, that the first time he saw telegrams from 'Ebenezer' – Lauwers – he drew attention to the fact that they were marked 'BLUFF CHECK OMITTED. TRUE CHECK OMITTED.' Everyone made reassuring noises; telegrams from 'Ebenezer' without security checks seemed to be part of N section's normal life, and Brook like everybody else got used to them.[238] Lauwers had a high opinion of the British secret services, in principle; supposed that his warnings must have got through; and inferred that N must keep sending men along to Holland to suit

---

235. Conversation with him, 8 November 1995.
236. *Enq.*, iv A. 840, and war diary, xlviii(i). 36–7.
237. *Ibid.*, 50, 14 November 1942.
238. Foot, *Holland at War*, 145–6.

some purpose too devious for himself to fathom. This mistaken view, set out in the epilogue to Giskes's book, is probably at the base of many later misapprehensions.

N sent nine more men in by the late October, and four by the late November moon. Most of these parties were for reconnaissance: two three-man teams, 'Celery' and 'Tomato', each including a wireless operator; 'Pumpkin' to work in southern Holland; 'Cucumber' to work in the eastern part of the country; 'Mustard' and 'Cress' to reconnoitre further; and three more wireless operators. Let us move out of the staff kitchen garden on to more personal terms.

Horst Steeksma who led 'Celery' had been born in Berlin in 1919, where his father worked as an electrical engineer; after Tilburg secondary school, he had been a company sergeant-major in the Prinses Irene Brigade, handling confidential papers. As a foil to his brightness, he had Meindert Koolstra to assist him, two years his senior, the stolid son of a Friesland baker who had helped in his father's shop before he joined the mounted police; and had volunteered for parachute training in the same brigade, before he joined SOE. Their wireless operator, Humphrey Macaré, was quite unlike either of them: physically much slighter, born at Bandoeng in 1922 and half-Javanese, he was the son of a railway inspector and had been conscripted into the Dutch navy – from a Bandoeng teachers' training college – as recently as July 1941. He was shy and keen.

Jan Hofstede ('Tomato') was a Dutch sailor, nearly twenty-four years old, who came from the large family – he had nine siblings – of a cattle dealer at Bilthoven. He showed promise both at Arisaig and at Beaulieu, and Rheam arranged a fortnight's special course for him and Steeksma on rail and telecommunications sabotage. He too had a foil, Peter Kamphorst, born as far back as 1894 at Ermelo, in farming country to the south-east of the Zuyder Zee, who had been a sergeant in the mounted police for nine years when Holland was invaded. He had only a limited command of English, but plenty of simple commonsense and patriotism. They too had a half-Indonesian wireless operator who had been a conscript sailor in the Dutch navy, the Sumatra-born Charles Christiaan Pouwels, whose father had worked in the telegraph office in Bandoeng. He had just turned nineteen.

Steeksma and Koolstra jumped together on 21/22 October 1942; Kamphorst went with them, and so did the thirty-year-old Michiel Pals ('Pumpkin'), another steady man from the Maréchaussée – a good talker, though not a man of much education – who was to have worked in the southern Netherlands wherever the secret army's leader (whoever that turned out to be) directed. Koolstra, Kamphorst and Pals had been friends and colleagues for years; they had all formed part of Queen Wilhelmina's escort out of Holland in May 1940.[239] Hofstede and the two young wireless operators, Macaré and Pouwels, followed three nights later.

Three nights later still, on 27/28 October, J. C. Dane ('Cucumber') and his W/T operator Jacob Bakker followed precisely in their footsteps. Dane was another recruit from the Maréchaussée, a twenty-five-year-old Protestant (Pals was a Roman Catholic) born near Terneuzen; he was highly thought of at Arisaig, and had recently married a wife in South Wales. (She bore him a daughter who never saw her father.) Bakker, also twenty-five, was a Batavian-born Dutch sailor, who made a much less favourable impact on the training staff; on their reports, N must have been short indeed of operators to take him on at all. These were two more tall men, each over six feet one. Dane had fought his way out in the summer of 1940, reaching England from Brest on 12 June. Bakker had escaped by trawler from IJmuiden in May 1942, acting as bodyguard to Arie de Vooys, who had master-minded Homburg's escape three months before. Dane was to have been the regional organiser in charge of sabotage in the three eastern provinces of Friesland, Groningen and Drenthe.

All these men left their dropping zone wearing German handcuffs.

Kaltenbrunner, who had taken over the leadership of the SD after Heydrich's death, reported gleefully to Himmler that, on the night of Dane's and Bakker's arrest, the Germans in Holland had collected eighteen tons of sabotage stores, at three different sites. De Jong comments on this report that it is a mark of N's remoteness from understanding what life in heavily populated and heavily policed Holland was like, that he should have supposed it possible for so

---

239. Rep, *op. cit.*, 217.

large a quantity of material to be spirited away out of sight in the few hours between dropping-time and dawn:[240] a fair comment. What could be done comparatively easily in France or Yugoslavia could hardly be dared in the Low Countries.

Through D/R, N's difficulties about getting someone back from Holland became known to Humphreys, who ran DF, SOE's western European escape section. In mid-1942 Humphreys found a dependable man who could be sent to run a land line from Belgium to southern France, and then extend it northward to serve Holland as well; ideally, he was to find a terminal also for a sea escape line on the Dutch, Belgian, or north French coast. He himself trained Alfred Schouten, a steady forty-year-old Flemish bank clerk, in the essentials of escape line work: these were caution, above all; reliance on priests, lawyers, minor civil servants, and a rigid system of passwords.

Schouten also had some training in boatwork. As he had a weak knee, he could not parachute and had to be sent in overland. He spent five horrible days and nights on a felucca, sailing from Gibraltar to the South of France,[241] and was received by DF's established 'Edouard' line, with the chief of which he stayed in Perpignan.[242] 'Edouard' went with him towards the demarcation line, but left him to cross it with a *passeur*; bad luck then intervened. Schouten's *passeur* saw him across the line, was paid 1,000 francs and said goodbye; the agent had not walked on another hundred yards before he was ambushed by a party of German customs officials, who had chosen that moment to hide behind a wall and pounce on the next passer-by. He had no satisfactory explanation for possessing two sets of papers, one French and one Belgian, in two different names; and was lucky to survive twenty-seven unspeakable months' hard labour at Oranienburg.[243]

It was a long time before Humphreys discovered he was missing. That ever-discreet staff officer sent a note to D/R on 19 November:

---

240. De Jong, *KdN*, ix(ii). 979.
241. MS note of 18 November 1942 by him in Clandestine Communications 27. Cp Richards, *op. cit.*, 569.
242. See Foot, *SOE in France*, 155.
243. His MS report, June 1945, in Clandestine Communications 27.

'I am extremely anxious that no Belgian Authority should know the real facts about Schouten's mission or where he has gone, as too many inexplicable things happen where the Belgians are concerned.'[244] DF therefore did not follow T section's drill of informing the Belgians in exile automatically about every agent dispatched.

The failure of Schouten's mission had an unhappy result for N as well as for DF section: for when N's repeated attempts to get an agent back from the Netherlands to report on current conditions came to nothing, the best that DF could do to help was, as we shall see, to provide an outlying 'Vic' line contact address in Paris.

Nobody in it ever wants to believe that a secret service can be completely taken in; but that is exactly what happened to SOE in Holland – for a time. Counter-espionage is much easier than espionage – as indeed one of the commentators remarked, when the time came to draw up a final account.[245] If the counter-espionage staff cover their tracks properly, they ought to be undetectable at the far end: this was how it turned out.

So four more N section agents found their way to Haaren at the end of November 1942, 'Mustard' and 'Broccoli' on the night of the 28/29th and 'Cress' and 'Chive' the night after. 'Mustard' was A. J. de Kruyff, Amsterdam-born in 1912, a quiet stonemason who had emigrated to South Africa in 1936, and had left his wife and baby son in Johannesburg when he enlisted in the Dutch army six years later. He too was supposed to reconnoitre possibilities for further sabotage, and to report them through 'Broccoli', his wireless operator, G. L. Ruseler, ten years his junior. Ruseler had been born in the Dutch East Indies – his father was a dry-dock technician at Batavia (now Jakarta) – and he came to SOE from six months as a sailor in the Dutch navy. He was not used to big cities, had indeed never been to Holland before;[246] and, again, his training reports suggest that N was still scraping the bottom of the barrel to find recruits.

As a survivor put it, who had seen only too much of the men who

244. Copy *ibid.*
245. Note by E. D. Stamp, 17 January 1945, 8, in Holland 16.
246. Rep, *op. cit.*, 219.

ran 'North Pole', 'German officers were indignant that such people were sent out to do such very important and dangerous work.'[247]

'Cress', H. J. Overes, another Amsterdammer, thirty-four years old, short, sturdy, and comradely in manner, had worked for seven years as a carpenter in South Africa. He mastered so completely the secret agent's gift for making himself unnoticeable that N section's historian, drawing up a list of the casualties of 'North Pole', forgot all about him.[248] He was to have helped to organise the secret army that was to grow out of the Plan for Holland; he had been a Dutch army NCO, so had some gifts for his task. He had been on the same Lysander course as Mooy.[249]

He and 'Chive' took off on the same night as 'Mustard' and 'Broccoli', but in a separate aircraft. All four had dined together at Gaynes Hall with Blizard, Snewing and Lieftinck. One of the two engines in 'Cress' and 'Chive's' Whitley became troublesome soon after take-off, and the pilot turned back. Bingham drove out to Gaynes Hall for the following night's farewell dinner, and after a brief telephone talk with London was able to reassure them that the other two had landed safely,[250] which, as far as it went, was perfectly true.

'Chive', who was 'Cress's' wireless operator, was John Bernard Ubbink, from Doesburg, on the IJssel east of Arnhem. He turned twenty-one a few days after SOE enlisted him, in May 1942; he was then described as an army sergeant, as which, for cover, he was dressed. He had been through the naval school at Delfzijl in 1936–40, and served as a junior officer in the captive Dutch merchant navy in the winter of 1940–1. He jumped ship in Stockholm, and reached England by way of Russia, Persia and India. He was trained at Gumley Hall, Ringway and Thame Park, but missed Beaulieu. He jumped – in plain clothes, of course – as a Dutch naval officer of the lowest grade. Poos collected him and his organiser. They were grilled, separately, for several days on end in the Binnenhof, and dispatched – drained of information – to Haaren, where they found 'Mustard' and 'Broccoli'.

---

247. Undated report by Ubbink on 'The Question Bingham', TSC in his PF.
248. His name does not appear in History cx.
249. War diary, xlviii(i). 60.
250. Report by Ubbink, 19 December 1943, TSC in his PF.

Untersturmführer Lahr, one of Schreieder's subalterns in the SD, interrogated Ubbink with a good deal of skill; persuading him – Lahr was by nine years the older man – that the Germans were completely informed about the whole of SOE's training and despatch arrangements. He quite convinced Ubbink, who after five days' recalcitrance told him everything he asked, codes and security checks included: 'it seemed the logical thing to do.'[251] Lahr's notional source in Baker Street had no real existence, but by this time the Germans had built up so big a fund of knowledge that the pretence of a well-placed spy carried conviction.

It was often said then – indeed, is still sometimes said today, in the teeth of the evidence – that there is but a single British secret service, of illimitable range and power. Several of N section's captured agents seem to have believed this; supposing the myth to be true, they cudgelled their brains for some devious yet rational explanation for their fate.

Only one solid benefit for the allied cause has ever surfaced. It appears that the ever-suspicious Hitler was disturbed enough by the reports that reached him during the winter of 1942–3 about SOE's attempts to work into the Low Countries and France to believe that a major allied invasion of that area might take place in 1943. His naval intelligence staffs were not competent to spot that there were still nowhere near enough allied landing craft for so vast a task; and towards safeguarding himself against this notional peril, he is supposed to have moved half-a-dozen divisions from the eastern to the western front.

Now a relief from the pressure of half-a-dozen divisions was no tremendous boon to the Red Army, which was trying to fend off almost two hundred; still, it was something. This small relief would have been quite enough to justify the sacrifice of a few score agents and a few score of their helpers, had SOE done it on purpose; as SOE did not.

Oddly enough, such divisional moves provided a bonus for both sides. The Germans concerned were vastly more comfortable; and the allies could feel, on balance, some relief. The almost inconceivably

---

251. De Jong, *KdN*, ix(ii). 980, tr.

intricate task of invasion would be a little harder still; yet the pressure on the eastern front, where the chances of war remained uncertain, would be a little less severe.

Hitler's order of 9 July 1942, with its specific mention of the southern coast of the Netherlands, shows how exercised the *Führer* was about a possible allied invasion, even that early; and shows also his readiness to move important units about, even at a critical stage in 'Barbarossa', his attack on the Soviet Union, when it was in its third week.[252]

---

252. Quoted by Captain S. W. Roskill in *Journal of the Royal United Services Institute* cix (February 1964), 28–9.

III

Dutch Catastrophes
1942–4

A pause eleven weeks long followed in N's drops of men; due not to suspicion, but to winter weather. His messages to Lauwers persisted in attempts to fix up a long-contemplated parachute drop into water; nothing came of this quickly. There were a few supply drops, but even these were hindered by storms; and, to simplify matters at their end, the Germans announced – and London believed – another notional casualty. Andringa was reported, falsely, to have died on 6 December from pneumonia contracted during a November night out at a reception committee.[1]

In Mooy's name, Giskes put up a plan for a Lysander landing on a new-built stretch of main road; this provided plenty of work for air and ground staff officers in England, while never coming near the stage of action.[2] N had hoped to use this means of inserting 'Asparagus' and extracting 'Kale'; he toyed too with a scheme for having an agent swim out to a seaplane in the Zuyder Zee,[3] an unpromising operation in midwinter.

In mid-February 1943 two SS men, never identified, nearly gave the whole ploy away. At a private dinner-party they had far too much to drink, and let out that they had helped arrest dozens of secret agents from England, with their weapons and stores, which kept on arriving. A Dutchman named Kik who was present at once passed this news on to Vorrink, who put it straightaway into a message to

---

1. War diary, xlviii(i). 54.
2. *Ibid.*, 60, 67.
3. *Ibid.*, 45–6.

London; but entrusted the message to the double agent van der Waals for dispatch, so it never got farther than Schreieder's desk.[4] Schreieder was furious that he could not identify and punish his subordinates.

All through the many months that the *Spiel* lasted, Schreider and Giskes remained aware that any slip, even quite a small one, on their part would be one too many. Robertson and Masterman, plying the same trade on the opposite side for over four times as long, were also perpetually aware of the same point: the enemy had to be taken in, not just once or twice, but all the time.

At this midwinter pause, it is time to recall that SOE did not develop its techniques for recording W/T operators' personal touch – called, or miscalled, fingerprinting – until the second half of 1943: too late to help the victims of the *Englandspiel.* Reception from western Europe was normally so bad that home station's operators had to strain their ears to the utmost to pick up any signal at all, let alone observe niceties of touch. All the same, every W/T operator was encouraged to believe that his or her touch on the key was distinctive. Certainly friends who had trained together got to know each others' touch; and even enemies, in the Y service that handled interceptions, got to recognise particular operators.[5] Now several of N section's captives worked their own sets, using texts laid before them by the Germans; affording nothing out of the ordinary to notice. When a victim was not ready to co-operate so far, an Orpo signals NCO stood in for him. May went on record: it was seldom necessary to listen to an N section operator more than thrice before he could be imitated perfectly.[6]

In any case, the sets available often sent such weak signals that most of the messages that SOE's home stations got from the field were more or less garbled. This in turn told against the usefulness of C's system of security checks, for accidental mistakes were as likely as deliberate ones.

4. De Jong, *KdN*, ix(ii). 960n.
5. Information from the author's sister, who spent the second half of the war as a rating in the WRNS, listening to Japanese submarines.
6. *Enq.*, iv B. 16; RIOD Doc. I-1103, typed report by May, 23 September 1946, 9.

There was one exception to this rule: by the autumn of 1942, traffic from the Netherlands seemed unusually clear. Marks said, forty years on, that he had developed doubts about Dutch traffic, and took time off from other work to go through the whole of what had passed, in both directions. He thus noticed that he had hardly ever had to call on his staff for a special effort to break an apparently indecipherable text from Holland: that traffic was almost word-perfect. He could see no technical reason why operators there should be working in less stress or discomfort than their colleagues in Norway, Denmark, Belgium, or France, whose traffic regularly arrived mangled. Was it possible that all the Dutch operators were under enemy control?[7]

He did not yet feel he had evidence solid enough to lay before the country section; and he knew how protective country section officers were always inclined to be about their own agents' reliability. But he managed, on his own initiative, to tamper with a message – that Bingham wanted cancelled, anyhow – to 'Spinach' so that it was indecipherable; and the lack of reaction from Holland convinced him that he was right.[8] Marks began by consulting Eric Heffer, whom Gubbins had recruited from the Ministry of Supply late in 1941; a suitable mentor, born in 1897, who had worked on intercept and decipher in mandated Iraq, and had a nose for SOE's sometimes intricate office politics. On Heffer's advice, he went to F. W. Nicholls,[9] the GSO1 (later head) of the signals section. Nicholls took him to see Gubbins, long his own personal friend.[10]

Gubbins enjoined on Nicholls and Marks complete silence, for the time being, except between themselves, on this subject; approved silence towards the country section; and directed that signals traffic should continue as usual.[11]

7. Conversation with him and (Sir) J. J. Astor, who had handled SAS signals in 1944–5, 14 November 1984; and his *Between Silk and Cyanide, passim*.
8. *Ibid.*, 204–9, 214–16.
9. See *DNB 1971–1980*, 629.
10. Wilkinson and Astley, *Gubbins and SOE*, 29.
11. Foot, *Holland at War*, 140–50; conversations with Marks, 22 January 1991 and 7 July 1995.

On 2 February 1943 the Germans had encountered their first crucial reverse since the battle of Britain, in their surrender at Stalingrad: proud as the British Commonwealth is of the victory at the second battle of El Alamein in the previous November, it must be admitted that a battle between two armies counted for less than the defeat of two army groups by three. On 18 February Gerbrandy called on Selborne to remark that his hitherto 'remarkably accurate' intelligence staff was 'now convinced that there was every chance of the German army collapsing within the next six weeks'; much to Queen Wilhelmina's concern, as she feared a 'premature explosion' of popular feeling in Holland, which might provoke ghastly reprisals.[12]

Early in 1943 N section took on an extra task, as travel agent for MI9, the escape service. Details were fixed between Blizard and Airey Neave, who had earned his place on 9's staff by a home run from Colditz. Neave wanted to start up a new escape line to run shot-down aircrew safely southwards out of the Netherlands, and thought he had found the ideal agent to take charge of it: Beatrice (Trix) Terwindt.

For what it may be worth, she – like Grace Darling – was a seventh child. Providence, or luck, looked after her: she was one of the five victims of 'North Pole' who were still alive at the war's end. She was born at Arnhem in 1911, to the Belgian wife of a Dutch father who ran a stone quarry; her family was comfortably off. She acquired fluent English and French at an English convent school in Bruges, and she also knew some German. She had been a KLM airline stewardess for some years, and the firm had found desk work for her when Dutch civil flying closed down in midwinter 1939–40.

She managed to walk out of Holland into Belgium, and out of Belgium into France in March 1942, with a young Dutch student. They got from Besançon into Switzerland at St Julien south of Geneva, running, helped by a customs guard who looked the other way. Thence she was allowed out to Lisbon, and so found a flight to England; where Derksema introduced her to Neave, and the rest followed.

---

12. Selborne to Churchill, with copy to Eden, 18 February 1943, TSC in Holland 1.

She took F section's paramilitary course at Wanborough Manor near Guildford, and spent a few days at one of the Beaulieu schools, where her 'very pleasant personality, quiet but forceful',[13] made its mark. She also did parachute training. She only stood a slender five feet six high, but was clearly a woman of capacity.

Early on 14 February 1943 she was dropped near Steenwijk, with the codename 'Chicory', and jarred herself in a heavy landing. A friendly Dutch reception committee chatted to her, and relieved her of her false identity card, describing it as bad. It came on to rain; they all went into a little shed.

As far back as 18 January, London in its 159th message to Lauwers had mentioned that 'Chicory' would be female,[14] but the Germans too had obsessions about security, and word had not reached Poos and Slagter; they were surprised to find themselves talking to a lady. Nevertheless, they coaxed out of her the address of her next secret contact. London, they explained, was often out of date with its addresses, and they could not take the responsibility of letting her go onward until they had made a check for her. London had told her to follow her reception committee's advice for the first twenty-four hours, so she complied: it was a shoe shop in The Hague belonging to C. T. J. Smit.

Then, brusquely, someone behind her threw a blanket over her head. She thought she was having her nerve tested, and told him not to play silly jokes; whereupon she was handcuffed.

Her training as an air hostess, prepared for sudden shocks, now stood her in good stead. She said nothing more she should not, through three days' and nights' continuous cross-questioning, during which Schreieder played the part of the soft man politely, alternating with a hard man who did not go beyond hard words.[15] The Germans did not discover that she did not belong to SOE. Smit, promptly arrested, also held firm; though he and a friend caught with him were shot next year, and another friend was murdered in Neuengamme.[16]

---

13. Typed and signed report of 24 January 1943 in her PF.
14. War diary, xlviii(i). 62.
15. Airey Neave, *Saturday at MI9* (Hodder & Stoughton, 1969), 205–13.
16. De Jong, *KdN*, ix(ii). 984.

Two packages had been dropped with Trix Terwindt. Lauwers's set reported her safe arrival, in his 124th message, on the 17th; but 'said that only one package, containing sets, had been recovered'. London duly arranged for a replacement package to be sent to her via de Haas, who was also – also quite untruly – believed to be safe.[17]

As nothing at all happened to develop her intended link, Neave realised that she must have become a casualty, but knew no details until the war in Europe was over. Word got through to him by August 1943 – May let it out[18] – that she had been arrested on arrival.[19]

Before ever she left London, Neave warned her against two men named Poos and Slagter – the very men into whose hands she fell.[20] It would be interesting to know how Neave knew, and whether he told SOE.

The survival intact – it is beautifully typed – of N section's war diary from July 1942 to December 1943, 160 single-spaced foolscap pages long, confounds those who maintain that the vast gaps in SOE's archive record were created to obscure past misdeeds. It now makes pathetic reading; and makes clear how entirely N and his superiors were taken in by Giskes and Schreieder. Extra care to be taken over 'Eureka' sets, to make sure they never fall into the wrong hands; special arrangements for the safe lodging of particular incomers; gentle rebukes for using single transposition in a code that demanded double, followed by the dispatch of a new code, complete with all transposition instructions; anniversary congratulations for Taconis and Lauwers when they completed a year in the field in November 1942; congratulations early in 1943 from Gubbins to Blizard on six months' excellent work; report from Rowlandson to Marshall-Cornwall in February 1943 that the 1,070 picked men for Phase A of the Plan for Holland are now *en poste*, and discussions with de Bruyne about what should be developed next; there is a whole clandestine cloud-cuckooland.[21]

---

17. War diary, xlviii(i). 71–2.
18. RIOD, Doc. I-1103, 21.
19. *Enq.*, iv A. 174–5.
20. Rep, *Englandspiel,* 246–8.
21. War diary, xlviii(i). *passim.*

This at least can be urged on N's behalf: he had sent several missions in separately, blind, in the spring of 1942, and had no idea how deftly they had all been run together by the competent police work of Giskes, Schreieder and Poos. Those he imagined to be at work separately were in hard fact all in prison together, apart from Dessing, who was on the run and out of touch.

N section and the RAF, unaware of Marks's doubts, sent seven more agents into the Netherlands later in the February moon, and seven more in March. All, at de Bruyne's insistence, went to reception committees; all, consequently, fell straight into enemy hands.

Three went on the night of 16/17 February: 'Endive' supposedly to 'Beetroot', who had – supposedly again – taken over from 'Turnip', and 'Radish' and 'Parsley A' supposedly to 'Catarrh'. 'Endive' was Klaus van der Bor, born in 1913 into a peasant family at Barneveld, east of Amersfoort; noted under training for the rude directness of his manner, as well as his genial heart.[22] He was an electric cable supervisor by trade, and had been trained in electrical sabotage; he had also had some clandestine experience already. He had been working for a large ardent group of amateur saboteurs and information-collectors, ill organised and full of double agents; one of whom, a German subaltern called Helmut Wetske, he had himself assassinated at Renswoude west of Ede.[23] As a result, van der Bor's description had been circulated all over Holland in the police gazette:[24] a weak start for a secret agent.

'Radish' and 'Parsley A' had a less usual journey than the rest: instead of dropping into a field, they dropped into water, and swam ashore. Wooler, SOE's parachuting expert,[25] had proved by personal experiment that one could drop into water and survive; for months past, N had been plotting to use this technique, and after many chops and changes – including the melting of winter ice – 'Catarrh' had been able to assure him (however falsely) that there was an unguarded strip of coast on the western side of the Zuyder Zee, just east of Hoorn.

---

22. Typed chit of 30 October 1942 in his PF.
23. RVPS report, 22–23 July 1942, 7; TS in *ibid.*
24. De Jong, *KdN*, ix(ii). 1030.
25. See Foot, *SOE in France*, 82.

On 18 February N expressed to Lauwers 'gratitude and admiration for the skill and patience that was shown in arranging for this most difficult operation';[26] Poos and Slagter had indeed had to work out a different drill.

'Radish' was Cornelis van Hulsteyn, a thirty year old born at Terneuzen, but brought up at the opposite end of the country beyond Groningen; his father was a protestant pastor. He had worked in Johannesburg as an architect; and had been a sergeant in the army in exile for a year before he joined SOE. Like Overes, he was to work on Phase B of the Plan for Holland, developing the bigger secret army that was to reinforce the 1,070 saboteurs for Phase A, supposed already *en poste.*

With him went C. C. Braggaar, an Amsterdam-born ship's officer, a few months younger than van den Bor, who had shipped petrol for Shell out of Rotterdam and knew about Dutch canals. SOE had trained him as a wireless operator, and he was to send for the OD.

He, and the next two agents to be sent, both had intelligence tasks also. SIS, not yet suspicious of SOE's teams in Holland, had no agents ready itself, and asked SOE to stand in for it.[27] Braggaar was to take up Jongelie's mission of liaison with the intelligence branch of the OD.

Both he and van Hulsteyn were quietly handcuffed as they stepped ashore.

Jan Christiaan Kist ('Hockey' – the first of the games codenames to go into the field) was dropped two nights later. He had worked as a classics master and a librarian in Leyden, his birthplace in 1913. After Holland's defeat he had some contact with the secret newspaper *Vrij Nederland,* and decided to escape: it took him ten months to reach Scotland via Gibraltar. By the time he joined SOE, early in November 1942, he had become a subaltern in the Dutch army. He was spared Arisaig, but had had three short spells at Beaulieu. He too was to work, replacing Jongelie, with the intelligence branch of the OD.

He boasted to Schreieder, shortly after capture, that he still had the

---

26. War diary, xlviii(i). 72.
27. *Enq.,* iv A. 506; de Jong, *KdN,* ix(ii). 981n.

worst hangover of his life, having drunk an English major under the table at his farewell dinner the night before.[28]

With him went Gerard van Os ('Broadbean'), born in 1914, a regular sergeant pilot in the Dutch air force before the war. His father kept a garage at Bloemendaal just south of Ijmuiden. He had been trained as a saboteur, as well as going through Arisaig and Beaulieu, and one of his tasks was to reconnoitre targets for the Plan for Holland teams, before training men in how to tackle them. Moreover, Schreieder dug out of him – for he and Kist were of course arrested on their DZ – that he was to collect intelligence from CID agents in Holland, and dispatch it to England by pigeon.[29] As a result of what they dug out of van Os, the Germans were able to roll up the 'Wim' intelligence group in Apeldoorn six months later.[30] Van Os and Kist both took with them Belgian, French, Swiss and Spanish money to pass on to travellers, as well as the usual supply of florins.[31] Moreover – trouble came of this – van Os was also to set up a chain of safe houses to form the Dutch end of a working escape line; down which, if all else failed, 'Kale' could return.[32]

The next effort, beyond Schouten's mission,[33] of DF, the escape section, to help N was made through van Os. It also miscarried, and brought more dangers with it; as will shortly become clear.

'Hockey' and 'Broadbean' each took a wireless operator, the brothers, Pieter and Willem van der Wilden ('Tennis' and 'Golf'). Willem, the elder, was a builder like their father, and had worked as such in South Africa; Pieter, born in 1914 and four years younger, was an artisan-bricklayer. Pieter had left a wife in Pretoria; Willem's wife was a clerk in van Kleffens's foreign office in exile in London. All these four agents were arrested as they landed.

The brothers' name turned out unfortunate; for, about the time they were dropped, the double agent van der Waals made a disastrous incursion into the high command of Dutch political resistance using

---

28. Schreieder, 296.
29. *Ibid.*, 296–7.
30. *Enq.*, iv B. 52.
31. *Ibid.*
32. Notes in History cx, under 1943; war diary, xlviii(i). 82.
33. See page 148.

the cover name, confusible with their real surnames, of 'Anton de Wilde'.[34]

Before we deal with this, it is just worth note that by March 1943 the Dutch government in exile had dropped its attempt to deal with the OD through SOE's agents, which had been neatly deflected by the Germans.[35] Instead, it was in touch with the OD through BI; one of whose operators once committed the enormity of staying on the air for three and half hours at a stretch[36] – clear enough proof that the Germans either controlled the OD, or regarded it as of no importance. Schreieder established which: he remarked in passing that another branch of the SD kept constantly up to date with the OD's activity.[37]

The Germans' deception of SOE now had a marked impact on Dutch politics. Queen Wilhelmina herself, in all innocence, had set in train the previous autumn an inquiry that now led to trouble.

Discussions with her were never easy, on points on which she was not fully informed. Gerbrandy, lunching with the Blands on 13 April, complained in private of the awkwardnesses he had with her, and mentioned that 'his own position was like that of Mr Gladstone with Queen Victoria. He said it was very difficult to deal with a woman who had been a Queen since she was a child and had never been contradicted. He and the Queen had "terrible rows"';[38] but he had at least found that she would respond calmly to written argument.

She was always conscious of the need to find out as much as she could about her country. So, in November 1942, she had asked Meyer Sluyser, who ran the Flitspuit, for help. She knew Sluyser must have friends in SOE; and invited him to see whether, through these friends, he could put her in touch with Vorrink, the socialist leader in occupied Holland. Sluyser passed this on to Dawson of N

---

34. The confusion became actual on 15 December 1943: appx IVa to 'Dutch investigation report' of that date in Holland 19, 2(TS).
35. See pages 30–1.
36. *Enq.*, ivA. 405–8.
37. Schreieder, 334.
38. Bland to Eden, 15 April 1943, in FO 371/34526.

section; and said that his old friend and colleague, Levinus van Looi, would certainly know where Vorrink was hiding. (Dessing had not yet reported that he and van Looi had worked together.) Sluyser also said that van Looi could in turn be reached through another journalist, Wins, whose address in Amsterdam he gave.

On 12 November N told van Hemert to follow this up, authenticating himself with a photograph of Sluyser's daughter Maryke which he had taken to Holland with him. Dessing had taken a copy of the same photograph, and left it behind with a friend; N broke his promise only to use it once.[39]

The Germans received the message for van Hemert, as a matter of course; equally, of course, Schreieder told van der Waals to take the photograph and try his luck.

His luck held. Wins and his wife, both Jews, had found life under nazi anti-Jewish rules unbearable, and had arranged to go underground. Van der Waals met them the day before they did so, and convinced them that he was a recently parachuted agent from England;[40] they postponed going into hiding, and put him in touch with van Looi, who came far enough out of it to meet him.

The photograph alone was not enough to convince van Looi. He asked for a broadcast from Radio Oranje, including the names he and Vorrink had used when writing (through a Portuguese address) to Sluyser in the previous year. Radio Oranje obliged, sending on 23 November: 'Here is a message for Fia and Koert: be trustful.'[41] Van der Waals thus met Vorrink, to whom he brought presents of tea, chocolate, cigarettes and small arms – all from SOE's captured drops.

Giskes and Schreieder played this big fish carefully.[42] They transmitted to London, mainly on the 'Cucumber' W/T channel, several long messages from Vorrink about politics, including some outspoken passages on the deportation of Jews. (Did N not notice how much 'Cucumber' endangered himself by staying on the air so long?) Late in February 1943 Vorrink asked for a set of his own. Through

---

39. De Jong, *KdN*, ix(ii). 969; cp *Enq.*, iv A. 471, and Rep, *op. cit.*, 221.
40. Rep, *op. cit.*, 222.
41. '*Hier is een bericht voor Fia en Koert: heb vertrouwen*' – de Jong, *KdN*, ix(ii). 974. N's war diary is silent on this point.
42. Cp Schreieder, 279–90, and Giskes, *op. cit.*, 115–16.

'de Wilde', Schreieder supplied one from his by now ample store. It broke down after the first message it sent. Vorrink did not know that it worked, not to England but to an Orpo set at The Hague.[43]

In mid-March 1943 Schreieder brought off a run of arrests, with the help of van der Waals, who had wormed his way, through Vorrink, into the confidence of several resistance leaders. On the 9th he caught Pahud de Mortanges, whose group – unconnected with SOE – had just sunk a minesweeper at Rotterdam. Its leader rose to the bait of an offer to supply SOE's limpet mines.[44]

Next morning the Germans arrested Kees Dutilh, who ran a busy intelligence group;[45] and, that afternoon, J. E. van Tyen, a director of Fokker's. Van Tyen believed he was on his way to an aircraft bound for England, and had a suitcase full of espionage material with him.[46] None of these three men survived, nor did several of their friends, and a source of van Tyen's in the Luftwaffe, traceable through one of the reports in the suitcase, was executed as well.[47]

That month, at least London advised 'Cucumber II' to paraphrase Vorrink's telegrams, to safeguard his code. N passed on to him an inquiry from the Dutch government in exile about who belonged to a National Committee that Vorrink had reported which was preparing inside Holland the queen's orderly return. Van der Waals carried the message. Vorrink gave him all six names, his own included.

The names were passed to London; but the Germans now struck. On 1 and 2 April they arrested all six of the committee, and over a hundred of their friends and relations.[48] Vorrink, his brother Adrian, van Looi and almost fifty others were taken to Haaren, where they were kept out of sight and sound of the 'North Pole' prisoners.[49] All but one of this political party survived the war.[50]

---

43. De Jong, *KdN*, ix(ii). 974–5.
44. Schreieder, 299–312.
45. There is a moving biography of Dutilh: Floris B. Bakels, *Wachter op de morgen*.
46. Schreieder, 315–19; de Jong, *KdN*, ix(ii). 974–5.
47. *Ibid.*
48. *Ibid.*, and war diary, xlviii(i). 80–1.
49. *Enq.*, iv B, 22–3.
50. Schreieder, 353.

A little news of this was allowed to seep through to N. On 7 April Lauwers's set reported, as if from de Haas, that Buizer had been 'surprised in The Hague and disappeared' on the 2nd; that van der Giessen suspected treachery; and that van Rietschoten said that Vorrink 'had also disappeared'.[51]

The enemy also seized the occasion to indicate that 'Hockey' was operating untroubled, except by 'Tennis's' inability to make his set work. Notionally, 'Tennis' was lent a set by 'Chive'; and, over it, arranged in the first week of April another dud broadcast by Radio Oranje, notionally to establish 'Hockey's' standing 'with important people'; which was duly done. 'Tennis' expressed prompt gratitude.[52] The same trick was played, yet again, through 'Parsley' as late as Michaelmas Day.[53]

The Germans' success in stifling early military resistance in Holland is only too well known. Outside Holland, it is less appreciated that by those arrests on 1 and 2 April 1943 they decapitated civilian resistance as well. Like the Hydra against which Hercules fought, civilian resistance instantly grew new heads, which Himmler, who was no Hercules, could not master; but this was a lamentable check, due to SOE's incompetence.

Meanwhile, N had sent in three more men, intended to help organise and train the secret army in Phase B of the Plan for Holland. 'Cucumber' carried all the traffic; London supposed 'Kale' to be in charge of the DZ. Exceptionally, this was to be a drop without a moon, guided by 'Rebecca' and 'Eureka'. Three men, all instructors, and seven containers, duly went in together on the night of 9/10 March; 'Cucumber' came through with his forty-fifth message on the 11th to report their safe arrival. Schreieder, to his annoyance, had to stay away from the drop, as he was busy with his run of arrests.[54]

These three men were 'Seakale', 'Kohlrabi' and 'Sprout'. 'Seakale' was Pieter Arendse, a thirty-year-old carpenter from The Hague who had been a sergeant in the Dutch army before the war, and seemed

---

51. War diary, xlviii(i). 89.
52. *Ibid.*, 96.
53. *Ibid.*, 144.
54. War diary, xlviii(i). 83; Schreieder, 314.

both gifted and reliable to his instructors at Arisaig. De Jong counts him as a wireless operator.[55] Boogaart ('Kohlrabi'), a few months younger, came from the village of Graauw, just inside the Dutch border on the left bank of the Scheldt, and had had nine years in the Dutch navy – rising to petty officer – before Holland entered the war. 'Sprout', the third Pieter in the party, also a regular sailor, was a tough called Dourlein, who was noted under training for the ferocity of his temper when roused. He came from Walcheren, where he had been born in 1918. After seven years in the navy, he had joined the mounted police in 1941; but had to flee when during a brawl he hit a member of the NSB so hard that the fellow died. He too managed to slip away in a small motor boat, and had spent over a year as a police corporal in the Dutch navy in exile before he volunteered for SOE.[56]

They had had two previous attempts at dropping, one in January and one in February; and an unexpected effect of dropping them without a moon was that they fell into a fir wood: troublesome, but workable, for Poos and Slagter. This DZ, between Ermelo and Putten – called number four in Baker Street – lay north-east of Amersfoort and WNW of Apeldoorn on the western side of the Veluwe; conveniently close to Driebergen for the Germans. These agents too found themselves in handcuffs before they had been at all long on Dutch soil; they too, after prolonged interrogation, joined the rest in Haaren.

It is worth a moment's pause to consider how they might have tried to behave during their relentless questioning.

J. C. A. Verloop, otherwise known as Leo de Bakker, born at The Hague in 1909, seaman, ex-Foreign Legionary and compulsive liar, managed under MI5 interrogation in the autumn of 1944 to provide a mass of unessential information; 'forgetting' exact names, exact addresses, the crucial points that might have been of use. The prisoners of the *Englandspiel* might have made much more use of this technique, well known in the subversive world; as a notorious example, the later nineteenth-century Irish 'lost' the accounts of Michael Davitt's Land League.

---

55. De Jong, *KdN*, ix(ii). 984.
56. Accounts of his escape and of his wartime naval service in his *Inside North Pole*.

In lapidary inscriptions, Dr Johnson once told Boswell, a man is not upon oath;[57] no more is he on oath when under interrogation. Unluckily for themselves and the cause they had volunteered to serve, North Pole's victims failed to take this in: they seem to have made hardly any attempts to mislead their interrogators. Even if they did try to do so, they could easily be undone, by more compliant comrades in captivity; who felt themselves compelled to tell the truth.

Here is a point to Lauwers's credit: that though he seems to have provided the Germans with an account nearly twenty pages long of the SOE training he underwent, he was vague about exact places and found himself unable to recall a single instructor's name.[58] Not all his fellow prisoners were anything like as discreet.

The prisoners who talked produced a cumulative impact: the pile of data in German hands got bigger and bigger, with less and less happy results for later victims. When the interrogator could describe the colour of the wallpaper in a Beaulieu classroom, and distinguish which of the staff there wore glasses, and which wore moustaches, which smoked cigarettes and which preferred a pipe, it was not easy for a newcomer to resist the belief that All was Known. No one seems to have succeeded with the simple counter, 'If you know so much, why bother me?'

Only those who have crossed that grim strait could ever describe – none, I believe, has – what it feels like to pass suddenly from believing one is *un dur des durs* to knowing one is *un lache des laches*.

It was through language that the first alarm was sounded in Baker Street at country section level: in April 1943, the same month as the overlooked report about Andringa and Dessing from Berne.[59]

In Holland, as elsewhere, there were then not enough wireless operators in the field – even notionally – to service each organiser separately; one operator often had to work for two organisers and

---

57. In 1775: L. F. Powell and G. B. Hill (eds), *Boswell's Life of Johnson* (1934), ii. 407.
58. Gestapo report of 14 January 1944 emanating from KGB files (see page 514); photocopied TS.
59. See page 126.

might have to handle more.[60] The Germans in charge of 'Kale' wanted – as part of their playing with Vorrink – to send nine long reports, for which they used, conformably to advice 'Kale' had been given before he left London, 'Cucumber II's' reserve poem.

Now 'Cucumber II' – Bakker – had been allowed to have a reserve poem in Dutch, to make quite sure that he remembered it. When the first message using this poem-code reached England, it could not at first be decoded.

Normal service routine, in such a case, was to ask for a repeat; not SOE's routine. The decoding staff never forgot that they worked, in reasonable ease and comfort, for operators who might be in acute danger; so they did their best to try every conceivable alternative before asking operators to put themselves at further risk by a repeat. In this case Bakker's poem included the word PRIJS, meaning price or praise; if it was spelt in the German fashion, PREIS, the code was soluble.

On such tiny points the fate of networks, indeed of kingdoms, can turn: 'For want of a nail, the shoe was lost.' In this case the warning went unheeded, though not unmarked; mainly because of the goose-swan syndrome – nobody but Marks could bring himself to envisage the worst case. Harvey, an expert lent by MI5 to SOE's special security section, got all the data he asked for from N, and drew up a paper nearly 5,000 words long on 'Bill and the OD', in which he included this odd spelling among other items; but attached no importance to it: because the agent had made the same mistake under training.[61]

Years afterwards, under cross-questioning by the British after his eventual release, Lauwers remembered that he had once, unnoticed by the Germans, slipped a German spelling into a code, and wondered whether doing so had done any good.[62]

All unconscious of the N agents' doom, SOE's planning staff and

---

60. Foot, *SOE in France*, 309–10, reports the case of a single operator working for twenty-three different agents in or near Paris. He did not survive, but fell victim to a different indiscretion.
61. 8–9 July 1943, in Holland 18; page 9 of TS. Cp Marks (who names Harvey), *op. cit.*, 335–41.
62. 30 May 1945, in his PF.

Bingham went ahead with discussing how the Plan for Holland was to develop. Bingham pointed out that the Dutch had only produced a dozen men, out of the five dozen who would be needed, to implement Phase B; and proposed the name of Phase C for 'the general rising of those members of the Orde Dienst not detailed for special tasks' in Phases A and B. De Bruyne was reluctant to release any more men until he could give his government 'more specific information as to the work they were to do'.[63]

Gubbins took the chair at an Anglo-Dutch meeting on 20 April, at which it was agreed that work was to start at once on plans to preserve Rotterdam's port facilities from enemy demolition; in which Rear-Admiral Taylor, SOE's D/Navy, took a willing hand.[64] On 8 May Gubbins sent Bingham a fresh directive: N section had so far restricted itself to *insaisissable* sabotage, but must now become more aggressive. It was to attack U-boat and fuel oil targets, canals and railways, bituminous (but not domestic) coal mines, shipbuilding yards working for the Germans, and other factories helping the enemy war effort – in that order of priority – without harming the local population, and if possible without using arms.[65]

On the night of 21/22 April 1943 N again sent a parachutist into water to swim ashore: at the same beach that van Hulsteyn and Braggaar had used in February. This agent, 'Lacrosse', was A. J. Wegner, a twenty-eight-year-old merchant seaman with a high forehead and green eyes, trained to be a secret army organiser (and dispatched to Holland a month too early by error in the section history). He had broken an ankle – hence the need to drop him into water – but pilot error put him down on the beach, where he was arrested.[66] He was so recalcitrant under interrogation that he was more roughly treated than was the SD's usual style with new arrivals on controlled sets. After some torture, he too succumbed obediently.

On the same night, to a separate DZ inland, the RAF dropped another pair of agents, Ivo van Uytvanck ('Gherkin') and F. W. Rouwerd ('Netball'). Van Uytvanck, almost six foot four tall, long an

---

63. War diary, xlviii(i). 87, April 1943.
64. *Ibid.*, 87–8.
65. *Ibid.*, 99.
66. TSC in his PF of 10 December 1943, in French: provenance unclear.

orphan, was almost twenty-five years old. Born at Bussum, east of Amsterdam, he had been working for some years as a secretary in South Africa, till called up into the Dutch army in January 1942. He had been trained as a railway saboteur, after he had volunteered for SOE, and was to have passed his knowledge on to the secret army. Rouwerd, five years older, had also been called up in South Africa early in 1942; he had left a wife in Pretoria. He had been a carpenter. His father had died when he was a boy of two in The Hague. He was a wireless operator, intended by N to provide communications for the secret army; but he and van Uytvanck were, as had become usual, arrested by their reception committee.

Meanwhile, 'Broadbean's' mission to set up an escape line had caused a seepage of German influence southwards out of Holland, that enabled a degree of enemy penetration – not as deep as they probed in Holland, but a degree – into both F, the independent French section of SOE, and the smaller, more discreet DF section, which dealt in escapes.

DF, one of the most efficient sections in SOE, built up in 1942 an agents' escape line – codenamed 'Vic' after Victor Gerson its originator[67] – which ran from Paris through Lyons, Perpignan and Figueras to Barcelona.[68] Most of its staff were, like its organiser, of Jewish descent; most of its safe houses in France were provided by members of the Ligue Internationale Contre l'Antisémitisme. Gerson, like Humphreys, his section commander, was a fanatic for security; one of his safest arrangements was that his safe houses were dead ends. Once a passenger arrived there, he was stuck: he could not move on till a courier came to fetch him.

For eighteen months the 'Vic' line worked smoothly, moving F and RF (Gaullist) agents and the occasional lucky shot-down airman across France and Catalonia. In the summer of 1943 Gerson, on one of his occasional visits to London, agreed with Humphreys that he might run an extension to Brussels; and in mid-September DF was asked to pass to N the address of a safe house in Paris.[69] When he did so, DF worked 'on the assumption, not that the Dutch line itself was

---

67. See M. R. D. Foot, *Six Faces of Courage* (Eyre Methuen, 1978), 75–88.
68. Clandestine Communications 21 to 24.
69. DFB to N, 16 September 1943, TSC in *ibid.* 23.

German operated, but that it would almost certainly be passing very "hot" bodies – i.e. bodies that were certainly blown and that might be German agents.'[70] The safe house, therefore, was as usual a dead end.

N passed the address on, in all innocence, to 'Broadbean'. It was 12 rue Peclet, not far from the Gare Montparnasse, the home of two maiden ladies called Fredin. Theirs was the door opposite the lift, on the sixth floor. If they happened to be out, one could try the door on the left on the same floor, Madame de Laprade's. At either door, the password '*Je viens de la part d'Alexandre*' should evoke the reply, '*Vous voulez dire Alexandre le Grand.*'

Before 'Broadbean' got this 'Vic' address, the Abwehr had already begun some degree of penetration into 'Vic's' working area. In May 1943 Christmann, purporting to be Dutch, turned up in Paris with a German companion in tow, who purported to be Dutch also. (Christmann was sent on this journey because Schreieder and Giskes thought him less likely to desert than van der Waals.)[71] They strode with little effort into the heart of the 'Prosper' circuit, and returned on 10 June, ostensibly for Christmann's companion to be taken to a Lysander. He was – apparently accidentally – arrested instead;[72] Christmann thus acquired merit, as a worthy if unlucky escape linesman, with several French resisters. But we must return to Holland.

On 21/22 May SOE's contributions in manpower to the *Englandspiel* came close to an end, with the dropping of 'Polo', 'Croquet' and 'Squash' – all three in a stick, with seven containers – at the third of N section's four regular dropping zones. It was not only N section that was making mistakes. This aircraft was also carrying seven containers for a different DZ, and dropped one of them by accident a mile short of this one: 'Cucumber' reported, in mock distress, that it could not be found.[73] An extra S-phone was supplied for each site, as well as the usual small arms and explosives.

---

70. Note by R. A. Warden, *ibid.*
71. Schreieder, 251–2.
72. Full account in appx IV B of Dutch investigation report of 15 December 1943, TS in Holland 19; in Foot, *SOE in France*, 312–4.
73. On 22 May 1943: war diary, xlviii(i). 105.

'Polo' was A. B. Mink, son of a marine sergeant, born at Den Helder in 1918, who had become a sergeant himself in the Dutch coastal artillery before the war; had had a brief spell as a customs officer south of Eindhoven, during the occupation; and had walked out through Belgium and France, reaching England by way of Curaçao (where he had a brother-in-law), Cuba, New York and Canada. 'Croquet', O. W. de Brey, had come out across France with him; and though three years younger, and from a rather different social layer – he had been studying mechanics at Delft – shared Mink's doubts about the competence of the Dutch clandestine authorities; both were anxious to come under the command of the British instead. 'Squash', L. M. Punt, just Mink's age, had also been a sergeant in the pre-war Dutch army; and had also taken several months to cross France.

De Jong describes him as a 'marconist'[74] – that is, a W/T operator – but there is no indication in his file that he ever did any W/T training: his schools are listed – Brede Hall, Arisaig, Manchester, Beaulieu and finally Gaynes Hall. De Jong's eighteenth line for the *Englandspiel* can therefore be dismissed as a myth; as if seventeen were not seventeen more than enough.

It is necessary to reiterate that a great many of the captured agents said a lot more than they should have done, in strict security theory. Indeed it is easy enough to suppose in retrospect that part of the blame for the disaster rests on them. So it does: part of it. Yet those who seek to condemn them must remember how tight a fix they were in. Dourlein tried to hold out against his German interrogator; who simply remarked that if, by refusing to speak, he compelled his enemies to put him up against a wall, 'we just send a telegram to England that you have been arrested by the Germans and no one will be any the wiser'.[75] Against this strength of pressure, only a hero of heroes could have thought of trying to hold out by remaining quite silent.

Yet Dourlein, though he had talked, remained a resourceful prisoner, looking out at least for a chance to pass word out about what was happening; and found one.

---

74. *KdN*, ix(ii). 986.
75. BSS/G to AD/P, 10 January 1944, in SOE Holland 21, quoting a report made by Dourlein to a Dutch official at Lerida, on his way through Spain; translator unknown.

The *Englandspiel* prisoners at Haaren were kept on an upper floor, under strict guard; other prisoners, on the ground floor, were less completely hemmed in. Dourlein made contact – by tapping in morse code on the heating pipes – with a merchant marine captain called Quant, in the cell below the one he shared with Boogaart; this officer managed to smuggle a message out.[76] In it Dourlein gave his real name, which his reception committee had wormed out of him; it got mutilated in transit. Boogaart, fearing reprisals on his family, gave the nickname by which he had been known at one of SOE's schools, because of all his seafaring stories: Drake.

De Jong traces the circumbendibus through which the message passed, reaching at last P. J. Six, the Chief of Staff of the OD. Six was a nobleman – a jonkheer – whose cover was that he cared a lot about horse-riding; his secret identity was known to few.[77] He passed the message on to MI6 on 10 June 1943 in these words: 'For Col. de Bruin eight parachutists among them Doulin and Drake arrested weeks ago code password friend Marius known.'[78] Atmospherics transmitted 'Drake' into what decoded as 'Arabc', and 'friend' – in English in the original – as 'vriend', the same word in Dutch. Such were inter-service jealousies in London that almost a fortnight elapsed before copies were sent to de Bruyne and to Bingham on the 23rd. De Bruyne at once spotted 'de Bruin' as himself and 'Doulin' as Dourlein, but was baffled (as well he might have been) by 'Arabe'. A check in SIS's signals office changed 'Arabe' to 'Drake'; this still meant nothing to de Bruyne, or to Bingham, or to anybody else he asked about it in N section (he must by accident have left out Boogaart's conducting officer).

Bingham at least understood the reference to 'Marius': he had told a few of his agents, Dourlein among them, that they could authenticate themselves to British or Dutch secret authorities in Switzerland, if they got that far, by saying, 'I am a friend of Marius.'

De Bruyne got Somer to tell Six that his message was unintelligible and to ask for more details. Six riposted: 'Message is from Haren

---

76. Rep, *op. cit.*, 258–60.
77. Schulten, *Verzet in Nederland,* 128.
78. '*Voor Kol.de Bruin acht parachutisten waaronder Doulin en Drake weken geleden gearresteerd code slagwoord* friend *Marius bekend*': de Jong, *KdN,* ix(ii). 993, tr.

must be enough for Colonel de B we know nothing more.'[79] Six may have known that the Haaren seminary had been taken over by the Germans as a prison, but was not going to waste precious secret wireless time saying so; to Bingham and de Bruyne it meant no more than 'Drake' did.

Bingham had a separate worry, about language. He minuted to Brook two days later that 'slagwoord', used for 'password' in Six's earlier telegram, was a word no Dutchman would normally use, which 'looks like a literal translation from the German "Schlagwort"'.[80] He thought it possible indeed that the Germans were running a major group of networks from the Netherlands to London, but supposed this group to form a penetrated wing of the OD, which was working to MI6 through a couple of sets C had had sent to Delfzijl from Sweden during the previous winter (now familiar in the literature in Dutch as the *Sweedse weg*[81]). OD's military traffic, he pointed out, 'though interesting never contains anything which either is not known, or the Germans would not want us to know'; while much of the rest was vague or even inaccurate.[82] This was sound reasoning by Bingham, but incomplete: he did not take in that it applied to his own section's traffic too.

In MI6, doubts about SOE's security in Holland had by now become serious. On 9 June Sporborg had a talk with Inglis, the head of Air Ministry Intelligence, who 'raised the point that "C" had written to him saying that a relatively recent incident in Holland had confirmed the VCSS [Dansey]'s suspicions that the Germans knew all about our work in Holland, and in fact almost had it under control.'[83] One of the reports that made Dansey's antennae twitch reached SOE, from SIS, on 9 June also. It came through MI9,[84] and originated with Flying Officer Clow of 138 squadron, who had been shot down on 28 March. He testified that his air gunner had

---

79. *Ibid.*, 994, tr: '*Bericht is uit Haren moot voor Kolonel de B voldoende zijn ons niet naders bekent*'.
80. N to D/R, TS 25 June 1943 in Holland 28.
81. *Enq.*, iv A. 174–96
82. As last note but one.
83. V/CD to AD/E, copies to CD and A/CD [Boyle], TSC in Holland 21.
84. For the method, see Foot and Langley, *MI9*, appx II.

been shown a chart of his track, and that the Germans understood SOE's simple three-red-torches reception committee signalling system.[85] Hinsley expounds SIS's conviction in the official history: 'from the summer of 1943 it was known [a strong phrase] that the Germans had penetrated the SOE's Dutch network since March 1942'.[86] Yet SIS then got on so badly with SOE that certainty took months to spread from the older body to the younger; and SIS's preoccupation with secrecy was such that not a word was said yet either to the JIC or the chiefs of staff.

Besides, the RAF had become worried at the rate of loss of extra precious aircrew, far more skilled than the bulk of Bomber Command at precise navigation, in special duty work over Holland. They lost twelve in the winter of 1942–3, one in every six sent: a loss rate of 18 per cent, far above the normal. In late May 1943 AI 2(c), the corner of the Air Ministry that ran special operations, banned all such flights to the Netherlands for the time being. The ban was continued, from month to month, until the end of March 1944.

In France the SD had an arrangement with the Luftwaffe: when the Germans were aware of an impending pick-up or parachute drop, they did nothing from the air to interfere with it. In the Netherlands, on the contrary, they made sure that the strong local night fighter forces, with their headquarters so conveniently near Driebergen, knew in advance of the drops they arranged, and were ready to pounce. They thus all but killed the goose that laid their golden eggs. They got some help from the RAF; as late as September 1942, pilots were still being ordered to wink their navigation lights several times on spotting the narrow triangle of three red lights on the ground.[87]

Since February, 'Kale' had been purporting to send back a friend whom he called 'Anton' to Baker Street to report on how work was going. Several attempts to move him by light aircraft, by seaplane or by small boat foundered. Finally 'Kale' sent word that he had secured a boat, and would return to England in it himself from the mouth of

---

85. Note by Sporborg to Mockler-Ferryman, 9 June 1943, TSC in Holland 21; details in JIC report of 22 December 1943, 7, duplic in *ibid.*
86. Hinsley *et al.*, *British Intelligence in the Second World War*, iii(i). 462.
87. Jotting in 'Cauliflower' orders in Holland 34.

the Scheldt, starting on the night of 14/15 July 1943. An RAF fighter patrol reconnoitred the area at dawn. It was an exceptionally fine, clear morning; no craft of any kind was in sight.[88] In retrospect it was clear that this was the Germans' way of wrapping up 'Kale's' traffic.[89]

N at once confided care of 'Kale's' subordinates to Drooglever Fortuyn, though that vigorous young man had not yet come of age; exactly what 'Kale's' fate had been remained a mystery for nearly two years. It may be presumed that N supposed he had been arrested on the way to his boat, or had in some other way fallen foul of the enemy; or even, was taking an unusually long time to find his way out overland. In retrospect N seems to have taken this loss a shade lightly; at the time it may have seemed a normal casualty of secret war.

It is still sometimes maintained in the Netherlands that the British sacrificed the victims of the *Englandspiel* on purpose, as part of a deception scheme so subtle that its purpose has never been revealed.[90] This is an illusion.

The war's most successful counter-espionage coup was run by section B1a of MI5, under T. A. Robertson,[91] jointly with the inter-service XX Committee that helped organise deception. As is now well known, these bodies ran back all the Abwehr's agents in this island who tried to send messages home; with disastrous effects for the Wehrmacht. Masterman's and Howard's books explain with how much finesse and attention to detail real deceptions were carried out; as do Euan Montagu's best-sellers, for a particular coup in Spain.[92] Their silence – Howard's silence, in particular – on the Dutch affair is conclusive. The comparatively haphazard bungles of N section fall into a different, lower class: cock-up rather than conspiracy.

---

88. Pencilled note timed 0705, 15 July 1943, in Holland 18.
89. Report by C. J. Miller, 15 December 1943, in Holland 19.
90. See for example P. H. Hoets, *Englandspiel ontmaskerd*, by an author with an eminent resistance record, based unhappily on unreliable sources.
91. See *Times* obituary, 16 May 1994.
92. (Sir) J. C. Masterman, *The Double-Cross System in the War of 1939 to 1945*; Ewen Montagu, *The Man Who Never Was* (Evans, 1953) and *Beyond Top Secret U* (Peter Davies, 1977); Sir Michael Howard, *Strategic Deception*.

An aspect of SOE's troubles in Holland that deserves attention can be perceived from B1a's success. As traffic with controlled agents developed, it became clear to MI5 that the Abwehr staff who supposed themselves to be in charge of them were to the last degree reluctant to accept the possibility that their agents might have been turned: exactly the fault of N section, and perhaps a usual *déformation professionelle* in the secret world. Indeed, Schreieder remarked, concisely and truly, when discussing with Giskes how secret case officers behave, that they cannot bear the thought that all is not in order within their own section; a weakness on which the Germans thought they could rely.[93]

There was, it is true – Marks has several times said so[94] – one deception that did work into Holland; but it had no bearing on the dispatch of agents, was unauthorised by (indeed, unknown to) the more than competent staff that handled major deceptions, and amounted to a private skirmish between Marks and Giskes: or rather, between Marks and May, of whom Marks had not then heard.

Briefing a party of W/T operators who were going, he was fairly sure, straight into enemy hands – an agonising task – Marks took care to appear sloppy in his methods, instead of his usual precise self; and pretended to be more interested in a crossword puzzle than in doing his job.[95] He sent another agent in, soon afterwards, with twenty-five spare poems;[96] believing that Giskes would not expect any really devious move from a section that was still fool enough to use poem codes. His own object seems to have been to conceal from the Germans the fact that SOE's signals section had rumbled them: as Giskes had feared from the start that they would.

It was indeed the signals section that mounted a practical test in the second half of June 1943. One of home station's operators sent immediately after she closed a routine schedule, HH. The instant response from Holland was another HH: for that was the habitual, automatic nazi signal clerks' farewell – it stood for 'Heil Hitler'. This

---

93. Schreieder, 394.
94. Conversations with him, 1995.
95. Marks, *op. cit.*, 176–81.
96. *Ibid.*, 276.

was clear enough proof that something was wrong.[97] It may be guessed that the solitary Orpo clerk who had been tricked into sending one HH too many, from force of habit, said nothing about his slip, lest he be posted to Russia.

Over fifty years later, again, Gubbins's Chief of Staff, Barry, recalled that he became aware on rejoining SOE in early July 1943 of some degree of unease about N section at Council level; but was not privy – or at any rate, aged eighty-five, could not remember having been privy – to any extra-secret information on this subject.[98]

Early in August 1943 Giskes arranged two ingenious conjuring tricks, to persuade N that Dutch sabotage had some real existence. Ras – still notionally at work after fifteen months in the field – reported on the 3rd that an ammunition train had exploded between Breda and Tilburg, starting a forest fire.[99] The forest fire, at that time of year, may have been real; and Giskes knew that the area was under constant photo-reconnaissance, because it included the important fighter air field at Gilze-Rijen, a constant thorn in Bomber Command's side.

Three days later, Lauwers's set came up with the tale – which was perfectly true – that a 1,000-ton barge loaded with aircraft parts had been sunk by an SOE limpet in front of the Maas bridge in the middle of Rotterdam.[100] The sinking, arranged by the Abwehr, delighted the large lunchtime crowds that were passing; the parts were all from crashed allied aircraft; and no one was hurt.[101] London sent its best thanks.

Leen Pot, a locally recruited intelligence agent – outside SOE – who had made a sensational escape after arrest a year before, turned up in London in August 1943; and testified that, so far as his own keen observation went, there had been practically no sabotage in Holland at all. Nobody believed him.[102]

---

97. *Ibid.*, 348–9.
98. Conversation with him, 4 August 1994.
99. War diary, xlviii(i). 133.
100. *Ibid.*
101. *Ibid.*, and Giskes, *op. cit.*, 112–14.
102. *Enq.*, iv B. 90.

N next proposed, on 19 August, a whole series of planned assassinations of notable collaborators, fourteen of whom he named in two telegrams to 'Catarrh'.[103] One of Lauwers's sets at once began to make difficulties: inquiries quickly showed that all the men named 'had armed bodyguards due to recent events',[104] and special teams would be needed for this task. Next month London replied that no special teams were available; but it was hoped that 'Catarrh' could get something done in November.[105] He could not; in spite of having asked for a couple of snipers' rifles on 6 October.[106] Arrangements were still under discussion in mid-December.[107] The contrast with the Gaullist 'Armada' team's decisive role in operation 'Ratweek' could hardly be more marked.[108]

Like most other groups of prisoners of war, the 'North Pole' captives in Haaren seminary thought and whispered from time to time about escape; but were tightly hemmed in. Trix Terwindt had a cell to herself; the others were grouped in twos or threes. The Germans took some care to keep like-minded prisoners apart.

The first to break out was van der Giessen – 'strong as a bear', in de Jong's phrase[109] – who wrenched off the bars outside his cell window by brute force, and clambered out; but did not manage to talk his way past the guard on the gate, to whom he pretended he was the boilerman. Thereafter the Germans reminded prisoners that if there were any more escapes, the promises that their lives would be spared might be withdrawn; and a new prison rule was introduced. At eight every evening, prisoners had to pile both their trousers and their shoes on stools in the corridors outside their cells.

Two prisoners in adjacent cells, Ubbink and Dourlein, decided to escape all the same. They had never met; but managed to make and to hide a small hole in the party wall, big enough to talk through.

---

103. War diary, xlviii(i). 134; names absent.
104. *Ibid.*: messages of 22 and 29 August 1943.
105. *Ibid.*, 140–1, 13 September 1943.
106. *Ibid.*, 150.
107. *Ibid.*, 152.
108. See Foot, *SOE in France*, 366.
109. De Jong, *KdN*, ix(ii). 1004, tr.

Their cell-mates agreed to help, though not to come out as well. They noticed that a noisy trolley brought round the last meal of the day, between six and six-thirty; and that thereafter, on weekends, only one sentry was left on duty. The sentries, whom Giskes did not wholly trust, were all Dutch SS men, unfit for the front.[110] On Saturday, 28 August 1943, a friend joined the solitary sentry; on the next evening he was alone. Just after the trolley had passed, the two escapers each got out of his cell through a gap above the door; and tiptoed round the corner, unnoticed, to hide in a cabin in the men's lavatory. The eight o'clock clothing check was perfunctory; nothing was noticed amiss. Deep in the night, which was mercifully rainy, Ubbink and Dourlein climbed clean out of the camp; aided by that luck without which escapers are helpless. A sentry walked right past them as they lay flat on the ground, and failed to notice them.[111]

They walked several miles, to Tilburg, where Kist had passed them an address to try; it was a shop, shut. It started to get light; they were both filthy, after wading through ditches, and Dourlein's clothes had got torn as they crossed the camp's barbed wire. Though both Protestants, they dived into the first open church they came to, which was Roman Catholic.

Their luck held. The priest heard their story, and handed them over to F. K. J. van Bilsen, a porter in a cloth factory, a former policeman and former NSB leader, who had gone over to resistance work.[112] Van Bilsen took them out by bicycle after dark to a farmhouse in Moergestel village nearby, while he launched some inquiries about them. These did no good – they led, through a double agent, to Schreieder – but van Bilsen's security was sound enough for Schreieder to be unable to track back to the inquiries' origin.

As the Germans knew their real identities, their parents' houses were carefully watched, and received unexplained Gestapo visits; the agents were too sensible to think of going home.

While they were on the run, N kept up a brisk exchange of messages by W/T with Holland, including routine traffic with 'Chive'; and again met somebody who had managed the passage over land.

---

110. Giskes, *op. cit.*, 125.
111. Dourlein, *Inside North Pole*, 126–7.
112. De Jong, *KdN*, ix(ii). 1006.

On 9 September 1943 a Dutchman called Hendrikus Knoppers ('Sergeant') reached London, having travelled across Belgium and France into Spain with the help of the 'Vic' line. He had served in the pre-war Dutch air force as a wireless mechanic, and was to have brought some papers out of Holland, which might have been of much interest. He said he had had to pass them over to one of 'Vic's' couriers; they never in fact turned up. He had been accompanied from his home at Blaricum, east of Amsterdam, to Brussels by a friend of his called Ridderhof – instantly recognisable in hindsight as the double agent – and from Brussels to Paris by a man whom he only knew as 'Arnaud', also instantly recognisable today as Christmann. Prolonged questioning by SOE and MI5 led to the conclusion that Knoppers was an innocent dupe. Only in November 1944 did SOE's security section spot the name of a close relative of his in a list of those helping Ridderhof to penetrate escape lines, and raise with N the possibility that he might even be an enemy agent;[113] in the end he was held not to be have been. For what it was worth, senior Abwehr agents exonerated him just after the war,[114] and MI5 also concluded that it was 'unlikely in the extreme' that he was a conscious spy.[115] They were wrong: he had been sent by Schreieder and Giskes.[116] But he had been sent on an impulse, with no sort of clandestine training and no means of telling the Germans anything useful to them that he discovered. He succeeded at least in wasting a great deal of officers' time. N trained him to go back; this mission was called off at the last moment. Having been made respectable by N, he was released to the Dutch forces; and was head of the wireless intelligence section of BI just after the war's end.[117]

N was more concerned about a party of his own agents who were supposed to have left for Spain in early September. Van Os, Pieter van der Wilden, Pals and a friend they were supposed to have accumulated in Holland, codenamed 'Steak', all set off – notionally – down the

---

113. Holland 18.
114. Holland 22.
115. Letter of 12 January 1945 in his PF.
116. De Jong, *KdN*, ix(2). 999–1000, 1033; Giskes, *op. cit.*, 111.
117. Kluiters, *De Nederlandse inlichtingen*, 365.

'Vic' line. Four actual Germans, Christmann among them, made this journey; two of them were given 'a very stiff security lecture' by 'Vic' himself for daring to slip out of the safe house in Lyons and get drunk.[118] They got beyond Perpignan, in a lorry loaded with oranges; which was, for once, stopped and searched by a road control as it neared the Pyrenees. The four men were – notionally again – arrested; 'Vic' did not re-employ the lorry driver; N was still without real news from the Netherlands.

However, his suspicions, and those of his superiors, were by now thoroughly aroused: 'we were aware of the penetration', as Selborne later put it to Churchill.[119] The ban on air drops into the Netherlands held; but N was able to make use of two sorties, one into northern France and one into northern Belgium, to send three agents on reconnaissance by the September moon. Their names were Cnoops, van Schelle and Gruen; they had decidedly different fates.

A. J. M. Cnoops ('Soccer'), then in his middle thirties, was a shopkeeper's son, who had been a riding instructor in South Africa. On 18/19 September 1943 he and two Frenchmen, from whom he promptly parted, were dropped to a reception committee near Rheims. He spent his second night in France at Mademoiselle Fredin's safe house in the rue Peclet in Paris, and then took a train for Rotterdam, bearing papers that showed him to be an OT worker on his way to a new job there from St Malo. By playing the stupid peasant, he got through an unexpectedly stiff control on the Dutch-Belgian border, where a German official told him his OT papers were out of order. His task was to sound out a particular businessman in Rotterdam, with whom – if he thought fit – he was to leave 30,000 florins for the secret army.

Cnoops did not care for the businessman, and left the money instead with an engineer called Bruintjes: a prudent decision, it turned out, as the businessman's name had been put forward by Lauwers's captured set. He arranged a password for releasing the money, and started back to England. He was lucky to avoid the same official at the Dutch-Belgian border; rejoined the rue Peclet; and

118. Foot, *SOE in France*, 368n.
119. 12 January 1944, copy in Selborne 1.

took the 'Vic' line over the Pyrenees, a long but 'not particularly hard' walk.[120] He was back in London on 12 November.

He brought back several pieces of interesting news, though – luckily for himself – he had met no other SOE agents when in Holland. He reported for example that 'The Dutch generally are very well dressed in clothes of good quality';[121] that there were not many train controls; that wirelesses, though forbidden, were common; that churches took regular collections for those in distress, which their congregations realised were to support young men living on farms; and that an English penny fell out of one of his trouser turn-ups when he unpacked his suitcase in Paris, a black mark for the security man at Tempsford.

Van Schelle was a twenty-eight-year-old Dutch farmer who had already done two odd short missions for SOE in prison in Brazil; his languages included Portuguese as well as Dutch, English, French, German and Spanish. The training schools in England thought him jumpy and unsociable; someone with better judgement saw that he was humorous and proud, and N took him on. He was codenamed 'Apollo', perhaps on account of his intellectual air, and sent on 18/19 September 1943 on operation 'Badminton'. In the same aircraft was 'Brutus'[122] on operation 'Rugger'. 'Brutus', still more intellectual, was Johan Gruen, a school teacher from Leyden. Gruen's task was to pass on advice from the Dutch government in exile to their population at home about how to behave during the forthcoming invasion; he was to distribute it through the underground press. Van Schelle's was to pass 20,000 florins to a Dutch and 100,000 francs to a Belgian escape line – he carried them concealed in his suitcase; to investigate an escape line of which London knew only that it had just moved a pilot from Holland to Switzerland; and then to come out through France. (Why on earth was SOE to do MI9's work for it?)

---

120. Cnoops interrogation, 18 November 1943, 4; TSC in his PF.
121. *Ibid.*, 5.
122. Distinguish from the 'Brutus' whose real name was Garby-Czerniawski, a Polish officer who played a leading part in the worlds of intelligence and deception; and from another, real name Hugh Fraser, who served with the SAS in the Ardennes (see page 375) and went on to a distinguished career in politics.

The two agents were to drop together, blind, on the Belgian side of the border, east of Antwerp, and to make their separate ways into Holland via an address they each memorised in Brussels. Gruen had a transmitter with him.

Close to their proposed DZ, their aircraft was attacked. The pilot managed a crash landing, in which no one was seriously hurt; but the aircraft caught fire. Both Gruen's transmitter and van Schelle's suitcase were consumed. The crew split up. Van Schelle and one of the dispatchers (an extra dispatcher had gone on the sortie for pleasure) walked off by themselves. Van Schelle hid him in a wood, went off to look for help, and had himself to hide from a close search: first, with a peasant boy's help, under a wood pile, and then for two foodless days in a haystack. He had to abandon the dispatcher, and reached Brussels on 25 October, to hear that 'Brutus' had already passed through.

The classics were not the longest suit of van Vliet, the Brussels escape line organiser who took van Schelle on; he called him 'Pollo'. Van Schelle thought van Vliet was 'Doing excellent work', with enormous energy, but was absurdly insecure; while the wife of a friend of van Vliet's, who gave a dinner party in van Schelle's honour, could be heard whispering to each guest in turn that he had just arrived from London.[123] The agent did not know that he was the temporary guest of his enemies: van Vliet was the Belgian alias used by Ridderhof. Van Schelle had common sense enough to see that this was clearly no company for a secret agent to keep for long; he left as soon as he could for Paris, Lyons, Perpignan and Spain, which he reached after some heavy walking on 1 December. He 'was greatly impressed by the high standard of security maintained throughout this line'.[124]

Well he might be: this is what saved it. He travelled under the auspices of Victor Gerson, DF section's principal star, who survived no fewer than seven missions into France. Neither he nor Gerson knew at the time that van Schelle's companion from Brussels to Lyons, who called himself 'Robert', was Christmann of Giskes's team: who went back three months later and arrested anybody he could catch. By that time Gerson himself and his more senior helpers had changed houses

---

123. Van Schelle interrogation, 22 December 1943, 2, 6, in his PF.
124. *Ibid.*, 7.

and identities; Christmann roped in some safe-house keepers and a girl courier, while an alternative set of safe houses prepared in advance kept the 'Vic' line going.[125]

Gruen met a farmer, near the site of the crash, who directed him to the nearest station; where his filthy clothes made him conspicuous beside everyone else's tidy ones. He got unmolested to Brussels, where 'van Vliet' – obviously in touch with London, and as obviously insecure – looked after him; saw him across into Holland with a *passeur* in Dutch police uniform; and settled him in a safe house at Doorn.

Based there, Gruen spent several busy weeks visiting editors of underground newspapers. The ever helpful 'van Vliet' arranged a courier service for him with the hapless 'Golf', whom he never met, through whose set all his W/T traffic with London passed:[126] all read by the Germans, who kept a close eye on him. Schreieder lists him as the last victim of the *Englandspiel*.[127]

Suddenly, on the morning of 3 January 1944, he was arrested as he walked into Doorn station to catch a train to The Hague. He made a rumpus, so that the village should know. This annoyed his captors, who gave him a rough ride during a fifty-six-hour session at the Binnenhof, which cost him two teeth.[128] He was moved to Haaren, where May – whom he thought extremely clever – cross-questioned him at more leisure. He gave May a lot of bogus information, received without comment. He was then bundled off to a forced labour camp near Hamelin, where he had the good fortune still to be alive when it was overrun on 5 April 1945.

He condemned N section for having briefed him woefully badly; they seemed to know far too little about actual life in the field.[129]

N sent something to Lauwers on 25 September 1943 that now looks gullible: why, he asked, had 'Brandy' (Bottema) sent him a message through an *Englandvaarder*, a traveller who managed the whole run from Holland to England, instead of sending it by

---

125. See Foot, *SOE in France*, 326–8.
126. War diary, xlviii(i). 152–8.
127. *Enq.*, iv B. 30, misdating his arrival back to July.
128. *Ibid.*, iv A. 513.
129. Interrogation, 29 May 1945, in his PF.

wireless?[130] A less ingenuous, less self-confident section head might have paused to think out the answer: that Bottema had no real connexion with Lauwers. N was gulled instead.

Though gulled, he was not purblind. Through 'Golf', London tried to warn its agents in Holland on 7 November that it had heard ill of van Vliet, alias Ridderhof; suspicions that 'Golf' protested a week later that he found 'absolutely unintelligible. The man was a great patriot and the best of comrades, although a somewhat pompous fellow prone to exaggeration.'[131] All the same, London's doubt must have indicated to Giskes and Schreieder that the sands were running out.

Let us revert to the fate of Ubbink and Dourlein hiding up on a farm at Moergestel.

They gradually convinced van Bilsen that they were genuine; Dourlein even wrote an article, about how high morale was in England, for a Tilburg underground newspaper (both he and van Bilsen are reproached by de Jong for letting it be signed 'PD'[132]). They were safe enough, within a few miles of their prison, if they stayed indoors in daylight.

They were exasperated to hear that only 500 florins (£50) were offered for their arrest – wanted for robbery with violence – by the police.[133] After a fortnight, when every house in Tilburg had been searched, they moved back there; and spent several anxious weeks more in hiding, until on 11 November van Bilsen was able with the help of some friendly policemen to see them over the Belgian border near Turnhout. Using van Bilsen's money, they took a bus to Turnhout, and a tram to Antwerp, where he saw them on to a train for Brussels and said goodbye. Help from a monk saw them across the next frontier, near Mons; and they travelled by express to Paris, sharing a carriage with German soldiers to whom they pretended they were going to work on an airfield near Marseilles. As they were chatting to Germans, nobody bothered to control their papers.

---

130. War diary, xlviii(i). 141.
131. *Ibid.*, 156.
132. De Jong, *KdN*, ix(ii). 1007. The article is in facsimile in Rep, *op. cit.*, 300–1.
133. Dourlein, *op. cit.*, 132: poster on the cover of Nicholas Kelso, *Errors of Judgement.*

In Paris van Bilsen's money ran out; but he had put them into touch with Ubbink's brother, who worked in a Dutch bank, and was able to telegraph to Paris a further sum which saw them through to Switzerland – once, after a weekend's delay, they had collected it. (He was duly repaid by SOE after the war.)[134] They had an inconvenient time of it when the banks were all shut, but had not been at SOE's schools for nothing: they spent it hiding in a brothel with an untalkative madame.

They took a train to Belfort, went on twenty-five miles southward by bus to Maîche, were looked after by a Dutch family there, and made their way next night – acting as extra porters for a band of smugglers – into Switzerland, where on 20 November they reported to the British and Dutch military attachés in Berne, Cartwright and van Stricht. Almost three months had passed since they escaped.

Schreieder had not failed to send N a message, back in August, that they had gone over to the Gestapo; so their welcome was not enthusiastically warm. Indeed Humphreys, alerted by the orange-lorry incident,[135] sent a Dutch DF agent, who had met one of them in training, to Berne to make quite sure they were who they claimed to be. This was one of Humphreys's stars, Guido Zembsch-Schreve, who had been born in Berne in 1916, the son of a Dutch doctor; he had travelled widely before the war, and was quick-witted and capable. He was in the process of setting up a line to carry contraband between Switzerland and Catalonia, as well as running the 'Pierre-Jacques' escape line between Paris and Brussels. Frontier crossings held no perils for him. When he got to Berne to verify the escapers' identity, he found that their evident sincerity had already cleared them.[136]

As soon as John Weidner's efficient 'Dutch-Paris' line which specialised in aircrew could arrange a convoy, Dourlein and Ubbink moved on across southern France – in German occupation for over a year – into neutral Spain.[137] There, at Lerida, they recounted their

---

134. Holland 38, 'Sprout' folder.
135. See page 182.
136. G. Zembsch-Schreve, *Pierre Lalande*, 104–5.
137. *Enq.*, iv A. 207–8; Herbert Ford, *Flee the Captor* (Nashville, Tenn.: Southern Publishing Association, 1966), 240–2.

adventures to a Dutch woman diplomat; they were back in England on 1 February 1944.

Schreieder, in retrospect, reckoned that the Germans had received, from a total of 95 drops, 3,000 stens, 300 brens, 500 pistols, half-a-million rounds of small arms ammunition, and 15,000 kilograms of explosives.[138]

On the other side, N section's accountant drew up at the end of the year, and slipped into the section history, a table showing the sums of money that had so far been poured out, most of them straight into the enemy's lap. This bears reprinting, as it shows the comparative importance the staff attached to each mission: 'Marrow', who carried the Plan for Holland, standing far out above the rest, with 100,000 florins (guilders) in his money-belt.

Operation	Guilders
GLASSHOUSE	3,000
CATARRH	12,000
CARROT	3,000
TURNIP	5,000
WATERCRESS	6,000
LETTUCE	17,000
LEEK	12,000
BEETROOT	12,000
SPINACH	5,000
MARROW	100,000
PARSNIP	5,000
LEEK A	3,000
KALE	6,000
MANGOLD	4,000
PARSLEY ·	10,000
PARSLEY A	2,500
CAULIFLOWER	4,000
CABBAGE	5,000
CELERY	7,500

---

138. Schreieder, 402.

Operation	Guilders
PUMPKIN	4,000
TOMATO	7,500
CUCUMBER	6,500
BROCCOLI	2,500
MUSTARD	2,500
CRESS	2,500
CHIVE	4,000
ENDIVE	10,000
RADISH	2,500
HOCKEY	5,000
TENNIS	2,500
GOLF	3,000
BROADBEAN	7,500
LACROSSE	4,000
KOHLRABI	4,000
SEAKALE	2,500
SPROUT	2,500
GHERKIN	4,000
NETBALL	2,500
CROQUET	4,000
SQUASH	4,000
POLO	4,000
SOCCER	31,000
BADMINTON	1,000
RUGGER	10,000
Gross Total:	355,500
Less amount recovered from Dutch Authorities:	128,750
Net Total:	226,750

On the intelligence front, 'North Pole' – the *Englandspiel* – was an undoubted German success, though a limited one. From doing for nearly six years in Great Britain against the Abwehr what the Abwehr almost did for fifteen months in Holland against SOE – taking *all* the other service's agents over successfully – MI5 was able to secure a large gain, operation 'Fortitude', the deception that went with operation 'Neptune': the assault phase of 'Overlord', the re-invasion that began through Normandy on 5/6 June 1944. 'Fortitude' convinced Hitler and the nazi high command that 'Neptune' was only a feint, because the main blow was going to come on the beaches south of Boulogne, a shorter way to Germany's industrial heart in the Ruhr. By pinning German forces on the right bank of the Seine, inactive, for the rest of June 1944, 'Fortitude' made Eisenhower's victory in the west certain.[139] The Abwehr got no such gain out of 'North Pole', for the agents they captured were neither senior enough, nor well enough informed, to provide the Germans with the data they sought about allied intentions.

On the other hand, the Germans did make a perceptible gain from 'North Pole' on the operational front: for it neutralised the main Dutch resistance effort for well over a year. Moreover, the Dutch government in exile's efforts to secure the untroubled return of their queen were a good deal hampered by the arrests that arose from SOE's mistakes.

It was not only SOE that suffered severely, of the secret services that worked into Holland; even if SOE did worst of them all. Somer produced a list for the Dutch post-war inquiry of forty-three agents whom BI had dispatched, from March 1943 to April 1945 (one of them went back): seventeen of those forty-three, nearly 40 per cent, did not survive the war.[140] That is, it was dangerous to try to work secretly in Holland, to do any thing at all more than keep one's head down as over 300,000 *onderduikers* did.

No one should be under any illusion: N section's early work into the Netherlands was disastrously bad. Some readers indeed will be tempted to say, 'But I would have done better myself' – forgetting whether they could possibly, at the time, have known enough to do so. The fog of war is proverbially dense; the fog of clandestine war is extra dense; in it N section's staff went astray. Yet the fault did not lie only with the section staff: the net of blame spreads a good deal more widely.

---

139. Details in Howard, *op. cit.*, v. 103–32.
140. *Enq.*, iv A, 325–8.

Some responsibility rests on the British government, especially on Churchill, Dalton and Selborne; of the three most on Dalton, who combined thrusting for results with inadequate practical grasp; but not all of the responsibility, even at ministerial level, is British. The Dutch must take some share; for such gullibility as the agents displayed – some of them displayed only too much – derived from Dutch as well as British recruiting policies. As the Dutch let few of their finest volunteers go anywhere near SOE, they are not well placed to complain at the behaviour of those SOE found instead. Moreover, it was the Dutch who insisted on drops to reception committees, whenever possible: a policy that turned out ruinous.

On the other hand, the results show that they were right to distrust SOE. Within that service, where does blame rest?

SOE's Council was far too far above the *mêlée* to help. General advice on principles of subversion could do nothing to sustain N section's staff over the details of whether its sets were in sound or in enemy hands. Gubbins it is true did remark, when the worst began to surface, 'AS YOU KNOW HOLLAND HAS ALWAYS BEEN SUSPECT BUT WE COULD GET NO EVIDENCE.'[141] He was a man of exceptional sensibility; his instincts suggested to him all was not well, but provided no basis for orders. Brook, Keswick's successor as D/R, had a great many worries about France in the midsummer of 1943, when the arrests of Delestraint and Moulin unhinged Gaullist resistance and the collapse of the over-extended 'Prosper' circuit led to hundreds of arrests and a major hiatus in the plans of the independent French section. Relations between London and Algiers also took up plenty of his time, as of his superior Mockler-Ferryman's (AD/E); and AD/E had weighty Scandinavian concerns as well, including SOE's successful attempt to stymie nazi research into atomic weapons. These preoccupations may help to explain why N section had been left to go its own way by itself.

Moreover, just when it became clear in SOE that something had gone very wrong in the Netherlands, Council had a good deal else on its collective mind. Gubbins had only just, in September, taken over

---

141. CD to V/CD from Cairo, 2 December 1943, deciphered tpt in Holland 4.

executive command as the new CD; his head was full of new and various responsibilities. He had to begin by resolving yet another command crisis in Cairo, where he was in early December when SOE's staff enemies mounted an attack on it in Whitehall. Operation 'Gunnerside', the attack on the Norwegian heavy-water plant that scotched Hitler's approach to an atomic bomb, and a major revision of SOE's strategy in Yugoslavia, both began that autumn.

Gubbins did not share the common failing of putting the blame of error on someone else. Yet even he inclined to include, among the possible causes for this disaster, the War Office's withdrawal of Blizard in February 1943. Here his usually sound judgement may have been at fault. For Blizard, advised by de Bruyne, insisted on always having his agents dropped to a reception committee: the main channel the enemy used to unravel N section's work. When Bingham took over, he tried to change the system, but was persuaded by de Bruyne and by his own staff to carry on as usual.[142] A note Brook sent to the JIC at an early stage of their inquiry stressed that 'the insistence of the Dutch' strongly influenced both Blizard and Bingham.[143]

Over-enthusiasm for one's agents seems endemic among amateur clandestine controllers; Laming, Blizard, Bingham and their staffs all felt it. Buckmaster, in the winter of 1943–4, was deaf to the fact that some of his sets in France had been turned; F's errors make no excuse for N's, though they provide company in the pillory.

A slice of blame must certainly be placed with MI6: for imposing on SOE an inadequate cipher system, and for employing an agent who explained all too clearly to the enemy how it worked. This cardinal error can be put in history's dock side by side with the cardinal error de Jong picked up long ago, about SOE's neglect of MI6's weak security checks.

MI5 too was not quite blameless; Giskes and Huntemann were clever enough to take in even the XX Committee's experts, and the signals and security staff missed a hint Lauwers managed to drop that he was under control.[144]

---

142. D/CE. G to AD/P, 15 December 1943, a preliminary survey of what had gone wrong, in Holland 19.
143. Brook to Capel-Dunn, 7 December 1943, TSC in Holland 14(i).
144. Page 144.

So tightly did the Germans control SOE's despatches to Holland that there is this at least to be pleaded, in mitigation of the disaster: the casualty total was not catastrophically high. Unlike F section's 'Prosper' circuit, centred in Paris, that snowballed till it extended from the Belgian border to the Vendée, and brought hundreds down in its fall, N section's supposed circuits never got off the ground at all. Teller who was arrested with Lauwers never returned. (After the war, Mrs Teller became Mrs Lauwers.) There were several score other consequential deaths, perhaps as many as seven score:[145] fewer than half the number of Italians shot in the Ardeatine cave massacre; fewer than a quarter of the dead of Oradour-sur-Glane; hardly a tenth of an average day's civilian casualties in Leningrad, in a siege that lasted 900 days; a drop in the ocean, compared to the millions of Jews killed in the Holocaust.

Month by month, SOE reported progress – or the lack of it – to the chiefs of staff. Month by month, from mid-April 1942 to 31 October 1943, these worldwide reports included a note of gentle but steady progress, with occasional checks, in the building up of an armed secret organisation in Holland, which would be of real use when the invasion began. The map that went with the report for mid-January 1943 showed the Dutch up with the Norwegians, the Poles and the Serbs: the most highly organised resistance groups in Europe.[146] So far as the Dutch were concerned, these reports were complete illusions; to this extent, the Germans did succeed in taking in the British high command. The reports were glanced at by the chiefs of staff, and pondered more carefully by C, who had three copies; they were also available to senior commanders visiting London from abroad, in a special information centre Churchill set up in the Cabinet war rooms in Great George Street – after the *Automedon* disaster – in an effort to limit circulation of highly secret papers.[147] The monthly report for the end of November 1943 put it glumly: the organisation 'had been penetrated several months ago and wiped out'; the JIC was to prepare a special report.[148]

---

145. Listed in de Jong, *KdN*, ix(2). 1028–30.
146. CAB 121/307.
147. Joan Bright Astley, who ran it, *The Inner Circle*, 66–76.
148. CAB 121/307, 30 November 1943.

That SOE's worst fears about SIS were unjustified is shown by the date of the telegram in which the secret service warned one of its star agents in Holland that the sister service was wholly penetrated in the field, and that the OD must also be handled with circumspection: 22 November 1943.[149]

It is time to go back to the fate of the agents captured in the *Englandspiel*, whom we left – after Ubbink and Dourlein escaped – cooped up on the upper floor of Haaren seminary.

They were not quite without resources. In some cells there were wireless receivers, tuned to the official channel, so that at Easter 1943 they had heard Bach's St Matthew Passion. Van Rietschoten had a more professional resource: he had managed, through all the searches, to retain a small MI9 hacksaw. He found himself in a cell with the recaptured, but still resolute, van der Giessen, and with Wegner.

The three of them determined to escape. They cut a hole in their ceiling with the little saw, hiding the marks with toothpaste. They then found an exit from the attic. They chanced their luck, which held, at the evening clothes parade; and made a rope out of their bed-strappings, anchored to a wrenched-off table leg. They got away on the stormy night of 23/24 November 1943; the storm covered any noise.

This second escape had disastrous results all round. The escapers misjudged the height of their attic: the rope was three metres too short. Wegner, who went first, misjudged the drop, hurt his foot badly and could only hobble. He heard hounds bay, as the Germans mounted a chase, but hid up to his neck in a ditch (just above freezing point); by luck he found a doctor who bandaged him up and gave him a bicycle.[150] He turned up, nearly a week later, at Drooglever Fortuyn's father's house in Maastricht. The banker was appalled at his scarecrow appearance; and greatly surprised to hear that his son, whom he had supposed safe in England, was a political prisoner in Haaren. He got Wegner help from another doctor,

---

149. Private information from the agent, who was able to secrete the texts of his telegrams.
150. Rep, *op. cit.*, 293–4.

and offered him money and clothes; both of which the agent refused.[151]

Instead, Wegner got in touch with his own wife, who lived in The Hague, and went to hide there till his leg had recovered. He tried to get in touch with d'Aulnis, with whom he had escaped over the Pyrenees; but d'Aulnis, warned off everybody in SOE by orders from London, could not respond. Wegner then set off for Switzerland, and on his way across Belgium fell in with an MI6 agent, to whom he entrusted a message for Blizard or Bingham that 'all organisation is in hands of the Germans during the last two years also ten men of I.S. The Germans are sending with code and wireless apparators all the reception landing are German and Dutch nazis.' The note, dated 10 December 1943, duly reached London[152] – but not till 2 March 1944.[153] It could only reinforce the impression made already by reports from Ubbink and Dourlein.

Wegner's luck then ran out. He was of course by now on the Gestapo wanted list; at a chance German control in Liège he was recognised and rearrested, and sent back to join his companions in misfortune, by now in Assen.

Van der Giessen and van Rietschoten parted at once from Wegner – what else were they to do? – and also avoided the hounds. They got clear away into the underground; van Rietschoten was ill with lung trouble for some weeks. They composed a report that the Germans were holding thirty-seven secret agents, to twenty-four of whom they gave training names. The message reached BI, via Berne, late in May 1944.

By then they had both been rearrested. This provides another example of the familiarity in which Dutch groupings tended to live. They could not use SOE's prearranged channels for escape, all already confessed to the enemy. Their discreet inquiries for a line to Switzerland or Spain led them to the huge and affable 'King Kong',

---

151. Statement by the elder Drooglever Fortuyn to K. de Graaf on 25 February 1945, reported by the latter two days later; TSC in Wegner PF.
152. TSC in his PF, headed 'DECODAGE DOCUMENT. MARCH.3.'
153. MI6 to Warden, of SOE's security section, in Holland 14(2).

Christiaan Lindemans, who took up their case with enthusiasm. They could not know that he had recently, secretly, changed sides.

He told them he had arranged for a submarine to pick them up off the Zeeland coast. They would need extra passes to enter the coastal area. He arranged for them to be photographed; and as a now normal routine showed the photographs to Giskes. Giskes at once recognised these well-known faces; a trap was set.[154]

On 5 May Lindemans and the agents set off by train from Rotterdam, and got out at Roosendaal, west of Breda: where they ran into a sudden SD control. They were driven off eastwards 'to have their papers checked'. Van der Giessen realised he was on his way back to Haaren, put up a moment's resistance, and was knocked out with a pistol butt. Lindemans vanished from their sight; they were again put behind bars.

Early in August May came to pass word to them, unofficially, that they were to be liquidated next day. They begged a few cigarettes off him. Next morning a small SD party called for them, marched them a little way out of Haaren and, as Deppner had ordered, shot them dead on the verge of the main road, 'while attempting to escape'.[155] Back in November, Wacker, the Haaren commandant, had been court-martialled for incompetence. Schreieder recorded his gratitude to Giskes, who by fantastic dexterity saved him from the same fate; but at the end of November 1943, Rauter transferred responsibility for captured agents from Schreieder to the iron-hearted Deppner.

Deppner left Trix Terwindt in Haaren till May 1944, when she was transferred to Ravensbrück. Her manner remained as demure as her spirit was unbreakable; she survived Ravensbrück, she survived Mauthausen, she survived the war.

Deppner kept on four wireless operators in Haaren, whom he judged the most useful to the Germans – Lauwers and Jordaan from SOE, and van der Reyden and ter Laak from SIS.[156] Lauwers and

---

154. Rep, *op. cit.*, 322.
155. May in *Enq.*, iv B. 21–2; de Jong, *KdN*, ix(ii). 1022–4. The charge is old: see Tacitus, *Annals*, ii. 67.
156. De Jong, *KdN*, ix(ii). 1025. Ter Laak, according to van der Stroom (*Nederlandse Agenten*, 18) had been in German hands since mid-February 1942.

van der Reyden survived Sachsenhausen and liberation by the Russians. Jordaan was sent to Mauthausen, where he died in the camp hospital on 3 May 1945, just after the camp was cleared of German guards. Ter Laak merged with the main body.

On 27 November 1943 Deppner sent all the other agents, blind-folded for the journey, to prison in Assen, within thirty miles of the German border; over which all fifty of them were sent in April 1944 to the concentration camp at Ravitsch in Silesia – like Auschwitz, originally an Austro-Hungarian army barracks. In early September nine of them were then moved on – nobody is quite sure where or when – probably to Gross Rosen, which even among nazi concentration camps had a dark name.[157] Wherever they went, they were all murdered.

The 5th of September 1944 is still fondly remembered in Holland as *Dolle Dinsdag*, Terrific Tuesday, when many towns in the south were beflagged in orange, and expected hourly the allied armies that had just run out of fuel. It was not so much fun in the camps.

On the morning of 6 September 1944 forty 'North Pole' prisoners reached Mauthausen from Ravitsch; a few F agents, and commandos captured in 1942 at St Nazaire, were with them. An SS NCO, Hans Gogl, organised their massacre. They were bullied and beaten, all day, without mercy, in the notorious granite quarry, from which had come the paving stones paced by Hitler in his Vienna art-school drop-out years. Half of them were shot to pieces before the day was out. The survivors, huddled into two small cells overnight, were put through the same mill again next day; none survived. Other prisoners noticed from afar how well they bore themselves under this final persecution.[158] One of them even attempted to bash a guard with the boulder he was carrying, a gesture he survived by a few seconds.

Twenty years later Gogl was traced by the tireless Simon Wiesenthal, put on trial at Linz, and acquitted. Tried again in Vienna in 1975, he said he was unable to remember any group of Dutch parachutists; and was acquitted again.[159]

---

157. Hermann Langbein, *Against all Hope* (Constable, 1994), 81.
158. Details in Rep, *op. cit.*, 331–9; not for the squeamish.
159. *Ibid.*

IV

Dutch Recovery
1943–4

Much of the winter of 1943–4 was spent by the Dutch authorities in exile in changing their minds about whether they wanted subversive operations into Holland restarted at all.[1] Meanwhile, a lot of British staff time was spent in London on 'Rankin', a plan for action if the German war effort suddenly collapsed. The staff who devised 'Rankin' much under-estimated Hitler's tenacity, and the Germans' will to fight, which Goebbels inspired and Himmler disciplined. They went into plenty of detail. 54 Division (Lines of Communication – that is, not a division at fighting strength) was to operate, directly under 21 Army Group, eastward out of Rotterdam into Germany, with an American regimental combat team under command. SOE and the Dutch government in exile were to provide guides and advice.[2] Blizard was prominent, on the civil affairs side, in these – as it turned out, useless – discussions. SOE in any case could not promise much. Rowlandson, a senior liaison officer, explained just before Christmas to the GSO 1 of 54 Division that it was 'impossible to guarantee that any particular plan or order will effectively be carried out'.[3]

Late in 1943 Dutch intelligence discovered that the Germans were about to introduce a new form of identity card, to be produced by a

---

1. Holland 4.
2. 'Aide-Memoire for Dutch Military Authorities', 2 December 1943, duplic in Holland 3.
3. M. A. W. Rowlandson to W. E. Underhill, 23 December 1943, TSC in *ibid.*

large and famous firm, the Enschedé printing works in Haarlem. In November Gerbrandy called on Selborne, and invited him to intervene. The target was a tempting one for SOE, and three N agents – the fiery Abraham Dubois and two friends – were trained to attack it; but never got started. They expected to leave by the December moon; but by then English and Dutch authorities alike were so alarmed by the latest news from Holland that all operations were at a stand. Last-minute efforts to get this one sortie authorised were wrecked on the rock of de Bruyne's refusal to agree to it;[4] on 20 December Mockler-Ferryman minuted to Gubbins that 'it is now too late to continue with the Haarlem project and it has been dropped'.[5] De Bruyne mis-remembered this affair as the last straw, which broke his confidence in SOE altogether;[6] and was not sorry soon to go back to a full-time career as a marine.

Hazelhoff, who knew him well – and took care not to work under him – said of him once, 'he didn't have a mean bone in his body'.[7] Yet he had some of the more tiresome mannerisms of the pre-war Dutch officer class, on points of military punctilio; his perfect uprightness was no defence against a Schreieder or a Deppner.

De Jong has some eloquent pages on how the London Dutch received the black news.[8] So far they had been sustained through the stresses of secrecy by the belief that they had been making important advances. The shock of finding that this was not in the least so was severe.

A few words are needed by the bye to conclude the tale of van Bilsen, who had put himself out so far to help Ubbink and Dourlein. He was a man given to sudden impulses and abrupt changes of mind. As a young man he had trained for the priesthood, but gave that up to become a policeman; was dismissed on returning from France, in late June 1940, for having run away there with his wife in May; and had a brief flirtation with the NSB before he went into resistance. SOE's security staff, puzzled by the various oddities that

---

4. Holland 4, N to D/R, 19 December 1943, TS with confirming MS by D/R.
5. *Ibid.*, AD/E to CD.
6. *Enq.*, iv A. 518–22.
7. *Soldier of Orange*, 132.
8. De Jong, *KdN*, ix(ii). 1012–19.

arose out of Ubbink's and Dourlein's reports, decided he had better be treated as a German agent, who had sent the two agents out of Holland to suit some still unrevealed German purpose.[9] By the time these notes were written, he was dead; for in Holland, too, he was regarded as so unreliable that a three-man party – two Jews and a policeman – shot him dead at Venlo on 20 January 1944; knowing nothing of how valuable he had been to the allied cause.[10]

Two conflicting strands in SOE's policy emerged after Ubbink and Dourlein sounded their alarm. Prompt notice was taken of it, both on the security and on the operational front; but for months yet the two men themselves were under suspicion, held indeed for a while inside a prison. Why was it necessary to treat two such brave men so sternly?

Unhappily for them, their German enemies had so thoroughly penetrated escape lines across Belgium that by mid-1943 MI5 had laid down a rule: anyone who turned up in England after crossing Belgian territory was assumed to have been helped by the enemy, until the contrary could be proved.[11] SOE had a sub-section, BSS, the Bayswater security section, to interrogate its own agents, once they were released by MI5 and had passed – if they claimed to have escaped – an interrogator from MI9.

It was at the MI9 hedge that Ubbink and Dourlein fell. Their expert questioner saw them separately. It was his job to be suspicious; he found too much to suspect.

They said they had escaped from Haaren seminary, but they each had trouble in finding the seminary on an air photograph, and still more trouble in detecting the wire barrier round it they said they had crossed. Remembering that they were less used to air photographs than he was, he pressed for detail. One said they crossed it at a support post; the other said, between the posts. One said the fence was straight at the top; the other, that it curved outwards. Which way did they then go? One said westwards; the other, south-eastwards. These

---

9. Notes of 30 March, 9 and 15 April 1944 in Holland 14(2).
10. Undated note in 'Chive and Sprout' folder. TSC in Holland 19; de Jong, *KdN*, ix(ii). 1007.
11. Security 1, History, 9 (16 July 1945).

were small points; but by the time he had accumulated a list of thirty-five contradictions, each small in itself, the cumulative effect was so strong that the MI9 man put in a hostile report.[12]

This was not until early February 1944, for the two escapers did not reach England till the first of that month. They had had to come out through Spain, where they had already been interrogated; it is easy enough to suppose that, after all they had been through, their memories of minute events had faded. On the other hand, all their MI9 interrogator's experience had been with men who showed exact recall of the tiniest details of their escapes;[13] hence his assumption that one at least of the Dutchmen could not be telling the truth. Security officers, in and out of SOE, continued for several weeks to take for granted that one of them must be a Gestapo plant.

N section had called in experts from SOE's security section in the last week of November 1943, and co-operated fully with them. One of them, Miller, produced a long analysis of how far the rot had spread on 15 December;[14] and the security section, in conjunction with MI5, produced a further paper on the role of Abwehr III.[15]

What, meanwhile, was to be done with the escapers? By mid-February 1944 they were angry men in a dangerous mood.

During three months in hiding, they had talked over what might have gone wrong; and reached an excusable, though false, conclusion. They noticed that each had been plied with questions about every member of N section's staff but one – Bingham; in whom the Germans hardly seemed interested at all. Bingham had mentioned to one of them that during the fighting in May 1940 he had been close to Captain Rost van Tonningen, whose banker brother was a leading collaborator. This helped to convince them that Bingham too sided with the enemy, and they denounced him to the security staff.

It was at once clear, both to MI5 and to SOE's security officers, that there was no sort of case against Bingham; whom the Germans

---

12. List of contradictions in Holland 13(1).
13. The poet Armel Guerne, who had worked closely with F section's 'Prosper' circuit, drilled himself not to remember such details as a security measure; but did not reach London till May (cp Foot, *SOE in France*, 320–1).
14. In Holland 19.
15. *Ibid.*, unsigned and undated TSC.

had looked over thoroughly, during his consular past in Holland in 1939–40. It was also clear that he would be in direct danger, if either Dourlein or Ubbink – trained in unarmed combat – met him again; and Mockler-Ferryman thought it prudent to post him away. Bingham had the good fortune to miss being chosen as liaison officer with the NKVD in allied-occupied Italy,[16] and went instead to join SOA, the Australian branch, where he proceeded to make the same mistake again. He took charge of operations into Timor, a Portuguese and Dutch island colony overrun by Japan. Allied decipher staff broke Japanese W/T reports from Timor to Tokyo, from which it was clear that all Bingham's agents were under enemy control; a fact he only admitted when a further agent, whom he had sent in blind, reported that he had watched a former colleague attend a supply drop with an armed Japanese soldier on either side of him.[17]

As one of Bingham's senior colleagues put it, not too kindly, Bingham's was not a personality that could have carried off so intricate an act of treachery for so long.[18] There is no other plausible candidate. In fact, there can be no doubt that there was no treachery: exactly as Schreieder testified to the Dutch post-war enquiry.[19] He also said as much to Rauter, when the two of them had a shouted cell-to-cell conversation in prison after the war, during their warders' lunch hour; forgetting that a fellow prisoner might speak German, and curry favour for himself by reporting what they had said to the Dutch.[20]

The other horn of the dilemma must now be thrust home: though there was no treachery, there was indeed incompetence, bungling even; and though Bingham did not begin it, he did not stop it either.

Care obviously had to be taken about whom Dourlein and Ubbink saw, and what they said. N section could be excused for not wanting them to mix with other agents, to whose morale they were not likely to do much good. They were kept for a while at one of SOE's many country houses, Tyting House near Guildford, under modified house arrest; they could go for walks, escorted by a guard,

---

16. Proposal of 22 March 1944 in Russia 4.
17. D. C. Horton, *Ring of Fire* (Panther, 1984), 195–7.
18. Private information.
19. *Enq.*, iv B. 45.
20. RIOD jotting.

but they had no access to the telephone or to the post. Dutch officials could, and a few did, visit them. As Selborne put it, as late as 16 June 1944, to the Dutch minister of justice, van Lidth de Jeude, the agents had had to be segregated, for a very complicated inquiry that was still not quite complete; they had not been interned.[21]

All the same, they were by this time inside Brixton prison. Correspondence between Selborne and the home secretary, Herbert Morrison, established that SOE had no powers to intern; that Morrison had, but was disinclined in this case to use them; that neither minister would contemplate running any sort of concentration camp; and that all things considered, the best place to keep the two young men would be a flat – in no sense a cell – inside the perimeter of Brixton prison. There would be no telephone; mail would be controlled; and there they could safely stay until the cardinal operation of 1944 – 'Overlord', the re-entry onto the continent – had securely begun.[22] Dourlein complained later that he had been more comfortable in Haaren.[23]

Giskes noticed a marked cooling-off in the tone of N's messages to Holland in the first ten days of December 1943, 'so dull and colourless compared with their usual quality that it did not need all our knowledge to enable us to guess that the enemy was trying to deceive us in his turn'.[24] N was indeed by then well enough informed to have grave doubts about the security of every set to which he sent; but turning doubt to certainty took time.

It was not till 5 January 1944 that the full reports by Ubbink and Dourlein, made in Spain, got to London; in Dutch. De Bruyne wrote next day to inform Mockler-Ferryman, and to draw one immediate conclusion: reception committees had, from the start, been ruinous.[25] He envisaged many possibilities as still open in the Netherlands, but for the time being, remained opposed to any activity at all. He then went off for three weeks to the United States on Dutch marine corps business; leaving his branch in charge of

---

21. Selborne 35. TS copy.
22. Selborne 8.
23. *Enq.*, iv C-11. 1941b.
24. Giskes, *London Calling North Pole*, 129.
25. Holland 4.

Lieftinck, the target of constant sniping from Somer, who seemed to SOE jealous that anybody but himself should have a finger in the clandestine pie. (Such by mid-war was the housing shortage in London that Lieftinck and Bingham shared a flat. They never talked shop there; but so abrasive was Bingham's manner, even in private, that on a day when he knew his flat-mate was out of town Lieftinck carefully searched his belongings. He found nothing.)[26]

In retrospect, the Dutch enquiry commission noticed that BI had made much less use of reception committees than had N section, acting with BVT and MVT; and remarked that no BI agent was arrested on landing – a fair comment.[27]

SOE in Holland indeed provides an example of the flywheel effect, familiar to many civil servants and managers: once a policy has been well launched, and is generally understood, it is hard to stop it and still more hard to reverse it. Though Dourlein and Ubbink escaped from enemy custody in August 1943, and testified to the fact in person at Berne in November, it took them over two months more to reach London; and it was not until mid-April 1944 that every relevant section in SOE had become convinced that every Dutch circuit SOE had started up since 1941 had fallen under enemy control.[28] Normandy D-day was by then less than two months distant.

Indeed over a year later, when the war with Germany was done, the ever-cautious Archie Boyle, who was SOE's head of intelligence, used the phrase 'how phoney the escape from prison sounded',[29] still impressed by the original doubts of the MI9 interrogator.[30]

The Dutch disaster provided an excuse for SOE's enemies – they were legion then, and not all of them are dead today – to combine to try to crush it. C, the Foreign Office, the Ministry of Information and Bomber Command all longed to see SOE buried; this seemed the moment to prepare the death certificate.

They were premature.

They chose the JIC as their instrument; that normally splendid

---

26. Rep, *Englandspiel*, 396.
27. *Enq.*, iv A. 448.
28. Holland 14(2), *passim*.
29. A/CD to BSS/A, 8 June 1945, initialled TS in Holland 14(6).
30. See page 200.

committee behaved rather oddly. On 1 December 1943 Ismay's assistant Jacob told Attlee, who was acting prime minister while Churchill was abroad, that most secret information – a usual euphemism for decipher – suggested that 'the whole SOE organisation in Holland has been penetrated by the Germans, and has been run by the Germans for at least a year'; the vice chiefs of staff – whose chiefs were abroad with Churchill – were greatly disquieted, and proposed an inquiry by the JIC.[31] Attlee concurred.

On 13 December Senter, SOE's head of security (AD/P), and Mockler-Ferryman appeared before Cavendish-Bentinck and Capel-Dunn, the JIC's chairman and secretary. A 'fair and friendly' trio from MI5 attended also: Liddell, Wethered and Rothschild.[32] But SOE was not present when Cavendish-Bentinck saw a delegation from MI6; nor was SOE afforded the usual courtesy of seeing the JIC's report in draft before it was circulated. Nor were any of the three officers who expressed the original disquiet present at any stage of the investigation.[33]

JIC(43)517(O) FINAL was dated 22 December, and considered by the chiefs of staff on Christmas Eve;[34] but no copy reached SOE until 4 January. In it the committee listed several weaknesses in SOE's general levels of security, particularly in Holland; oddly enough, hardly instancing the case of Ubbink and Dourlein. A disaster in Belgium had been retrieved; it was clear that the disaster in Holland had not.[35]

Ismay wrote to Attlee on 3 January 1944 – with a copy to Selborne – that the chiefs of staff 'find the situation highly disturbing', and believed a 'closer integration of the work of SOE and SIS to be essential to our war effort'.[36] Selborne protested by telegraph to Churchill, who responded, 'We will certainly go into this on my return.'[37] Selborne put up a paper to the defence committee on 11 January, for

---

31. TSC in Holland 21.
32. AD/P to A/CD, 14 December 1943, initialled TS in *ibid.*
33. D/R to AD/E, 8 January 1944, TS in HQ 199.
34. V/CD to CD, 28 December 1943, Holland 21.
35. Duplic *ibid.*
36. TSC *ibid.*
37. Note by Peck of 8 January 1944, *ibid.*

its meeting three days later, in which he stressed the need for 'the daily work of a Minister' in charge of SOE, 'because constant adjustments have to be made between political and military considerations'; this was the context in which he remarked that '80% of my time is devoted to SOE'. 'Notable special operations', he went on, 'already stand to its credit, and all that it asks is that it should be given the confidence which it deserves and be freed from the feeling that any setback which the fortunes of war may bring is going to be made the occasion by other Departments for immediately demanding its dismemberment.'[38]

Churchill was still away, ill. Attlee chaired Eden, A. V. Alexander, Lyttelton, Sinclair, Bridges and Ismay on the 14th; this time Selborne was heard. He emphasised that 'SOE's principal function was to fight', and pressed without success for a firmer footing for SOE in the chiefs of staff machine.

Eden, quite apart from being C's friend and official sponsor, had long-standing reasons for distrusting SOE,[39] and was not regarded within it as a likely supporter. Nevertheless, he now came to its rescue. It was he who shot down at this meeting a plan to amalgamate SIS and SOE, and strongly supported Selborne's plea for extra help to patriot forces in the coming invasion.[40] Ismay concluded this deplorable incident with a minute: 'There must be an end to the JIC practice of preparing a charge sheet in the absence of the defendant.'[41]

Bingham was posted out of N section on 26 February 1944. The next and last N was Ivor Dobson, then thirty-eight, brought over from T section where he had been a successful conducting and operations officer. He had managed a shipping firm in Antwerp before the war, knew that city – where he had been born – like the back of his hand, and was fluent in Dutch as well as in French. The air force's continuing ban on secret flights into Holland, hardly relaxed before June, gave him time to settle in. He was thoroughly indoctrinated in SOE's methods already.

It was a curious irony that February 1944 saw both SOE's greatest

---

38. Duplic *ibid.*, 5–6.
39. See Lady Ranfurly, *To War with Whitaker* (Mandarin, 1995), 81–2.
40. DO(44) 2nd meeting, most secret, duplic in Holland 21 and HQ 199.
41. Initialled typescript in CAB 121/305, 1 March 1944.

triumph, the sinking of a ferryload of heavy water on Lake Tinnsjo that scuppered Hitler's effort to secure an atomic bomb,[42] and the arrival in England of the two successful escapers from Haaren, whose news of the extent of the Dutch disaster almost put paid to SOE altogether.

De Bruyne's departure from the secret world enabled the Dutch to make a fresh start at a subversive staff, with van Oorschot's BBO under a head with pre-war intelligence experience and a chief of staff – de Graaf – who had just escaped from occupied Holland. Fresh personalities transformed the scene, in spite of security suspicions about de Graaf, who had come out of Holland along a line that was known to be at some points under close German control.[43]

N section got on much better with van Oorschot's BBO than it had done with de Bruyne's BVT or MVT. To start with, van Oorschot was an old friend of Somer's and got on with him; and convened a meeting at which BI, BBO, SIS and SOE were all represented. Johns and Dobson represented SOE, 'expressed the wish for real co-operation', and explained what tasks SOE would be likely to be called on to perform during 'Overlord'. There was a useful follow-up meeting between Cordeaux, Johns and Dobson. 'Our relations with the BBO', the section history continued, 'remained exceedingly good throughout the whole period of relationship with them. They had very little knowledge of the inner workings of our clandestine methods and, apart from looking after the interests of their agents, they were satisfied to leave the whole matter to us.'[44]

Partly for sound professional reasons, partly because personalities clashed, relations between SOE and SIS were sometimes rough. As was noted above, the two services needed contrary conditions in occupied Europe – where SOE sought to stir mayhem, SIS longed for quiet[45] – so no wonder they sometimes got on badly. Through the spring and summer of 1943, the two bodies' sections working into Holland – SIS's under Cordeaux and Seymour, SOE's under Brook and Bingham –

42. See Charles Cruickshank, *SOE in Scandinavia* (Oxford University Press, 1986), 198–202, and Knut Haukelid – less official but more vivid – *Skis against the Atom* (tr. F. H. Lyon, Kimber, 1955), 143–58.
43. Holland 14(I). *passim.*
44. History cx, March 1944, 2.
45. Page 35.

were notably at daggers drawn.[46] During the prolonged inquiry into SOE's Dutch affairs that followed on Ubbink's and Dourlein's appearance in Berne, SOE's files are peppered with jottings of the type, 'I wonder how long C had known that.' Cordeaux and Seymour played their cards as close to their chests as they could; an unhappy, though perhaps unavoidable, *déformation professionelle*, exacerbated by the personal dislike they both felt for Bingham.

Once Bingham had left, relations improved: so far indeed that during the last winter of the war SIS agents going into Holland usually went to SOE receptions, and the SIS liaison officer was welcome as a full member of SFHQ.[47] As early as 24 May 1944, Johns was able to tell the security section that N section staff and their opposite numbers in SIS co-operated so closely that they were almost 'two halves of the same organization'.[48]

Some of the credit for these improved relations was undoubtedly due to Johns, who took up his duties as LC in February 1944;[49] for as a recent employee of C's in a key post, he knew how to manage the sister service with tact.

Relations between SOE and SIS improved as the war went on, in most areas of work, as the two got to know each other better and to acknowledge the need for each others' existence. In the Low Countries, on the contrary, relations between the Abwehr and the SD got worse as the war went on: they moved from fairly cordial co-operation to such a degree of hostility that by the spring of 1944 – when the Abwehr had, technically, been absorbed into the SD – Giskes felt that he and his colleagues 'now had to face an additional front'.[50]

Though N's drops of agents to enemy-controlled circuits had stopped in late May 1943, half a year before Dourlein and Ubbink reached Berne in November, wireless traffic with the infected sets continued on into the spring of 1944. The RAF's ban on parachute operations into Holland was here a positive blessing to SOE; it could blame the air force for the lack of real activity, while a notional

---

46. All four of these names figure frequently in *Enq.*, iv.
47. History cx, March 1944, 2; written after April 1945.
48. BSS/A to AD/P, TSC in Holland 14(3).
49. Cp page 334.
50. Giskes, *op. cit.*, 153.

exchange of ideas went on with circuits that – Baker Street took in rather slowly – belonged to the other side.

This provided a fine chance for active counter-espionage, that is, for deception: the task of the London Controlling Section, deeply suspicious of SOE – even though Selborne and Masterman were old friends[51] – rather than of SOE itself. There are a few traces on file of N section's reports of exploitable contacts with the enemy, but no trace that any of them were taken up.[52] Again, Sir Michael Howard's silence on this point is conclusive.

The results of SOE's remaining work into Holland, in the few weeks before 'Overlord' began, can be summed up in four words: too little, too late.

Yet before they are recorded, a few words are needed on what the Dutch were able to do, on the occupied spot, to help themselves. Those of their officer corps who had been taken prisoner at the moment of conquest, in May 1940, were all sent home two months later on the condition that they took an oath to play no part at all, direct or indirect, in resistance to the new regime. As gentlemen as well as officers, they took this oath seriously: an important and lasting handicap to Dutch resistance.

What, meanwhile, were the Dutch in Holland achieving for themselves?

Severe repression – remember the dead from the Wilton-Feyenoord sabotage, early in 1941 – had cowed some, but only some of them. There had been two great strikes, neither of which SOE had anything to do with; for in February 1941 it had no agents present, and in April–May 1943 all the agents it had present were in enemy hands.

The intricacies of the Dutch constitution have ensured a multiplicity of Dutch parties, reflected in the way the Dutch set about resistance. There were almost always several groups in being, rivals to each other, in one of which a would-be resister could try to enlist; their rivalries did not always advance the common cause, and sometimes retarded it.

The Ordedienst (OD), mentioned several times already, was both

---

51. Private information; and Selborne to J. Davidson-Pratt, 9 July 1942, Selborne papers 23.
52. In Holland 14(3), 19, 29, 31 July and 24 November 1944.

widespread and, from SOE's angle of sight, unsafe: it had early attracted enemy attention, and the warning Jambroes's captive set sent back to London – that its highest command was riddled with informers[53] – was perfectly true. Nevertheless, N section, egged on by the Dutch authorities who sympathised with the aims of the OD, continued attempts to work with it right through to the end.

The Landelijke Organisatie (LO), or countrywide organisation, covered even more of the Netherlands than the OD did, but it had no offensive potential. It provided care, food and cover for refugees – many of them Jewish – from nazi rule, but its task was to hide people, rather than to fit them to fight.

Besides several small groups of resolute individuals, there were two rival sabotage bodies that tried to work on a national scale: the Raad van Verzet (RVV), council of resistance – not to be confused with the much stronger Conseil National de la Résistance in France, or with such bodies as the National Liberation Councils of Algeria or the Yemen – and the more left-wing Knokploegen (KP), or combat groups. The RVV and the KP both badly needed touch with SOE to secure arms and explosives: this touch had yet to be established.

Dutch churchmen and academics had already had practical experience of anti-nazi propaganda. The Rector Magnificus of Leyden university, Huizinga, had presided as early as April 1933 over an international conference there which discussed the nazi threat to academic freedom.[54] By the summer of 1944, Leyden had long been closed – for protesting too ardently at the exclusion of its Jewish staff – and the other universities were subsisting as best they could under Goebbels's distant dictatorship. There was no Dutch equivalent of the university-inspired electrical sabotage Groupe G in Belgium.[55]

On the staff side, as has been shown, useful progress was made in spring 1944: a competent Anglo-Dutch team was now ready to run operations. Yet before the Normandy landings began, results in the field remained meagre.

Seven agents were dispatched on the last night of March, when the

---

53. See page 134.
54. Schulten, *Verzet in Nederland*, 28–9.
55. See pages 278–9, etc.

RAF at last consented to re-start flying. One refused to jump; four more got into prompt, deep trouble with a double agent; the two survivors, on a mission to the clandestine press, were of no use on the arms supply front. No more agents went out until two were dispatched on the last night of May; the aircraft carrying them was shot down and there were no survivors.

The career in SOE of N. J. Celosse, whom his friends called Bob, shows that the secret war did not get much more straightforward after the end of the *Englandspiel.*

Celosse was a Dutchman, born in 1917 in Java where his father worked, and after brief spells in the Dutch army and in the German-controlled compulsory labour force (the *Arbeitsdienst*) secured a post as a food inspector. This carried with it a permit to travel all over the Netherlands. He began to smuggle extra food, systematically, to refugees who were living illegally on farms.[56]

Through a cousin, he got in touch with a small resistance movement called CS.6 (sometimes spelled CS VI). This was supposed by the half-informed to be the sixth attempt at forming a centre for sabotage; in fact it was named after Corellistraat 6, the Amsterdam address – opposite van Hemert's old school – of two of its leading members. Its core consisted of Amsterdam university students, some of them with communist leanings, but it was not under communist control.[57] It had been active through most of 1943, attacking Dutchmen who worked with the Germans and sabotaging railways.

One of its more junior members – he still believed the Centre for Sabotage story,[58] an instance of how confused resisters often were between appearance and reality – was Kas de Graaf, nearly two years older than Celosse and a colleague in the food inspectorate. He determined to go to London, to pursue arms and money and to press for central direction of sabotage. He claimed, without authority, when he got to London to be speaking for the much larger and more powerful RVV, which did not take CS.6 seriously.[59] Celosse travelled with him.

---

56. RVPS report, 14 February 1944, TS in Holland 14(2).
57. Schulten, *op. cit.*, 135–7, de Jong, *KdN*, vii(ii). 957–60.
58. *Enq.*, iv A. 555.
59. De Jong, *KdN*, viii(ii). 969; RVPS report on de Graaf, 12 February 1944, TSC in Holland 14(2).

They got away from Holland late in November 1943 and got as far as Paris. There they fell in with Christiaan Lindemans, the enormous Dutchman nicknamed 'King Kong'. He was tremendously helpful to them, entertaining them, helping them to hide safely in Paris and to travel safely through to Spain; they felt much indebted to him. This is the sort of bond a man never forgets.

At about this time, Weidner, who ran the Dutch-Paris escape line, also met Lindemans, and gave him 50,000 French francs to help him run friends through Paris to safety; but was so appalled at King Kong's careless manners, which ran to dropping a revolver in a station waiting-room, that he determined to have no closer touch with him.[60]

On 24 January 1944 N sent a chit to DF to say that he was 'very anxious to get in touch' with de Graaf and Celosse; who were in England within a fortnight.[61] Warden, of the security staff, thought highly of Celosse; so did Dobson; and the latter proposed that he should be sent straight back, after parachute training only. He did two jumps at Ringway, excellently; was given the codename 'Faro'; and went back to Holland armed with an SD *Kennkarte* and 50,000 florins for CS.6, with which he was to act as liaison officer.

During his absence, CS.6 had attracted German attention; it was known in London that some of its leaders had been arrested. Hence the spine-chilling warning at the start of his operation orders: 'We have reasons to suspect this organization may have been partly penetrated by the enemy.'[62] The Dutch enquiry indeed picked it out as a serious fault that Celosse was sent to work with CS.6 at all; and blamed de Graaf by name for allowing it.[63]

De Graaf was regarded by SOE's security staff as 'completely blown', because he had already had so many brushes with the Gestapo.[64] He moved at once onto van Oorschot's staff; Celosse returned to danger on 31 March.

---

60. Ford, *op. cit.*, 242–4.
61. Celosse PF, copy.
62. *Ibid.*
63. *Enq.*, iv A. 564.
64. BSS/A to D/CE, 28 February 1944, TSC in Holland 14(2).

He led a party of five, who were to drop blind onto the Wieringermeer polderland, newly reclaimed, at the north-west corner of the Zuyder Zee. With him were his assistant Johan Seyben ('Ping-pong') and his W/T operator Aart Penning ('Skittles'). Seyben had been trained, with du Bois, for the cancelled attack on the Enschedé printing works.[65] Penning, a Dutch gendarme who had managed to escape in the summer of 1940, had since married a Welsh wife, who had borne him two children; he had spent time with her, instead of mugging up his cover story, before he emplaned, and as the green light went on he announced that he would not drop. The others went without him; he spent the next six months at Inverlair.[66]

Celosse was glad of the help of the other men in his party – Seyben, Cnoops (now 'Cricket') on his second mission and Huub Sanders ('Curling'), his twenty-one-year-old operator, a Java-born sailor – for their baggage was scattered over both sides of a canal. They got, with some trouble, to Amsterdam, where Celosse went to live with his wife Mies in the Jekerstraat and the other three boarded together in the busier P. C. Hooftstraat.

Celosse's mission was to CS.6, as liaison officer with SOE and finder of dropping zones; Cnoops was to perform similar tasks for the much larger and more formidable RVV, once he had got in touch with it. SOE understood already that both CS.6 and the RVV had been to some extent penetrated by the Gestapo;[67] how far, Celosse and Cnoops would have to find out. Sanders could send for both. SOE's security staff later deplored this arrangement as a 'cardinal error',[68] but what else were the agents to do?

Sanders at least was in a more secure mode than the W/T operators N had earlier dropped into Holland, because he had no poem code; he carried one-time pads, reinvented by Marks in 1943, but originally discovered by the Germans in the 1920s (and in use by the Foreign Office – who did not mention them to SOE – 'throughout

---

65. *Enq.*, iv A. 553.
66. Note of 1 April 1944 in his PF. See also Eddy de Roever, *Zij sprongen bij Maanlicht*, 45.
67. BSS/A to BSS, 16 March 1944, TS in Celosse PF.
68. E.g. BS to AD/P, 24 May 1944, 12, TSC in Holland 14(1).

the war', according to Robin Denniston).[69] After he had used a strip of letters, he could burn it, leaving the enemy nothing but gibberish to decipher. Moreover, he was equipped with a more elaborate system of security checks than the previous ones; and he had a personal question-and-answer code ('What do you know?' was to evoke the reply, if he was not in enemy hands, 'American sailor').

Two other N agents parachuted into Holland on the same night, also blind, from a different aircraft: Tobias Biallosterski ('Draughts') and his wireless operator Jan Steman ('Bezique'). They landed west of Breda, buried their W/T set as well as their parachutes, released a pigeon at dawn, walked into Etten to catch a bus, and got on with the job; of which more in a moment.

None of them knew of the consternation in Baker Street on the day they arrived, All Fools' Day; for this was the day chosen by Giskes to pull N's leg. He offered the following telegram, in clear, to ten of SOE's channels, six of which accepted it:

```
L

WEL 8996 JTB

SRL B2725 (1)     FROM HECK BLUE          1 APRIL 44      309

TOR 1020

GROUPS . 72

MESSRS. BLUNT BINGHAM ANQ SUCCS LTD LONDON IN THE LAST TIME

YOU ARE TRYING TO MAKE BUSINESS IN NETHERLANDS WITHOUT OUR

ASSISTANCE STOP WE THINK THIS RATHER UNFAIR IN VIEW OUR LONG

AND SUCCESSFUL COOPERATION AS YOUR SOLE AGENTS ✗ STOP BUT

NEVER MIND WHEN EVER YOU WILL COME TO PAY A VISIT TO THE

CONTINENT YOU MAY BE ASSURED THAT YOU WILL BE RECEIVED WITH

SAME CARE AND RESULT AS ALL THOSE YOU SENT US BEFORE STOP

SO LONG.


TP AT 1119 GMT 1 APRIL 44 DLAD +÷4W

C AT 1119HRS GMT 1ST APRIL 1944JA

OK  RATE 1120 .
```

N class D
18
Repeated by GOLF 4.4.44

---

69. *Churchill's Secret War* (Stroud: Sutton, 1997), 27.

MESSRS. BLUNT BINGHAM ANQ SUCCS LTD
LONDON IN THE LAST TIME YOU ARE TRYING TO
MAKE BUSINESS IN NETHERLANDS WITHOUT OUR
ASSISTANCE STOP WE THINK THIS RATHER UNFAIR
IN VIEW OUR LONG AND SUCCESSFUL COOPERA-
TION AS YOUR SOLE AGENTS STOP BUT NEVER
MIND WHEN EVER YOU WILL COME TO PAY A VISIT
TO THE CONTINENT YOU MAY BE ASSURED THAT
YOU WILL BE RECEIVED WITH SAME CARE AND
RESULT AS ALL THOSE YOU SENT US BEFORE STOP
SO LONG.[70]

Giskes and Huntemann had cooked this up between them – doing so
reminded Giskes of a game of 'Consequences'[71] – without bothering
Lauwers for his help. By this time Giskes was no longer on speaking
terms with Schreieder,[72] and how he got access to the transmitters is
a minor puzzle; old friendships in the Orpo, and Berlin's hard-won
authority to send the message, probably sufficed.

It was a sharp rebuff to N, sharp as a slap in the face; and felt as
such, for all its gentle wording. It was an equally sharp rebuff for N's
superiors, D/R and AD/E; for Council; and for the RAF.

At least it should have cleared Ubbink and Dourlein from suspicion of double-dealing (though Johns was still expressing doubts
about them as late as 18 April);[73] but the security section also read it
with gloom. Moreover, it raised at once a further security flap: how
did the Germans already know that Bingham had been superseded?
This was put down at first to indiscreet talk among the Dutch – to
whom of course the message had had promptly to be confessed –
which had spread to a BI agent before he left, only to fall too
promptly into enemy hands.[74] Later, the security section concluded
that the Germans had probably penetrated the courier line that the
Dutch knew as the *Zwitzerse Weg*, the Swiss Way. This ran with

---

70. Tpt in Holland 14(2), item 309; HECK BLUE (i.e. 'Leek') the sender.
71. Giskes, *op. cit.*, 135.
72. *Ibid.*
73. Holland 14(2).
74. D/R to AD/P, 17 April 1944, TS in Holland 14(2).

clockwork regularity, every six days, between The Hague and the Dutch legation in Berne, and may well have carried in interceptible form the news that Bingham had left.[75]

For a few hours there was also a flap about the two parties of agents dropped on the last night of March; until practical men remembered that both parties had dropped blind, 100 miles apart, and could hardly have been rounded up in time to be covered by the message from 'Leek', transmitted at ten on the morning of 1 April.[76]

To these parties we now return.

Within a day or two of landing, Celosse met his friend Lindemans again – Mies Celosse had encountered him while her husband was abroad. Lindemans, helpful as ever, got hold of a car, and drove the Celosses back to the Wieringerpolder to rescue some cached kit.[77] He introduced his friend 'Jackie' to them, who came to live in the Jekerstraat house in south Amsterdam; so did Cnoops, when he found his digs were being watched, after he had moved Sanders to a safe place. Cnoops did not care for 'Jackie': sensibly, because 'Jackie' was a double agent called Adrian Breed, planted on the circuit by Lindemans, who had changed sides while Celosse was in England.

Now Lindemans had a way with women. When yet there was no fear of AIDS, he disliked sleeping alone; his wartime career was littered with discarded mistresses, one at least of whom bore him children. He shopped some, but not all, of them to the Abwehr; it was a convenient way of getting them out of his orbit.

At seven in the morning of 9 March 1944 the Gestapo had raided a small hotel, the Montholon, in south-west Paris. Probably they had been tipped off by one of the *femmes de chambre*, who was walking out with a man in the SD. They arrested thirteen guests, among them a good-looking French dancer who was pregnant with a child of Lindemans. After they had left, the manageress went round the hiding-places she knew of in the vacated rooms, making a small haul of arms, passports and stamps for forged papers.[78]

75. BSS/A to AD/P, 24 May 1944, TSC in Holland (2).
76. *Ibid.*
77. De Roever, *op. cit.*, 46.
78. Appx D to report of 11 January 1945 in Lindemans PF, vol. 4.

Somebody telephoned word through to Lindemans, who was in Brussels that day; he was much upset.

He was extra fond of Mademoiselle Filou the dancer, who had borne him one daughter already and was to bear another in Fresnes. His younger brother Jan had been arrested in Holland during the winter. Always a man of impulse, even more so than van Bilsen, he abruptly decided to turn double agent.

He had a friend in the NSB, Willy van der Meer of Leyden, who also happened to be in Brussels; and was able to put him in touch at once with a junior Abwehr employee they both knew as Nelis. Nelis's real name was J. C. A. Verloop, another Dutchman, who had turned double already. He had been a merchant seaman in the 1930s, and had left Holland abruptly to join the French Foreign Legion; in which he had fought at Narvik in 1940. His battalion's survivors were taken to Liverpool, where he turned down a chance to join the Free French, and moved on to Brest. There he was greeted by a young German officer, who recommended him to return to Holland. Rearrested near Lille as a suspected spy, Verloop had been turned loose on the understanding that he would work with the Abwehr; Kup was among the men with whom he dealt. He was living in Brussels, on a German-paid salary of 6,000 francs a month, trying to break into escape lines. On being approached by Lindemans, Verloop took a train to Driebergen, and at once managed to set up an interview between Lindemans and Giskes.

To Giskes's astonishment, this gorilla-like figure strode into his office and poured on to a table in front of him a thick briefcase full of forged travel documents and identity papers, together with some of the Wehrmacht and OT rubber stamps used to forge them, and wads of foreign currency.[79] Thereafter, he was Giskes's man.

According to a fellow traitor, 267 arrests followed from Lindemans's change of sides in the spring of 1944:[80] a stiff obstacle for revisionists to cross as they seek to prove that his heart was 'really' on the side of the allied, not of the nazi, cause.

Just before the war, he had had a bad accident when testing a motor bicycle. This seems to have left him not only physically but

---

79. Giskes, *op. cit.*, 144–5.
80. De Jong, *KdN*, 10a. 418–19.

emotionally scarred, liable to gusts of temper and sudden changes of judgement as well as to epileptic fits. MI5 found him particularly hard to interrogate, for sharp questioning tended to bring on a fit, or at least the appearance of one. The plea of diminished responsibility, which epileptics can make in courts of law, carries less impact before the bar of history; but at least one writer has been found to plead the cause that Lindemans was not at heart a traitor.[81] There is perhaps an analogy here with Henri Déricourt, the double agent highly thought of both by the Gestapo in Paris and by F section of SOE in London; and more recently presented – in the teeth of the evidence – as a tool of MI6 rather than of his own ambition.

Lindemans at least secured his brother's release from prison – the young man was sent off to work in Germany instead. The Germans kept Mademoiselle Filou, as a means of keeping her lover under some degree of control. He busied himself with betraying to them as many of his ex-colleagues as he could catch; including Celosse's nascent circuit.

Celosse and Cnoops were both busy, hunting for dropping zones for arms, seeing to reliable reception committees who would have safe storage spaces, and reporting progress to London through Sanders. So was Seyben, who lived and worked independently, but was also bound to the same W/T set. Cnoops was also able to pass some SOE directives to the RVV; who put up a plan for an attack on Dordrecht power station, which fell through because the RAF found itself unable to drop flares to illuminate the target.[82]

On Friday/Saturday night, 19/20 May, Celosse was away. Next morning Mies went out shopping, early. Cnoops, dead tired, decided to take an extra hour in bed. He was awake, not yet up, when the obliging 'Jackie' looked in and took away his shoes to clean. A few minutes later the doorbell rang; heavy boots then sounded downstairs. Cnoops reached for his revolver, which he kept overnight by his shoes; it was not there. An SS party overpowered him, arrested Mies when she returned, and quietly collected Celosse also, later in the day. There was a prearranged danger signal, a particular way of hanging the curtains; no one who knew it got a chance to display it.

---

81. Anne Laurens, *L'Affaire King Kong*.
82. History cx, April 1944, 1.

Both Celosses were taken to Haaren. She was released late on 5 September; Bob was shot, earlier that day, at Vught. Cnoops escaped from Sachsenhausen right at the end of the war. Seyben and Sanders were also promptly arrested, by Lindemans's agency; Sanders was shot in September, Seyben survived Oranienburg and Landshut.[83]

Sanders showed skill and resource in enemy hands. He was captured with his set, and worked it back under German orders; but much more slowly than had been his usual style, and fiddling so oddly with his security checks that London quickly realised something was up.[84] Direction-finding, asked to place his set, put it first at Driebergen, then in Utrecht, instead of in Amsterdam; and when he was asked 'What do you know?', he replied, 'American soldier'.[85] It was thus early clear to his friends that his enemies held him: a refreshing change.

Extra confusion was added to the clandestine scene in Holland in mid-May 1944, right at the time of these arrests; it arose from muddles within the German secret services, and from Lindemans's notorious lack of security. His flamboyant behaviour caught the eye of some policemen in the SD, who were unaware that he was an Abwehr agent. In a scuffle with them, he was wounded and taken to a hospital in Leyden, from which he was cut out a fortnight later by an Abwehr squad in plain clothes led by Willy Kup, who pretended to be resisters.[86] Word of this coup crept out round resistance circles, as it was meant to do, and did his standing in them good.

Let us revert to All Fools' Day 1944 to describe the separate mission that went in on the same night as Celosse's party. Tobias Biallosterski, born at Bloemendaal in 1920, had already had plenty of brushes with danger before he joined SOE. His father, a Polish Jew by origin with a Dutch Christian wife, was a diamond polisher by profession, like three of his sons, including the future agent. The father escaped to England in May 1940. Tobias, not a practising Jew himself, enabled

---

83. PFs, and de Roever, *op. cit.*, 45–52.
84. HQ 179, signal security.
85. BSS/A to AD/P, 24 May 1944, TSC in Holland 19.
86. De Jong, *KdN*, 10a. 419–20; appx I to progress report on Giskes, 5 June 1945, xxxi, duplic in Holland 22.

over forty Jews to hide from the Germans. He and his friend Rein Bangma undertook the perilous task of carrying packets of *Het Parool*, one of the leading underground newspapers, round the suburbs of Amsterdam by bicycle: the link between the press and the distributors in detail. At the paper they were known as 'Tom and Popeye'.[87] Moreover, he hid three evading RAF aircrew as well. By October 1943 he judged his home district too hot to hold him, and escaped with some friends on a Rotterdam potato barge, which broke down in the North Sea. HMS *Campbell* met and rescued the party;[88] N section was delighted to take him on.

As he was already a figure in the world of the underground press, he seemed a suitable man to go and repair the damage that must, London thought, have resulted from Gruen's unhappy connexion with 'Golf'.

He found indeed, when he and Steman had moved off – troubled only by barking dogs – from their DZ near Breda to his mother's home near his birthplace, and he had regained touch with his clandestine friends, that Gruen's misadventures were already widely known. That agent was generally thought to have over-estimated his own importance, and to have approached too many people.[89]

On first arriving, Biallosterski and Steman thought it safer to bury their W/T set than to carry it about with them; but when Steman went back a week later to collect it, there was no trace of it beyond a few bits of its packing. Evidently a passer-by had noticed the disturbed earth, dug it up, and made off with it; a policeman would not have dropped the packaging.[90] Nothing more was ever heard of the set.

Biallosterski soon got in touch again with the editors of *Het Parool*, and on 27 April 1944 the paper's front page reproduced a signed message from Wilhelmina which he had brought over with him.[91] In it the queen reassured her subjects that she and they stood shoulder to shoulder in the struggle for truth, law and liberty.

---

87. Madelon de Keizer, *Het Parool 1940–1945* (Amsterdam: Otto Cramwinckel, 1991), 332.
88. RVPS report 17, 107, 14 October 1943, TSC in his PF.
89. Report by Biallosterski, 13 July, 4–5; tr. unknown; *ibid.*
90. *Ibid.*, 3–4.
91. Facsimile in de Keizer, *Het Parool*, 402.

The agent by this time had already left Holland, on the 19th; having distributed 50,000 florins round the clandestine press, and heard many tales about 'Brutus' and how little use that unhappy man had been. A priest helped Biallosterski cross into Belgium, wearing a customs armlet; before another priest found him a bicycle, which he rode right through to Paris. He reached England, through Spain, on 9 July.[92]

In the summer of 1944, as in the summer of 1943, Bomber Command displayed anxiety about special duties drops into the Netherlands, which were more than once suspended for sound airmen's reasons. Air staff officers felt, intelligibly enough, that airmen's lives ought not to be risked flying Halifaxes or Stirlings at low level near the major Luftwaffe night-fighter base at Gilze-Rijen, or anywhere else where the Kammhuber line was dense. The line was the second – second only to Berlin – most formidable barrage of AA guns in the world, and was intended ('sanguine!' Mr Gladstone would again have added) to make the Reich impenetrable by air from the west. This was not country over which any aircrew would care to hunt long, at a few hundred feet, for the dim lights of a reception committee.

Up till 1944, reception lights in Holland had not been all that dim; indeed, numerous reports from returning special duties pilots had remarked on how bright they had been.[93] Hindsight, but hindsight alone, makes these reports suspicious: at the time, they were thought to reflect Dutch rather than German competence.[94]

Agents in Holland showed a waiting reception committee by putting out, in the middle of the dropping zone, three red lights in a narrow triangle, with its point down-wind. Close to the point, the man in charge flashed an agreed morse letter on a white torch.[95] This made a mark easy enough for a sharp-eyed pilot to pick out, and the letter provided a degree of security: not a guarantee – it might have

---

92. Details in his PF.
93. Air 27/956, 138 squadron ORB, *passim*.
94. Conversation with Robin Brook, 24 June 1996.
95. Holland 34, appx II of operation orders for 'Cauliflower', 19 September 1942, page 3 of TSC.

been prearranged, by mistake, with the enemy. If it had been, the orders given as late as September 1942 to the pilot – that, when he saw the lights, he was to 'wink his navigation lights several times'[96] – would have made it all the more easy for a lurking night fighter to pounce; this may help to account for the RAF's rate of casualties over Holland.

On the last night of May 1944 two more N agents left for Holland, Cornelius Dekkers ('Poker'), a twenty-four-year-old subaltern wireless operator, and Gerrit Kuenen ('Football'), a slightly older sergeant sabotage instructor. Before the war Dekkers had been a student at Breda, and Kuenen an engineering draughtsman at Beverwijk. Dekkers, one of ten children, spoke eight languages, three of them fluently. They had each left Holland, separately, in 1941, and reached England by way of Perpignan, a Spanish prison, and the new world.

They were to have been dropped east of Eindhoven, but the Hudson that carried them flew too close to Gilze-Rijen and was shot down. There were no survivors.[97]

In fact the Dutch recovery, that forms this chapter's heading, had taken place *in posse*, on the staff. *In esse*, in the field, on Dutch ground, there was still a woeful shortage of arms and no reliable W/T liaison with London. Steman, the only free operator, currently had no set.

---

96. *Ibid.*
97. Their PFs; and de Roever, *op. cit.*, 53–61.

V

Belgian Disasters
1940–2

'Le Belge a horreur de la discipline. La désobéissance est
chez lui un réflexe spontané.'

Le Soir, Brussels, 16 September 1944

Holland, we have seen, was by no means the same as France. No
more was Belgium; though there were more similarities between
Belgian and French than between Dutch and French reactions to
occupation. As the Belgians had been German-occupied before, well
within living memory, they knew more about how to behave than
the Dutch did; more also than the French, who had more remote
memories of the partial occupations of 1870–1 and 1814–18.

Some Belgians were inclined to let it all slide over them, and wait
for better times: as had been the case a century and a quarter before.
As Fanny Burney, the novelist, wrote when she fled from Paris to
Brussels on Buonaparte's return from Elba in 1815, 'The Belgians
have for so many Centuries been accustomed to sanguinary conflicts, and violent, or mercenary, change of masters, that I really
thought, from the placid state in which, when here seeking an
asylum, I found them, that they were utterly indifferent to the result
of the neighbouring struggle, and would just as willingly have fallen
again into the hands of Buonaparte as not.'[1] Others were, from the
first, inclined to be more combative. In 1940 elderly men retained,
and passed on to their sons, vivid memories of how disagreeable
German occupation had been. Even if many of the atrocity stories

---

1. 3 July 1815, quoted in Eva Figes (ed.), *Women's Letters in Wartime 1450–1945*
(Pandora, 1993), 123.

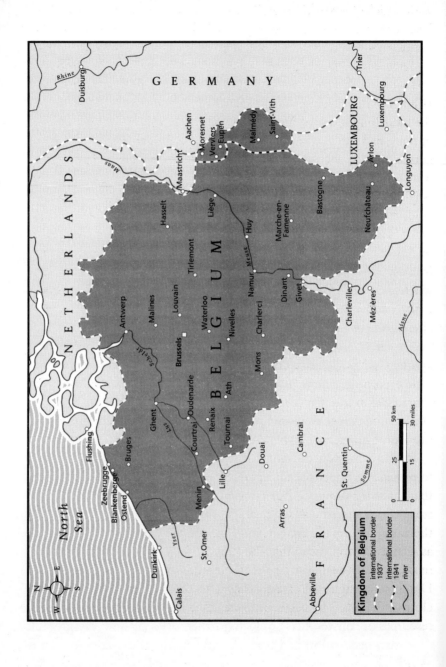

with which the world's press had rung in the autumn of 1914 had been untrue, being run by imperial Germany had been nasty: the nation that had quite liked Buonaparte did not care for Kaiser Bill.

Les braves Belges became proverbial with the English public in 1914, but the army has never forgotten nor forgiven what the Belgians who were supposed to be in combat beside it had done on the hard-fought day of Waterloo, almost a century before. Too many of them had run away at the first salvo from Buonaparte's eighty-gun battery, and spent the day hanging about in the Forêt de Soignes, waiting to join whichever side won. This did not augur well for Anglo-Belgian collaboration in arms; and, behind the scenes, Dansey made a remark which the politically correct would today denounce as racist. He had had some disillusioning experiences with Belgians during the 1914–18 war, and believed their national character to be irredeemably faulty. This disinclined him to help SOE in any way where work into Belgium was concerned: 'It is many years ago since I first had to deal with Belgians and their intrigues. They have not altered one bit in twenty five years.'[2]

This is but one example of a widespread disdain for Belgians among the ruling class in London about 1940. Clerks in the Foreign Office complained of 'miserable weaklings' and 'chicken-hearted characters' in the Belgian embassy during that year's summer crisis,[3] and another wrote them off collectively – 'they are a poor lot' – in a dismissive minute in March 1941.[4]

In this world war, Belgium's role in German strategy was, initially, to provide the space for the opening move of *Sichelschnitt*, the stroke that shattered the allied front in May 1940; then, to provide airfields from which the air onslaught on Great Britain could be fought; and thereafter to provide factories and labour for German war industry, as well as communications into France. An eventual allied advance into Germany would be far more likely to cross Belgian than to cross Dutch soil; might well start, where the air cover would be densest, close to Belgium's western corner; and would certainly need the port resources of Antwerp in the closing stages.

2. Dansey to Knight, 28 September 1942, initialled TS in Belgium 229.
3. PRO FO 371/24276.
4. FO 371/26342, f. 116.

On 10 May 1940, with no warning, Germany invaded Belgium as well as Holland, Luxembourg and France. That day, the Belgian security authorities arrested both Leon Degrelle, the rexist leader, and Joris van Severen, the 'very capable' leader[5] of Verdinaso. Degrelle was put straight over the frontier into France, where the police interned him as an undesirable alien; he was back in Belgium by August, full of complaints. Van Severen, after five days in a cell in Bruges, was deported westward also; and shot dead at Abbeville on the 20th, in a small massacre of suspects by drunken French soldiers. Staf de Clerq who ran the VNV survived for the time being; only to die in the middle of the war. By then it had become clear that, in Belgium as in Holland, those inclined to favour nazism had only one role to play for their current masters: to drum up volunteers for the fight against bolshevism.

Yet in May 1940 the bolsheviks were still the nazis' allies; this *Blitzkrieg*, like the Luftwaffe's effort in the battle of Britain, was partly fuelled by soviet petrol. The German army and air force overran Belgium with wholly unexpected speed: less than three weeks passed between the first attack and the surrender. Calvocoressi's *Total War* includes a map that shows the stages of the German advance quite clearly:[6] the expanding torrent of armour advocated by the tank experts.

The king of the Belgians was in a horrible dilemma, for which his ministers and his allies had no sympathy. They held that he should follow his father's example, and continue to head a Belgian army – even an army in exile – that went on fighting Germany. He was still more sharply pricked by the dilemma's other horn: he thought his duty lay in sharing his people's sufferings. So Belgium in May 1940 endured a constitutional as well as a military crisis.[7]

Bad as the military results of the German onslaught were, the political results were hardly better. Not only was the army swiftly

---

5. FO 371/26342, f. 306 v.
6. Peter Calvocoressi, Guy Wint and John Pritchard, *Total War* (2 edn, Viking, 1989), 135.
7. PRO WO 197/127 contains copies, sent by Beaumont-Nesbitt to the War Office's historical section on 23 July 1940, of correspondence between Churchill, Gort and Keyes in May and June of that year; they provide the core of Keyes's son's defence of Leopold III.

overwhelmed, but Leopold III and his ministers fell out irretrievably. He used his powers as commander-in-chief with little reference to them. When they joined in the panic which carried most of the motor-car-owning population of Belgium away south-westwards in mid-May 1940, hampering the movement of troops, providing the Luftwaffe with opportunity targets, and setting a deplorable, though promptly followed, example to the population of north-east France – not the most creditable page in the history of the western European bourgeoisie – he declined to follow them. He judged it his duty to stay with his occupied people.

The Belgian parliament, like the Dutch, had gone into recess for Whitsun. Most deputies, like most of the rest of the ruling class, bolted. Enough of them cast up in Limoges on the last day of May for an extempore, emergency session,[8] which echoed Pierlot the prime minister's denunciation of Leopold's surrender, made in a broadcast from Paris on the evening it was made, 28 May.

The cabinet broke up. Two ministers, Jaspar (health) and de Vleeschauwer (colonies), turned up in London, where they fell out with each other. On 28 June Jaspar put out an appeal, similar to de Gaulle's now celebrated appeal of ten days earlier, for Belgians who wanted to continue resistance to join him.[9] De Vleeschauwer had already been granted, by decree of his cabinet colleagues, administrative and financial powers over the Belgian Congo, a trump card.[10] They had with them – though in no sympathy with them – Camille Huysmans, absentee mayor of Antwerp, yet also chairman of the Second International: another usable advantage. Moreover, Huysmans was an old friend of Dalton's, who thought highly of his intellect;[11] and was of Jewish descent.[12]

For months these two were the only ministers resident in London; and Jaspar's colleagues disavowed him from a distance. Gutt, the minister of finance – an Alsatian Jew by ethnic origin, who disliked

---

8. Fifty-four senators and eighty-one deputies were present: Aveling to Halifax, no. 3, 14 June 1940, print in FO 371/24274.

9. *Keesing's Contemporary Archives*, 4136.

10. *Ibid.*

11. Dalton to Halifax, 11 October 1940, signed TS in FO 371/24276.

12. Jotting in FO 371/24274, f. 180.

Huysmans[13] – visited London by air occasionally from Lisbon. The Foreign Office offered the whole cabinet asylum in London as early as 16 June;[14] irresolute ministers dithered in southern France.

Formally, it is worth recall, it had been the Belgian army – like the Dutch, but unlike the French – that had surrendered to the German army; leaving the cabinet free to continue the war, if it would or could. The cabinet's second thought, after repudiating the king, was to rejoin him in captivity; a step forbidden by the new authorities in Brussels. London was thus a haven of last resort, to which the least irresolute ministers picked their way. Pierlot and Spaak, the prime and foreign ministers, were marooned for some days on the Franco-Spanish border, without visas either to re-enter Vichy France or to enter Spain; where, once admitted, they were put in house arrest. They escaped while their guards' backs were turned, slipped illegally into Portugal, and turned up in London – bringing Gutt with them – late in October.[15]

The Belgian government in exile thus got off to a late and shaky start. Meanwhile, the Foreign Office had fended off, with some difficulty, efforts by Huysmans and others to set up a Belgian National Committee in parallel with de Gaulle's Free French.[16] A further weakness in Pierlot's small team was that it consisted almost entirely of Walloons, and included no leading figure who could appeal to Flemings.[17]

Local authorities in Belgium returned to – a few had remained at – their posts; and adopted what they called a *politique du moindre mal*: they tried to follow whatever course would do least harm to their citizens, their equipment, and themselves.[18]

Belgium was emphatically not one of the countries in which SOE's first task was to stimulate resistance. From the moment of the Belgian surrender on 28 May 1940 a few officers began to plan how

---

13. FO 371/24277, f. 310: Aveling to Halifax, 18 October 1949, TS.
14. FO 371/24275, f. 75.
15. FO 371/24276, *passim.*
16. *Ibid.*
17. FO 371/26342, f. 149.
18. Many details of the Germans' administrative system are set out in E. Dejonghe (ed.), *L'Occupation en France et en Belgique 1940–1944.*

to get rid of the Germans; by the end of the year a fairly well articu-
lated body, the Légion Belge, had got a little way beyond the opening
stage of deciding who was reliable. There were also several other
smaller and wilder groupings, with some strength in particular areas.
While the ministers in exile tried to decide where to settle, most of
the survivors of the Belgian officer corps buckled down at once to the
tasks of resistance; beginning by counting up who was available, and
for what. Claser, for one, saw as early as the day his army surrendered
the width of the Channel, the strength of the navy, and the need to
resist.[19]

Could anything be done, by the world's leading naval power, on
the forty-two miles of the Belgian coast? Section D found a man
with an intimate knowledge of this coastline, René Burggraeve, a
junior customs official, born in 1896 and still bursting with energy.
He selected the open beach a few miles north-east of Ostend; four
attempts were made to set him down on it. On the most successful of these, on the night of 10/11 July 1940, an MTB took him
over, and he was rowed the last hundred yards to land from a
dinghy. He had hardly stepped ashore when a couple of Very lights
went up, the local platoon opened fire, and Burggraeve prudently
re-entered his dinghy, rejoined the MTB and returned to Dover.[20]
Further efforts to land him were still being made in late August; all
failed.

The Belgian shoreline soon formed part of the most heavily
defended coastline in the world, next to the Channel Islands: it ran
from the mouth of the Scheldt to the mouth of the Somme, and
landings on it were all but impossible. T long continued to press for
them; two attempts were mounted, and called off, in May 1941.[21] In
January 1942, imitating F section's attempts to moor containers of
arms offshore for fishermen to collect,[22] T contemplated attaching
some to an uncharted wreck off the Belgian coast;[23] nothing came of
this.

---

19. H. Bernard, *L'Armée Secrète 1940–1944*, 8.
20. D/I to D, 12 July 1940, copy in van Riel PF.
21. Whole world war diary, v(i). 873, 876, 21 May 1941.
22. Foot, *SOE in France*, 472.
23. TSC jotting of 16 January in Belgium 102.

Next month an operation called 'Ferret' was prepared. An MTB from Felixstowe was to meet seven Belgians, one of them an SOE wireless operator on the run, at a buoy nine miles north of Blankenberghe, to which they were to find their own way.[24] The Germans arrested most of them before they could leave the shore, and 'Ferret' stood down.

Combined Operations put a small commando party ashore on Christmas Eve 1943 on one of these all but impenetrable beaches, twenty miles west of the Belgian border by Gravelines, and two sturdy survivors from it marched through to join a 'Marksman' maquis in the Jura foothills next spring; but the MTB that bore them returned to Dover empty of soldiers.[25] After all their failures, SOE's staff sensibly tried no more in practice; though both staff and agents in T and in DF, as in N, sections continued to hanker after contact by sea in theory. Late in February 1942, after 'Ferret's' collapse, instructions to a departing agent included some hundreds of words on how to conduct a sea pick-up:[26] wasted effort.

Governments in exile can easily turn into hotbeds of intrigue: there is often so little left for their members to do but conspire. This affliction settled both on the Poles and on the Belgians. In both cases, rival departments – one military, one civil – strove for control over internal resistance, within the homeland. As SOE monopolised control of arms supply, it was necessarily much involved.

The principal authority on the history of SOE laid down in 1948 that it could do nothing without political implications.[27] In Belgium this was particularly noticeable: all its early attempts to get work under way were bedevilled by officials or ministers of the government in exile in London.

Just as the clandestine affairs of the Polish government in exile were bedevilled by rivalries between the ministries of defence and the interior, so were those of the Belgians between two rival bodies, each of which sought to control resistance activity. These were the Sûreté,

---

24. Belgium 167; not mentioned in Richards, *Secret Flotillas*. Cp page 264.
25. Personal knowledge.
26. Passelecq PF.
27. Mackenzie, *Secret History of SOE*, 346.

the security service in exile, and the Deuxième Section, the intelligence branch of the exiled general staff.

SOE's staff had no desire to work against the Belgian government in exile, any more than they wanted to work against any other body recognised by the crown; but to work with it was for some months impossible. SOE worked into Belgium under constraints that made Heller's Catch-22 look simple. In its earliest days the whole body was obsessed with security: but the more perfect the security, the smaller the actual gains. On security grounds, Eric Dadson, the first head of T section, was forbidden any contact on SOE business with any representative of the nascent Belgian government in exile.[28] Until such contact started, recruits were all but unfindable; once it had started, they were all but unusable.

For the Sûreté announced that it would only co-operate with T if fully informed, in advance, of every agent's intended role. MI5 and MI6 agreed that any such step would be dreadfully insecure. That MI6 was managing, all the same, to co-operate closely with the Sûreté only gradually became clear to T. On the other hand, the Deuxième Section announced that it would only co-operate with T if T had no dealings with the Sûreté at all.

T section persevered as best it could. Dadson and his successor Claude Knight in turn resolved to see whether they could mount operations without referring to any Belgian officials in London; and Knight enlisted Keswick's and Gubbins's approval and aid. Keswick and Gubbins, in a number of interviews with the key Belgian figures, reserved SOE's right to send agents into Belgium without clearing them in advance with any Belgian authority, in exile or not; while taking care not to reveal whether T section had done, or was going to do, anything of the sort. Hanbury-Williams and Playfair, in their report, observed that SOE might well need to work with 'Allied nationals who may not be identified with or may even be in political opposition to' a government in exile; and added only the proviso that SOE must 'ensure that their agents do not encourage any particular political faction or participate in intrigues carried on in opposition to the Government recognised by HM Government'.[29]

---

28. History lxv, T section, 3.
29. 18 June 1942, 5; in HQ 60.

The Belgian government in exile realised that its political hold over Belgium, however sound in law, was weak in fact. This led quite fast to fears of widespread unrest, or even of civil war, once the allies overran nazi Belgium. No wonder they were anxious to control the way weapons were distributed round their country for subversive purposes; they lived in constant alarm that private armies would spring up, aimed at overthrowing themselves. Whether danger impended from the fascist right or the communist left they were unsure.

Hence the weight they gave to their security branch, the Sûreté, which wished to have a finger in every secret pie: greatly to SOE's annoyance. Its civilian head, Fernand Lepage,[30] was the only member of the Belgian magistracy to have effected an escape as far as London; this gave him standing in the eyes of his fellow-countrymen in exile. A Belgian army captain, Nicodème, headed his small staff at 27 Eaton Place, round the corner from the government's main offices in Eaton Square; with an assistant called Aronstein, a former Lufthansa employee but of German Jewish origin, thus reliably anti-nazi. They were later lent, by the friendly millionaire who owned it, 38 Belgrave Square, where Robin Brook had once worked as private tutor to the millionaire's daughter.

The Deuxième Section – later in the war renamed the Deuxième Direction – was formally part of the general staff of the Free Belgian army. Its first two heads, Colonels Diepenrykx and Trieste, were trained staff officers with no previous knowledge or experience either of clandestine or of intelligence work. They too worked near to the exiled cabinet's offices in Eaton Square; settling in 34 and, later, 40 Eaton Place.

There were three points at issue – political, organisational and personal.

The political trouble was that ministers in exile feared that SOE would arm bodies in Belgium who could use the arms, not against

---

30. A Paris gunsmith called Le Page made the pair of pistols Buonaparte carried to Waterloo, but abandoned in his coach when it was stuck in a traffic jam during his flight; they now rest in the Rijksmuseum. The coincidence of names may only be an accident.
    Photograph of Fernand Lepage in George de Lovinfosse, *Au Service de leurs Majestés*, 47.

the Germans but against the returning exiles: a delicate, even embarrassing matter, on which SOE could produce plenty of assurances, but could not be sure the exiles would believe them.

Organisationally, Gubbins – who here took the lead – had endless trouble in trying to convince the Belgians that SOE's active role, inciting sabotage and subversion, was quite unlike MI5's or MI6's – providing security or intelligence; so that the excellent relations between Lepage's Sûreté and both MI5 and MI6 did not entitle Lepage to be kept fully informed about SOE's entirely separate work. Lepage's task, Gubbins argued, should be restricted to clearing T section's Belgian recruits as unlikely to be traitors or troublemakers, after which he should leave them to get on with their jobs.

The personal trouble was simple, but dire: Lepage and Keswick did not trust each other, nor did Lepage and Knight.

T section believed this was a transient trouble; none of them took in that it was going to last for years, as it did.[31]

That bugbear, the quarrel between Flemings and Walloons that has so often riven Belgian politics, mercifully played no part in this story. Indeed, a well-informed Belgian reckoned in early 1941 that the German occupation had produced a miraculous Walloon-Fleming entente.[32] Yet though there were no racial quarrels within T section, or indeed within Belgian resistance – the enemy was too fierce for local difficulties to be allowed to get in the way of resisting him – there was one important impact that the racial problem made on T section's task. Many Flemish-speaking schoolmasters had taken care not to teach French at all well; so that a great many Flemish-speaking Belgians felt they had not got adequate French to sustain themselves in the journey across France that had to come first if they wanted to get out of Belgium to join the forces in exile. Many more of the recruits available to T were of Walloon than of Flemish origin; this was a datum of the war's geography, not a reflection on Flemish patriotism.

The German counter-espionage triumph in Holland is notorious. It is less well known that, for a while, they did almost as well in

---

31. History lxv. 7.
32. Enclosure in O'Malley to Makins, 4 March 1941, 3; TS in FO 371/26342. f. 196.

Belgium, where for their first three years of occupation they had only too large a share in running armed resistance. Troubles for SOE were not as traumatic as they were in Holland, but were not slight; crossed wires with MI6 made them worse. Recruiting, again, was difficult; most of T's early agents were of low quality, and their morale – even before dispatch – was generally bad.[33]

The government in exile provided a lasting difficulty also. Financially it was one of the strongest, for – thanks to British sea power – it continued to command the resources of the Belgian Congo; morally it was one of the weakest. Its ministers often hesitated to sanction any steps at all; Gubbins, just after the war, complained of their pusillanimity[34] – the vice attributed to them already in the summer of 1940 by Aveling, chargé d'affaires at the British embassy to Brussels, who had followed them to Bruges, to Poitiers and to Bordeaux, and had offered them air or sea passages to England, which they had first proposed and then refused.[35] One of their senior civil servants, much embrangled with SOE, could not recall in distant retrospect that he had received any orders from the exile cabinet; he had simply got on with his job.[36]

SOE was not only sometimes in rivalry with SIS; rivalries between its own sections were endemic. T section, remembering that Belgian independence dated back to a war of liberation against the Dutch in the early 1830s, distrusted N section. F section, less historically minded, remembered it had originally been formed to look after Belgian as well as French affairs. When on 19 December 1940 T was set up as an independent section, F did not release to it several Belgians whom it was already training.[37]

T's first head, Dadson, had been the managing director of the Antwerp gas company. He was a tall, thirty-seven-year-old bachelor with a sound head for business, an extensive knowledge of Belgian commerce, fluent French, fair Dutch, and a small collection of rare

---

33. Mackenzie, *op. cit.*, 299.
34. In a peppery minute of 26 October 1945, prefixed to History lxv.
35. Aveling to Halifax, 16 July 1940, print in FO 371/2475.
36. Conversation with Baron Lepage, 18 November 1988.
37. Whole world war diary, i. 37.

coins. Like Nelson, the first CD, he is said to have belonged in the late 1930s to Dansey's now well-known Z organisation, which had doubled up for C's agents abroad. It is not known how many others from Z were absorbed into SOE. Dadson's name was put up to Nelson by Guy Vansittart, also Z, whom his elder brother Sir Robert described as knowing Belgium 'better than any other Englishman living in this country'.[38] Nelson's first impressions were favourable.[39] Unhappily Dadson's discretion did not match some of his other abilities. In the autumn of 1941 he fell foul of SOE's security branch, and resigned sooner than be dismissed. His offence seems to have been to have written a lampoon about some fellow officers which he forgot to lock up overnight.[40]

He had a few months as security adviser to an electricity firm, but then – his *Times* obituarist missed this – was able to join the Belgian section of PWE, and occasionally make himself useful to T.[41]

He was replaced by Claude Knight, who had already spent over six months in the section, originally as a conducting officer. Knight came into SOE from the War Office's military liaison staff, where he had dealt with Belgian, French and Dutch troops. He was a Coldstreamer, already a major at thirty, with fine manners, good French, knowledge of the world, and a place in Society – both sides of the North Sea, for his wife was a peer's daughter, and one of her grandfathers had been Sylvain van de Weyer, long the Belgian envoy in London.[42] A stammer only served to enhance his earnestness and his charm; but fine manners, in the longer run, were not enough to convince the London Belgians that he was reliable. He knew no more of the actualities of clandestine war than they did; less, even, than Pierlot and Spaak, who had undergone interrogation and escape. Indeed, as the section history recorded, none of T section's

---

38. TS of 6 October 1940 in FO 371/24276, f. 322. Nelson and Vansittart are named in Read and Fisher, *Colonel Z*, 176.

39. Nelson to Jebb, 20 December 1940, TSC in Dadson PF.

40. Conversation with C. T. Knight, 3 July 1990.

41. *The Times* obituary, 9 March 1995, 21d; jottings in Belgium 113, and elsewhere in SOE's Belgium files.

42. Obituary in *The Times*, 29 November 1993. Conspiracy theorists will note that Colonel J. H. Bevan, who ran the deception service in 1942–5, was also a close connexion of van de Weyer's.

officers 'had any practical previous knowledge of clandestine work. They gained it by experience which can only be described as bitter.'[43]

One of these officers, Duff Torrance, was a friend of Dadson's, whom he had known in Antwerp in the late 1930s. He had fought in France and in Salonika in 1915–17, and had had a brief spell in MIR under Jo Holland, early in 1940; but he was no more discreet than Dadson, and left with him.

Another early conducting officer who could not stay the course was Jocelyn Clark, who came to SOE via the fifth battalion of the Scots Guards, a unit of skiing volunteers for service in Finland who mercifully never got there. His mother was Belgian; he was a captain in the Gordon Highlanders; he had done well reading economics at McGill just before the war. If he had a fault, it was to be over-enthusiastic, thus rubbing his seniors up the wrong way. Accident put his sister at Pierlot's elbow, as a secretary; this in turn led to sus-picions, as the perhaps over-sensitive Knight was 'trying to steer some sort of course through the very heavy waters of SOE/SIS/MI5/ Belgian relationships'.[44] He had to go back to ordinary soldiering when the Germans arrested his parents in Belgium in the spring of 1942.

R. L. Raemakers was more than a conducting officer – he was first taken on, in August 1942, as an 'Operations Adviser'. He was Dutch by birth – his father was the leading cartoonist of the Great War – and trilingual in English, Dutch and French; and so capable that he moved on after a year to the task of liaison with COSSAC (the chief of staff to the supreme allied commander) and then with SHAEF.

Briefly, T section's conducting officers included a friend of Knight's, the second Lord Howard of Penrith, great-grandson of the twelfth Duke of Norfolk. He had been at Trinity, Cambridge, and at Harvard while his father was ambassador in Washington. He felt that in his middle thirties he ought not to be a staff officer, and moved across to March-Phillips's Small Scale Raiding Force. In September 1942 he was badly wounded, and taken prisoner, on operation 'Aquatint' on the west Norman coast, which was fatal to his commander.

---

43. History lxv. 8
44. Post-war jotting by Norman Mott in Clark PF.

Another of them was André M. F. J. Robinson, whom Ian Fenwick – *Punch* cartoonist; then commandant of STS4; destined for an early death with SAS – described in March 1943 as 'just what a conducting officer should be'.[45] Born in 1916 to an Anglo-Belgian marriage, he was bilingual in English and French, as well as having fluent Dutch and German. He had been a clerk in Aachen in the winter of 1934–5 before becoming a railway clerk in London; entered SOE through the field security police; and had the great gift of being 'never in the way, and never out of the way'.[46]

Albert Vennix also had a Belgian mother. He was born in Glasgow in 1915 and brought up in Antwerp, where his British father died in 1930; he was trilingual in English, French and Dutch. He had worked as a claims clerk for Lever Brothers, and enjoyed a spell as a field security police sergeant-interrogator at the RVPS. He joined T section in August 1942, but was posted out seven months later, as more suited to interrogation work than to a conducting officer's task. Another conducting officer was E. A. Cuthbert, a sub-lieutenant RNVR, who had spent a year as a sea-going junior officer before SOE took him on in April 1942; he too did not stay long.

R. I. Dobson, whom readers have met already as the last N,[47] was for years the section's operations officer, charged with all the details of confirming dropping zones, keeping in touch with the RAF, ordering equipment: a mass of tedious, necessary tasks. His assistant and successor was G. J. Kidd, born of British parents in Antwerp in 1903 and brought up there as a child – so that he had fluent French and Dutch; he had worked as a junior accountant in India and in Egypt, and came into SOE as a field security lance-corporal, watching over T's trainees. He was a steady, competent, good-humoured man, not easy to rattle. Planning was in the hands of Hardy Amies, who later become T himself.[48] They were helped in the donkey-work that goes with running a unit of this kind by Graeme Thompson, who had just turned thirty when the war began; he had acquired fluent French during eight years as a real estate agent in France, before he became

---

45. Signed TS chit in Robinson PF.
46. *Ibid.*
47. Page 206.
48. See pages 333–40.

a captain in the Intelligence Corps, which reclaimed him in autumn 1943. Mrs Cameron, a WAAF officer, looked after agents' welfare at the training stage and helped people prepare their cover stories. Peter Belgeonne succeeded Thompson, and stayed on at work after the end of the war to bear the burdens of tidying up.

W. A. Murphy, an early member of SOE in the Balkans, had sold petrol over much of Europe for fifteen years before the war. He joined T section, from Cairo, at the end of 1943 as planning officer, and went forward into Belgium – promoted major – with SPU47. At six feet four, with a long nose, he was a readily recognisable personality, and did useful work writing SOE histories as the organisation wound down.

For training purposes, T section shared STS4 at Winterfold with N; Flemish was then regarded simply as a dialect of Dutch, so that Flemish-speaking Belgians and Dutchmen could follow the same lectures. The paramilitary, parachute, sabotage, signals and security schools were also as described above.

Reception committee drill was the same for Belgium as for Holland. At least two men were needed for each expected container; spades, or a convenient pond or canal, were needed too, to dispose of the containers; not to speak of somewhere safe to store the supplies received. For a small reception, to meet a single agent and a package or two, it might be worth carrying passes to break curfew; larger parties simply took their chance and hoped to dodge police patrols.

Belgium's status was different from Holland's in nazi constitutional theory. Instead of being a *Reichskommisariat*, under direct colonial rule from Berlin, it was meant to be a client kingdom. Nazi theorists had a smattering of ancient history, and thought that Belgium might stand to the Third Reich much as Pontus or Numidia had stood to the Roman Empire. The administrative headquarters in Brussels that had made itself world-infamous by shooting Edith Cavell in 1915 was set up again, alongside the continuing Belgian civil service.

The catch in this system was that the king, though present in his palace at Laeken, refused to reign. Power was therefore exercised by the German commander-in-chief, General von Falkenhausen, previously the German adviser to General Chiang Kai-shek. The general left most decisions to the president of the military administration,

Eggert Reeder, who held brigadier-general's rank in the SS. As the war went on, Himmler tried harder and harder – through Reeder – to elbow the military authorities out of the way and run Belgium through his own cohorts. Unluckily for the historians, we have no Schreieder in Brussels to provide an almost day-to-day account of Section IV F's activities.

The Abwehrstelle in Brussels, established in the rue de la Loi as early as 18 May 1940, was commanded till the end of 1941 by Lieutenant-Colonel Dischler; then by the tall, monocled Colonel Servaes, who was said to look like a high dignitary of the Church of England; and from April 1943 to March 1944 by Colonel Scholtz. Under them, Major Möhring ran the counter-espionage section III F, aided by Otto Weil and a number of highly competent Belgian traitors.[49] After March 1944 the Abwehr was absorbed into the SS; most of its men went into reconnaissance units, and from SOE's angle it ceased to be a menace.

A routine interrogation of a captured agent in Belgium would include German assertions that they knew all about his employers in London; he was only a filthy spy, who would be disavowed. As there was no hope for him from his former employers, he might just as well save himself further brutalities by changing sides.[50] Good agents held out against this sort of pressure; others succumbed.

Though Giskes was long the senior Abwehr counter-espionage personality in Belgium as well as in Holland, his great success with operation 'North Pole' led him to concentrate rather on the Dutch than on the Belgian aspects of his responsibilities. The comparatively gentle, but firm tone that he and Schreieder of the SD took with their Dutch captives does not seem to have been copied south of the Dutch-Belgian border, where prisoners had a rougher ride.

Two points in wartime political geography are worth mention, though SOE took little notice of either. The two northernmost French *départements*, Nord and Pas-de-Calais, were administered by the German occupying authorities – to suit their own convenience – from Brussels, rather than from Paris or Vichy. Frontier controls

49. Bernard, *op. cit.*, 37–8.
50. Details in long report by Brion, 5 June 1945, signed TS in Belgium 108.

between them and Belgium remained, as an obstacle to movement – always something a dictatorship seeks to maintain; with German police and customs officials standing by at the elbows of the locals, who did the donkey-work of questioning and case-rummaging. And secondly, the areas round Moresnet, Eupen, Malmédy and St Vith, south of Aachen on the Belgo-German frontier, ceded by Germany in 1920 as a first instalment of the detested reparations for damage caused in the previous world war, were on 18 May 1940 re-annexed to the Third Reich. Hitler had incessantly denounced the Versailles settlement, of which this cession formed a part,[51] and reversed it by a personal order. SOE's inter-section boundaries followed pre-war geography, not Hitler's decrees; with at least one tragic conse-quence.[52]

The Foreign Office noticed a turn in Belgian opinion, in the autumn of 1940. As England did not give in to Germany after all, it was no longer necessary to make the best of a bad job and settle down simply to endure occupation.[53] Personally, one might well not yet want to take an active part in resistance, but at least one could hope for Germany's eventual defeat. When, a year or so later, it emerged that the *Blitzkrieg* had not brought swift victory over Russia either, one could hope more strongly.

As a background to what follows – tales too often of betrayal and disaster – readers need to recollect the profound unpopularity of the occupying forces in Belgium. For every honestly mistaken far right-winger, there were scores of right-minded citizens, who longed for the enemy to be gone; and the longer the war went on, the more likely each individual was to take the anti-nazi side in a sudden crisis.

By the summer of 1941 it was clear, mainly through reports from refugees, that Belgium was facing famine:[54] no wonder, as the food that used to reach it from Holland and France went to Germany instead, though German propaganda blamed the British blockade. The appearance of prosperity in independent – if divided – Belgium

---

51. C. Parry (ed.), *Consolidated Treaty Series* (New York: Oceana, 1981), cccxxv. 210–12.
52. See page 375.
53. FO 371/26342.
54. FO 371/26343, *passim*.

in the late 1990s must not obscure the state of crisis in which prostrate, conquered Belgium lay in the early 1940s.

Prostrate and conquered though Belgium was, it was not inert.
There were several active small groups of friends, more of them collecting intelligence – which they had no means of transmitting –
than attempting sabotage, for which they had no tools. Several larger
underground movements were also organised, two military and
nine – leaving aside such purely intelligence groups as the Dame
Blanche – civilian.

The military two, which in the end combined, were the Armée
Secrète (AS) and the Légion Belge (LB), both initiated by, and largely
composed of, officers of the Belgian army who had survived the
fighting and escaped becoming – or escaped from being – prisoners
of war. Most of the Flemish officers the German army took prisoners were soon released, as a propaganda gesture. Each movement had
an intelligence as well as a subversive wing: a fruitful source of complications between SOE and SIS.

Some of the nine civilian groupings had military names. The
largest was the Front de l'Indépendance et Libération (FIL), which
had two subsidiaries, the Partisans and the Armée de Milice
Patriotique (AMP). There were also the Movement National Belge
(MNB), the Organisation Militaire Belge de Résistance (OMBR),
and the Armée de Libération (AL), as well as three groups devoted to
sabotage: Group G, of which much more later; Hotton, which
sprang from the AS; and Nola.[55]

All of these movements arose spontaneously in Belgium, except for
'Nola', which was, as will be shown, a creation of SOE's.[56] FIL and
its subsidiaries were certainly more radical in outlook than was the
government in exile; FIL was the body that the small but influential
Belgian communist party did its best to infiltrate, after Hitler's attack
on the USSR on 22 June 1941 persuaded it to change sides. The
OMBR, in spite of its French name, worked mainly in northern –
that is, Flemish-speaking – Belgium. The AL, a Christian Democrat
body, was Walloon-centred, with no perceptible class base; it worked
mainly in and round Liège. Its strength by 1944 was estimated as

---

55. Listed in History xxxiv. 19.
56. See pages 305–6.

high as 20,000 to 25,000, about thrice the size of the OMBR, and it included effective saboteurs at work before the liberation as well as armed parties who fought in early September that year. Yet it had no links at all either with SOE or with the government in exile; such arms as it had, had been successfully hidden in 1940 or stolen or bought from the enemy later.

There were in fact too many, rather than too few, underground movements in Belgium – nothing has been said, for example, of the numerous escape lines, equally prevalent and equally dangerous. Multiplicity of movements made it more easy for double agents to creep in somewhere, and do harm. Moreover, the difficulties that attend any operation of war in which the chain of command is unclear were all too common. Leaving aside the local troubles, with their probabilities of too many cooks spoiling the broth, agents sent into the field by T were often uncertain whether they were commanded by him, or by the Sûreté, or by the Deuxième Section, or by Pierlot, or by Churchill, or by King Leopold. This did not make for swift decisions.

It is time to see what these agents were trying to do.

Section D had managed to dispatch a single agent towards Belgium, before ever SOE was founded: a thirty-seven-year-old businessman called Maurice Simon, burly of build and emphatic in manner, who had been the Brussels sales manager for HMV gramophones and had developed a taste for intelligence work for the French Deuxième Bureau. He was hurriedly briefed, on a river trip between Westminster and Kew, by a man whose name he never knew, handed 5,000 French and 40,000 Belgian francs in cash, and packed off on 18 June – after the French had asked for an armistice, but before one had been concluded – to the Biscay coast of France. His cover was that he was seeking to regain touch with his wife and their two little boys; his tasks were to collect ration cards, and so on, and to look into how to restart an underground newspaper (an active resistance role in Belgium in 1914–18).

No proper system of communication with him was arranged. He managed to rejoin his family, to return to Belgium, and to get a job as a nazi-sponsored distributor of seeds. His various attempts to get some sort of resistance work going attracted German attention, and in mid-July 1941 he was arrested. He made himself so agreeable to his captors that they enlisted him in the secret field police, the geheime Feldpolizei, on whose behalf he travelled frequently between Belgium and France; always taking steps to warn his victims before he arrived to arrest them, and only picking up those who ignored his warnings. He turned up in London again late in August 1942, to set a number of problems to the security authorities,

By mid-August 1940 some 350 Belgian soldiers who had escaped their country's military downfall had gathered in a camp at Tenby in west Wales.[57] Section D recruited half a dozen of them, who were handed over to T; a total of twenty-eight more had been recruited by the end of March 1941, but few of them turned out suitable.[58] T section did not get an effective agent launched until 'Opinion's' mission in July 1941; out of over fifty dispatched in 1941–2, only one ('Collie') came back at all fast, and only three others ('Mandamus', 'Lemur' and 'Toad') could also be classed as entirely successful. The rest were more or less – usually less – glorious failures. Their adventures will be set out roughly in the order in which they were dispatched; readers of pro-allied sympathies must now expect a run of disappointing vignettes.

At least T had more dignified codenames than N section. After a random start, it settled to names of animals; followed by characters from Shakespeare and from classical literature; and, suitably for a section by then run by a couturier, names of fashion accessories for W/T sets. The lists twice overlapped with SAS; in the cases of 'Brutus' (also the name of a Polish triple agent) and 'Regan'.[59] Among the far too numerous targets of top priority laid down for SOE in its first directive from the chiefs of staff were 'Communications and supplies of enemy forces in France, Belgium and Holland'.[60] Not much could yet be done towards attacking them.

In January 1941 Dadson proposed to send a business acquaintance of his own to act for him in Switzerland. This was Herbert Schneider,

---

57. Morton to Churchill, TS in FO 371/24276, f. 94.
58. History 1xv. 3.
59. Pages 375 and 379.
60. Mackenzie, *op. cit.*, 92, in a paper on 'Subversive Activities in Relation to Strategy' arising from COS(40)386th item 2 of 12 November.

a British subject both of whose grandfathers had been born German; his father's mother was Swedish, his mother's father had become Belgian. He spoke perfect German and fluent French and Dutch.[61] Nothing seems to have come of this proposal, presumably because of transport difficulties. Similarly, a Belgian ship's wireless operator called Levaque was dispatched at the end of March 1941 to Jamaica, whence he was to make his way to neutral Cuba, seeking repatriation to Belgium. He fell ill, moved on to South America, and was dropped.[62]

On 3 March 1941 an SOE appreciation began: 'Germany has every inducement to attempt an invasion of the United Kingdom at an early date.'[63] This opinion is now known, from ultra-secret information unpublished until the 1970s, to be incorrect: Hitler had already given up the idea of invading England, in order to concentrate on invading Russia.[64] Even on the German side, few people yet knew this; fewer still on the British, none of them in SOE. Moreover, the German news media continued to write and broadcast as if England was the main and imminent enemy; useful cover for the impending eastward move.[65]

In 1941 Belgium pullulated with would-be resisters, bereft either of weapons or of security sense, who congregated in cafés to conspire; and with would-be informers, who haunted the same cafés in search of gossip they could pass over to the Germans, and thus curry favour for themselves. T sent several agents onto this confused scene; some directly by parachute into Belgium, others obliquely, through Iberia and/or France. Most of these men knew each other; for Belgium, like Holland, suffered from the small-country syndrome, the tendency for all those of like mind and background to be acquainted. Consequently, as in Holland, missions meant to be separate got mixed up together; and, as in Holland, the Germans sometimes made confusion worse confounded. This syndrome is not confined

---

61. T to AD/A, 17 January 1941, TS in Germany 153.
62. Belgium 13; History lxv. 3.
63. In Belgium 170, 'Claribel'.
64. Hinsley *et al.*, *British Strategic Intelligence*, i. 185–90.
65. Cp Charles Cruickshank, *Deception in World War II* (Oxford University Press, 1979), 207–11.

to the Low Countries; it was perceptible, for instance, in the Israel of the 1960s.[66] In the war against Hitler, the battle of Britain was the only major early success. Instead, there were several hitches and some disasters. For example, the next of T's missions, mounted as early as 15 April, was an entire failure.

Gaston Hermie, a Belgian merchant navy officer who had lost an arm at Dunkirk, had been doing odd jobs since for the Belgian military attaché in London, and was therefore acceptable. He had a wife in south-west France and owned an hotel in Normandy, so might have cover for travelling. He did no SOE training at all, but was given the codename 'Independence', a private code, and a mission. He was to join the many Belgians who were being repatriated through Iberia and Vichy France, and to look into communications problems for Dadson, on which he could report slowly by post until a wireless operator joined him later. He sailed from Liverpool to Gibraltar under his own name.

However, on reaching Spain he made no secret of his passionate anti-British sentiments; got back to Belgium bearing packets and messages from friends he had made in the German embassy at Madrid; and appears simply to have used SOE to pay his passage home. A proposal by Buckmaster, later head of F section, to have him assassinated was not taken up;[67] T dropped him.[68]

In mid-May 1941 the navy tried to put a T section agent called Mann ashore on the north Breton coast, with a pair of F agents – one of them the formidable Pierre de Vomécourt – from whom he was promptly to part. As usual with F's attempts at cross-Channel sea operations, this one failed;[69] and T did not use the Breton coast again till 1944. Mann volunteered to parachute instead, and went off to Ringway, but broke his hip in a practice jump. When he had recovered, he was released to Lepage's office.[70] He did not fall entirely under his new master's spell; at a moment when relations between Knight and Lepage were extra strained, he volunteered to photograph

66. See Isser Harel, *The House on Garibaldi Street* (Deutsch, 1975), 222–4.
67. FM to F, 21 November 1941, initialled TS in Hermie PF.
68. Belgium 86.
69. Cp Richards, *op. cit.*, 96.
70. Note of 7 June 1941 in his PF; and Belgium 166.

for Knight the contents of Lepage's safe, to which he had a key. This offer too was not taken up.[71]

T's first drop took place, within a week after F's, on 12/13 May 1941: a single agent, Emile Tromme, who was to have been dropped with a single container that carried his clothes and his W/T transmitter. He had been born close to the German frontier, at Grand Halleux ten miles south-west of Malmédy, on the eve of the German invasion of his country at the start of the Great War: 2 August 1914. He was a mechanic and an electrician, who had served for several years in the Chasseurs Ardennais; SOE promoted him from private to sergeant while he was under training, and he was given the code-name of 'Caesarewitch', after the Newmarket horse-race.

He chose a dropping zone near his birthplace, but the aircraft overshot it: he was dropped into Germany, close to Düren which is nearly twenty miles east of Aachen. By a further error, the navigator forgot to press the switch which released the container; so Tromme had neither a change of clothes, nor a W/T set. Moreover, he had fallen into a prisoner-of-war camp. He coped with these difficulties as best he could, escaping promptly from the camp, getting across the frontier undetected and getting himself organised; but four months passed before T heard from him.

Jean Pierre Absil made an abortive sortie. He had worked in Belgium, before the invasion, with de Saumarez of the Ministry of Information, who introduced him to Dadson. Dadson briefed him on how to set up a passive resistance organisation, but sent him to none of SOE's schools. His codename, 'Silkmerchant', was transparent: it described exactly what he was. He had been managing director of Bianchini Ferrier, a Brussels silk firm. He flew to Lisbon on 28 May 1941, ostensibly on a visit to Lyons on business before he returned to Belgium as a refugee. He spent some months in Lyons, but got no nearer Belgium than Berne. (The war diary reported his arrival in Belgium in error.)[72]

Absil met some of Pierlot's colleagues, who were still in Vichy France. He did manage to send two emissaries into Belgium, who brought back a little useful intelligence on possible railway targets,

---

71. Note by T of 8 April 1943 in Belgium 244.
72. Whole world war diary, x(ii). 2751, 22–24 January 1942.

and threw up some useful data on how to cross from Belgium into France. But the man with whom he had expected to work most closely in Belgium, Section D's Maurice Simon, came down to Lyons to warn him that he had himself had to become a Gestapo agent to save his own skin, and that Absil had aroused the suspicions of both the German and the Vichy police. To try to allay these suspicions, Absil married a dressmaker from Paris; and returned to London, in late July 1942, with nothing more positive to report. Eventually he was found a post as liaison officer between the Admiralty and the Free Belgian navy, and left SOE.[73]

Dadson realised that tacit support from the Roman Catholic hierarchy would be a great advantage to any groups he could set up in Belgium. He called on a Belgian Jesuit acquaintance, Fr Jourdain, who had been at the Belgian college at Buxton; and, after due arrangements about secrecy, asked for advice. Fr Jourdain at once volunteered to go himself.

The Abbé, as SOE's staff knew him, though already forty-three years old and at five feet four (163cm) hardly an imposing figure, took his parachute training, and spent three weeks at Beaulieu imbibing SOE's doctrines of subversion. The staff understood that his cloth would keep him from work as a saboteur; none of his fellow students knew that he was a priest. He was codenamed 'Opinion'; and introduced to his proposed wireless operator, Armand Leblicq ('Moonshine'), some nine years his junior.

They were both ready to leave by the July moon, and indeed took off from Newmarket late on the 5th; but were brought back by the pilot, who was not quite sure he had found the right blind dropping zone. Next day they went off again.

A macabre accident followed.

On the way by motor car to Newmarket, Leblicq suddenly demanded to be shriven before take-off. There was no chaplain at the racecourse; the rector and the vicar of the two local parishes were of course Protestant; and the conducting officer, (Sir) Douglas Dodds-Parker, knew of no nearby Roman Catholic chapel. Fr

---

73. Belgium 157; his PF.

Jourdain felt that he had now to admit his clerical identity to his colleague; Dodds-Parker knew already, and the driver could be trusted. In a corner of the briefing shed, the two were at least out of earshot of others present; Jourdain heard Leblicq's confession and absolved him.

Leblicq remained highly excited, and somehow got wrongly strapped up in his harness. This time the pilot found the DZ, south of Marche-en-Famenne in the Ardennes; Jourdain jumped first, making a bad exit. When Leblicq followed him through the Whitley's hole, his static line did not work; his parachute, jammed into the tail wheel, did not open. The combined strength of everyone on board, including Dodds-Parker, did not suffice to tug him back in, against the slipstream. By the time the aircraft got back to Newmarket, terror and cold had killed him.[74]

There could be no explaining all this in a coroner's court, with press and public present. His body, suitably weighted, was loaded into a Whitley's bomb bay, and committed to the sea outside the three-mile limit. Dodds-Parker had to go and recount what had happened to Spaak; who took it calmly. After the war, one of SOE's rear party made a clean breast both to the dead agent's widow and to the Registrar-General who issued a death certificate, putting the death at Great Bradley, the next village south of Newmarket. This enabled Madame Leblicq to claim a pension.[75]

Fr Jourdain landed with his face covered in blood, because he had hit it on the far side of the hole as he jumped; he was also encumbered with his parachute – the two of them only had one spade between them, and Leblicq had carried it. Moreover, he was close to a hamlet – people were coming out of their houses to look at the Whitley, which was still circling, and a gypsy cycled off to warn the police that he had seen a parachute. No one came to investigate till nine in the morning, by which time the Abbé had hidden his parachute in some bushes, washed his face in a stream, walked into Marche, and gone to ground in the house of a doctor, who was brother-in-law to an old pupil. The doctor disposed of his

---

74. Misleading account in Foot, *SOE: An Outline History*, 135; misdated one in A. D. Dodds-Parker, *Setting Europe Ablaze*, 93–4.
75. Conversation with Dodds-Parker, 1990; Leblicq PF.

parachute, and the Abbé got on with his missions; not knowing that his wireless operator was dead, but realising he was unavailable.

He had two tasks, one political, the other clandestine. On the political front, he saw Cardinal van Roey at Malines and Mgr Kerkofs, the Bishop of Liège, and Baron Goffinet, who was a personage at court; though as he said himself when he returned to England a year later, opinions in Belgium were so changeable that not much reliance could be placed on the pro-allied assurances he had collected from them.

On SOE's front, he found three likely leaders of resistance: his friend and old pupil André Hanin at Marche, who ran a cutlery business; George Canivet, a lawyer at Tournai; and in Brussels, René Watteau, who under cover of his furniture-making business had already organised groups to suggest bombing targets and groups to prepare for sabotage.

Jourdain was in touch with one of SIS's agents in Brussels and understood that SIS would arrange for an aircraft to return him to England: vain hope. After several weeks' hanging about he and this agent set off together, overland; crossed occupied and unoccupied France without undue incident; and reached Barcelona, where he made touch with fellow Jesuits. He had got beyond Valladolid, on his way to Portugal, when on 29 December he was arrested by a suspicious policeman; got packed off to Miranda; and did not get out until August 1942.[76] SOE released him to the Free Belgian forces, where he became almoner to a parachute unit. He returned to Belgium on SAS's operation 'Noah' in 1944.[77]

In Belgium, as elsewhere, there were several small groups of friends who wished the nazis and their sympathisers harm. Sometimes they had, or acquired, arms; sometimes they dared to act. In the late summer of 1941 one such group, which called itself 'Phalange Blanche', began violent operations in north-western Hainaut. On 11 August, after dark, two young men – Paul Houbar and Robert Lelong – called on a rexist at Leuze, midway between Tournai and Ath. He was out. His wife, under menace from their revolvers, let

---

76. Interview, 27 August 1942, in his PF.
77. Belgium 171; see page 373.

them wait for him; when he returned home, they shot him down and walked away. On 17 September three men – one of them Lelong – shot another rexist dead at Tournai. On the same evening, in the same city, another 'Phalange Blanche' party led by Henri Talboom – who alone was armed – called on a third rexist, also out. This time the intended victim's wife was able to telephone him a word of warning, and he came home escorted by three German policemen; two of whom Talboom shot dead in his porch, while the rexist bolted over his neighbour's roof.

German reaction was this time prompt. Twenty hostages were arrested overnight, most of them Tournai notables. All were released shortly; for the police had a useful clue. Someone left behind in the porch a briefcase containing two Colt magazines, and Houbar's full name and address. Though Houbar had alibis for the Tournai raids, he was arrested (with the help of a double agent) in northern France on 5 October; was repeatedly interrogated; was taken to Germany for trial and sentence; and was beheaded there in March 1944, aged twenty-one. Lelong too was cornered in November 1941, at a friend's farm in the country, by a force of sixty *Feldgendarmes*; and shot himself sooner than be taken alive. The police never caught Talboom; he got away to Switzerland in July 1942. Those of the 'Phalange Blanche' who were not arrested merged into the secret army.

A memorial to Lelong near where he died – at Brasmenil, a few miles south-east of Tournai – calls him a 'Partisan'; which neither he nor any of his colleagues were. Equally, there is no clear evidence of a connexion with SOE; though Lelong sometimes said he was under the orders of an English major in Brussels, and he may have had some means of communicating with Talboom through the BBC's *messages personnels*.[78] The brief life of the 'Phalange Blanche' at least shows that there were resources in Belgium which SOE might exploit, if it could find out how to do so.

---

78. This account rests on Etienne Verhoeyen, '*Un groupe de résistants du Nord-Hainaut: La Phalange Blanche*', in *Cahiers-Bijdragen* 12 (May 1989), 163–205, published by the Centre de Recherches et d'Etudes historiques de la Seconde Guerre Mondiale. None of the agents named are traceable in SOE's files. Brief summary in *Livre d'Or de la Résistance Belge* (hereinafter *Livre d'Or*), 126–7.

The high-level German reaction to these killings boded no good either to the Belgians or to SOE. On 20 October 1941 *Le Soir* at Brussels carried a new decree by General von Falkenhausen, threatening '*the most vigorous measures*' and declaring that all political internees were henceforth being held as hostage for the nation's good behaviour.[79]

In the Netherlands, as has long been only too clear, the Germans made ample use of double agents; so they did in Belgium, though not with quite such startling success. J. C. Masterman, past master in the handling of such men and women, began his account of their use by MI5 in 1939–45 with the remark that 'They have been used frequently and extensively in most wars and in many places.'[80] A few of them passed through SOE in the Low Countries; here is an early example.

By the August moon, two more agents parachuted into Belgium, on the 12th: Armand Campion ('Periwig') and Octave Fabri ('Chicken'). Their fates were as different as their codenames.

Campion, born at Nivelles in 1910, was a soldier's son and a metal-worker, who had joined the French Foreign Legion in 1936. Serving in it, he won a Croix de Guerre in Norway in 1940. He had been a signaller, with fluent morse; he sailed through Winterfold and Arisaig, and Beaulieu thought well of him also.[81] He had made three sound jumps from Ringway; but broke his ankle badly when he landed in Belgium near Silly, north of Mons. He hobbled to the nearest curé's house. The curé found him a doctor, who put him in a convent hospital, but the nuns started to talk. Campion discharged himself, and tried to get on with organising some sabotage; he seems to have had an intelligence task as well.[82]

He recovered enough to visit his older brother Leon in Brussels. Leon was a food inspector, therefore able to travel widely; they collected a reception committee. Campion did not transmit his first message until 1 December; a steady flow of traffic did not start till mid-January 1942.

---

79. A. F. Aveling tr., in dispatch to Eden, 29 October 1941; FO 371/26343, f. 227c.
80. *Double-Cross System*, 1.
81. Typed chits in his PF.
82. Knight to Nicodème, 9 January 1942, photocopy TS signed, in Belgium 144.

The flow was too steady: on 28 January Campion was arrested at his set, at his brother's house at Evere in north-eastern Brussels. SOE did not discover this for over a year; and not till the autumn of 1944 did T find out, from one of Campion's prison guards, that on being arrested he had denounced everyone he could think of except the curé. He betrayed to the Germans his brother, his sister-in-law, his nieces, the doctor who had set his ankle, the mother superior of the convent, everyone he had met during his training and all the reception committee. The guard described him as the nastiest piece of work he had ever come across, and a friend of the doctor's wife called him '*le parachutiste dénonciateur*'.[83]

Retrospectively, 'Our Signals Section stresses the fact that it would have been impossible for PERIWIG to inform the Home Station if he were working under duress, because no reliance could be placed on the identity checks issued at that time':[84] a sign that one lesson at least had been learned from 'North Pole'. Campion's treachery did severe harm: not only did his now notional group receive several drops of real stores, but several agents fell, through his duplicity, straight into enemy hands.

One of these, Alphonse Delmeire ('Canticle'), was a barely literate gypsy, who had been called up into the Belgian army in 1939 at the age of nineteen, fought with his regiment in May of next year, did not like Germans, and got away to Great Britain. 'Not such a fool as he looks' was the comment on him by one of the Scottish schools, and Rée noted at Audley End that he 'might be useful as an agent amongst the dregs of society in Belgium, where other people would not have the same entrée'.[85] He claimed to know most of the gendarmeries of northern France, inside whose prisons he had briefly done time.[86] As he had spent a whole peacetime winter smuggling across the Franco-Belgian border, he had skills useful to SOE. He was to have been courier to the Belgian end of a line T intended to set up to move agents from France into

---

83. Photocopied note of 15 October 1945, *ibid.*
84. Note by P. E. Belgeonne, 22 December 1945, signed photocopy TS, *ibid.*
85. TS jottings in his PF. This was Harry Rée, later one of F section's stars, then a lance-corporal in the field security police.
86. Undated TS note in Belgium 33.

Belgium,[87] but Campion made the arrangements for dropping him with the Germans' connivance.

By a stroke of luck, the aircrew carrying Delmeire could not find the prearranged dropping zone. The agent dropped elsewhere,[88] and so had a few more days of freedom. But as soon as he attended a pre-arranged meeting with Campion in mid-March 1942, he was arrested; and did not return.

A party of three tough sergeants, called Deflem, Kaanen and Picquart – Mule, Sable and Lamb by codename; mechanic, butcher and student in peacetime – dropped together near Lessines on the last night of April 1942. Kaanen, like Campion, had spent four years in the Foreign Legion; he and Picquart (the wireless operator) were both single thirty year olds. Deflem, nine years older, had left a wife and two children at Diest when he escaped to England in 1940; he had had a spell with the Free French. Their task was to do what damage they could to rail, canal, oil and Luftwaffe targets in and near Antwerp; but all the arrangements to drop them were made, with his ready connivance, on Campion's captured set. The Germans were waiting for them.[89]

The dropping zone was surrounded with soldiers; one of whom was so excited at seeing the parachutists land that he let off his rifle. The three sergeants at once drew their pistols and returned fire. Hopelessly outnumbered, they were all three dead within minutes.[90] This was from both sides' point of view a bungled operation. German intelligence and counter-espionage authorities much preferred live prisoners, from whom information might be extracted, to dead ones; T much preferred his agents not to be captured at all.

Campion's last victim was Sergeant Pierre Vliex ('Marmot'), born in 1906, a publishers' traveller round Liège before the war, who fought in May 1940, was back at home by mid-June, and determined to ignore his mother's entreaties to stay there. He left Belgium late in February 1941, spent six months in Miranda on his way to England, volunteered for special service, and was directed to work as a sabotage

---

87. See page 261.
88. See page 275.
89. Their PFs; Belgium 102,122 and 154.
90. 1947 interrogation of Weil, Stinglhamber PF, vol. 2.

assistant for the circuit T still supposed Campion was running round Mons.

He was promoted *adjudant* (sergeant-major) on the night he left for the field, 18 September 1942; several containers of stores went with him; all the parachutes were seen to open, near Grammont. He was still entangled in his parachute harness when he found himself confronted by a German officer, revolver in hand: his mission was over before it had begun. The Germans shot him, in Brussels, on 8 June 1943; he had spent the previous night in prayer, refused the customary blindfold before the firing squad, and cried '*Vive la Belgique*' as his last words.[91]

Fate caught up with Campion. He was long held in Etterbeek prison in an inner suburb of Brussels. He was in the next cell to the heroic Baron Greindl of the 'Comet' escape line when they were both killed, on 7 September 1943, by the same allied bomb.[92]

Napoleon used to say that a general, to be any use, must have luck. So must an agent; as the career of Octave Fabri shows. He was born in 1903 in Hoboken, by Antwerp; and was an electrical engineer for the Sofina combine. In 1940 he escaped across France to Bayonne, took ship for Casablanca, and reached England in August; he was an early recruit to SOE. His instructors all thought him bright, though he did not mix well with his fellow students. On 12 August 1941 he parachuted, blind, into central France; and survived several beginner's gaffes, such as producing in a café a sandwich he had brought in his pocket from the aircraft, made of much whiter bread than anyone local had seen for months. A fortnight later, with a well-placed friend's help, he got into Belgium; where his troubles multiplied.

His mission was to sabotage an aircraft engine factory near Antwerp; but as his father had been boasting to all the family's friends that Octave had got away to England, he had to invent a new identity for himself. All the plans to send him a wireless operator, and so some stores, broke down. He met, by accident, an agent with whom

---

91. German almoner's statement to his father, 28 June 1943, reported in letter of his father's of 30 October 1944, TSC in his PF. Other details in Belgium 115. Photograph in *Livre d'Or*, 107.
92. Cp Foot and Langley, *MI 9*, 136–8.

he had trained, called Scohier, of whom more in a moment; and managed to slip away when Scohier arrived to keep a rendezvous with him in a Gestapo car. During the winter he tried to walk into Switzerland from France, but the snow was too deep. He got back to Brussels with the last of his money; did odd jobs; and fell in with a small, secure communist group, who recruited him as a sabotage instructor. They were not quite secure enough; their leaders were arrested in April 1944, and Fabri not long afterwards. He had so much compromising material on him that he swallowed his lethal tablet.

His luck had still not run out: he was given a strong emetic, survived, and came round in hospital; where a nurse took pity on him, smuggled him into her flat and kept him there till Brussels was liberated.[93]

Another agent with whom Fabri had trained and whom he met by chance was Achille Hottia ('Marmoset'), twenty years old when he was dropped near Mons, on the very night of Campion's arrest – 28 January 1942 – to act as sabotage assistant. He soon found out that his organiser was under arrest, and attempted to get to Spain, narrowly escaping an ambush in France. He returned to Belgium and met Fabri, who was a friend of his mother's and took charge of him; but they found no useful work to do. Hottia tried the overland route again, this time in company with three escaping aircrew. They were all arrested on the Franco-Belgian frontier on 27 April 1943; and Hottia was shot by the Germans on 30 September.[94]

As Tromme's and Campion's sets were so long silent, T needed to send another agent to Belgium to try to make touch with Fr Jourdain; and picked a young man of whom Jourdain had thought well when they were both at Beaulieu. This was Jean Scohier, codenamed 'Conjugal' though still a bachelor. He was a nineteen-year-old student of ancient history when his country was invaded, and got away promptly to England.

On 3/4 September 1941 he and a wireless operator Lheureux ('Lacquer') jumped back into Belgium, near Dinant. Scohier took a

---

93. Fabri PF.
94. According to Fabri's report of 25 October, duplic in Belgium 114; the only document left in that file besides Hottia's cover story.

train to Brussels, and rejoined his parents there; they told the neighbours he had come back from France. He also rejoined a student
girlfriend, on whom he lavished time and money as well as affection.
His orders were to work in Liège; he ignored them.

He met the Abbé, and acted as cut-out between him and the
wireless operator; and Jourdain introduced him to his Brussels contact Watteau ('Sealyham'). Watteau in turn produced a Brussels
professor called Hoffman, who was able to mend Lheureux's defec-
tive set.[95] Nobody seemed to bother much about secrecy. A
shot-down pilot, passed on by the body of young toughs who were
Lheureux's reception committee near Verviers to the Scohiers,
reported that the agent 'had secret information and files littered all
over his apartment and made no attempt to observe the most elementary security rules'.[96]

No wonder that in mid-February 1942 'Conjugal' was arrested;
perhaps on a tip-off from a resentful sub-agent he had decided no
longer to employ. Watteau and Hoffman, with Lheureux to keep
them in touch with SOE, were happy to try to keep a sabotage circuit running. Lheureux became quite widely known among resisters
round Brussels and Liège, under the cover name of 'Charlier'. It was
he who handled Tromme's traffic, for example, in mid-September
1941; and he survived unarrested when Tromme fell into enemy
hands three weeks later, after the last-named agent had re-started
transmitting himself: a direction-finding team caught him near
Verviers.[97]

The nazi regime was known, in principle, to be corrupt; the rot
spread to many of its underlings, rather more in Belgium than in
Holland: the Dutch civil service, under occupation, tried to preserve
impeccable standards. A useful side result of the corruption was that
a captured agent could sometimes quickly be bought out, if he had
resolute companions still at liberty. Even at this early stage, Lheureux

---

95. Some details in Belgium 46(i).
96. TJ to T, 1 May 1942, para. 12 of TS in Scohier PF; report of an interview the
    day before at the Great Central Hotel, Marylebone – an MI9 centre – with J.
    A. McCairns, who shortly joined the Lysander flight of 161 squadron (see the
    many references in Hugh Verity, *We Landed by Moonlight*.
97. TSC of Lisbon report of 3 July 1943 in Belgium 256.

contemplated trying to buy off Tromme's jailers, but was neither brisk nor rich enough: Tromme was shot on 25 February 1942.[98]

On 18 March 1942 Lheureux rang the bell of Hoffman's house, where he kept a set, to meet a schedule with home station; he had two enciphered messages in his pocket. A stranger answered the door; behind him, Lheureux glimpsed a Gestapo man in uniform. Murmurs that he had made a mistake in the house number did not carry conviction; several Germans came out to speak to him. He moved away; they followed; he ran. Hearing steps close behind him, he turned, and shot his nearest follower down. While the rest dithered, he leapt on to a tram and escaped.

A few weeks later, on 14 April, he was himself arrested, in Liège, by a stroke of bad luck. He was staying with the Laport family, who were active in escape work, in the rue des Anges. Madame Laport came to warn him that the block was surrounded by Germans. He at once went up on the roof. But a German spotted him there, opened fire, and wounded him. He fell through the skylight of the house next door; passed out; and came to to find himself being bludgeoned into wakefulness in a room full of people, among whom he recognised a fellow operator, Brion ('Majordomo'), whose transmission had attracted the Germans to the spot. Neither agent gave any sign that he recognised the other; Lheureux still did not know, three years later, whether Brion was at that moment a captive, or playing the innocent bystander.[99]

Luckily for Lheureux, the Liège Gestapo did not recognise him as the Brussels gunman. But they discovered his set, with his fingerprints on it, in the house next door, and invited him to play it back; which he refused to do. He was bundled off to Germany on forced labour, and had the good fortune to survive. Indeed, he retained enterprise and energy enough to escape in mid-April 1945, as Germany foundered, during a forced march from Ichtershausen, a sub-camp of Buchenwald.[100]

Scohier also survived – just. Under interrogation, he went out of his way to smile and be polite to those who questioned him; he

98. TSC note in Belgium 241.

99. See page 279.

100. Interview, 4 May 1945, TS in Belgium 46(i).

seems also to have answered truthfully some at least of their inquiries. But he fell ill, with tuberculosis, and was dispatched to a hospital at Potsdam, where Soviet troops overran him at the end of the war. He cast up, almost moribund, in hospital in Derby, where Fabri had a few words with him in late June; it was not till 12 October 1945 that his doctors would let him write a report. In it he was full of praise for Canivet and Hanin – the former arrested, and supposed dead; the latter most active, but never caught. Mgr Kerkhofs and William Ugueux had been helpful also – the Monseigneur had brought him into touch with the formidable Charles Claser, who ran the Légion Belge – and he spoke highly of Wampach; of the circumstances of his own arrest he said nothing.[101] SOE's security staff had the compassion to leave him alone.

Before the police got on to him, Scohier managed to make one useful recruit on the spot, Marcel Leclercq ('Corgi'), who, according to Lheureux, was a more skilled W/T operator than he was himself. Leclercq collected a few reliable friends, and on a single night in October 1941 brought off three simultaneous cuts on railway lines, one at Ensival just west of Verviers and the other two at Herstal and Vivegnis in the northern suburbs of Liège.[102] The cuts were soon mended.

Liège was an important railway, road and waterway junction, therefore a neighbourhood likely to attract SOE's attention; indeed, the first thing Tromme did on getting back to Belgian soil after his unhappy drop in Germany[103] seems to have been to organise a pylon-felling party in the countryside round Liège, which did a lot of work during the winter of 1941–2.[104]

Tromme had managed, without any difficulty, to meet Lheureux, who handled some W/T traffic for him; exciting some suspicion in Baker Street, and still more in Broadway. There, Dansey observed that he used language similar to that of an SIS operator who was under suspicion.[105] Keswick laid his finger on the difficulty a few

---

101. TS in Belgium 241. For Wampach, see pages 259–63.
102. History lxv. 6.
103. See page 246.
104. Undated report by Julien Deschesne in Belgium 48.
105. 20 December 1941, TS note to AD/P [then Boyle] in Belgium 48.

weeks later: Belgian resisters 'only knew of *one* organization in England', and found Lheureux more easily approachable than SIS's men.[106]

A further difficulty was that many of SOE's and of SIS's wireless operators had trained together, or at least had known each other at Tenby. Several times over, in the winter of 1941–2, SOE agents encountered SIS agents in Belgium, asked for help, and did not get it. T section history complains about this;[107] though in retrospect C's agents can be seen to have been prudent in safeguarding their own missions by not getting embrangled with others. Such incidents made bad blood between the two services, both sides of the water.

Several times over, T also sent his agents into Vichy France, unoccupied by the Germans until November 1942; the case of 'Chicken' was noted just now. Agents could find their feet there, outside the close watch of the Gestapo, and then move forward into Belgium to work. Many groups of Belgian refugees were scattered over southern France, in which Baker Street supposed they could mingle without being conspicuous. There were two catches in this system, not yet clear to T. The first was that C and the Sûreté both had numerous informants, scattered round these groups, in touch with London; the second was that the Vichy police forces were efficient, inquisitive, and on the look-out for strangers.

This was the undoing of Jacques Detal ('Gypsy'), whose mission was another failure, foreshadowing worse to come. He had been born near Paris of Belgian refugee parents in 1915; his father died a few years later, and his mother remarried. He was a Belgian army subaltern in 1937–40; survived the May campaign; and worked for ten months in France for Belgian intelligence before escaping to England. He joined SOE in August 1941, and after little clandestine training beyond a parachute course jumped into central France on 10/11 September. His W/T operator, Frederic Wampach ('Vermilion') jumped with him. Wampach, a dozen years older than Detal, had been an efficient signaller in the Belgian army, but had

---

106. MS note on TJ to D/R, 16 January 1942, *ibid.*
107. History lxv. 15.

been badly shaken by a rough passage through Dunkirk.[108] Detal's task was to organise courier lines into Belgium, which were to help the section – once it had got better organised – by passing instructions in and bringing out such documents as specimen ration cards.

Detal had a struggle, like every other agent in the field, to keep his clandestine identity secret; he had some extra troubles as well. One was that Wampach's nerve had so far gone that he could rarely be persuaded to transmit at all, and then only if his organiser stood over him. Another was that the Belgian refugees in France, collectively, turned out a feeble source of recruits: most of them seemed to Detal to be low in both courage and enterprise.[109] He recruited a few reliable French sub-agents instead.

It was more awkward for him still that he had a recent past as an intelligence agent, and was known as such to some agents of the Sûreté; while the Sûreté had not been informed of his new mission. Lepage soon found out.[110] Seven months later, Lepage was evidently circulating rumours to Detal's discredit, which were quite untrue; and was strongly suspected of having tipped off the French police to the existence of seventeen sub-agents of what he presumably regarded as a rival service.[111]

There was also a misunderstanding with SIS, in February 1942, about a message Detal passed to London through intelligence channels at Annemasse and Geneva, and was misdirected; this produced a handsome apology from Dansey to T, who was told 'that we were to receive full co-operation and that we should consider ourselves as "people from whom no secrets were hid"'.[112]

One of Knight's difficulties over Detal's work in France was that Lepage at the Sûreté was far better informed than anyone in T section about where the Belgian staging-posts in France were, and which of the exiles were reliable. The Sûreté had its own channels for communicating with these parties, which Lepage did not dream of

---

108. Jottings by Rée in his PF.
109. Two TS pages, copying a report sent by courier on 11 January 1942, in Belgium 149(i).
110. Lepage to Dadson, 30 October 1941, signed TS *ibid.*
111. T to D/R, 11 May 1942, TS *ibid.*
112. T to D/R, 18 February 1942, TS *ibid.*

sharing with Knight; any more than SIS would readily share with SOE its channels into the intricate Vichy police system.

Most of T's agents, it will be noticed, seemed to take an unconscionable amount of time travelling round western Europe. William Ugueux boasted to the Liège conference in 1958 that, as early as 1942, he had made the circuit Brussels-Lisbon-London-Brussels in as little as five days;[113] but it was not for SOE that he was working. Verity's French edition, which identifies him as '*Espion Belge*', explains that he came back by Lysander;[114] presumably he flew on the first two stages of his journey also, thus overflying both Pétain's and Franco's police forces, either of which were ready to make trouble and impose delays on those less well connected.

Detal had so busy a winter, based on Châteauroux, that on 1/2 March 1942 T sent him – separately – a courier and an extra operator. The courier went directly into Belgium, to handle the frontier crossings; but was the unlucky Delmeire, for whom all the arrangements were made with Campion.[115]

Not all the refugees who fled westward from Belgium at the start of the Great War crossed the Channel: Edmond Courtin's mother was at Fécamp on the east Norman coast when he was born early in 1918. As he had five younger siblings, he was exempt from call-up; and was a bank clerk in Brussels, where his father was by then a senior policeman, when the next world war reached Belgium. He made an adventurous escape to England, which included stowing away on a steamer from Marseilles to Oran; joined the little force at Tenby in May 1941; and joined SOE that August.

He was bright and enthusiastic, and quickly learned morse; he was trained as a W/T operator, codenamed 'Mouse', and dropped into central France late on 1 March 1942, to act for Detal. He had two sets with him, one for himself and one for Wampach. By aircrew error, he was dropped about twenty miles beyond his intended DZ; but shortly met Detal, and gave Wampach his set. He returned to Châteauroux from a short spell away on 16 March, at six in the morning; booked into an hotel; and had just got his aerial spread out

---

113. *European Resistance Movements 1939–1945*, 176.
114. *Nous atterrisions la nuit* (France: Empire, 1982), 206.
115. See pages 252–3.

round his room for a schedule at ten o'clock when two policemen called. Theirs was a routine call, to see who the newcomer was; but they at once noticed the aerial, found the set under Courtin's jacket, and arrested him.[116]

Detal and Wampach were arrested next day. Courtin was frequently questioned by the French police, but given no formal trial. He had over eight disagreeable months in prison, in Châteauroux, Périgueux and Bergerac in turn. Detal joined him in the last-named jail, and on 9 December the two of them and a party of communist stonemasons escaped through a hole the masons made in the prison wall. Courtin detached himself from the rest, and managed to join a group evading through Andorra. He reached Gibraltar on 21 January and London on 11 February 1943; and did not yet volunteer to resume secret work.[117]

Detal had talked so freely to his captors that when he turned up in Spain he was coolly received by the British authorities to whom he appealed, as they thought he had changed sides. However, SOE – always short of manpower – snapped him up again; F section sent him back to France (as 'Delegate') by parachute on the last night of February 1944. F did not then understand that some of his sets, like too many of N's and T's earlier, were in German hands. Detal was arrested on his DZ, and murdered in Buchenwald in September 1944.

In May 1943 Wampach also escaped from his French prison with the help of a resolute party of Gaullist fellow-inmates and a warder. He went back to Belgium, because he had not seen his wife for three years; but after a brief family reunion, thought he should return to England for whatever duties T next required of him. His luck then ran out: he picked the wrong escape line. The plausible mistress of the still more plausible Prosper de Zitter, the notorious double agent who had passed for an escaping Canadian squadron-leader,[118] persuaded

---

116. Belgium 123.

117. His PF; and ten-page signed TS in Belgium 123.

118. For de Zitter, see Jacques Doneux, *They Arrived by Moonlight*, 123–4. Doneux was not sure whether he really existed, or was a Gestapo myth. I have spoken to an evading airman who met him, and was betrayed by him. He had thirty-one aliases known to SOE, and a missing finger joint; no two sources seemed to agree on which joint. (His PF.)

him that he had only to wait in a Brussels flat – not far from his own home in Woluwe-St-Lambert – with a party of fellow-escapers, till a convoy was ready to take them through Spain to freedom. He and his companions were all suddenly arrested by the Gestapo in September; and on 10 December 1943 Wampach was shot dead at the Tir National, where Edith Cavell had been executed in 1915.[119]

The mission of Guy Stinglhamber ('Musjid') began unsteadily, flourished briefly during the winter, and collapsed early in 1942. He was a gold-mining engineer, son of a Belgian army colonel; he reached England from South Africa in July 1940, eager to play some part in the war. Finding the Belgian government in exile '*en pleine pagaille*',[120] he joined Captain (later General) Bergé's party of Free French parachutists, who worked with – indeed helped to found – SOE's RF section.[121]

He caught Sporborg's attention at Beaulieu, and Sporborg forwarded to Dadson on 1 August 1941 a paper Stinglhamber had written about how full Belgium was of sabotage targets, compactly near each other, which he could use his own family connexions to approach.[122] He was transferred from RF to T section, and on Michaelmas Day was parachuted – though already forty years old – into Belgium.

Or rather, he was dropped by pilot error just inside France, in a village east of Givet. He managed to collect his belongings and slip a few miles down the Meuse to the village of Hastière, where he recruited an old friend, Emile Binet, the secretary to the commune, whose son Jean and another student acted as his couriers. His task was to start organising sabotage in Flanders, preferably from a base he was to set up at Bruges.

He found out a lot about possible targets among factories working for the Germans, but seems to have had no impact on the flax industry of West Flanders, which T described on 19 September as

---

119. Belgium 150 and his PF.
120. Report by his assistant Jean Binet, September 1945, TSC in Belgium 127.
121. Foot, *SOE in France*, 153–4. Bergé went on to help found SAS (see his *Times* obituary, 20 October 1997).
122. TS and TSC in Stinglhamber PF.

'probably the most important target in Belgium'.[123] A wireless operator Oscar van Impe ('Arboretum') dropped in to join him on 8 November. Twenty years his junior, born in northern France to a Belgian mother, van Impe was a bright but impetuous young man whose presence should have provided plenty of warlike stores.

This did not work out, for two reasons. One was quite common in resistance: bad weather or difficulties of navigation too often kept the RAF's aircraft and reception committees apart. According to young Binet, Stinglhamber complained that he had wasted eighty-seven nights hanging about in the Ardennes for aircraft that never appeared.[124] Less commonly, he got on badly with his wireless operator, whom he found frivolous, idle, careless, obstinate, a liar, and under-motivated.[125]

There were also troubles about money. Stinglhamber had brought 45,000 Belgian francs with him, borrowed 30,000 more from the Binets (duly repaid after the war), and 75,000 from his mother; there still did not seem to be enough.

Of van Impe's carelessness one example can be given. He lived with the Binets, and worked his set from their AC mains. On 9 February 1942 he plugged it into a DC socket in Brussels; it at once burnt out. The moment was extra unfortunate: he supposed he was on his way back to England, as his organiser had found (he believed) an efficient sea escape line working out of Blankenberghe, and had determined to seize this chance of getting rid of him. This was the origin of operation 'Ferret', which, the reader may remember, came to nothing.[126]

Four days later, Stinglhamber – on orders from London – went to call at an address in Brussels with some money for an agent who had run short of it; but this agent was Campion, who was accompanied by a Gestapo team. They at once arrested and searched Stinglhamber, and found in his pockets the addresses of both the Binets at Hastière and Jean Guillini, a noted swimmer, who was running the Blankenberghe escape (and had lent Stinglhamber another 123,000 francs, then worth £1,000, also repaid to his heirs).

---

123. Belgium 127.
124. *Op. cit.*, in Belgium 127.
125. *Ibid.*
126. Page 230.

Both Binets were arrested; young Jean, who admitted nothing, was released seven months later, as nothing could be pinned on him, and saw out the war working for a Belgian intelligence circuit.[127] Guillini and most of his team were arrested also. Van Impe was left *plaqué*; without a set that worked – his spare set was captured at the Binets' – he could effect nothing, and he did not attempt the long journey overland to Gibraltar. He too fell into German hands in August.[128]

London normally put these arrests of wireless operators down to efficient German direction-finding. D/F was in fact often the cause; but so was careless talk, and so sometimes – as Campion's example shows – was treachery. It suited the Germans to have the British believing in D/F, rather than realising how widespread were the Germans' informers, conscious and unconscious, in resistance circles. One contemporary account put down denunciation as responsible for 98 per cent of the arrests in Belgium.[129]

The aircraft that carried Stinglhamber went on, after dropping him, to drop two more agents into south-eastern Belgium, 'Outcast' and his wireless operator 'Balaclava'.

'Outcast' was J. N. L. Maus, a Luxembourger who had been in the Belgian army since 1930 – volunteering at the age of eighteen – and had risen to sergeant-major rank (*adjudant*). 'Balaclava', also an *adjudant*, six years younger, was André Fonck, a village blacksmith from Grapfontaine, close to Neufchâteau, midway between Bastogne and Sedan. Both were strong, steady-tempered men, who had served in the same regiment, the Chasseurs Ardennais; Fonck had been a signaller.

They stayed one night with a brother of Maus's near Arlon, but Maus then went off to live with his wife near Namur, leaving Fonck to fend for himself; which he did by settling in with his parents by the forge in Grapfontaine. He told the neighbours he had come back from France. Twice a week, all through the winter, he took a train to Namur, met Maus in a café, handed over and received messages,

---

127. *Op. cit.*, in Belgium 127.
128. Belgium 11, consisting wholly of photocopies, is weak on information.
129. Misdated note in Houten PF, TSC.

and returned home. They received a couple of drops of stores, and carried out one effective piece of sabotage: a factory producing wood alcohol for Germany at Marbehan, a few miles south-east of Neufchâteau, was put out of action for three months.

Fonck was undone through always transmitting from home: direction-finders caught him. On 2 May 1942 his mother came up to the attic during one of his schedules – she was his only look-out – to tell him that there were Germans all round the forge. He hid his set and codes inside a truss of hay beside him, and went downstairs. The Germans held him and his parents and searched the building thoroughly; after three hours, they had the set and codes.

He was badly beaten up, and assured that he would have to watch his parents being shot if he continued to refuse to talk; he called this bluff, and stayed fairly silent. A few days later, he was confronted with a letter a sub-agent had been fool enough to send him by post, which mentioned 'Leon' – 'Outcast's' field name – in a context that undercut a fiction Fonck had launched about who 'Leon' was. Through the letter's postmark the Germans caught the sub-agent; through whom in turn they got 'Outcast's' home address. Maus was arrested at his own hearth on 13 May, tried, condemned to death, and shot the same day – 8 July – near Arlon.

Fonck was dispatched, after nine months in solitary in Namur jail, back to Arlon, where his parents (who had been released) were summoned to be present at the military tribunal that condemned him too to death. They were released again, under threat of lasting imprisonment if they said anything about the trial; he was sent off to Germany as a slave labourer instead of sharing Maus's fate. He survived brief spells in Sachsenhausen, Auschwitz and Buchenwald; 'it seemed a miracle that he was still alive', so ill he looked, at the end of the war.[130]

For much of 1942 the Germans had been using the 'Balaclava' set, which they had captured, codes and all, in the truss of hay at the forge; they secured several drops of stores and one of two men, and the London security staff, when once they discovered this,

---

130. Comment by Miss Gilliat-Smith on interrogating him, 8 May 1945, TSC in Belgium 17.

were suspicious of Fonck, until he came back to clear his own name. To the two men, 'Bull's' wireless operators, we will revert later.[131]

The 'Hireling' mission, formally a disaster, had some useful results. It was led by J. P. E. Cassart, a regular engineer officer who knew a lot about aircraft engineering; and was therefore well equipped to direct sabotage. His ambitions, and his mission, ranged much more widely. He was an indiscreet but useful agent.

As he had been an officer for seventeen years before the war hit Belgium, had survived the few weeks' fighting, had escaped into unoccupied France and had several times gone back into Belgium on intelligence missions, he was disinclined to listen to much of what he heard at Beaulieu; for he could not help thinking that he understood both the trade of war and the actual state of occupied Europe better than his instructors. He therefore did not bother much about security, which they all tried to impress on him as any agent's necessary first care. He was indeed amazingly indiscreet; but his indiscretions were not useless to the allied cause. For, because he talked so much and so widely, word spread round Belgium that an officer had come over from London with serious instructions from the government in exile about sabotage and the setting up of fighting groups; and that he could even summon arms by air.

He had indeed a wireless operator, the twenty-year-old Henri Verhaegen ('Rhomboid'), sturdy, energetic and determined; moreover, his set worked. Twice they set off to fly to Belgium, but were brought back to base. At the third attempt, on 3/4 October, they jumped successfully, some twenty miles ESE of Liège, a mile away from the intended spot.[132] They arranged for a single drop of containers, also deep in the Ardennes, early on 8 November; and were able to use them for a little serious sabotage. They claimed seven Luftwaffe aircraft destroyed by SOE's altimeter-set bombs, and one severe rail crash that killed forty-three German soldiers. Verhaegen spent a lot of time distributing stores and training men in their use, as well as working his W/T set; and claimed that they had also assassinated

---

131. On pages 292–3.
132. Belgium 152.

seven Gestapo agents, some German and some Belgian, as well as mounting attacks on German lorries and on Belgian pylons.[133]

Besides supervising all these arrangements for sabotage, Cassart was busy talking, mainly to fellow officers in Brussels. Many of his friends were no more discreet than he was. He and Verhaegen began to feel Belgium was too hot to hold them, and proposed a Lysander pick-up: at Poulseur, south of Liège. The RAF refused the site (which the Luftwaffe soon thereafter turned into an airfield), because it was too near some high-tension cables. They fell back on their second choice, a deserted small airfield at Neufchâteau.

Unknown to either of them, one of their friends was a double agent, and was keeping the Germans informed of the plans of which they made no particular secret. They had also forgotten about weather: after they had fixed the pick-up date, it started to snow. They drove down to Neufchâteau in daylight on 8 December, and Cassart insisted on being driven round the landing-field, to assure himself that the snow was not lying too deep: a reconnaissance that left tracks and attracted local attention. When, after dinner, they were driven back to the field, and their driver had helped them to set out the torches, Germans sprang out of the surrounding hedges to arrest them.

They caught Verhaegen. Asked what letter was to be flashed to their aircraft, he gave the wrong answer. Flight Lieutenant Murphy arrived punctually; saw the lights; and took in that he had been flashed the wrong signal. Having come so far, he thought he might as well land, to see what was up, but landed a quarter of a mile away from the little flarepath instead of on it. The Germans at once opened fire on him; he took off again instantly, and returned to Stradishall with thirty bullet-holes in his Lysander, as well as one in his own neck; from which he managed to staunch the flow of blood with the lucky charm that he carried (as so many airmen did). His charm was indeed lucky: one of his future wife's silk stockings; it saved his life.[134]

Verhaegen and the sole sentry guarding him were separated from the others during the brouhaha of Murphy's landing and take-off.

---

133. *Ibid.*
134. See Verity, *op. cit.*, 9–10, 45–7.

Verhaegen suddenly wrested his captor's rifle from him, shot him with it, and scarpered. Cassart also had been briefly in German hands; he too suddenly ran away – leaving a suitcase-full of reports for London, in clear, that gave the Germans only too much information about the Légion Belge.[135] Pursuit almost caught up with him. He lay down in a pile of nettles against a churchyard wall. A German soldier stood within touching distance of him, did not notice him, and trudged away.

Cassart and Verhaegen happened to take the same train out of the neighbourhood next morning, and met on it; but Cassart was not free for long. Within a week, he was picked up in a café in Brussels. He will reappear in these pages later.

His lightly wounded wireless operator, by now without his own set, tried to report his organiser's capture and his own escape through Lheureux; and set off for Spain. He too had a spell in Miranda, where he met Fr Jourdain; and, like him, returned eventually to England. The perpetually suspicious Dansey supposed him to have been allowed to escape by the Gestapo;[136] Knight knew better, and used Verhaegen as conducting officer to explain to agents under training what the real difficulties of life in Belgium were. Several men of weight who later came over from Belgium testified to how well he had done.

Unhappily for his parents, the Germans had secured his identity card, and traced them through it. The elderly couple were taken away to Germany. Mrs Verhaegen died in prison; her husband returned weighing less then seven stone (38kg).[137]

London, Tenby and Malvern – to which the free Belgian army moved – were not T's only sources of recruits. Sometimes he got help from SOE's anchor-man in Lisbon, John Beevor, who under the cover of assistant military attaché at the legation was well placed to interview arrivals from Belgium. He was several times able to steer likely men towards T; till Portugal got too hot to hold him, and he was recalled. As he had held the almost legendary post of Prefect of

---

135. Bernard, *op. cit.*, 23.
136. Initialled TS minute, 18 April 1942, in Verhaegen PF.
137. Dobson to MO1(SP), 1 April 1946, signed TS in Belgium 243.

Hall at Winchester, he could carry responsibility; and as he had been a partner in Slaughter & May, the City solicitors, he knew how to be discreet. His judgement was usually sound, but even he could be deceived.[138]

Vergucht's mission can be disposed of briefly. He was a Belgian merchant marine officer, born in 1917, who knew morse. Duff Torrance took charge of him. It was simple to introduce him (code-named 'Duncan') into occupied Europe: he sailed as a seaman from Gourock on a Glen line cargo boat on 28 October 1941, went ashore with the rest of the crew when she docked at Setubal in Portugal a fortnight later, and did not rejoin his ship. His captain, who was in the know (the crew were not), reported him missing; he took care to keep clear of the Portuguese police, but reported – at once, and against orders – to the German consulate in Lisbon. There he was of course cross-questioned about convoy drills and English morale; and was flown on to Berlin, whence he was released to Antwerp. There, he reconnoitred a power station at Merksem and some possible ship-yard targets at Hoboken, while awaiting the W/T set that was to reach him by messenger, so that he could arrange for sabotage stores to be dropped.[139]

As the messenger with the set was Delmeire, whose drop was arranged by Campion,[140] Vergucht too was left *plaqué*. Eventually he decided life would be more agreeable in England than in occupied Belgium, turned up in Irun in October 1943 pretending to be an American, and was back in the United Kingdom at the end of the year.[141] He had so odd a set of stories to tell about his relations with the Germans, his arrests, escapes, trials and re-arrests, that he was put away on the Isle of Man until July 1944. He then went back to his pre-SOE career, while SOE and the Belgians wrangled about who owed him his back pay. During these wrangles, Belgeonne

---

138. Example in whole world war diary, ii. 104, 28 January 1941. Entries *ibid.*, ii. 127–8, 31 January, iii. 350, 31 March, and iv. 602–3, 15 April 1941, fore-shadow operations back into Belgium; none took place. See Beevor's undervalued *SOE: Recollections and Reflections 1940–1945*, 30–43.
139. Belgium 56.
140. See page 253.
141. Belgium 56.

The three CDs:

Nelson

Hambro

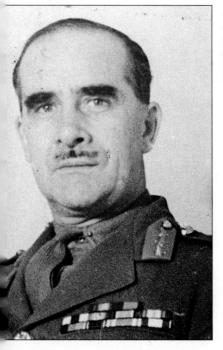

Gubbins

Some London staff: Keswick   Knight

Bingham   Dobson

position: Rauter   May

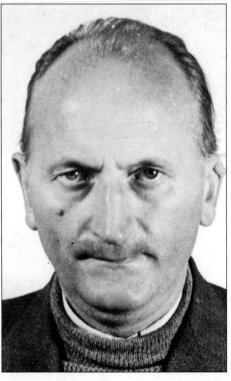

os   Giskes

Some victims:

Ras

van

Beukema toe Water

onis

Lauwers

Terwindt

ink

Dourlein

'King Kong'

Celosse

Tazelaar

Faber

ll'

Floor

io

Todd

nkgreve

Austin

Del Marmol (far left), Pire (next) and others, secret army HQ near Brussels, July 1944

Containers in polderland: near Amsterdam, mid-May 1945

wrote him down as 'a "bad egg" who has hardly done any work for us'.[142]

When at the end of November 1941 Gubbins asked for reports from every country section in his charge about their current results, he got two closely spaced foolscap pages of lament from Laming, who had no useful contacts at all to report; while Knight in a single page could recount contact with a secret army body near Liège, that he was trying to bring under T's and the Belgian government's control, plus three established groups of saboteurs, one of which had begun work.[143]

PWE's split away from the rest of SOE was not perfectly smooth. At the end of 1941 Taylor had to express himself strongly, at a joint PWE-SOE meeting, on the compilation of a PWE plan for Belgium on which SOE had not been consulted at all. Bruce Lockhart gave him immediate and unhesitating promises of prior consultation in future; noted in SOE's war diary,[144] but difficult to fulfil.

The next mission T mounted was primarily a propaganda one; though its leader, Sergeant Oscar Catherine ('Manfriday'), had been through Rheam's sabotage school, and had mugged up before he left a long list of possible sabotage targets, all in his province of Hainaut.[145] He had been wounded in mid-May 1940, and had the luck to be put on a hospital train to England; where he married an Englishwoman who worked in the Ministry of Information, besides volunteering for special service. He was commissioned into the Belgian army on the day he went back into action, 28 January 1942. He was then twenty-six; his wireless operator, Gaston Aarens ('Intersection'), four years younger, jumped with him.

Fabri's friend Hottia was in the same aircraft, and was to have dropped separately. After discussion, in flight, with the Whitley pilot, they all three agreed to drop together, near Mons. By a slight error, they were let go just south of the frontier, near Maubeuge; not, as it

---

142. 1 March 1946, to a suppressed correspondent, photocopy in Belgium 249.
143. HQ 45, 26 and 27 November 1941.
144. 1–2 January 1942, page 2523, quoting minute of 30 December 1941 about meeting the previous day.
145. Four-page appx D to his operation orders, at start of Belgium 103.

turned out, the worst of their troubles. Catherine himself landed on the roof of a barn. The ground turned out to be too hard for them to bury their parachutes; two friendly colliery night watchmen provided a brazier. Catherine added to the bonfire much of the store of leaflets he had brought with him, sooner than have them discovered in a customs search; but on second thoughts, marched northwards through the night with Aarens, crossed the frontier without a check, and came to his own parents' house at La Bouverie, south-west of Mons, by seven next morning. Hottia, in keeping with his codename of 'Marmoset', slipped away by himself.

Catherine went into Mons at once, and introduced himself to the Goormaghtigh family, one of whose sons he had met in Lepage's office. This connexion raised a difficulty for T: Jocelyn Clark reported to him on 4 April (a shade late) that papers taken off Catherine, just before he left Newmarket airfield, included a mass of names and addresses – the Goormaghtighs among them – with which the agent had been supplied by the Sûreté, without informing T.[146] Endless vistas of confusion opened up for T; though, by an odd paradox, it was through one of the missions of which T had not been forewarned that his eyes were eventually opened.

Aarens's field career was short. He could not at first make his set work. Scohier, with whom Catherine early made touch – through 'Sealyham' – arranged for Leclercq to announce Catherine's safe arrival. But Scohier was soon arrested; and Aarens too was picked up, at his set near Mons, on 27 March. From the run of further arrests that followed, which included the Goormaghtighs and his own parents, Catherine assumed that Aarens must have talked.

A further proof that he talked is a pile of messages from him, mostly marked IDENTITY CHECK GIVEN, in a surviving file;[147] all purporting to come from 'Manfriday', though in fact written – in French – by the Germans. This pile bears out a remark Marks made in forceful retrospect: 'Identity checks were 99% useless; their security was negligible, and they were almost totally invalidated by morse mutilation.'[148] The messages are interspersed with still more

---

146. Initialled TS. Followed by five pages of MS jottings, in Belgium 103.
147. Belgium 103.
148. Undated paper on SOE field ciphers, appx K, History xx (Signals), para. I(2).

numerous replies from T; and the file – even after laundry – will present an interesting exercise for anyone who wants to work over in detail the intricacies of playing back a captured set. For six months, T was completely deceived.

There are a few written reports from Catherine in the same file, sent through a church-organised courier service into Switzerland. Though deprived of his own wireless operator, he tried to organise railway sabotage in Hainaut; he had one useful meeting with a courtier, and reported that King Leopold III looked for some act of apology from the ministers who had denounced him, but would not set his face against re-employing all of them after the Germans had gone.

A master plan to bring all Belgium's railways to a standstill when the allied invasion took place came to nothing, but Catherine was able to get some minor factory sabotage going in the Mons area; for instance, 'a workman spent his time carrying bearings in a barrow and throwing them into the marshes', and the same firm manufactured several thousand iron spikes, used with effect against Wehrmacht rubber tyres in the summer of 1944.[149]

Catherine had a particularly useful friend from before the war, a Namur lawyer called André Ranwez; Ranwez had a brother-in-law who was a priest in Brussels, who put Catherine up for his first night there, and another friend of Mme Ranwez put him in touch with Watteau and so with Scohier. He made several friendships with priests, one of whom undertook to forward to London his report that Aarens had been taken; this message never got through. Moreover, he stumbled against a frequent – though seldom noticed – obstacle on the fringe of the resistance world: small-mindedness.

Shortly before he left England, Catherine had been summoned by Pierlot, who told him to tell the journalist Marc Delforge that Pierlot would be glad of his help in London. Catherine knew Delforge already, and promptly passed on the message. Delforge, knowing no better, mentioned it to a colleague, adding how it had reached him. The colleague, jealous perhaps at not yet having been invited himself, went out of his way to make difficulties for Catherine; spreading false rumours about indiscretions the agent never committed, and

---

149. Summary of activities by Catherine, 16 July 1945; signed TS in Belgium 104.

repeatedly blocking his access to escape lines. As Ranwez later remarked, in normal conditions such incidents would have been negligible; but, underground, everything hinged on confidence, and such stories could only harm Catherine.[150]

He did manage to inspire a few one-day strikes in coal mines, and one in a steelworks, in the Mons area, and got twenty locomotives put out of action there in the first week of September. He also organised an underground newspaper called *Les Compagnons de la Résistance*, which came out now and again in Hainaut;[151] but normally he lived in Brussels, with a family called Wolf. After he heard of his parents' arrest in September, he only went out of doors after dark; for they of course had photographs of him. Aarens had also had a snapshot of him.

Next time he did venture out in daylight, he was arrested. On the morning of 17 January 1943 he took a teenage son of the Wolfs to call on a Jesuit priest, who said he had a pair of shoes for the boy; he and young Wolf were seized in the street as they left the priest's house. Catherine was much less helpful a prisoner than his wireless operator had been.

Another pair of agents, dropped on 1/2 March 1942, had their mission ruined through London's blindness to 'Intersection's' arrest: these were 'Incomparable' and his wireless operator 'Mastiff'.

'Incomparable' was Valere Passelecq, a student friend of Scohier's who was reading law, and had been learning to fly a glider in his spare time. The two of them trained together, finding some of their Special Training School (STS) companions rather uncouth.[152] His first task was to report to London the state of opinion in Brussels, so far as he could discover it, of both the Belgians and their occupiers. He was then to set about organising pro-allied propaganda as best he could. As he had attended Station XVII, where he made an extra good impression, he was also (when he had time) to encourage men whose names he was given to embark on industrial sabotage, in Brussels, Antwerp, Ghent, Huy, Mons, and elsewhere.[153]

---

150. Page 8 of a 35-page signed report, 10 May 1945, TSC in Belgium 104.
151. *Ibid.*, 14.
152. TS jotting of 12 June 1941 by Rée in Passelecq PF.
153. Lengthy incomplete *ordre de mission*, TSC in Belgium 85.

Moreover, he was to be the first emissary of 'La Justice', a purely notional secret society, illimitable in its range, inexorable in its grip, which was about to busy itself with the execution of quislings. He was to spread the rumour that this body existed, and was provided with leaflets and coffin-shaped stickers to associate it with any assassinations that happened to take place while he was in Brussels. Prodigious results were expected.[154]

It was not to be. He took a wireless operator with him, René Copinne ('Mastiff'), nearly ten years older than himself, who had been a stockbroker's clerk in Brussels before the war. Delmeire travelled with them. A 'Periwig' reception committee was to have received them, but the pilot did not see its lights (which may indeed not have been there); they jumped blind, in a stick of three, followed by packages holding their luggage.

The parachute with 'Mastiff's' set in it landed so heavily that the set was unusable. 'Mastiff' reported this by barn code in a letter to a Stockholm address. News did not reach Baker Street until the second half of May.[155] When it did, T instructed 'Intersection' to write to 'Mastiff' at the latter's father's address:[156] trouble duly followed for 'Mastiff' and for 'Incomparable', who were arrested in early July.

A spare set for 'Mastiff' was sent by hand of 'Koala':[157] another failure. Victor Lemmens, who bore the codename, was a stocky Flemish labourer, good-humoured, tenacious, not bright. He had been born in 1900, and had both a brother and a son in his late teens at work in a large modern coal mine at Beeringen (which has now dropped its first e) near his home. He had worked in the mine himself, and was to organise go-slow sabotage there, as well as tackling larger targets – if the chance offered – at nearby Hasselt or on the Albert Canal. As all the arrangements for dropping him were made with 'Intersection', he was arrested on landing on 25 June 1942; and shot dead four months later.[158]

---

154. Closing paragraph of two-page '*MISSION SPECIALE*', TS in *ibid.*
155. Address in Belgium 117; Belgian section progress report of 26 May 1942 cited in whole world war diary, xiv(ii). 4049.
156. *Ibid.*, 4035–6, dated 23 May 1942.
157. Whole world war diary, xv. 4356–7.
158. Belgium 90 and his PF.

Eugene van Loo, fourteen years his junior, was to have been his wireless operator, as 'Ocelot'. He had survived the May 1940 campaign in the rank of sergeant (Lemmens, during six years in the army, did not rise above private); lost his wife in an air raid in August; left his eight-year-old daughter in Brussels with his parents; and escaped through France and Spain in 1941. He too was dropped, on 29 August 1942, by arrangement with 'Intersection'; he too was arrested on landing; and the sparse surviving files suggest he was presumed shot.[159]

The Germans soon put 'Mastiff's' new set on the air, beginning with a large demand for money on 31 July; on this and several other telegrams the correct identity check was given. At least no other agents were sent to this set while the enemy was working it.[160]

Felicien Moreau could not even spell his own first name;[161] but he was tough, and detested the Germans – they had killed his brother, and several of his cousins, in a small massacre of civilians on the Sambre in 1914, when he was a boy of fourteen. He had left school at nine, and spent ten years as a farm labourer before learning about motorcars; he had plenty of common sense, and became a garage mechanic. He served with an armoured car unit in May 1940, had a week as a prisoner of war, got a job as a lorry-driver and promptly drove into France. Five months in Miranda delayed his arrival in England, where the Sûreté passed him over to SOE.

T section gave him the task of damaging motor transport in Brussels, on which he was given a fair amount of information; and was duly parachuted into Belgium on 25 May 1942, as 'Cayote' – a suitably misspelled codename – taking another wireless set for Vergucht with him. Vergucht was to identify him, at a brasserie outside the Gare de Midi, by a piece of pink sticking-plaster Moreau was to put on his chin.[162]

Unhappily, this drop too was arranged with 'Intersection'; so Moreau's spell as a free man on Belgian soil ended on his DZ. He was taken away to Cologne, where he was shot in mid-December.

---

159. Belgium 134 (all photocopies) and his PF.
160. Belgium 117; some telegrams singed, some laundered.
161. The affirmation of secrecy he made for SOE on 8 May 1942 is signed 'Felecem Moreau', rather hesitantly, in his PF.
162. Belgium 38.

One more unhappy agent sent to an 'Intersection' reception, as late as 27 August, must be noted: P. R. Osterrieth ('Platypus'), a bright and promising envoy from the Belgian government to several leading Belgian firms, which he was to persuade to adopt a go-slow policy in the dealings they would necessarily have with the Germans; producing as little for the Germans as they could, while maintaining Belgians in jobs that would preclude their being packed off to Germany as forced labour. There are traces in the file[163] of tiffs between the Sûreté, PWE and SOE about exactly how this mission should be set up, but the tiffs were all resolved, and off Osterrieth went: to be handcuffed on his DZ.

He was taken to St Gilles prison in Brussels, from which he managed to smuggle out a message, with a fellow prisoner's help; it reached Baker Street, but could not be deciphered.[164] He was sent away to Germany, where he had the misfortune to be in Bochum prison in June 1943 when it was hit by a major allied air raid, which killed him.

As late as 23 September, Knight said in a chit to D/R: 'Personally, I feel sure that Manfriday and Intersection are alright.'[165] However, 'Intersection' was unable to provide answers to two simple trick questions T put him; and T had to accept the evidence of Delforge, given in London on 22 September, that 'Intersection' had been arrested before Easter.[166]

Catherine at least survived imprisonment – he even survived Dachau; Aarens, far more useful to the Germans, did not. These provide two further examples of the erratic, not to say capricious, course of nazi justice.

On the same night as Oscar Catherine another, and a far more successful, agent dropped; on the first of three missions, all of which he survived. A. J. Wendelen (this time christened 'Mandamus'), born in 1915, had been an officer in the Belgian Carabiniers till illness forced

---

163. Belgium 132.
164. *Ibid.*
165. Typed, initialled note in Belgium 103.
166. Unsigned TS by Delforge, and initialled TS note of interview with him by Dobson on previous day, 23 September 1942, in Belgium 104.

him to resign early in 1940 to start a career at the Brussels bar; this was interrupted by the German invasion. He managed to flee to England in May, went briefly back to France, and with Polish help returned to England again; he did not join SOE until July 1941. All the schools he attended – he began at the F section paramilitary school at Wanborough Manor below the Hog's Back – thought highly of him; Roger de Wesselow, the perceptive commandant there, noticed how mature he was, Arisaig judged him 'really first class', and a Lysander course found him 'flawless'. He became one of T's stars, acclaimed indeed in 1944 as 'certainly our most distinguished agent'.[167]

On his first mission he went, with a wireless operator, to work partly on propaganda, partly on electrical sabotage, round Liège.[168] The latter task brought him in touch with Groupe G, of which he was practically the co-founder.

Groupe G, the strongest of the small groups, was a don's dream of how resistance should be conducted; and had close connexions with SOE.

It was conceived by Jean Burgers,[169] who graduated from a five-year course in electrical engineering at the Free University of Brussels in October 1940. In all proper secrecy, he consulted several professors, and several fellow students, whom he trusted. Gently, gradually he put together sabotage teams fit to cripple German communications, by rail, by canal, by telephone and by power line.

He and Wendelen had known each other when they were both undergraduates – Wendelen, much his senior, had read law – and it was Wendelen's arrival in 1942 that brought Burgers' dreams of major sabotage organisation a great deal nearer practical reality, by providing explosives and expert advice on sabotage techniques.

Groupe G prided itself on its independence; and yet sometimes described itself as Groupe G(WO), using the War Office's English initials; which it would never have adopted, had it not appreciated how much it depended on the War Office's MO1(SP) – one of SOE's covers – for stores and advice.

---

167. Typed chits in his PF; Murphy to Amies, 15 November 1944, TSC in Belgium 20.
168. Parts of *ordre de mission*, undated TS in Belgium 107.
169. Photograph in *Livre d'Or*, 311.

Groupe G needed a good deal of money. Most of it came from what the group's final report called necessary banditry:[170] raids on banks, railway stations or post offices; where the staff were, as often as not, quite happy to hand over Belgian francs by the thousand for resistance purposes, succumbing willingly to a show of force and taking care not to be too diligent in helping the police with their inquiries. There was a solid clandestine precedent for this: Lenin in exile, earlier in the century, had been kept in decent comfort by his party on the proceeds of raids on Russian banks, the most successful of them conducted by Stalin, who thus came to his leader's notice.[171]

Wendelen's wireless operator was Jean Brion ('Majordomo'), the son of a Brussels chauffeur, born under German occupation in 1916; a cabinet-maker by trade, and an army lance-corporal when he joined SOE after a spell as a gunner on a merchant ship. He kept well away from Brussels, where his wife lived and he had many friends; and settled in a house in Liège, ostensibly as a doctor's servant – the house, indeed, in which Lheureux was arrested in April.[172]

Two months later, on 16 June 1942, he was caught nearby himself, by direction-finders – he had had a protracted and difficult sked, which had lasted for an hour and a quarter. He behaved with exemplary skill under prolonged, brutal interrogations, sticking to the story that he knew nothing of his organiser, and received all his outgoing traffic – already enciphered – from a fictitious courier to whom he handed any incoming traffic as he received it. Two elderly ladies called Durieux, from whose house he was working, also said nothing they should not; the Germans assured him that they had been known spies during the previous world war. Brion was held for some months in Liège in prison, and then bundled off to forced labour in Germany; he too survived Dachau.[173]

On 2/3 March 1942 Sergeant Jacques van Horen, formerly of the Belgian artillery, jumped back into Belgium, alone, south-west of Marche-en-Famenne: into eighteen inches of snow, so dense that he

170. Belgium 160(3).
171. Dmitri Volkogonov, *Lenin* (Harper Collins, 1995), 54–6.
172. See page 257.
173. Belgium 108 and his PF.

had to struggle to hide his parachuting gear.[174] Codenamed 'Terrier', he was to have been Absil's wireless operator; but discovered, by a telephone call to Absil's office, that his intended organiser was still in Lyons. He resumed his peacetime job, as a Brussels hospital electrician – pretending to have just got back from France; and lived with his own parents, who became his W/T protection team. He had no trouble getting a new identity card in his own name.

He told T, by wireless, that he could not reach Absil; and was sent instead to see Binet at Hastière. Asking for him in a café, he heard of his arrest; which he reported. T next sent him to see Dr Lespagne ('Spaniel' or 'Negus'), at Dinant, a helper of Stinglhamber's who told him of that agent's arrest as well. They planned a rescue; van Horen was on the air for an hour, from ten to eleven on the evening of 3 April, with a message about it.

An hour was too long: a direction-finding team caught him, and took him and his parents to jail. He was roughly treated – hung up for a quarter of an hour by a rope passed through the handcuffs that held his wrists behind his back – and had the texts of several of his messages read back to him, as the Germans had captured his code with his set. As he still refused to play his set back, he had to watch while an Orpo sergeant played it back for him at his next schedule, remarking that his style was easy to imitate. Home station made no comment.

In St Gilles prison, van Horen was put in the next cell but one to a man who had trained with him, called Cerf; of whose downfall more shortly. They exchanged tapped messages through the man in the cell between them; to whom Cerf confided all sorts of secrets, not having taken in that the man was a German stool-pigeon.

Before leaving England, van Horen had mentioned to T section that his brother-in-law, Philippe Dinne, was a reliable trained post-office wireless operator; but had been too busy, in the month before his arrest, to approach him. When his German interrogators asked him, out of the blue, who Dinne was, he told them the whole story.

---

174. This was one of the nights on which, on account of the snow, Andringa and Molenaar refused to drop into Holland: see page 122 above. It is quite unclear from SOE's files whether his name was van Horen or van Hoven.

London codenamed Dinne 'Weasel', and from the end of June exchanged traffic with him – or so London thought – for several months. This was notional traffic: 'Weasel' was entirely under German control – how entirely, the case of 'Mink' will show.

'Mink' was Willy Bernaerdt, born at Antwerp in 1903, and a ship's steward by trade. His ship was interned at Casablanca in July 1940. Fifteen months later he escaped, with a few acquaintances, in one of her rowing boats; was picked up off Gibraltar by a British warship; and was released straight from the RVPS into SOE.[175]

After training, he was sent back to work in his home city; partly to organise industrial sabotage and passive resistance, partly as another rumour-spreader about the secret society called 'La Justice'. He was to assemble sub-agents for sabotage, but not to carry out any until a wireless operator reached him to arrange the supply of stores.[176] He was the only agent SOE sent to Belgium by the late March moon, on the 23/24th.

Unhappily, London sent 'Weasel' the bogus operator to help him.[177] An Abwehr agent, briefed with the proper passwords, called on him on 27 July, identified him, and at once arrested and searched him. Worse, he had an address in his pocket, from which the Germans secured 200 more arrests in the neighbourhood.[178] He was long held prisoner, and killed in April 1944.

Three agents, 'Mongoose', 'Chamois' and 'Lynx' their wireless operator, were dropped near Neufchâteau on 26/27 June 1942, to organise the arming of the secret army in Hainaut and to reconnoitre the bridges on the Meuse, in case any of them later needed to be sabotaged. 'Mongoose' and 'Chamois' were a pair of Belgian army subalterns, called Wouters and Houben, bright and nimble young men who had got on well together under training. 'Lynx' (Flotte), born near Neufchâteau in 1917, had been an ordinary seaman, RN, and had a boisterous, extrovert character. At Thame Park he was

---

175. Jotting in his PF. Distinguish him of course from A. B. Mink, alias 'Polo', N agent.
176. Extensive orders in Belgium 126.
177. T war diary, xxii. 10–11, July 1942.
178. Etienne Verhoeyen, '*Abwehr appele Londres*', in *Jours de Guerre* (Brussels, 1994), 92.

notable for his quick reactions; but he could not make his wireless set work in the field.

T therefore asked van Horen to look out for them,[179] not knowing that van Horen was in enemy hands. Moreover, Flotte was reported later by Houben to have been indiscreet in his friendship and conversation in Liège, where all three settled temporarily in a flat. There on 15 August they were all arrested by the field police, handcuffed, and marched out to a waiting car to be driven to Brussels.

The moment his feet touched the pavement, Houben bolted; like Leen Pot,[180] he was out of pistol range before the guards had recovered from their surprise, and escaped into a park; where, with difficulty, he applied the technique he had learned at Beaulieu for escaping from handcuffs. He did better: he escaped from Belgium altogether, and spent ten months making himself useful to a different resistance body in France. There he fell again into hostile hands, in June 1943; and was eventually packed off to Buchenwald. Even Buchenwald he was tough enough to survive. SOE never heard a word of Wouters again, and he was presumed dead.[181]

SOE did hear of Flotte again; for, even before his arrest, van Horen's set told England that 'LYNX landed in marshy ground, and it is, therefore, possible that his set requires attention'.[182] 'Lynx' himself purported to come up on 23 August, asking for 300,000 francs – and using his correct identity check. His third message, of 5 September, was so mutilated that the signals staff could not tell whether the security check was present or no. On 14 September he was asked whether he needed soap; and replied on the 20th, '*il y en a assez des poires*': nearly, but not quite the correct reply. This gave T pause for thought; something more solid followed.

Van Horen discovered that his mother had been released from prison; and that his neighbour on the other side from Cerf was able to send laundry home once a week. Through this safer neighbour, he smuggled out a letter to his mother, in which he included a brief

---

179. War diary, xxii. 10, July 1942.
180. See page 178.
181. PFs on the agents concerned.
182. Note of 14 August 1942 by T on signal to 'Lynx'; photocopy TS in Belgium 93.

Playfair message to go to his Swedish safe address. It was dated 15 October and read simply 'SUIS EN PRISON'.[183]

This convinced SOE's security staff, by the end of November, that both 'Terrier' and 'Weasel' must be under enemy control.[184] 'It would be of the greatest assistance', their report concluded, 'in the investigation of this type of problem if a summary of operations were kept up to date for each agent';[185] they had found the interlocking of agents almost too complicated to unravel. Indeed 'Terrier', who survived over three years in German prisons, told Miss Gilliat-Smith at his final interrogation that inside St Gilles he had seen, as well as Cerf and Lespagne, Stinglhamber, Brion, Copinne, Delmeire, Passelecq and van Impe.[186]

By July 1942 DF section had found an anchor point in Paris – J. M. E. Carrier, 90 rue de Cambronne – with whom, after an exchange of passwords, T's couriers could leave mail; a courier from London was to call for it monthly. Unluckily, T passed this address straight on to 'Terrier', who had been in enemy hands for three months, and to 'Intersection', arrested a week earlier still.[187] Soon thereafter, Carrier's arrest followed; he survived the occupation, but was of no more practical use to SOE.[188] It was through the captured 'Terrier' set, also, that London unwittingly settled the hash of van Impe, left setless by his own mistake shortly before his organiser had been arrested.[189] The section war diary for July, August and September 1942 reports long discussions with 'Terrier' and 'Weasel' about 'Arboretum', including ways of reaching him;[190] the Germans picked him up quietly, through an address London had given as far back as April,[191] four months later. Like Flotte, he never returned.

*

---

183. Belgium 161.
184. DCE/G to D/R, 30 November 1942, TS *ibid.*
185. *Ibid.*
186. 8 June 1945, TS *ibid.*
187. MS jotting below D/F to T, initialled TS, 3 July 1942, in Belgium 161; and war diary, xxii. 4.
188. Note of 25 February 1945 in his PF.
189. Page 264.
190. xxii. 9, 29–30, 39.
191. Verhoeyen, *op. cit.*, 93.

The popular view of war is that it must be two-sided, Us against Them. Yet several aspects of the world wars of 1939–45 were many-sided: consider the case of Poland, overrun by its two principal enemies as they fought each other, or the still more intricate case of Yugoslavia. Polygonal campaigns were, as they remain, common; and Knight as T felt he was fighting one in the summer of 1942. Not only were the axis powers his enemies, but he was sure he could not call the Sûreté his friend; nor did he feel safe with C. T section rejoiced when on 1 June 1942 SOE took charge of its own signals traffic, because it would no longer be easy for C to pass copies of all T's signals to the Sûreté; as the section believed had hitherto been the case.[192] As late as 17 November, the security section agreed with T that 'Lepage is opposed to and has actively hindered' SOE's policies of sabotage and the raising of a Belgian secret army, and instanced five cases of T's agents for whom Lepage seemed to have made trouble.[193] T was still complaining of Lepage six months later.[194]

Relations with the Sûreté's rival, the Deuxième Section, flourished in the spring and early summer of 1942, when Bernard took charge of it. Henri Bernard, born in 1900, son of a general, brother of a professor of law, regular engineer major and an instructor before the war at the Belgian staff college, had done his best for several T agents, particularly Cassart, whom he had housed and helped. After Cassart's arrest, he felt Belgium too hot to hold him, and managed the journey to London in four months. To his surprise, for he knew nothing of the subject – except what he had picked up in eighteen months' experience as a resister in Belgium, most of it devoted to the 'Luc' escape line – he found himself at once made head of the Deuxième Section.[195]

His friend William Grisar, an older regular major – and a close friend of Prince Charles – who had fought with distinction through the Great War, had also been among Cassart's helpers, and also thought that the agent's arrest made it advisable for him to flee.[196] He

---

192. History lxv, 14.
193. Belgium 244, D/CE, G to T, TSC.
194. T to D/CE, 8 April 1943, TS *ibid.*
195. His PF.
196. Note in Grisar PF.

and Bernard were soon on first-name terms with Claude Knight; each did what he could to forward T's efforts, and each felt as keenly as Knight did that they must regard the Sûreté as their enemy rather than their friend. A battle here impended: only a staff battle, but on it agents' lives were at risk.

Madame Bernard's feat is worth separate mention: she came out of Belgium to England across the Pyrenees, making her own arrangements, and bringing her eight-year-old daughter with her.

Roger Cerf ('Tiger') had a brutally brief career in the field, largely by his own fault. He was born in Brussels in May 1920; his parents were well off (they shared a house with Spaak's mother), and had sent him to England to learn the language before the war. He was a sergeant in the First Guides Regiment during the invasion, was briefly imprisoned, released, and found his own way to Portugal; moving thence via Glasgow into SOE. An instructor at Arisaig noted that 'he is probably the most intelligent of the group but he knows he is and makes the others feel it'.[197] At the W/T school at Thame, Rée found him 'a very bad co-operator, extremely egoistical' and 'entirely unamenable to discipline';[198] at least he learned his job.

He parachuted back into Belgium on 2/3 March 1942, 'made his way straight home, let himself into his parents' home with his own latch key,'[199] told all his friends he was on a very, very secret mission, and was arrested within a week of landing, having passed on a family message to a fellow agent's father, who at once denounced him to the Germans. His family appealed to the Prince de Ligne, who went to see von Falkenhausen; the queen dowager's help was invoked as well, on the grounds that 'the wicked English had turned the boy's head, and that he was too young to realise the seriousness of what he was doing'.[200] The general received the prince politely, said he would do what he could for the young man, but then declared that nazi justice must take its course; and Cerf was shot in mid-August. De Ligne's

---

197. TS chit in his PF.
198. TS, 15 January 1942, *ibid.*
199. TS of interview with the younger Prince de Ligne, 14 October 1942, *ibid.*
200. *Ibid.*

son observed that the English were 'asking for trouble' if they sent out such young and irresponsible men.[201]

On the other hand, the man for whom Cerf was to have worked did well: on the first of three successful missions. He was Philippe, Comte de Liedekerke, then aged twenty-six; a Belgian aristocrat, a regular gunner officer who had escaped from a prisoner-of-war camp to find his own way to England, through Marseilles and Algiers, by October 1941. He was bright, well-read, well-connected, adventurous, assertive; Knight saw at once how he could make touch with conservative circles in Belgium, codenamed him 'Collie', and dispatched him.

He dropped, with Cerf – from whom, luckily for himself, he parted at once – on 2/3 March 1942, with a mission to sound out those circles in the capital; 'to study the existing clandestine organisations and popular resistance to the occupant';[202] and to probe the Légion Belge, one of the strongest existing movements. He went first to stay with a family friend, Madame Paul Lippens ('Astride'), one of the directors of the Belgian Red Cross, who often attracted German attention, but by 'living a perfectly open and what she termed virtuous life'[203] always deflected it. De Liedekerke did exceptionally well, and was back in England by mid-July, bringing one of the founders of the Légion Belge with him.

This was Captain-Major Charles Claser,[204] codenamed 'Bull' on sight by T: a stocky, determined, forty-year-old regular officer who had been a term-mate of Prince Leopold, the future king, at the Ecole Militaire.[205] Unhappily, Claser's presence in England coincided with a major row between SOE and the Belgian government, and at one moment made it worse.

These quarrels worsened during the spring, and came to a climax in the summer, of 1942. T bombarded D/R with protests and complaints about the Sûreté;[206] a 'most cordial' meeting on 20

---

201. *Ibid.*
202. Undated TS in his PF.
203. Interrogation of her by Bodington in Belgium 20, 3, TSC.
204. Often mis-spelt Glaser in T's files.
205. Bernard, *op. cit.*, 268.
206. Belgium 266, *passim.*

February between Pierlot, Gutt, Gubbins and Keswick[207] brought no useful results at the working level. By 12 April Gubbins was minuting to Hambro that 'The time has come to put the definite screw on the Belgian authorities and I propose to do it.'[208] In mid-May, Hambro warned the Foreign Office that he doubted whether SOE would be able, as things stood, to organise any resistance in Belgium at all.[209]

Aronstein was then caught by Amies frightening off a squad of nine potential recruits for SOE, all of whom withdrew at the last minute. Knight jotted at the footnote of Amies's report on this an ominous phrase: 'the rumour is that the Sûreté send over [to Belgium, by secret carrier] Photos and descriptions of our men so that they are always caught'.[210]

Gubbins noted down for Selborne, on 30 May, the core of the case against the Sûreté:

Lepage admits that he:-
(a) Does not consent to any activities in Belgium which are not controlled by him.
(b) Does not desire sabotage: at least if involving the risk of life.
(c) Does not approve of Para-Military work, or of contact with [clandestine] Army Groups.
(d) Does not envisage Military action in Belgium, either by the British or by the Belgians themselves.
(e) Does not wish Belgian industry damaged, even in war time.
He has announced that he will get wind sooner or later of any activities of which he is not informed, in advance.

Moreover, Nicodème his assistant had been heard to refer to SOE as 'murderers'.[211]

---

207. TS *ibid.*
208. TSC *ibid.*
209. Minute by Makins, 15 May 1942, in FO 371/30816A.
210. MS on TH to T, 27 May 1942, TS in Belgium 266.
211. TSC *ibid.*

A further complaint SOE had against the Belgians was that T's parties seemed to get held up in Miranda – Jourdain, for instance, had been pinned there for months – while Lepage's protégés seemed to be released quickly. Eden himself put this complaint to Spaak on 4 June;[212] Spaak shrugged it off. Nevertheless, de Liedekerke and Claser were shortly thereafter released, and Jourdain soon followed. (What leverage had the Belgians in Spain? A little – they controlled supplies of surplus cotton from the Congo.)

On 9 June Gubbins lunched, alone, with Pierlot; and seized the occasion to complain of Lepage's intrusions into the sphere of action, which ought to have been outside his remit as head of security. Pierlot put it bluntly: '*Lepage, c'est moi*'[213] (he had used the same phrase to C not long before). Gubbins protested that he had his orders from the chiefs of staff, and must carry them out; Pierlot reiterated, amicably but firmly, that he had to have one man in charge of secret work into Belgium, and that man had to be Lepage.

Pierlot and his colleagues may have been feeling their oats, after supplying the British treasury with the gold that made it possible to continue buying arms from the United States until the arrangements for lend-lease were complete.[214] Their attitude to SOE soon turned truculent. A friend in MI5 told Knight, within a week, that Lepage regarded SOE as a transient body, much less important for him and for Belgium than MI5 or MI6. The same friend suggested what turned out to be the solution to the imbroglio: bringing out of Belgium a man of whom Lepage stood in awe, Ganshof van der Meersch, a senior judge;[215] but this lay in the future.

On Friday, 10 July, Selborne and Gubbins had a formal confrontation with Spaak and Rolin, under-secretary at the Belgian Ministry of Defence. Gubbins rehearsed the case against Lepage set out a page or two ago. Selborne added that with the Belgians, and with the Belgians alone, he was failing to get the co-operation from exiled authorities that was available to him everywhere else in

---

212. Makins to Oliphant, 4 June 1942, *ibid.*
213. TSC of M to CD, 10 June 1942, *ibid.*
214. Correlli Barnett, *The Audit of War* (Pan, 1986), 144.
215. T to D/R, 15 June 1942, initialled TS in Belgium 266.

occupied western and northern Europe. Rolin said nothing; Spaak hedged.[216]

Claser's brief presence in England brought the pot to the boil. He, Bernard and Grisar all went down to Beaulieu for a few days, and hammered out together – in occasional consultation with Knight and the staff – what they thought the Légion Belge ought to try to do next. They were far too optimistic: they proposed tasks for it in support of an imminent allied landing. Grisar typed the resulting document up himself.

Only one man in SOE – CD, who sat with the Chiefs of Staff when matters that vitally affected SOE were discussed – had any idea in the summer of 1942 whether there was any prospect of invading the continent soon. He knew for certain that there was none; but many staff officers beneath him, like many other staff officers in Whitehall and in Washington, ignorant of the colossal pile of staff work that lay ahead, supposed that 1942 was a conceivable and 1943 a probable year for a major cross-Channel operation. The tragedy of the raid in force at Dieppe on 19 August 1942, which hoped for so much and achieved so little at so high a cost in life, helped to clear junior planners' heads.

Waste, error and war all go together. A French proverb, attributed to Marshal Turenne, says that the general who has never met defeat has fought in very few actions. Marlborough and Wellington, rare exceptions to Turenne's rule, were long dead. Even Montgomery, conceited enough to cherish his own undefeated myth, had been on the losing side in Ireland in 1921 and at Dunkirk in 1940, as well as approving the disastrous plan for the attack on Dieppe just before he left to command the Eighth Army and become famous.

Claser was to prepare a series of armed groups to attack German headquarters and observation posts on and near the Belgian coast, by cutting off their telephone and wireless systems, and to prevent German destruction of aerodromes, all over the country; as well as standing by to guide allied forces, and taking any other measures the moment might demand. He was also to work with Houben and Wouters, should they be available – as they were not; to arrange

---

216. Note of meeting, TSC *ibid.*

reception committees; and to prepare hide-outs for a staff of a dozen, with a dozen liaison officers, whom the Belgians in London meant to send over; besides assembling documents for Lepage's courier to collect.[217]

The *ordre de mission* was finally signed on 5 August 1942 by Rolin – Pierlot himself, at this moment, was abroad on a visit to the Congo. A muddle ensued.

A month after the signals change-over, SOE's whole world war diary closed; from 1 July 1942 country sections were to keep their own.

For sheer fantasy, as well as for beauty of typing, T section's war diary for the next seven months rivals N's;[218] entire incomprehension in Baker Street that the wireless operators to whom all sorts of secrets are confided are, in fact, NCOs in the Orpo who stand in for captured agents of SOE. T's diarist records at length exchanges with 'Balaclava', 'Intersection' and 'Terrier', all of them by then firmly in German hands, as if they were free to work in secret. He even mentions that Knight 'had not the same faith in LACQUER as he had in the others'[219] when 'Lacquer' too had been the Germans' prisoner for three months, though with less disastrous results.

Knight proposed, to 'Periwig' as well as the four operators just named, a combined or rather a simultaneous attack on electricity plants on the night of 20/21 July;[220] needless to say, the actual results were nil, and only 'Periwig' even pretended to have secured any. In the autumn, T launched another great scheme, 'Mapplewell', for railway sabotage to be conducted by 'Periwig' and 'Corgi',[221] again without useful result.

Yet some use can be made even of what this tainted source says, when it recounts events in this island; to which the long arm of the Abwehr did not reach, though the Abwehr (deceived in turn) thought it did.

A lengthy extract can illustrate both this point, and the staff muddle; and help to light up Claser's character:

---

217. This has been in print for a dozen years: Bernard, *op. cit.*, 283–8.
218. Cp page 158.
219. War diary, xxii. 14, quoting report of 20 July 1942.
220. *Ibid.*, 1–3, 8, 11–13.
221. *Ibid.*, 88–92.

Just before his departure BULL made out some notes in the presence of MAJOR KNIGHT, MAJOR AMIES and MRS. CAMERON. These notes began, '*Suite à mes méditations dans le calme le plus absolu, voici les conclusions auxquelles je suis arrivé*'.[222] These calm meditations dealt with the question of BULL's interview with representatives of the Belgian Government. As it had been suggested that he had never wished to meet CAPITAINE NICODEME he put on record that he had not been able to arrive before 6.55 p.m. at the rendezvous at the Ritz on August 5th because he had been detained at a meeting with LE PAGE, SPAAK, ROLLIN and COMMAN-DANT BERNARD at Park West. He had waited at the Ritz until 7.40 at which time, thinking he had waited long enough for NICODEME, he had permitted himself to go and have his supper. As regards the rendezvous the following day for 6.10 p.m. at 25, Edgware Road he had indicated that a car was going to fetch him at 6.30 as he had to catch a train. He had waited until 6.35 when he had left without having seen the person concerned. This was unimportant as he had no need of their directive. He had been very much surprised (because he had fought for clear cut duties for everyone and for the military authority alone concerning themselves with military affairs) that ROLIN had found it necessary to read LE PAGE an *ordre de mission* that had been given to BULL by the action service: this was because ROLIN wished to concern himself with military problems with which he had nothing to do. BULL stated that he had 'un grave défaut' which was that he wished to speak perfectly clearly before he attacked a problem and it was impossible to work with complete confidence with persons who could not give him anything positive. BULL proceeded to deal with the pretensions of ROLIN that the Sûreté had had more success than any other country in dealing with escaping parachutists: the result, from his own experience and from what he had found out, was that their arrangements almost invariably led to Miranda prison, showing that the service was very badly organ-

222. TSC of French original in Belgium 27, dated 7 August 1942.

ised. He could not see the point of giving 50,000 or 100,000 francs to each team in order to get them into Miranda when it would be much simpler and cheaper for them to hand themselves over to the first civil guard they met after crossing the Pyrenees: furthermore this method would save time as it would involve passing through fewer prisons. In conclusion he said that he intended to work on the following lines. He would work only on the military side and later he would send a delegate to discuss internal political affairs and a member of the Légion Belge as his liaison officer on such questions in the occupied territory, and it was to the latter that he would communicate information of interest to the Sûreté. There were only two ways of working, either hand in hand (which is always impossible) or that each one should have his own separate work. None of this would prevent him from doing everything in his power to achieve as rapidly as possible a victory in which the Belgians would have their glorious part.[223]

Late on 6 August, 'Bull' was taken away to an SOE safe house to be clothed and prepared for his journey. Pierlot at this juncture returned from the Congo; heard about 'Bull' from Rolin, whom he disliked and distrusted; and demanded to see the agent before he left. SOE replied that it was too late. Pierlot thereupon blew up, and disavowed 'Bull's' mission. He distrusted regular army officers, because of some indiscreet far-right-wing remarks made by refugee officers in England in the autumn of 1940 – men who knew nothing of the stalwart work done by those who stayed to face the music in occupied Belgium, but who exercised a negative impact on Belgian history all the same.

Claser was sequestered in an SOE safe flat, to have his clothing checked and to run through his orders one last time; and then moved down to the west country to await a flight to Gibraltar. He finally left the country on 10 August.

In Belgium, he was to have not one wireless operator, but two: 'Wallaby' and 'Springbok', two students, who jumped together southeast of Givet on 27 August. 'Wallaby' was Jean Sterckmans, son of a

---

223. War diary, xxii. 23–4, August 1942.

railway manager, born in 1920; 'Springbok', a year younger, was Nestor Bodson,[224] son of a schoolmaster. One was to be based on Liège, the other on Namur; each had elaborate instructions about how to make touch with 'Bull', who would be using the identity of 'Mr Rose'. Each also had a subsidiary mission, only to be attempted if security and work for 'Bull' allowed: they were to collect identity cards, ration cards, driving licenses, *Ausweise*, all the documents an agent might need in his wallet; and to report on the packaging of German imports into Belgium, in case SOE's camouflage department could fake labels on packages of arms.[225] Unhappily, they were sent with a planeload of containers for 'Balaclava': after that agent, the blacksmith of Grapfontaine, had fallen into German hands. They were therefore doomed to trouble: briefer in Bodson's case than in Sterckmans'.

Bodson took the high line on being arrested: gave his name, his sergeant's rank and army number, and refused to co-operate in any way with his captors. Fourteen months later, they shot him dead. Sterckmans was more pliable: up to a point. He agreed to play his set back, and revealed his codes; but in six of the ten messages he sent, he left out his true security check; and when home station asked him whether he needed any soap,[226] he made no reply at all. He had a disagreeable time in prison in Belgium, and a horrible time in labour camps in Germany; which he survived, only to be arrested on his return to Belgium on a capital charge of treason, for having worked with the enemy at all. Adelin Marissal was distressed to hear of this case, and appealed to the War Office;[227] SOE testified to Sterckmans's more or less correct behaviour, but everyone on the English side was nervous of any appearance of trying to interfere with the course of Belgian justice. Grisar and Bernard felt morally responsible for Sterckmans, but unable to produce in open court any of the messages exchanged with him. Discreet pressure from London persuaded the Belgians to drop the case.[228]

---

224. Photograph in *Livre d'Or*, 104.
225. Notes in their PFs.
226. See page 69.
227. Marissal to T. M. Stevens, signed TS, 22 November 1945, in Sterckmans's PF.
228. Dobson to Belgeonne, 13, and Belgeonne to Dobson, 15 May 1946, signed TS and TSC in Belgium 243.

The fundamental trouble about relations with the Belgian government in exile was that its timid ministers long doubted whether
the allies could beat Germany. Other politicians in exile, however
gloomy in private, took a more robust anti-German attitude, and
were cherished for doing so by those who had to work with and for
them; the Belgians' fear was sometimes contagious.

In mid-August 1942 the Belgian government in exile, in the
person of Spaak, broke off official relations with SOE altogether.
The Deuxième Section, conscious of responsibilities to agents
already in the field, did not follow Spaak's instructions closely; so
late in October Commandant Bernard was dismissed from it,
specifically on the ground that he was too pro-British. Hambro
and Selborne wrote on 29 October to Brooke to complain that 'the
Belgian Government, as constituted in this country, is irreconcil-
ably opposed to effective para-military action in Belgium, whether
this be directed towards immediate sabotage or towards secret army
activities'. Yet such news as came out of Belgium made it clear
that 'the Belgian people themselves earnestly hope and pray for
signs of a more active policy against the common enemy'.
Therefore,

> Lord Selborne does not feel justified in abandoning to darkness
> and despair those elements in the Belgian Army and people
> which look to us for guidance, encouragement, instruction and
> more practical aid.
>
> It is monstrous that a so-called Allied Government should
> deliberately procrastinate in this way on an important war
> issue.[229]

Brooke took the matter to the chiefs of staff, and in the Foreign
Office it attracted the attention of Cadogan, the permanent under-
secretary; who put forward a workable solution – a fresh Belgian
minister might be able to sort out the trouble.[230]
Selborne and Delfosse, the new Belgian defence and justice
minister, were able to work out a formula, of which Hambro sent a

---

229. Supplementary papers 17, signed TS.
230. War diary, xxii. 53, September 1942.

copy to Brooke on 26 November, with a cautious note[231]. The Belgians proposed, and SOE agreed to try to work with, a separate sub-section within their Sûreté branch, which was to handle military activities, jointly with their Deuxième Section and with T. SOE would continue to handle transport and signals.

In a progress report of 29 September 1942, T section confessed it was not quite certain that 'Terrier' was not in German hands: busy as he had been in linking up various contacts, this was proof of activity but not of loyalty.[232] On 4 November it indicated that 'Intersection' was definitely 'working for the Germans', as his reports did not tally with 'Manfriday's'.[233] Several reports passed over from C had also cast doubt on 'Terrier', before his Playfair message came through.

By Christmas 1942 T had had enough. Hardly before time, he sent identic messages to 'Intersection', 'Terrier', 'Weasel', 'Mastiff', 'Ocelot' and 'Lynx' – agents who, as his war diary put it, 'were thought to be compromised'.[234] He told them all, quite falsely, that he had decided to abandon action in Belgium, to protect its population from reprisals; they were each to destroy his set, and to come out through Spain or remain in Belgium as they chose.

Relations between SOE and Lepage remained so tense that Knight, speculating in mid-December 1942 about Stinglhamber's fate, said he had 'hopes, which may or may not be justified, that Lepage, objecting to a Free Frenchman working in Belgium, had him arrested on a political charge, where he will be much safer than if loose'.[235]

By late October 1942 T had dispatched forty-five agents to Belgium, of whom thirty-two had fallen into enemy hands, ten of them – including three killed in action – on their dropping zones. Besides Leblicq, who had never landed, eighteen of these forty-five were wireless operators. Among these, Verhaegen had returned safely, Vergucht had no set, and all the rest were already dead or were in enemy hands: in most cases, unknown to T. It may help the reader to

---

231. Supplementary papers 17, signed TS.
232. T section war diary, xxii. 61, September 1942.
233. *Ibid.*, 93, October 1942.
234. *Ibid.*, 123, December 1942.
235. T to D?CE, 2, 16 December 1942, initialled TS in Stinglhamber PF, vol. 1.

have these unhappy results set out in the table on the following page; which adds two relevant agents from DF and one from the NKVD to T's tally. Houben, who was momentarily in German hands in 1942, is left out of the captures listed above, though he figures twice in the table of troubles.

It was usually assumed by SOE's security branch that when a wireless operator was captured, he would be quite likely to be forced soon to give a recent address for his organiser: for instance, Detal's arrest (and Wampach's) had followed a day after Courtin's. Yet though the table shows repeated arrests following on an operator's, it was not always the operator's fault. We have seen that Campion and Aarens seem to have co-operated quite readily with their captors; van Horen and Fonck did not. The arrests that followed theirs arose from mistakes in Baker Street; Houben and Wouters, for example, fell into enemy hands because T gave the already captive 'Terrier' an address at which he could reach them. It was easy for some Belgian equivalent of Poos to turn up at the address and beguile the agents into captivity.

The Germans were both ingenious and assiduous in playing back their captured sets. T's war diary is full of imaginary tales of minor acts of sabotage, with a few major ones – undetectable from the air – thrown in; T dutifully reported all this to higher authorities, and it was generally understood in the secret world in Whitehall that Belgian resistance showed great promise. This was all illusion: T had so far achieved very little.

His eyes were opened in the autumn of 1942, when the main tide of the war changed.

T's Runs of Trouble
April 1941–October 1942
agents dispatched who did not start work:

Hermie	Leblicq

Campion ('Periwig') arrested 28 January 1942,
hence arrests of:

Stinglhamber	Deflem
Delmeire	Kaanen
Vliex	Picquart

Aarens ('Intersection') arrested 27 March 1942,
hence arrests of:

Lemmens	Passelecq	Carrier (DF, in Paris)
Van Loo	Copinne	
Moreau	Osterrieth	

Van Horen ('Terrier') arrested 3 April 1942,
hence arrests of:

Houben (who at once escaped)	
Wouters	van Impe
Flotte	Bernaerdt

Fonck ('Balaclava') arrested 2 May 1942,
hence arrests of:

Maus	Bodson
	Sterckmans

arrested independently:
in France:

Courtin	Schouten (DF)
Detal	Claser
Wampach (1st)	

in Belgium:

Tromme (1941)	Brion	Lheureux
Cassart (1941)	Cerf	
Scohier	[Kruyt (NKVD)]	

returned safely to UK:

Absil	Verhaegen
Jourdain	de Liedekerke

at work:

Wendelen	Catherine

on the run:

Fabri	Houben
Hottia	Vergucht

VI

Belgian Recovery
1942–4

It was as well to set out T's troubles in detail, sometimes minute; they compare with N's difficulties at the same time against similar enemies. T's successes can be depicted with a somewhat broader brush.

After his eyes had been opened to the enemy's deceptions of him, and the rows with the government in exile had been composed, he was able to press on with serious work. Four agents left by the November moon of 1942, before the storm in the political stratosphere was quite over; four more in December. All began to show results in the new year.

T decided to dispatch a British officer, with an assistant, who would be answerable directly to himself, not to either the Sûreté or the Deuxième Bureau: hence one of the section's most successful sorties, the first mission of 'Lemur' and 'Toad'.

'Lemur' was an international man, born in Hampstead late in 1916 of Anglo-Belgian parents, trilingual in English, French and Dutch with fluent German and fair Spanish as well; at school in Albany, New York (he had an American stepfather) as well as Havana and Antwerp; and claiming to run 100 metres in eleven seconds. His name was Louis Livio; late in the war, he changed his name to Latimer, his stepfather's name. Before he joined SOE, in March 1942, he had been a private in the army medical corps, working as a laboratory assistant.[1] 'Toad', his W/T operator, seven

---

1. His PF.

years his junior, was a bright Belgian called Joseph Pans, who had
left school at fourteen to work in the family dairy in a Brussels
suburb, and had had a little experience of the secret war already: he
and his brother had printed and distributed a few anti-German
leaflets, based on texts dropped by the RAF.[2] He had escaped to
France to avoid having to work for the Germans; and had spent
some months in a French concentration camp.[3]

'Lemur' was also a trained W/T operator and found it convenient – though also exhausting – to send most of his own messages
himself, using 'Toad' as his assistant, porter, messenger and whipper-
in. They dropped north-east of Tournai on the evening of 16
November 1942, and soon settled down to work in the triangle of
Courtrai-Renaix-Tournai. There were several empty châteaux in the
area, no longer leased as they had been before the war by French
businessmen; 'Lemur' took a year's lease on one, installed a lady
there who pretended to be his sister, transmitted from it, arranged a
DZ in its park, and cached the resulting arms in its potting shed and
a nearby monastery. He stuck firmly to his orders: his task was to
receive and store arms, not to engage in any other form of resistance
activity; of course, if a nugget of intelligence came his way, he was to
pass it on, but he was expressly forbidden to make touch with any
existing Belgian group.[4]

He and 'Toad' between them, with a few helpers, received a total
of thirty-six containers, in eight different drops to five different DZs;
stored all the contents; hid all the empty containers – rescuing them,
in one case, from a pond just before a *Feldgendarme* drained it; and
arranged passwords for releasing the arms into whatever hands T
chose when the right moment came. One group of saboteurs with
which they made accidental touch seemed to them so promising
that they let it have some plastic; with which it severely damaged a
signal box on the main line at Liège, causing the enemy marked
inconvenience.[5]

'Lemur' had the usual troubles establishing satisfactory contact by

2. RVPS report of 26 July 1942, TS in his PF.
3. RVPS report of 21 July 1942, TSC in his PF.
4. Mission order, 23 October 1942, TS in Belgium 91.
5. Report, 1 August 1943, duplic *ibid.*

W/T. One of his texts, picked almost at random, will give some idea of how mangled even a good operator's traffic could be:

> TOR 0944 GMT   26 MAY 43
> 56 FIFTS SIX STOP URGENT FONFIRM IS TRUE TWO
> CHAPS DROPPED NIGHI OF APRIS THIRTEEN TO
> FOURTEEN   BW   POLILH   PILOT   BY   ERROR
> UTLAPLAIENE INSTEAD OF LAPINTE STRANDED
> THEY WANT INSTRUCTIONS IF OA SHALL I CON-
> TAFT STOP NEXT MOON OPS NINE TEN FOLLOWED
> BU ELEVEN STOP PIGEONS RELEASED DAWN
> TWENTY FIVE CHEERIO
> TRUE AND BLUFF CHECKS PRESENT[6]

London could not confirm the story of the two parachutists, and on 2 June 'Lemur' signalled: 'AN DROPPING MATTER OF TWO FHAPS FISHY';[7] it was perhaps an attempt by the Abwehr, which had heard rumours of his group, to break into it. He and 'Toad' came out safely in the second half of July, via a safe house in Paris, which saw them through to a Hudson.

With Mrs Cameron's help Livio produced an unusually long report, two-dozen foolscap pages crammed with detail about an agent's daily life.[8] Woolrych, the commandant of Beaulieu's Group B, read it with delighted interest – 'of the utmost importance', 'a first class document, excellently drawn up', and the first long full report of its kind he had ever had. Naturally he complained of several points where he thought Livio and Pans had broken Beaulieu's rules unwisely, in particular the case of a drop of which a whole village was aware; the report remained of great help for future training.

M. van Dorpe, a Belgian businessman nearing forty, dropped the night after 'Lemur' late on 17 November 1942; hid overnight behind a haystack; and walked next morning to call on a cousin near Courtrai. The cousin's house was full; van Dorpe went briefly to stay with his own parents in Courtrai. He got a shock when he

---

6. Belgium 91, tpt.
7. Tpt *ibid.*
8. Duplic *ibid.*, 1 August 1943.

unpacked: his toilet case bore a large label reading 'BABOON', his codename – another black mark for the security man at Tempsford.[9]

His main mission was to inhibit the cultivation of colza (rape) and flax in western Belgium. The Germans encouraged colza, a comparatively new crop, needing the oil to make margarine for themselves (though they told the Belgians it would be for them). Before the war, the bulk of the flax crop had gone to Belfast to become linen; the Germans wanted it for uniforms. Many farmers whom van Dorpe approached directly or indirectly were delighted to get any guidance from the London regime, and agreed to plough in as much colza and spoil as much flax as they discreetly could.[10] After three months, van Dorpe made his way to Switzerland, whence he came back to England.

Belgium too had its *onderduikers*. A vast rag-bag of citations compiled after the war instances Antoine Lessines, who distributed enough money to keep them going to some ten thousand men in Hainaut who went into hiding, sooner than work in Germany.[11] SOE's role here was simply to act as conduit for the money, dispatched by the government in exile. Sometimes it could incite men to join these parties in hiding directly; as the case of 'Dingo' shows.

'Dingo' was Leon Harniesfeger, born at Bruges in 1908, who had left school at fourteen to become a steelworker at Charleroi. He therefore had French enough to sustain him across France when he absconded in May 1941; but it took him almost a year to reach England, because he was stuck for so long in Miranda. As an ardent socialist, he much disliked the nazis. He dropped back into Belgium, two nights after 'Baboon', to provoke go-slow in the Charleroi factories and to encourage the clandestine press. He took nearly a million and a half Belgian francs with him.

In three months' hard work he secured considerable success. Though no sort of intellectual, he started up a small clandestine weekly called *Relève*, helped four other local underground journals, persuaded key men in several factories to give up work and go into hiding, and left a solid group of friends behind him when he set out

---

9. Interrogation, 16 December 1943, in Belgium 16.
10. *Ibid.*
11. Citation for King's Medal for Courage, TSC in HQ 215(i).

to return overland in February. This journey also took him almost a year, part of it spent in Switzerland; he was not back in Great Britain until 1 February 1944.[12]

The tradition, started up under Dalton when SOE was founded, that SOE was to appeal constantly to the socialist left in Europe, was thus clearly still alive. Pierlot, himself to the left of centre, approved it in Belgium; but not every instance succeeded, as the case of 'Alsatian' – taken a little ahead of its place in chronology – can show.

To give agents confidence, during their training they were taken to see girls getting their parachutes ready at long benches, beneath a huge notice that read 'REMEMBER A MAN'S LIFE DEPENDS ON EVERY PARACHUTE YOU PACK.'[13] Yet no one is perfect. When 'Alsatian', the thirty-three-year-old trade unionist Désiré Brichaux, was dropped on 20 April 1943, on a mission for the Sûreté, his parachute never opened. A farmer found his body in a field, north-west of Charleroi, next morning.[14]

As part of their training at Beaulieu, students had it impressed on them that they must learn to be taciturn; must drop any habit they had acquired of chattering to chance acquaintances; above all, must be reticent – silent, even – about exactly where they lived or where they had just come from. One T section agent under training remarked that this would not be difficult for him, because before the war he had been a novice in a Trappist monastery. This was Louis Stroobants ('Borzoi'), who had had a hard eighteen days' campaign in May 1940 as stretcher-bearer to an artillery regiment; had been captured, and escaped back from Germany to Belgium; and after a string of further adventures, including a spell of over four months in Miranda, turned up in the Belgian army camp at Malvern and volunteered for special service.

He did particularly well at his SOE schools, was given extra training in propaganda, and left by parachute on 20 December 1942 with 'Gibbon'. He made an even worse exit from his aircraft than Fr Jourdain had done, and reached the ground bleeding profusely and

---

12. His PF.
13. Personal knowledge: though never in SOE, I was trained at STS 51.
14. Battle casualty form in his PF. Belgium 8 therefore had no bearing on operations.

half-conscious. 'Gibbon' was able to give him first aid and calm him down. After three weeks' convalescence, 'Borzoi' carried out his mission with success: he spent two months at work with the Flemish clandestine press, for which he was carrying a welcome half a million francs.

He worked closely with the FIL, and was assured that London was wrong to believe that organisation was communist-inspired; its sole aim, he was assured, was 'to unite all Belgians for driving the "boche" out of the country'.[15] He saw the money he had brought sensibly laid out on paper, ink, and printing machinery; felt iller and iller, with a misdiagnosed attack of scabies; had a run-in with some *Feldgendarmes* in Brussels over being out after curfew; knocked out his nearest captor and ran away, but left his identity card behind; so thought it was time to leave Belgium. An escape line saw him as far as Belfort in early March. There he had another hitch with *Feldgendarmes*, but talked his way out of it; and was seen on to a path through the Jura by two children, aged twelve and fourteen. He got back to England in September, to emphasise that the FIL was anxious for the means to embark on sabotage.[16]

'Gibbon' was less lucky. He was Sergeant T. J. L. Ceyssens, born in Egypt in 1910 and manager of a sugar factory there when the war began; he joined SOE in the summer of 1942, and took an advanced propaganda course as well as the usual paramilitary training. He went into Belgium with a complicated task: he had to organise – with the help of a pigeon-loft owner – a regular news service between Brussels and London, which was to include propaganda films parachuted in to him and microfilmed copies of current Belgian newspapers sent out by pigeon. The pigeons were to reach him by parachute, twenty-five a month, with their food. His '*centre colombophile*', at the Château de Mont-Saint-Jean on the battlefield of Waterloo, was run by Raymond Demanet, from whose son-in-law he brought messages to prove his own good faith.[17]

He found a reception committee leader in Robert de Keersmaecker, to whom – with Maurice Lebbe – he handed over the whole project in March 1943, and set off for Switzerland (he had

15. 'Report on interview with Borzoi', 3 October 1943, 8, duplic in Belgium 15.
16. *Ibid.*, 7.
17. Section IV of *ordre de mission* dated 23 October 1942, TS in Belgium 66.

been ordered to leave after three months). He had the misfortune to be stopped at a control in Besançon, because he was carrying no papers at all, and imprisoned. Instead of being swept into the pool of labourers for Germany, he was sent back to St Gilles, where he was recognised and denounced by a former sub-agent. He did not survive Oranienburg and Belsen.

His circuit produced a lot of inessential information during the summer of 1943 – Aronstein later remarked that most of what they sent was known already, from other sources[18] – but eventually got entangled with de Zitter,[19] and so ceased to be of any use to SOE.

The case of Maurice Durieux ('Caracal') provides a fine example of triumph over unexpected obstacles. Born in Nivelles on 23 February 1910, he had worked before the war as a publicity agent for Lever Brothers, and had developed plenty of self-assurance allied with good manners. In the army (he was a gunner), he rose swiftly to the rank of *adjudant* and did invaluable work as Belgian liaison man at Gibraltar; from which he moved on into SOE in autumn 1942. His capacities as a propaganda agent were well thought of at Beaulieu, where Henry Heffinck, his wireless operator ('Shrew'), was noted by the commandant as 'an imperturbable, single-minded, independent and determined worker'.[20] Heffinck, seven years older then Durieux, was a chauffeur from western Flanders.

When the two jumped into Belgium, also on 20 December 1942, Durieux had a parachute accident, never fully explained to T (though the RAF at once modified that type of parachute).[21] He hit the aircraft's tail as he left it, and landed so badly that he broke a shoulder, an arm – in eight places – and both his legs.

He was still fully conscious. He handed his money and his memorised orders over to Heffinck, and told Heffinck to get on with the task. He was found early next morning by a couple of peasants, who took him on a barrow to a cottage;[22] one of them sent for a niece

---

18. Note of 16 February 1944 of conservation with Lebbe, TSC *ibid.*
19. Interrogation of Lebbe, 15 March 1944, TS *ibid.* Cp page 262.
20. Finishing report by Woolrych, 26 August 1942, signed TS in Heffinck PF.
21. Chit from T to D/FIN, TS, 9 March 1944, in Durieux PF.
22. Photographs in *Livre d'Or*, 229.

who was a nurse. A series of strokes of better luck produced an ambulance, with Viscountess de Lantsheere on board, to intimidate any German who might care to stop it; he was taken to a clinic in Brussels, where two surgeons called Coryn, father and son, amputated his right leg.

Albert Hachez, who had taken over the 'Zero' intelligence organisation from Ugeux in the previous March, claimed to T section when he reached England that it had been himself – in breach of all the rules of clandestine prudence – who had provided Durieux with the false papers necessary to cover his stay in the clinic;[23] but does not appear in Durieux' own book, which gives all the credit to a deliciously beautiful nurse at the clinic, the de Lantsheere family, the Coryns and Elizabeth Sacré, who visited him every day.[24]

Even from his hospital bed, Durieux pressed on with his task, which was to hamper the export of Belgian labour to Germany. Through sub-agents organised and trained by Heffinck, he had the registers of four different branches of the Office National du Travail destroyed, and campaigned against that organisation so effectively, all through Wallonia, that the Germans abandoned its use, and set up their own *Werbestelle* to hold labour records.[25] 'Caracal' had therefore succeeded at least in wasting enemy time and causing trouble in the supply of forced labour; and did so from a clinic more security-minded than the convent hospital that had gossiped about Campion.[26]

Moreover, still from his bed, through one of the peasants who had originally found him, he began to organise the 'Nola' sabotage group. This was never large – it did not run to as many as 250 members – but it was secure; Heffinck trained it so it was competent; and it was kept in regular touch with England for parachuted supplies. Eventually,

23. Interview with Hachez by Mrs Cameron, 20 September 1943, TS in Belgium 256. For an outline of Belgian intelligence circuits during the war, see H. Bernard, *La Résistance 1940–1945*, 60–78.

24. Guy Weber, *Capitaine Caracal SSA 2690*, 127–56.

25. Draft citation for Durieux, who eventually received the MBE; TSC signed by Mockler-Ferryman in January 1943 in Durieux PF.

   Many details of the Germans' administrative arrangements can be found in E. Dejonghe (ed.), *L'Occupation en France et en Belgique 1940–1944*.

26. Cp page 251.

when his health had recovered enough, Durieux moved in the autumn to stay south of Valençay, in central France, at Henri Bernard's mother's château; and reached England by Lysander next spring.[27]

He entrusted 'Nola' to Georges Gérard,[28] and by dint of sheer common sense Gérard succeeded in keeping a group of competent saboteurs together, silent – a rare gift among Belgian sub-agents – awaiting orders from London about how and when they were to start work. This small investment paid a handsome dividend.[29]

Bingham, at one of Mockler-Ferryman's weekly planning meetings, 'saw no means of preventing the Germans carrying out prearranged Demolitions':[30] which, *pace* Bingham's shade, became an SOE speciality. Bodies like 'Nola' and Groupe G, as well as resisters in Rotterdam, were getting ready to prove him wrong.

The escapade of 'Coal' and 'Turtle' reads more like a weak thriller than hard fact, but is true.

As far back as 27 May 1942 a small meeting in the Air Ministry, including the formidable R. V. Jones, contemplated sending a party to the Low Countries or to northern France to steal a radar-equipped night fighter, so that Jones could examine and counter its air interception plant.[31] Eventually T found two Belgians to take this on, Legrand and van Dael ('Coal' and 'Turtle' respectively), air force officers who were old friends and competent, after some refresher training, to fly a Messerschmitt 110.

They jumped blind, on 18/19 January 1943, wearing RAF uniform – if caught, they were to pass themselves off as shot-down aircrew. Elaborate arrangements were made with Fighter Command to ensure their safe return by air, by night. So transparent were some resistance circles in Belgium that Dessing, on the run from Holland, hoped to get a lift with them,[32] but was disappointed. They went to Brussels, where van Dael's wife found them Belgian identity papers

---

27. See page 323.
28. Photograph in *Livre d'Or*, 313.
29. Cp pages 348, 365.
30. HQ 14, 10 June 1943.
31. Unsigned TS, perhaps by TD, in Belgium 42.
32. Berne to SOE, 20 April 1943, tpt in *ibid.*; for Dessing, see pages 125–7 above.

and a safe flat; and they got within a hundred feet of an AI-fitted Me 110 – Legrand brought back a drawing of its nose aerials.[33] But the aircraft were too closely guarded for the pair to think of stealing one; instead, they persuaded a fitter in the repair shop at Evere (close to Brussels) to steal one of the AI sets, which reached Jones through another channel. They returned to England separately, Legrand down a fast and van Dael down a slow escape line.[34]

The success, in the teeth of stiff obstacles, of the 'Caracal' mission helped to prove to T that it was going to be perfectly feasible to work into Belgium, even if the Sûreté saw all the papers beforehand. Yet hitches with the Sûreté were still liable to occur; as the case of 'Labrador' and 'Calf' was about to prove.

They were dropped on the same night as 'Coal' and 'Turtle'. 'Calf', J. P. Janssens, was injured in the drop, and took a few weeks to recover before he opened up W/T traffic. He was a young sailor, who would have preferred a life at sea. His organiser, Edmond Maréchal ('Labrador'), five years his senior, was a hairdresser by trade – he had left school at fourteen – and a cycle-borne light cavalryman by military training. They were sent by Marissal to improve liaison with the Légion Belge, of which they found the high command in disarray – as will soon be shown; and fell victims to at least one piece of double crossing after they had received a few drops of stores.

They were approached by some shot-down Canadian airmen, who were in hiding and in search of an escape line. 'Calf' gave the airmen's particulars – which were genuine – to home station, and asked for help. The Deuxième Direction gave them a safe address, which they passed on to the airmen, and were rash enough to visit themselves. It was not safe at all; it was controlled by the notorious de Zitter: as the Sûreté in London knew, but had not told Marissal's staff.

De Zitter met 'Labrador', and quite took to him; he tried to enlist 'Labrador's' help in running his bogus escape lines. 'Labrador' remembered, a shade late, Beaulieu's warnings against mixing different

---

33. Belgium 42; closely akin to a later mark photographed in plate 18b of R. V. Jones's *Most Secret War.*
34. Interrogations of Legrand, TSC, 16 and 18 June 1943, and report by van Dael, signed TS, 2 February 1944, in Belgium 42.

kinds of resistance work together; so de Zitter had 'Calf' arrested at his set, and a few weeks later betrayed the demoralised 'Labrador' also. 'Calf' promptly escaped, but was soon recaptured. At least they survived their concentration camps.

Walthère Gauthier[35] ('Griffon'), a steel factory storekeeper, was already thirty-nine when he entered SOE in August 1942. He was sent to Thame to be trained as a wireless operator, but was plucked away halfway through the course to go to Beaulieu and learn to be an organiser instead. (The change of intended mission was made on Belgian, not British, initiative.) Beaulieu found him shrewd, determined and hard-working; and he went to the field, on a blind drop south of his birthplace at Liège, on 13/14 February 1943.

Raymond Holvoet ('Badger'), his wireless operator, half his age, jumped with him, but they missed each other on the DZ: Gauthier had hurt himself on landing, and hobbled off at once in search of help instead of collecting his kit. Holvoet, a conceited young man hardly out of school – he had just won an annual literary prize for Flemish adolescents – did no better: in fact he did worse. He was unable to make W/T contact with home station at all; and a string of indiscretions included having himself photographed in parachuting gear.

Gauthier did what he could, without fast touch with London, to encourage Légion Belge adherents west of Brussels, but soon decided to try the return overland. He picked an escape line so bad that he was arrested on the French frontier. He was packed off eventually to Dachau, where he was put into a penal unit – as if Dachau itself were not punishment enough – and beaten up daily, instead of occasionally; he narrowly survived.

Holvoet, disguised as Flight Lieutenant Kingsley, RAF, picked a better escape line, and was back in England at the end of July, only to be packed off to the cooler.[36]

*

---

35. A pencil note on SOE's copy of his MI5 clearance form reads 'real name Jean René <u>CUDELL</u>' but the whole of the rest of his PF, including his citation for a king's commendation for courage, treats him as Gauthier.
36. Their PFs.

By spring 1943 local resistance, some of it wholly unconnected with SOE, was beginning to make a marked impact on the German-run economy of Belgium. The communist-inspired Partisans claimed, for example, to have raided the marshalling yard at Louvain late on 3 April, blown up with dynamite 2,200 gallons of fuel oil, and destroyed 272 Westinghouse brake tanks (also one of Groupe G's favourite targets).[37]

Yet as late as April 1943 T was still locked in W/T converse with the false 'Periwig'; though, by the end of the month, MI5 and SOE's security section had convinced him that that operator 'must be considered to be in German hands'.[38] Drops were still being made to 'Corgi', 'Lacquer's' supposed successor; by mid-May he too had come under suspicion, and by July had been dropped.[39] All through May, again, T was exchanging messages in good faith with 'Ocelot', who had been arrested on landing eight months before; slender W/T touch was maintained with him into July.[40] Improvements were at last at hand.

T was by now attracting less disaffected and more competent agents from the Belgian army: for instance, Henri Frenay, a twenty-eight-year-old miner's son, motor mechanic turned gunner sergeant, whom the Sûreté introduced to SOE in midsummer 1942. He was a quiet, persistent, steady worker, who absorbed all SOE's schools could teach him, and made friends with Jean Lambert Woluwe, another miner's son from his own home town, Herstal, which is just below Liège on the Meuse.

Frenay and Woluwe ('Mouflon' and 'Jerboa') went into Belgium on 13 April 1943, after full training as saboteurs, with the mission of attacking a factory at Ghent; which they found unapproachably guarded. So they moved to Hainaut, and applied their sabotage techniques to such targets as they could find. They sank a couple of barges and a dredger on the Mons-Tournai canal, blocking it; they blew up seven canal locks, causing a good deal of further disruption;

---

37. *The Underground Press in Belgium* (1944), 32.
38. War diary, xxiii. 162, 1, 8, 26 April 1943. Cp pages 251–4.
39. War diary, xxiii. 162, 174–5 (May) and 193 (June) 1943, and xxiv. 490–9, a confession by 'Corgi'.
40. *Ibid.*, 212, 359.

they made eleven attacks, of varying weight, on railway targets. They found a factory at Ath – one of only two in Belgium – making ply-wood for the Germans, and broke up all its machine tools. Finding thirty wagon-loads of flax and colza in a railway siding, and having thirty incendiaries by them, they burnt the lot.[41]

When they had run out of stores, they set out for Spain; both returned safely to England in February, and volunteered at once to set out again.

'Porcupine' and 'Mandrill' dropped together on 14 April. 'Porcupine', Jean Coyette, was a thirty-six-year-old doctor of law at Brussels university. 'Mandrill', Henri Filot, eight years younger, his assistant, was a Belgian locksmith (he must have enjoyed the burglary module at Beaulieu),[42] whose mother had fled to Holland at the start of the previous world war. The aircraft that carried them failed to return. 'Dormouse', Leon Bar their wireless operator, followed three nights later.

This was one of several missions SOE ran jointly with PWE: its object was to demoralise German soldiers, by using leaflets and lamp-post stickers or even by chatting them down in bars. The main tide of the war had by now turned against Germany. Staff officers in London, who had not taken in how desperate the trio of Hitler, Himmler and Goebbels had become, believed that the ordinary Fritz could be persuaded to see reason and stop fighting. 'Porcupine' was reckoned reasonable enough to persuade him. His team received several loads of parachuted propaganda, and distributed it as best they could; results were meagre. He and 'Mandrill' got away into Switzerland in July; 'Dormouse', still at work for another organiser, stayed in Belgium. He will reappear in a few pages' time.[43]

The tale of the Rat, the Goat and the Vole is too colourful to be omitted. Its principal villain was once succinctly described by Amies as 'our agent GOAT (a bad hat)'.[44] For discretion's sake it was left out

---

41. Citation for Frenay, 18 March 1944, TSC in his PF; and see Belgium 105.
42. Cp Cunningham, *Beaulieu*, 72–3, 108–10.
43. See page 318 below.
44. 29 February 1944, Belgium 147.

of *SOE in France*, as it did not directly affect any of SOE's several sections that worked there. Indeed, had DF been allowed a say, things would no doubt have turned out differently; but T, recalling Detal's lack of success,[45] wished to set up a wholly independent escape network, with no help from the Belgians or anyone else – except the RAF – at the start. Once it existed, use of it was to have been offered to those who needed it; but there were hitches.

The three agents were all British officers, the Vole as organiser, the others to help him. Their escape line was to run from Brussels to Lysander landing grounds in south central France, perhaps with an extension to the Riviera coast. (Did T know that Lysanders from Tangmere could barely reach Lyons?) The Rat and the Goat dropped together, blind, into the Aveyron on 14/15 April 1943, each with a W/T set and a .32″ pistol. The short, sturdy Vole followed on the next night, by Lysander.[46] They failed to meet him; when they did foregather, a few days later, he quarrelled with them. According to the Rat, the only survivor, the Vole had a nervous breakdown, and hid for weeks in his room at his own sister-in-law's small country hotel. He was last seen alive towards mid-May, walking away from the hotel between the Goat and the Rat.[47]

Some weeks later the Goat reached Paris, alone, with plenty of money. In September the Rat organised his own airborne extraction. No one then connected the Goat with the discovery on 23 June, not very far from where he had landed, of an unidentified fresh corpse in a well: the body of a short sturdy man with four .32″ bullet holes through his chest, fired from behind.

The Goat had boasted to a friend while under training that he had already enjoyed nearly a thousand mistresses; hence, no doubt, his codename. He ignored, or had never heard of, the principle laid down by Hanbury-Williams and Playfair: 'it should be emphasised constantly to officers in SOE that they must be like Caesar's wife.'[48] He had taken plenty of money to France with him; raised plenty

45. Pages 259 ff.
46. T section war diary, xxiii. 163, April 1943.
47. *Ibid.*, 171, May 1943.
48. 18 June 1942, 35, in HQ 60.

more in the Aveyron; and settled down in a flat in the west end of Paris to spend it, principally on women, sometimes one, sometimes two at a time. To some of them he boasted that he was a spy, now and then producing his W/T set – even calling up home station – to prove it. One of these girls, with more sense of security than he had, ventured to remind him that her companion that night was a Gestapo nark; whereupon the Goat strangled the alleged nark with a silk stocking. He did not dispose of her body deep enough. A dog soon found it; the police recognised it, and called on the victim's madame. She had last seen the girl when booking her out to Monsieur Goat, who had not bothered to move to another flat. He was shot at Mont Valérien, or – more probably – polished off by his SS gaolers after a bungled attempt to escape.

After the war, the Vole's French wife recognised his exhumed body. The Rat, cornered by Inspector Skardon, confessed that he had watched the Goat shoot the Vole, and helped to drop the body down the well; he lived abroad thereafter. The only redeeming feature of this story is that two French businessmen, who were conned out of over two million francs by the Goat before he left the Aveyron for Paris, were repaid in full out of SOE's post-war surplus.[49]

T sent two two-man parties by the May moon, 'Muskrat' and 'Vampire' to Antwerp and 'Bullfrog' and 'Gofer' to the Ardennes, as well as 'Macduff's' three-man party, which was to prepare the way for 'Civet/Stanley', to whom we shall turn shortly.

'Muskrat', Jean van Gyseghem, was working on a second degree in philosophy at Ghent when the war reached Belgium; he was then twenty-four. He left Belgium, with some friends, in July 1941, and had several months in Spanish prisons before he was released. Rheam taught him how to be a saboteur. Many of his instructors thought him bright as well as pleasant. He was teamed up with 'Vampire', François Beckers, two years his senior, a garage hand before he joined the army, who had spent five years as a regular soldier and airman

---

49. Belgium 147; PFs on the three agents; note by T of 12 September 1944 in Security 57(ii). Rat's account in the war diary – xxiii. 360–71, July-September 1943 – needs to be taken with a pinch of salt.

and was a fully trained W/T operator before ever he went to Thame: a small lively man, secure even when in his cups.[50] They dropped on 22/23 May.

Like Livio and Pans, they were to reconnoitre possibilities rather than to do anything active; Antwerp was the area round which they were to explore. They achieved one arms drop, of ten containers, near Turnhout. One of the reception committee boasted of having been present, and the Germans consequently captured most of the arms; with them was a royal gamekeeper, who had also helped with the reception and who preserved exemplary silence under questioning. The area was so comparatively quiet that Beckers once stayed at his set for two hours without trouble, and only once even heard of a D/F car in the neighbourhood. Both he and his organiser complained that they far too often got BBC messages warning them of impending drops that never took place; and van Gyseghem added the complaint that Antwerp was far too full of VNV for his taste.[51]

On 21/22 May, the night before 'Muskrat' and 'Vampire' left, Francou ('Bullfrog') and Paul Goffin ('Gofer') jumped into the Ardennes. Fifteen pages of conversation with Mrs Cameron survive from the 'Bullfrog' party.[52] They landed in the wrong place, somewhere near Belgium's south-easternmost corner; confided in the first level-crossing keeper they met; and were relieved to see the Union flag on his mantelshelf. They twice put out of action the wood alcohol factory at Marbehan that their predecessors had wrecked before;[53] they burnt some colza; they derailed several trains; they received, in two drops, a total of ten containers of warlike stores; and Francou, who was twice arrested, twice escaped – once by jumping out of a train, and once by knocking out all three of the *Feldgendarmes* who stopped him. Francou warmly praised Goffin, his W/T operator, for skill and discretion. Goffin's rexist past had caused a moment's hesitation before SOE took him on;[54] his case is a good

---

50. Notes in their PFs.
51. Interrogations *ibid.*
52. Belgium 24, TS, 12 November 1943.
53. Page 266.
54. TS jotting of 18 June 1942 in his PF.

example of how a man can change his mind entirely over politics, and turn out well.

As we have seen, Pierlot distrusted Belgian regular army officers, on political grounds.[55] Moreover, as Bernard put it at the start of a long letter to Knight on 22 November 1942, '*Le Gouvernement ne veut pas d'action en territoire occupé.*'[56] Yet during the late autumn Pierlot was brought, by a private accident, to change his mind about the reliability of the Légion Belge, and even about the advisability of active resistance. His brother-in-law, François de Kinder,[57] had reached London by late October 1942, and was able to recount to him a long talk he had had in the previous July with Colonel Jules Bastin,[58] who was running the Légion. Jean del Marmol, called '*l'ami Jean*' in the Légion, and one of Bastin's closest helpers, had arranged and been present at this talk, at his own family's château at Falaën north-west of Dinant. De Kinder had been won over by Bastin's and del Marmol's manifest honesty and respect for the Belgian constitution, and was able to persuade Pierlot that no sort of danger to the exiled regime could result from a body run by such men.[59]

On 30 December 1942 Pierlot, as minister of defence, wrote a long letter to Bastin, to explain why his government had hesitated so long to pick a military commander in occupied Belgium, and then to offer him the post, with strict warnings against exposing civilians to reprisals, or adopting any attitude that might provoke civil war. Otherwise, Bastin was to have a free hand, and was urged to decentralise as much as he could.[60] The letter, dispatched by a secret service courier, took nearly seven weeks to reach him. He accepted at once.

Bastin, whom SOE called 'Osric', had had some experience of secret war as a young man: captured as a cavalry troop commander, and wounded beneath his dead horse, in mid-August 1914, he had

---

55. Page 292.
56. TS in Bernard PF.
57. Portrait in *Livre d'Or.* 96.
58. Portrait *ibid.* 118.
59. H. Bernard, *Jean del Marmol,* 27–8.
60. Text in Bernard, *L'Armée Secrète,* 285–7.

escaped from Germany at the eleventh attempt, to serve with distinction in Flanders.[61] He had worked closely with Claser ('Bull'), right from the start, and was eagerly awaiting the results of de Liedekerke's mission; but these were slow to arrive.

Poor 'Bull': he was in deeper trouble than he knew. He could not find either of his wireless operators; both of them had gone to an enemy-controlled reception.[62] So he cast back into France, in the hope of finding an operator there. On 6 November 1942 he was arrested, on a trivial charge, on the demarcation line; was recognised, while a prisoner, by an alert member of the Abwehr; and was transferred in February 1943 to St Gilles prison in Brussels. Four days later he was released, and taken for a ride by people he thought friendly, to a garden in the suburbs, where he met an affable English officer who entertained him with English cigarettes; to whom he boasted about where he had hidden the microfilms he was trying to take to London. The officer saw Claser and his secretary onto an escape line; they were again picked up in France, near the demarcation line, and this time shut away more thoroughly. The affable officer's Englishness was as notional as his commission: he was an Abwehr sergeant whose English happened to be perfect. Through Claser's assistant Major Stiers, commander of the Légion Belge's active groups in Flanders, who was also completely taken in, the Abwehr secured only too much knowledge about the Légion's leadership. The top men were shown stocks of captured weapons, not knowing they had been captured; through a captured set, they thought they corresponded with London; when asked, on that set, for a list of their subordinate officers, they provided it. Meanwhile, the BBC was tricked, through another captured set, into sending a message which meant that Claser and his companion had reached London.[63]

There was even an ugly story, reported later by de Liedekerke 'from a para-military source which he believed thoroughly trustworthy', about Claser 'sitting in a car with two men in plain clothes' and

---

61. *Ibid.*, 273.
62. Page 293.
63. Abwehrstelle Belgien report to Berlin on 'Taurus' organisation, 8 November 1943, TS tr. (anon.) in Belgium 23; Bernard, *L'Armée Secrète*, 38–49.

recommending those who knew he was a patriot, and came to speak to him, to another rendezvous; where they were all arrested.[64]

'Bull' had further failed to endear himself to the secret high command in London by showing enthusiasm, while he was still at large, for reorganising intelligence-collecting as well as stimulating paramilitary action. This led to a protest from C himself to CD, requesting that SOE stop 'Bull' from causing any further damage; a justified but unfortunate flurry.[65]

Possibly incited to do so by 'Bull', who was unaware how closely he was being watched by the Germans, several senior Belgians who were eminent in resistance committed the imprudence of holding a conference in Liège just after Easter, in late April 1943: called by Colonel Siron, who mistook three Gestapo acquaintances for English officers. Siron's object was to form a united resistance movement; the Germans' object was to arrest as many leading men as they could.

Bastin, after much hesitation, attended the meeting, but took care to arrive alone. He had hardly done so when the doors burst open and a Gestapo party rushed in, firing sub-machine-guns at random; they arrested everyone there. Bastin, lightly wounded, stuck to the story that he had been invited to a meeting to discuss how to make sure the communists did not seize power; he had even bothered to have in his pocket some forged letters of menace from communist bodies he had made up. None of his friends betrayed him, and the Germans let him go; he was able to tell the story to 'Civet' in August 1943.[66] 'Civet' offered to arrange his escape to England; he thought it his duty to stick it out with his men.[67]

Frederic Veldekens ('Samoyède') had an important propaganda task, but had done some paramilitary training as well. When his mission began, with a blind drop near Enghien on 12 March, he was twenty-nine years old; he had been a planter in Sumatra before the war.

---

64. War diary, xiii. 280, July–September 1943.
65. *Ibid.*, xxiii. 130–2, December 1942.
66. 'Civet's' report, as 'Stanley' of January 1944, TSC in Belgium 29. For 'Civet', see below, pages 327–30.
67. Bertrand, *L'Armée Secrète*, 58.

A few weeks later, late on 19 April 1943 – by coincidence, the day the Warsaw ghetto rising began – three desperate members of Groupe G, headed by George Livchitz who was a Jew, stopped a train in a cutting near Tirlemont. The train had just left Malines for Auschwitz and was crammed with Jews, under an armed guard. Livchitz had a revolver, his party's sole armament. They stopped the train simply by putting a red lantern on the track. Two or three hundred passengers were persuaded to leave the train, through a random shower of bullets; about a hundred got away. Twenty were shot down on the spot. Livchitz was caught and shot later, with his brother.[68]

The incident served at least to alert the surviving Jews in Belgium to their probable fate if they did not go into hiding.[69] Veldekens heard of it promptly, and reconnoitred the hospital at Tirlemont in which about fifty wounded Jews were being kept under a solitary sentry's eye. Before he could mount a discreet rescue party through the back entrance, which was close to the Jews' ward, the hospital was surrounded by a force of local maquisards – *onderduikers, refractaires* who had come out of hiding for the purpose – waving weapons. Someone rang up the Gestapo; the maquisards were chased off, and the Jews dispatched to Germany and oblivion.[70]

For ten more busy weeks Veldekens got on with his mission: to identify the sites of German wireless-jamming stations, and to tell parties off to wreck them – this was duly done, but London cancelled the order to wreck; to discover and destroy the Germans' lists of owners of wireless receivers – done; to prepare the seizure of broadcasting stations from the Germans, at the moment Belgium was liberated; to secure cinemas from enemy destruction; and to discover what stocks of paper, printers' ink and typefaces would be available to the returning Belgian government.[71]

By the end of June, he had achieved most of the large programme London had set him, but was too hopelessly compromised with the enemy to stay safely at work. He fled to Switzerland, and was back in London in November. For the rest of the war he worked at

---

68. Photographs in *Livre d'Or*, 363.
69. William Ugeux, *Histoires de Résistants*, 17–28.
70. Veldekens interrogation, 9 and 14 February 1945, TSC in his PF, 11.
71. *Ibid.*, 1.

Aronstein's elbow for the Sûreté, in spite of the doubts he had rightly thrown on the cover story provided for him before he left London. He was to adopt the name of a man who really lived in Brussels, about whom, for safety's sake, he made a few inquiries: to find he was doubling with a man who 'already had six sentences for various offences including assault and battery'.[72]

He left a working organisation behind him under a Brussels friend, Frans Mertens ('Samoyède II'), who had pulled strings in the Ministry of Justice to get him adequate papers. Mertens ensured that 'Samoyède' kept in W/T contact with home station till liberation; but Veldekens' own operator did not. This was Leon Bar ('Dormouse'), shared with 'Porcupine': a twenty-four-year-old army regular sergeant, and a good operator.[73] Bar was set up, as Brion had been, ostensibly as a domestic servant: a role that did not much appeal to him. Veldekens found him a protection team, and made sure that he never used the same house twice running; but he got bored with security. Off his own bat, he leased himself a flat; took a spare set there, alone; settled down to work off a backlog of minor messages; and on 27 August was duly caught by a direction-finding team, with whom he exchanged shots. They took him away, wounded, and tortured him. Torture got nothing out of him; next February they shot him dead.[74]

It is time to introduce Ides Floor, a Belgian businessman long resident in London who happened to be a friend of SOE's lynchpin Gubbins. From August 1941 to February 1942 he had spent a useful six months in Gibraltar, with Durieux to help and succeed him, handling Belgian liaison.[75] Gubbins persuaded Lepage to take on Floor as liaison officer with T. Unhappily, when he joined SOE Floor's Belgian army rank was only lieutenant (he was promoted major later). He was therefore viewed askance from the start by Colonel Marissal, a stickler for military etiquette who was unimpressed by Floor's role in

---

72. *Ibid.*, 2. For a summary of 'Samoyède's' achievement, see brief tribute by Ugeux in *Memo from Belgium*, 56–7.

73. Photograph in *Livre d'Or*, 99.

74. Belgium 57: Bar PF.

75. Weber, *op. cit.*, 69–71; photograph in *ibid.*, 73.

rescuing Belgian gold in 1940.[76] Floor's enterprise, business sense and good manners vastly improved T section's relations with the Sûreté, made more convenient by the installation of a direct telephone link between Baker Street and Belgrave Square.

Moreover, an important arrival from Belgium in late July 1943 overshadowed Lepage, and further eased the personal friction T had found so tiresome. This was a senior judge, Ganshof van der Meersch, who had already taken so active a part in intelligence work that it seemed prudent to him to turn to an escape line and evade the Gestapo. The Belgian community in London welcomed him. Pierlot and Delfosse persuaded him to take on oversight of the Sûreté; and, to make sure that he outranked the rank-conscious Marissal, he was made a lieutenant-general.

After the war, Gubbins went on record: 'It is not too much to say that without General Ganshof and Major Floor nothing of any significance would have been achieved in Belgium.'[77]

Ugeux, like Ganshof, found Belgium too hot to hold him, came out down one of his own lines, and – being his senior already – was installed over Lepage's head at the Sûreté. This too improved Anglo-Belgian secret relations. So did the appointment of Captain-Major the Comte de Borchgrave as operations officer to Marissal; he was as competent as he was polite, and his beautiful manners both raised the morale of agents, and soothed the prickliness of staff officers.

Co-ordination was often a bugbear in resistance. Over-centralisation was dangerous; if someone near the centre got caught, it might ruin thousands. Over-diffusion was dangerous in another way: it might well lead to waste of effort, as several groups devoted themselves to a single target (compare Veldekens's attempt to rescue Jews).

In Belgium, as has been shown, there were several strong underground movements, some local, some national: with the king a self-proclaimed prisoner, and most ministers abroad, there was yet one personality strong enough to impose order on potential chaos. When Walthère Dewé organised his intelligence circuit, 'La Dame Blanche', during the Great War, he insisted that its members kept clear of all other resistance activity; and was just as rigid with the

---

76. *European Resistance Movements 1939–45*, 265–6.
77. CD to D/HIS, 1, 26 October 1945, initialled TS prefixed to History 1xv.

members of 'Clarence', the intelligence circuit he organised next time round. He was a big enough man to break his own rule.

Through Jean del Marmol, Dewé arranged a pact between the Armée de Belgique, as the Légion Belge currently called itself, and the Armée de la Libération; it was signed at Liège on 20 April 1943, and ratified by a further note signed in Brussels on Trafalgar Day the same year; he countersigned both.[78] This ensured that neither body interfered with the work of the other.

Thanks to Dewé's group, which had plenty of experience from 1914–18 to guide it, and included such agents as the well-placed railway clerk at Namur,[79] C did substantially better in Belgium than CD could.

This is perhaps the place to insert an odd undated fragment from Colonel Marissal's post-war memoir, preserved in the Belgian archives. He alleged that the Germans managed to send over to London a retired Belgian officer called Meukerman; warmly recommended to him for employment by Lepage, but rejected by Marissal on advice from men who knew Meukerman better. The newcomer found himself a niche in the Belgian embassy in London; where he was caught by Special Branch in the act of composing a message for the enemy. He was tried in secret and hanged.[80]

By midsummer even Humphreys, the head of DF, with his long views, became aware that Schouten's mission must have aborted.[81] Of 'Rat', 'Goat' and 'Vole' he had not yet heard. He arranged for Gerson, who ran his best line ('Vic') from Paris to Barcelona, to lay on an extension to Brussels;[82] and he arranged two more lines of his

---

78. Text in Bernard *Un Géant de la Résistance*, 39–40.

79. See Foot, *Resistance*, 24.

80. J. Marisall, *Historique*, 127. SOE once held a file on a man called Neukermans, 'rejected by 2e Section'; but it has been destroyed. P. C. R. Neukermans, despised by his captors, was executed on 23 June 1944: see *Camp 020*, 62, 283–4, 368.

81. Page 148.

82. Cp page 170.

own that were meant to affect the Low Countries, 'Pierre-Jacques' and 'Greyhound/Woodchuck'.

'Pierre-Jacques' – they jumped near Fontainebleau on 23 July 1943 – had a dual task. Not only were they to run an escape line from inside the Dutch border across Belgium and France into Spain; but they were to run a separate line, carrying parcels rather than men, from Geneva to Barcelona. 'Pierre' was Guido Zembsch-Schreve – whom we have met before, travelling to Berne to authenticate the two successful 'North Pole' escapers.[83] He has written an authoritative war autobiography, *Pierre Lalande* – one of his cover names – to which any reader is referred who seeks an answer to that always interesting question, What did it feel like at the time?[84] Though born on Swiss soil of a Dutch father, he could pass without a tremor for French, and settled in Paris, leaving 'Jacques' – Jacques Planel, his French W/T operator – safely ensconced in the country.

There was a hitch. They handed Planel's papers over to an early acquaintance for improvement, a process expected to take a few weeks; it took six months. Impressed by Humphreys with the need to do everything gently, carefully, and quite right, they marked time till Planel had a wallet-full of documents that would survive a stiff control; by then, it was early 1944. Not much had been done towards organising either task when a worse hitch ensued. Zembsch-Schreve was ordered by W/T to hand over a spare set to another circuit, at a bar rendezvous in Paris. Instead of sending a sub-agent, he undertook this task himself; and was arrested. He had the strength of character to stick to his cover story, which his interrogators never broke; they packed him off all the same to the horrors of the concentration camp called Dora, where he devoted himself to sabotaging the V2s he was supposed to be manufacturing – and survived. Over half the V2s made in Dora mis-fired: an interesting side effect of using intelligent men as slaves. Planel, on orders from London, returned quietly through Spain.[85]

---

83. Page 187.
84. Leo Cooper, 1996.
85. Planel's end of the story, with a wealth of detail, is in Clandestine Communications 11; he thought his organiser over-cautious.

'Greyhound' had better fortune. He was George (de) Lovinfosse,[86] who could trace his ancestors back to the middle ages at Herstal; he was born in 1896, the same year as Gubbins, had been twice wounded in the Great War, had been a friend from boyhood of Colonel Piron, who commanded the free Belgian brigade in exile, and was also a friend of Henri Bernard. He had done useful liaison work with the BEF in 1940, escaping from Bordeaux to Falmouth and joining the Home Guard in the west country. In June 1942 he was suddenly summoned to London, and found himself a prospective T section agent with a British commission. In spite of his age, he volunteered to parachute.

A first attempt was made at despatching him in April 1943, with Courtin ('Mouse') on his second mission as his W/T operator. Lovinfosse liked Courtin, but thought him unsuited for DF work; moreover, Courtin was to organise two or three lines to carry packets between Paris and Spain, which Lovinfosse thought an unsuitable burden to lay on an operator.[87]

On 11/12 August, with a fresh companion, he parachuted into the Indre, in central France, and was warmly received at the Château d'Entraygues, not far from Châteauroux, by Bernard's formidable mother,[88] who lived there with her daughter Madame Bouchardy.

His wireless operator, who jumped with him, was Dominick Kelly ('Woodchuck'), who came into SOE from the City police; only revealing later that his father had been shot by the Black and Tans during the Troubles. His family came from Co. Clare, where he had been born in 1915; he had lost a younger brother in the RAF. He had been brought up in France, and was bilingual, with French too perfect for him to be able to pass as a Belgian; that would not be needed.

Lovinfosse settled him in an isolated farm, where the family were happy to have him; he made friends with a local Vichy police wireless expert, whom he trained to be his successor. This man in turn was kept fully informed of all German W/T direction-finding efforts in the *département* of the Indre; so Kelly never had any troubles on that score. By this stage in the war, and in this part of France, he

---

86. He added the 'de' after the war.
87. Robinson to Knight, 17 April 1943, TS in Courtin PF.
88. Photographs in Lovinfosse, *Au Service de Leurs Majestés*, 57; cp *ibid.*, 157–62.

found indeed that 'The French people today are willing to help in any way they can, the furtherance of the allied action. Their sense of patriotism which had disappeared since the last war is returning with a vengeance. With complete disregard for their own personal safety they will undertake any work.'[89]

He found also that his organiser 'always gave me full details as to where to go, whom to see, and even exactly what to say; nothing was left to chance by him. He took even more than the necessary precautions for my personal safety, and, I have learnt since, sometimes at the risk of his own.'[90] Lovinfosse secured himself cover as clerk of works to a local builder, and made useful friends at Châteauroux, in Paris, in Bordeaux, in Périgueux and in Perpignan, besides making touch with Brussels.[91] By December he had a line working through to San Sebastian, and sent Kelly down it with success. He stayed on himself to look after various passengers.

When Wendelen did eventually get back to England, in summer 1943, he had a lot of useful, elementary points to make – for instance, would it not be as well to waterproof containers? And ought not W/T operators to have been warned – his had not – of the need to have at least one look-out man during every schedule? He had happened to be wheeling his bicycle past the house in which Brion was arrested, at the moment of arrest; and had had time to spot both the D/F van and the German back-up team.[92] Soon he was in action again.

Two major missions left for Belgium in the summer of 1943: two men, each with a first-class operator, from the Sûreté to look into the affairs of the FIL, and two more – one preceding the other, also with two operators – to attend to the affairs of the army. The Sûreté's mission was to have been headed by an agent caller Kherkoff ('Mercutio'), who has vanished entirely from SOE's surviving archive; except for two war diary entries, one of which gives his name, while the other says baldly, 'It appeared that C. objected to the choice of

---

89. Report of 14 February 1944, 8, TS in his PF.
90. *Ibid.*, 2.
91. War diary, xxiii. 367–74, July-September 1943.
92. Notes dated 17 June 1943, TS in Belgium 107.

MERCUTIO. Meanwhile the Sûreté were concentrating on plans for this most important Mission';[93] on which they sent one of their own staff.

This was the Comte de Liedekerke, on his second sortie; now codenamed 'Claudius'. He had probably heard already of his brother Raphael's arrest;[94] this did not lessen his readiness to risk his own life again. He took with him as his W/T operator A. G. A. Blondeel ('Pointer'), who must be distinguished from Colonel Eddy Blondeel, who commanded the Belgian SAS unit.[95] 'Pointer', another child of a refugee of 1914, had been born in Bristol a fortnight before Christmas of that year. His parents returned to Antwerp, where he had been working in the late 1930s for a Swedish metal firm. He was captured as an army subaltern in May 1940, but escaped into unoccupied France; which he left in late summer 1942 with a party of F agents who got out of Mauzac.[96] (He already knew Bodington of F's staff, formerly a Reuter's man in Paris.) SOE promptly recruited him. The training staff thought highly of him; their trust was borne out in the field. He and 'Claudius' landed safely, dropping blind, near Gembloux on 15/16 July, and settled in private houses in Brussels – much safer than hotels.

They were followed on 11/12 August by Wendelen, now 'Tybalt', also with a W/T operator, 'Hillcat' – that is, Jacques Doneux, whose only fault was that he spoke French with a light English accent: once fashionable in the best quarters of Paris, but a shade conspicuous in wartime Brussels, where an SOE agent from a different group who had a brief meeting with him took him for an Englishman. Doneux has left a splendid account, in his war autobiography,[97] of what the life of a clandestine wireless operator in western Europe was like by this stage of the war.

They had an awkward start to their mission – Wendelen hurt himself on landing, and was confused for a few hours; moreover, they

---

93. xxiii. 167, May 1943.
94. According to the *Livre d'Or*, 93, Count Raphael was arrested on 15 October 1942, and shot in an old fort at Utrecht on 9 October 1943.
95. Photograph of Colonel Eddy in *Livre d'Or*, 16.
96. See Foot, *SOE in France*, 203–4.
97. *They Arrived by Moonlight.*

were in that frequent parachutists' trouble, they did not know exactly where they were – they too had dropped blind. Common sense and helpful villagers soon sorted their problems out, and they too made for Brussels.

'Pointer' and 'Hillcat' were both sound operators, devoted to security; each had a small but sound protection team, who carried their sets for them to the many different transmission sites they used, and kept careful watch while they were at work – watching the sky as well as the streets. A Fieseler Storch aircraft, flying low, often appeared about ten minutes after an operator had started to transmit: part of the Germans' efficient D/F system, and a strong inducement to message-writers to be brief. 'Hillcat' had a further arrangement with the local police, who warned him of any German raiding parties anywhere near either his lodgings, or his working sites. Moreover, he had first-class camouflage for one of his sets: it was disguised as a portable radiogram, which would pass muster at any control – unless someone demanded to play it.[98]

'Claudius's' tasks were to seek out the leaders of the FIL, Groupe G, and the MNB, give them some money, and discuss their policies.[99] He fulfilled them rapidly; yet a draft citation for 'Tybalt' is here in point:

> The importance of the CLAUDIUS mission cannot be under-estimated, but CLAUDIUS himself was only able to establish a few initial contacts; it was TYBALT who really carried out the main part of the work. His experience as MANDAMUS gave him immense knowledge of technical details, of practical sabotage, reception committees, etc. The report he made on his return[100] shows that not only has he dash and courage, but a lucid and orderly mind due, no doubt, to his early legal training.[101]

Wendelen in short was able to follow up the leads provided by de Liedekerke, and by his own knowledge of the leading men in the

---

98. *Ibid.*, 106.
99. Interrogation, 23 October 1943, TSC in his PF.
100. [Duplic in Belgium 160(iii).]
101. Enclosed in T to AD/E through D/R, 4 January 1944, TSC in Wendelen PF.

field; both to get some short-term sabotage done, and to prepare a much more significant effort whenever a main allied invasion of north-west Europe was going to call for it. When he returned to England, late in the autumn, he left 'Hillcat' in Belgium to provide a message link between the FIL and London.

Whether the FIL was, as SOE's agents were often told,[102] a non-political body of earnest resisters, or whether it was a front organisation of the Belgian communist party, was a point about which T section remained in the dark. After the war, Belgian communists were proud of their influence in it; but, just as happened with the communist-inspired Franc-Tireurs et Partisans in France, it often happened that a wider membership had ideas of its own.

Blondeel had joined Wendelen when de Liedekerke went back to England in the early autumn; and the two of them went to Paris together in November, where they elected to take different escape lines. Wendelen's went through Spain, where he created a secret furore. Having managed a tiresome crossing of the western Pyrenees, he telephoned a British consulate, and to make clear who he was mentioned that he worked for SOE; having forgotten both that telephones in Franco's Spain were tapped, and that to mention SOE at all on an unscrambled telephone line was regarded as a grave breach of security. He had a lot of explaining and apology to do before he was forgiven.

Meanwhile, 'Pointer' pinned his hopes on an MI9 line called 'Felix', so secret that Langley never mentioned it to Foot when they were writing their book on MI9. Secrecy and efficiency do not always coincide. When two months had passed, during which three Lysander pick-ups and two MTB pick-ups arranged by 'Felix' had each broken down in turn, 'Pointer' thought he would be more use to the war if he resumed work; the more so, because in January 1944 'Hillcat' handed over to a locally trained operator and started a six-month return trek overland.

Wendelen had used the codename of 'Hector' in the field, and had handed FIL liaison over to 'Hector II', Arnold Withold-Lobet, for whom (with London's leave) 'Pointer' did another solid four months' work.[103]

---

102. Cp page 303.
103. See also page 341 below. Photograph of 'Hector II' in *Livre d'Or*, 98.

Wendelen's own report fills twenty-five pages of T's war diary.[104] One or two points in it are worth extracting: the MNB's device, for example, for getting abrasives when none could be parachuted – use flint crushed under locomotive wheels.[105] The MNB, largely recruited from the civil service – including the police and the nationalised industries – was primarily concerned with the problem of maintaining public order when the Germans left, but Wendelen recommended sending it a dozen sabotage instructors as well. He put a senior man from the MNB, and one from the FIL, in direct touch with Burgers, who turned out far too devoted a resister to betray any of his acquaintance, when the Germans did catch up with him.

The Partisans – 'who were by origin essentially Communist'[106] – had by now fused with the action groups of the FIL; and were recovering after a heavy series of arrests. Wendelen found their security excellent, and thought their members sound; they ran their own sabotage school. Like Groupe G, they were painfully short of explosives. Careful plans for railway, telephone and canal sabotage, to coincide with the allied invasion – whenever it happened – had already been made.[107] Everybody complained at the lack of adequate stores drops: a point Wendelen emphasised when he got back to London in December – by which time weather had, for the moment, closed down supply.

After long debate, Marissal determined to send his younger brother Adelin across to find out what was really going on with the secret army. The Belgians called him 'Stanley'. Knight, who could not stand him,[108] codenamed his mission 'Civet'. The main lines on which he was to act were set out in his *ordre de mission* and are in print.[109] He was formally to offer to Bastin's successor, Colonel Yvan Gérard, alias Latour, the nomination as commander of the secret forces in Belgium, and to pass on to him – or whoever took the

---

104. xxiv. 416–41, October/December 1943.

105. *Ibid.*, 426.

106. *Ibid.*

107. *Ibid.*, 431–1.

108. Belgium 267 is peppered with hostile references to him by Knight.

109. Bernard, *L'Armée Secrète*, 297–8.

job instead of him – the government's and SOE's joint wishes about how he was to act.

These were set out in a pamphlet, of which 'Stanley' took several copies with him, called *Le Cheval de Troie* by Captain Y.[110] It bore a false imprint (Algiers 1941), and seemed at a glance to be a Vichy officer's ramblings about the Trojan war; that was only the cover to get it past a cursory police inspection. It bore plenty of traces of the doctrine of the Belgian staff college, through which the elder Marissal, Cassart, Bernard, Claser and many others had passed. It laid down that the secret army was to consist of officers, NCOs and men of the active or the reserve list of the Belgian army, and discussed how it was to be organised, recruited, paid, disciplined and – if occasion arose – decorated. Paramilitary bodies could join it, on condition that they laid aside every political object; were secure and fit; accepted the army's regulations; and took orders from an officer. A particular clause laid down that there could be a commander in chief, named by the king; or if the king could not act, by the minister of defence. The army's general staff was specified to be in general command, under the king and the minister. It was thoroughly imbued with pre-war regular army orderliness, often anathema to resisters; yet it was drawn up in an idiom quite familiar to the men to whom 'Stanley' brought it.

As for what they were to do, once activated, he also brought a plan for secret military action in Belgium dated 31 March 1943, and signed by Pierlot, Gubbins, Jean Marissal and Knight.[111] The usual distinction was made between current sabotage, which should aim discreetly at disrupting the enemy's road, rail and water communications, and the phase of active operations that would begin when land fighting re-started in earnest. Even then, care was to be taken to spare the civilian population reprisals, so far as could be done: isolated headquarters, for example, were to be attacked, rather than major headquarters in city centres. The secret army was particularly charged to be on the alert for passing on, to the first allied troops it met, all the information it had about precise

---

110. Summary *ibid.*, 288–91; cover reproduced in *Livre d'Or*, 232.
111. First and last pages in facsimile in Bernard, *L'Armée Secrète*, 293–4; extracts in *Livre d'Or*, 233–8.

enemy locations and defences; and to be ready to provide guides across tricky areas, whether polder land, forest or back alleyways. Gubbins slipped in a final paragraph about the value of false rumours of roads cut and bridges blown, as a means of disconcerting the enemy.

Most of the secret army's leaders dreamed of taking the field again, commanding troops in action; forgetting that they had neither the artillery, nor the supply columns, nor the air support, let alone the armoured fighting vehicles, without which an army of the 1940s could not fight. Latour and Bastin, when released, divided Belgium up into five zones; the map they made of the zones included a start line for operations well outside Belgium, in case of a landing in France, which ran past Calais, Arras and St Quentin to Rethel.[112] This was dreamland indeed.

'Civet' was preceded not only by two wireless operators, 'Seal' and 'Ibex', but by an energetic assistant, 'Macduff'; they all jumped together on 21/22 May 1943. 'Macduff' was another Belgian aristocrat, Baron C. A. de Montepellier de Vedrin; his original task was to find a Lysander ground on which 'Civet' could be brought in, as the RAF had agreed after all to contemplate further Lysander operations into Belgium.[113] He looked at over a dozen possible sites; none turned out suitable,[114] so 'Civet' had to go via France.

He did so by Lysander on 21/22 July, took a train next morning to Paris, and was in Belgium a week later. 'Seal' turned out unable to make contact with England; 'Ibex'[115] worked for him instead. He took his next elder brother Julius's identity papers, as a *grand mutilé* from the previous world war; Julius stayed at home while Adelin travelled. He met all the inner high command of the Légion Belge, which at this time called itself the Armée de Belgique; it will be convenient to call it in future by the name it eventually adopted, L'Armée Secrète, the secret army.

*

112. See map on page 364, taken from *European Resistance Movements* (1960), 262.
113. War diary, xxiii. 159, 8 April 1943.
114. *Ibid.*, 218–19.
115. Photograph and brief eulogy in *Livre d'Or*, 247.

'Ibex' was caught at his set on 9 August (and killed not long there-after by an allied bomb). '*L'ami Jean*' del Marmol at once conjured up two more wireless operators from England for 'Stanley', called 'Lear' and 'Buckhound'. 'Buckhound' too was caught, close to his set, in late September. 'Lear', once he had got over some starting troubles about reclaiming a pair of sets that fell into a farmyard, was able to carry on.

After less than three months, 'Civet' returned to England – again by light aircraft from France – and prepared a long report.[116] He was loud in his praise of the man who looked after him in Paris on the way back to England, who was the brother of one of his principal helpers in Belgium, Laurent Wolters, '*l'ami Laurent*'.

Laurent Wolters's brother, Leon – Russian-born, like himself: their mother was Russian – lived in Paris, where he joined the French army in 1939. Leon was wounded and captured during the next year's fighting, and was released to Paris – as unfit to fight – in 1941. He tried to resume work as an engineer. By chance, he ran into Pierre de Vomécourt, the mainspring of F section's original start in France, for whom he provided a flat in April 1942 when de Vomécourt was on his second mission.

The Abwehr knew only too much about de Vomécourt's acquaintances, and arrested Leon Wolters on 24 April. He broke down at once under questioning, and informed them of a café rendezvous he had with de Vomécourt next day; at which de Vomécourt was caught. De Vomécourt went on to trial and a long spell in Colditz; Wolters was let off with a caution.[117] He kept clear of resistance work for a year, but longed to atone for his initial error. He had compounded this error by handing half a million francs of de Vomécourt's operational funds over to Sergeant Bleicher of the Abwehr; that may have been one reason why the Abwehr left him alone thereafter. Another was that he got work for a Vichy government-sponsored firm. For a year, from mid-1943 to mid-1944, through his brother Laurent, he made himself useful to Belgian resisters. He provided a Paris safe house, where a number of senior

---

116. Nearly twenty pages of single-spaced foolscap, TSC in Belgium 29.
117. Foot, *SOE in France*, 193.

members of the secret army spent a week or two on their way to or from Belgium; several of them were indignant when Leon Wolters was arraigned by the French in the spring of 1945 for the damage he had done to de Vomécourt's 'Autogiro' circuit.[118]

When 'Civet' withdrew, 'Lear' ceased work and came out also, by the more laborious method of the trek overland through France and Iberia; it took him more than three months longer.

Colonel Bastin ('Osric'), though released by the Germans in the summer, and able as has been seen[119] to talk to 'Civet', was still under fairly close enemy supervision. He was rearrested in October, and sank into the full darkness of '*Nacht und Nebel*'; he perished in Gross Rosen.

'Macduff' by contrast had been enjoying himself quietly in casinos when off duty – unsuitable conduct for an agent, because such places were often full of Germans – and in the war diary's words was 'far too compromised to remain in Belgium';[120] he too came out through France and Spain.

After Bastin's arrest, London continued for convenience to use 'Osric' as the codename of the head of the secret army: a task taken on at once – '*ami, si tu tombes, un ami sort de l'ombre te remplacer*' – by Colonel Yvan Gérard.[121] Gérard was well described by a subaltern friend of Bastin's as '*un type épatant mais pas fait pour le clandestin*'.[122] This subaltern, Alexander de Winiwater, captured in 1940, had brought off the rare feat of an escape from Colditz in September 1943, and was sent over to England through Spain next winter to report to Marissal on how the secret army was getting on (operation 'Simplon'). He emphasised the need for arms, money, and stores, and asked for over a hundred wireless sets, not at all an easy request to fulfil.[123]

In the spring, Gérard felt the Gestapo's breath far too hot on his own neck for safety. With his government's leave, he came to

---

118. Leon Wolters PF.
119. Page 316.
120. xxiii. 233.
121. Photograph in *Livre d'Or*, 341.
122. RVPS note of talk with T on 7 March 1944 in de Winiwarter PF.
123. *Ibid.*

England through the sea escape line MI9 ran from Brittany, followed a few nights later by his wife and their two children. Command passed to one of his regional chiefs, Lieutenant-General Pire ('Pygmalion'),[124] an arrangement satisfactory to everyone except the Germans.

The fate of 'Seal' – Guy Christiaens – deserves mention to round off this part of the tale. He eventually found a set and crystals that worked. After 'Ibex' had been arrested, and 'Civet', 'Lear' and 'Macduff' had set off on their different journeys back to England, 'Seal' remained on duty: the sole link, for months, between the exiled government and its secret army. Like so many W/T operators who attempted long spells at work, he began to overlook the need to keep his spells on the air short. He was caught on 10 January 1944, and put through a succession of prisons and camps, some of them infamous. He was still alive in Mauthausen when it was overrun, but succumbed on 1 July 1945.

Michel Losseau ('Othello'), T's only agent to travel by the June moon, jumped early on the 14th. He was a twenty-four-year-old gentleman farmer, large, sturdy, a good shot, well known and well connected. 'Intelligent and astute under a bluff and almost gross personality, redolent of the soil' was one training school's comment; another was reminded of a Newfoundland puppy. On his way out of Belgium he had met Absil in Lyons, and thus got recommended to SOE.[125]

There was nothing puppyish about his behaviour in the field. He had a general mission to the Belgian peasantry, which he carried out with aplomb. He began by using his friendships to acquire a post as inspector on the Belgian state railways, which carried with it a pass valid for first-class travel on any train and a chauffeur-driven car. After a few weeks' travel, he went to the man at the top: de Winter, the permanent under-secretary at the Ministry of Agriculture, whom he persuaded to work for his constitutional masters in England as well as his occupying masters in Belgium. Among the results were small increases in the national bread and fat rations, destruction of quite four-fifths of the

---

124. Photograph in *Livre d'Or*, 94.
125. Jottings in his PF.

colza crop, rations for *réfractaires*, and some reduction in the flourishing food black-markets. 'Othello' incorporated 'Baboon's' circuit in his own; indeed, 'Baboon's' brother Frans van Dorpe became 'Othello II' and carried on with organising sabotage on farms after 'Othello' left. 'Tybalt' arranged him a safe journey back, down the 'Comet' line, about which he quite properly refused to reveal anything to his SOE interrogators; he was back in England on Christmas Day.[126]

Knight was zealous, conscientious, and the soul of honour, if not of efficiency; fate placed him in an impassable fix. He longed to get his section working properly, but men more slippery than himself seemed constantly to sow obstacles in his path, which he was unable to remove. For a time he was a *bête noire* to most of the Belgian government in exile in London; and when he fell ill in the summer of 1943, SOE found it convenient to post him out to work for the political intelligence department. Gubbins admired his loyalty and recognised 'he had done his best';[127] it was time for a change. Amies took over from him – formally, on 11 August, though he had stood in for him several times already.[128]

Sir Hardy Amies – he was knighted in 1989 – joined SOE in spring 1941, as an acting captain in the intelligence corps. His gifts included bilingual German, for he had managed a factory in Germany for some time – during the *Nazizeit* – so he also had some knowledge of the enemy, as well as fluent French. After a few months as an instructor on the German army at Beaulieu, he joined T section in November 1941, to look after training and recruiting. He came to know so much about the section's problems and methods, and was so calm in manner and so quick to take points in, that he seemed an eminently suitable successor to Knight. He was made acting head of the section in August 1943, an appointment not confirmed till February next year; he said once, long afterwards, that it always seemed to himself that a couturier must be ill equipped to head a section in a secret service, and he supposed his superiors felt the same.[129]

---

126. Interrogation 13 January 1944, TSC in *ibid.*; war diary xxiii. 299–312.
127. Note of 20 January 1943 in his PF.
128. War diary, xxiii. 199.
129. Conversation with him, 1990.

Their reports on him were by no means hostile, but he was left as acting head till P. L. Johns took the section over in November 1943, with Amies as his deputy. When Johns moved on, next February, to the new post of DR/LC, in charge of all the Low Countries under Brook, Amies resumed charge of the section, this time confirmed as its head. He remained T till he was posted out in July 1945, apart from six months as head of SPU 47 – the forward mission on Belgian soil – from September 1944.

The American share in the allied subversive effort in the Low Countries was slight. Though the president of the United States had a Dutch surname, his Dutch descent was remote – it went back to a Roosevelt who had settled in New Amsterdam in 1649, before ever it became New York. No such vital American interest existed in Holland or Belgium as drew the attention of the Office of Strategic Services to France or Germany. OSS was unaffected by the wireless games that tarnished SOE's reputation; only with the 'Jedburgh' teams did it start to cast even light weight into the scales. We shall come to them in the next chapter.[130]

Meanwhile, it is worth mention that an American – Captain Alfred C. Rogers of OSS – joined T's staff in the autumn of 1943. Like Mortlock, his opposite number in N section, he gave OSS a toe-hold in the affairs of the Low Countries, which that service never needed to exploit.

A useful result of the 'Stanley' mission was that the Deuxième Direction and T section between them settled down to providing the secret army with better communications with London, through the dispatch of liaison officers who could advise on sabotage methods and W/T operators who could pass messages to and fro; ideally, of course, arms supplies would follow. Readers who care to turn to appendix 4 will find a list, which the author hopes is complete, of the agents sent to Belgium under SOE's auspices. A few are worth particular mention.

Fr Carez, a priest in an Oblate monastery in Hainaut, had already

---

130. See pages 387–9, 392–6.

done a lot of work with 'Lemur' and 'Toad' before he came out with them in late July 1943. He had helped to organise reception committees, and with his father superior's leave had stored arms in his monastery's outhouses. He was an unusually bright man in his middle twenties, who earned golden opinions in SOE's schools, and jumped back into Hainaut on 18 October with the repeatedly misspelt codename of 'Manelaus'.

His cover for being away was that he had been to France to look into the progress of boy scout movements there. He had been active in his local scout movement, and indeed at one moment had been taking a scout class when the Germans came to search his monastery; they apologised for interrupting him, and withdrew, not knowing they had been within a few feet of the containers they were seeking, which the scouts had helped drag across from the DZ.[131]

Sometimes he kept his own priestly identity; sometimes he pretended to be a businessman; latterly he passed himself off as a farmer.[132] He lived as a rule in Brussels, with a safe friend who asked no questions; communicated through couriers – girls were safest; and went down to zone I when he was needed. By the spring of 1944, he found that most of the Belgian gendarmerie were perfectly ready to help, but his sub-agents constantly had trouble with the Gestapo. He sub-divided them carefully enough for the group not to unravel altogether if one was caught.

The main obstacle to arming the secret army, through Fr Carez or anyone else, was weather, rather than the enemy. Flying conditions over Belgium were so bad that there were no drops of men or even of stores between 21 October and 19 January.

'Philotus', a courier, had been safely dropped on 20 August, but was arrested within a month. 'Flaminius' and 'Guineapig', Vekemans and Joakim, dropped two nights after Fr Carez, also on a liaison mission to a secret army zone – their zone was III, in Flanders, and Joakim had a W/T set that worked. But weather apart, Flanders was an excessively awkward area in which to contemplate parachute drops, because it bristled so with anti-aircraft defences.

Just after Christmas, Gubbins had a long informal talk with

---

131. Interrogation, 11 August 1943, 2, TSC in his PF.
132. Interrogation, 10 February 1945, 2; TS *ibid.*

General Ganshof, who pressed – exactly as Knight had pressed a year earlier – for larger deliveries of stores; for the moment, this was impracticable. Ganshof added that he had been nobbled by C, 'who had suggested to him that he should go no further with SOE in preparing actual operations as this would definitely affect the flow of information':[133] a suggestion Gubbins of course did his best to counteract, taking it up with C direct.

With a little help from SOE, the FIL brought off a famous propaganda coup on 9 November 1943. The principal Belgian evening newspaper, *Le Soir* – corresponding to London's current *Evening Standard* – appeared in a clandestine edition, indistinguishable at a glance from the nazi-dominated one, full of a bogus Wehrmacht communiqué and a mass of anti-nazi jokes. Fifty thousand copies of this splendid spoof were printed; some soon changed hands for 1,000 francs each.[134] A sabotage coup at the printing works held up production of the official edition for just long enough to get the fake to the news stands.

Verhaegen got bored with being a conducting officer, and wrote (in excellent English) to Knight on 8 January 1943 to ask to go back to more active work.[135] Exactly a year later, there was a tragic consequence.

He received a Belgian Croix de Guerre and a British Distinguished Conduct Medal for his first mission; was promoted to captain's rank; and with the codename of 'Thersites' prepared for his second. He was to go back to Belgium by parachute to be adviser on communications to the head of the secret army; and was equipped with several different identity cards, one of them blank, rail passes and workmen's passes of various kinds, and plenty of money. This time he had his own W/T operator, Hector Goffin ('Fortinbras'), but their luck ran out.

They took off from Tempsford, with two other W/T operators, in a 138 squadron Halifax on the evening of 7 January 1944. At 0125 next morning the aircraft reappeared over Tempsford, flying on only three engines, evidently having failed to find its DZ; jettisoned its

---

133. War diary, xxiv. 384.
134. Parts in facsimile in *Livre d'Or*, 67–8. War diary, xxiv. 424, 462. For details, see Doneux, *op. cit.* (2001 edn), 90–2.
135. Signed TS in his PF.

containers; crashed, and burned up. 'Armadillo' escaped lightly and
'Polonius' was badly wounded; everyone else on board was killed.[136]
Indeed, 'Polonius' was so badly hurt that he remained unfit for operations till the war was over (his name was Hiersoux); 'Armadillo',
once he had recovered, tried again.[137]

Chance, often the leading factor in war, in secret war is sometimes
paramount: consider what happened to Cassart, arrested late in
1941.[138]

He survived to report that after several months' imprisonment in
Aix-la-Chapelle (Aachen) and a further year of it in Berlin, in
September 1943 he was sent for trial in that capital, before a military
court in the Witzlebenstrasse. He was one of several cases to be heard
that day. Hanging about in a waiting-room, he asked to go to the
lavatory; nobody bothered to go with him, so he walked straight out
into the street. There he had the luck to meet a party of French prisoners of war, one of whom bought his wristwatch for eighty marks.
With sixty of these, he bought tickets on no fewer than seventeen
local trains, which in four days' and nights' travelling brought him
back to the Belgian border near Aix. He ate in station buffets on the
way. None of the trains he took had a police control; at stations, the
military police controlled only those in uniform – he was in plain
clothes – and the civil police controlled only those leaving the station
in towns – he got out in a village. By a further stroke of luck, a good
Belgian family he met near Aix saw him across the border to
Plombières; thereafter he was soon among friends, and found the
'Comet' line down to Spain.[139]

This provoked a furious telegram, perhaps Dansey's, to MI9's
'Monday' at Madrid: 'INFORM COMET ONCE MORE THAT
THIS TYPE BARGAIN WITH SOE WILL RESULT COM-
PLETE DISASTER'.[140] Cassart did not mind. He had got away, and
was soon in England: 'a little stiff-built man about 5'4" high, with

---

136. *Ibid.*
137. See page 379.
138. Page 269.
139. Thirty-five-page MS by him in his PF; undated, but spring 1944.
140. 16 January 1944, *ibid.*

broad slightly stooping shoulders, bad sight, pointed nose, and thin, scarce sandy hair' reached Paddington station on 24 January 1944.[141]

The escape and security services were so busy that several weeks passed before anyone was free to interrogate him properly; meanwhile he was held, incommunicado – like Ubbink and Dourlein – at Tyting House.[142] It was more comfortable than any of his prisons, but he did not feel a free man. 'If he had known how he was going to be received,' he said on 7 March to his joint MI5 and SOE interrogators, 'he would not have returned to the UK.'[143] A week later, one of the SOE security men commented that the tale of how he had got away from Berlin 'is almost incredible, but of course nearly all escape stories are'.[144]

His Belgian friends in London, restive at the long delay, all spoke up for him; MI5 agreed to let him have the benefit of the doubt; and late in March he was released to Lepage, on the understanding that he would only be employed on regimental duties, and he kept clear of intelligence work. He had a row with Amies, returning a carefully chosen present of books; and turned up, still exuding bad temper, under the inappropriate cover name of Courtois, with the SAS Belgian unit in Ayrshire in April. Strict instructions came that he was to be kept clear of all D-day preparations, to which the whole SAS brigade was then devoted.[145] He made himself useful to the unit; and commanded a small SAS operation, 'Bergbang', which lasted from 2 to 11 September and armed a few maquisards south of Liège; he then became the unit's planning officer.[146]

Groupe G reckoned that, all told, it lost Belgian industry working for the Germans between twenty and twenty-five million man-hours of work; ten million of them in a single coup, on the night 15/16 January 1944. Multiple, simultaneous demolitions that night ensured that on the following day (a Monday) there was no electric

---

141. Report that day by the sergeant-major who took charge of him, *ibid.*
142. Cp pages 202–3.
143. His PF.
144. Note of 16 March 1944, *ibid.*
145. Personal knowledge.
146. Jean Temmerman, *Acrobates sans importance*, 61–73, 85.

power available in Belgium whatever, unless from searchlight-generators or private emergency plants. Mines in the Borinage, for example, could get no underground work done at all for nearly a week; and steam engines had to be found from other lines to run any train service at all between Brussels and Antwerp.

This splendid stroke was bound to attract Gestapo attention: pursuing clue after clue, they found their way back to the originator, Burgers.[147] He was arrested in mid-March, and hurried away to Buchenwald; where he was murdered, with many other resisters – none quite as successful as himself – six months later.[148] His young wife remained at such liberty as occupied Belgium afforded, and helped Groupe G to carry on: stricken, but not struck down. It had, in the end, over 4,000 agents; of whom some 800, like its leader, did not survive. (These casualty figures are oddly close to those of Marie-Madeleine Fourcade's 'Alliance' intelligence circuit in France.)[149]

Groupe G's men and women were well above average quality as agents. Their cellular system was as shock-proof as such systems ever can be; and, once caught, they knew their duty to hold their tongues. Richard Altenhoff for example, chief of their supply system,[150] was captured on 31 July and tortured, but said nothing.

Henri Neuman ('Caesar'), another leading member of the group – its canal sabotage expert, among other things, and a personal friend of his contemporary Wendelen with whom he had read law – reached England just before Christmas, as the Gestapo had been closing in on him in Brussels. He reinforced Wendelen's report with more first-hand knowledge. 'Recruiting is done *only* on a basis of *personal* knowledge of the new member' – a sound recipe for any secret group. Moreover, 'absolutely unconnected with its other sections', Groupe G had a security service of its own, staffed in part by retired policemen; only Burgers himself (whose real name Neuman did not divulge) knew who ran it. This service watched out for, and disposed of, would-be traitors.[151]

---

147. Photograph in *Livre d'Or*, 311.
148. Bernard, *La Résistance 1940–1945*, 88–9.
149. See her *Noah's Ark* (Allen & Unwin, 1973), 362–70.
150. Photograph in *Livre d'Or*, 133.
151. Interrogation, 4 January 1944, TS in his PF.

Neuman reckoned on thirty men to form a parachute reception committee – twenty to handle the stores, and ten on watch; he too remarked how inconvenient it was to mobilise so many people on nights when no aircraft appeared.

After a few weeks in England, he parachuted back into Belgium on 8/9 February 1944, with a W/T operator, Henri Dendoncker ('Yapock'), and a propagandist, Emile van Dyck, who had a mission to the MNB, largely spoiled by the wave of arrests that afflicted that body in the spring.[152] Dendoncker seemed to Neuman indiscreet – he was dainty enough to refuse to use the lodgings first found for him, because there was no bathroom – and fell into enemy hands next month.

Neuman did not: he spent six useful weeks in the field, tuning up Groupe G's saboteurs for their imminent tasks in aid of the invasion, and making himself useful to two important colleagues who dropped one on the same night and the other soon after. He was classified as 'A very high class agent' when he got back to London in May.[153]

His colleagues were de Liedekerke, on his third mission (now codenamed 'Iago' in London and 'Scipio' in the field) and Commandant Guillery ('Vergillia/Nelly'). De Liedekerke had a series of important missions from the Sûreté: above all, he was to arrange for the counter-scorching – that is, protection from German sabotage – of Antwerp. When he revisited Antwerp he met Reniers, a sapper subaltern in the secret army, who had been wrestling with precisely this problem for years; liked and trusted him; and gave him official blessing to do what he chose. This had weighty results.[154]

'Iago' took his own operator with him, W. C. Waddington ('Regan'), an officer in the South Wales Borderers who spoke excellent French and had spent some time in occupied Europe before this journey began. He stayed on in Antwerp, after 'Iago' left to pursue the rest of his tasks, and so provided Reniers with a link to London.

'Iago' was of course in touch with 'Hector II', who spent his

---

152. For a summary of the MNB's composition and troubles, see Bernard, *La Résistance 1940–1945*, 81–4.
153. MS note in his PF.
154. See pages 379–82.

mornings as a coal merchant and his afternoons and evenings helping to manage the FIL; this important figure fell into German hands
by mischance. His office telephone number was captured with
Burgers; who said nothing to explain what it meant. From his office
the Gestapo extracted what the office thought was his home address.
In fact it was his parents' house; he slept elsewhere. But he had not
gone completely underground – that would not suit his cover as a
coal merchant – and occasionally dined with his parents, who suspected he might be doing secret work but knew nothing of it. On the
evening in March that the Gestapo called on this transparently innocent elderly couple, the dining-table was laid for three. Who was the
third? They said they were expecting a friend. When their guest
arrived, visibly their son, he was arrested; and under the shock of
arrest, admitted to being a resister, but gave no one away. His arrest
caused a fair amount of dislocation in the FIL's communications
with London, reknitted deftly enough by de Liedekerke, Neuman
and Guillery, aided by the tireless 'Pointer' and, as we shall soon see,
by Marchand and Floor.

Among several other missions to Belgium this spring, only a few call
for particular notice. One was the second mission of Livio and Pans,
now with the grander codenames of 'Pandarus' and 'Agamemnon'.
Pans was not the only T section W/T operator to go on a second mission. Those who volunteered for one, if not already officers, were
commissioned, as he was: a moment's excursus may be allowed on
army bureaucracy.

SOE did its best to run itself simply, with a minimum of paper;
and its offices were physically outside Whitehall, in Marylebone. Yet
in some respects it was tied to the apron-strings of devotedly bureau-
cratic departments: as exemplified by the case of Pans.
Mockler-Ferryman, who in the autumn of 1943 might be supposed
to have enough work on his mind, had had himself to sign and forward to SOE's administrators, for transmission to the War Office, six
separate army forms, four of them in duplicate, to secure Pans the
rank of second lieutenant.[155]

---

155. AD/E to AQ, 16 September 1943, TSC in Pans PF.

They next jumped on 3/4 March. Their first task was to distribute the arms they had collected and hidden, with Fr Carez's help, in Hainaut; they then settled down in Brussels, where they set up a battery shop at 130 rue des Beguines – partly for cover, and partly to supply batteries to any SOE W/T operators who needed them, as several did. Livio ran small classes, in an upper room, for local W/T operators under training, who were to be used by L'Armée Secrète. Through '*l'ami Jean*', he was brought into touch with the high command of that army himself; and did not think much of their security. 'All you had to do was to knock at the door' where a big headquarters meeting was being held, 'and you could go in if they recognised you.'[156]

His own security was not perfectly watertight; there were too many comings and goings at the rue des Beguines, and the local German D/F team noticed the training broadcasts.[157] On the afternoon of 24 May, Livio was up in the training room when he heard a scuffle and shots downstairs. He went down, to find three men lying wounded on the ground – one of them was Pans – among a party of armed strangers, who at once arrested him.

Pans was left for a week in a cellar before anyone even bound up his wounded thigh. Livio was put through an intense, violent, prolonged interrogation, including a bogus firing squad and the revolting bath-tub torture; but gave away nothing of any importance.[158] Pans, no more lightly treated, was equally unforthcoming.

They were put away in St Gilles prison, but not forgotten. On 2 September they joined a large party of fellow prisoners who were crammed, eighty to each forty-man truck, into a train at Brussels south station; which set off for Germany, but did not get far. The Gestapo filled the train, but omitted to crew it. The engine-driver took it twenty miles out of Brussels; waited for daylight: and reversed back into a Brussels siding. Those who had not escaped overnight were released by the railwaymen in the yard, to find the capital *pavoisé* to receive its liberators: but we anticipate.

*

156. Interrogation, 29 November 1944, 2; TSC in his PF.
157. *Ibid.*, 12.
158. *Ibid.*, 4–10.

Gustave Marchand's mission – he parachuted in on 11 April – made an important supplement to de Liedekerke's and Neuman's. Like Neuman, he was a founder member of Groupe G; he was a civil engineer, at thirty-two a little older than most of the group. He had only left Belgium in December. As news only reached London just before he left that Burgers, the head of the Groupe, had been arrested, as had 'Hector II', he was sent into the field without any *ordre de mission*, charged simply with doing what he thought best. He jumped, as 'Varro', with two companions, 'Tamora', the wireless operator, and the almost indispensable Ides Floor ('Dardanius'). 'Tamora' fell almost instantly into a German drive for forced labour from which he had not got the papers or the *savoir faire* to extricate himself, was in Germany by 3 May, and was never spotted as a clandestine.

Neither were Floor nor Marchand, in the five weeks and nearly five months respectively that they spent in the field. It was brave to the verge of rashness on Floor's part to go at all, because he knew so much that might have been tortured out of him had his enemies discovered who he was; but he felt the state of Belgian civilian resistance to be so critical that he had to go and judge for himself on the spot. He wrung leave to go from Ganshof and Gubbins; Amies weighed in with facilities.

In a long report on his return[159] – he was back in England, on a light aircraft from France, on 20 May – he explained what he had discovered, as 'Agnes', during his few weeks in Belgium, most of them spent in Brussels. He and Marchand had agreed, once Marchand had again made touch with leading survivors in Groupe G, that those wily and experienced saboteurs had better turn to railways (particularly railway telecommunications), telephones and canals as their principal invasion targets. London was to provide, through 'Nola', a million francs a month to support this; which was duly done. Floor and Marchand had brought $125,000 over with them to cover immediate needs (though $50,000 of this vanished en route: as late as 14 December, Marchand was reporting it as still untraced).[160]

---

159. Belgium 52.
160. Mission report, 13, duplic in his PF.

Part of the trouble about arming either the secret army, or Groupe G, or any other body with which T was in touch was the familiar one of shortage of air lift. From mid-February 1944, SOE's air liaison section maintained two registers of all secret drops made for it from England, one for successful and the other for unsuccessful sorties.[161] In the former, page after page is filled with drops into France, while hardly any other country gets anything at all. Certainly, as it was into France that the invasion went, some priority for France made sense; can it also have been that Buckmaster and Dismore had more trenchant personalities than Dobson and Amies?

From the spring of 1944, the 'Carpetbagger' squadrons of the 8th USAAF, flying out of Harrington, joined Bomber Command's two Tempsford squadrons and Transport Command's 38 Group in providing dropping aircraft; but Harrington's vast Liberators could only carry twelve containers each. The smaller and slower Stirlings, flown by 138 squadron from May, could each carry twenty-four.

The secret army was sent fifty-nine containers of arms by the March moon, 128 in early April, over 340 by the April/May moon, and nearly 200 more before Normandy D-day: say eighty tons of weapons and explosives. Hardly a tenth as much was dropped in the same period for Groupe G; there were a few drops for 'Nola' and others as well. This did something, if nothing like enough, to meet the most crying need for armed resistance: arms.

The next most crying need was for money: to sustain, with food and rent, the hordes of *réfractaires* who had been persuaded to go into hiding rather than into a German forced labour camp, as well as the smaller but more important number of men and women who had gone into full-time resistance and so forfeited their normal salaries or wages.

Oversight of resistance finance was placed, by the government in exile, in the hands of a Brussels banker called Scheyven, codenamed 'Socrates'. T took for granted 'Socrates' would need wireless touch with London, and sent him on 2/3 June Leon de Winter ('Enobarbus'), a twenty-three-year-old gendarme's son who had been studying to go to the Ecole Militaire before the war reached Belgium.

---

161. Air 26 and 27.

'Socrates', it turned out, hardly needed a W/T operator, and passed de Winter on to the 'Samoyede' network, which had plenty of work for him. The package with his set in it could not be found after his drop, but his new friends provided him with another; he never transmitted twice from the same house, and returned full of praise for the security of the group he worked with.

Scheyven, though technically never a member of SOE, was a pillar of strength for all T's and the exiled government's efforts towards resistance. Still in his early thirties, he was already well known in society and in the business world in Brussels; was a patriotic Belgian; had a strong vein of common sense; and was uncommonly ready to take risks. He took over, and transformed, the FIL's organisation called 'Solidarité'. He dealt personally with its provincial heads, all of whom were old friends of his – they included the mayor of Liège and the brother of the mayor of Namur; he insisted that they should each appoint a deputy, whose identity he took care not to know himself, so that funds could continue to be distributed in case of important arrests. His man in Charleroi was the official responsible for issuing clothing and food ration cards, whom the Germans supplied with a list of those from whom such cards were to be withheld: a great clandestine convenience.[162]

A. G. J. Goffin ('Ventidius'), who dropped into the Ardennes on 6 March 1944 to provide the secret army's fifth zone with W/T contact, was then aged twenty-three; he had been trained as a mining engineer in Morocco before the war, and had started to learn to fly. He dropped with another W/T operator, Renaut, who went off at once to Zone I, and with Bultot his own organiser, from whom he kept well clear. The papers he had brought with him were brushed aside at a glance as worthless by his new friends, who at once provided him with a fresh set. Madamoiselle Elizabeth del Marmol, of Namur, went out of her way to be helpful to him; and his career shows that T's wireless operators had learned from the errors and indiscretions of their predecessors. He kept his sets buried in large boxes in gardens; kept codes and crystals hidden at a different

---

162. Interrogation by de Guélis, 18–19 December 1944, 3; TSC in Scheyven PF.

address; never carried his set himself.[163] His case can stand for an example of how sensible SOE agents were able to benefit from the more foolish mistakes of others.

The 'Vic' escape line, run (readers will recall) by Victor Gerson for DF section, ran from Brussels to Barcelona, usually through Paris, Lyons and Perpignan. In the first seven months of 1944, forty-two T section agents took it, without loss (the line's boast was that it never lost a genuine passenger); as well as eight aircrew and ten agents from other sections in SOE.[164]

Frenay and Woluwe, busy in Hainaut the previous summer, jumped back into Belgium on their second mission, this time as 'Balthasar' and 'Lavinia', on 13 April 1944. Previously they had only had tenuous touch with London; now they took with them a British subaltern, A. W. Gardiner ('Titus'), as their W/T operator. All three landed, by an airman's mistake, on the wrong dropping zone, but were luckily received by a friend of Woluwe's. As they had proved themselves so capable at canal sabotage already, their aim this time was to attack a canal lock at Menin, east of Ypres: an important waterway link between Belgium and northern France. Their attack went in a fortnight later, on the 20th.

Unhappily, the lock was under alert armed VNV guard. Frenay was wounded, trying to help one of his team who was under fire, and Woluwe, betrayed by a passer-by, was taken prisoner. Frenay died next day in hospital at Courtrai. But the team effort worked: two charges went off, where they should, and the lock was closed to traffic till late June.

Woluwe's luck was out: after almost a year in enemy hands, he was shot dead a few days before the end of the war. Gardiner's, comparatively speaking, was in. He was arrested at a chance control on 6 June, but managed to pass himself off as an escaping airborne officer; the Germans never rumbled his connexion with SOE, and he survived.[165] His personal file includes reports of some grisly tortures inflicted on one of the little group's girl couriers; who survived them.

---

163. Interrogation, 11 January 1945, TSC in his PF.
164. DF/Rec to DF/WT, 13 September 1944, in Clandestine Communications 23.
165. Belgium 18, 92; Frenay PF; Gardiner PF.

In October 1944 Frenay's widow and a representative of SOE were present when his body was reburied, with full military honours, near his birthplace. The military medal he had been awarded for his first mission, but had never received, was pinned on to the pall over his coffin.[166]

Groupe G was undoubtedly the leading body of saboteurs in Belgium; Ugeux, by 1944 head of the Sûreté, spoke of it forty years later as if it had been the only one,[167] but was wrong. He forgot 'Nola', and the MNB, and the considerable number of private acts of sabotage that individual Belgians carried out; he also forgot, or suppressed, the secret army. That body, still dreaming of a formal military role, hived off its main sabotage groups into a separate organisation, codenamed 'Hotton'; to which, in April 1944, T sent Mathot ('Saturnius') and Berten ('Glamis') as advisers and instructors, with 'Cominius' to help arrange drops.

Michael Blaze ('Cominius') was a most efficient W/T operator. He was a law student from Tournai, born in 1920, who had been as far as Montpellier with the relics of his unit in the summer of 1940; had quitted Belgium in April 1941; and had had spells in French prisons, both sides of the Mediterranean, and in the Foreign Legion before joining SOE's 'Brandon' mission in Tunisia.[168] SOE's schools thought well of him; he was tall, handsome and energetic. He dropped into Belgium on 10/11 April 1944, with 'Glamis', and from late April till late August handled with unusual success a large quantity of traffic, at first at Pire's headquarters and after 'Overlord' had begun for the secret army's central region IV, round Brussels. Busy though he was, the Germans never managed to catch him, or either of the instructors.

For some of T's other agents who had been less fortunate, such judicial process as nazism boasted also dragged on for years, but led to a more summary conclusion. Stinglhamber, van Impe his too frivolous wireless operator, Binet his senior assistant and Guillini his proposed sea escape organiser were all beheaded on 22 May 1944.[169] Scohier was made to watch.

---

166. Typed chit of 7 November 1944 in his PF.
167. *Memo from Belgium*, 53–4.
168. For 'Brandon', see Richards, *Secret Flotillas*, 582–93.
169. Belgium 127

Even as a prisoner, Passelecq lived up to the codename of 'Incomparable'. In a camp at Esterwegen, he organised the building of a crystal set that could receive British and Swiss news bulletins, and passed word round his fellow prisoners, doing marvels for their morale; but the set was found, and the whole camp punished. He and Delmeire attempted an escape, but were caught; the Gestapo's patience then ran out. They were tried, condemned, packed off to Wolfenbuttel and beheaded a day or two after the Normandy landings.[170]

In April 1944 Jean de Lantsheere, of 'Nola', secured an audience with King Leopold, and was able to open to him during a walk in the park at Laeken – thus out of earshot of German ears and microphones – the prospect that 'Nola' might arrange to cut him out and take him to a waiting aircraft. The king replied that, having chosen to be a prisoner and to try to be of some use to his people, he could not initiate such a scheme; but showed keen interest. In the next few days, the guards round his palace were much strengthened; and on 5 May the emissary had to agree the coup would be impossible.[171]

There were still occasional difficulties between SOE and Leopold's ministers in exile, but the quarrels of 1942 were over. Pierlot continued to refuse to nominate a single personage through whom SOE could deal both with the Deuxième Direction and the Sûreté; but T now, as a matter of routine, sent to each of these two still distinct bodies a copy of every telegram he received from the field. Neither, therefore, could accuse T of dealing with the other behind its back.

Pierlot kept trying – without any success – to pump Selborne or Gubbins about the time and place of the impending re-invasion of the continent. As late as 12 May, Johns warned Brook that he remained opposed to any SAS operations into Belgium at all, lest they led to premature disclosure to the Germans of Belgian resisters who came forward to help.[172] Eisenhower's staff was also resolutely opposed to any uniformed airborne incursion before the main descent.

---

170. Belgium 101, interview with 'Lacquer', 4 May 1945, 7; TS.
171. Weber, *Capitaine Caracal*, 163, 166.
172. France 216.

Prolonged negotiations between the Foreign Office, the government in exile, and SHAEF – summarised by Professor Warner for the fortieth-anniversary conference – resulted in an agreement on 16 May 1944, by which the Belgians accepted the necessity of the commander-in-chief's powers on the spot, as allied forces arrived in Belgium, and the commander-in-chief in turn undertook to hand responsibility over to the government as soon as the state of the war allowed.[173]

Two agents' adventures rather far out of the common run, Blondeel's and Masereel's, can bring this chapter towards a close.

Blondeel – 'Pointer', that prince among wireless operators – was ordered in May to take a fortnight's holiday, and took it in Paris, where he had a shock. He was accosted in the rue St Honoré by a woman who spoke French with a Belgian accent, and insisted he went with her to a café to meet a man who spoke likewise. They declared themselves to be counter-espionage agents working for the Germans, who could see which way the war was going, and wanted to change sides. They knew his current codename in Brussels, 'Bernard'; worse, they knew where he had hidden his set when he left, because – they said – the man in whose empty house he had left it was another double agent, working for the Germans. He was on his way at that moment to have a drink with that very man at the Ritz. They pointed out to him, round the corner in the rue Cambon, the Mercedes into which he was then to be bundled for later interrogation in Brussels.

He did not keep his appointment in the Ritz; nor did he return to his hotel. He bought himself a new razor, toothbrush and so on, and found another hotel; taking extra care to make sure he was not being followed. He took the risk of one further meeting with his two acquaintances of the rue St Honoré – to tell them that he had not yet had a reply to their request to join the allies, without mentioning that he had done nothing to forward the request. At the end of his fortnight's leave he reported back for duty in Brussels, but was at once

---

173. FO 371/35234, 38873 and 40388, summarised in *Memo from Belgium*, 154–8.

ordered home. His escape line again failed him; he tried to press on beyond Perpignan on his own account, and ran into a communist maquis, which held him on suspicion for three days. His luck held, and he was rescued by an opportune staff officer newly arrived from Algeria. He was back in England on 9 September 1944, in time to volunteer for a mission to the Far East. He earned his MBE.[174]

Gaston Masereel ('Andromache') came into SOE early in 1944 from a previous career in Belgian resistance. He had been one of the two watchmen who kept look-out for an SIS wireless operator in Brussels; who, in spite of their vigilance, was arrested in September 1943. Masereel at once made himself scarce; got to Switzerland in a fortnight; and was in Gibraltar in mid-November.[175] SOE's schools and Belgian security alike thought well of him; at twenty-seven, and with his experience, he was already mature.

He set off for Belgium late on 2 June on an important mission: he was to be chief liaison officer between the Belgian government in London and the left-wing FIL, of which the government remained deeply suspicious. He took with him detailed orders about short-term sabotage, aimed at rail and road targets, intended to make the Belgian transport system as unusable as could be for the Germans in the invasion that was clearly now imminent – yet re-usable for the allies, if it promptly succeeded.[176]

He also memorised the BBC messages that were to trigger action: '*La Cousine Bette est mon roman favori*' for railway and '*On s'est bien amusé à l'Ecole*' for general sabotage. He had two assistants with him, Stroobrants ('Priam') and Filot ('Aeneas'), both on their second missions. For all their splendid Trojan codenames, their luck was out. The Halifax of 138 squadron that was carrying them was shot down west of Bergen op Zoom after crossing the Dutch coast; Masereel, wounded, was the only survivor.

He left the blazing aircraft unconscious, and came to to find himself sitting in several feet of water, and unable to see. One eye was full of blood; he was very short-sighted and had lost his spectacles. He vaguely recalled having laid out, by silent killing, some German

174. Belgium 133 and PF.
175. Interrogation, 26 January 1944, TS in his PF.
176. Belgium 4.

sailors who approached him by boat; passed out again; and recovered enough to find himself being carried naked through a Dutch village by a party of Armenians in German uniform.

He had two months in solitary in a Breda prison hospital, followed by a much more comfortable month in St Gilles prison in Brussels; successfully misled his interrogators; was put onto the famous train for Germany on 2 September, but was released next day.[177]

In secret war the rule holds fast that whom you know counts for more than what you know. The best informed SOE agents who had to work in central Brussels knew that, just off the Grand Place, there was a small café called the Coq du Jemappes, where Monsieur Desterbecq who ran it could be relied on (even if he seemed a shade fond of the bottle): not only for food, but for shelter, for false papers, for smuggling messages in and out of St Gilles. No fewer than eleven agents survived to testify to his help, which dated back to his hiding an escaping officer for a fortnight in August 1941.[178]

On 2 June 1944, when it was clear to everybody that the long-heralded invasion would shortly be attempted, Himmler put out an order to the SS in Belgium: counter-terror was to be maintained in every possible way.[179] The SS were prepared; so were the Belgians.

---

177. *Ibid.* Cp page 343.
178. Citation, TSC in Belgium 215.
179. Nestler, *Europa unterm Hakenkreuz*, iv. 248, document 165.

VII

Luxembourg
1940–5

Luxembourg provided one of the grandest houses of Europe in the late middle ages. John of Luxembourg who became King of Bohemia died at Crécy; hence the Prince of Wales's feathers familiar today. Charles of Luxembourg became the Emperor Charles V. The fortress that dominates Luxembourg city, on a bluff between two rivers, was for centuries reckoned the strongest in Europe after Gibraltar.

The grand duchy of Luxembourg was included in the Congress of Vienna's kingdom of the Netherlands, as the personal possession of King Willem I; it also belonged, as the rest of his kingdom did not, to the amorphous Germanic Confederation, which included Austria, Prussia and a score of smaller states. Lord Palmerston's treaty bisected the grand duchy, of which the western half became part of Belgium. At the close of the German civil war of 1866 Luxembourg, which had played no part in it, became a bone of contention between Prussia and France. The emperor Napoleon III offered to buy it from Willem I's grandson, Willem III. The Prussians, who had a garrison in Luxembourg fortress – under a barrier treaty of 1816 – would only agree to withdraw it if the grand duchy was declared neutral; as it was, by a treaty of London in May 1867. This treaty only provided a collective guarantee; the joint and several guarantee of Belgium was stronger.[1]

Under the Salic law, which was ancient when Charlemagne revised it, women could not hold land. Willem III's sons both died before

---

1. M. R. D. Foot, 'Great Britain and Luxembourg', in *English Historical Review* lxvii (1952), 352

him. His kingdom of Holland passed on his death in 1890 to his only daughter Wilhelmina; but the grand duchy of Luxembourg went to the next male heir, Adolphus of Nassau-Weilberg, and again became an independent state. Adolphus's son Wilhelm succeeded him in 1905. Wilhelm had six daughters, but no sons; a family treaty of 1907 arranged to set aside the Salic law.[2] His eldest child Marie-Adelaide succeeded him in 1912, and abdicated in 1919 in favour of her next sister Charlotte; who was still on the throne in 1940.

By the twentieth century, Luxembourg had given up all claims to militancy. On 2 August 1914, as on 10 May 1940, the German army occupied it in a single day, without any need to fight for it. Grand Duchess Marie-Adelaide indeed welcomed the conquerors; and so, when Germany had lost the Great War, had to abdicate.

Soon thereafter, on 25 July 1921, Luxembourg and Belgium formed a customs union, which has been in effect from May Day 1922. The grand duchy was admitted to the League of Nations, but played no prominent part in international affairs. As late as 1938, France proposed to offer a further guarantee to Luxembourg, but did not go ahead with the proposal; and the British government seized the occasion to indicate that it no longer felt itself bound by the treaty of 1867, though it would give Luxembourg such general support as a fellow member of the League deserved.

The one country that did offer the grand duchy a fresh guarantee was Germany, whose minister on 26 August 1939 promised it inviolability in the event of war:[3] a promise that went the usual way of Hitler's promises.

Renaissance scholars, and geographers, both reject the thought of hilly Luxembourg as one of the Low Countries; but, beyond the authority of the treaty of Vienna, it figures in these pages for more practical reasons. As late as July 1941, Hambro allotted care of it to T section.[4] Moreover, most of the refugees from Luxembourg who reached England fit to fight found their way to the Belgian troop of 10 commando, or to the free Belgian forces at Tenby or Malvern; where they found themselves called '*sales Boches*' if they spoke their

---

2. *Almanach de Gotha* (Gotha: Justus Perthes, 1912), 58.
3. FO 371/24274, fo. 224v, print.
4. Whole world war diary, vi. 1219–20.

own language to each other. The free Luxembourg army in exile consisted of no more than an artillery battery, part of the free Belgian brigade. Artillery was chosen as an arm of ground service not too likely to lead to capture; for the German police forces were inclined by 1944 to treat men of military age and Luxembourger origin as deserters, due for prompt hanging.

MIR spotted a possible sabotage target, the great railway viaduct to the east of the old city, opposite the fortress bluff; and even provided Ironside, the CIGS – under whom Gubbins had once served at Murmansk – with some technical details to take over to France.[5] Like so much else, this project got swept aside in the tumult of May 1940.

Grand Duchess Charlotte had no wish to follow her elder sister's example. She and her husband, Prince Felix of Bourbon-Parma, simply drove out of their palace on 10 May 1940; their chauffeur, unused to taking orders from anyone else, ignored the gestures of German soldiers who tried to stop them, and they evaded safely. She stayed for a time with her mother's family in Portugal, paid a brief visit to London in August, and then moved to Canada; coming over to stay in England in 1943. Her minister, the energetic Bech, ran a small government in exile near London. Her husband and her eldest son both took commissions in the British army.

So far as SOE was concerned, T was normally too preoccupied with Belgian affairs to have time left over to attend to the grand duchy. Tactically, as well as diplomatically, Luxembourg remained on the margin of great affairs; nobody foresaw its future role in the EEC.

Just as Eupen and Malmédy were thrown in with the Gau of Aachen, the nazis threw Luxembourg in with the Gau of Moselland; its Gauleiter, Gustav Simon, was declared Governor of Luxembourg, and set out to incorporate it by stages into the Third Reich. French – hitherto the language of government – was forbidden as early as 10 August 1940; French street signs and French shop signs disappeared. The local dialect, Letzeburgesch, was banned as well.

---

5. MIR war diary, appx B 13, in HQ 71.

The Luxembourgers recalled, in their folk memory, the *Klöppelkrieg* – the war with bludgeons – of 1798: a popular uprising against a detested regime, most firmly put down by revolutionary France.[6] The sufferers' descendants had enough sense not to try again. But when their new enemy presented them with an easy chance of making a mass protest, they took it.

On 7 September 1941 the Nuremberg Laws against the Jews – forbidding them to marry Germans, to sleep with Germans or to hold professional posts – were extended to Luxembourg. Some five weeks later, on 10 October, a census required every citizen to state his or her nationality and mother tongue – German was expected to be the answer. Ninety-seven per cent put down Luxembourger and Letzeburgesch instead.[7]

Simon was nazi enough to persist. He cancelled the concordat with the Roman Church that dated back to the early nineteenth century, expelled some two thousand monks and nuns, and forbade the remaining clergy to enter schools. On 30 August 1942 he forbade the use of the acute, the grave or the circumflex accent; and, more significantly, announced that with Hitler's agreement the province was henceforth to be annexed to the Reich. Like many other leading nazis, he was a bully, and did his worst to intimidate his new subjects.[8]

A brief general strike was the result. Twenty-five executions on 31 August helped to quell it. Thereafter, Luxembourg became one of the smaller fields on which nazi racial theorists started to work out population transfers. It became fully part of the police state against which the allies fought.

The great railway viaduct in the capital apart, there was only one sabotage target in Luxembourg that attracted SOE's attention: the steel industry, concentrated in the grand duchy's south-west corner, which was producing over two million tons a year before the war, using ores from Lorraine and coke from the Ruhr. This was about a

6. Arthur Herchem, tr. A. H. Cooper-Prichard, *History of the Grand Duchy of Luxemburg* (Luxembourg: P. Lindon, 1950), 148.
7. Henri Bernard, *Histoire de la Résistance Européenne* (Verviers: Gérard, 1968), 190; FO 371/26345.
8. Cp Henri Koch-Kent, *Sie boten Trotz* (Luxembourg: Hermann, 1974), 13–19.

twelfth of Germany's annual production. The steel works themselves were supposed to be well guarded, but T drew the attention of Maus, the first agent sent to the neighbourhood, to the usefulness of attacks on the railways that fed them raw materials.[9] He settled near Namur instead, and made no impact in the grand duchy.

The grand duchy's government in exile took even longer than the Belgian to settle down after its flight, and has been sharply accused of doing too little for its citizens who were trying to join the allied forces.[10] Its direct impact into resistance, if any, has left no traces in SOE's archive.

A despairing note in T's war diary for the summer of 1943 records that his section 'had made many attempts to gain contact with the Luxembourgers but no recruit had actually materialised'.[11]

A few more or less heroic individuals managed at least to set up efficient escape lines, useful to French prisoners of war who had got out of their loosely guarded camps and were trying to rejoin France, or to join the Free French. Even among these *passeurs*, one of them noted 'far too much petty jealousy and rivalry':[12] a constant theme among part-organised and amateur resisters, all Europe over.

This man, Emile Krieps, was a twenty-year-old school teacher under training when the Germans burst in; was made to join the VNV, as a condition for getting a job; and was then sent to teach in Germany, where his failure to indoctrinate nazism into his charges brought on his arrest, six months in a concentration camp, and dismissal. He escaped, down one of the principal Belgian lines for airmen, in late October 1942; was stuck for four months in Miranda; and after various other adventures parachuted back into Luxembourg on 4 July 1944 to reorganise the local branch of the 'Vic' escape line.

This he did, quietly and unobtrusively, till during the security flap that attended the Germans' failed Ardennes offensive in December 1944, he was bundled off to Paris for three highly uncomfortable days in the hands of American counter-intelligence. Thence

9. Note of 23 September 1941, TS in Belgium 129.
10. E.g. Koch-Kent, *op. cit.*, 166–72.
11. xxiii. 208.
12. Note of 18 July 1950 in E. H. Krieps PF, TSC.

he was released to be with his English wife when their first child was born.

Jules Dominique also did not approve of the German occupation, and took to the hills. He found a few friends to join him *en maquis* in south-eastern Belgium in the autumn of 1942, when German demands for forced labour began to bite on Luxembourg youth; and had a robust way of securing weapons. He tried to be first on the scene when USAAF heavy bombers crash-landed, as they quite often did on their way back to England from attacks on Germany; and to see what he could salvage in the way of re-usable machine-guns and ammunition from the wrecks. He provides a splendid example of self-propelled resistance. SOE knew of him, late in the war; but no records survive to show whether or how he and T section could work together.[13]

As a coda to SOE's affairs in Luxembourg, mention deserves to be made of three agents who had each carried out a short mission for T in summer 1944, and volunteered to go on a second for X into Germany next spring. Corbisier (now 'Benedict') was their leader, the other two were both W/T operators, Morel and de Winter. Their tasks would have been to make touch with the Belgian forced labourers round Kassel, to organise such sabotage as they could, and to pass on any orders they got from the allied high command. De Winter had a relative there, through whom work might start.[14] But the Hudson carrying them was shot down, just north of Clervaux, on the first night of the March moon, 20/21st; there were no survivors.

---

13. See Koch-Kent, *op. cit.*, 285–90.
14. Lengthy *ordre de mission*, TSC in de Winter PF.

VIII

'Overlord' and 'Market Garden'
1944

'C'était imprudent. Follement imprudent. Mais toute la résistance à l'occupant, toute la guerre clandestine n'étaient-elles pas, du point de vue de la raison, une folle téméraire?'
William Ugeux, *Le Passage de l'Iraty*, 217

Ever since SOE had been founded in 1940, a strategic use for it had been prominent in the minds of Churchill and of the chiefs of staff: it was to cause maximum disruption and dismay to the enemy's rear areas, whenever a major seaborne landing was launched, above all when the main thrust went in. 'Neptune', the assault phase of 'Overlord', was this main thrust: the invasion of western Normandy by allied forces on 5/6 June 1944, now remembered – not quite accurately – as 'D-day'.[1] The need to keep SOE intact and competent for the support of 'Overlord' was a principal reason for preserving it against its enemies.

Yet the fact that the landing was in France, not in the Low Countries, put the Low Countries out of the centre of the frame for invasion planning. The Low Countries' part in the allied victory, and SOE's share in it there, could not help being minor – ancillary – subordinate. Yet it deserves to be remembered that the Low Countries' role was as difficult, as dangerous as anyone else's; and that the Low Countries' casualty rates – notably among SOE's agents, as among captured Jews – were often higher than the French.

---

1. D-day and H-hour were convenient planners' phrases used to mark the start of many operations besides 'Neptune'. For a general account of this D-day, see Stephen E. Ambrose, *D-day 6 June 1944* (Simon & Schuster, 1994).

The success of the plan hinged on a major deception, 'Fortitude';[2] here Belgium at least was able to play a part, as will soon be shown.

By the time 'Neptune' began, SOE's forces in western Europe came directly under Eisenhower, the allied commander in chief. Robin Brook, formerly D/R, had been at his elbow since May, with Special Force Headquarters (SFHQ) alongside the main Supreme Headquarters, Allied Expeditionary Force (SHAEF). SFHQ left a rear link in London, and with it there was another rear link, from the Special Force Detachments (SFDets) with the army groups and armies. A table of these may be of use:[3]

1	SFDet with Second British Army
2	SFDet with First Canadian Army
3	SFDet with Twenty-first Army Group
4	SFDet with Seventh US Army
10	SFDet with First US Army
11	SFDet with Third US Army
12	SFDet with First US Army Group
13	SFDet with Ninth US Army

Each of these detachments consisted of a handful of staff officers, fully informed of the location and capacities of SOE agents on their formation's front, with adequate clerical and signalling staff. Each, like the still more secret Special Liaison Units from Bletchley, was at the disposal of the relevant commander and chief of intelligence. Each could provide, in periods of static warfare, a few nuggets of information; and when battles turned mobile, most were able to secure resistance help in protecting specific bridges from demolition, and so on. They constituted an extra facility for making war, not then described in any staff college's curriculum; and, for security's sake, left out of most of the official histories – just as most deception was.

Yet the business of secret war was by now complicated enough for Mockler-Ferryman to issue a booklet on operational procedure for SFHQ and its detachments that ran to over a hundred pages, many

---

2. Sir Michael Howard, *Strategic Deception*, is decisive.
3. Appx F to SFHQ monthly report, August 1944, in CAB 121/319.

of them double-sided single-spaced duplicated foolscap:[4] a monument to staff college punctilio.

The start of 'Overlord' of course put both T and N sections on their mettle, but there was little immediate that N could do, for lack of organisers on the spot. T had many more men available, but some of them were not ready to do the right thing. A vast amount of staff time had gone into efforts to appease Colonel Marissal, and set out the tasks that L'Armée Secrète might have been asked to perform, had the chance arisen for it to take part in proper battles. An example is in appendix 6: a scheme for interrupting the advance of German armour to repel a landing on the Belgian or northernmost French coast that never took place. This in turn was only an appendix to a long document drawn up by T, consulting with SOE's planning staff; all this effort, alas, was wasted time.

In March and April 1944 senior staff of SOE had had to reassure, in turn, 21 Army Group, SHAEF and the Home Security Executive that it was indispensable for SOE to transmit large blocks of *messages personnels* by the BBC shortly before the invasion took place; and that there was no possibility that these messages would carry any actual information to the enemy, beyond reminding him 'that D-day is shortly to follow'.[5] SOE did thus compel the allied high command to forfeit surprise over the precise timing of the landing, but luck was with the allies. By an office slip – much more probably than by a diabolically clever plot by the deception staff – the BBC broadcast a great wodge of preparatory messages on 1 May, thus warning hundreds of agents in error that the invasion would happen in the next fortnight. This had an after-effect: it blunted the sensitivity of the Germans to the real messages, several of which they had by now discovered from captives who had chosen to talk.[6]

On 8/9 June German radio-detection teams in Belgium picked up a warning order from T to Belgian resistance, to be prepared for an imminent national rising: sent in pre-one-time-pad codes to several operators. Like so many of SOE's codes, they read this one

---

4. HQ 204.
5. Mockler-Ferryman to SHAEF, bigot, 7 April 1944, TSC in France 222.
6. Conversation with Goetz, formerly the SD's wireless expert in Paris, 1984; he claimed to have known fifteen of the messages, wrung out of captured agents.

easily, and reported it. Colonel von Roenne, head of Fremde Heere West – foreign armies west, the main German army intelligence staff facing SHAEF – telephoned it through at once to Hitler's supreme headquarters, currently at Berchtesgaden. This report seems to have played a cardinal part in persuading Hitler to cancel a move of reinforcements westwards across the Seine that he had ordered on the evening of the previous day: the troops, already on the move, turned round and went back to guarding against the landing on either side of Boulogne that the German general staff continued to expect.[7]

It was not only the SOE message that turned this trick for the allied deception staff. The now celebrated double agent 'Garbo' sent another that told in the same sense,[8] and the combined impact of both reports on Hitler was big enough to change a mind that might have been unmoved by one alone. SOE can claim a little credit for this, but only a little; T section simply served as a vehicle for cleverer men's ideas.

It did so at some moral cost to Lord Selborne. On 17 May he had assured Pierlot that the Belgian secret army would only be called out 'when their chances of survival were good';[9] D+3, while the whole landing still teetered in the balance, was far too early to make any such claim. Selborne evidently held that the needs of the grand alliance overwhelmed his assurances to a minor ally. Pierlot did not complain.

The Poles did succeed in not having their sizeable secret contingents round Lille, which had some small overlaps into Belgium, called into action yet:[10] an interesting example of the relative standing of the Polish and the Belgian governments in exile.

Apart from this T section message, there has long been a rumour that one or more British agents – usually specified as SOE agents – were deliberately parachuted to the field, primed with false information about the impending invasion, in the hope that they would be captured, have this falsehood tortured out of them, and so deceive

---

7. Sefton Delmer, *The Counterfeit Spy* (Hutchinson, 1973), 17–22.
8. Masterman, *The Double-Cross System*, 157–8.
9. TSC in Selborne 1; further exchanges, March-May 1944, in Selborne 34.
10. Cp page 390.

the enemy further. This rumour received its most elegant expression in a novel by Larry Collins, manifestly fiction.[11]

The nearest that anyone has ever produced to hard evidence for it came in a *Times* obituary on 23 June 1998 of Norman Jordan-Moss. He was there stated to have sent several wireless operators on just this hopeless task; and was in 1944 on the staff of MEW. He was certainly not in SOE (or if he was, all trace of him has been disappeared); and it is more than likely that his obituarist was mistaken.

'Overlord' was a doubly decisive operation. It helped ensure the defeat of Hitler's Germany; and provided an Anglo-American presence on the continent, once it had succeeded, of which even the victorious Stalin had to take heed. In its success SOE played a hidden but significant role; and part of that role – admittedly, a lesser part – was played out in the Low Countries.

The German army in western Europe in 1944 was dependent, to a degree three-quarters forgotten today, on rail as well as horse transport for supplies – for the ammunition, the reinforcements, the clothing, food and fuel without which an army cannot fight. Rail transport was largely denied it by French, Dutch and Belgian railwaymen. In France, the responsible German agreed, 'it was the permanent attitude of non-co-operation and go slow of the railway staff, even when they were not on strike, that made it impracticable to clear up enough of the mess for trains to run';[12] the Dutch railways went on a strike on 18 September that lasted to the end of the European war. The troubles were intensified by railway sabotage in Belgium, much of it using SOE's plastic and SOE's advice.

The main line from the Ruhr to Normandy ran through Liège, Namur and Charleroi towards Paris and Rouen; all three Belgian cities had active teams of railway saboteurs. So active were those teams that, Henri Bernard claims, cases were known of German units in Holland that were eventually ordered to move to the fighting front in France taking the detour round through the Reich instead of taking the risk of trying to cross Belgium by train.[13] This,

---

11. *Fall from Grace* (Granada, 1985).
12. Foot, *SOE in France*, 411.
13. Bernard, *Jean del Marmol*, 68–9.

though not easily perceptible, was a definite gain: a delay imposed on enemy deployment by SOE.

One day it will be worth a railway historian's while to inquire what the knock-on effect was on the domestic traffic of the Reichsbahn that so many trained German railway workers had to be diverted to the Netherlands. In that almost unimaginably awful last winter of the war, while the cities of the Reich were being pounded flat by Russian artillery in the east and by American and British Commonwealth bombers in the west, movement in and out of them, as well as between them, was being made harder by the striking rail-waymen of Holland.

Groupe G, following its now arrested leader's original decision to concentrate on German communications as well as electric power supplies, began a systematic and largely successful attempt to paralyse the Belgian railway system. Remembering their power coup earlier in the year,[14] they made eleven major railway cuts, all on the same day, 9 June; and by the end of August had made nearly 500 more, sometimes by cutting off electric current, which blocked traffic between Brussels and Antwerp, sometimes by more conventional means.[15]

Yeo-Thomas's unforgettable remark in 1943, that the effort so far made to arm French resistance was 'like a man filling a swimming pool with a fountain pen filler',[16] may have been a shade extreme; yet its force carried outside France into the Low Countries as well. Most of the arms dropped into Holland had gone straight to the enemy; far too few had gone to Belgium at all. It was nevertheless possible for enough patriots to come forward on Belgian soil, as on French and on Dutch, to make supplying the army at the Normandy front an extra difficult and exasperating business for the enemy.

A final assessment of SOE's value in the supreme commander's sphere, drawn up at leisure in SHAEF after the fighting was done, laid emphasis on the usefulness of resistance action against railways; apart from the actual delays and diversions, troops who did get

---

14. Pages 330–9.
15. Notes in Belgium 160(iii).
16. Mark Seaman, *Bravest of the Brave* (Michael O'Mara Books 1997), 120.

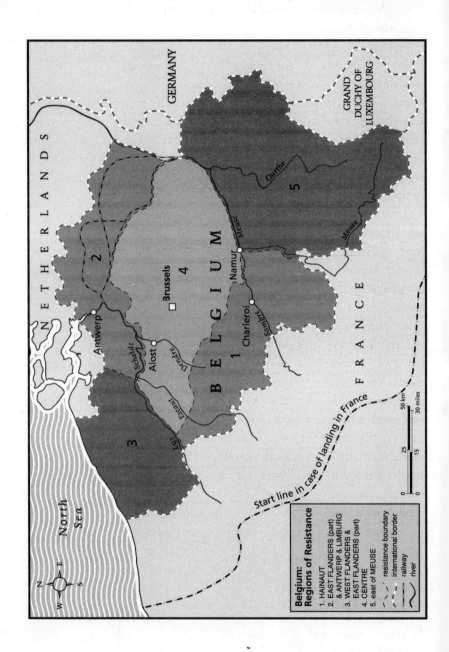

Belgium:
Regions of Resistance

1. HAINAUT
2. EAST FLANDERS (part)
   & ANTWERP & LIMBURG
3. WEST FLANDERS &
   EAST FLANDERS (part)
4. CENTRE
5. east of MEUSE

— · — resistance boundary
— — — international border
railway
river

through to the front 'arrived in a state of extreme disorganisation and exhaustion'.[17]

For about a year past, the joint planning staff, the JIC and the chiefs of staff had received a weekly report on SOE's activities. SHAEF was added to the distribution list as soon as SFHQ joined it; so that Eisenhower's senior staff knew, for example, by late May that the Belgian secret army's effective strength on Normandy D-day was likely to be between 7,000 and 8,000.[18] The same source reported for the week ending 18 July seventeen railway cuts and five turntables destroyed in Belgium, as well as the delivery of nearly thirty tons of warlike stores to eastern Belgium (a drop in the ocean compared to what had gone into France).[19] Repeated resistance activities were reported from Belgium, culminating in a big petrol fire in the Yvoir tunnel, south of Namur, started by secret army saboteurs, which was expected to block the main line on the right bank of the upper Meuse for six weeks.[20]

By mid-July a note from Amies to Floor could mention that SHAEF was very pleased with the obstacles that SOE was helping to place in the way of Belgian waterway traffic[21] – Groupe G had made eleven major canal blockages too, to complicate Frenay's fatal effort at Menin,[22] that was only just now cleared. Rail traffic in Belgium was by this time down to 30 per cent of what it had been in May.[23] On 12 July Eisenhower signed a short secret note of 'sincere congratulation' to Belgian resistance for the success of its sabotage so far, singling out the FIL, 'Nola', Groupe G and the MNB for praise.[24] 'Tybalt' took several copies of this generous document back to the field with him in August.

---

17. HQ 201, 3, duplic, dated 13 July 1945.
18. SOE weekly review, 15–21 May 1944, 7; top secret, duplic in CAB 121/319.
19. SOE (44) 5.36, 6 and appx C, *ibid.*
20. SFHQ monthly progress report for July, 10 August 1944, appx: top secret, duplic *ibid.*
21. TSC, 15 July 1944, in Belgium 169(v).
22. See pages 346–7.
23. Report by Rolin written before his arrest, received on 10 July 1944, in Belgium 160(viii).
24. Photocopy in Belgium 160(i).

Before the invasion had been launched, T section had had a lot of trouble trying to find out precisely which rail – and other – targets which group in Belgium was going to attack. Part of Guillery's task had been to establish this, and report; but Guillery found the business of keeping out of the hands of the enemy police took up too much of his attention to give him leisure to complete long reports on intentions. Valuable as his mission was for providing liaison, and preventing over-lapping, on the spot, it did not bring London the hoped-for target lists.

The results, all the same, turned out worth having. L'Armée Secrète threw off the unit codenamed 'Hotton', which was to con-centrate on sabotage. Mathot and Berten had been sent in in April to reinforce it. A few lines on Mathot can help to show what work with the 'Hotton' groups could be like.

François Mathot, an orphan from infancy, had been a Belgian regular gunner; he did not care for life in occupied Belgium, nor for several Spanish prisons through which he passed on his way to England; which he reached, aged nearly twenty-five, in late summer 1943. He dropped as 'Saturnius' on 9/10 April 1944, and cast up in early June near Chimay, in wooded country near the French border south of Charleroi.

He was out on his own – no wireless operator, no readily available source of warlike stores; but a friendly population, a helpful local police force, and a few reliable friends. With them, he got explosives from some French tank traps dating back to the spring of 1940, and set out to make trouble. They destroyed, or at least damaged, a dozen locomotives. The Germans sent an armoured car patrol against them; they demolished three armoured cars and even destroyed a tank. On 3 September they took three officers and forty-nine German sol-diers prisoners. In short, 'Saturnius' ran an ideal pinprick operation, calculated to exasperate a retreating enemy; and survived to receive a distinguished conduct medal.

None of L'Armée Secrète's parties were in a state to stop a panzer division; for they had neither air reconnaissance, nor air support, nor serious anti-tank artillery. A few hand-held anti-tank weapons, British PIATs and American bazookas were available; with them a very brave man might damage the track even of a heavy German tank, but that was all. Still, delays might be imposed, even on the unstoppable, by sudden cunning tree-felling; exasperating delays could be imposed even on a crack SS panzer division by tampering with its tank transporters, as the heroic 'Alphonse' teams had shown round Montauban in June; and petrol stores were at once essential to the enemy, and vulnerable to saboteurs.

Success at this sort of action depended on a mixture of foresight, courage and luck; planning could seldom provide for it. Baron Rolin ('Messala'), another of the Belgian aristocrats who put himself forward to help as the Comte de Liedekerke had done in adjusting and co-ordinating the plans of the resistance, had jumped into Belgium on what turned out to be D-3 for 'Neptune' – the night of 2/3 June – with a wireless operator, Hautfenne, who had the bad luck to stumble on a police patrol that very night. Rolin made touch with Guillery, and helped him with his liaison work, which was by this time complicated as well as dangerous: so dangerous that Rolin was himself arrested within a month of landing. At least both he and his operator survived.

They had been among ten agents dropped into Belgium on 2/3 June; a further cascade of eleven followed on 4/5 August, and six more the night after; listed in appendix 4. Brief though the field careers of all the post-D-day Belgian agents were, a few of them deserve notice, now or later in the chapter.

As late as 7 July 1944, when 'Cato', 'Diomedes' his W/T operator and 'Mardian' his assistant landed by parachute not far from Marche-en-Famenne, the contrast between planning and result was marked. Through a mistake by the reception committee, the party – and the dozen containers and five packages they accompanied – missed the intended field, and landed in a wood. By dawn, the men and the containers had all been gathered on the field; four packages were still missing, one of which – with 'Diomedes's' money and spare clothes in it – took a month to find. They had dropped from a Liberator;[25] their containers left the field in two carts, one drawn by a carthorse, the other by a pair of oxen.[26]

By now, Belgian opinion was much more solidly pro-allied than it had been when Father Jourdain had dropped into the same area

---

25. SOE Air 26, 50a.
26. Interrogation of S. H. Gardiner ('Diomedes'), 6 March 1945, 1, TSC in his PF; cp last photograph but three in Foot, *SOE in France*.

three years before. The local midwife took a leading part in organising 'Cato's' reception. 'Of the few collaborators there were in the
area, none dared say anything', as they knew their farms would be
burned down if they did.[27] Moreover, the whole group, an FIL one,
had acquired a proper standard of discipline for secret work: 'If at any
time any of the men or a girl courier, did anything foolish, or
betrayed the others, they knew that they would be liquidated immediately.'[28] This was a mood in which serious work could get done; the
usual hitches hampered it.

'Diomedes' was a twenty-four-year-old Intelligence Corps subaltern called Stuart Gardiner (he was A. W.'s brother), who was an
electrical engineer before the war. Having served in the field security
police, he took extra care about security; 'he had had no wish to be
cognisant with the organization as he felt it would be better to be
completely ignorant in case of capture'.[29] He settled in Brussels, and
arranged to transmit from one or another safe house, prepared in
advance by his protection team, ten miles out in the country to the
north-east at Kampenhout. But the FIL insisted on transporting his
sets and his crystals, separately, through their own channels instead of
letting him carry anything so compromising himself; and the transport took seven weeks.

'Cato' and 'Mardian' his assistant, two Belgians called Lepoivre
and Corbisier, got on quietly with their task of liaison with the FIL's
leaders, untroubled by contact with London.

On the day after the Normandy landings, King Leopold and most of
his family were deported to Germany. Five weeks later, Hitler at last
authorised a change of regime in Belgium; *Reichskommissar* Grohé
took over from General von Falkenhausen. The new system lasted
less than seven weeks before the allied advance swept it away. A new
Befehlshaber der Sicherheitspolizei, Jungclaus, was appointed early in
August; his reign was even shorter.[30]

*

27. S. W. Gardiner, *ut supra*, 2.
28. *Ibid.*, 6.
29. *Ibid.*, 5.
30. Dejonghe, *L'Occupation en France et en Belgique*, i. 89.

Brute facts of geography and logistics kept Dutch resistance from playing a prominent part in 'Overlord' at the start; quite apart from the obstacles of internal dissensions, lack of arms, continued pressure from strong hostile police, and the dark shadow still cast by 'North Pole'. By mid-June, N was able to reassure SOE's ever-suspicious security staff that, through two SIS operators who worked with it, SIS believed the RVV at least to be mainly sound. A meeting on the 16th, chaired by Warden, with representatives from SIS and the free Dutch as well as Johns and Dobson present, concluded that the Germans had only broken into the fringes of the RVV. 'All organisations are bound to be penetrated to a greater or less extent';[31] and work ought to go ahead.

Accordingly, seven agents were sent into Holland on 5/6 July, to establish firmer touch with the KP and the RVV; but four of them were shot down on the way, and only one of the remaining three – de Goede ('Rummy') – escaped arrest.

Bert de Goede was a Dutch merchant marine officer who had managed to stow away on a Swedish ship, and thus evade occupation.[32] L. G. Mulholland ('Podex'), who jumped with him, also a sailor, had been born in Sumatra twenty-three years before: of Dutch parents, in spite of his English name. He too had escaped through Sweden, by swimming ashore while his ship had stopped to drop its pilot. He and de Goede had separate liaison missions to the four main Dutch organisations – KP, RVV, OD and LO. Moreover, Mulholland was to try, gingerly, to find out what had become of Celosse;[33] a task he sensibly did not attempt. He settled in Rotterdam, where he pretended to be on leave from work in Germany, and held several useful classes in sabotage work and the elements of safe clandestine behaviour (such as: do not recognise your co-workers in the street; do not pile all your bicycles outside the house where you attend a secret class). A third sailor, Arie van Duyn ('Cribbage'), was to transmit for them both; he had come into SOE from the Dutch navy, in which he had been fighting since 1940. He had a longer run than was usual for a W/T operator, but was arrested

---

31. TS in Holland 14(iii).
32. De Roever, *Zij sprongen bij maanlicht*, 159.
33. Lengthy undated operation orders in his PF. For Celosse, see pages 211–19.

in December; five weeks after Mulholland had been swept up in a
razzia and packed off to work in Germany. All through the fighting
in France this summer, N was hoping to get the Dutch properly
organised to help, but hardly ever had any positive success to report.

Late in July 1944 the prospect was raised, from Belgium, that SOE
might bring out the king's brother Prince Charles; who was already
on the run from the Gestapo, and moreover suffering badly from sci-
atica, so that he did not travel easily. The foreign secretary thought
the scheme important, and urged action;[34] the chiefs of staff
agreed.[35] Wendelen was sent in by the August moon to reconnoitre.
He took with him van der Spiegle ('Donalbain') as his W/T operator,
who settled quietly in Brussels with a landlady who knew what he
was doing, and acted as his bodyguard;[36] and a courier, Elaine
Madden ('Imogen'), who only once 'had any trouble of any kind' –
when she had to shed a follower. 'I found the work much easier than
I anticipated and all the people I tried to contact were most helpful.
The only regret I have, is not having arrived sooner and being able to
work more':[37] for Belgium was overrun before anything could
happen.

For quite suddenly, the beachhead built up in over eight weeks'
hard fighting in western Normandy by the allied armies – including
British, American, Canadian, Polish and French units – broke open:
the German army opposed to them cracked. As late as 28 July 1944
the operations branch of SHAEF laid down that though 'The calling
out of resistance in the ARDENNES may, in due course, be of considerable military value', it would not be needed 'for at least two
months, probably much longer'.[38] Within a week, Patton had broken
through past Avranches, and begun the right hook that was to carry
his army into the Vosges; and within a month, resistance in the
Ardennes briefly became crucial.

In the second half of August 1944 a wave of euphoria swept over

---

34. (Sir) F. K. Roberts to Johns, 4 August 1944, TS in Belgium 169.
35. LC to AD/E, 10 August 1944, TSC *ibid.*
36. Belgium 51.
37. Single-page report, 22 November 1944, duplic in Belgium 84.
38. Copy in Belgium 171.

the allied staffs in western and southern Europe that were waging war on the axis: it really looked as if the German army was on the run, so that victory was nearly in sight. No one foresaw the horrible last winter that lay ahead; the end of the war suddenly seemed near. There was an exodus (*quorum pars minima fui*) of staff officers from London on missions to the continent: they could no longer face themselves in their shaving-glasses until they had met more danger than lay in being bombarded by buzz-bombs. Two of these men went to the Ardennes – Whitehead and Hubble of RF section; Hubble was murdered in Buchenwald, Whitehead evaded safely. One, Mills of F section, talked his way onto a 'Jedburgh' team and jumped on 'Market Garden'; he came back.

Outline history has quickly absorbed the rapid dash across the Belgian plain; and has forgotten that in south-eastern Belgium, in the hillier parts of the country, the course of battle did not run so smoothly. Both SOE and SAS were hotly engaged in the Ardennes for a fortnight, in a series of brushes with bodies of Germans who were trying to fight their own way home into the Reich along by-ways and side roads. They varied from formidable SS Panzer units, still with their tanks and armoured cars, who shot at anything that moved, to groups of clerks and laundry staff who hardly knew how to hold a rifle, and a few teams of mere marauders who planned to lie up in the woods and prey on villagers.

L'Armée Secrète had a few parties who acquitted themselves manfully; SOE's inter-allied missions provided a few more. During these protracted skirmishes, the secret army indeed incurred 1,100 battle dead, on top of 350 members shot after arrest in Belgium and 4,500 who died after being deported to Germany: a formidable count of casualties.[39]

The Special Air Service (SAS) was part of the army, in no sense part of SOE; but SAS and SOE needed to co-operate closely, for they were often likely to want to operate in the same areas at the same time. In the SAS regiment's earliest days, in the Western Desert, it had made useful friends among SOE's signals staff in Cairo; similarly, the 'Phantom' squadron allotted as a signals unit to the newly formed

---

39. Bernard, *La Résistance 1940–1945*, 105.

SAS brigade made friends in Baker Street in the spring of 1944. At a more exalted level, there was more room for confusion.

General Morgan, chief of staff to the supreme allied commander – whoever that was to be: hence the acronym of his headquarters, COSSAC – had been working on allied invasion strategy since the spring of 1943. Yet not till the last week of April 1944 did senior officers either at SHAEF, which had succeeded COSSAC, or at Baker Street start to approach the problem of SAS's role in the battle. This was only a week before the target date of 1 May, fixed at Teheran, and only five weeks before the actual D-day, 5/6 June.[40]

The SAS brigade, then containing two British and two French regiments, a Belgian company (which later became a regiment), and a Phantom signals squadron using SOE's 'Jedburgh' sets, numbered some 2,200 men, highly trained and highly motivated parachutists, *gonflés à bloc*, longing to start or re-start a fight. They were stationed south of Glasgow, in Ayrshire. Tactical brigade headquarters lay in huts alongside HQ Airborne Troops at Moor Park, close north-west of London, now a golf course club-house. In those days SAS troops were forbidden to operate in plain clothes; and neither SHAEF nor SOE welcomed the presence of uniformed parties anywhere in north-west Europe before 'Overlord' began.

In the event, the first SAS parties went into France on the night of 5/6 June, and during the next three months practically the whole brigade became engaged, troop by troop, in active operations in France, well beyond the regular fighting lines. Planning these in detail had been complicated by the large number of authorities involved, and by the apparent impossibility of admitting either the French or the Belgians – half the brigade, after all – into the planning process at all until after D-day. SAS jumped the gun to this extent, that a select party from the Deuxième Régiment de Chasseurs Parachutistes (alias 4 SAS) was screened off from the rest, and briefed for a jump into Brittany: which took place about midnight on the critical night.[41]

Whether the Belgian component of the brigade was to be allowed to operate outside Belgium was a point in dispute between SOE,

---

40. France 216, 'SAS Operations under SHAEF control'.
41. Personal knowledge, and see Foot, *SOE in France*, 402–9.

SAS, SHAEF, the War Office and the government in exile during the spring. Cassart, who had not added much discretion to his other attributes during his long spell in enemy hands, made confusion worse confounded by a muddled statement about the unit's intentions to Colonel Marissal in early May: based on nothing firmer than gossip he had picked up in mess.[42]

Small parties of Belgian SAS were used on road-watching in northeastern France in July and August, providing useful tactical intelligence; road-watching had been one of SAS's earliest tasks in the desert. No one in the brigade was privy to Bletchley's ultra secret product, to which road watching could not add much beyond cover.

Eventually, the week before Brussels fell, Blondeel was able to secure the slow leave of his superiors to act, and took off into Belgium on operation 'Noah', with six companions. Renkin,[43] grandson of a Belgian prime minister, had preceded him, on 15 August, with an advance party nine strong to form a base near Givet; he had verbal orders from Blondeel, contradicting the hesitation of the high command, to get in touch with any maquis he could find nearby in Belgium, and arrange a drop there.[44] They were proud to be the first troops of the invading army to reach Belgian soil.

Along the Franco-Belgian border in the Ardennes maquisards took advantage in the summer of 1944 of bad co-ordination among their enemies. If patrols from within Belgium threatened them, they skipped to France; and vice versa.[45]

EMFFI, for no reason stated, gave an emphatic, specific order to the 'Andrew' Jedburgh team – which was to operate alongside 'Citronelle' mission in the tongue of France that reaches north of Charleville into Belgian territory – that it was on no account to cross the frontier into Belgium or to have any contact with Belgian maquis at all.[46] This order was all the more awkward because one of

---

42. AD/M to AD/E, 11 May 1944, in France 216.
43. Photograph, *en maquis*, in *Livre d'Or*, 298.
44. Sixteen-page report on 'Noah' by Blondeel, 1, undated, duplic in Belgium 171; and see Temmerman, *op. cit.*, 9–43.
45. Temmerman, *ibid.*, 12.
46. Report on 'Andrew' by Major – later Monsignor – A. H. S. Coombe Tennant, 1, duplicated in France 173(7).

'Andrew's' officers, Edmond d'Oultremont – who had switched teams – was a Belgian nobleman whose *savoir vivre* would have been of great value in a liaison role. As his team commander Coombe Tennant put it, his 'blood is so blue that he never feels at a loss'.[47] There was nothing, though, that either of them could do except act as extra infantrymen for 'Citronelle's' commander 'Prisme', because their wireless set did not survive its drop. Messages they sent to London through 'Citronelle's' set took a fortnight to travel from Bryanston Square to Baker Street, hardly a kilometre away: another instance, if one was needed, of EMFFI's incompetence.

Orders or no orders, the 'Andrew' party wandered with their companions to and fro across the frontier as tactical necessity dictated; one of their more successful ambushes, in which they killed several Germans and took a couple of prisoners, was near Nafraiture in Belgium, a dozen miles north-east of Charleville, late in August. Normally of course maquis did not take prisoners – how could they guard and feed them? – but this couple 'were quite tame' and did fatigues, helpfully, till the American army arrived in early September.[48]

'Citronelle', an inter-allied mission dispatched to northern France in April 1944, was meant to work in the French Ardennes *département*; in fact, it confined itself largely to the tongue of French territory north of Charleville-Mézières, which reaches out to Givet. A verbose operation instruction included these remarks: 'The security of the Belgian Troupes Secretes is a matter of some doubt at the moment, and the French Maquis should have the fewest possible contacts with them. The members of the mission should not have any dealings whatever with the Belgian Troupes Secretes or any other Belgian Resistance Groups in the vicinity.'[49]

'Prisme', the mission commander – much later well known as General de Bolladière, who objected to French counter-terrorism in Algeria and joined a nuclear protest group – was too sensible to be hidebound by his orders, and found in practice that frequent advantage was to be found in crossing over into Belgium when a hunt was up for him in France.

---

47. *Ibid.*, 6.
48. *Ibid.*, 9.
49. 11 March 1944, para. 1(f), in France 63.

SAS's northernmost party in the Ardennes was under Hugh Fraser ('Brutus'), younger brother of Lord Lovat the commando brigadier and future first husband of Lady Antonia the historian. A furious telegram from him, of which the first four words have passed into regimental legend, is worth quoting in full. He sent it on 13 September from his Ardennes hideout some twenty miles south of Liège.

GOD ROT GUBBINS GUTS STOP HAS SF ANY CON-TACT IN THIS REGION STOP BLUNT[50] MET ONE HALF WITTED SF BOY WHO ASKED HIM FOR ORDERS STOP IS SF AWARE OF FRONTIER CHANGES AND UNARMED BELGIANS IN THE GREATER REICH SINCE 1940 STOP IS SF AWARE OF ATROCITIES AND GERMAN BANDITS IN WOODS STOP IS SF AWARE THAT THE PREVENTION OF RE-INFILTRATION IS A MAQUIS RESPONSIBILITY STOP DID SF ORDER TOTAL MOBILISATION HERE ABOUT SEPTEMBER FIRST KNOWING THAT THERE WERE NO ARMS STOP AN ACT AMOUNTING TO MASS MURDER.[51]

SOE had its parties scattered round the secret army's Region V as well. Let us move from the Scottish aristocracy to the Belgian prole-tariat.

Maurice Bertrand (no connexion of Henri's), born at Verviers in 1921, left school at fourteen, and worked as a pastry-cook; he was his mother's sole support. He was in trouble enough with authority to be sent to a reformatory school early in 1940; took part in the exodus into France, got back home again, and – for lack of any other source of income – worked for a year in Germany at his trade, hating it. He absconded while on leave, in May 1942, and at the price of ten months in Miranda turned up at the RVPS in October 1943.[52]

---

50. Nothing to do with Blizard or with the art historian: the cover name used in the field by Eddie Blondeel, who commanded the Belgian SAS unit.
51. Copy in Belgium 171.
52. RVPS report, 20 October 1943, TSC in his PF.

An SOE school, STS44 at Gumley Hall in Leicestershire, transformed him, teaching him to fire ten different weapons and giving him a thorough knowledge of unarmed combat;[53] Rheam had already taught him sabotage techniques. As 'Bianca', he parachuted safely south of Liège on 2/3 June 1944, to help L'Armée Secrète do sabotage; and did wonders. With plenty of willing local help, he carried out a major demolition on the 23rd near Visé, of the main railway between Maastricht and Liège, and another a month later on the branch line between Visé and Plombières – which the Germans had been using to supplement the main line from Aachen to Liège; and in August he imposed constant delays on German train traffic between Liège and Verviers. Early in September he even got embrangled in a skirmish with some Tiger tanks, from which he escaped with a light wound; and was soon overrun by the Americans. 'He showed great resource and daring', in the words of his citation for the MC, 'and his ability to control and command when in the field exceeded all expectations.'[54]

Alexander Goffin, lying up in a remote Ardennes village south of Liège, observed two Belgian Gestapo clerks who had forgotten that they were as vulnerable as a pair of Napoleon's policemen in occupied Spain, and came to look the place over. He sent word to his Russian maquisard neighbours in the woods nearby; and saw the two Gestapo men hanging there, dead, within two hours.[55]

Even in the closing stages of a campaign, agents could still be alert for new tricks in tradecraft, or old tricks reapplied. Servais, a forty-year-old bank manager from Montmédy, who worked briefly and successfully training peasants near Gembloux, brought back a tale from his region IV. A party of six Germans, who had stopped him, seen his papers, and let him go, went on to search a château nearby for a W/T set. They never found it, for they were shown round by a maid who 'had it wrapped in some towels she was carrying under her arm', and gave it back to the operator when the visitors had gone.

Mrs Olga Jackson ('Emilia') was by birth Belgian, but had married an English husband and had lived in England since 1935. She had a

---

53. Signed report, 30 May 1944, TS *ibid.*
54. TS *ibid.*; cp also Belgium 21.
55. Interrogation, 11 January 1945, in his PF.

strong, self-confident, humorous personality, and was a junior FANY officer. She joined SOE in March 1944, and was dropped into Belgium on 4/5 August, with an odd mission: though she spoke not a word of German, her task was to introduce herself to as many senior German staff officers as she could, and proceed to rot their morale by explaining to them that Germany had already lost the war. In the few weeks that turned out to be available to her, she set about her task with such aplomb that she was mentioned in dispatches for courage and enterprise; concrete results were necessarily slight.[56]

Van Gyseghem and Beckers, renamed 'Aemilius' and 'Rosencrantz', went on a second mission, this time to zone III (west Flanders) of the secret army, on the last night of August. Van Gyseghem's parachute did not open fully, and he was badly hurt. Beckers took him to a maquis hospital; almost at once, the province was overrun. Beckers had a few exhilarating days helping to clear out pockets of Germans who did not retreat fast enough; the mission was soon successfully over.

When Lovinfosse brought Durieux back to England in March, he had handed 'Greyhound' over to a Belgian army friend, called Adam; who had the services of Kelly's friend, the Vichy policeman, as his W/T operator. But Adam was arrested near the Spanish frontier of France in May (he was released two months later). Humphreys decided to set up a new line running from Belgium to Spain, run by a man he had trained himself; and dispatched for this task, on 12 June, Hans Felix Jeschke, with Paul Goffin on his second mission as his wireless operator. They were flown to Gibraltar, and were soon in Spain.

Jeschke was a full-blown enemy national – he had been born in Leipzig in 1906 – but was passionately anti-nazi. His colourful past had included a violent escape from SS custody and service with the republican army in the Spanish civil war. This time he crossed Spain without incident, with Goffin; who got left behind by accident during the walk across the Pyrenees, and never regained touch with his organiser. Jeschke pressed on to Paris, met the 'Loyola' line run by

<hr />

56. Her PF.

the Polish Popiel,[57] and set out to extend it to Brussels; finding it convenient to steal a German army motor bicycle, which he rode with papers he forged himself, making himself out to be a lieutenant in the transport corps entitled to wear plain clothes on duty.

Little notice can be taken of diplomacy in this book, which is about war; but one diplomatic event commands notice.

4 September 1944, as will shortly be shown, was the brightest day in Belgian resistance. On the following day, the 5th, the Belgian, Dutch and Luxembourg governments in exile all signed the Benelux treaty: an act of political and economic faith in each other, the acorn from which the oak of the present European community has sprung.

It was the sudden fall of Brussels that alarmed the German secret high command so much that the massacres of agents, already noted, in Mauthausen, Buchenwald and other camps followed in the next few days. Alarm spread quite far down the German security forces.

It was, for example, the fall of Brussels that convinced May, the Orpo code expert, that the allies would soon be in Driebergen; for once his usually sound judgement was at fault. He made a bonfire of all the messages exchanged during the *Englandspiel*, and broke its ash up carefully when it had burned out.

A junior officer in the Household Cavalry remarked, on being ordered to France in 1914, that he 'hadn't reckoned on going farther out of Town than Windsor'.[58] Thirty years later, his regiment led the Guards Armoured Division into Brussels, five years to the day after the next British declaration of war on Germany.

Next day the last wave of this advance swept on to Antwerp.

Horrocks, the corps commander, said on the 3rd, in the park at Laeken, to Lovinfosse, who was at hand for any co-ordinating tasks that might be needed, 'this is not my victory, it belongs to Belgian resistance; without that, I could not have advanced so fast.'[59]

---

57. Foot, *SOE in France*, 366; Jeschke had there to be called Hilton, one of his many cover names, to protect relatives still living in Saxony.
58. Private information.
59. *Livre d'Or*, 315, tr.

By this time the German forces in the west gave onlookers the impression of being an entirely beaten army, on the run, looting as it went. Shops in towns in southern Holland through which this rabble passed, in a ludicrous miscellany of vehicles – cars, military or civilian; lorries, ditto; flat-bed farm carts; perambulators – found their windows broken, by soldiers who helped themselves to anything that took their fancy in them; any visible typewriter or bicycle was liable to be seized. One bystander was reminded of the Thirty Years' War.[60]

Gubbins, SOE's mainspring,[61] was fond of saying, 'The problem is not simple.'[62] He devoted much thought to the question of how best resistance activity could be correlated with the tactical needs of an allied invading commander. Once – once, in the Low Countries, though more often elsewhere – he solved this equation satisfactorily, in Antwerp; with tactically brilliant success, of which no strategic use could be made for some months.

Elaborate arrangements had been made by both sides about Antwerp docks, which the Germans meant to disable and the resisters to preserve. The resisters caught the Germans off balance, and won. SOE's team on the spot consisted of two rival groups of resisters, the stronger from the left and the weaker from the right in politics; both were prepared, for the nation's good, to accept orders from a regular Belgian engineer subaltern, Urbain Reniers, whom the secret army's chiefs had picked to take charge of counter-scorching. For months past he had gradually secured the allegiance of many of the senior port authorities, who by this time preferred working with the allies to working with the Germans: a military instance of the familiar political technique, 'boring from within'. The chief of the fire brigade, for example, put all his resources at Reniers's disposal, including passes to travel anywhere in the harbour.

SOE provided two wireless operators, brothers, to keep Reniers supplied with orders and stores: 'Regan', who had arrived with de Liedekerke in February, and 'Armadillo', H. J. T. Waddington, who had recovered from the air accident that had killed Verhaegen, and parachuted in to join his senior on 6 August. He was received by an

---

60. De Jong, *KdN*, x(a). 121–8, 176–7.
61. Foot, *SOE in France*, 18.
62. Gubbins in *RUSIJ* xciii (May 1948), 212; conversations with him, 1963–8.

FIL party in the Ardennes, who undertook to send his sets forward separately; they did not arrive in useful time. His brother had two, which they used indifferently; taking care to keep themselves well apart from the locals, with whom they kept in touch through a woman who ran a café near the main railway station.[63]

The truth is that at Antwerp the Germans, by tradition so methodical, had not made up their minds in time how much damage they wanted to cause; and were rushed, at the last moment, by the advancing British army and the local resistance combined, so that they caused very little.

The simplest way to ruin the port would have been to blow up the few lock gates that led directly onto the Scheldt, so that at low tide the docks dried out; whereupon many old dock walls would have collapsed, bringing down with them the cranes that stood on them. The Germans did damage three lock gates leading on to the Scheldt, two of which were at once repaired by using spare gates, kept waiting for an emergency; in the third a hole about ten feet square caused a fall in the water level of a couple of feet, nothing like enough to endanger the old walls, before it was stanched.[64]

Resisters, all of one mind, had under Reniers's direction provided a small counter-scorching team for each object – dock gate, power station, floating crane or what not – that needed to be secured, and equipped each team with a small armed covering party, ready to beat off any interference. The Germans started one or two fires at the last moment; they were promptly put out.

Care was taken to keep the port area quiet during August; all the acts of sabotage that took place in that province – there were many – were out in the countryside, or in other towns than Antwerp. This showed sound resistance discipline, and may have lulled the local Germans into a false sense of security.

They decided, rather late, to cripple the port by digging pits in the quays, some eighty metres apart, each to be filled with a concrete tube a metre in diameter and as deep as low-water mark; at the bottom of each tube an explosive charge was to be tamped. In mid-August work

---

63. Interrogation of 'Armadillo', 5 December 1944, in his PF.
64. Many details in Belgium 269; summary at back of HQ 226, counter-scorching report.

began on the pits, and on making the tubes; on 25/26 August a raid on the two concrete factories destroyed the tubes.[65]

On 4 September the leading armoured cars of 11 Armoured Division approached from the south. German engineers were standing by to blow up the main road bridge at Boom; by a deft resistance coup, they were outflanked and overpowered.[66] At noon, all Reniers's parties went to their action stations. One group rapidly threw up a wall, to block the Germans' plan to let the city's sewers flow into the tunnel under the Scheldt. Others seized both the main power station, and all the key electrical switching points for moving dockyard equipment. Out of 602 dockyard cranes, the Germans only managed to destroy three; counter-scorching parties collared the rest.[67] The telephone exchange, railway station and town hall were seized as well, and by two o'clock the Waddington brothers were explaining to the intelligence officer of 23 Hussars exactly where the Germans' defences lay.

Even in this symphony of triumph, there was one discordant note. Marine Captain E. Colson ('Harry') claimed in an eleven-page report three months later that his private navy had been the real liberator of the port – he had himself cut the wires that the Germans had laid leading to their explosives; and he did not see why this man Reniers, who said he had orders from Eisenhower but never produced them, should get all the credit. But nobody else wanted to give Colson and his friends credit, because they belonged to the then unpopular Mouvement National Royaliste.[68] Colson took part, as 'leader of Antwerp Docks Resistance Group', in an Imperial War Museum conference on Belgian liberation in 1984.[69]

His friend Reniers had in fact been acting as his own good sense determined – he had been wrestling with the problem since 1940 – and on verbal orders from de Liedekerke, who dropped Eisenhower's

65. Bernard, L'Armée Secrète, 183.
66. Useful sketch map ibid., 185; many details in Memo from Belgium (1985), 88–93.
67. Gubbins in RUSIJ xciii (May 1948), 219.
68. Document 1055 10 R3, TSC in Brussels archive. For the MNR, over 2,500 strong nationally, see Bernard, La Résistance 1940–1945, 85.
69. Memo from Belgium, 10, 93–6.

name without any authority from the general. Pire issued, for the record, a formal order to Reniers to do what he had done; it did not arrive until 9 September, by which time teams from the Royal Navy had already been at work for four days in the port, checking that all was well, and Reniers's troops had secured for light casualties the northern suburb of Merksem.[70]

Before ever Antwerp went critical, Reniers had had a few dealings with the enigmatic Lindemans ('King Kong'), the man who had seen de Graaf through Paris.[71] During the spring and summer they had met several times, usually in Antwerp cafés. Reniers's doubts about Lindemans's reliability, reinforced when the Dutchman pulled a revolver out on hearing a German policeman had just entered the café, were appeased when he, Lindemans and a girl he recognised as a clerk working for the Germans all stayed at the same Brussels hotel, and Reniers was not betrayed. Lindemans constantly pressed him for money, of which he provided a little; and sometimes for warlike stores. He gave Lindemans some explosive, specifically for a rail cut between Malines and Tirlemont; duly carried out. During the crisis, 'King Kong' fought well in some skirmishes on the left bank of the Scheldt.[72] From all this it is fair to conclude that Lindemans's heart was not as wholly devoted to the German cause as his conduct in Holland in the spring had suggested;[73] he clearly enjoyed adventure.

L'Armée Secrète and several other Belgian resistance movements proved their worth in the next four days, by doing exactly what SOE's council had long prayed resisters would do: they mopped up whatever odd pockets of German troops were left on the flanks of the main advancing allied columns, taking them prisoner when they could and killing them when they were obstinate. The haul included two generals and several thousand prisoners of war: at a high cost in resistance casualties.

Language difficulties allowing, resisters were also available to help the allies in all sorts of ways. A Polish lancer commander reported, for

70. TSC of orders, and further notes, in Reniers PF.
71. Page 212 above.
72. Report of 24 November 1944, signed TS in Reniers PF.
73. Pages 216–19 above.

example, that as his tanks approached the Dutch frontier north of Ghent a resistance company joined them, 121 strong including seven officers. 'Very useful people they were because they knew the terrain, they could tell our tank commanders where the ground was hard and where not, they did patrolling and sentry service during the night thus relieving our troopers weary of driving and fighting.' This sort of aid was widely available: 'extensive mopping-up operations' are credited to the secret army as well.[74] Hence Horrocks's remark to Lovinfosse.

One instance of the kind of confusion that could follow on so sudden a liberation[75] is too odd to omit.

The reader may recall that Jeschke had been busy building a DF line between Brussels and Paris, disguised as a lieutenant in the German army. He happened to be at the Brussels end of his line when the allied armies arrived, and slipped away to a flat he thought safe on the Brussels side of Ghent. He got a chit of sorts from the new occupying authorities, and lay low for a few days; but was denounced to the local occupying troops, who were Poles, by suspicious neighbours who produced his German motor bicycle as evidence. The Poles were about to shoot him when one of the firing squad recognised him: they had been in the same platoon in Spain.[76]

Eisenhower seized the occasion of the liberation of Brussels and Antwerp to issue another order of the day, this time distributed widely from 3 October, without security grading; in which he thanked Belgian resisters for the magnificent help they had given to assist his rapid conquest of Belgium. He added that he would be proud to have them continue under his command, if they cared to enlist; but that those who did not should promptly hand in their arms.[77]

---

74. SOE (44) 5–48, 6, weekly report for 4–10 September 1944, duplic in CAB 121/319.
75. On the ambiguity of this word, see Norman Davies in Dear and Foot (eds), *Oxford Companion to the Second World War*, 688–9.
76. Conversation with Jeschke – by then an antique dealer in St John's Wood – in 1970. He glossed over this incident in his formal SOE interrogation of 18 September 1944 (photocopy TS in his PF).
77. Facsimile in *Livre d'Or*, 339.

This last point he presumably inserted at Pierlot's request. The Belgian cabinet returned from exile on 8 September: such was the muddle on the spot that there was nobody waiting for them at the airport, and the accounts of their reception are oddly contradictory.[78] They returned to a country on the verge of political anarchy and of social chaos. The Germans had bolted from most of it, but were not yet defeated; trade and industry were not far from standstill; food was short; fuel was shorter; even means of secure communication were scarce. On this last point, SOE was able to lend a hand.

Secret services normally then held to a strict rule: they forbade their agents in the field to send each other messages by wireless. R/T was thought far too easy to intercept. W/T was also easy to intercept, and the provision of enough secure ciphers was thought insuperably hard. Why provide the enemy with more points at which he could break into circuits?

One large, and largely notional, circuit in France got as far as coaxing at least thirty transmitters out of SOE, but never used any of them.[79] In Belgium, as in Holland, something on these lines turned out feasible because a man on the spot had the knowledge, the courage, and the enterprise to see it through.

René Verstrepen, a reserve captain in the Belgian army, had studied wireless in detail for twenty years before the war, and ran a radio shop in Antwerp. He was recalled in 1939 – then aged thirty-eight – to establish a wireless system for the Belgian army staff. He was captured in May 1940, but released next July, on account of his reserve status and Flemish birth. He at once settled down to form a resistance signals unit, working from a nucleus of his recent companions in arms. He became a regular source of spare parts – from his shop – and of further training for SOE wireless operators who needed either.

He knew the leaders of the secret army, well. For security's sake, he sent no messages at all on his network before Normandy D-day; but from then till the end of October the Verstrepen Group, as they were called, passed brief messages by W/T between secret army headquarters – which Pire settled in the country, not far from Brussels – and all five zonal headquarters. Long afterwards Marks recalled

78. *Memo from Belgium*, 160–1.
79. Foot, *SOE in France*, 105.

having provided them with codes, replaced soon after D-day by one-time pads.[80] It may have been Livio who brought the codes over in March.[81] Blaze worked their central station, on top of all his other work.[82]

In the joyous confusion that followed liberation, the Verstrepen Group provided government with a secure means of communicating with its provinces. Verstrepen himself worked with 2 SF detachment to send five valuable W/T operators into the still-occupied western Netherlands.[83] The identifiable four of these five are listed in appendix 4. They provided tactical intelligence for the First Canadian Army.

In Holland, with Philip's vast works at Eindhoven to provide expertise and advice on the quiet, both the OD and the RVV invented W/T nets for themselves. They did not have the benefit of Marks's advice; both, the OD particularly, suffered from enemy penetration as well as enemy direction-finding. One 'Jedburgh' team 'Edward', on operation 'Market' – we turn to 'Jedburgh' teams in a moment – met a Dutchman who claimed he had one of a group of thirty W/T sets, linked all over Holland to gather information.[84]

On 9 September, the day after Pierlot returned to Brussels, Prince Bernhard followed him, to set up the external headquarters of the Binnenlandse Strijdkrachten (BS), forces of internal Dutch resistance, of which the prince had just been appointed head; the name evidently borrowed from the Forces Françaises de l'Intérieur.

Allied commanders and staff all remembered from what they had read of the Franco-Prussian war of 1870–1 the trouble and confusion then caused to the winning side by the *Schlachtenbummler*, the hordes of noblemen and their servants who went to war as if to a hunting meet, crowding roads needed for the prompt passage of troops with the horses and carriages that conveyed them to what they

80. Conversation with Marks, 22 January 1991.
81. Bertrand, *L'Armée Secrète*, 126.
82. Jottings in Blaze PF.
83. Citation, signed by Gubbins, for the MBE (Mil) Verstrepen received in 1947. I have seen hardly any other papers on him.
84. Undated report, 5, duplic in Holland 4.

regarded as a spectator sport.[85] Montgomery, not much given to changing his mind, put Prince Bernhard into this category: one of his errors. It was not widely known of the prince that he had a brother serving in German uniform on the eastern front; but his German origin, like his RAF training, was enough remembered for many senior soldiers to suspect that he would only get in the way.

Though his father had been a German prince, of Lippe-Biesterfeld, English had been his nursery language because his nanny was Anglo-Chinese;[86] and he had mastered Dutch on marrying Princess Juliana. A staff officer from N section, A. G. Knight, and two SOE sergeant wireless operators called Spence and Hannaford, went with him.[87] He worked from various châteaux in and near Brussels, later moving forward to Breda; at the end of the war he moved to his wife's palace of Soestdijk by Baarn.

The prince, who had hoped to be commander of the forces invading Holland, had accepted this lesser appointment in agreement with Eisenhower; who also appointed Yvan Gérard as the external commander of the Belgian forces of the interior, over whom Gérard does not seem to have exercised much control.

The allied high command distrusted, from professional habit, men of low rank or none. Dutch resistance threw up in September 1944 a man in whom princes and resisters alike could have trust, with both rank and personality: Henri Koot,[88] a retired colonel of the East Indian army. Koot had been born in Bali in 1883, of a Dutch father and a Chinese mother.[89] He had spent his working life as a staff officer; he had run Dutch cipher and decipher in the 1920s,[90] and so knew how to keep his mouth shut. He was resolutely anti-nazi, and had twice been imprisoned briefly by the occupiers.[91]

---

85. Cp (Sir) Michael Howard, *The Franco-Prussian War* (Rupert Hart-Davis, 1961), 62–3.
86. De Jong, *KdN*, i. 577.
87. History ix, September 1944.
88. Photograph in De Jong, *KdN*, x(i). 689.
89. *Ibid.*, x(ii). 564.
90. Kluiters, *De Nederlandse . . .*, 367.
91. De Jong, *KdN*, x(ii). 565.

There was an unhappy hitch about confirming his appointment with the government in exile, which lasted five weeks: Prince Bernhard confirmed it on 20 October.[92] Koot had by then already said goodbye to his wife and abandoned his house in The Hague, and settled in digs in Amsterdam; whence he undertook the cumbrous and intricate task of persuading the RVV, the KP, survivors of the OD, and any other live subversives he could reach to pool their efforts and to work together.

From time to time, he received orders from Prince Bernhard. Many of those he commanded in the BS were barely prepared to accept orders, but respected his judgement enough to follow his advice. By early 1945 he was able, often with the help of SOE agents, to produce armed parties at particular spots, to attempt particular tasks of sabotage or counter-sabotage.[93] Van Oorschot of course knew him well. His headquarters was called Delta-Centrum: there was nothing fourth-class about it.

Teams codenamed 'Jedburgh', of several nationalities, played a key part in stiffening and supporting resistance during 'Overlord'. Some scores of teams worked in France; others were available for the Low Countries.

Their origin can be traced back to (Sir) Peter Wilkinson's initiative. He had been one of the stalwarts of MIR, and was an eyewitness both of the German airborne attack in Crete in May 1941, and of the swiftness and ferocity of civilian reaction to it.[94] He appreciated how much use lively minded agents would have been, had they been on the spot to harness and co-ordinate this civilian ardour. He put up a paper to Gubbins, who was able to develop the idea a year later at a meeting with Mountbatten, then chief of combined operations, and Weeks, the deputy chief of staff, Home Forces.[95] They met to discuss how to carry out the role which the chiefs of staff had just

---

92. *Ibid.*, 570.
93. Citation, 7 January 1946, by Gubbins for award of CBE, TSC in Headquarters 216, (iv); award gazetted 11 June 1947.
94. See Antony Beevor, *Crete* (John Murray, 1991), 116–17, 139–40, 176, 185, 208.
95. History xii(ii). 1–3.

allotted to SOE in future major assaults: to organise and arm patriot forces for attacks on rail and signal communications, and on aircrew, on the night of the assault; and later to lay on guards, guides, labour and raiding parties, as required.[96]

'Jedburgh' teams were recruited accordingly. Each was normally to be three strong: one American, from the SO branch of OSS; one British, from SOE; and one local – French, Belgian, Dutch or Norwegian – found through SOE channels. (They do not seem to have operated in Denmark.) One of the three was to be a wireless operator, probably a sergeant; one a subaltern; and the team commander was to be a captain or a major. SOE designed a light portable transceiver for them, excellent in every way but one – it was often damaged by being parachuted.

The men were selected at Stodham Park, near Liss on the Hampshire-Sussex border. Those chosen moved on for training to Milton Hall near Peterborough, where they formed themselves into teams.[97] For this sort of journey, travelling companions had to get on well together; hence a number of single-nationality teams.

The officers were all trained to be fit to command an infantry company, whatever their rank. They and the sergeants also passed parachute courses (at Ringway) and learned the elements of sabotage. A 'Jedburgh' team was thus likely to prove itself a formidable reinforcement for any group of resisters with whom it came in contact. Even if its set did not work, so that it could not summon stores in or pass intelligence out, it could provide valuable training; and at least one of its members should have no language problems. They jumped in uniform, so that wherever they went they could provide ocular witness that liberation was coming near; though often enough the first reaction of their reception committees was to insist that they went – for a few days, at any rate – into plain clothes.

Five 'Jedburgh' teams were standing by to go to Belgium. They were held back till the allied armies reached the Seine. The advance from the Seine to the Scheldt then turned out so swift that they

---

96. *Ibid.*, quoting COS(42)133(0), 12 May 1942.
97. Van der Stroom was wrong to remark (*Nederlandse agenten*, 13n) that they trained at Jedburgh, which was simply their codename.

never went at all: a minor instance of the waste of war.[98] More formidable bodies of armed men were standing by as well, most of them outside SOE.

One 'Jedburgh' effort had just begun before the major action started. Henk Brinkgreve, born at Utrecht in 1915, was a Dutch reserve artillery officer, recalled from business for service with his anti-tank battery in May 1940. He managed to evade surrender, retreating across Belgium and northern France to Cherbourg, whence he took ship to England that June. He had a spell with March-Phillips's Small Scale Raiding Force, and took part in one of its Channel Island raids; after it was disbanded, he worked at Lieftinck's elbow at Dutch army headquarters.

Headquarter work seemed tame to him; he got accepted as a 'Jedburgh'. With another major, the American Olmsted, and Sergeant Austin of the Royal Berkshire Regiment, he formed team 'Dudley', which jumped – at the fifth attempt – into Overijssel province on 11/12 September 1944. They had been given no inkling that First Airborne Division was going to land, as it did, some thirty miles south of them on 17 September, in its attempt on the world-famous 'bridge too far' at Arnhem.[99] Yet they were well placed to try to hinder the movement of German counter-attacking forces; they had done nothing so far beyond getting themselves reliably housed and clothed.

That another major airborne operation, somewhere into the Low Countries, aimed at bringing the war to a swift close, impended in September 1944 could hardly be counted a secret. Old men forecast it, in pubs and in clubs; airborne troops, some of them too long idle, longed for it; in an RAF transport squadron that would certainly be involved in it, it was all but an accepted fact.[100]

The allied armies that fought in 'Overlord' included four airborne

---

98. Mackenzie, *History of SOE*, 604. The Belgian officers involved were Comte Edmond d'Oultremont, E. de Selys Longchamps, C. Bachelart, W. Shreurs, and A. A. E. de Winiwarter (note in History xii(iii)). Winiwarter was taken on at a late stage to replace Francou, who left SOE in July (notes in their PFs).

99. Cornelius Ryan, *A Bridge too Far* (Hamish Hamilton, 1974).

100. Ralph Campbell, *We Flew by Moonlight* (Ontario: Orillia, 1995), 94.

divisions, elite troops, three of which had taken part in the 'Neptune' landings in Normandy. The British First Airborne Division, held back from 'Neptune' in reserve, was briefed for fifteen other operations, for two of which troops were actually emplaned, each of them cancelled in turn, before going to its doom on operation 'Market Garden' at Arnhem. It was determined to go *somewhere*, or be disgraced.

Several of these cancelled operations raised headaches for SOE as well; such as 'Linnet'. This was a plan to put all four divisions down in western Belgium in early September, to seize an airhead including Courtrai, Oudenarde, Ath and Tournai; thus inhibiting any German attempt to stabilise a front west of it. Resisters inside the airhead were to do no more than register their presence, unless called on locally for guides, news, or labour. Resisters in a belt twelve miles wide outside it were to harass enemy counter-attacks. 'By direction of C-in-C 21 Army Group [Montgomery] NO demolitions will be carried out which are in any way likely to interfere with the forward movement of ALLIED troops.'[101] The 'Bardsea' parties, highly trained Polish parachutists whom Gubbins judged the finest body of fighting men he had ever seen,[102] were also to take part, mobilising 'Monica', the Polish miners' resistance group across the French border, on 'Linnet's' western flank.

As it turned out, hardly any of the plans made for this sort of resistance work in Belgium, in immediate touch with the advancing allied armies, were needed. For the German army did not try to defend Belgian soil; it ran back fast into the shelter of the Siegfried Line. Eisenhower and Montgomery conquered Belgium west of the Meuse in less than a week in 1944, three times as fast as Manstein and Guderian had conquered it in 1940.

SOE in Belgium had, as we have seen, a share in one triumph, the seizure of Antwerp docks almost intact – exactly the sort of task its founders had had in mind for it since 1940. Faulty strategy by Eisenhower and Montgomery failed to exploit this remarkable gain – nearly three months passed before the mouth of the Scheldt was

---

101. SFHQ Preliminary Instructions, 29 August 1944, <u>TO BE PASSED BY HAND</u>, duplic in Belgium 209; paper 2.
102. Conversation with him, 1965.

cleared of Germans, so that Antwerp was usable – but that was their mistake, not SOE's.[103]

'Bardsea' also, promising though it had been, never left the starting gate; frantic efforts by the Poles in exile to dispatch it into beleaguered Warsaw, instead of north-eastern France, shattered on the immovable logistic and diplomatic obstacles. Even 'Monica', round Lille, was not called out: the advance flashed past it too fast.

SOE had made an attempt at contact with 'Monica', also mistimed, through F. Chalmers Wright. He had come into SOE from the political warfare angle; he had carried out a PWE mission in Grenoble in the winter of 1942–3, so securely that he had little to show for it.[104] He suffered severely in Spanish camps on the way out, but returned to France – on foot over the Pyrenees – in the spring of 1944 with a quite different task. The Polish government in exile in London and SOE's EU/P section sent him to reorganise the large Polish community round Lille so that it could play an effective part in 'Overlord'. In this he succeeded; he again had a horrible Pyrenean passage out. For his third mission he parachuted into the Belgian Ardennes on the night of 1/2 September 1944. By pilot error, he dropped from only 250 feet, and injured his spine on landing. This did not keep him from taking part in several days' sharp fighting before he went to see a doctor. He then moved westwards to Lille to visit 'Monica', which had already been liberated.[105]

'Market Garden' was Eisenhower's and Montgomery's left hook, intended to outflank the bulk of the German forces in the west and encircle the Ruhr. It began on 17 September 1944 with 'Market' – the simultaneous landings of most of three airborne divisions along the line Eindhoven-Son-Veghel-Nijmegen-Arnhem – and 'Garden', the advance overland along the same line of Horrocks's XXX Corps, which started from the Meuse-Escaut canal, almost sixty miles from Arnhem; and did not quite arrive in useful time.

Chickens hatched during 'North Pole' came home to roost during 'Market Garden'. Such news about secret service affairs as filtered

---

103. Cp Noel Annan, *Changing Enemies* (Harper Collins, 1995), 112–13.
104. Foot, *SOE in France*, 100, 208–9.
105. Poland 112. He died, aged eighty-six, in July 1990.

through to allied airborne forces' intelligence staffs indicated that Dutch resistance had been penetrated by the enemy to a hopeless degree; so that any approach by men claiming to be Dutch resisters was liable to be treated with reserve, even suspicion. It was the task of the 'Jedburgh' teams to dispel suspicion and replace it with confidence – if they could.

Their trouble, like their colleagues' in other airborne forces, was lack of means of communication. None of their specially designed sets worked. The only one of the seven W/T operators among them who could raise England at all was the most experienced of them, who took a trusted B Mark II set with him as part of his private baggage; and he was not at Arnhem. There, a telephone engineer called Deuss had a complete clandestine telephone network in full working order; but was unable to make useful touch with the staff of First Airborne Division, who had landed west – too far west – of the town, to whom these lines would have been invaluable.[106]

Four 'Jedburgh' teams took part in 'Market': 'Edward' with the airborne corps headquarters, 'Daniel' with the 101st and 'Clarence' with the 82nd US Airborne Division, and 'Claude' with the British First Airborne Division.

The operation was planned in a tremendous hurry, in a single week. The 'Edward' team at Moor Park, where most of the airborne planning was done, was able to provide useful data to the planners about Dutch terrain and the probable enemy forces on the spot.[107] Staal, its leader,

also established with intelligence Officers and Civil Affairs Officers a more clearly defined field of activities for the whole liaison mission. These activities were designed to:-

(a)   Further the success of the operation through employment in the military field of local Dutch Resistance Forces as required by the local commander.

(b)   Provide intelligence on various levels from local resistance groups inside the air head and from resistance groups infiltrating into the air head from outside.

---

106. Conversation with Deuss in Paris, 5 June 1984. For these networks in general – there were several – see de Jong, KdN, x(ii). 487–97.

107. Report on 'Edward', unsigned and undated, 2, duplic in Holland 4.

(c)   Assist in vetting of resistance members who were to be used as guides, guards, patrols and in any other field of military activity.

(d)   Provide labour from resistance sources for all work of a military nature, e.g: landing strips.[108]

In hindsight, many critics have deplored the diversion of aircraft from the main object of 'Market' – seizing bridges – on to the conveyance of General Browning and a retinue of staff officers to form a corps headquarters that hardly exercised any influence on the battle. They forget that Browning too was determined to jump *somewhere* before the war was over.

His headquarters, right on the German border south-east of Nijmegen, was so ineffective because little of the airborne signalling equipment worked. The only 'Jedburgh' operator who made contact with base at all was one of 'Edward's', using his B Mark II (his Jed set did not work). This operator was Len Willmott, who had joined the Royal Corps of Signals in his middle teens and had had plenty of experience behind the lines already – he had been one of SOE's operators in Greece as far back as the autumn of 1942.[109] He sang the praises of the B II, as thoroughly robust; it certainly worked well for him.

Staal and his team, like the others, found they could provide useful liaison between the fighting troops, the local underground forces (who were often at odds with each other) and the many willing civilians. In Nijmegen, as soon as it was liberated, he made a discovery of vital intelligence importance. He called at the electric power station – he was in Dutch army uniform – and found out that it was in touch by telephone with many other power stations in Holland, on a private network unknown to the Germans.

Through this network, communication of a sort could be set up with First Airborne at Arnhem, unreachable by wireless; in the long run, vast amounts of news could be collected from all over the country. Staal was far too sensible to hug this secret to himself; he told XXX Corps I staff, as soon as they arrived, and word reached all the

---

108. *Ibid.*
109. See Simpson and Adkin, *The Quiet Operator*.

proper authorities. This invaluable source was extinguished a few weeks later by a fool journalist, who slipped an account of it past an inattentive censor; within a week, the Germans closed down the net.

Meanwhile, the 'Edward' team, working jointly with their neighbour in 'Clarence', had assembled a force of 100 Dutch volunteers to help build a landing strip at Malden, south of Nijmegen – 250 men turned out to do the work – and done plenty of translation and liaison.

The 'Clarence' Jedburgh team dropped with the American 82nd Airborne Division near Nijmegen. All its stores, including Sergeant Beynon's W/T sets, were dropped by error into woods full of German troops; and the other American in the party, Verhaege, was badly wounded. A. D. Bestebreurtje was also wounded, but remained at duty.

Bestebreurtje, born on 12 April 1916, was the son of a general manager of Unilever; as such, his Grand Tour included a year at Yale, though as he did not stay to take a degree he does not figure in Robert Winks's scintillating book on Yale men at secret war.[110] He had also attended the universities of Zürich and Geneva, studying law, and held some Swiss skating records; something of an all-round man, and a good one to have beside one in a battle. He was busy in making arrangements for the local underground to help in the crossing of the Waal, the southern branch of the Rhine, and helped to supply them with arms, besides constantly exposing himself to danger. Beynon recorded that 'his coolness under fire was the talk of the division';[111] this among men noted for their courage.

The 'Daniel' team jumped with the first wave of 101 US Airborne Division near Son; but two of their three aircraft were already on fire when the parachutists left them, and most of their kit – including all their wireless – was lost. Major R. K. Wilson of OSS was the commander; Abraham Dubois, late of N section, was the team's main inspiration. He had escaped from the Dutch ministry of defence in exile to 12 Commando, then to a parachute unit, and then to SOE. He was to have led the attack that was cancelled on the printing works

---

110. *Cloak and Gown* (Collins Harvill, 1987).
111. Report in Holland 32, undated, duplic.

at Haarlem.[112] Dobson recognised that his lively temperament would be better fitted to 'Jedburgh' work than to long-term work in secret.

Dubois spent the first two days of 'Market' at General Taylor's elbow, as his interpreter, and then settled a quarrel between the KP and the OD at Uden. The 506th Parachute Regiment captured the bridge over the Dommer at St Oedenrode with invaluable help from the KP; and the KP, again, provided guards over 400 captured German soldiers at Veghel, under Wilson's supervision. On 26 September Taylor dismissed the team. They drove to Brussels in a captured car, and were back in London next day. Two of them, Dubois and Lykele Faber – one of the team's two W/T operators, who had both lost their sets – had a second mission ahead of them.

One 'Jedburgh' team, 'Claude', was in the thick of the fight at Arnhem. They had a perfect drop on to the Oosterbeek DZ, at about 1400 on 17 September. Captain Jacobus Groenewoud, a twenty-five-year-old shipping clerk from Amsterdam, was in command. He and Harvey A. Todd, US infantry, set off with the leading elements of First Airborne Division for the main bridge, providing useful touch with locals on the way. By nightfall they were established in a house at the north-west corner of the bridge. From the attic, Todd sniped Germans and directed anti-tank fire, till he was himself wounded by a sniper next day. Carl A. Scott, the W/T operator, was still hunting the DZ for his set; he never found it. M. J. Knottenbelt, a Dutch subaltern lent to the team from 10 Commando, who had made his first jump on the 17th, organised civilian labour round the main DZ. He started to disband it on the 20th, by when it was clear that the division was bottled up in its bridgeheads and had gone over to the defensive. Slightly wounded, he evaded across the Rhine. Sergeant Scott stayed behind; the Germans caught him, and shot him on 2 November.

Groenewoud had been shot dead on 19 September, on his way out of the inner bridgehead with news for divisional headquarters. Todd had by this time recovered from his face wound and was back in action, first as an artillery observer, then again as a sniper. He was wounded twice more on the 20th, being blown out of his attic on to

---

112. See pages 198–9.

ground level; and spent the next two nights up a tree, out of ammunition, in a street full of passing German soldiers. He was finally captured on the 27th, and had a rough time as a prisoner of war. One of his nastiest shocks came when an interrogator who had posed as a Dutch civilian at 82nd Airborne Division headquarters mentioned Bestebreurtje's name, but only as that of the interpreter.

Small parties of resisters, inspired by 'Dudley', were able to hamper the flow of German troops and supplies up to the Arnhem front, by tree-felling and nightly rail cuts; but not to any marked extent. Brinkgreve had not been on the ground long enough to make a major impact; nor were either arms, or previous agreement to work together, available for the locals who had leanings towards activity.

On the day 'Market Garden' began, Radio Oranje broadcast an order from the government in exile: the Dutch state railways were to strike. Though listening to Radio Oranje was – by nazi law – illegal, word got through fast: all trains had stopped by midnight. Stations did not reopen next day; indeed, Dutch civilian railway traffic north of the Rhine never restarted till the Germans surrendered next May. Most of the strikers *dijkten onder* (went underground); all received strike pay, most of it supplied secretly from London from the earnings of the Dutch mercantile marine. Not a *doppeltje*, not a farthing, went astray.

The appalling consequence had not been foreseen by Gerbrandy, who gave the order; for which the proposal – according to N section's history – had originated in the field.[113] The Germans brought in their own railwaymen to move and supply their own troops; traffic to sustain Dutch civilians had to go by road or by barge, and as a reprisal to the strike the Germans thereupon banned barge traffic. The horrors of the Hunger Winter, still unforgotten, followed: ending in nearly sixteen thousand deaths from starvation, in one of the most fertile countries on earth.[114]

Before we leave 'Market Garden', we must look again at 'King Kong', whose shadow fell momentarily across the rescue of Antwerp.

---

113. History cx, September 1944, 2.
114. See Henri van der Zee, *Hunger Winter* (Jill Norman and Hobhouse, 1982), and recall the siege of Leningrad (page 193).

Vulgus vult decipi, et decipiatur, says the proverb: the mob wants to be, and is, deceived. There is no need for scholars or other sensible men to go along with it. The popular press, the *Daily Mirror* in the lead, has long maintained that 'King Kong' betrayed 'Market Garden': an accusation disposed of as long ago as 1950. We have the word of General Student, the German commander on the spot, that no word of warning reached him. Chapter XVII of the report of the Dutch parliamentary commission of inquiry into the conduct of the Dutch government in exile established that Lindemans did indeed cross from allied into German-occupied territory, but on 15 September 1944, at which date no plans for 'Market Garden' had yet left England (planning did not begin till the evening of the 10th). The agent is supposed to have seen, or heard of, the plans – accounts vary – at Prince Bernhard's headquarters; again, the committee established that Lindemans never went there at all until several days after 'Market Garden' had begun, when he had picked his way back from the neighbourhood of Eindhoven through the still fluid fighting lines.[115]

His open face and plausible manner captivated male staff officers as well as what was then regarded as the frailer sex. In particular Peter Baker, 'Harrier' of IS9 (WEA),[116] the escape service's forward unit, housed in a requisitioned *maison de rendezvous* in Brussels, thought highly of him. Baker engaged Lindemans as his driver; together they went on several missions to infiltrate escape agents through the lines. Lindemans thus rapidly became familiar with many allied headquarters locations in Belgium, Prince Bernhard's office eventually included. He even claimed access to a room in which he could read up the allies' future plans; probably an empty boast.

In the prince's entourage he met de Graaf, whom he had looked after in Paris; de Graaf knew that some doubts were being expressed about him, and interviewed him at length, emerging on 16 September with the conclusion that he 'certainly was no traitor', but was 'rather a dreamer', suitable for subordinate posts.[117]

---

115. See Hinsley and Simkins, *British Intelligence . . .*, iv. 378–8.
116. Airey Neave, in *Saturday at MI9*, 285–92, omitted Baker's name out of respect for his parents, then alive; so did Foot and Langley, *MI9*, 220–1. After the war, Baker became an MP and was disgraced. De Jong names him: *KdN*, x(i). 421.
117. Note in Lindemans PF.

Paradoxically, it was on this very day – the eve of the 'Market' drop – that Lindemans was issued at Driebergen with an *Ausweis*, a German pass to see him through controls (reproduced below).[118] It reads as follows:

Darf nur deutschen Kontrollen und Streifen vorgezeigt werden.

O.U., den 16.9.1944.

A U S W E I S !

Der holländische Staatsangehörige mit Kennkarte A 35 Nr.096953 Christiaan B r a n d steht im Dienste des Sonderstabes OKW, Driebergen. Brand ist mit allen Mitteln zu unterstützen und bei Rückfragen Sonderstab OKW,Driebergen, über WV Utrecht anzurufen. Inhaber ist berechtigt, eine Schusswaffe zu führen.

Major und Dienststellenleiter.

May only be shown at German control and contact points
In the field, 16 Sep 1944

PASS!

Christiaan <u>Brand</u>, Dutch subject with identity card A35 nr. 096953, is serving with the Highest Command's special staff, Driebergen. Brand is to be supported in every way. For further inquiries, Highest Command's special staff, Driebergen, can be called via Army Headquarters, Utrecht. Holder is entitled to carry a firearm.

Kiesewetter
Major and Bureau Leader

[stamp:] Front Reconnaissance Troop 365.

For some weeks more he continued to bemuse de Graaf and to fascinate Baker, but various security staffs began to run restive about him. Oreste Pinto, early in the field of inaccurate story-writing after

---

118. *Ibid.*

the war about intelligence affairs, has this to be said for him: instinct told him Lindemans was a traitor. Suspicions accumulated far enough for him to be pulled in for interrogation on 28 October. He was expected to resist arrest fiercely, or to bluster; on the contrary, he at once confessed. He was sent over to London for protracted interrogation by MI5;[119] which established, beyond any doubt, that he had become a German agent in the spring of 1944, and had been acting as one – a few anti-German freaks apart – ever since.[120]

The check at Arnhem and the 'King Kong' affair between them left a bitter after-taste on the staff; nothing with the Dutch seemed to be going quite right.

119. *Ibid.*

120. After this book had been completed, some of MI5's files were opened to research. Glancing in a file on Camp 020, I found that Nelis – not the most reliable of sources – had accused 'King Kong' of betraying 'Market Garden'; that Giskes had been asked whether this was so, and had replied, 'Of course.' Most probably, what 'King Kong' betrayed was operation 'Comet', a project for the seizure of Eindhoven by First Airborne Division, which was cancelled; and of which the double agent may have heard staff gossip.

IX

Follow-through and Aftermath
1944–5

There was a sharp contrast between the swift release of the Belgians – almost all over in a week – and the protracted agony of most of the Dutch. The southerners too were swiftly liberated, but a front was then drawn between them and the rest, who endured the agonies of the Hunger Winter. So far as Belgium was concerned, suddenly the fighting seemed all but over: the occupiers vanished, and vast crowds in the big towns welcomed the incoming allied armies. Beyond tying up loose ends, paying off debts, and discussing decorations, two tasks remained for SOE. The Verstrepen W/T network proved, in the short run, a great help to government, for it was the fastest and most secure way by which ministers could communicate with their provinces. And something – not much, but something – could be done about sending agents forwards into the Netherlands and Germany.

Besides lending a hand with communications, SOE was able to help solve for the Pierlot government the problem that had long perplexed it, of how public order was to be maintained through the near-anarchy of liberation. Earlier in the year the Germans, suspecting rightly that the bulk of the gendarmes by now sympathised with resistance, had disarmed them. SOE arranged for the RAF to fly in 18,000 stens, with plenty of 9mm ammunition;[1] the guns were passed out to the gendarmerie; and there was only one trace of trouble.

---

1. Amies to Floor, 13 September 1944, TSC in Belgium 234; details of sorties in Air 26.

Several communist-dominated FIL units refused to follow Eisenhower's order, and either enlist in the armed forces or hand in their arms. Difficulties with them culminated in a riot in Brussels on 25 November; the gendarmes opened fire on the rioters, wounding forty-five of them, none fatally. By the end of the month, these troubles were over: as General Erskine, the British commander in Brussels, made it clear that his troops would support Pierlot's regime.[2]

Notoriously, Holland is low-lying, much of it below mean sea level. Centuries of effort and intellect had gone into protecting it from the sea. In the spring of 1944 both SIS and SOE became aware that the Germans envisaged opening some of the dykes, and precipitating major floods; the government in exile had constantly been aware of the danger.[3] Yet it was the British, not the Germans, who first created new floods.

Before any use could be made of Belgian resistance's crowning achievement, the delivery of Antwerp almost intact, the mouth of the Scheldt had to be cleared: this took several weeks' bitter fighting by the First Canadian Army, interference by the RAF with the sea defences of Walcheren, and a major combined operation. On 1 November 1944 bombing from the air breached Walcheren's dykes, so that in Toby Graham's phrase, 'the island was like a saucer full of water'.[4] This hampered German attempts to reinforce the garrisons of Flushing and Westkapelle; an allied commando force was able to fight its way ashore; the conquest of Beveland followed. Minesweepers then cleared the estuary; and the first allied supply ship docked in Antwerp on 26 November.

The Germans hung on to Holland north of the Meuse and Rhine. One reason why they did so was that the coastline from the Helder to the Hook of Holland provided convenient bases for the bombardment of London by V2 rockets. Some staff time was spent, at SHAEF, at SOE and at SAS headquarters, in seeking to devise attacks

---

2. Bernard, *La Résistance 1940–1945*, 124–6.
3. HQ 5, 29th meeting of SOE-SIS-FO liaison committee; statements by C and by Boyle.
4. Dominick Graham, *The Price of Command* (Toronto: Stoddart, 1993), 185.

on V2 sites, or at least on the rockets' supply of liquid oxygen. As any large level slab of concrete or sound road surface could be used as a launch pad, and the Germans tended to move around quite often from one pad to another, it was hard to mount specific attacks; attacks on liquid oxygen factories held a little more promise. SAS toyed with the idea of cutting out a technician; no one could see how to get him away, even if one was captured, and the Air Ministry could not provide a parachutable expert to interrogate him on the spot. Agents were alerted to the importance of attacks on rockets in transit, and on telephone and survey equipment at unused launch pads; useful results were few.[5]

One rocket technician did appear in mid-January – a deserter – and was enthusiastically received, until he turned out to be a double agent, sent through the lines by the SS to mislead the allies.[6]

Elderly Londoners still pride themselves on how well the capital stood up to a cascade of V1s and V2s during the last eleven months of the war in Europe. Few know that Antwerp, Liège and Brussels were hit in the closing months of the war by even more V1 pilotless missiles – doodle bugs, as Londoners call them – than ever fell on England: over ten thousand were discharged at targets in Belgium.[7] V1 sites were thus eminently suitable for attack by saboteurs; but I have found no trace in SOE records of any successful attack on them from the ground. This was an aspect of war on which SOE had to defer to the air force as the more competent arm for the task. Much resistance effort, and some effort of SOE's, went into reporting where V1 sites were, so that they could be strafed; a separate story.

Antwerp suffered trouble comparative to London's. It had to endure 4,248 V1s and 1,712 V2s, which between them killed 4,229 people, 714 of them in allied military service. In the worst incident, on 16 December 1944, a V2 landed slap on a full cinema, killing 296 servicemen and women and 271 civilians.[8]

*

5. Planning discussions in Holland 9, December 1944–January 1945.
6. History cxi, 6 March 1945.
7. Holmes, *Fatal Avenue*, 190.
8. Summary drawn up on 25 May 1945 by HQ 7 Base sub-area, British administrative HQ in Antwerp; duplic in Belgian archive, W12 suppl 6.

Amies remarked with authority, on looking back at the struggle, that 'Clandestine work, both in the field and at an HQ, brings out the worst in men's character.'[9] There were only too many illustrations of this during the war's last winter, in which T had little to do: not only, though principally, on the German side.

The nazi secret police fastened such a grip of terror on the population of the Third Reich that only the bravest dared put a toe out of line. The Soviet secret police was quite as fierce.[10] The Germans, notoriously, did their best to kill all the Jews and gypsies they could catch, and imprisoned Jehovah's Witnesses and male homosexuals under atrocious conditions. The NKVD, practised during the *Yezhovshchina* in scouring out foreigners, deported whole communities of Germanic ethnic origin to the wastes of Siberia, where they were dumped, to survive if they could on subsistence farming.

In the lands overrun by the westbound Red Army, a welcoming soldiery had hard on its heels much less welcoming police units from the NKVD, whose object was to persecute all who had helped the Germans; and whose members were strict in their arrest.

The SD in the Netherlands, plentiful and only too well informed, intensified their reign of terror during the war's last winter, keeping right down to the standards of the NKVD. Giskes had by now been eased out of secret service proper, though he retained his rank of lieutenant-colonel, in command of a new unit: 307 *Frontaufklärungskommando*, a counter-espionage unit, mainly composed of his former Abwehr colleagues. With it he saw out the war.

Dutch armed resistance on the ground, such as it was, continued to do its best, in spite of internal rivalries, which usually remained acute, and shortage of weapons, which SOE and the RAF did what little they could to remedy. At least France no longer provided the principal drain on air supply. Yet the RAF remained uneasy, as well it might, at the prospect of operating at low level over an area so brimming with anti-aircraft defences as Holland.

---

9. History xlvi, paper of 27 April 1945, 12, TSC.
10. Startlingly frank account of the NKVD's reign of terror, by some French escaped prisoners of war who had been subjected to it, dated 9 September 1941, in Security 20.

Ten agents, nevertheless, were dropped in August – Postma and Reisiger on the 7th/8th, Frans Hamilton and his sister on the 9th/10th, and the rest at the end of the month. Postma ('Sculling') worked round Utrecht, where he and Reisiger ('Turniquoits'), his wireless operator, got an efficient team of resisters assembled. Unhappily, in late November through a chance courier's arrest the Germans caught Postma and several of his friends,[11] and D/F was Reisiger's undoing a month later; neither returned.

Antonia Hamilton, though like Mulholland with a British surname, was Dutch by birth (in her case, in 1910); and when she jumped with her brother Frans on 9/10 August, she had a parachuting accident: she broke her leg and ankle, badly. Frans succeeded in getting her first aid, and then moving her into a clinic, without indiscretion; but she could not walk properly till after the Germans had been chased out of Holland, and made no attempt to imitate Durieux and run a circuit from a hospital bed.

Her brother, much distressed at her injury, moved on once he had seen her safely settled, and is described in the section history as having done 'an extremely good job' in North Holland province, training 'a large number of potential instructors in sabotage and reception committee work'.[12]

Two parties of three were dropped on 28/29 August, one into the Veluwe: Luykenaar ('Shooting'), Hinderink ('Hunting') and Beekman ('Charades'), their wireless operator. Luykenaar got himself organised promptly enough to cut the railway between Amersfoort and Apeldoorn during the fighting at Arnhem, but then retired to Rotterdam, where he 'did a magnificent job' training saboteurs during the winter;[13] he managed an evasion southward in mid-March. The young Hinderink moved east, instead of west, and spent the winter training saboteurs in Overijssel. Jacob Beekman, the W/T operator, went with him, so he had some chances to secure stores.

While under training at Thame Park, Beekman – whom Beaulieu found 'practical and cunning'[14] – had met and fallen in love with a

---

11. De Roever, *Zij sprongen bij maanlicht*, 74.
12. History cx, August 1944, 1.
13. *Ibid.*, 2.
14. Note in his PF.

Swiss fellow-student, Yolande Unternahrer. She had already gone to France, early in 1944, to work for the unforgettable Guy Bieler, and had been arrested with him, at her set in St Quentin, in March. Her husband already knew of her arrest when he jumped; but did not learn till 1946 that she was murdered in Dachau in early September.[15]

They soon met the 'Dudley' 'Jedburgh' team, who were working in the same area; the two parties divided the work between them.

The other party of three – van de Meer, Buitendijk and Kroon ('Stalking', 'Fishing' and 'Skating') – were to have parachuted in, in all innocence, right in the path of 'Market Garden' near Eindhoven. Their aircraft was damaged by flak, and had to make a forced landing near the DZ. Van de Meer and Buitendijk survived the crash with nothing worse than bruises; Kroon was quite badly hurt. They found a safe house for him, but it was not safe enough: the Germans caught him, and he died in enemy hands right at the end of the war. The other two, after a few weeks' work with local resistance, came out through the nearby fighting lines on 10/11 November.[16]

Tobias Biallosterski ('Draughts') went in on his second mission ten days later, on 8/9 September, dropping east of Alkmaar with a new W/T operator, Pieter de Vos ('Backgammon'). The Stirling that had carried them was shot down over Texel on the way home. 'Draughts' was no longer to work for the clandestine press: he was to act as linkman between the RVV and the Dutch in exile, a role soon changed for a still more important task: he and de Vos were to provide Koot's principal link to Prince Bernhard. Both agents found safe houses in Amsterdam, where de Vos had four separate transmitting stations.[17]

Biallosterski organised North Holland province so well that he was able to import arms for over a thousand men into Amsterdam, hidden in the false bottom of a barge. He had a second wireless operator to help him: Paul Polak (whom de Roever calls Peters),[18]

---

15. Foot, *SOE in France*, 106, 223, 268, 294, 368, 428–32, and de Roever, *op. cit.*, 84–8.
16. History cx, August 1944, 2.
17. De Roever, *loc. cit.*, 116, has a photograph of one of these in a hospital basement.
18. *Ibid.*, 112, with handsome snapshot.

alias 'Boating'. Polak was dropped, only thirty-six hours before 'Market Garden' began, with three other agents: Maarten Cieremans ('Cubbing'), who went to work with Postma near Utrecht, and Wim Hoogewerff ('Coursing') and Gerard de Stoppelaar ('Monopoly'), who went to Rotterdam. Hoogewerff came from the East Indies; Stoppelaar had been a merchant seaman who jumped ship in Sweden.[19] They all three dropped, at their own request, in uniform; on local advice, they changed at once into plain clothes.

From one or other of the SOE agents in Rotterdam, the workmen at the Wilton Feyenoord shipyard who had provided resistance's early martyrs in 1941 secured some explosive, which they used to sink at their moorings four blockships they had been made to prepare for obstructing Rotterdam harbour: a triumph of counter-scorching. They were still active early next year, when they sank a large floating crane.[20]

In spite of the reputation that French resistance had built up over the years, it is worth record that one SAS captain, Gilbert Kirschen ('Regan', then 'Fabian'), a Brussels barrister who had joined Blondeel's unit, found after two muddled sorties into France that his third drop, into the Veluwe in September, got much calmer and more efficient local help than he had met before, from the RVV.[21] This may simply have been a matter of luck and personalities; and in Holland, as in France, the Gestapo was always close on resisters' heels, so that there was a constant run of arrests.[22]

A useful result of the cross-posting of Johns from SIS to SOE now emerged. Reports from both services' wireless operators were making it more and more clear how hard it was becoming to move about at all in Holland, let alone when encumbered with a clandestine transmitter. Johns was able to effect a reform that would have been inconceivable three years earlier. The report for the week ending 24 September laid it down: 'SIS and SOE W/T channels have been

19. *Loc. cit.*, 174–5. Different landing date *ibid.*, 11.
20. CAB 121/319, reports of 15 October 1944, 5 October 1944, 9 and 28 January 1945, 3, duplic.
21. G-S. Kirschen, *Six amis viendront ce soir*, 95–8.
22. E.g. *ibid.*, 151–5.

pooled in the field and distributed throughout Holland.'[23] Henceforward, after a proper exchange of passwords, agents of either service could use any set that was available: a great help on the ground, whatever awkwardnesses had to be got over at home station.

Moreover – another change from the past – the supply of arms overland was no longer out of the question. Prince Bernhard arranged for the Hudsons of 161 squadron to fly fifty tons of small arms and explosives into Brussels airport, and did his best to forward them into safe BS hands in occupied Holland, while the lines were still fluid.

In parallel, the supply of arms by air went on, not always smoothly. De Jong prints a detailed account, from the ground end, of a drop near Putten, north-east of Amersfoort, on the last night of September.[24] Seven containers (out of twenty-four) burst in the air; instead of a neat drop onto the DZ, the goodies were spread out over nearly 3,000 yards. No wonder the KP organiser of the reception committee was furious.

The neighbourhood of Putten was extra dangerous because on the same night as that unfortunate drop, an ambush on the edge of that village shot up with a bren gun a Luftwaffe lorry with two officers and two NCOs of the Hermann Goering division inside it. The bren gun came through an SAS channel, and was fired by 'Tex' Banwell, a platoon sergeant from First Airborne Division who had been captured at Arnhem and escaped, had fallen in with an active RVV party, and was glad to help them. He survived (he turned up at the 1989 London conference);[25] many inhabitants of Putten did not, because German reprisals were prompt and fierce: the men all went to Neuengamme.[26]

Hardly had Dubois returned from 'Daniel' when MI9 borrowed him, renamed him 'Ham', and had him dropped back into Holland with a Belgian W/T operator, Raymond Holvoet ('Bacon'). Holvoet had grown up, and grown penitent, during three months in the

23. CAB 121/319, SOE (44)S.50, 6.
24. De Jong, *KdN*, x(b). 612–13.
25. Foot, *Holland at War*, 117–18.
26. De Jong, *KdN*, xb(i), 46–58.

cooler;[27] but his luck had run out. His set did not survive the drop; and the Germans arrested him ten days later. Dubois was hard at work, with Kirschen of SAS – whom MI9 had also borrowed – helping to organise 'Pegasus I', the successful rescue of over a hundred stranded members of First Airborne Division. He also tried to spring Holvoet. After the much less effective 'Pegasus II', he mentioned his contacts with the Germans who held Holvoet to Kirschen; who, backed by London, implored him to break them off. They were too late. Early in December Dubois was trapped at a farmhouse west of Ede by an *agent provocateur*, wounded, and captured. On 9 March 1945 he was among a crowd of prisoners shot dead in reprisal for a botched attack on Rauter; and Holvoet had the same fate a month later.[28]

The 'Clarence' team had made itself so useful round Nijmegen that it was invited back, and returned – overland – on 3 October, renamed 'Stanley II'. Bestebreurtje who had only been lightly wounded again led it, with Beynon of OSS as his wireless operator and Vickery, a young sapper subaltern, in place of the more severely wounded Verhaege. They were able to make some use of S-phones to direct artillery fire; but the battle was settling down for the winter, and in a few weeks they were released.

Herbert Morrison, the home secretary, read Selborne's report on SOE assistance to 'Overlord',[29] and bothered to write to say that 'It is a fascinating record of human courage and first-class organisation.'[30]

On 9 November 1944 the chiefs of staff issued their last directive to SOE.[31] It began in a tone at once formal and anodyne: 'It is essential that subversive activity should be planned in close co-ordination with strategical policy and operational plans. Similarly, our strategy and current plans must take account of the contribution which subversive activities can make towards the military and economic offensive.'

---

27. See page 308.
28. See pages 416–17.
29. WP(44)570.
30. 23 October 1944, signed TS in Selborne 8.
31. COS(44) 957(0), top secret. C wrote it (CAB 121/305).

SOE was therefore to remain in constant touch with the three other fighting departments; with the Foreign, Colonial and India Offices (the dominions, oddly enough, were left out); with MEW, with PWE and with SIS; and with 'the Controlling Officer', who ran deception. Each of these in turn was enjoined to aid and consult SOE as need arose. SOE was specially instructed not to clash with SIS, but to supply it with intelligence on request. It was to intensify sabotage, and to use guerillas to keep German forces dispersed.

In the field, the supreme allied commanders in north-west Europe, in the Mediterranean and in south-east Asia were to control SOE's operations; only Poland, Czechoslovakia and Sweden lay outside this remit. No action was called for in countries not named in the directive; this amounted to standing at ease, if not quite standing down, SOE's missions in America, Africa and Russia.

The high command still believed it could exercise some control. A meeting on 16 November 1944 between Prince Bernhard, several brigadiers from 21 Army Group, and Brigadier-General Howell, the deputy head of SHAEF's mission to the Netherlands, settled that requests by the allied forces for action by the Dutch were all to pass through that mission; except for anything to do with action in territory still in enemy hands, which was to go through Rowlandson's 3SF detachment. When the prince opened a small advance headquarters in Breda, as he did a few days later, he was to keep in daily touch with Rowlandson by liaison officer. Everyone was to call on the prince's headquarters, in Brussels or in Breda, rather than have the Dutch visit them; as Rowlandson set out in a letter that day, to which he added a postscript, 'It is superfluous to say that this letter should NOT be shown to any Dutchman.'[32]

So confident was the high command that 'Market Garden' would succeed that the 'Dudley' 'Jedburgh' team in Overijssel, forty miles beyond Browning's 'bridge too far' at Arnhem, was ordered on 17 September to seize bridges and keep civil traffic clear of the main roads, to facilitate the allied advance into Germany – supposed imminent.[33] It was an order Brinkgreve, the team's commander, had the good sense to ignore. As the team was not after all relieved by a

---

32. 3 SF Det to 1 and 2 SFDets, signed TSC in Holland 4.
33. Report on 'Dudley' in Olmsted PF, c. 1 December 1944.

rapid allied advance, Brinkgreve had to do what he could in Overijssel province; though neither Olmsted nor Austin could pass as Dutch. Austin – nicknamed Bunny, like the tennis player – moved round from farm to farm, communicating with Brinkgreve mainly by courier; he must have had a lonely autumn. Olmsted came back through the lines, bearing a long assessment by Brinkgreve of the prospects of resistance if the war did not end quickly. He missed 'Pegasus I' on 22/23 October, the successful transit – organised by 'Fabian' and others, received by Airey Neave and Hugh Fraser – of a party of 138 airborne troops and escapers; and was lucky to be one of the seven survivors of 'Pegasus II', a month and a day later. Most of this party were ambushed, and either shot or captured, west of Arnhem.[34] Olmsted and a few companions got safely over the Rhine.

The whole right bank of the river in Holland was thickening up with German fighting men, prepared to meet a renewed allied attack. Brinkgreve's 'Jedburgh' training had encouraged him to expect contact with an advancing allied army in a matter of days, or a few weeks at most, after he landed. He now had to undertake the tougher tasks of a longer-term SOE organiser. His role might be compared to Claude de Baissac's running F section's 'Scientist' circuit in south Normandy in June and July 1944;[35] save that he had neither of de Baissac's main advantages, two previous missions to lend him experience, and short odds that he would soon be overrun. He must have had a lonely autumn of a different sort from Austin's: mixing often with fellow-resisters to whom he could not tell too much, and rubbing shoulders in the streets of towns he had to visit with Germans to whom he could not tell anything at all. He organised numerous supply drops, which put weapons into the hands of 1,200 Dutchmen, and had reserves laid by for twice as many more; Olmsted reported that the province could raise 12,000.[36]

Hardly had Brinkgreve dispatched Olmsted to start his journey through the lines when five members of the KP, armed and instructed by him, brought off a bank raid in Almelo on 14

---

34. Useful map in de Jong, *KdN*, x(ii). 526, with variant dates. Those in text are from Neave, *op. cit.*, 291–2, 296; he was present on both occasions.
35. See Foot, *SOE in France*, 344, 382, 398, 408–9, 440–1.
36. Report of 14 December 1944 in his PF.

November: 46,000,000 gulden sequestrated by the Germans, on their way to the Reichsbank's coffers in Berlin, were cut out by the raiding party, who hoped to use the money for local railwaymen's strike pay.[37]

This coup was reported in Austin's last message, received three days later. He was caught by bad luck. He happened to be in Luttenberg, midway between Zwolle and Almelo, when the SD stumbled on an RVV arms depot – nothing to do with him – elsewhere in the village, and proceeded to search every house. As he could not answer questions in Dutch, he was arrested;[38] leaving Brinkgreve with plenty to do, but no wireless to help him do it.

Intensive searches by the SD pulled in a member of the LO carrying papers that led them in turn to two of the KP bank raiders. These young men were persuaded that if they would reveal where the money was buried, they would be released. The SD – here is nazi justice again – secured the money, and packed the young men off to concentration camps they did not survive.[39]

By a considerable feat of diplomacy, Brinkgreve managed to persuade the rival groups of resisters in Overijssel – as usual, KP, RVV, and OD – to act together, instead of competing. He had some temporary help from Jacob Beekman. His feats included repeated railway cuts, and a block on the Twente canal at Delden, west of Enschede.[40] N sent him a more lasting assistant in January 1945, Sjoerd Sjoerdsma ('Squeak'), a merchant marine wireless operator whose war had included sitting out the July 1943 firestorm in Hamburg on board his ship in the harbour.[41] Not much was going to frighten him after that. He matched Brinkgreve for steadiness of nerve, and survived. (The last set he used is on show in the Amsterdam resistance museum.)

Had Giskes and Schreieder not handled the *Englandspiel* so deftly, SOE might have done much better in canalising Dutch resistance as Brinkgreve and Sjoerdsma managed to do. They did not both survive.

---

37. N section war diary, 19 November 1944.
38. Austin PF.
39. De Jong, *KdN*, 10(ii). 616–17.
40. CAB 121/329, report of 7 January 1945, 3, duplic.
41. Sjoerdsma PF.

On the afternoon of 5 March 1945 three Dutch SS men, making a routine check for unlicensed slaughter of cattle, turned up at a farm near Overdinkel, close to the German border east of Enschede, to which Brinkgreve and Sjoerdsma had just moved their headquarters. The farmer's daughter, who knew nothing of Beaulieu's warnings against conspicuous hurry, rushed into Brinkgreve's office to warn him, and thus drew SS attention to the room. In the ensuing scuffle Brinkgreve was shot dead at close quarters. The rest of his party escaped, and rescued their few papers later.[42] The SS supposed they had shot a truculent farmer, and remained unaware that they had taken out one of the most gallant of the 'Jedburghs'.

A parallel mission to Brinkgreve's north-west of it in Friesland was run by Pieter Tazelaar ('Necking'), who parachuted in on 18/19 November 1944. He was unusually well placed to work for SOE, for almost three years earlier – late on 23 November 1941 – Hazelhoff Roelfzema had put him ashore near the casino at Scheveningen, in white tie and tails and reeking of brandy, so obviously a gentleman that he could stroll past all the sentries unchallenged.[43] He had then been working for Dutch and British intelligence; both thought highly of him. To have had previous experience of what it was like to be a secret agent in occupied territory was indeed a boon.

His wireless operator, who jumped with him, was Lykele Faber, born in 1919, who had not been called up for military service by the Dutch because he was a Seventh Day Adventist, and so did not believe in shooting anybody. He left school at fifteen, and ran through a series of odd jobs – poultry farmer, window-dresser, carpenter's mate, seller of tombstones and of sewing-machines – before he was called up for forced labour in Germany in October 1941. After nine months as a window-cleaner in Chemnitz, he was allowed to return to Holland, and became a post-office clerk in Amsterdam, where he learned morse. He met at chapel Anne-Marie Weidner, a nurse, to whom he became engaged; she encouraged him to escape. Her sister Gabrielle in Paris sent him on to their brother John at Annecy, where Faber spent some months learning French

---

42. Brinkgreve and Sjoerdsma PFs; N section war diary, 7, 14 March 1945.
43. *Soldier of Orange*, 110–16.

and helping Weidner run his now well-known escape line;[44] down which he moved, walking into Andorra with a group of pilots, in mid-October 1943. SOE welcomed him when he reached England in March 1944, and trained him as a parachutist and wireless operator; his shy, determined personality made an impression.

He jumped as a member of the 'Daniel' 'Jedburgh' team on 'Market Garden', but was of little use to his friends as his set never turned up. A few weeks later he jumped into the Netherlands again, with Tazelaar. They worked in the open country south of Leeuwarden; so well organised that they soon received seventy-two containers, delivered by three Stirlings, on a single night.[45]

In the autumn of 1944, a team of Dutch telephone engineers wired up the SD commandant's office in Leeuwarden, under the Germans' noses, so that resistance got advance notice of intended major SD raids, and knew something of where the Gestapo's principal suspicions lay.[46] This was a priceless gift of local intelligence; it is tempting to think it was done on Tazelaar's suggestion, but he probably arrived too late to propose it. He may all the same have had access to the results.

One chance raid was almost the ruin of him. He never forgot an afternoon in Friesland early in 1945. A party of Germans arrived, unannounced, at the farm where he was staying. He just had time to notice that they were armed only with machine pistols, no use beyond a range of forty yards, before he and the farmer slipped behind a rare hedge to hurry off to the next farm. Glancing back, he saw a German astride the roof of the farm they had just left, searching the countryside with binoculars. The party chased him from farm to farm till nightfall, never quite getting within range, and never thinking to send for a single rifle, which could easily have brought him down.[47]

It was merely a matter of luck that Friesland lay off the axis of the main allied advance into north-west Germany, so that the men

---

44. See Ford, *Flee the Captor.*
45. Air 26, page 139: 23/24 November 1944.
46. Note of interrogation, 27 June 1945, of Dr Evne of Beekbergen near Apeldoorn; in History cxii.
47. Conversation with him, 26 February 1989.

Tazelaar had trained were not there to assist it. He had 2,000 armed men waiting, who provided priceless assistance to the Canadians when they eventually arrived.

He had one unexpected source of help, besides Faber. Flight-Sergeant Alfred Springate, RAF, had the good fortune to get ashore when his bomber was shot down into the Zuyder Zee off Stavoren. Aircrew were ordered to lie low, and escape when they could, sooner than join resistance movements; Springate had the courage to disobey this order. Being already a fully trained wireless operator, he thought he would do the allied effort more good by sharing Faber's load – and danger – than by embarking on the long trek home. All three of them survived.

In February 1945, during a hard winter for Belgium, Pierlot's government at last fell. Achille van Acker constructed a new one, which made no difficulties for SOE. Pierlot, as the continuator of free Belgium, was made a count; Lepage, by the bye, died a baron.

In the spring of 1945, Dobson took most of N section's staff across to Brussels, leaving a rear link in Baker Street under C. F. Dadley, a fifty-year-old travel agent who was 'an extremely good mixer' and had been a GSO3 on SOE's staff for a year already.[48] T had been in Brussels since September with an advanced headquarters called SPU 47; he moved back to London in March.

Proverbially, the dykes are vital to the security of Holland. Both the government in exile and the occupying authority gave occasional thought to them; they remained under the supervision of the pre-war Dutch water authority. Not till 5 December 1944 do SOE's surviving records show any interest in the problem. On that day Mr Akermann, a land-drainage official who had reached London, had a talk with Dobson and others to discuss some proposals signalled by 'Draughts'. The agent proposed seizing and opening the lightly guarded sluices on the Afsluitdyk, which closed in the Zuyder Zee. Akermann observed that to do this in winter might well let the sea in, and so make worse a 30cm rise in the water level 'Draughts' had observed; that there were several reserve sluices available; and that it

---

48. Dadley PF.

was always vital to review Holland's water problem as a whole, however strongly local opinion urged some such striking action. He added that the Afsluitdyk was exceptionally strong, and would need 'very heavy bombs to damage it'. Dobson agreed to tell 'Draughts' to take no action.[49]

'Draughts' himself had been in the field since mid-September, on his second mission. (Dansey used to say that no agent could be relied on to last longer than six months.)[50] The Gestapo caught up with him on 10 February. He and several friends were stopped at a chance road control; one of the friends had some compromising papers on him. A scuffle broke out, during which Biallosterski was shot through the chest; he died of this wound, in a German military hospital, a fortnight later, having said nothing he should not.

SOE's staff were wise enough to learn from experience, when the secrecy in which the whole organisation lived made it possible to do so. N section was able to pick up some useful lessons from F's and RF's telephone sabotage in France in June 1944, some of it highly successful. These were embodied in orders sent to agents in the Netherlands in the spring of 1945.[51]

The object of telephone sabotage was to overburden the system, rather than to break it down entirely; for the allies would need to have it working as perfectly as possible, the moment they had driven out the Germans. Therefore, telephone stores were not to be attacked; on the contrary, care was to be taken to make sure the enemy did not demolish them. Friendly staff could no doubt be found to explain what steps the Germans had in mind, so that these could be countered. Nor were exchanges to be damaged. Instead, agents were to attack trunk cable lines, well away from towns. Felling three or four telephone posts together, preferably at a corner, was recommended; so was carrying away as much fallen wire as possible. Buried trunk cable should be dug up, and a yard at least of it cut out; one of the cut ends should be stuck in a bucket of water. As the Germans were short of skilled telephone maintenance men, it would

49. H. Saunders to AD/E, 6 December 1944, in Holland 6.
50. M-M. Fourcade, *Noah's Ark*, 255.
51. Undated TSC in S. Sjoerdsma PF.

be worth mounting an ambush as well, to eliminate a German repair party, or to convert a Dutch one.

Richard Barmé ('Trapping') and Piet de Beer ('Snooker') had gone in, to meet their different fates, a few days before Tazelaar and Faber. Barmé, who had bicycled into Belgium aged seventeen in 1942, and found his long way to England over the Pyrenees, was the youngest agent N sent to the field; his family was Jewish. He parachuted in to de Goede, with twenty-four containers, on 1/2 November; also bringing with him a wireless set, which SOE had trained him to use. Through the winter, he ensured communication between Rotterdam and London; not soon enough to save van Duyn. He too was caught at his set on 2 February, and murdered five weeks later.[52]

De Beer had been resisting since the summer of 1940, and had had ten weeks inside Haaren over Christmas 1942. He lay low for a while on being released, and then went back to secret work; by May 1944 he was a leading KP figure in Rotterdam. He came out across the Waal on 22 September 1944, had a long interview with Prince Bernhard near Brussels, and was dropped back into Holland at the second attempt on 10/11 November. (De Roever has him drop from a Lancaster;[53] it was in fact one of 644 squadron's Halifaxes, from Tarrant Rushton.) He went back to work in Rotterdam, survived van Duyn's arrest on 19 November, but thought it prudent to escape down the line through the marshes of the Biesbos in mid-January.

Two generations later, it is easy to forget who the enemy was against whom SOE and all the allies fought: a team false as Malory's King Mark, who would swear not to do a thing, and straightway do it. One of Giskes's strongest cards, when he wrestled with the hapless *Englandspiel* captives of N section, was his promise to spare their lives: a promise honestly given that the system under which he worked betrayed. A further grisly instance of nazi justice follows.

On the night of 6/7 March 1945 resistance caught up with Rauter: by accident. Four men from a BS unit in Apeldoorn, armed with sten guns and dressed in stolen Waffen-SS uniforms, prepared – against orders – to mount a road block on the Wuste Hoeve heath

---

52. Sympathetic memoir by Eddy de Roever (1995).
53. De Roever, *Zij sprongen bij maanlicht*, 181.

on the main road from Apeldoorn to Arnhem. They wanted to steal an army lorry, in which they could carry off next day three tons of pork – already earmarked for the Wehrmacht – from an abattoir in Epe. At about midnight they heard a loud vehicle approach from the south, and lit their stop sign. In the vehicle, an open BMW touring car, sat Rauter, beside the driver, who was a stranger to him. He knew, the moment he saw the sign, that this was an ambush, for he had lately ordered that cars were only to be stopped at night in built-up areas. He cried an alarm, and reached for his machine pistol as the driver pulled up. His machine pistol jammed; the stens did not. Rauter's driver and the officer on the back seat behind him were killed; he, shot through cheek and lung, was left for dead.

A German patrol found him at dawn, and took him to hospital in Apeldoorn, where Schöngarth, his deputy, saw him briefly later in the day. Between them, with Berlin's approval, they concocted a terrible revenge: 243 bullet holes were counted in Rauter's car; 243 prisoners held by the Germans were therefore shot dead, with twenty more thrown in for bad measure. Some were resisters; some were minor criminals; none had yet been tried. One was a boy of fifteen, found carrying a suitcase in a part of The Hague that had just been bombed, and therefore accused of looting. A single Orpo policeman ventured to query the order to shoot; he was arrested and joined the victims, on the spot. Some of the shootings were done secretly, in the dunes; others publicly, in market-places. Several agents were among those shot: Austin, Hoogewerft, Holvoet, Barmé and Dubois;[54] so was de Jong's resistance hero Thijssen.[55]

When OSS started to get its London SO branch organised, its staff had indicated that they 'did not think they could offer any substantial help in France or the Low Countries'.[56] They did in the end operate into France; but talk of attaching OSS to either T or N section came to nothing; and no OSS went to Belgium.

---

54. De Jong, *KdN*, x(i). 418–27; Austin P.F. May's process-verbal (21 October 1949 in RIOD Doc. I-1103) gives the date and place of Austin's death as 4 April 1945, on the Geldersche dyke near Hattem just south of Zwolle.
55. De Jong, *KdN*, x(ii). 602.
56. HQ 12, 13 January 1943.

A. B. Schrader ('Bobbie'), the only agent – 'Jedburghs' apart –
OSS sent into the Netherlands, born at Soerabaya in 1917, had run
escape groups – with equal zeal and indiscretion – in the middle of
the war, from his cover as a senior man in the food supply office. He
managed to escape by sea in October 1943; was carefully investigated
by MI5, who were convinced of his patriotism; and was parachuted
into Friesland on an intelligence mission on 10 November 1944.
Three months later, to the day, he was arrested near the coast, north-
west of Groningen. The Sipo said he 'made a full confession', but
there was not much in it – he never mentioned SOE, and only gave
away half-a-dozen names the Germans must have known well
already.[57] Nor were the Dutch authorities in London told anything
about Schrader's mission.[58]

May, in retrospect, supposed that while the Sipo thought they
were playing with Schrader, Schrader was playing with them.[59]

SOE and SAS had had a little practice in Normandy, with such
operations as 'Helmsman' and 'Swan', in running informants
through the lines to provide tactical intelligence in more or less static
warfare.[60] Whether this practice would be of any help when the war
turned more fluid was uncertain; and in any case, the pursuit hurtled
across Belgium so fast that there was hardly time to get much useful
done. SOE's necessary habits of secrecy prevented N section from
finding out much, if anything, from F section's experience in western
Normandy: as usual, the Dutch were on their own.

The section history has several reports, in the spring of 1945, of
useful intelligence brought in by line-crossers; more, it turned out,
could be achieved by wireless. The Verstrepen group of W/T operators, who had been of such essential use to the returning government
in exile,[61] were of some further use to the secret war. At least five of
them were infiltrated into western Holland, under SOE's auspices, to
provide tactical intelligence for the First Canadian Army.

---

57. His PF.
58. Van der Stroom, *Nederlandse agenten*, 11,
59. *Enq.*, 48, 19–20.
60. See Foot, *SOE in France*, 405–9.
61. Page 385.

The first to go in, as a test case, was van de Spiegle, active already in Belgium as 'Donalbain'. He was infiltrated over the lower Maas, with his W/T set, on 19 November; still bearing the codename 'Foxtrot' he had used at his set on his earlier sortie. A citation in his thin PF praises his 'great resource, daring and initiative' during the further six months he remained on this dangerous duty.[62] A paragraph in the section history mentions that he worked at first near Dordrecht, and then from somewhere midway between Zwijndrecht and Rotterdam.[63]

By February 1945 there were four Verstrepen operators at work, all presumably sent overland, codenamed or named Foxtrot, Bock, Gueuze and Kriek. Kriek was Beckers, who had done two missions for T already. In March Bock had been replaced by Orval; and is recorded returning on 6 April. As there are no surviving SOE operational papers on them, and their tasks lay outside the present writer's remit, their history is pursued no further here.

By early December SOE was able to estimate the number of Dutch resisters who were already armed at 11,700, and reckoned on arming another 10,000 during the next quarter,[64] forgetting that winter weather might inhibit supply. There were no drops of men between 19 November and 27 February, with the solitary exception of Sjoerdsma.

SOE had no role to play in the sudden and savage fighting in the Ardennes, commonly called 'the battle of the Bulge', that raged from 17 December to early in the new year. SAS, much better suited to sudden tactical assaults, distinguished itself.[65]

In mid-March 1945, with Germany's collapse in sight, McLeod left the SAS brigade for an appointment in the Far Eastern theatre; Calvert who had made a name for himself on Wingate's expedition in Burma took over from him.[66] He had what McLeod lacked, plenty of recent first-hand knowledge of irregular combat; but in mountainous jungle terrain, rather than the flat urban landscape of north-west Europe.

---

62. TSC of 8 January 1946, prepared for Gubbins's signature.
63. History cx, November 1944, 2.
64. Table in History cx, dated 3 December 1944, TS.
65. See references in Temmerman, *Acrobates sans importance*.
66. See J. M. Calvert, *Fighting Mad* (Jarrolds, 1965).

When 'Fabian' was eventually withdrawn early in 1945, he was summoned by Calvert, who pointed out to him on a map a patch of woods between The Hague and Utrecht, and inquired how long an SAS party could hold out 'in this bit of jungle, here'. 'About a quarter of an hour, sir,' was 'Fabian's' reply;[67] SAS did not move into northern Holland till the third Reich was in its death-throes.

One more N agent parachuted in on the last night of February, eight more in March, and a final fourteen in April 1945, beside two 'Jedburgh' teams: the war now clearly in its closing stages.

There were nearly a million forced labourers from the Low Countries in Hitler's Germany by 1944, about twice as many Dutch as Belgian: a tempting resource for N, T and X (SOE's German section) to exploit, if only links could be established with them. As early as July 1942, T was credited with having inserted propaganda, at least into western Germany;[68] though this may have been one of the many occasions on which the Brussels Abwehrstelle was leading T by the nose.

OSS seems to have recruited a lot of Dutch agents to be dropped into Germany, during the war's last winter, some equipped with a less cumbrous W/T set than the S-phone; to provide intelligence rather than to create mayhem.[69] SOE's X section prepared a feasibility study on whether Hitler could be killed, and concluded both that the practical obstacles were insuperable, and that he was by now so bad a strategist – he was in an early stage of Parkinson's disease – that he was more use to the allies alive than dead.

X also sent some fifty agents into the Reich, few of whom returned. N and T sections were of a little use in helping to train them. Pans, for instance, was a conducting officer with the Belgian sub-section of Templer's German directorate, much liked for his high spirits and genial character; he could explain only too clearly some of the consequences of capture.[70]

---

67. Kirschen, *Six amis . . .*, vii.
68. Progress report, 21 July 1942, 4, TSC.
69. See William J. Casey, *Secret War against Hitler* (Washington DC: Regnery Gateway, 1988), *passim*.
70. Cp page 343.

N made one unavailing attempt to penetrate Germany, through Jos Gemmeke, the third woman agent the section parachuted. Though still under age when her country was occupied, she went early into resistance, and by the autumn of 1943 had become a key figure in the world of clandestine press. Her father was a paper merchant; the first man for whom she worked turned out to be the editor of *Je Maintiendrai*, one of the greatest of underground newspapers. It became Miss Gemmeke's job to ensure its secret distribution throughout the Netherlands; she did it so well, and so securely, that she became responsible for looking after several other journals' distribution as well.[71] After the failure of 'Market Garden', she came out – with difficulty, by bicycle, charming a *Feldwebel* into giving her leave to cross the Waal – and reported to Prince Bernhard at the end of October. He at once sent her over to England, where the RVPS noted that 'she is a very level and cool-headed young woman, completely unemotional, very reserved and very determined'.[72] Beaulieu also found her outstanding, and she qualified at Ringway. FANY recruited her.

She was dropped on 10/11 March, in the hope that she could go forward into Germany – under cover of being secretary to a businessman – and get on with organising Dutch workers. Yet by the time she arrived normal communications between Germany and Holland had pretty well broken down. She accumulated some awful accounts of foreign workers' treatment, which she sent out by courier;[73] her mission was aborted by the course of the war.

Marinus van der Stoep ('Scrape'), the agent dropped at the end of February, took up his former friendships in the Rotterdam KP energetically; and was killed in action on 11 April in a raid – so aggressive had the KP become – on a German-held villa in Kralingen, in east central Rotterdam.[74] He was reported wounded to SOE that afternoon, and Sjoerdsma – hardly back from Overijssel – parachuted in again that night with a leg-bag full of medicines for him: too late.[75]

---

71. Interrogation, 13 June 1945, TSC in her PF; conversation, 1990.
72. Report of 6 November 1944, 7, TSC *ibid.*
73. They too are in her PF.
74. De Roever, *op. cit.*, 209–11.
75. *Ibid.*, 223–4.

Bobby ten Broek ('Ping'), dropped in mid-March, was one of several SOE W/T operators who assembled in and around Rotterdam, where resistance activity was by now becoming intense. He went in the same aircraft as Peter Borghouts ('Swish'), nominated by Prince Bernhard as chief of active resistance, who soon had a still more important role to play.[76]

Some double agents tried, towards the twelfth hour, to reinsure with the allies;[77] others persevered. As late as 7 April 1945, Ridderhof, doggedly pursuing a three-year-old instruction of N's to the recently captured Lauwers to get in touch with Bottema, succeeded in mounting a big police raid at Makkum, just inside the eastern end of the Afsluitdijk. A lot of BS weapons were captured, and seven resisters were shot dead.[78]

A vast amount of undercover work was done by Dutch resisters, as it had been done in the autumn by Belgian, as the advance swept forward from Wesel towards the Baltic: providing up-to-the-minute information on where the enemy was and what he was doing, mopping up parties not disposed of by the main advance, guarding – eventually, herding – prisoners, preserving bridges and locks. 'In nearly all the liberated towns and villages', SOE's reports for the week ending 15 April remarked, 'order has been maintained by Resistance leaders who have taken over control of their respective areas.'[79]

Two more 'Jedburgh' missions dropped in the first week of April: 'Gambling' on 3/4 and 'Dicing' on 7/8. J. S. S. Menzies, 'Gambling's' W/T operator, had been in one of Gubbins's independent companies as far back as 1940; had served nearly three years in Gibraltar, as a secret wireless operator; and had been on one 'Jedburgh' mission already, into the Indre et Loire, on which – as in 'Gambling' – he behaved calmly under pressure. His commander, A. H. Clutton, born in 1898, was old enough to be his father; had fought as a gunner officer on the western front in 1916–18; and had passed the 'Jedburgh' training board with a plus mark for every quality except 'He is fond

---

76. *Ibid.*, 212–13, and see page 425.
77. Cp page 349.
78. De Jong, *KdN*, ix(ii). 952, 1029.
79. CAB 121/319, 5, duplic; several reports in HQ 248.

of risk and adventure.'[80] Knottenbelt, who had made his first jump on the first day of 'Market Garden' with the 'Clarence' team, was their interpreter. They dropped east of Amersfoort, with three SAS companions; they all had a fairly hectic fortnight before the allied armies overran them.

Robert Harcourt, who had been up at Cambridge before he went into the Royal Armoured Corps, led 'Jedburgh' team 'Dicing'.[81] He had an interesting, but rather accident-prone, war. He had been with a 'Phantom' squadron, signals specialists, in Sicily; and had dropped into the Var with the 'Cinnamon' team the night before operation 'Dragoon', the Franco-American invasion of the Riviera coast of France. It was a bad drop; Harcourt broke both his legs, and could only be a liability to his friends.[82] They hid him safely; he recovered, and went up to Ringway to do one more jump to make sure he was fit to go back to the field.[83]

'Dicing' was to have dropped into the Veluwe on the same night as 'Gambling', to a nearby field; which was surrounded by German troops that evening, so the reception committee had the good sense to go back home. 'Dicing' was rapidly re-briefed, to land near Assen on 7/8 April 1945 with an awkward task: to act as a sort of connecting file between the local resistance groups and two squadrons of French SAS, who were to operate (as 'Amherst') in the same area of Drenthe at the same time.

Harcourt's thirteenth drop was not his luckiest. One of his companions, Bestebreurtje, on his third mission, broke an ankle on landing. Harcourt happened upon him at the edge of the DZ, hid him a few yards away in a wood, but shortly thereafter was boxed in by German patrols and taken prisoner. He narrowly escaped being shot at once, and was despatched to Marlag/Milag Nord near Bremen, which was soon overrun by the Guards Armoured Division. His bad luck continued to dog him: his captors removed the 15,000 gulden he had on him. ('I omitted', he reported wryly afterwards, 'to

---

80. Jottings in their PFs.
81. Snapshot in Noel Annan, *Changing Enemies,* after page 114; sharp comment *ibid.*, 213.
82. France 173/26.
83. STS 51 report, 25 March 1945, Holland 26.

obtain a receipt.')[84] At least he was still alive when Marlag/Milag Nord was overrun.

The third officer in the team, Ruysch van Dugteren, kept – against orders, of course – a diary, which is in print.[85] With stout local help, including that of the police, he managed to hide Bestebreurtje; helped Somers the wireless operator, who had been on team 'Simon' in France, to report the local states of chaos; had three days' street fighting in Groningen; and emerged having liberated a motorcar of Seyss-Inquart's with bullet-proof windows.

The French SAS teams who operated into the north-eastern Netherlands in the closing stages were all on their second mission, and were all disagreeably surprised to discover that working beside these Dutch civilians was quite unlike working beside the French, their comrades on their previous venture. They inclined to blame their heavy casualties on Dutch treachery or Dutch cowardice;[86] not having taken in that those with whom they now had to work had become cautious, after twice as long an occupation as Vichy France had known, and under much closer Gestapo watch.

One of N's last drops was a tragedy. On 11/12 April Johan Greydanus ('Jingle') and his W/T operator, Frans Dekker ('Whistle'), jumped south-west of Hilversum, with a Dutch intelligence agent named by de Roever as E. W. Janzen.[87] Dekker fell, up to his neck in water, into a polder ditch, from which the reception committee hauled him out. Greydanus's body was found some days later in the nearby lake, his parachute still packed on his back; Janzen's body, also drowned, turned up a day later. Dekker worked at de Vos's elbow for the few remaining days of occupation.[88]

Another drop, on the same night, was much more of a clandestine success. Hendrik Geysen ('Scream') was to see what he could do to save the great bridge over the Maas at Moerdijk. He rapidly talked his way so deep into the confidence of the local Gestapo that he was able

---

84. His report of 12 May 1945, *ibid.*
85. De Roever, *op. cit.*, 250–3.
86. Report by Harcourt of 'Dicing', 12 June 1945, in Holland 26.
87. De Roever, *op. cit.*, 232.
88. *Ibid.*, 234–5; Greydanus PF.

to discover their plans to blow the bridge up, to form local teams that were able to counteract them, and to provide valuable data for allied counter-intelligence teams after the liberation.[89]

Anton Gehrels ('Grunt'), who had already done a short mission into the Achterhoek, the back corner of Holland east of Zutphen, from 17/18 March till he was overrun on All Fools' Day, went back again by parachute on St George's Day, 23 April, to work near The Hague. He found all the local resisters more interested in politics than war. 'No material was dropped to them and GRUNT felt extremely disgruntled.'[90] He was not the only one: the war in Holland ended not with a bang, but a whimper.

In mid April 1945, in a gesture of infantile bravado – compare the Iraqi firing of Kuwaiti oil wells in 1991 – the Germans pierced the dykes at the north-west corner of the Zuyder Zee, to flood the Wieringer polder: then the newest and richest patch of land reclaimed from the sea in the kingdom. They created lesser floods also east of Amsterdam and north of Zwolle, in attempts to use back against the allies the tactics of flooding on which the Dutch had relied, with equal lack of success, in 1940.

Right at the end, in April 1945, SOE's effort into Holland brought in a dividend that mattered. SOE provided the channel – Borghouts – through whom Eisenhower negotiated direct with Seyss-Inquart the conditions under which the German garrison in the western Netherlands was to surrender unconditionally. There was no repeat this time of the fumbling that had dragged on for weeks (again, much of it through an SOE channel) over the Italians' sur-render:[91] the Third Reich was crumbling too fast. The Germans' bluff, in the full Rauter tradition, that they would flood out North and South Holland, and most of the province of Utrecht as well – leaving the three million inhabitants to survive in the dunes if they could – was called.[92]

---

89. De Roever, *op. cit.*, 220–2.

90. History cx, April 1945, 4.

91. See Dodds-Parker, *Setting Europe Ablaze*, 136–42; C. M. Woods, 'A Tale of Two Armistices', 1-6, in K. G. Robertson (ed.), *War, Resistance and Intelligence* (Barnsley: Leo Cooper, 1999).

92. Telegrams in HQ 248.

At the very end, internal and external resistance met. With a faint echo of Leclerc's armoured division liberating Paris, the Prinses Irene Brigade provided the first allied troops to enter The Hague. At every point of importance, they found a uniformed German soldier, with a resister beside him; usually with one weapon between them – who carried the weapon depended on individual character.

There was a severe final awkwardness between Prince Bernhard and General Foulkes, the allied corps commander on the spot. The prince was of course anxious that his resisters, who had suffered for so long, should have their moment of triumph; the general, aware how cut off the German forces were by now from any reliable news or orders, was anxious to avoid trouble. The general won: resisters were ordered not to carry weapons for a couple of days. This caused much heart-burning, but could not be helped. 'They should realise', the prince wrote later, 'that as soldiers they, as well as us, had to carry out orders issued to us, however unpleasant they might be.'[93]

On 21 August 1944 Gubbins had sent a circular to all his country section heads. He was most anxious, he said, that the fate of all those who had worked 'so devotedly and gallantly' for SOE, and had fallen into enemy hands, should be cleared up; this was to take second priority only to actual operations. 'I want every effort to be made so that we should not fail those who have served us so well'; for the dead deserved eventual recognition as much as the living deserved rescue.[94]

There was nobody in N or T section with the energy, the character or the personality of Vera Atkins, who spent many months in the ruins of Germany ferreting out who had done what to the missing agents of F section, many of them her personal friends. The fate of the missing Dutchmen and Belgians remains, in a few cases, obscure.

Repeatedly, in chaotic Europe at the war's end, contradictory reports came in about the whereabouts, even the fate, of particular agents; to the confusion of dwindling staff and to the distress of their families and friends.

---

93. History cx, May 1945, 5.
94. 21 August 1944, copy in North Africa 32.

This happened, for instance, with Jordaan ('Trumpet'), who for some reason now obscure had been separated from the main body of the victims of 'North Pole' and put into Sachsenhausen, west of Kassel. He was mis-reported to have been in Oranienburg in April 1945. In fact he had been packed off by train to Mauthausen, in a cattle truck with 180 men in it, without food or water: nine of them died during the six-day journey. He missed the executions in Mauthausen, but had the ordinary run of bestial bullying and over-crowding. In a foul-mouthed community, he continued to follow Christ's advice, and swore not at all.[95] Exhaustion and dysentery carried him off on the night of 2/3 May 1945, shortly before the Americans freed the camp.[96]

Cnoops, who was in all three, reported in the summer of 1945 that the camp at Vught was a great deal worse than the nearby camp at Haaren; and that Sachsenhausen was a great deal worse than either. Sachsenhausen indeed, though less of a name in this country than Belsen or Auschwitz, was down on that level of iniquity; as was Mauthausen, to which the bulk of the 'North Pole' victims were dispatched, *Rückkehr unerwünscht* – not required back. None of them had the personality of Brigadier 'Trotsky' Davies, captured on an SOE mission in Albania, who talked the commandant at Mauthausen into treating him and his batman as prisoners of war.

The truth about how frightful the concentration camps had been was at once apparent. When Belsen and Buchenwald main camps were liberated by British and American forces in April 1945, there was an instant, worldwide, major sensation, which resounds to this day. How such camps were run, indeed what they were for, are more complicated questions, to which the answers have taken longer to emerge. Two of the world's most powerful propaganda organisations are still currently involved: the ex-Soviet bloc, seeking to play down the part that communist prisoners took in governing the camps, and world Jewry, seeking to stress the sufferings of the Jews – which were indeed appalling, far worse than anyone else's – to such an extent as to obscure the very existence of non-Jewish prisoners.

---

95. Matthew v. 34.
96. TSC of letter from his father to W. E. Mills, 26 October 1945, in his PF, quoting evidence of C. Vroligk his camp companion.

Those who survive this sort of ordeal are never quite the same again. Even if they have the cultural energy of a Trix Terwindt, who retired from a further career as an air hostess to try to carve herself out a place as a novelist, they will go through agonies, as she did; many subside into a lasting gloom, broken by occasional tempests of rage.

Todd took part in a long march across Germany, from Schubin in Poland to Hammelburg, north of Würzburg; was liberated by an American tank unit on 27 March 1945; went straight back into action with them that evening; and was at once recaptured. He finally escaped on the last night of April.[97] Everyone who had dealings with him testified to his bravery and resource; among many brave men, he remained undecorated.

The shower of DSOs that descended on F's agents did not fall on the Low Countries; for intelligible reasons. A single DSO went to a Belgian subaltern, Antoine Lambrecht, who had been the secret army organiser in Limburg, with 7,000 men under his command; had stormed Hasselt prison on 10 June 1944, at the cost of thirty-five German and five resisters' lives, releasing many Belgian political prisoners; and had lost his own father and two brothers when his headquarters was attacked by the Germans on 30 June.[98] Floor also had a DSO; de Liedekerke, Wendelen, Livio, Reniers and del Marmol all received well-earned military crosses.[99] So, in N section, did Mulholland.

There was a much brisker distribution of awards in the Order of the British Empire, and of King's Medals for Courage; and the two general officers who were deep in resistance, Pire and Ganshof van der Meersch, both became honorary Commanders of the Bath.

There is an absurd story, once touted in the press on the authority of E. H. Cookridge, that Christmann received a British decoration for the work he was supposed to have done moving escapers from Holland and Belgium down to Spain. Christmann

---

97. Reports by Todd, 26 May 1945, and Knottenbelt, undated; both duplicated on Gronewoud's PF.
98. TSC of citation in HQ 215(i).
99. Rea to Belgeonne, copy to Gubbins, 13 February 1946; TS in Belgium 243(i).

himself, whose profession it had been for some years to tell lies – he was a *Sonderführer* in the Abwehr, used by Giskes to penetrate several resistance movements – modestly admitted to the French in the course of a long deposition that he had been awarded the Victoria Cross.[100] There is not a shred of evidence in the British files that the British ever awarded him anything. Amies, Brook and Gubbins, cross-questioned twenty years later, all agreed that they had never heard of such a thing;[101] and it may be written off as another of the resistance myths that sensible readers can discard.

Christmann said, under questioning by the French at the end of the war, that the SD in France watched the arrivals and departures by Déricourt's supposedly secret air line with care, but made no arrests: in order to protect the security of 'North Pole': until Gilbert Norman was arrested by an over-zealous clerk in mid-June 1943. This would carry more conviction had Christmann not claimed, almost in the same breath, to have been in charge of 'North Pole' himself; and had several F section agents not been arrested before Norman, on leads-in presumably provided by Déricourt. The incident may also be written off as one of the false trails laid by captured German secret service officers who felt the truth was better left hidden.[102]

On 8 May 1945 Prince Bernhard sent a teleprint to Mockler-Ferryman:

> SPLENDID RESULTS ACHIEVED BY OUR INTERIOR FORCES ARE DUE TO VERY LARGE EXTENT TO THE ORGANISATION AND GUIDANCE FROM YOUR HQ COMMA FOR WHICH THESE FORCES AND I ARE EXTREMELY GRATEFUL ALSO ON THEIR BEHALF I SHOULD LIKE TO EXPRESS OUR APPRECIATION TO ALL YOUR PERSONNEL FOR THE GREAT WORK THEY HAVE DONE STOP THE COOPERATION WITH

---

100. 17 May 1946, page 29 of a 41-page sworn statement; copy in his PF.
101. Note by Boxshall to Foreign Office, 3 June 1966.
102. Audition chez le Capitaine Trossin de Christmann, cote 57; photocopy TS, no date; a reference owed I believe to Pierre Reynaud.

YOU WAS ALWAYS IDEAL FOR WHICH I WANT TO
THANK YOU PERSONALLY STOP

On the last day of the month Eisenhower wrote to Gubbins, praising
the 'very considerable part' resistance had played in the allied victory
and expressing his 'great admiration for the brave and often spectacular exploits of the agents' working under SFHQ.[103]

Though the war in Europe was over, Japan went on fighting. For
the Dutch, as well as the British, there were large imperial assets still
at stake – a point on which the passionately anti-imperialist
Americans did not see eye to eye with their allies. Several of SOE's
agents in Europe, such as 'Pointer' and the tireless 'Toad', volunteered for further secret service in Asia. One of them, Vickery who
had been lightly wounded on 'Stanley II', was killed in a take-off
crash on 1 April; the rest came back.

On 4 August 1943 Hambro had laid down, at one of his weekly
meetings of directors and regional heads, that it was going to be
essential for SOE to retain, or rebuild, an effective underground
organisation in each liberated territory, at least 'until all danger of re-
occupation by the enemy or internal disturbances were past'.[104] If
anything got done on this front in Belgium or Holland, no trace
remains in the surviving papers.

Cost-effectiveness, that accountants' shibboleth, is not to be valued
solely in terms of cash. Yet after SOE was disbanded, in January
1946, its tidying up party handed over to the Treasury a sum of several million pounds,[105] clear profit: perhaps, in the secret service
world, unexampled. It can be said with confidence that none of this
profit was earned in the Low Countries, which – financially as well
as tactically – were more often a liability than an asset.

Much of the wartime tension petered out in squabblings over
pension rates, how much back pay was due, and who ought or ought
not to be decorated. One of the best of DF's W/T operators, for

---

103. Tpt and duplic in HQ 248.
104. HQ 12.
105. Private information.

example, Robert Chapman, who had worked with distinction for 'Vic', turned out in spite of his English name to be a Belgian citizen, born in Antwerp in 1901, and some of DF's time in the spring of 1945 was taken up with listening to Chapman's complaints, supplying him with clothing coupons and arranging his demobilisation.[106]

In the late 1940s, a sub-branch of the Belgian Ministry of Defence filled three fat files with letters to former heads of resistance movements, with their replies; inquiring, on duplicated or printed forms, why particular sums of money – specified down to the last centime – had been stolen during the war by bodies of armed men from particular post offices, post vans or railway stations. As Mr Gladstone would have said, Bureaucrats are.

One T agent gave another a lift down to the French Riviera for an autumn holiday, travelling in uniform so that they could use service petrol. They were unable to explain satisfactorily either to the French customs authorities, or to service police, how they came to be driving a smart little red sports car that had belonged to a leading collaborator; this was a row that rumbled on for months after the end of the war.[107]

In the general joy that came with the end of the war in Europe, the plight of the western Netherlands got overlooked. By mid-April 1945 the entire official food ration for a day supplied only 400 calories. In the words of a bleak official inquiry by a team of Oxford doctors immediately after the liberation, 'This was inadequate for existence.'[108] (In the Warsaw ghetto, two years earlier, the official ration supplied 184 calories a day; life on boiled hay turned out just to be liveable, for a while.)[109] Sixteen thousand Dutch citizens died of hunger during that last winter and spring. Moreover, the end of the war did not bring the end of suffering.

The very last food ration – a kilogram of potatoes a head, and a little bread – was issued on 29 April. The Germans did not surrender till 4 May; not till 10 May were local officials, themselves debilitated

---

106. Clandestine Communications 41.
107. PF of one of the agents concerned.
108. Dr H. Sinclair quoted in *Malnutrition and Starvation in Western Netherlands* (The Hague, 1946), 155.
109. Joe J. Heydecker, *The Warsaw Ghetto* (I. B. Tauris, 1990), 4.

by hunger, able to arrange to distribute the food that various allies – the British especially – had anxiously provided. Hundreds of men and women who had survived to the bitter end thus perished as a freer age dawned.

SOE was able to take a part in the arrangements for food to be dropped in from the air, by daylight; 161 squadron was delighted to play a part in this.[110]

Wars often bring on revolutions; even in steadfast Great Britain the war brought a marked political shift to the left. In Belgium by contrast the war's aftermath tended to the conservative side, once the forces of the FIL had been confronted and disarmed by Pierlot's returning cabinet, backed by a gendarmerie just armed by SOE and by Erskine's army of occupation. Martin Conway's summary repays study.[111]

At the war's end, the Republic of Indonesia was proclaimed in the Dutch East Indies. The new British government, strongly anti-imperialist, had as one of its main aims the winding-up of British rule in India; and did not go out of its way to afford facilities to the Dutch to attempt to regain their own Asiatic empire. This has left some lasting resentment in the Netherlands, the main bar to close and placid Anglo-Dutch relations; and had an odd repercussion on resistance history and myth-making.

By a displacement of anxiety, some Dutchmen transferred their anger at British inactivity in Indonesia into all sorts of accusations about British misbehaviour in secret affairs during the war. The finest Dutchmen, it was said, had been lured to their deaths – deliberately betrayed to the Gestapo – to secure Britain's predominance over Holland in times to come. This odious fabrication, eagerly taken up by some journalists, was given an extra twist by the allegation that SIS knew all about the *Englandspiel*, but had sacrificed SOE's agents to safeguard its own: another odious fabrication, that particularly exasperated Cordeaux.[112]

---

110. Telegram in HQ 248.
111. Gill Bennett (ed.), *The End of the War in Europe 1945* (HMSO, 1996), 117–38.
112. Private information.

At least the Low Countries were spared civil war, which ravaged pre-war Spain, wartime Yugoslavia and post-war Greece. Antagonisms, though strong, were not pursued beyond the flash-point of violence: a tribute to the equable temper of most of the citizenry, to placid Christian belief and to parliamentary monarchy.

Gubbins retired, with a KCMG, to a new career in textiles and to unobtrusive caring for his former agents. Barry, his chief of staff, was for many years joint master of the Hampshire hunt. Nelson never recovered full health. Hambro went back to business, and flourished; Sporborg, general manager of Hambro's bank, flourished also, as did Brook. Amies became Queen Elizabeth II's dressmaker.

Of the surviving agents, Wendelen became an ambassador; Kirschen, doyen of the Brussels bar. A few calm and stout-hearted men, such as Zembsch-Schreve, whom not even Dora could daunt, can say like the Abbé Sieyès '*Moi, j'ai vécu.*'

A deal of mud had been thrown at van 't Sant by the Dutch press in the middle 1930s, when he was covering up for the queen's husband (who died in 1934); some of it stuck. Even during the war, rumours spread round Holland that there was a traitor in Wilhelmina's entourage, and then that it was he who was to blame. He hesitated to go back after Germany's defeat, and was upset that he was not given full clearance by the parliamentary commission of inquiry. He remained close to the royal family, as a private friend; and died in 1966.[113]

Degrelle escaped into Franco's Spain. He was tried *in absentia*, and sentenced to death at the end of 1944;[114] but survived many years, to publish books on the epic of the Waffen-SS, dying eventually on 31 March 1994 – still in Spain.

As a counterweight to the suggestion that some captured N section agents talked too much, when Giskes's wireless expert Huntemann – who no longer had a Reich to defend – gave himself up in Germany in April 1945, he sang as loud as a tame canary: there seemed to be

---

113. De Jong, *KdN*, ix(ii), 811–36.
114. *Grote Winkler-Prins*, vii. 167 (Amsterdam: Elsevier, 1980), dated his sentence on 29 December. *The Times* of the previous day carried a three-line column fill on its third page, giving Reuters' authority for the 27th.

nothing at all that he held back from the Americans or from the British.[115] The junior American officer who had first go at him reported on 4 May 1945, with true professional caution, that 'Subject, who is himself an expert in penetration technique, may now try to penetrate personally the Allied Intelligence Service', and recommended that 'he be watched extremely closely for a long time'.[116]

As Germany collapsed, in mid-April 1945 Giskes dissolved what was left of his FAK, and went to stay with his sister-in-law at Wiehl, a few miles east of ruined Cologne. She went to Wiehl town hall to get a ration book for her guest; and, knowing no better, mentioned to the mayor that he had been quite senior in the Abwehr. That afternoon, 24 April, the American army arrested him; to them, and later to the British, he too talked quite freely.[117] He had done all that a competent security officer should, without ever going beyond the limits of legal or decent conduct; and so was released, without trial, to the Dutch. They held him for a time, and then also released him.

Dutch post-war policies hardly affect this book. After the trauma of occupation, public opinion was ready to accept a new law, which reinstated the death penalty – retrospectively to 1940 – for treasonable activities and for mass murder, if proved before a special court. Under this law, both Ridderhof and van der Waals – after protracted trials – were executed. Lindemans killed himself, and a fresh girlfriend, while awaiting trial.[118]

Seyss-Inquart, a defendant at the principal trial of major war criminals at Nuremberg in the autumn of 1945, was one of the eleven leading men sentenced to death by hanging.[119] Goering cheated the hangman by committing suicide the night before the execution; Seyss-Inquart went with the rest. Christiansen, at the age of sixty-nine, was given a twelve-year sentence for three proved atrocities, carried out by men under his command.

The Dutch also tried some of the lesser fry. Mussert for example,

---

115. Lengthy interrogations in Holland 22.
116. *Ibid.*, page 10 of a 28-page duplicated report issued by First US Army.
117. His PF.
118. Some old hands believe his sudden death was not suicide (conversation with Zembsch-Schreve, June 1998).
119. Nuremberg Trial, xxii. 519–21, 529.

captured by the British at Utrecht, was found guilty of high treason on 12 December 1945, and shot in the dunes by Scheveningen, where so many Dutch had been murdered by the nazis, on 7 May next year. Harster, Rauter's subordinate in charge of security and Jew-baiting, was perhaps lucky to escape with a twelve-year sentence; while May the wireless expert was perhaps unlucky to encounter one as severe as ten. Both had been captured at the surrender of The Hague.

May claimed he went back to Haaren, just in case, at the end of the first week of April 1945, and burned all the remaining papers he could find;[120] the exploit is improbable, as the area had for some months been in allied hands.

The Dutch tried and condemned May for an offence that had nothing to do with coding or with SOE. It was proved against him that in April 1942 he had formed one of a small execution squad under *Obersturmbannführer* Deppner, who told him he must behave as an SS-man too and needed toughening up. The squad shot some seventy Mongol prisoners of war from the Red Army, four at a time, down into a ditch near Amersfoort. May had taken care, on the way to the killing ground, to make his own sub-machine-gun unusable, and did not himself fire a shot; but had to admit he had been present.[121] In 1949 he was given a ten-year sentence, backdated to 1945.

Poos and Slagter – both now dead – were each sentenced to twenty years, and each served twelve.

Giskes himself, in retrospect, thought that resistance had played a large part in the defeat of the German armies in France and Belgium.[122] His own and Schreieder's counter-espionage skills had ensured that Holland was not added to that list. The opinion, from one of Europe's leading experts on the subject, is worth more attention than it is ever likely to get from staff college lecturers still obsessed by Clausewitz's obsolete opinions of the low value of amateur patriot forces.

Schreieder was found hiding in North Holland province by the Canadian army in late May 1945. He turned out even more talkative than Huntemann or Giskes, rattling off the names and particulars of former colleagues by the score. When the Canadians and the British

---

120. *Enq.*, iv B. 19.
121. RIOD Doc. I-1103.
122. Camp 020 interim report on Giskes, July 1945, 12; duplic in Holland 22.

had quite finished with him, he was handed over to the Dutch; who heard him at length at their commission of inquiry.[123] They then put him on trial; where his friends in the SD, and even his enemies, stood by him. Harster, with whom he had worked in close contact for seven years, testified that he had taken part in no atrocities – not in the *Kristallnacht* of November 1938, the nazis' dress rehearsal for worse things to come, or in any persecutions of Jews or of prisoners, of whatever nationality. From the other side, Beatrix Terwindt bore witness that his behaviour to her had been entirely correct; he had even attended to a complaint from her about the food at Haaren. Thereafter, for all the *Englandspiel* prisoners, it had improved. He too was brought before the special court; on 31 January 1949 it let him go free.[124] He was still in good voice when BBC television interviewed him forty-five years later.

Rauter's fate was different.

The Canadian army found him in a hospital in north-west Germany, still prostrate after the attack on the Wustehoeve for which he had exacted such a price. The Canadians handed him over to the Dutch; who, once he had recovered, assembled the special court to try him. All through his trial, though he had little doubt of the sentence, he remained an unrepentant nazi. Harster was allowed a quarter of an hour with him the afternoon before he was shot, and noticed he was perfectly self-composed. At his special request, early on 25 March 1949 he went to his death neither bound nor blindfolded, and gave the order to the firing-squad himself.[125]

Churchill, relaxing out of office after six years' severe strain, visited Holland in May 1946, with his wife and his youngest daughter. They went at the queen's invitation, and stayed with her, calling also on Princess Juliana and Prince Bernhard in their country palace at Soestdijk. Everywhere, they were rapturously received. On the 9th he went to the Binnenhof at The Hague, where the SD had planted their headquarters; and became the first foreigner ever to address the States-General. Next day he went to Leyden, where he received an honorary doctorate of laws. Did anyone then remember that it had been Taconis's university?

---

123. See appx 5.
124. RIOD Doc. I-1529 ab.
125. *Het proces Rauter, ad fin.*

Appendix 1
Chronology

DATE	GENERAL	HOLLAND	BELGIUM
30 Jan. 1933	Hitler in power in Germany		
17 Feb. 1934			Leopold III king
10 Dec. 1936	George VI king		
11 March 1938	Germany annexes Austria		
29 Sep.	Munich agreement		
14 March 1939	Czechoslovakia dismembered		
22 March	Germany annexes Memelland		
23/24 Aug.	Nazi-Soviet pact		
1 Sep.	Germany attacks Poland		
3 Sep.	Great Britain and France declare war on Germany; U-boat sinks liner *Athenia*		
27 Sep.	Germans in Warsaw		
28 Sep.	Nazi-Soviet friendship treaty		
9 Nov.		Venlo incident	
11 Jan. 1940			Malines incident
9 April	Germany attacks Denmark and Norway		
10 May	Churchill prime minister		Germany attacks Low Countries

DATE	GENERAL	HOLLAND	BELGIUM
13 May		Queen moves to England	
15 May		Dutch army surrenders	
28 May			Belgian army surrenders; king stays in Belgium
31 May	Dunkirk evacuated		Limoges meeting denounces king
3 June			
11 June	Italy declares war on France and Great Britain		
14 June	Germans in Paris		
17 June	French request armistice		
18 June	De Gaulle founds Free French movement		Maurice Simon sails
22 June	Franco-German armistice		
29 June	USSR occupies Bessarabia		
10/11 July			Burggraeve's landing fails
14 July	USSR annexes Baltic states		
19 July	Chamberlain signs SOE's charter	CID set up under van 't Sant	
22 July	War cabinet approves SOE		
Aug.	Nelson CD		
27/28 Aug.		van Driel sails	
3 Sep.		Gerbrandy cabinet sworn in	
12 Sep.	Italy invades Egypt		
17 Sep.	Hitler postpones 'Seelöwe'		
25 Oct.			Pierlot reaches London
11 Nov.	Battle of Taranto		
18 Nov.	Gubbins joins SOE		

DATE	GENERAL	HOLLAND	BELGIUM
9 Dec.	Wavell attacks in Egypt		
19 Dec.			T set up under Dadson
20 Dec.		N set up under Laming	
22 Jan. **1941**	Australians in Tobruk		
6 Feb.	British in Benghazi		
15/16 Feb.	SOE's first air drop, into Poland		
25–26 Feb.		Strike	
11 March	US congress approves Lend-Lease		
15 April			Hermie sails
27 April	Germans in Athens		
12 May			Tromme drops
20 May	Germans attack Crete		
24 May	*Hood* sinks		
27 May	*Bismarck* sinks		
22 June	Germany attacks USSR		
1 July		'Rhodium' fails	
6/7 July			Fr Jourdain drops
11 Aug.	Atlantic Charter signed		
12 Aug.			Campion drops
19 Aug.		Derksema heads CID	
7/8 Sep.		Homburg & Sporre drop	
19 Sep.	Germans in Kiev		
3 Oct.			Cassart & Verhaegen drop
7/8 Nov.		Taconis & Lauwers drop	

DATE	GENERAL	HOLLAND	BELGIUM
1 Dec.			Knight T
7 Dec.	Japanese attack Pearl Harbor		
8 Dec.	USA & Great Britain declare war on Japan		Neufchâteau incident
10 Dec.	*Prince of Wales* sinks		
11 Dec.	Germany declares war on USA		
19 Dec.		Blizard N	
20 Dec.		BVT set up under de Bruyne	
20 Jan. **1942**	Wannsee conference		
28 Jan.			Wendelen drops
5 Feb.		De Bruyne also heads CID	
17 Feb.		Homburg in Yarmouth	
23 Feb.	Dalton succeeded by Lord Wolmer (soon Lord Selborne)		
27/28 Feb.	Bruneval raid	Dessing drops	
1/2 March			Passelecq drops
2/3 March			De Liedekerke drops
6 March		Lauwers arrested	
9 March		Taconis arrested	
March	Hambro CD		
27/28 March	St Nazaire raid	Baatsen drops	
28/29 March		Andringa & Jordaan drop	
1 April		Plan for Holland in draft	
30 April			
27 May	Heydrich mortally wounded		Deflem's party killed in action

DATE	GENERAL	HOLLAND	BELGIUM
1 June	CIGS circular on SOE	Van 't Sant heads CID	
2 June	Battle of Midway begins		
4 June	Lidice massacre		
9 June	Germans in Tobruk		
21 June			
26/27 June		Jambroes drops	
1 July	First battle of El Alamein begins		
4 July	Convoy PQ17 scatters		
10 Aug.		Lovink heads CID	Claser flown to Gibraltar
12 Aug.			
19 Aug.	Dieppe raid		
22 Aug.			
24/25 Sep.		'Kale' drops	compulsory labour instituted
18 Oct.	Hitler's commando order		
24 Oct.	Second battle of El Alamein begins		
8 Nov.	Anglo-American landings in NW Africa		
11 Nov.	Germans invade southern France		
16 Nov.			Livio drops
28 Nov.		BI (Broekman) replaces CID	
29/30 Nov.		Ubbink drops	
20 Dec.			Durieux drops
23 Jan. **1943**	British in Tripoli		
2 Feb.	Germans in Stalingrad surrender		
13/14 Feb.		Trix Terwindt drops	

DATE	GENERAL	HOLLAND	BELGIUM
24 Feb.		Blizard outposted	
9/10 March		Dourlein drops	
1 April		Bingham N	Frenay & Woluwe drop
13 April	Warsaw ghetto rising		
19 April			
late April		Strike	
3 May	Allies in Tunis		
21/22 May		Last *Englandspiel* drop	
5 July	Battle of Kursk begins		
10 July	Allies land in Sicily		
15/16 July		Somer heads BI	De Liedekerke's second drop
21 July			'Stanley' mission begins
25 July	Mussolini deposed		
Aug.			Amies acting T
11/12 Aug.			Wendelen's second drop
17 Aug.	Peenemünde raid		
23 Aug.	Russians retake Kharkov		
29 Aug.		Ubbink & Dourlein escape	
3 Sep.	British land in Italy	Dessing reaches UK	
Sep.	Gubbins CD		
8 Sep.	Italy changes sides		
9 Sep.	Salerno landings		
18/19 Sep.		Cnoops drops into France	
18 Oct.			Fr Carez drops

DATE	GENERAL	HOLLAND	BELGIUM
6 Nov.	Russians retake Kiev		Johns becomes T
20 Nov.		Ubbink & Dourlein in Berne	
22 Jan. **1944**	Anzio landings		
1 Feb.			De Liedekerke's third drop
8 Feb.		Ubbink & Dourlein in UK	
26 Feb.	Johns becomes DR/LC	Dobson N	Amies T
3/4 March			Livio's second drop
15 March		BBO replaces MVT	
31 March		Biallosterski & Celosse drop	Frenay's & Woluwe's second drop
1 April		Giskes pulls N's leg	
10 April	Russians retake Odessa		
11/12 April			Floor drops
20 May			Floor in UK
4 June	Allies in Rome		
5/6 June	'Overlord' begins		
8 June			secret army called up
13 June	V1 attacks begin		
13 July	Russians in Vilna		
20 July	'Valkyrie' fails		
1 Aug.	Warsaw rising begins		
4 Aug.		Frank family arrested	
4/5 Aug.	Franco-American landing in Riviera		
15 Aug.			Wendelen's third drop
19 Aug.	Paris rising begins		

DATE	GENERAL	HOLLAND	BELGIUM
25 Aug.	Allies in Paris		
29 Aug.	Slovak rising begins		
3 Sep.			Allies in Brussels
4 Sep.			Allies in Antwerp
5 Sep.		'Mad Tuesday'	
5 Sep.		Benelux treaty signed	
6–7 Sep.		Mauthausen massacre	
8/9 Sep.	V2 attacks begin	Biallosterski's second drop	
10 Sep.		Brinkgreve drops	Allies in Liège
14 Sep.		Allies in Maastricht	Allies in Luxembourg
17 Sep.		'Market Garden' begins	
26 Sep.		Arnhem evacuated	
3 Oct.	Warsaw rising ends		
21 Oct.	Americans in Aachen		
12 Nov.	*Tirpitz* sinks		
18/19 Nov.		Tazelaar & Faber drop	
28 Nov.			Antwerp port reopens
16 Dec.			Ardennes attack begins
27 Dec.			Degrelle sentenced to death *in absentia*
17 Jan. **1945**	Russians in Warsaw		
7 Feb.		new Dutch cabinet	
23 Feb.		Brinkgreve shot	
5 March			new Belgian cabinet

DATE	GENERAL	HOLLAND	BELGIUM
6/7 March		Rauter wounded	
7 March	Americans take Remagen bridge		
10/11 March			
23 March	Battle of Wesel	Jos Gemmeke drops	
3/4 April		'Gambling' drops	
4 April		Canadians in Zutphen	
7/8 April		'Amherst' & 'Dicing' drop	
12 April	Roosevelt dies		
16 April		Canadians in Groningen	
28 April	Mussolini shot		
30 April	Hitler kills himself		
4 May	Lüneburg Heath surrender		
7 May	Reims surrender		
8 May	Berlin surrender		
26 July	Attlee prime minister		
6 Aug.	Hiroshima bombed		
9 Aug.	USSR declares war on Japan		
14 Aug.	Japan surrenders		
2 Sep.	Tokyo Bay surrender		
15 Jan. 1946	SOE disbanded		
7 May		Mussert executed	
17 Oct.		Seyss-Inquart hanged	
March 1947		Ridderhof executed	

DATE	GENERAL	HOLLAND	BELGIUM
May 1948		Christiansen sentenced	
25 March 1949		Rauter executed	
26 Jan. 1950		Van der Waals executed	
31 March 1994	T. A. Robertson dies		
14 May			Degrelle dies in Spain

Appendix 2

Partisan Leader's Handbook

[This pamphlet, of forty small pages – it measured four inches by five and a third (106 × 134mm) – was written by Gubbins in the spring of 1939 as a tactical guide to sabotage agents.[1] The spelling is his compositor's. He never needed to revise the text. It was translated into many languages, and copies of it have travelled all over the world.]

PRINCIPLES OF GUERILLA WARFARE AND SABOTAGE.

1.   Remember that your object is to embarrass the enemy in every possible way so as to make it more difficult for his armies to fight on the main fronts.

You can do this by damaging his rail and road communications, his telegraph and postal system, by destroying small parties of the enemy, and in many other ways which will be explained later.

Remember that everything you can do in this way is helping to win freedom again for your people.

2.   You must learn the principles of this type of warfare, which are as follows:—

    (a)   Surprise is the most important thing in everything you undertake. You must take every precaution that the enemy does not know your plans.

    (b)   Never engage in any operation unless you think success is certain. Break off the action as soon as it becomes too risky to continue.

---

1. HQ 64, MI(R) Functions and Organisation.

(c)   Every operation must be planned with the greatest care. A safe line of retreat is essential.

(d)   Movement and action should, whenever possible, be confined to the hours of darkness.

(e)   Mobility is of great importance; act therefore where your knowledge of the country and your means of movement — i.e., bicycles, horses, etc. — give you an advantage over the enemy.

(f)   Never get involved in a pitched battle unless you are in overwhelming strength.

(g)   Never carry incriminating documents on your person nor leave them where they can be found.

The whole object of this type of warfare is to strike the enemy, and disappear completely leaving no trace; and then to strike somewhere else and vanish again. By these means the enemy will never know where the next blow is coming, and will be forced to disperse his forces to try and guard all his vulnerable points. This will provide you with further opportunities for destroying these small detachments.

3.   **Types of Operations.** — Operations can be divided into two main types:—

(a)   Those of a military nature which entail the co-ordinated action of a certain number of men under a nominated leader.

(b)   Individual acts of sabotage, of sniping sentries, etc., for which men can be specially selected to work individually in certain areas.

For action of a military nature the choice of suitable leaders is of great importance. A leader must have courage and resource, he must be intelligent and a good administrator and be a man of quick decision. He must know intimately the country in which he is operating, and should be able to use a compass and map. The sort of man required is the type whom other men will willingly accept to lead them in dangerous actions, and whose personality will hold them together.

The size and composition of guerilla parties must depend on the nature of the country and the hold which the enemy has over it. It must be remembered that the speed of modern communications, i.e., motors, wireless, etc., and the presence of aeroplanes make it very difficult for a large party to remain concealed for any length of time. Parties should therefore number between 8 and 25, depending upon the work to be done; such parties can move quickly and yet hide themselves fairly easily. Under specially favourable conditions, it may be possible to collect several parties together, up to 100 men or more, for some important undertaking. In such cases, however, the arrangements for dispersal after the operation must be made with special care.

4.   Modern large-sized armies are completely dependent on roads, railways, signal communications etc., to keep themselves supplied with food, munitions and petrol, without which they cannot operate. These communications therefore form a most suitable target for guerilla warfare of all kinds, and any attack on them will at once force the enemy to disperse his forces in order to guard them. Communications are open to attacks both of the military and sabotage type. Attacks can also be directed against small detachments of the enemy, stocks of food, munitions, etc., and many other objects.

5.   Military action is employed when it appears that damage can only be inflicted if force has to be used first:

The following are types of military action:—

(a)   Destruction of vital points on roads, bridges, railways, canals, etc., when action by an individual employing secret means would not be effective. If a hostile guard has first to be overpowered, or work preliminary to destruction requires a considerable number of men, the project must be undertaken as a military operation.

(b)   The raiding and destruction of hostile mails, either in lorries or trains.

(c)   The destruction of enemy detachments and guards.

(d)   The organization of ambuscades of hostile troops and convoys travelling by road or train.

(e)   The destruction of stocks and dumps of food, petrol, munitions, lorries, etc., by first overpowering the guards on them.

(f)   The seizure of cash from hostile pay-offices etc. ETC. ETC.

6.   Military action is greatly facilitated by the support of the local population. By this means, warning can be obtained of all hostile moves, and it will not be possible for the enemy to carry out surprise action. It is therefore important to endeavour not to offend the people of each district, but to encourage their patriotism and hatred of the enemy. Successful action against the enemy will breed audacity and force the people to take note and respond. Their response in the first instance should be directed to the supply

of information about the enemy, his strength, movements, etc., and to assistance in the concealment of compatriots who are taking part in guerilla warfare. In effect, the people must be taught to boycott the hostile troops completely, except as may be necessary to obtain information. This can best be done by convincing them that the enemy's occupation is only temporary, that he will soon be ejected, that those of the people who have helped will then be rewarded, but that those who have fraternized with the enemy will be ruthlessly punished. The question of 'informers' and traitors who are in league with the enemy is dealt with later.

7.   The areas most suitable for military action are those where cover, such as rocks, trees, undergrowth, etc., give a concealed approach to the object or detachment to be attacked. Such cover not only provides an opportunity for attack without discovery, but also for getting away safely when the attack is completed. In all such attacks, it is important that sentries should be posted on all approaches to give warning of any possible surprise by the enemy; it is not necessary that all these sentries should be armed men, in fact it will frequently be of advantage to use some women and children, who are less likely to be suspected. A simple code of signals must be arranged.

Every operation of this nature must be most carefully planned. When some particular operation has been decided upon, the locality must be thoroughly reconnoitred, and the enemy's movements in the vicinity should be systematically studied and noted over a period of days, with special reference to such points as the following, where applicable:—

(a)   Hours when sentries are relieved, and how relief is carried out.

(b)   Total strength of guard or detachment.

(c)   How and when do supplies for the guard arrive? Are civilians allowed to enter the post?

(d)   Where do men not on sentry-go keep their rifles? Are these rifles chained up or in plain racks?

(e)   Are men allowed to leave the position for short periods?

(f)   How often are guards inspected, by whom and at what times?

(g)   What means of communication for the post exist, i.e., telegraph, motor-cycle, or cycle messengers, carrier pigeons, etc. Can these be destroyed?

(h)   Do mails or small detachments of men follow regular routes at fixed times, giving opportunities for ambushing?

(i)   Do these detachments have sentries, advance parties, etc., or do they proceed in one group?

(j)   Are motor vehicles fitted with bullet-proof or puncture-proof tyres, armoured sides, etc.?

(k)   What special tools and explosives, if any, are required for the operation, and what amount?

Examples of such operations are given at the end of the book.

8.   Sabotage deals with the acts of individuals or small groups of people, which are carried out by stealth and not in conjunction with armed force. These undertakings, however, frequently produce very valuable results and, like military action, force the enemy to disperse his strength in order to guard against them. The following are examples of this type of work:—

(a)   Jamming of railway points.

(b)   Destructive work on roads, railways, canals, telegraphs, etc., where this can be done by stealth.

(c)   Firing of stocks of petrol; burning garages, aeroplane hangars, etc.

(d)   Contamination of food, of forage, etc., by acid, by baccilli, poison, etc.

(e)   Contamination of petrol by water, sugar, etc.

(f)   Destruction of mails by burning, acids, etc.

(g)   Shooting of sentries.

(h)   Stampeding of horses.

(i)   Use of time bombs in cars, trains, etc. ETC. ETC.

9.   Sabotage to be effective requires the same degree of careful preparation as does military action. The first point is to choose an objective which has some value, even if it is only the sniping of a sentry or the firing of a stack of forage. Such shootings mean that the enemy must double his sentries or risk their loss; such destruction means more guards. So more troops have to be used, and this is one of your objects.

The next step must be to study the place and conditions, so that the most favourable moment for success can be selected. A sure line of retreat, or an alibi, must be arranged beforehand. Often it will be necessary to wait a fortnight or longer before the right opportunity presents itself. At the same time, however, it may be necessary at times to carry out sabotage on the spur of the moment without previous preparation, for example when a convoy of lorries arrives unexpectedly in a village, and there is a chance of setting one on fire. Such opportunities should not be missed. It is certain that the enemy will force a proportion of the inhabitants to work for him in mending roads, loading and unloading trains, and other works of a military nature. Such working parties provide good opportunities for sabotage by time bombs, by acids and other devices.

10. **Organization:—**

(This particular pamphlet is intended simply for the use and instruction of guerilla 'parties'. The higher organization of guerilla warfare throughout a whole country or region is dealt with in the manual 'The Art of Guerilla Warfare').

In the early stages of guerilla activities, before hostile counter-measures have become intense, it will be possible for the members of a party to live independently in their own villages and homes and carry on their normal occupations, only collecting when some operation is to be undertaken. The longer they can go on living in this way the better. When the enemy begin to take active measures to prevent guerilla warfare by raids on suspected houses, by arresting suspects, etc., it will eventually be necessary for the guerillas to 'go on the run' — i.e., to leave their houses and live out in the country, hiding themselves by day, and moving at night. The number of men 'on the run' in any one party must depend on the nature of the country. If it is wild, hilly, and forested, it may be possible for parties of up to 100 strong to avoid detection for long periods. If the country is flat and featureless and cultivated, it may be difficult for even one man to remain undetected for long. The organization must therefore depend on the country; the wilder it is the closer can the organization be — i.e., the leader has his men closely under control all the time, and the party moves from place to place, as necessary, to carry out operations or avoid capture. In less favourable country, the organization must be looser and men must be collected for action by secret means. If and when the enemy's activities make it too dangerous, for the time being, to continue, the men should leave their area, and join parties operating in more favourable conditions. These latter parties must always serve as a rallying point for men who have been forced by danger of arrest to 'go on the run', for deserters from the enemy, and escaped prisoners.

The 'leader' is responsible for the organization; the importance of selecting only men who are reliable and resourceful is thus paramount.

11. **Information:—** If you can keep yourself fully informed of the enemy's movements and intentions in your area, you are then best prepared

against surprise, and at the same time have the best chance for your plans to succeed. The enemy is handicapped in that his men must wear uniform and are living in a hostile country, whereas your agents wear ordinary clothes and belong to the people and can move freely among them. Therefore, make every use of your advantage in order to obtain information. Suitable people must be selected from among the inhabitants to collect information and pass it on; these should be people who are unfit for more active work, but whose occupations or intelligence make them specially suitable for the task. The following are types who can usefully be employed:—

(a)   Priests.

(b)   Innkeepers.

(c)   Waitresses, barmaids, and all café attendants.

(d)   Domestic servants in houses where officers or men are billeted. These are a very useful source.

(e)   Doctors, dentists, hospital staffs.

(f)   Shopkeepers, hawkers.

(g)   Camp followers.

These people must be trained to know what sort of information is required; this is most easily done by questioning them on further points whenever they report anything, as they will then learn to look for the details required (see example at the end of the book). They must also be trained to be on the look-out for enemy agents disguised as compatriots.

It is important that as little as possible of this information should be in writing, or, if it is in writing, that it should not be kept any longer than necessary. All papers, documents, etc., dealing with intelligence or your organization in any way, must be destroyed immediately you have finished with them, or kept in a safe place until destroyed.

It has been proved over and over again in guerilla warfare that it is the capture of guerilla documents that has helped the enemy most in his counter-measures. These have been captured either on the persons of guerillas, or seized in houses that have been raided. The utmost care is therefore necessary.

12.   **Informers:—** The most stringent and ruthless measures must at all times be used against informers; immediately on proof of guilt they must be killed, and, if possible, a note pinned on the body stating that the man was an informer. This is the best preventive of such crimes against the homeland.

If it is widely known that all informers will be destroyed, even the worst traitors will hesitate to sink to this depth of perfidy, whatever the reward offered.

If a person is suspected of being an informer, he can be tested by giving him false information, and then seeing if the enemy acts on it. If the enemy so acts, such evidence is sufficient proof of guilt, and the traitor must be liquidated at the first opportunity.

13.   **Enemy Counter-Measures and their frustration:—** The best means of defeating the enemy's counter-measures is by superior information which will give warning of his intentions — i.e., of raids against suspected houses, of traps he may lay, of regulations he proposes to enforce in the territory he occupies, etc. Attempts to bribe the people must be met by the measures shown in paragraph 12 above.

Certain counter-measures, however, can only be met by special action; for instance, the use of identity cards, which the enemy is certain to introduce when guerilla warfare becomes active, in order to assist him in tracing the guerillas. It will then be necessary to obtain or copy the official seals and stamps so as to provide identity cards for the guerillas.

When the enemy finds that passive means are insufficient to defeat guerilla operations, he will resort to active measures. These will probably take the form of mobile columns of considerable strength, horsed or in motors, including armoured cars and tanks, with which he will make sudden sweeps, often by night, through the various parts of the country. The bigger the column, the easier it is to obtain information about its projected movements, and it may even prove possible to combine several parties together and destroy it. If, however, the enemy's measures are so comprehensive as to lead to unnecessary risk, it will often be better for the guerillas to lie quiet for a month or so, or move to another district.

14.   **Conclusion:—** All guerilla warfare and sabotage must be directed towards lightning strokes against the enemy simultaneously in widely distant areas, so as to compel him to weaken his main forces by detaching additional troops to guard against them. These strokes will frequently be most effective when directed against his communications, thus holding up supplies and eventually preventing him from undertaking large scale operations. At the same time, however, action should be taken against detachments, patrols, sentries, military lorries, etc., in such a way that the whole country is made unsafe except for large columns and convoys. This will hamper the enemy's plans effectively.

The civil population must be made to help by refusing to co-operate with the enemy, by providing information about the enemy, and by furnishing supplies and money to the guerillas. If they suffer inconvenience from your activities, either directly or as a result of enemy counter-measures, it must be explained to them that they are helping to defeat the enemy as much as their army at the front. The bolder the activities of the guerillas, and the greater the impunity with which they can act, owing to their careful planning and superior information, the more will the population despise the enemy, be convinced of his ultimate defeat, and help the guerillas.

Remember that you are fighting for your homeland, your mother, wife and children. Everything you can do to hamper and embarrass the enemy makes easier the task of your brothers-in-arms at the front who are fighting for you. As your activities develop, the enemy will become more and more ruthless in his attempts to stop you; the only effective reply to this is greater ruthlessness, greater courage, and an even wider development of your operations. Your slogan must be 'Shoot, burn and destroy'. **Remember that guerilla warfare is what a regular army has always most to dread. When this warfare is conducted by leaders of determination and courage, an effective campaign by your enemies becomes almost impossible.**

ROAD AMBUSH   Appendix I.

1. **Planning.**

   (a)   Find out by what roads small detachments and patrols of the enemy are accustomed to move. Select on one of these roads a locality which offers a good opportunity for ambushing.

2. **Locality.**

   The following points should be looked for in selecting the locality for the ambush:—

   (a)   A line of retreat must be available which will give all the men a safe and sure way of escape. A thick wood, broken and rocky country, etc., give the best cover.

   (b)   Firing positions are required which enable fire to be opened at point-blank range. When there is no chance of prior discovery by the enemy, it may sometimes be of advantage to improve the position by building a stone or sandbag parapet. This should not be done, however, unless it can be concealed from aircraft.

(c)   The locality should provide at least two fire positions and it is often better if these are on opposite sides of the road.

(d)   It is best if the fire position enables the approaching enemy to be in view for three or four hundred yards. By this means it can be discovered in time if the enemy is in greater strength than expected; in such a case the enemy should be allowed to pass without being attacked.

3.   **Information.**

Then get the following information:—

(a)   Do the detachments move on foot, mounted, or in motor vehicles?

(b)   What is the average strength of these detachments? How are they armed? How many vehicles?

(c)   Do they use armoured cars and light tanks to patrol the roads?

(d)   At what times do they pass the place you have chosen?

(e)   Do they move in one block, or do they put men out in front and behind to guard against surprise? How do these men move, and how far from the main body?

(f)   How will they try to summon assistance if attacked? Where is the nearest place such assistance can come from?

(g)   If the detachment is carrying supplies, are those supplies of a type which can be easily destroyed by you, or be of use to you?

(h)   What sort of troops are they, active or reserve, elderly, young, or what? Is there an officer with them? Can he be picked out and shot by the first volley? Can the N.C.Os be picked out as well?

4.   **Action.**

(a)   The men must get into position without any chance of discovery. If there is any doubt, the position should be occupied by night.

(b)   Sentries must be posted to give warning of the enemy's approach. They must be in sight of the firing position. It is not necessary to use guerillas for all sentry posts; a woman or child can sometimes be employed with advantage as they need not be in hiding.

(c)   A simple system of signalling by sentries must be arranged. This can be the removal of a hat, doing up a shoelace or any natural action of that nature.

(d)   If the enemy detachment is preceded by scouts, or a scouting vehicle, these should be allowed to pass on and not be fired at. Sometimes, however, it may be advantageous to place one or two guerillas further on from the firing position to shoot these scouts. **They must never be fired on, however, before the main attack begins; the guerilla leader must make certain this is known and understood.**

(e)   The leader must give the signal to open fire. This can either be pre-arranged or given at the moment. Fire must be rapid fire, so as to have an immediate overwhelming effect.

(f)   Two or three of the best shots must be detailed to shoot any officers or N.C.Os. If these cannot be recognised by their uniform, they can be discovered by noting who is shouting orders, etc.

(g)   If the enemy appears to be destroyed, and it is intended to destroy or loot any cars or lorries, men for this task must be detailed beforehand. The rest must remain ready to open fire in case enemy are concealed in the lorries, or reinforcements arrive.

(h)   The leader must give the signal to retire, and this signal must be unmistakeable.

To judge the correct moment to break off the action is the leader's most difficult task. If the opening volleys of fire have not disorganized the enemy, it will probably be better to retire immediately, and be content with the damage done. If, however, the enemy detachment is completely destroyed, the opportunities should always be taken to seize all rifles, ammunitions, etc., and destroy or loot all other material. All papers and documents found should be taken away for examination. The dead must be searched for anything that may be useful.

(i)   Remember that soldiers will always face the direction from which they are being fired at. It is usually best therefore to divide the party into two groups, on different sides of the road, of which only one group should fire first. The enemy will then face towards this group and start to attack and fire. The other group must then shoot the enemy in the back.

(j)   **Sentries must remain in position until the leader gives the signal to retire.**

(k)   Retirement when begun should be as rapid and dispersed as possible, i.e., the party must break up, and collect again as the leader may have ordered. Make full use of the time until the enemy hears of the attack to get right way from the scene.

(l)   All wounded guerillas must be carried away if possible. It may be useful to have a few horses hidden at a short distance to carry wounded.

5.   Road Blocks.

The use of road blocks by means of trenches, felled trees, rocks, etc., in conjunction with an ambush must be carefully considered.

At the commencement of guerilla warfare, before the enemy has had experience, it may be useful to have a block at the place of ambush, so as to force lorries to halt. When, however, the enemy is experienced, he will use scouts and patrols on all roads, and these will be warned by the blocks and so warn their detachments. A stout wire rope fastened across the road after scouts have passed, at a suitable height to catch the motor driver, is a useful device.

If it can be arranged to have mines or bombs buried in the road which scouts will not see, these are of great assistance in demoralising the enemy. Fire should not be opened until the mine has been exploded under the enemy. Here are details of road mines:—

(1) **Crater or Land Mine:**— 60 lbs. of high explosive buried 5 feet deep and fired electrically will produce a crater 25 feet across which will wreck a tank, armoured car, etc., completely. All traces of the digging must be obliterated carefully to avoid the enemy locating the ambush by scouts on motor-cycles. The digging for this reason should be done outside the tarred area of the road but close to it. If done overnight and watered as soon as filled in, the traces of excavation can best be obliterated. The debris from the explosion will be thrown as far as 200 yards. Men in ambush 100 yards away, behind cover, are sufficiently protected, however. A crater so formed, if in a defile, is an impassable obstacle to tanks. The method of laying the charge is as follows:—

A hole 5 feet deep is dug and 60 lbs. of explosive in its paper wrapping is placed in the bottom. The paper wrapping of one packet is broken and an electric detonator is inserted, dug well into the explosive itself. Two wires, 100 yards in length, are joined to the two ends of wire projecting from the electric detonator. If the ground is wet, these joints must be protected with insulating tape or some other covering. Care must be taken that the two joints do not touch. The long wires are then led away to a distance and hidden where necessary in a shallow trench. When the two outer ends of the wire are connected to the terminals of an ordinary car battery the charge will be exploded.

(2) **Small Land Mine:—** A charge of 10 lbs. of high explosive with not more than 6 inches of earth covering will blow the track off a tank or the wheel off a lorry passing over it. The road should therefore be partially blocked by a broken-down farm cart or other means so that all traffic is forced to proceed through a very limited gap. The charge should be placed as in the preceding paragraph, but may be fired from a distance of 25 yards. Care must be taken to judge the exact moment the wheel of the vehicle passes over the charge.

(3) **Hand Bombs:—** These are of two sorts, those with a 7 second time fuze and those which go off on impact. The impact bomb is essentially for throwing. The thrower should locate himself behind a wall or other cover, preferably within 10 yards of where the enemy vehicle will pass. The bomb will smash through any metal it is in contact with on impact, but will have little effect on a vehicle elsewhere. It should therefore be thrown to hit the side or tracks of a tank or the wheel of a vehicle. The time bomb is most effectively used for the destruction of any machinery or vehicles in which it is placed or thrown.

6. **Remember:—**

   (a)   Let scouts pass.

   (b)   Use your best shots to kill any officers, N.C.Os and drivers of vehicles immediately.

   (c)   Armed sentries must remain at their posts until ordered to retire.

   (d)   Any looting or destruction must be protected by men ready to fire.

RAIL AMBUSH. **Appendix II.**

In general the rules for road ambushes apply to rail ambushes, so read them and make certain you understand them.

The difference between a rail ambush and a road ambush is that in a rail ambush you must combine some plan to wreck the train, either by derailing it, by blowing a mine under the engine, or other means. **It is not sufficient merely to shoot at the train; this would do more harm than good and must be avoided.**

   (1)   The principle is first to derail the train and then shoot down the survivors.

(2)   Choose some place which is suitable for wrecking, for example a high embankment where the falling engine will drag the coaches down with it; or a bridge, where the train will, with luck, fall into the river.

(3)   Do **not** choose a place where trains run slowly; the faster the train is going, the better results you will get.

(4)   The coaches at the rear of the train will probably suffer least damage; your first volleys should be directed against them.

(5)   It is best to dispose your party in two groups, as in a road ambush, on opposite sides of the train.

(6)   The signal to shoot will be when the wrecking starts or the mine is exploded. Everyone must start firing immediately.

(7)   The train must not be looted until you are certain that all resistance by the enemy is at an end. After looting, it should be set on fire.

(8)   If the train is armoured, and the wrecking has not been severe, it may be better to retire immediately. An armoured train will usually have many machine-guns with it.

Read again the rules for a Road Ambush and apply them to this case.

Here are some methods of derailing a train:— To derail a train with certainty, both rails must be cut. This can be done very easily in the following ways:—

(1)   One pound of high explosive pressed hard against the side of each rail.

(2)   Three pounds of high explosive placed against the under side of each rail.

(3)   Ten pounds of high explosive buried under the ballast not more than 4 inches from each rail.

(4)   A single charge of fifty pounds of high explosive buried three or four feet deep between the rails. This will lift the locomotive ten feet into the air and is the best way where no bridge or steep slope can be found.

If the derailing is done by methods (3) or (4), or where the ballast has been allowed to come close up under the rails by method (2) as well, it will be possible to lay the charge so that it will be undetected by day. Care must be taken not to show any signs of digging. A tin of water should be carried to wash down the stone ballast and clean it of earth adhering to it when using methods (3) or (4).

In all cases, it is best to fire the charge under or just in front of the front wheels of the locomotive. This can be done in two ways:—

(a)   By means of an electric detonator with long wires leading to a battery where a man is concealed to operate it at the right moment.

(b)   By means of a striker machine which is buried under a sleeper next to a rail joint. The weight of the locomotive passing over releases a striker which fires the charge by means of an instantaneous fuze.

In both cases, the detonator must be buried firmly in the explosive. When a battery is used, great care must be taken that the battery does not come near the ends of the wire till the last moment, to avoid accidents.

A length of wire up to 100 yards may be used leading away from the explosive to a hidden spot where it is fired. Insulated wire such as is used for electric light in houses must be used. The accumulator battery out of a car is best but a good hand torch dry battery will do.

Diagrams of methods (1) and (2) of cutting rails:—

Method (1).

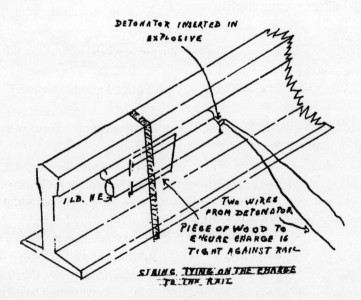

Method (2).

Detonator and wires to battery should be arranged as in Method (1).

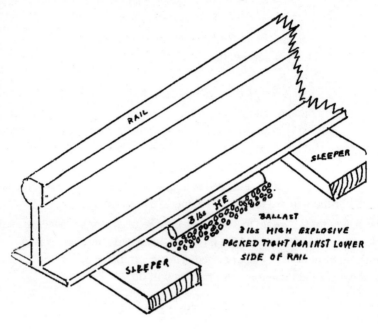

Method of connecting electric detonators.

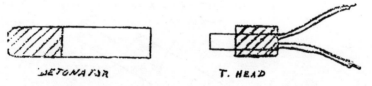

The electric detonator is in two parts:—

(1)   The detonator, which is a small copper tube closed at one end and open at the other.

(2)   The T head, which has two wires sticking out of one end and a very thin bridge of wire like the filament of a lamp the other. The filament end of the T head is pressed into the open end of the detonator. When an electric current passes through the filament it gets red hot and burns away completely but in doing so ignites the detonator.

When wires are joined together or to the T head or battery, the covering must be cut away and the metal cleaned bright by scraping with a knife. The wires may then be twisted together. The bare wire at a joint must never touch anything, especially another joint. It is best to bind insulating tape or a piece of cloth round the joint. The joining of the wires for two charges fired by one battery is shown below.

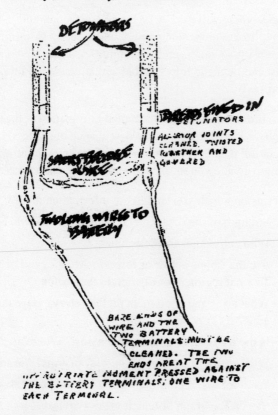

Destruction of Railway Engines:—

(1) If you have no explosives, run off most of the water in the boiler and bank up the fire. The fire box, no longer cooled by the water, will get red hot and the steam pressure will bend it in.

(2) If you have explosives, make it up into one pound packets each with a hand bomb time striker mechanism. This mechanism will explode the charge six seconds after the pin is pulled out. The best places to put these charges are on any of the large machined portions of the engine which the hand bombs will cover and are not more than 1″ thick. If the engine is cold, open the smoke box in front and put a charge just inside one of the tube openings.

THE DESTRUCTION OF AN ENEMY   Appendix III.
POST, DETACHMENT OR GUARD.

1.   The object of this can be either to inflict casualties on the enemy, or to carry out the destruction of some place which the detachment is guarding.

2.   The detachment will usually be housed in a small house, hut, or tents, and will have taken steps to try and make these safe against attack. Remember, however, that if you use cunning, patience, and determination, no small post can be made impregnable and at the same time do its job of protection properly.

3.   **Information:**— You must get detailed information of the posts in your area, and then decide which offers the best chance of success. It may not be possible to get full details of all, but you will get enough information about some of them to enable you to select one and carry out a successful attack.

4.   The points on which you should get information are:—

(a)   Strength of the detachment, number of officers, N.C.Os etc.

(b)   Who commands the detachment?

(c)   Are the troops active or reserve? Are they old or young men? To what regiment or district do they belong?

(d)   What arms and equipment do they carry? Have they machine-guns?

(e)   Is there a reserve of arms in the post? Where are they kept?

(f)   What are the orders for safe custody of arms? Are any locked up?

(g)   What means of communication has the post got — i.e.

(i)   Telegraph or telephone or wireless.

(ii)   Signal flags.

(iii)   Rockets.

(iv)   Pigeons.

(v)   Sirens, hooters.

(vi)   Messengers.
ETC.

Can any of these be destroyed when necessary?

(h)   What sentries does the post provide —

(i)   On the railway, bridge, or store it is guarding?

(ii)   On the post itself?

(i) At what hours are sentries relieved —

(i) By day?

(ii) By night?

(k) How is relief carried out?

(l) Is there a group of men in the post always ready for immediate action? How strong is it?

(m) How long is each sentry's beat? What are its limits?

(n) What places can these sentries not see except by going to them?

(o) Are any civilians allowed to approach or enter the post, selling food, papers, etc.? Can you use any of these civilians to get information?

(p) Are there any searchlights in position?

(q) Is the post protected with barbed wire? Is this wire electrified? How do soldiers get in and out?

(r) Where does the post get its water supply from? Can the source of water be destroyed?

(s) How often is the post and its guard inspected by someone from outside?

(t) How far away is the nearest reinforcement, and how long would it take to come? Can it be ambushed on the way by another party?

(u) Can your destructive work be undertaken while the post is being fired at, or must the post first be destroyed completely.

(v) Can the post be blinded by smoke bombs for long enough to allow the destruction to be done?

(x) Are there watch-dogs, alarm traps, etc.?

ETC. ETC.

5. **Plan:**— This must depend on the information collected regarding the daily life and habits of the post, the state of alertness of the guard, its strength, armament, etc.

If the post is very small — say six to eight men — it may be possible to capture it by getting one or two men inside to seize the arms and hold up the guard at the moment the sentries are shot; on the other hand, it may be possible to rush the post from outside after shooting the sentries, to surround it and cut all communication, and shoot down all the men inside. It will also frequently be practicable to carry out destruction by one group while the other group of the party prevents the enemy of the post interfering. This depends to some extent on how long the destruction will take.

If the post is large, it will probably not be possible to destroy it. In such cases, if you wish to carry out some really important destructive work, it should be attempted by masking the post with heavy fire, smoke, etc. Such an attack has usually most chance of success when carried out by night.

In every case of an attack on a post, your first care must be to arrange for the destruction of means of communication — i.e., telegraph, wireless, etc. — unless you have a plan to ambush reinforcements.

Do not alarm any post that you mean eventually to attack — i.e., do not allow men to snipe it, to cut off its water supply, etc. Leave it absolutely quiet until the moment for attack comes. This will put the enemy off his guard.

CONCEALMENT AND CARE OF ARMS AND EXPLOSIVES.   Appendix IV.

Try and get your arms before the enemy invades your country, so that you can conceal them more easily and at leisure.

1.   One of the first acts of the enemy will be to demand the surrender of all arms held by the civil population.

2.   All arms, bombs, etc., which are concealed must be protected against damp, rust, etc.; remember that your life and that of your friends may depend on a weapon in good order. The best way of preserving rifles, revolvers, etc., is to cover them with mineral jelly or vaseline, and wrap them in greasy paper or cloth. They may then be safely buried.

3.   Places where arms can be concealed are:—

    (a)   In the ground by burying. Choose a place where the earth has already been turned, or else go far away into a wood, etc.

    (b)   In the thatch or roof of a house.

    (c)   In a well-shaft, by making a chamber in the wall six feet or more down the shaft.

    (d)   In the banks of streams, in hollow trees, behind a water-fall, etc.

(e) In haystacks, potato or turnip heaps, ditches, culverts, etc.

(f) Do **not** use places like cellars, wooden floors, cattle sheds, etc., which the enemy is bound to search.

(g) As a last resort, give them to your women if caught unexpectedly.

4. You must make every effort to obtain arms and ammunition from the enemy during ambushes, raids, sniping, etc., as it will be difficult in time of war to replenish your stock by other means. Boxes of rifles and ammunition are frequently transported by rail and in lorries, inadequately guarded: find out when these are being carried and try and get them.

Be very cautious of buying arms from a supposed enemy traitor. This is a common way of inducing you to walk into a trap.

THE ENEMY'S INFORMATION SYSTEM AND HOW TO COUNTER IT.
Appendix V.

As soon as guerilla warfare or sabotage commences, the enemy will set up an information organization in order to try and find out your organization, leaders and intentions.

The methods he will employ are as follows:—

(1) Local agents, selected from amongst the inhabitants, and either bribed or compelled to act for him.

(2) Agents recruited from his own or other countries and imported into your area.

These two types of agents can only be discovered by very careful work on your part, by getting information regarding arrivals of unknown people, by laying traps for suspected agents, etc.

(3) Special information branches that he will form.

(4) Captured prisoners and their interrogation.

(5) Captured documents which may reveal details of your organization, plans, names of partisans, etc. It is most important that no documents should be kept unless absolutely essential, and these should never be carried on the person for longer than necessary. This is usually the enemy's best source of information.

(6) Censorship of civilian letters.

(7) By placing agents among captured partisans. This is a difficult thing to counter and can only be met by strict discipline among the partisans in the prisons and concentration camps. They should be trained never to talk about their military matters, to mention names, or to give away any information at all. Steps must be taken within prisons by the partisans to test and try out every prisoner who comes in, to make absolutely certain that he is not an agent in disguise.

(8) **Listening sets:—** These will also be placed in prisons and camps, so all conversation must be restricted to general matters and nothing said which might lead to the capture or death of your compatriots.

(9) Men who are captured must at once organize themselves in the prison to censor all their own letters that they are writing to friends outside, and to censor all incoming letters to individual prisoners.

(10) The best method of dealing with informers is their ruthless extermination when discovered, as described in the main part of this book.

(11) Prisoners who are being interrogated may be tempted by the fact that there is only one enemy in the room to give away information if pressed, as they may feel that only one person will know it. All men must know that this is not correct; not only will the enemy instal listening sets in the room in which the prisoners are interrogated in order that two or three people may hear any confession, but also all the information a prisoner gives, and his name and district, will be taken down in writing and distributed everywhere. His comrades would then eventually discover his treachery and he would be dealt with suitably when the enemy has been defeated.

You must try and break up or hinder the enemy's information organization by all means. The most effective is the destruction of the personnel engaged on that work. Intelligence officers, N.C.Os, etc., frequently work individually and move about the countryside. Opportunities must be sought to kill them and destroy or carry off any papers they are carrying.

HOW TO COUNTER ENEMY ACTION.   **Appendix VI.**

The enemy will make use of his superior armament to try and break up guerilla activities. Here are some of the methods he will employ, and ways for you to counter them.

(1)   **Aeroplanes:—** These will be used to search the country for guerilla parties, and possibly also to attack them. The best counter is concealment, therefore move as much as you can by night. By day, on the approach of an aeroplane, men must be taught to get under whatever cover is available, **and to lie still with faces to the ground**. Movement and human faces show up to aeroplanes at once.

Do not fire at an aeroplane unless actually attacked by it. Remember that an aeroplane, if it sees you, will at once report your position to the nearest military detachment who will come out after you. Therefore, if you think your party has been seen, move off at once to some other place, and keep a good look-out.

(2)   **Tanks, armoured cars, armour-plated lorries etc.:—** Do not shoot at these haphazardly, it will have no effect unless you have anti-tank rifles and bombs, etc. You must lay a proper trap if you are trying to destroy them — i.e. a road mine or block, or the vehicle must be halted. Remember that these vehicles shut down their windows when attacked, and are then very blind; it will then be possible for bold men to crawl close enough to bomb them or set them on fire with petrol.

(3)   **Gas:—** The enemy will only use gas if he gets you in a corner and other methods fail.

Therefore your first precaution must be to avoid being caught where you cannot get away. Your information of the enemy's plans and proper posting of sentries and look-outs when the party is collected will prevent you being caught. If you hear that the enemy intends using gas against guerillas, all men should provide themselves with gas-masks.

(4)   **Shells, bombs, grenades:—** Against these weapons the best protection is to be down flat behind any cover available, such as a bank, ditch, etc.

(5)   **Machine-guns, etc.:—** Smoke bombs can be used to create a smoke screen between yourself and the machine-gun so as to enable you to get away.

GUERILLA INFORMATION SERVICE.   **Appendix VII.**

1.   Early information of the enemy's moves, strength, intention, etc., is vitally important. You must therefore impress on all your compatriots the necessity of passing on to some members of the party the information they hear. The following, owing to their occupations, are in a good position to get news:—

  (a)   Innkeepers, hawkers.

  (b)   Waitresses, barmaids, etc.

  (c)   Postmen, telephone and telegraph operators.

  (d)   Station-masters, railway porters and staffs.

  (e)   Doctors, priests, dentists, hospital staff.

  (f)   Domestic servants, barbers.

  (g)   Shopkeepers, newsagents.

  (h)   Contractors, camp followers, camp sanitary men.

  (i)   All people who have access to military camps, establishments, etc.

  (j)   Discontented enemy soldiers.

2.   Domestic servants and café attendants are particularly valuable agents; they must be encouraged to gain the confidence of the enemy soldiers, and be on easy and intimate terms with them. Suitable agents of this type should be introduced into houses where enemy officers are billeted, etc. It is a natural weakness of soldiers in a hostile country to react favourably to acts of courtesy and kindness from women; such men will frequently drop unsuspecting hints that they are shortly going on patrol, etc. The agent must then find out as much detail as possible and pass it on at once.

3.   Discontented soldiers must be discovered, i.e., those who have recently been punished, have had their pay stopped, etc. These, if encouraged, may give useful information.

4.   Information should be passed by word of mouth unless that is impossible. If impossible, it must be written and sent by messenger (children frequently make good messengers) or placed in a pre-arranged place, and then destroyed by the recipient.

SABOTAGE METHODS.   **Appendix VIII.**

Sabotage means any act done by individuals that interferes with the enemy and so helps your people to defeat him. It covers anything from the shooting of a sentry to the blowing-up of an ammunition dump. The following are various acts, and the best way of carrying out the difficult ones:—

(1) **Lorries, cars, tanks, etc.:—** Burn them by knocking a hole in the bottom of the petrol tank, and setting fire to the escaping petrol.

If you can't burn them, put water or sugar in the petrol tank, or remove the magneto, etc. This will temporarily disable the vehicle.

(2) **Munition Dumps:—** The best method is to lay a charge of explosive among the shells and then explode it, but it will be rare that you will get an opportunity to do this unless you are disguised as an enemy soldier. There are other ways. If the dump is in a building, a good way is to set fire to the building. Use oil-soaked rags, shavings, thermite bomb.

If the dump is in an open field or by the road, throw a special bomb into it (this must be a bomb with at least one kilo-gramme of explosive in it, and you must hit a shell or it will not be effective).

(3) **Cement:—** Open the sacks, and pour water on them, or leave them for rain and moisture to get in.

(4) **Hay, Forage:—** Burn or throw acid or disinfectant.

(5) **Petrol stocks:—** Use a special bomb or thermite bomb.

(6) **Refrigerator sheds, and refrigerator railway vans:—** Destroy the refrigerating apparatus.

(7) Sniping and killing sentries, stragglers, etc.

Get a rifle or revolver with a silencer, but use a knife or noose when you can. This has a great frightening effect. Don't act unless you are certain you can get away safely. Night-time is best and has the best effect on enemy nerves. Get used to moving about in the dark yourself. Wear rubber shoes and darken your face.

(8) **Telegraph lines on roads and railways:—** Cut these when-ever possible. When you cannot reach them, throw over a rope with a weight on the end and try and drag them down. Cut down a tree so that it will fall across them.

(9)   **Railways:**— Jam the points by hammering a wooden wedge into them. Cut signal wires.

Set fire to any coaches and wagons you can get at. If you can use explosive, try and destroy the points. Remember that railways can carry very little traffic if the signalling apparatus is interfered with, and this traffic must go very slowly.

(10)   **Water Supplies:**— Contaminate water which is used by the enemy. Use paraffin, strong disinfectants, salt, etc.

(11)   Destruction of leading marks, buoys, lightships, etc., in navigable waters.

(12)   **Burning of soldiers' cinemas, theatres:**— Cinema films are highly inflammable. The cinema should be fired during a performance by firing of the films in the operator's box. This should easily be arranged.

(13)   Time bombs, cigar-shaped, are very suitable for placing in trains, lorries, etc. They are made of lead tubing, divided into two halves by a copper disc. Suitable acids are put in each half, and when they have eaten the copper away, the acids combine and form an intensely hot flame, which will set fire to anything with which it comes into contact. The thickness of the copper disc determines when the bomb will go off. Get some of these bombs.

FINIS

Appendix 3

Action Agents Sent to Holland

Almost all these agents went by parachute. Two, Driel and de Haas, went by sea instead. One 'Jedburgh' mission, 'Stanley II', went overland; so did the Belgian W/T operators of the 'Verstrepen' group. SAS are excluded.

All who returned to England before September 1944 did so across Belgium, France and Iberia; except for Homburg, who came by sea.

Those marked R were among the hundreds executed in reprisal for the botched attack on Rauter.

NAME	CODENAME	DATE SENT	ROLE OR REGION	FATE
J. VAN DRIEL[1]		17/18 Aug. 1940	reconnaissance	arrested, released, retired
H. A. HOMBURG	Glasshouse	7/8 Sep. 1941	sea ferry	arrested, escaped; returned Feb. 1942; killed in action in RAF 1 April 1945
C. J. SPORRE	"	"	"	presumed drowned 13/14 Nov. 1941
T. TACONIS	Catarrh	7/8 Nov. 1941	sabotage organiser	arrested 9 March 1942; killed in Mauthausen Sep. 1944
H. M. G. LAUWERS	Ebenezer	7/8 Nov. 1941	his W/T operator	arrested 6 March 1942; survived
		* * *		
G. DESSING	Carrot	27/28 Feb. 1942	reconnaissance	returned to UK Sep. 1943
A. A. BAATSEN	Watercress	27/28 March 1942	sabotage	arrested on landing; killed in Mauthausen Sep. 1944
T. C. ANDRINGA	Turnip	28/29 March 1942	reconnaissance	arrested 28 April 1942; killed in Mauthausen Sep. 1944
J. MOLENAAR	Turnip II	"	his W/T operator	killed himself on landing
G. H. G. RAS	Lettuce	28/29 March 1942	Utrecht	arrested 1 May 1942; killed in Mauthausen Sep. 1944
H. J. JORDAAN	Trumpet	"	his W/T	arrested 3 May 1942; died in Mauthausen 3 May 1945

1. Section D, not N.

NAME	CODENAME	DATE SENT	ROLE OR REGION	FATE
B. KLOOS	Leek	5/6 April 1942	Overijssel	arrested 1 May 1942; killed in Mauthausen Sep. 1944
H. SEBES	Leek II	"	"	arrested 9 May 1942; killed in Mauthausen Sep. 1944
J. H. M. DE HAAS	Potato	18 April 1942	sea ferry	arrested 28 April 1942; killed in Mauthausen Sep. 1944
H. PARLEVLIET	Beetroot	29/30 May 1942	Limburg	arrested on landing; missing, ? killed in Gross Rosen
A. VAN STEEN	Beetroot II	"	his W/T	"
N. KRUYT[2]	Barsac	21/22 June 1942	unknown	survived
J. J. VAN RIETSCHOTEN	Parsnip	22/23 June 1942	S. Holland	arrested on landing; escaped Nov. 1943; recaptured May, shot Aug. 1944
J. J. C. BUIZER	Spinach	"	his W/T	arrested on landing; killed in Mauthausen Sep. 1944
G. L. JAMBROES	Marrow	26/27 June 1942	OD liaison	"
J. BUKKENS	Marrow II	"	his W/T	"
G. J. VAN HEMERT	Leek A	23/24 July 1942	Overijssel	"
K. W. A. BEUKEMA TOE WATER	Kale	24/25 Sep. 1942	OD Liaison	"

2. NKVD, not SOE.

NAME	CODENAME	DATE SENT	ROLE OR REGION	FATE
C. DROOGLEVER FORTUYN	Mangold	"	his W/T	"
R. C. JONGELIE	Parsley	"	OD liaison	"
A. K. MOOY	Cauliflower	"	Lysander ops	arrested on landing; missing, ? killed in Gross Rosen
A. C. VAN DER GIESSEN	Cabbage	1/2 Oct. 1942	S. Holland	arrested on landing; escaped Nov. 1943; recaptured May, shot Aug. 1944
H. R. STEEKSMA	Celery	21/22 Oct. 1942	sabotage	arrested on landing; killed in Mauthausen Sep. 1944
M. KOOLSTRA	Celery II	"	his assistant	"
M. PALS	Pumpkin	"	South Netherlands	"
P. KAMPHORST	Tomato II	"	sabotage	"
J. HOFSTEDE	Tomato	24/25 Oct. 1942	sabotage	
C. C. POUWELS	Tomato III	"	his W/T	arrested on landing; missing, ? killed in Gross Rosen
H. M. MACARÉ	Celery III	"	W/T	"
J. C. DANE	Cucumber	27/28 Oct. 1942	eastern Holland	arrested on landing; killed in Mauthausen Sep. 1944
J. BAKKER	Cucumber II	"	his W/T	arrested on landing; missing, ? killed in Gross Rosen

NAME	CODENAME	DATE SENT	ROLE OR REGION	FATE
A. J. DE KRUYFF	Mustard	28/29 Nov. 1942	reconnaissance	arrested on landing; killed in Mauthausen Sep. 1944
G. L. RUSELER	Broccoli	"	his W/T	"
H. J. OVERES	Cress	29/30 Nov. 1942	secret army organiser	arrested on landing; missing, ? killed in Gross Rosen
J. B. UBBINK	Chive	"	his W/T	arrested on landing; escaped 29 Aug. 1943, returned 1 Feb. 1944
P. KUZNETSOV[3]	Burgundy	"	unknown	arrested July 1943; suicide
		* * *		
BEATRIX W. M. A. TERWINDT[4]	Chicory	13/14 Feb. 1943	escape	arrested on landing; survived Ravensbrück
K. VAN DER BOR	Endive	16/17 Feb. 1943	sabotage	arrested on landing; killed in Mauthausen Sep. 1944
C. E. VAN HULSTEYN	Radish	"	secret army	"
C. C. BRAGGAAR	Parsley A	"	W/T for OD	"
J. C. KIST	Hockey	18/19 Feb. 1943	OD liaison	arrested on landing; missing, ? killed in Gross Rosen
P. VAN DER WILDEN	Tennis	"	his W/T	arrested on landing; killed in Mauthausen Sep. 1944

3. NKVD, not SOE.
4. MI9, not SOE.

NAME	CODENAME	DATE SENT	ROLE OR REGION	FATE
G. VAN OS	Broadbean	"	escape	"
W. VAN DER WILDEN	Golf	"	his W/T	"
P. A. ARENDSE	Seakale	9/10 March 1943	secret army	"
P. C. BOOGART	Kohlrabi	"	"	"
P. DOURLEIN	Sprout	"	"	arrested on landing; escaped 29 Aug. 1943; returned 1 Feb. 1944
A. J. WEGNER	Lacrosse	21/22 April 1943	"	arrested on landing; escaped Nov. 1943; rearrested in Belgium early 1944; killed in Mauthausen Sep. 1944
F. W. ROUWERD	Netball	"	W/T	arrested on landing; missing, ? killed in Gross Rosen
I. VAN UYTVANCK	Gherkin	"	secret army	arrested on landing; killed in Mauthausen Sep. 1944
O. W. DE BREY	Croquet	21/22 May 1943	"	arrested on landing; killed in Mauthausen Sep. 1944
L. M. PUNT	Squash	"	"	"
A. B. MINK	Polo	"	"	"
(1) A. J. M. CNOOPS	Soccer	18/19 Sep. 1943	deliver money	dropped in France; reached Holland; returned 2 Nov. 1943
J. D. A. VAN SCHELLE	Apollo	"	"	shot down in Belgium; escaped; returned 20 Dec. 1943

NAME	CODENAME	DATE SENT	ROLE OR REGION	FATE
T. GRUEN	Brutus	"	press	shot down; escaped; arrested 3 Jan. 1944, released 5 April 1945, overrun
		* * *		
(1) T. BIALLOSTERSKI	Draughts	31 March/1 April 1944	"	returned 9 July 1944
J. A. STEMAN	Bezique	"	his W/T	arrested Feb., released April 1945
N. J. CELOSSE	Faro	"	CS6	arrested 20 May; shot 5 Sep. 1944
J. H. SEYBEN	Ping-Pong	"	his assistant	arrested 10 May 1944, survived
H. A. J. SANDERS	Curling	"	his W/T	arrested 20 May; shot 6 Sep. 1944
(2) A. J. M. CNOOPS	Cricket	"	RVV	arrested 20 May; escaped from Sachsenhausen April 1945
C. M. DEKKERS	Poker	31 May/1 June 1944	railway sabotage	shot down and killed
G. J. KUENEN	Football	"	his W/T	"
L. MULHOLLAND	Podex	5/6 July 1944	RVV	arrested 11 Nov. 1944; sent to Germany; survived
L. A. DE GOEDT	Rummy	"	KP	returned 24 Feb. 1945
A. VAN DUYN	Cribbage	"	his W/T	arrested 19 Dec. 1944; survived
P. J. KWINT	Fives	"	RVV	shot down and killed

NAME	CODENAME	DATE SENT	ROLE OR REGION	FATE
P. VERHOFF	Racquets	"	"	"
J. A. WALTER	Bowls	"	W/T	"
J. BOCKMA	Halma	"	RVV	"
S. POSTMA	Sculling	7/8 Aug. 1944	liaison	arrested 22 Nov.; shot 2 Dec. 1944
H. G. REISIGER	Turniquoits	"	his W/T	arrested 27 Dec. 1944; killed in Neuengamme March 1945
F. L. J. HAMILTON	Rowing	9/10 Aug. 1944	press	survived
ANTONIA M. F. HAMILTON	Tiddlywinks	"	"	injured on landing; survived
J. H. LUYKENAAR	Shooting	28/29 Aug. 1944	Veluwe	came out mid March 1945
J. R. HINDERINK	Hunting	"	Overijssel	came out 5 April 1945
J. BEEKMAN	Charades	"	their W/T	came out 5 April 1945
J. M. VAN DE MEER	Stalking	"	Eindhoven	came out 10/11 Nov. 1944
K. BUITENDIJK	Fishing	"	"	came out 10/11 Nov. 1944
G. KROON	Skating	"	their W/T	injured on landing; captured, died 2 May 1945
(2) T. BIALLOSTERSKI	Draughts	8/9 Sep. 1944	Amsterdam	arrested 10, died of wounds 26 Feb. 1945
P. DE VOS	Backgammon	"	his W/T	overrun May 1945

	NAME	CODENAME	DATE SENT	ROLE OR REGION	FATE
	H. BRINKGREVE	Dudley	11/12 Sep. 1944	'Jedburgh' in Overijssel	shot 5 March 1945
	J. M. OLMSTED[5]	"	"	"	escaped 24 Nov. 1944
R	J. P. AUSTIN	"	"	their W/T	arrested Dec. 1944, shot 4 April 1945
R	W. H. HOOGEWERFF	Coursing	15/16 Sep. 1944	Rotterdam	arrested 2 Feb., shot 8 March 1945
	M. CIEREMANS	Cubbing	"	Utrecht	arrested late Nov. 1944, escaped at once, survived
	G. DE STOPPELAAR	Monopoly	"	Rotterdam	survived
	P. POLAK[6]	Boating	"	Amsterdam	came out March 1945
	J. STAAL	Edward	17 Sep. 1944	'Jedburgh'	soon overrun
	M. C. SOLLENBERGER[7]	"	"	with airborne corps HQ	"
	R. MILLS[8]	"	"	" (W/T)	"
	L. R. D. WILLMOTT[9]	"	"	" (W/T)	"
	J. BILLINGSLEY[7]	"	"	" (W/T)	"
(1)	A. D. BESTEBREURTJE	Clarence	"	'Jedburgh'	wounded, soon overrun

5. OSS.
6. Called Peters by de Roever.
7. OSS.
8. Ex F section staff.
9. Earlier missions elsewhere; later mission for MI9.

	NAME	CODENAME	DATE SENT	ROLE OR REGION	FATE
	G. M. VERHAEGE	"	"	round Nijmegen	"
(1)	W. W. BEYNON[7]	"	"	" (W/T)	soon overrun
	R. K. WILSON	Daniel	"	'Jedburgh'	"
(1)	A. DUBOIS	"	"	round Eindhoven	"
(1)	L. FABER	"	"	" (W/T)	"
	G. W. MASON	"	"	" (W/T)	"
	J. GROENEWOUD	Claude	"	'Jedburgh'	killed in action 19 Sep. 1944
(1)	M. J. KNOTTENBELT	"	"	round	wounded, escaped Sep. 1944
	H. A. TODD[7]	"	"	Arnhem	wounded, captured Sep. 1944, escaped April 1945
	C. A. SCOTT[7]	"	"	" (W/T)	shot 2 Nov. 1944
			* * *		
(2)	A. D. BESTEBREURTJE	Stanley II	3 Oct. 1944	'Jedburgh'	returned Nov. 1944
	P. C. H. VICKERY	"	"	near Tiel	returned Nov. 1944; killed in India 1 April 1945
(2)	W. W. BEYNON[7]	"	"	"	returned Nov. 1944
R (2)	A. DUBOIS[10]	Ham	16/17 Oct. 1944	escape	arrested Dec. 1944, shot 9 March 1945

7. OSS.
10. With MI9.

NAME	CODENAME	DATE SENT	ROLE OR REGION	FATE
R (2) R. HOLVOET[11]	Bacon	"	"	arrested 27 Oct. 1944, shot 10 April 1945
R R. BARMÉ	Trapping	1/2 Nov. 1944	Rotterdam W/T	arrested 2 Feb., shot 8 March 1945
P. DE BEER	Snooker	10/11 Nov. 1944	"	returned late Jan. 1945
(2) P. TAZELAAR[12]	Necking	18/19 Nov. 1944	Friesland	overrun late April 1945
(2) L. FABER	Bobsleigh	"	his W/T	"
(2) J. P. L. VAN DE SPIEGLE[13]	Foxtrot	"	tactical W/T	returned April 1945
(1) S. J. SJOERDSMA	Squeak	5/6 Jan. 1945	Overijssel W/T	overrun early April 1945
(3) F. BECKERS[14]	Kriek	8 Feb. 1945	tactical W/T in Veluwe	overrun 18 April 1945
BOCK[14]		Feb. 1945	tactical W/T	soon returned
GUEUZE[14]		"	"	overrun April 1945
(1) ORVAL[14]		"	"	soon returned
M. VAN DER STOEP	Scrape	27/28 Feb. 1945	Rotterdam	killed in action 11 April 1945
R. L. BANGMA	Whimper	2/3 March 1945	Veluwe	overrun April 1945
J. VAN DER WEYDEN	Snort	"	his W/T	"

11. With MI9; earlier mission for T.
12. Earlier mission for Dutch intelligence.
13. Earlier mission for T; now in Verstrepen group.
14. Verstrepen group.

NAME	CODENAME	DATE SENT	ROLE OR REGION	FATE
B. JOS GEMMEKE	Cackle	10/11 March 1945	workers in Germany	overrun May 1945
(1) A. M. J. GEHRELS	Grunt	17/18 March 1945	Achterhoek	overrun 1 April 1945
(1) W. PLEYSIER	Rumble	"	"	"
J. J. F. BORGHOUTS	Swish	"	western Holland	overrun May 1945
J. TEN BROEK	Ping	"	Rotterdam W/T	overrun 5 May 1945
J. J. WEVE	Hoot	30/31 March 1945	"	overrun May 1945
A. H. CLUTTON	Gambling	3/4 April 1945	'Jedburgh'	overrun 17 April 1945
(2) M. J. KNOTTENBELT	"	"	in	"
J. S. S. MENZIES	"	"	Veluwe (W/T)	"
J. M. CHRISTIANSEN	Hiss	"	N. W. Holland	overrun May 1945
C. DEN DEKKER	Rap	"	his W/T	"
(2) ORVAL[15]		4/5 April 1945	tactical W/T	overrun 6 May 1945
R. A. F. HARCOURT	Dicing	7/8 April 1945	'Jedburgh' in	arrested on landing; released May 1945
(3) A. D. BESTEBREURTJE	"	"	Drenthe	injured on landing; overrun 17 April 1945
C. J. L. RUYSCH VAN DUGTEREN	"	"	"	"
C. C. SOMERS[16]	"	"	" (W/T)	"

15. Verstrepen group.
16. Earlier mission into France.

	NAME	CODENAME	DATE SENT	ROLE OR REGION	FATE
	J. GREYDANUS	Jingle	11/12 April 1945	Hilversum	parachute did not open
	F. DEKKER	Whistle	"	his W/T	overrun May 1945
	W. S. BISSCHOP	Howl	"	Rotterdam	"
	H. GEYSEN	Scream	"	"	"
(2)	S. J. SJOERDSMA	Squeak	"	"	"
(2)	A. M. J. GEHRELS	Grunt	23 April 1945	The Hague	"
	F. J. STUVEL	Fizz	"	"	"
(2)	W. PLEYSIER	Rumble	23/24 April 1945	Amsterdam W/T	"
	W. BOUMA	Gurgle	"	Amsterdam	"
	W. DINGER	Grind	"	"	"
	F. E. M. VAN DER PUTT	Splash	"	"	"
	B. J. A. NIJDAM	Yelp	"	"	"

Appendix 4

Action Agents Sent to Belgium

All but eleven of these agents went by parachute.

Those marked F went into, or at least towards, France, intending to go forward by land.

Burggraeve attempted direct entry by sea. Simon took ship to the west coast of France; Levaque took ship to the West Indies. Hermie and Vergucht went by sea, and Absil by air, to Portugal; Hermie and Absil went on overland, Vergucht went on by air to Berlin and then by land. Claser and Schouten went from Gibraltar to the south coast of France by sea, and then by land. Jeschke and P. Goffin went from Gibraltar by land. Marissal went to France by light aircraft, and then by land.

All but Burggraeve who returned before September 1944 did so through France and Spain; except for about a score, marked A, who came by light aircraft from secret landing strips in France; and for Coyette, who began and ended his second mission overland from Switzerland. SAS, again, are excluded.

Almost all of them had a four-letter code number, preceded by T, with which the reader need not be bothered; listed in Belgium 256.

NAME	CODENAME	DATE SENT	ROLE OR REGION	FATE
F M. J. F. G. SIMON[1]	033	18 June 1940	reconnaissance, propaganda	arrested mid July 1941; joined GFP; absconded mid July, returned 22 Aug. 1942
A. L. BURGGRAEVE[1]	Douane	10/11 July 1940	coast	withdrew after a few steps ashore
J. E. D. LEVAQUE	Association	late March 1941	general	faded out
F G. M. HERMIE	Independence	15 April 1941	communications	changed sides
E. M. J. TROMME	Caesarewitch	12 May 1941	sabotage	arrested 4 Oct. 1941, shot 25 Feb. 1942
F P. J. ABSIL	Silkmerchant	26 May 1941 by air to Lisbon	political warfare	only reached Lyons and Berne; returned 20 July 1942
FR A. JOURDAIN[2]	Opinion	6/7 July 1941	organiser	returned 27 Aug. 1942
A. J. LEBLICQ	Moonshine	"	his W/T	killed in parachute accident
A. CAMPION	Periwig	12 Aug. 1941	sabotage and W/T	arrested 28 Jan. 1942, changed sides, killed in air raid 7 Sep. 1943
F O. FABRI	Chicken	"	Antwerp	arrested June 1944, soon escaped, overrun
J. A. SCOHIER	Conjugal	3/4 Sep. 1941	sabotage	arrested mid-Feb. 1942; survived, ill

1. Both these agents were Section D's, not T's.
2. Later mission with SAS.

NAME	CODENAME	DATE SENT	ROLE OR REGION	FATE
A. J. C. LHEUREUX	Lacquer	"	his W/T	arrested 14 April 1942, escaped April 1945
J. T. J. M. DETAL	Gypsy	10/11 Sep. 1941	courier lines	arrested 17 March 1942 in France, escaped, returned summer 1943; on fresh mission as F agent, arrested on landing 29 Feb. 1944, murdered in Buchenwald 14 Sep. 1944
F F. J. WAMPACH	Vermilion	"	his W/T	arrested 17 March 1942 in France, escaped May 1943, rearrested, shot 10 Dec. 1943
G. STINGLHAMBER	Musjid	29 Sep. 1941	Flanders	arrested Feb. 1942, executed 22 May 1944
J. N. L. MAUS	Outcast	30 Sep. 1941	Luxembourg province	arrested 13 May 1942, shot 8 July 1942
C. A. FONCK	Balaclava	"	W/T	arrested 2 May 1942, just survived Buchenwald
J. P. E. CASSART[2]	Hireling	3 Oct. 1941	organiser	arrested 13 Dec. 1941, escaped from Berlin late 1943, returned 31 Jan. 1944
(1) H. P. VERHAEGEN	Rhomboid	"	his W/T	returned 30 July 1942

2. Later mission with SAS.

	NAME	CODENAME	DATE SENT	ROLE OR REGION	FATE
F	F. VERGUCHT	Duncan	28 Oct. 1941 by sea to Lisbon	W/T	returned 29 Dec. 1943
	O. M. VAN IMPE	Arboretum	8 Nov. 1941	Musjid's W/T	arrested Aug. 1942, executed 22 May 1944
			* * *		
	A. HOTTIA	Marmoset	28 Jan. 1942	Hainaut	arrested 17 April, shot 30 Sep. 1943
(1)	A. J. WENDELEN	Mandamus	"	general	returned 28 May 1943
	J. BRION	Majordomo	"	his W/T	arrested 16 June 1942, survived Dachau
	O. CATHERINE	Manfriday	"	propaganda	arrested 17 Jan. 1943, survived Dachau
	G. M. C. AARENS	Intersection	"	his W/T	arrested 27 March 1942, beheaded 4 or 9 Dec. 1944
	A. DELMEIRE	Canticle	1/2 March 1942	Detal's courier	arrested mid March 1942; executed 7 June 1944
F	E. A. L. COURTIN	Mouse	"	Detal's W/T	arrested in France 16 March 1942, escaped Dec. 1942, returned early 1943
	V. M. PASSELECQ	Incomparable	1/2 March 1942	political warfare & sabotage	arrested 9 July 1942; executed 7 June 1944

NAME	CODENAME	DATE SENT	ROLE OR REGION	FATE
R. COPINNE	Mastiff	"	his W/T	arrested July 1942; shot 18 Jan. 1943
(1) COMTE P. DE LIEDEKERKE	Collie	2/3 March 1942	political warfare	returned 17 July 1942
R. CERF	Tiger	"	his W/T	arrested early March, shot 4 Aug. 1942
J. VAN HOREN	Terrier	"	Absil's W/T	arrested 3 April 1942; survived
W. G. H. C. BERNAERDT	Mink	23/24 March 1942	Antwerp sabotage	arrested 27 July 1942; killed 19 April 1944
J. V. DEFLEM	Mule	30 April/1 May 1942	sabotage	killed in action on landing
L. KAANEN	Sable	"	his assistant	"
J. PICQUART	Lamb	"	Mule's W/T	mortally wounded on landing
J. KRUYT[3]	Burgundy	24/25 May 1942	unknown	injured on landing; soon arrested and shot
F. J. G. MOREAU	Cayote	24/25 May 1942	MT sabotage	arrested on landing; killed 17 Dec. 1942
V. J. LEMMENS	Koala	25/26 June 1942	coal go-slow	arrested on landing; shot 8 Oct. 1942
R. M. WOUTERS	Mongoose	26/27 June 1942	arm secret army	arrested mid Aug. 1942; believed shot late Aug. 1944

3. NKVD, not SOE.

NAME	CODENAME	DATE SENT	ROLE OR REGION	FATE
M. M. F. HOUBEN	Chamois	"	"	arrested and escaped 15 Aug. 1942; rearrested in France 11 June 1943; survived Buchenwald
U. G. A. F. FLOTTE	Lynx	"	their W/T	arrested 15 Aug. 1942; wounded; vanished
F C. CLASER	Bull	10 Aug. 1942 by sea via Gibraltar	co-ordinate secret army	arrested Dec. 1942; died in Gross Rosen 12 Dec. 1944
J. STERCKMANS	Wallaby	27 Aug. 1942	Bull's W/T	arrested on landing; survived
N. A. G. BODSON	Springbok	"	"	arrested on landing; shot 5 Dec. 1942
P. R. OSTERRIETH	Platypus	"	go-slow	arrested on landing; killed 13 June 1943 by allied air raid on Bochum
E. J. VAN LOO	Ocelot	29 Aug. 1942	Koala's W/T	arrested on landing; presumed died in enemy hands
P. J. L. H. VLIEX	Marmot	10 Sep. 1942	sabotage	arrested on landing; shot 8 June 1943
F A. SCHOUTEN[4]	Worthington	mid Oct. 1942	escape line	arrested in France c. 20 Nov. 1942; survived Oranienburg
A (1) L. A. LIVIO	Lemur	16 Nov. 1942	Tournai	returned 23 July 1943

4. DF's agent, not T's.

NAME	CODENAME	DATE SENT	ROLE OR REGION	FATE
A (1) J. M. PANS	Toad	"	his assistant	returned 23 July 1943
J. M. VAN DORPE	Baboon	17/18 Nov. 1942		returned 16 Nov. 1943
(1) L. F. HARNIESFEGER	Dingo	19/20 Nov. 1942	Courtrai peasantry trade unions, Charleroi	returned 1 Feb. 1944
(1) L. J. STROOBANTS	Borzoi	20 Dec. 1942	propaganda, in Ghent	returned early Sep. 1943
J. J. L. CEYSSENS	Gibbon	20 Dec. 1942	pigeon service for political news	arrested 17 March 1943; died in Belsen 15 March 1945
A M. D. G. DURIEUX	Caracal	20 Dec. 1942	destroy papers	badly injured on landing; returned 3 March 1944
(1) H. HEFFINCK	Shrew	20 Dec. 1942	his assistant	arrested 31 Jan. 1944, escaped at once, returned 22 March 1944

*   *   *

NAME	CODENAME	DATE SENT	ROLE OR REGION	FATE
E. MARECHAL	Labrador	18/19 Jan. 1943	liaison	arrested 10 Sep. 1943, survived concentration camps
J. P. JANSSENS	Calf	"	his W/T	arrested 22 Aug. 1943, also survived KZs
J. M. N. LEGRAND	Coal	"	purloin aircraft	returned 12 June 1943
M. A. C. VAN DAEL	Turtle	"	his assistant	returned 2 Feb. 1944
W. J. GAUTHIER	Griffon	13/14 Feb. 1943	liaison	arrested early May 1943, survived Dachau
(1) R. A. HOLVOET[5]	Badger	"	his W/T	returned 29 July 1943

5. Second mission for MI9 in Holland.

NAME	CODENAME	DATE SENT	ROLE OR REGION	FATE
F. M. F. G. VELDEKENS	Samoyede	12 March 1943	propaganda	returned 16 Nov. 1943
(1) H. FRENAY	Mouflon	13 April 1943	sabotage	returned 1 Feb. 1944
(1) J. L. WOLUWE	Jerboa	"	his assistant	returned 22 Feb. 1944
(1) J. E. M. G. COYETTE	Porcupine	14 April 1943	demoralise German army	escaped to Switzerland July 1943
(1) H. A. L. FILOT	Mandrill	"	his assistant	returned 7 January 1944
F A	Rat	14/15 April 1943	Vole's W/T	returned Sep. 1943
F	Goat	"	"	arrested 9 Nov. 1943 in Paris, shot there later in year
F	Vole	15/16 April 1943	escape line	murdered by 'Goat' in France May 1943
L. BAR	Dormouse	17/18 April 1943	Porcupine's and Samoyede's W/T	arrested 27 Aug. 1943, shot 10 Feb. 1944
D. BRICHAUX	Alsatian	20 April 1943	trade unions	parachute did not open
(1) J. VAN GYSEGHEM	Muskrat	22/23 May 1943	Antwerp	returned 1 Feb. 1944
(1) F. BECKERS	Vampire	"	his W/T	returned 1 Feb. 1944
(1) L. H. J. FRANCOU	Bullfrog	21/22 May 1943	Ardennes liaison	returned 26 Oct. 1943
(1) P. E. J. GOFFIN	Gofer	"	his W/T	returned 1 Feb. 1944
(1) BARON C. A. DE MONTPELLIER DE VEDRIN	Macduff	21/22 May 1943	Lysander grounds	returned 2 Nov. 1943

NAME	CODENAME	DATE SENT	ROLE OR REGION	FATE
G. A. M. J. CHRISTIAENS	Seal	"	his W/T	arrested 10 Jan. 1944, just survived Mauthausen (d.1 July 1945)
L. C. VAN DER MEERSCHE	Ibex	"	his assistant	arrested 9 Aug. 1943, killed in air raid 7 Sep. 1943
M. A. E. M. LOSSEAU	Othello	13 June 1943	peasantry	returned 25 Dec. 1943
F G. ZEMBSCH-SCHREVE[6]	Pierre	23 July 1943	escape line	arrested in Paris late March 1944; survived Dora
F J. M. C. PLANEL[6]	Jacques	"	his W/T	stayed in France; returned late May 1944
(2) COMTE P. DE LIEDEKERKE	Claudius	15/16 July 1943	FIL	returned Oct. 1943
A. G. A. BLONDEEL	Pointer	"	his W/T	returned 9 Sep. 1944, sent to Far East
F A A. R. E. M. MARISSAL	Civet/Stanley	21 July 1943	secret army	returned 18 Oct. 1943
(2) A. J. WENDELEN	Tybalt/Hector	11/12 Aug. 1943	FIL	injured on landing; returned 6 Dec. 1943
J. G. R. DONEUX	Hillcat	"	his W/T	returned 5 June 1944
F A G. A. R. LOVINFOSSE[6]	Greyhound	"	escape line	returned 3 March 1944
F D. KELLY[6]	Woodchuck	"	his W/T	stayed in France; returned 4 Feb. 1944

6. DF's agent, not T's.

NAME	CODENAME	DATE SENT	ROLE OR REGION	FATE
J. G. V. FLACON	Lear	19/20 Aug. 1943	assist Civet	returned 1 Feb. 1944
L. HUYSMANS	Buckhound	"	Civet's W/T	arrested 26 Sep. 1943; presumed killed
J. H. WARGNIES	Philotus	20 Aug. 1943	courier	arrested 14 Sep. 1943; escaped; shot 7 July 1944
R. TYTGAT	Gratiano	19 Sep. 1943	Samoyede's W/T	returned 7 April 1944
FR E. G. CAREZ	Manelaus	18 Oct. 1943	secret army	twice arrested June 1944, soon escaped; overrun
P. J. G. VEKEMANS	Flaminius	20/21 Oct. 1943	secret army	arrested 15 May 1944, returned via Odessa
G. M. H. JOAKIM	Guineapig	"	his W/T	arrested mid-May 1944, escaped, returned 22 Sep. 1944
		* * *		
(2) J. E. M. G. COYETTE[7]		Dec. 1943	supply money	returned March 1944
(2) H. P. VERHAEGEN	Thersites	8 Jan. 1944	W/T for Osric	killed in air crash
H. GOFFIN	Fortinbras	"	W/T Hainaut	"
R. P. E. MICHAUX	Lucius	"	W/T for Tybalt	"
R. N. A. HIERSOUX	Polonius	"	W/T	wounded in air crash
(1) H. J. T. WADDINGTON	Armadillo	"	W/T	"
J. B. SCHOOLS	Hortensius	10 Jan. 1944	sabotage	returned 9 May 1944

7. Mission overland to and from Switzerland.

	NAME	CODENAME	DATE SENT	ROLE OR REGION	FATE
	J. F. FLOUR	Horatio	"	W/T for Vergillia	arrested 22 May, overrun 3 Sep. 1944
	L. H. ENGELEN	Caphis	"	sabotage	arrested 17 March 1944, survived Buchenwald
	A. J. DELPLACE	Nicanor	6/7 Feb. 1944	"	arrested late May, killed early Sep. 1944
	M. F. GRUNER	Flavius	"	his W/T	arrested c. 8 Aug. 1944, vanished in Germany
	J. H. NEY	Marcius	"	secret army W/T	arrested 12 Aug. 1944, died in Neuengamme early 1945
(3)	COMTE P. DE LIEDEKERKE	Iago/Scipio	8 Feb. 1944	counterscorch	returned late May 1944
	W. C. WADDINGTON	Regan	"	his W/T	overrun in Antwerp 4 Sep. 1944
	H. O. NEUMAN	Caesar/Montano	8/9 Feb. 1944	political intelligence	returned 20 April 1944
	H. DENDONCKER	Yapock	"	W/T for Tybalt	arrested March 1944, survived Buchenwald
	E. J. E. VAN DYCK	Volumnia	"	propaganda coordination	returned 25 May 1944
F	J. E. C. E. GUILLERY	Vergillia/Nelly	10 Feb. 1944		overrun
(2)	L. A. LIVIO	Pandarus	3/4 March 1944	arm secret army	arrested 24 May, escaped 3 Sep. 1944

	NAME	CODENAME	DATE SENT	ROLE OR REGION	FATE
(2)	J. M. PANS	Agamemnon	"	his assistant	arrested, wounded, 24 May, escaped 3 Sep. 1944
	C. A. F. HOYEZ	Cawdor	5/6 March 1944	secret army LO	arrested in Pyrenees 25 May 1944; vanished
	G. G. BULTOT	Apemantus	6 March 1944	secret army zone V	overrun
	A. J. G. GOFFIN	Ventidius	"	his W/T	"
	J. J. J. G. RENAUT	Agrippa	"	secret army W/T zone I	"
	R. A. DEPREZ	Lucullus	30/31 March 1944	secret army zone II	shot down en route
	A. GIROULLE	Troilus	"	his W/T	"
(2)	H. FRENAY	Balthasar	"	canal sabotage	mortally wounded 28 April 1944
(2)	J. L. WOLUWE	Lavinia	"	his assistant	arrested 28 April 1944, shot 26 April 1945
	A. W. GARDINER	Titus	"	their W/T	arrested 6 June 1944, survived as prisoner of war
	F. B. F. MATHOT	Saturnius	9/10 April 1944	'Hotton' sabotage	overrun
	A. B. J. M. MELOT	Aufidius	10 April 1944	secret army zone IV	arrested 14 June, rescued mid July 1944
	A. D. BERTEN	Glamis	10/11 April 1944	'Hotton' sabotage	overrun
	M. G. BLAZE	Cominius	"	his W/T	"
F	I. FLOOR	Dardanius/Agnes	11/12 April 1944	co-ordination	returned 20 May 1944

NAME	CODENAME	DATE SENT	ROLE OR REGION	FATE
G. MARCHAND	Varro	"	his assistant	arrested 6 Sep. 1944, at once released, overrun
A. J. DELVINGT	Tamora	"	W/T for Dardanius	arrested 14 Dec. 1944, survived
J. J. G. MICHAUX	Mutius	30 April/1 May 1944	secret army W/T	arrested 13 June, escaped 2 Sep. 1944
A. WOUTERS	Antenor	30 April/1 May 1944	secret army W/T zone III	killed 5 Sep. 1994
P. J. M. L'HOEST	Chiron	"	secret army HQ W/T	arrested 6 July, rescued 3 Sep. 1944; joined Verstrepen group
M. A. BUFKENS	Coriolanus	"	secret army W/T zone V	overrun
A. G. SCHAEPDRYVER	Publius	"	secret army W/T zone IV	arrested 30 Aug. 1944, died in Mauthausen 1 Feb. 1945
A. J. A. FALESSE	Velutus	"	secret army zone II	arrested early July 1944, survived
M. I. J. BECQUAERT	Patroclus	"	his W/T	"
A. J. J. MABILLE	Bassianus	6/7 May 1944	sabotage	arrested 26 June 1944, survived
T. ANDRIES	Roderigo	"	"	overrun
A. E. J. G. BAYET	Euphronius	"	FIL sabotage	arrested 26 June 1944, survived
P. J. M. DAVREUX	Menecrates	"	sabotage	killed in action 1 Sep. 1944
L. J. J. JOYE	Sempronius	"	"	arrested late May, killed early Sep. 1944

	NAME	CODENAME	DATE SENT	ROLE OR REGION	FATE
	J. F. J. G. LEURQUIN	Junius	28 May 1944	secret army W/T zone IV	arrested 17 June 1944, survived
	G. J. G. ANDRÉ	Lodovico	28/29 May 1944	sabotage zone I	overrun
	BARON J. A. ROLIN	Messala	2/3 June 1944	co-ordination	arrested 26 June 1944, survived
	H. HAUTFENNE	Lepidus	"	his W/T	arrested 2 June 1944, survived
	M. A. T. BERTRAND	Bianca	"	sabotage zone V	overrun
	L. G. DE WINTER	Enobarbus	"	W/T for Socrates	overrun; shot down on later mission for X section
(2)	H. A. L. FILOT	Aeneas	"	FIL liaison	shot down en route
(2)	L. J. STROOBANTS	Priam	"	"	"
	G. L. E. MASEREEL	Andromache	"	"	shot down en route but survived; arrested at once, rescued 3 Sep. 1944
(2)	L. F. HARNIESFEGER	Ligarius	"	assist Varro	arrested 6 June, rescued 3 Sep. 1944
	J. J. LOMBA	Canidius	"	his W/T	arrested July, rescued 3 Sep. 1944
	G. L. E. G. COLIGNON	Alarbus	"	W/T for Velutus	arrested early July 1944, survived
(2)	H. HEFFINCK	Sicinius	5/6 June 1944	help Nola	arrested Aug. 1944, survived
	A. A. PAULY	Silius	"	his W/T	arrested 29 Aug. 1944, survived

* * *

	NAME	CODENAME	DATE SENT	ROLE OR REGION	FATE
F	H. F. JESCHKE[8]	Daniel	12 June 1944	escape line	overrun near Ghent; escaped Polish vengeance
F (2)	P. E. J. GOFFIN[8]	Lawrence	"	his W/T	arrested in Spain; released; overrun in France; on to Far East
(2)	BARON C. A. DE MONTPELLIER DE VEDRIN	Bernardo	4/5 July 1944	help Osric	overrun 13 Sep. 1944
	M. L. GREGOIR	Taurus	6 July 1944	W/T zone I	overrun
	C. L. E. D. LEPOIVRE	Cato	6/7 July 1944	FIL liaison	overrun
	G. J. F. CORBISIER	Mardian	"	his assistant	overrun; shot down on later mission for X section
	S. H. GARDINER	Diomedes	"	their W/T	overrun
	L. E. CHABART	Menas	4/5 Aug. 1944	help Samoyede	overrun
	L. C. H. SERVAIS	Phrynia	"	sabotage zone IV	overrun
	R. A. R. DUBY	Alcibiades	"	sabotage, Groupe G	overrun
(3)	A. J. WENDELEN	Brabantio	"	sabotage; Crossbow	overrun
	ELAINE M. MADDEN	Imogen	"	his assistant	overrun; became Mme Blaze
(1)	J. P. L. VAN DE SPIEGLE	Donalbain	"	their W/T	overrun; later mission into Netherlands

8. DF, not T.

NAME	CODENAME	DATE SENT	ROLE OR REGION	FATE
R. J. THONON	Helenus	"	sabotage with 'Nola'	wounded 16 Sep. 1944, overrun
Z. E. G. BRAIBANT	Trimon	"	sabotage, Groupe G	overrun
L. P. E. DE COENE	Eros	"	W/T and sabotage, zone II	overrun late Sep. 1944
E. M. G. PLISSART	Cimber	"	communications	overrun
OLGA JACKSON	Emilia	"	demoralise senior Germans	overrun
(2) H. J. T. WADDINGTON	Armadillo	6 Aug. 1944	W/T in Antwerp	overrun there 4 Sep. 1944
R. R. V. TRUYENS	Caius	"	assist Rolin	arrested 30 Aug., escaped 2 Sep. 1944
A. M. J. LIMBORG	Calpurnia	"	his W/T	overrun; later mission for X section
H. DE RADIGUES	Menenius	"	liaison with FIL	overrun
V. A. DIRICKX	Dolabella	"	his assistant	overrun
A. G. J. J. GUISSART DE BEAUSAINT	Servelius	"	sabotage	overrun
R. M. CAUSIN	Scarrus	7 Aug. 1944	W/T for Rolin	overrun; later mission for X section
J. J. L. MOREL	Voltimand	31 Aug./1 Sep. 1944	"	quickly overrun, shot down on later mission for X section

NAME	CODENAME	DATE SENT	ROLE OR REGION	FATE
J. L. G. VAN GASTEL	Hecate	1/2 Sep. 1944	"	quickly overrun
M. F. DE SELYS LONGCHAMPS	Reynaldo	1/2 Sep. 1944	secret army organiser	quickly overrun
(2) J. VAN GYSEGHEM	Aemilius	"	sabotage, zone III	injured on landing; quickly overrun
(2) F. BECKERS	Rosencrantz	"	his W/T	quickly overrun; later mission into Netherlands

Appendix 5

German Directive for Interrogation of Captured Agents

[The following list of a hundred questions, a tribute at once to proverbial German thoroughness and to the excellence of Schreieder's memory, was appended to the second interim report on him, issued by the combined services detailed interrogation centre on 19 November 1945 and preserved in a duplicated copy in his personal file. He produced it again later for the Dutch commission of inquiry.[1] The translator is unknown.]

Like any other police interrogation, the interrogation of agents fell into two main parts:

  (a)   Personal and life history.
  (b)   Interrogation to obtain the facts of the case.

In order to obtain certain basic facts from every interrogation, the following questions were used as a guide by the interrogators. Apart from these questions, which had to be answered fully, others to suit each individual case were put.

  1.   Length of stay in ENGLAND before the agent set out on his mission.
  2.   Had the agent fled from HOLLAND or where did he originally come from?
  3.   To which Resistance Organisation did he belong in HOLLAND?

---

1. *Enq.*, iv B. 40–2.

4.   What position did he hold in the organisation and what were his duties?

5.   Why did he escape from HOLLAND?

6.   When did he escape?

7.   Name, description, last and probable present residence of refugees, who might, even if only temporarily, have gone with him.

8.   Detailed description of escape route.

9.   In which transit camps for refugees did he stay on his journey?

10.   Did he meet any persons known to him in any of these camps?

11.   What organisations or individuals aided him in his flight, either financially or by other means, e.g. providing him with contacts, etc.?

12.   When did he arrive in ENGLAND?

13.   To which or by what British or Dutch officials did he report or was he expected on arrival? (Name and address of such officials and location of such offices including a description of the personnel employed there.)

14.   Did he meet any Dutch or other refugees whom he knew personally at these places?

15.   Did the agent, before being sent to a screening camp (Ueberprüfungslager), come into contact with any officials other than those he had reported to or was met by in the first place?

16.   Name and location of screening camp. (Was it under English or Dutch supervision?)

17.   Length of stay at the screening camp.

18.   How many people of Dutch or other nationality lived in such a camp?

19.   Did he personally know any of the inmates of the camp? If so, name, address and probable present residence.

20.   Who interrogated him?

21.   What questions were put to him?

22.   Place of residence and occupation after he left the screening camp.

23.   When, where, by whom and under what circumstances was he asked to become an agent?

24. When and where did he agree to become and sign on as an agent? (British or Dutch Office?)
25. What other persons, there for the same purpose, did he meet on that occasion? (Name, description, residence.)
26. After signing on, was he at once sent to a school for agents, or was he given a place to live in (flat, house) and told to await further orders? (Name and location of school or residence.)
27. Names and descriptions of any other persons with whom he shared a flat or house, during the waiting period.
28. Were these people also waiting for further orders?
29. When was he first sent to an agents' school?
30. How and through whom did he get his orders?
31. By what means and by whom was he taken to the school?
32. Was he taken to the school alone or did he travel with others?

The number of schools attended by the agent were to be given in chronological order and for each school the following points had to be covered:

33. Name and/or number of school.
34. Name of town, village, etc.
35. Other details of location.
36. Description of school building (external appearance, internal layout).
37. Name and description of CC and instructors. What subjects were taught by individual instructors?
38. The name under which agent was known at the school.
39. Number and names of his co-pupils (real name, any alias, nickname, term of endearment or school name). Description of his co-pupils. What does the agent know about the individual pupils?
40. Did he get to know members of any other course?
41. Details of school curriculum.
42. What was taught in each subject?
43. What were the practical exercises like?
44. What apparatus or materials were used for such exercises?
45. Give the daily routine from Reveille to Lights-out.
46. Length of time spent in each school.

47. Was the agent conveyed from school to school singly or with other pupils? If so, names.

48. Who was in charge of such transport?

49. Where did the agent live in the intervals between courses (schooling) if one course did not immediately follow the other.

50. If any of his co-pupils left in the middle of a course or did not arrive at the next school, give their possible employment.

51. Give description as in No. 39 of any newcomers to the school.

52. Where did the agent live after completion of schooling and before going on operations? (If he did not stay at a holding school.)

53. Which other agents lived with him?

54. With which British or Dutch authorities or officials did the agent come into contact before going on ops?

55. When and who handed the agent his written operation orders? When and to whom did he return these orders after learning them by heart?

56. Repeat verbatim such orders (orders to be written out by the agent by hand in the second person.)

57. Did the agent have any knowledge of the orders given to other agents?

58. In connection with the first part of the agent's mission, did he get any addresses of contacts in HOLLAND?

59. Were agents supplied with contacts outside HOLLAND and if so, why?

60. Name and description of agents with whom he was to work. Were the latter already at work or were they to be dropped with him?

61. Date on which he commenced operations.

62. Had the agent been dropped or had he been sent ashore from a boat? (The latter method was no longer in use after April 1942.)

63. Were British or Dutch officers or any other people present at the farewell dinner?

64. Name and description of any agent at these farewell dinners. (When did they go on operations?)

65. Who took the agent to the starting point?

66. Which other agents started the same evening in other aircraft? (Names, descriptions.)

67. Does the agent know anything else about the operational use of other agents?
68. Cover-name used by the agent while on board the aircraft.
69. Name, description and mission of other agents travelling on the same aircraft.
70. Exact time of start.
71. When and where were the agents dropped?
72. When and where and with whom had the agent been dropped?
73. Were any WT or DF sets dropped and where are they now?
74. If these sets were not used by the agent or agents, for whom were they intended?
75. Was it part of the duty of the agent or agents to deliver letters or parcels (disguised objects) to addresses given to him in ENGLAND?
76. Was the agent received in the dropping area?
77. What passwords did he have to exchange with the person who met him?
78. What was the text of his message reporting his successful landing? Did such message contain a check (control).
79. How was the report sent? By pigeon or by WT?
80. Where was the agent taken after he landed?
81. Where were any others who jumped with him taken?
82. Name used on the agent's personal pass.
83. Names used on other agents' personal passes.
84. Name used by the agent and his assistants in the WT messages.
85. Did the agent have a WT operator with him or did he transmit himself? In the first case did the agent have his own code?
86. Number and make of WT sets.
87. Name and location of the transmission site. Next time for transmission.
88. Brief description of basic code used (book-code, poetry-code, transposition tables, etc.).
89. Brief description of other coding methods to be used by the agent (letter-code, Playfair, Platzbestimmung).
90. The possible use of an agent's number or key cipher. (Detailed interrogation on WT technicalities and ciphers was done by officials of the Orpo and Kriminalobersekretär MAY-Controls.)

91.   How much money did the agent or agents carry and for what purpose was the money to be used?

92.   Did the agent or agents receive any orders other than the written orders?

93.   What did the agent do until his arrest and what part of his mission had he accomplished?

94.   Had the agent collaborated with any resistance organisation and to what did his collaboration amount?

95.   What channels for contacting his assistant were used by the agent and how could he get hold of his assistant in a case of emergency?

96.   Number and contents of WT messages sent and received by the agent until his arrest. (Who drafted and encoded these messages?)

97.   Name and description of any other agents whom he met after he had been dropped. (How could he get in touch with them?)

98.   Did the agent contact any of his relations, e.g. parents, wife?

99.   With whom, where and at what time has the agent appointments which he has not yet fulfilled?

100.   Has the agent or his assistant received orders to return to ENGLAND within a certain time, or is he expecting someone from there?

Appendix 6

Notes on the Means of Dealing with the Movement of Armoured and Motorised Forces by Road to Reinforce Coastal Sectors[1]

In the following notes the ways of interfering with the successive stages of the movement into action of an Armoured Division are considered.

1. *Period from the 'Alert' until columns move off*
   (a) Attacks on Headquarters responsible for the transmission of the 'Alert'.
   (b) Attacks on the telecommunications of such Headquarters. The Telecommunications Section has detailed intelligence as to the communications system, in the areas where the Armoured Divisions are stationed.
   (c) General interference with electricity supplies (of particular value should the 'Alert' occur at/by night).
   (d) Attacks on officers and men in their billets.
   (e) Attacks on D.R.'s in the course of distribution of orders.
   (f) Attacks on Company and Detachment Headquarters.
   (g) Destruction of sign-posts and misdirection of traffic.

2. *Refuelling*
   (a) Attacks on petrol dumps.
   (b) Attacks on ammunition dumps.
   (c) Attacks on food supply lines.

---

1. From war diary, xxiv, after page 516.

3. *Movement by Road*
    (a) Misdirection of traffic, including the use of misleading traffic signs, such as those indicated in the Annex to this Appendix.
    (b) Laying of anti-tank mines. (A small quantity of British anti-tank mines can be used in every area, supplemented by dummies which can be made locally. The effect of these, coupled with suitably placed and worded notices, should be considerable.)
    (c) Use of Molotov and similar bombs. (It is suggested that these stores should be capable of local construction. If possible, they should be supplemented by Anti-tank weapons, such as the Bazooka, if stocks can be made available.)
    (d) Attacks on administrative vehicles.
    (e) Use of tyre-bursters and other devices, such as nails, for puncturing pneumatic tyres.
    (f) Blocking of routes by improvised road-blocks, such as felled trees, stretched wires, etc.
         It is the practice of armoured formations to move by night as much as possible, and it is likely that the divisions which are NOT stationed in the immediate area of the landing will make their approach march by night. In this case, opportunities of ambush en route and attacks in laager are likely to occur.

4. *Movement by Train*
    (a) Harass troops and transport en route for entraining platform, by means of snipers, ambushes, tyre bursters, etc.
    (b) While troops are waiting at entraining platform, keep them on the alert by intermittent sniping.
    (c) If possible, arrange for local railway employees to be slow and make muddles over entraining arrangements.
    (d) When trains are on move interfere with their progress by causing derailments.

5. *Forming Up*
    (a) Continue to use harassing tactics as in 3 above.
    (b) If possible, attack Regimental Headquarters before its sub-units go into action.

(c) Harass D.R.'s and thin-skinned vehicles by sniping, ambushes and other similar activities.

It is emphasised that the attacks referred to above should be carried out by small parties of men who should, on no account, allow themselves to be engaged in a stand-up fight. It is therefore important that the site of such attacks should be chosen with a view to the attackers being able to make a safe withdrawal.

Appendix 7

Sources

(a) *Archives*

As Bradley Smith remarked early in his study of the young Himmler, 'No matter how complete the documentation may be, it is always spotty, while the possible inferences are limitless.'[1] In SOE's case, the archive is not so much spotty as shattered: about seven-eighths of the *paperasserie* it created is thought now to have been destroyed; some by accident, some on purpose. The purpose was to clear archive shelves, even if one of the results of the clearance may have been the vanishing of evidence of old scandals. Some 15,000 files survive, a largely haphazard collection, about half each personal and operational; many slender, a few huge. Luck, always important in war, has a part to play in history as well.

Moreover, there is a double initial difficulty: some of SOE's work was so secret that nothing was ever put on paper about it at all, and some other authorities in the inner circle of Whitehall conformed. Among these was the chiefs of staff committee, of which one of the assistant secretaries, Hollis, wrote to Jebb on 7 May 1941 – they were by then on first-name terms – 'As you know, we do not, I think rightly, take minutes at the meetings when your organisation is discussed.'[2] From a security aspect, this was no doubt a sensible decision; maddening though it is for historians.

The present writer was once, by accident, at a meeting at which the speaker believed he was only addressing civil servants. On behalf of

---

1. Bradley F. Smith, *Heinrich Himmler* (Stanford, California, 1971), 5.
2. CAB 121/308, TSC.

the Public Record Office, he – who was old enough to know better – explained that in transferring documents from original to microfilm or microfiche, or even direct to computer screen, the PRO would have no trouble in suppressing one forename among several; or one name in a list; or one clause in a sentence; or one sentence in a paragraph; quite imperceptibly to the reader in the new medium.

Luckily, none of SOE's papers have yet undergone this treatment; but not all that survive are originals. At some stage, probably in the 1970s while files were being sorted, the scrappiest papers were replaced by neat typescript top copies: careful, perhaps perfect, transcriptions, but not the originals on which a perfectionist would insist. Several of these files have only been available to me in photocopy.

Of nearly 300 files created by N section, forty-six survive. For T section, 269 files survive even after losses in the Great Fire of Baker Street in 1946. The papers of SOE's higher echelons, in western Europe at least, survive in a haphazard rather than a systematic way; there are no Council minutes, for example, in the winter of 1942–3.

Boxshall, then keeper of SOE's archives, told de Jong in 1978 that he could not produce an N section war diary for him;[3] whether because he had mislaid it, or because he was ashamed of it, I do not know. Both N and T sections kept lengthy war diaries, the first largely and the second partly fanciful, because of German counterstrokes; they remain useful sources for points over which the Germans had no say.

The surviving Dutch and Belgian operational files have now gone to join the HS series in the PRO (where they will be traceable from the file numbers given in footnotes above). They provided part, perhaps half of the story. The rest came either from personal files, or headquarters or security or clandestine communications files, not yet released; or from other sources indicated in the notes. Among these other sources Lord Selborne's SOE files, sequestrated from the rest of his personal archive (which is in the Bodleian) after his death, were among the most significant.

---

3. De Jong, *KdN*, ix(ii). 1034n.

The air historical branch, ministry of defence, besides providing the operational record books of 138 and 161 squadrons, RAF, made some more detailed papers available, which helped to clarify problems; though no records from 419 Flight or 1419 Flight surfaced.

Eddy de Roever, one of the leading Dutch historians of this subject, most kindly passed to the foreign office's SOE adviser in 1994 some papers bearing on it he had secured from Moscow. They purport to be Gestapo comments on N section's performance during the *Englandspiel*, and sworn statements by several of their captives, picked up by Soviet investigators in the ruins of Germany in 1945 and never thrown away. They are of considerable interest; whether any papers that lay for so long in the hands of the Soviet secret police can also be authentic is a separate question. Their RIOD reference number is: collection 206, 500.1.1283.

I am particularly grateful to the RIOD for letting me browse among the files left behind by Rauter, and for other substantial help. The Belgian Centre de Recherches et d'Etudes historiques de la Seconde Guerre Mondiale (now renamed the Centre d'Etudes et de Documentation Guerre et Sociétés Contemporaines) has also been particularly helpful.

(b)   *Printed Books*

Espionage, subversion, deception, all forms of secret service are of lasting interest to journalists and scarifiers. The Fat Boy in *Pickwick Papers* who liked to make his hearers' flesh creep would have revelled in current news media interest in these subjects. It is past time for historians to make a disjunction between writers who seek to advance knowledge, and sensation-mongers who seek to excite their readers: even if, by exciting them, they poison the wells of history. Several familiar titles, some of them best-sellers, are therefore left out of the list below; their evidential value is nil.

Books were published in London, if no other place is given.

ADKIN, see SIMPSON

AENEAS TACTICUS, *Works* (Cambridge, Mass.: Illinois Greek Club for Loeb, 1928), Greek and English on facing pages, full of still useful hints.

AINEIAS THE TACTICIAN, *How to Survive under Siege*, ed. and tr. David WHITEHEAD (Oxford: Clarendon Press, 1990), a more modern version of the same.

AMERSFOORT, H., and KAMPHUIS, P. H., *Mei 1940* (The Hague: SDU, 1990), an admirable collection of Dutch historians' essays, with maps and photographs, about the ground battle in their country, 10–14 May 1940.

AMIES, Hardy, *Just So Far* (Collins, 1954)

—, *Still Here* (Weidenfeld and Nicolson, 1984)

Each of these autobiographies includes a modest and discreet section on his war career.

ANDREW, C. M., *Secret Service* (Heinemann, 1985), valuable on Venlo, handles the infant SOE briefly.

ASTLEY, Joan Bright, *The Inner Circle* (Hutchinson, 1971), insights into SOE's origins in MIR and into the working of the War Cabinet's military machine. See also WILKINSON.

BAKELS, Floris B., tr. FRIEDHOFF, Herman, *Nacht und Nebel* (Cambridge: Lutterworth Press, 1993), an appallingly vivid account, now in clear English, by a Dutch solicitor of what run-of-the-mill imprisonment was like in the hands of the SS; he was lucky to survive Natzweiler. First published in Dutch in 1977.

—, *Wachter op de morgen* (Kampen: J. H. Kok, 1988), a life of C. C. Dutilh (1915–44) and his friends engaged in wartime espionage.

BARNOUW, D., see FRANK, Anne

BEEVOR, J. G., *SOE: Recollections and Reflections 1940–1945* (Bodley Head, 1981), admirable summary by a senior staff officer.

'Belgium, September 1944', see *Memo from Belgium*

BERNARD, Henri (ed.), *Guerre totale et guerre révolutionnaire* (Brussels and Paris: 6v, Brepols, n.d. [1960]), a formidable analysis, by a military historian with practical experience of his subject, ranging from ancient times to the mid-twentieth century.

—, *La Résistance 1940–1945* (Brussels: La Renaissance du Livre, 1968), a brief introduction in the collection 'Notre Passé' to the history of Belgian resistance to nazism.

—, *Un Maquis dans la Ville* (same, 1970) deals mainly with escapes run by the milices patriotiques of Schaerbeek, the northern quarter of Brussels; includes brief, valuable passage on sabotage.

—, *Un Géant de la Résistance: Walthère Dewé* (same, 1971), a sympathetic biography.

—, *Jean del Marmol: une grande figure de l'armée secrète* (Brussels: Pierre de Meyere, 1972), sympathetic brief biography by a contemporary of a heroic figure in the world of secret liaison.

—, *L'Armée Secrète 1940–1944* (Paris and Gembloux: Duculot, 1986), a valuable history.

BLAKE, Lord, see *Dictionary of National Biography*

BROWNING, Christopher R., *Ordinary Men* (Harper Perennial, 1993), an account of the work in Poland in 1942 of a single German reserve police battalion; raises awkward questions about the Orpo in particular and human behaviour in general.

Camp 020: MI5 and the Nazi Spies (PRO, 2000), details of British interrogation techniques.

CLIFF, Ann, see DOURLEIN

C[OWELL], G., *The SOE Archive: UK Establishment* (np: 1992), a useful if incomplete list of SOE's headquarter and training locations in Great Britain.

CUNNINGHAM, Cyril, *Beaulieu: The Finishing School for Secret Agents* (Leo Cooper, 1998), full of local detail; includes lists of staff and summaries of the courses taught.

DALTON, Hugh, *The Fateful Years* (Muller, 1957), has a chapter on the origins and early years of SOE.

The Second World War Diary of Hugh Dalton 1940–45, ed. Ben PIMLOTT (Cape/LSE, 1986), informative and revealing. And see PIMLOTT.

DEAR, I. C. B., and FOOT, M. R. D. (eds), *The Oxford Companion to the Second World War* (Oxford University Press, 1995), a summary guide to most aspects of the history of the war.

DEJONGHE, Etienne (ed.), *L'Occupation en France et en Belgique 1940–1944* (2v, Lille, 1987–8), two special numbers of the *Revue du Nord* recording a conference at Lille in April 1985.

Dictionary of National Biography

1961–1970, ed. (Sir) E. T. WILLIAMS and C. S. NICHOLLS (Oxford University Press, 1985).

1971–1980, ed. BLAKE and C. S. NICHOLLS (same, 1988).

1981–1985, same eds (same, 1990).

Missing Persons, ed. C. S. NICHOLLS (same, 1993), includes several characters from the worlds of intelligence and subversion.

1986–1990, ed. C. S. NICHOLLS with Sir Keith THOMAS (same, 1996).

DODDS-PARKER, Sir A. D., *Setting Europe Ablaze* (Windlesham: Springwood Books, 1983), a series of inside stories by an early and senior SOE figure.

DONEUX, Jacques, *They Arrived by Moonlight* (Odhams, 1956; St Ermin's Press, 2001), a particularly clear and helpful wireless operator's war autobiography.

DOURLEIN, P., tr. RENIER, F. G., and CLIFF, Ann, *Inside North Pole* (Kimber, 1953), an exemplary victim's account of the fate of most of SOE's Dutch agents in 1942–3.

DURIEUX, M. D. G., see WEBER, Guy

ELLIOTT-BATEMAN, M. R. (ed.), *The Fourth Dimension of Warfare* (Manchester: University Press, 1970), includes *inter alia* a lecture on SOE by Gubbins.

—, *Revolt to Revolution* (same, 1974).

Enquête commissie Regieringsbeleid 1940–1945, iv (The Hague: Sdu,

1950), deals in minute detail with the relations between the Dutch secret services in exile and their British and German opposite numbers. Testimony on oath from witnesses of all three nationalities; some of it mistaken.

European Resistance Movements 1939–1945 (Oxford: Pergamon Press, 1960) contains the proceedings of the conference organised at Liège by Henri Michel in 1958.

European Resistance Movements (same, 1964) covers the conference at Milan in 1962. Both volumes include both expert and official accounts.

FAIRBAIRN, W. E., and WALBRIDGE, D. N., *All in Fighting* (Faber and Faber, 1942), elements of unarmed combat and the use of the fighting knife.

FOOT, M. R. D., *SOE in France* (HMSO, 1968), deals primarily with F section.

—, 'Reflexions on SOE', in *Memoirs and Proceedings of the Manchester Literary and Philosophical Society* cxi (1969), 1.

—, *Resistance* (2 edn, Eyre Methuen, 1977).

—, 'Was SOE any good?', in *Journal of Contemporary History* xiii (January 1981), 167, answers with an emphatic yes.

—, *Holland at War against Hitler* (Cass, 1990), proceedings of a tercentenary conference on Dutch resistance in London in 1989.

—, *SOE: An Outline History 1940–46* (4 edn, Pimlico, 1999).

— and LANGLEY, J. M., *MI9* (2 edn, Boston: Little, Brown, 1980), an account of the British escape service, 1939–45. And see DEAR; MACKENZIE.

FORD, Herbert, *Flee the Captor* (Nashville, Tennessee: Southern Publishing Association, 1966), an account of the Dutch-Paris escape line run by John Weidner; much *oratio recta*.

FRANK, Anne, *Het Achterhuis* (Amsterdam: Contact, 1947), often translated. Nothing to do with SOE, but a world best-seller: a remarkable worm's-eye view of life in nazi-occupied Europe.

Authenticated by parallel-text edition BARNOUW, D., and STROOM, G. van der (eds), *The Diary of Anne Frank* (Viking, 1989).

FRIEDHOFF, Herman, *Requiem for the Resistance* (Bloomsbury 1988), partly fictional war autobiography of a junior Dutch resister, who worked under Bickman from May 1940, ran evaders into Belgium in 1942, came out himself in 1943 and returned in the Prinses Irene Brigade. Invaluable for atmosphere. And see BAKELS.

GEYL, C. M., see JONG, Louis de

GISKES, H. J., *Abwehr III F. De duitse contrespionage in Nederland* (Amsterdam: De Bezige Bij, 1949), tr. as *London Calling North Pole* (William Kimber, 1953), with appendix by H. M. G. Lauwers, the first account to be published in English of the *Englandspiel* by a participant, explains how it looked to the Abwehr; honest and straightforward.

GUBBINS, Sir C. MacV., 'Resistance Movements in the War', *RUSIJ* xciii (May 1948), 210–23, clear lecture outline of SOE's main achievements. And see ELLIOTT-BATEMAN; WILKINSON.

HALPERN, Samuel, see PEAKE

HAZELHOFF ROELFZEMA, Erik, *Soldaat van Oranje '40–'45* (The Hague: Stok, 1972), tr. and abbreviated as *Soldier of Orange* (Hodder, 1972), lively account of his secret war and later RAF operations.

HINSLEY, (Sir) F. H., *et al.*, *British Intelligence in the Second World War* (3v in 4, HMSO, 1979–88), deals mainly with decipher.

HINSLEY, (Sir) F. H., and SIMKINS, C. A. G., *Security and Counterespionage* (HMSO, 1990), equally authoritative, occasionally refers to SOE.

HOETS, Pieter Hans, *Englandspiel ontmaskerd* (Rotterdam: Dontzer, 1990), by an early resister who escaped to England, worked in secret intelligence, and lost many friends; unhappy in its sources, which have led him astray.

HOLMES, Richard, *Fatal Avenue* (Cape, 1993), puts the battlefields of the Low Countries in their historic context.

HOWARD, (Sir) Michael, *Strategic Deception* (HMSO, 1990), decisive.

HOWE, Ellic, *The Black Game* (Michael Joseph, 1982), reveals a great deal about black broadcasting and the forging of pamphlets and passes. The author, expert on printing techniques, claimed not to know for which secret services he worked.

JOHNS, P. L., *Within Two Cloaks* (Kimber, 1979), describes in detail yet with no indiscretions, his work for SIS in Lisbon and for SOE into north-west Europe during the war.

JONG, Louis de, tr. Geyl, C. M., *The German Fifth Column in the Second World War* (Routledge & Kegan Paul, 1956), an early strike of revisionist history-writing which seeks to dispel many hardy myths.

—, *De Bezetting* (Amsterdam: Querido, 1966), a long and fully illustrated book, written to accompany a series of television programmes on the German occupation of Holland; many comments by survivors.

—, *Het Koninkrijk der Nederlanden in de tweede Wereldoorlog* (14 v in 27, The Hague: Staatsuitgeverij, 1969–91), the most complete and comprehensive account of any occupied country's history in this war; ranges far outside the Netherlands as well. Now and then fallible in detail, but an admirable life's work.

—, *The Netherlands and Nazi Germany* (Cambridge, Mass.: Harvard University Press, 1990), the Erasmus lectures at Harvard in 1988, on the holocaust, on Dutch wartime resistance, and on Queen Wilhelmina's role.

—, 'The "Great Game" of Secret Agents', in *Encounter* liv (January 1980), 12–21, deals mainly with the *Englandspiel,* concluding that it was caused by error rather than treason in London; covers MI6 as well as SOE, and touches on Belgium and France also.

KAHN, David, *The Codebreakers* (Weidenfeld and Nicolson, 1966), a comprehensive treatment of code and cipher breaking from the earliest recorded times; unluckily for the author, written before the Ultra secret went public. His second edition (1996) remedies this solitary defect in a final section. And see LORAIN.

KELSO, Nicholas, *Errors of Judgement* (Robert Hale, 1988), the established view of 'SOE's Disaster in the Netherlands 1941–44', based on published sources.

KIRSCHEN, G. S., *Six amis viendront ce soir* (2 edn, Brussels: Presses de Belgique, 1983), describes three SAS missions, two to France in 1944 and one to Holland in 1944–5; vivid recreation of what it felt like.

KLUITERS, F. A. C., *De Nederlandse inlichtigen – en veiligheidsdiensten* (The Hague: Sdu, 1993), a detailed set of check-lists covering many different Dutch intelligence and security organisations, with some notes on their British opposite numbers and on SOE; running from 1912 to 1992, with much attention to the years 1939–45, masses of addresses, and numerous personal details; some odd omissions.

KOCH-KENT, Henri, *Sie boten Trotz* (Luxembourg: Hermann, 1974), a hard-hitting account of those citizens of the grand duchy of Luxembourg who took an active part in resistance.

LANGLEY, J. M., see FOOT

LAURENS, Anne, *L'Affaire King Kong* (Paris: Albin Michel, 1969), tries to depict Christiaan Lindemans as a double agent acting in the allied, not in the German, interest. Extensive quotations, unacknowledged, from Giskes; many conversations in *oratio recta*; inconclusive.

LAUWERS, H. M. G., see GISKES

LINDEMANS, C., see LAURENS, Anne

Livre d'Or de la Résistance Belge (Brussels: Leclercq [1948]), official testimonial drawn up soon after the war under the auspices of the Belgian ministry of defence; lavishly illustrated; includes a roll of honour covering over 50 pages, with some 8,000 names. SOE archive holds a copy as History lxvii.

LORAIN, P., ed. KAHN, D., *Secret Warfare* (Orbis 1983), an invaluable set of annotated sketches of the arms, aircraft and wireless equipment available to SOE in France, plus detailed notes on pre-OTP coding; applies also to Low Countries.

MACKENZIE, W. J. M., ed. FOOT, M. R. D., *The Secret History of SOE* (St Ermin's Press, 2000), virtual in-house history; indispensable.

MACRAE, Stuart, *Winston Churchill's Toyshop* (Kineton: Roundwood Press, 1971), clear and useful account of M. R. Jefferis's branch of the ministry of defence, based first in Portland Place and then near Aylesbury, which invented secret weapons and devices – most of them explosive – and soldier-proofed them.

MARKS, Leo, *Between Silk and Cyanide* (Harper Collins, 1998), a brilliant summary of SOE's agent cipher problems; appeared almost too late to affect this text.

MASTERMAN, (Sir) J. C., *The Double-Cross System in the War of 1939 to 1945* (Yale University Press, 1972), explains in detail how deception was really carried out.

Memo from Belgium (Brussels: ministry of foreign affairs, 1985), no. 195 of 'Views and Surveys', reports an Imperial War Museum symposium in London on 21–22 August 1984 on 'Belgium, September 1944'. Ganshof and Ugeux were among those present.

NICHOLLS, C. S., see *Dictionary of National Biography*

NUREMBERG TRIAL, see *Trial*

PEAKE, Hayden B., and HALPERN, Samuel (eds), *In the Name of Intelligence* (Washington DC: BICC, 1994), a *Festschrift* for Walter L. Pforzheimer; contains much of interest, but seldom touches on SOE.

PIMLOTT, Ben, *Dalton* (Cape, 1985), a political biography. And see DALTON.

RENIER, F. G., see DOURLEIN

REP, Jelte, *Englandspiel* (Bussum: van Holkema & Warendorf, 1977), long fluent popular account, based partly on *Enquete-commissie*, partly on de Jong, and partly on interviews with families, giving the Dutch point of view; no references.

REVUE DU NORD, see Dejonghe, E

RICHARDS, Sir F. Brooks, *Secret Flotillas* (HMSO, 1996), a wonderfully complete account of clandestine sea operations in north-west Europe and the western Mediterranean, 1940–5.

ROEVER, Eddy de, *Zij sprongen bij maanlicht* (Baarn: Hollandia,

1985), valuable and well-illustrated chronicle of the agents parachuted into Holland, by the BBO and SOE jointly, from 1 April 1944 to the end of the war.

—, *Richard Barmé* (same, 1995), a brief affectionate memoir.

SCHREIEDER, J., *Das war das Englandspiel* (Munich: Walter Stutz, 1950), a much longer account than Giskes's, which goes into more detail; tone self-satisfied.

SCHULTEN, Dr C. M., *Verzet in Nederland 1940–1945* (The Hague: RIOD/Sdu, 1995), a most useful outline of Dutch resistance history, covering politics, intelligence and escapes as well as subversion.

SIMONI, Anna, *Publish and be Free* (The Hague: Nijhoff, 1975), a catalogue of the British Library's Dutch clandestine holdings, shows the versatility of the Dutch intelligentsia under occupation.

SIMPSON, John, with ADKIN, Mark, *The Quiet Operator* (Leo Cooper, 1993), a short life of Len Willmott, covers both his sorties into Holland (the second was for MI9).

STAFFORD, David, *Britain and European Resistance 1940–1945* (2 edn, Macmillan/St Anthony's, 1983), SOE's effort as seen through the chiefs of staffs' eyes.

STROOM, G. P. van der, *Nederlandse agenten, uitgezenden door geallieerde geheime diensten te London. Een chronologisch oversicht* (Amsterdam: RIOD, n.d.), duplic. A brief, invaluable list. And see FRANK, Anne.

TEMMERMAN, Jean, *Acrobates sans importance* (Grivegnée-Liège: Lemaire, 1984), lively and accurate account of the Belgian component of SAS and its war work.

Trial of Major German War Criminals (22 v, HMSO, 1946–51), a verbatim record of the proceedings at Nuremberg from 20 November 1945 to the sentences on 1 October 1946; powerful, if sometimes slanted, evidence on nazi atrocities.

UGEUX, William, *Le 'Groupe G' (1942–1944)* (Paris and Brussels: Elsevir Sequoia, 1978), memorial sketches and numerous details of circuit.

—, *Histoires de Résistants* (Paris and Gembloux: Ducrulot, 1979), striking anecdotes of attempts at active resistance in Belgium.

—, *Le Passage de l'Iraty* (Brussels: Didier Hatier, 1984), retrospective sketch of a courier line working from Belgium and France into Spain and Portugal.

The Underground Press in Belgium (Lincolns-Prager, 1944), pamphlet by Belgian ministry of information in exile; quotations and illustrations, and a copy of *Le Soir* for 9 November 1943.

VERITY, H. B., *We Landed by Moonlight* (Wilmslow: Air Data Publications, 1994), covers most of the clandestine landings by light aircraft of 161 squadron, RAF, in which the author served with distinction. First published by Ian Allan, 1978; now usefully expanded; little reference to Low Countries.

'Views and Surveys', see *Memo from Belgium*

WALBRIDGE, D. N., see FAIRBAIRN

WEBER, Guy, *Capitaine Caracal SSA 2690* (Dinant: Bourdeaux-Capelle, 1989), a life of DURIEUX with plentiful extracts by the agent himself.

WILKINSON, Sir P. A., and ASTLEY, Joan Bright, *Gubbins and SOE* (Leo Cooper, 1993), invaluable.

WILLIAMS, (Sir) E. T., see *Dictionary of National Biography*

WILLMOTT, L., see SIMPSON.

ZEMBSCH-SCHREVE, G., *Pierre Lalande* (Leo Cooper, 1996), accurate and detailed description of his SOE training and activity, and of life as a prisoner in Dora.

Index

This index is made on English rules, not on Dutch: ij comes between ii and ik, not after y; professorates and degrees are omitted. So are most service ranks. To save space, holders of peerages created before 1940 are indexed under their titles alone. Composite and double-barrelled surnames are entered under their first letter: Beukema toe Water under B, Hazelhoff Roelzema under H, Mockler-Ferryman under M.

The following prefixes are none of them used in fixing the place of an entry: D', de, den, der, du, 's, 't, ter, van, van de, van der, van 't.